Jos van Doormaal

Nonlegal Sanctioning in Private Legal Systems

Limits in US Antitrust Law and EU Competition Law

Nomos

The Deutsche Nationalbibliothek lists this publication in the Deutsche Nationalbibliografie; detailed bibliographic data are available on the Internet at http://dnb.d-nb.de

a.t.: Bremen, Univ., Diss., 2021

ISBN 978-3-8487-8164-5 (Print)
978-3-7489-2624-5(ePDF)

British Library Cataloguing-in-Publication Data
A catalogue record for this book is available from the British Library.

ISBN 978-3-8487-8164-5 (Print)
978-3-7489-2624-5 (ePDF)

Library of Congress Cataloging-in-Publication Data
van Doormaal, Jos
Nonlegal Sanctioning in Private Legal Systems
Limits in US Antitrust Law and EU Competition Law
Jos van Doormaal
518 pp.
Includes bibliographic references.

ISBN 978-3-8487-8164-5 (Print)
978-3-7489-2624-5 (ePDF)

1st Edition 2021

Published by
Nomos Verlagsgesellschaft mbH & Co. KG
Waldseestraße 3–5 | 76530 Baden-Baden
www.nomos.de

Production of the printed version:
Nomos Verlagsgesellschaft mbH & Co. KG
Waldseestraße 3–5 | 76530 Baden-Baden

ISBN 978-3-8487-8164-5 (Print)
ISBN 978-3-7489-2624-5 (ePDF)
DOI https://doi.org/10.5771/9783748926245

Onlineversion
Nomos eLibrary

Wirtschaftsrecht und Wirtschaftspolitik

edited by
Prof. Dr. Florian Bien
Prof. Dr. Ulrich Schwalbe
Prof. Dr. Heike Schweitzer

founded by
Prof. Dr. Dr. h.c. mult. Ernst-Joachim Mestmäcker

Volume 306

Preface

This work was accepted as a doctoral dissertation by the law faculty of the University of Bremen. The literature and case law are current to January 2020.

First and foremost, I would like to thank my doctoral supervisor Prof. Dr. Gralf-Peter Calliess. He has inspired and supported me throughout my work and has given me the academic freedom to complete my dissertation. I would also like to thank Prof. Dr. Christoph Schmid for writing a second expert opinion (*Zweitgutachten*).

Special thanks also go to all my family and friends who have so strongly supported me throughout my dissertation. They were especially important at the end of my dissertation and motivated me to finish the process.

Lastly, I would like to thank my parents and my wife who have given me all the support and assistance possible. They were there when I needed them the most.

Bremen, February 2021 *Jos van Doormaal*

Table of Contents

Part IV: Summary, Conclusions and Best Practice Guidelines

List of abbreviations and principal concepts

Commission	Directorate General for Competition of the European Commission
GC	General Court (constituent court of the EU which allows parties to the proceedings to lodge a complaint against a Commission decision; formerly known as the CFI before the entry into force of the Lisbon Treaty on 1 December 2009)
ECJ	European Court of Justice (constituent court of the EU which handles second level appeals by reviewing a GC judgment; before 2009 it was the appellate body to uphold, modify or reverse the findings of a CFI judgment; for reasons of clarity, court judgments before 1989 are also mentioned as coming from the ECJ in this research
CJEU	The Court of Justice of the European Union (the collective term for the judicial arm of the EU, consisting of the GC and the ECJ despite this definition dating from 2009, for the purpose of elucidation the CFI and the ECJ combined are mentioned as the CJEU in this research
CFI	Court of First Instance of the European Communities (precursor of the GC before the entry into force of the Lisbon Treaty on 1 December 2009)
PLSs	Private Legal Systems
NCAs	National Competition Authorities
Members	Member undertakings of the trade associations researched
ICA	International Cotton Association
ADB	Antwerp Diamond Bourse
DDC	Diamond Dealers Club
GAFTA	Grain and Feed Trade Association
FCC	Federation of Cocoa Commerce
LME	London Metal Exchange
FOSFA	Federation of Oils, Seeds and Fats Associations
BIMCO	Baltic and International Maritime Council

Guidelines on Horizontal Co-operation Agreements	Guidelines on the applicability of Article 101 of the Treaty on the Functioning of the European Union to horizontal co-operation agreements
Guidelines on Inter-State Trade	Guidelines on the effect on trade concept contained in Articles [101 and 102 TFEU]
The Commission Recommendation on SMEs	The Commission Recommendation concerning the definition of micro, small and medium-sized enterprises or any future recommendation replacing it
The De Minimis Notice	Commission Notice on Agreements of Minor Importance which do not Appreciably Restrict Competition under Article 101 (1) TFEU
1999 White Paper	White Paper on Modernisation of the Rules implementing Articles 85 and 86 of the Treaty (now Articles 101 and 102 TFEU)
RDBER	Research & Development Block Exemption Regulation
SABER	Specialization Agreements Block Exemption Regulation
Commission's Guidance	Commission's Guidance on the Commission's enforcement priorities in applying Article 82 of the EC Treaty [now Article 102 TFEU] to abusive exclusionary conduct by a dominant undertaking
Discussion Paper	Commission's Discussion Paper on the application of Article 82 [now Article 102 TFEU] to exclusionary abuses
Rome Treaty/ EEC	Treaty Establishing the European Economic Community

Introduction

For a society to exist at all, law, more than only national defence must be provided by the government.[1] This postulates that a public legal system is non-rivalrous[2] and non-excludable.[3] However, these seemingly rigid truisms can be undermined by even a cursory glance at history. In ancient, medieval and modern times many instances of pluralistic legal systems existed in which multiple sources of law were in competition within the same geographic area.[4] These systems created social order in the absence of a single centralized hierarchical legislature. In some instances, an ineffective government even resulted in the formation of private legal systems ("PLSs") – non-governmental institutions intended to regulate the behaviour of their members.[5] While one could say that non-State legal sys-

1 B. Chaplan, "The Economics of Non-State Legal Systems", *Libertarian Alliance* 1997, p. 2; See also T. Hobbes, "*Philosophicall Rudiments Concerning Government and Society (De Cive)*", London: J.C. for R. Royston 1651, p. 85. Therein, *Thomas Hobbes* asserts this idea by stating that it pertains to the sovereign to establish the content of natural laws and organize their enforceability. He adduces this by stating that, what is to be called injury to a citizen, is not to be determined by natural, but by civil law.

2 M. Kolmar, "*Principles of Microeconomics: An Integrative Approach*", Cham: Springer International Publishing AG 2017, p. 140.

3 D. Robbins, "*Handbook of Public Sector Economics*", Boca Raton: CRC Press 2005, p.185.

4 In the medieval society that Prof. Berman investigates, canon law, royal law, feudal law, manorial law, mercantile law and urban law co-existed. None was automatically supreme over the others. See H. J. Berman, "*Law and Revolution: The Formation of the Western Legal Tradition*", Cambridge/London: Cambridge University Press 1983, p. 519; P. S. Berman, "*Global Legal Pluralism: A Jurisprudence Of Law Beyond Borders*", New York: Cambridge University Press 2012, p. 13. Such systems often existed in an uneasy relationship with the State legal system.

5 See A. Aviram, "The Paradox of Spontaneous Formation of Private Legal Systems", *John M. Olin Law & Economics Working Paper No. 192* 2003, p. 1-3 for an example of a Private Legal System that existed at the end of the 10th Century AD. In his work *Aviram* explains that due to the decline of the Carolingian Empire, a political vacuum emerged in which private warlords consolidated power and raised terror in the absence of an effective central government. In response to this situation, one of the world's first decentralized peace movements, Pax Dei (Latin for 'Peace of God') gained importance. Private warlords voluntarily observed rules regulating warfare,

tems are historical anomalies, in modern times parallels have sprung up, albeit in a less dramatic form.

Even in fully developed market economies with a high degree of division of labour, formal legal rules, which are enforced by a branch of government in which judicial power is vested, "the judiciary", do not comprise the total picture. It is immediately evident that there are unmet legal needs in society, as an omniscient, infallible, omnipotent, and benevolent government that guarantees perfect enforcement does not exist. This utopia can especially be rebutted by looking at industry-wide arbitration systems established by some trade associations which represent the interests of industry actors in particular commodities industries such as the agricultural, cotton, cocoa, diamond, metal, and oilseeds, oils and fats trade.[6] Together with their members these institutions have set up very complex systems of specialized commercial arbitration which operate in the shadow of the law.[7] The most salient features of these systems share four similarities. First, fellow merchants are selected as arbitrators to decide industry disputes which originate from standardized contracts. Second, the arbitration system presumes to have authority over all industry conflicts. Third, these conflicts occur in industries in which a good reputation is crucial to operate on the market. Fourth, extrajudicial measures/

---

and – in the event of non-adherence – were punished by means of social and religious ostracism; A. Marciano, "*Law and Economics: A Reader*", in: T. J. Zywicki (ed), "The Rise and Fall of Efficiency in the Common Law: A Supply-Side Analysis", Abingdon/New York: Routledge 2009, p. 364. It should, however, be noted that the dichotomy between private and public legal systems is not always that clear throughout history. An example would be 'The Statute of Staple' enacted in 1353 by the King of England, which provided for the establishment of arbitral merchant courts to resolve disputes arising in the markets of the most important articles of commerce in England, namely lead, tin, wool and woolfells. These courts applied the privately formed Law Merchant (or *Lex Mercatoria*) and customs, whereas common law courts were prohibited from hearing disputes arising from contracts on the staples markets.

6 These trade associations were perceived as operating in non-State legal systems by *Dietz*. See T. Dietz, "*Global Order Beyond Law: How Information and Communication Technologies Facilitate Relational Contracting in International Trade*", Oxford/Portland: Hart Publishing 2016, p. 192.

7 C. R. Drahozal, "Private Ordering and International Commercial Arbitration", *Penn State Law Review, Vol. 113:4* 2009, p. 1032.

nonlegal sanctions[8] are used to punish non-compliance with arbitral awards.[9]

Even though specialized commercial arbitration is a less adversarial procedure to accommodate repeated-dealings and offers a more efficient, cost-friendly and secretive form of dispute resolution as opposed to public court adjudication,[10] not all of the aspects of such a system are without controversy. Extrajudicial measures to punish recalcitrant industry actors for not paying an arbitral award have an enormous impact on them.[11] Often, such industry actors are subject to (enormous) reputational harm and can even have their access to the services provided by the relevant trade association cancelled. This can cause targeted industry actors to lose access to the relevant commodities market. While extrajudicial measures are necessary to deter industry actors from failing to pay arbitral awards and are a more efficient method of enforcement as opposed to enforcement in public courts, every time trade associations impose such measures, these institutions as well as their members and – arguably – non-members for their role in the execution could violate US Antitrust Law and EU Competition Law.[12] More specifically, with regard to the US legal system, nonlegal sanctioning "can" make all three actors liable under Section 1 of the Sherman Act, which prohibits "*every contract, combination in the form of trust or otherwise, or conspiracy, in restraint of trade or commerce among the several States, or with foreign nations*". In addition, it has the potential to attribute liability to trade associations and their members under Section 2 of the Sherman Act when extrajudicial sanctioning classifies, as an illegal monopoly, an anti-

8 For the purpose of this research, the terms extrajudicial measures and nonlegal sanctions are used interchangeably.

9 *Posner* refers to the enforcement of arbitral awards as private substitutes for judicial protection. See R. A. Posner, "*Economics Analysis of Law*", New York: Wolters Kluwer Law & Business 2014, par. 8.6.

10 P. Newmann, "*The New Palgrave Dictionary of Economics and the Law: Three Volume Set*", London: Palgrave Macmillan 2002, p. 93.

11 *Ellickson* describes this reliance on extralegal mechanisms as an alternative to, not an extension of, formal legal sanctions as "socials norms" or "order without law". See R. A. Posner, "*Law and Social Norms*", Cambridge/London: Harvard University Press 2000, p. 172. In *Ellickson's* empirical study of cattle ranchers and farmers in Shasta County, California even though rural neighbours did not rely on the law, they were cooperating in order to prevent lawsuits (*e.g.* payment of debt(s), payment of damage by landowners to the property of others). *Ellickson* interprets this as a rule requiring the "informal resolution of internal disputes", but argues that social norms are only efficient in close-knit groups.

12 A. Aviram, "The Paradox of Spontaneous Formation of Private Legal Systems", *John M. Olin Law & Economics Working Paper No. 192* 2003, p. 6-7.

competitive attempt to monopolize, or as an outlawed conspiracy to monopolize any part of the trade or commerce among several States, or with foreign nations. Under EU Competition Law, trade associations, their members and – arguably – non-members engaged in nonlegal sanctioning can infringe Article 101 TFEU if such measures classify as "*agreements between undertakings, decisions by associations of undertakings and concerted practices which may affect trade between Member States and which have as their object or effect the prevention, restriction or distortion of competition within the internal market*". Furthermore, the first two actors can breach Article 102 TFEU if extrajudicial sanctioning classifies as an abuse of a dominant position.

Even if, at present, nonlegal sanctioning has never been subject to antitrust scrutiny by the responsible enforcement authorities of the USA (*i.e.* the FTC) and the EU (*i.e.* the Commission) and US courts and the CJEU, this does not preclude future prosecution under these laws. This is regardless of the discussion whether such silence is a metaphor for inaction, or entails that the responsible authorities and courts condone extrajudicial sanctioning. What matters is not whether these authorities and courts are willing to examine the potential anti-competitiveness of trade associations, their members and – arguably – non-members, but whether these actors transgress the bounds of US Antitrust Law and EU Competition Law. If so, their participation in this type of enforcement, in spite of its (at first glance) pivotal role in maintaining an efficient system of specialized commercial arbitration in which awards are adhered to, is illegal. This could make all three actors liable for excessive fines and sometimes even criminal charges under both legal systems. To alleviate or even prevent such repercussions, legal clarity and guidance should be provided to trade associations, their members and non-members when those actors impose extrajudicial sanctions on disloyal industry actors for not complying with arbitral awards. This is not only important for these actors, but it also contributes to the general understanding of whether non-State orchestrated sanctions are permissible and offers the responsible enforcement agencies and courts with useful guidance on how to treat such conduct. A change of the purpose of US Antirust Law and EU Competition Law over time and a potential (but unlikely) future swing in the antirust pendulum does not change these benefits.[13] An increase in legal clarity and transparency

13 It is difficult to predict how the definition, scope, nature, purpose and objective of US Antitrust Law and EU Competition Law will change in the future. A com-

for all parties involved in nonlegal sanctioning under both present legal systems is more than appropriate.

To reach the conclusion that trade associations, their members and non-members violate US Antitrust Law and EU Competition Law for their participation in nonlegal sanctioning, the research is organized as follows. Part I (consisting of five Chapters) explains present-day PLSs by focusing on the salient features of six modern trade associations that provide systems of specialized commercial arbitration in which recalcitrant industry actors are extrajudicially punished for not complying with arbitral awards. Part I also introduces the central research question. To start this discussion, Chapter 1 maps out that private initiatives and PLSs are not present-day anomalies, but have occurred throughout history, such as with regard to self-regulation within the Oikos in classical Athens, the flexibility and the allocation of risk pertaining to lease contracts in the agriculture sector in the Roman Empire, *Lex Mercatoria* in Medieval Times and the Industrial Revolution in Modern Times. Subsequently, some general characteristics of present-day PLSs as well as the six types of nonlegal sanctions are briefly discussed. To this extent, the typology of extrajudicial measures describes the practice of blacklisting, withdrawing membership, refusing to re-admit expelled members on the basis of an additional entry barrier, refusing to deal with ostracized members, entering the premises of wrongdoers without a warrant and effectively limiting adequate access to public courts prior to arbitral proceedings and after an award.[14] Chapter 1 ends with stating the reasons for the existence of present-day PLSs by focusing on the inefficiency of the court system, increased demand for contractual security and a decrease in transaction and distribution costs.

In Chapter 2, six trade associations which operate in PLSs are selected from a plethora of other institutions which provide their members with specialized commercial arbitration and punish disloyalty of industry actors following non-compliance with arbitral awards with nonlegal sanctions. These include (i) the International Cotton Association ("ICA")[15]; (ii) the Diamond Dealers Club ("DDC")[16]; (iii) the Grain and Feed Trade Associa-

---

plete overhaul of both legal systems is not impossible, which would subsequently prompt institutional change.

14 Whereas this last measure is not a nonlegal sanction/extrajudicial measure, as it is not imposed on a disloyal industry actor for not complying with an arbitral award stemming from specialized commercial arbitration, it will be treated as fitting within both terms throughout this research.

15 For the website of the ICA, see http://www.ica-ltd.org/.

16 For the website of the DDC, see http://www.nyddc.com/.

tion ("GAFTA")[17]; (iv) the Federation of Cocoa Commerce ("FCC")[18]; (v) the London Metal Exchange ("LME")[19]; and (vi) the Federation of Oils, Seeds and Fats Association ("FOSFA").[20] For each of them, the trade association's history, legal form, institutional structure, membership requirements, system of specialized commercial arbitration, types of available nonlegal sanctions as well as the rationale for extrajudicial enforcement is explained. This contributes to a better understanding of how present-day trade associations which are active within PLSs function and to what extent these institutions opt out of the legal system. Furthermore, it broadens and increases the degree of congruence regarding the general characteristics of these trade associations. In an absence of such a case- based review, the purpose of this research, which is to examine the illegality of trade associations, their members and – arguably – non-members for their participation in nonlegal sanctioning under US Antitrust Law and EU Competition Law, cannot be achieved. Any different approach would contradict one of the most pronounced features of contemporary legal research which stresses the importance of a case-based review. Here, this case-based review is a study of different trade associations.[21]

In Chapter 3, the broad overview of Chapter 2 is summarized. The focus is on the legal form of the trade associations researched,[22] access to membership and the system of specialized commercial arbitration by looking at the structure and composition of the arbitration board (*i.e.* first-tier arbitration, second-tier arbitration and the qualification criteria for candidate arbitrators), the place of arbitration and applicable law and the finality of arbitration or the possibility of (some) legal redress in public courts. Furthermore, all types of nonlegal sanctioning which are used by the trade associations researched are highlighted as well as the reasons for such measures are outlined. This comprehensive overview is necessary to summarize the most critical issues and make the reader well aware of all similarities and differences between the trade associations researched in order to contribute to a better understanding of how trade associations active within present-day PLSs function. Without such a broad discussion, it is impossi-

---

17 For the website of GAFTA, see http://www.gafta.com/.

18 For the website of the FCC, see http://www.cocoafederation.com/.

19 For the website of the LME, see https://www.lme.com/.

20 For the website of FOSFA, see http://www.fosfa.org/.

21 The approach to this Chapter is to identify similarities and differences and does not require the author to provide his own opinion.

22 The six trade associations selected are referred to as the "trade associations researched" throughout this research.

ble to understand the limits of nonlegal sanctioning in the diverse arena and would make this research rely on meta-theoretical assumptions rather than facts.

In Chapter 4, the boundaries of nonlegal sanctioning are explained by focusing on US Antitrust Law and EU Competition Law. This is done by discussing three aspects. First, the reasons for the selection of both legal systems. Second, an explanation why nonlegal sanctioning is a good method to resolve the prisoner's dilemma and the adverse impact of opportunistic behaviour. Third, a short discussion on which actors are involved in extrajudicial enforcement to clarify the addressees of potential antitrust liability. After narrowing down the focus and scope of the research subject, the central research question is introduced. In Chapter 5, the research design and research methods are discussed. Both topics feature critical issues which are crucial in this research, such as the reasons for the selection of the six cases (trade associations), a delimitation of what will be discussed pertaining to US Antitrust Law and EU Competition Law, a reflection on the central research question and the objectives of the research which pertain to increased transparency and guidance for all actors involved in nonlegal sanctioning to understand when they infringe the core provisions under both legal systems and to promulgate best practice guidelines for the actors that infringe these laws to escape from antitrust liability.

After this broad overview, Part II (comprising two Chapters) features a discussion of the hypothesis that the six trade associations researched, their members and – arguably – non-members breach US Antitrust Law every time the former actors impose a nonlegal sanction on a disloyal industry actor for not complying with an arbitral award stemming from specialized commercial arbitration. To do so, in Chapter 6 the six nonlegal sanctions are reviewed against the yardstick of Section 1 of the Sherman Act, which prohibits agreements in restraint of trade or commerce. To stimulate a thorough review, four main aspects are highlighted. First, which actors involved in nonlegal sanctioning can be held subject to antitrust scrutiny under Section 1 of the Sherman Act is discussed. Second, whether the trade associations researched, their members and non-members, satisfy the collusion requirement for their separate role in the participation of extrajudicial sanctioning is reviewed. Third, anti-competitiveness of all six types of nonlegal sanctions when they are imposed by the trade associations researched and executed by their members and – arguably – non-members is examined in detail. Fourth, whether the actors that impose anti-competitive nonlegal sanctions can use a rule-of-reason defence to exonerate their participation is probed. This then stimulates a broader understanding of whether such measures are permissible and what the actors can do to alleviate the risk of antitrust liability.

After this descriptive review of Section 1 of the Sherman Act, the intention of Chapter 7 is to reflect on the investigation into the illegality of the trade associations researched and their members due to their participation in nonlegal sanctions under Section 2 of the Sherman Act. With regard to the former group of actors, whether their role in the imposition of nonlegal sanctions amounts to unlawful monopolization and attempted anticompetitive monopolization is described. Owing to a plethora of problems, this is not an easy task. This is because it is unclear whether the trade associations researched hold monopoly positions or specifically intend to monopolize the markets for regulation and private ordering and it is unsure whether extrajudicial measures felt on adjacent second-tier commodities markets are considered anticompetitive conduct and are sufficiently causal.[23] Concerning the members of the trade associations researched, the focus here is on an unlawful conspiracy to monopolize. After establishing whether the trade associations researched and their members can be held accountable for a violation of Section 2 of the Sherman Act for their participation in nonlegal sanctioning, a rule-of-reason analysis is conducted. This will also contribute to the debate on whether nonlegal sanctions are allowed and, if not, how they can be structured so that the trade associations researched and their members can avoid antitrust liability.

In Part III (consisting of four Chapters) a comparable, but more thorough review is conducted with regard to the illegality of the trade associations researched, their members and – arguably – non-members, when they orchestrate nonlegal sanctions as opposed to US Antitrust Law. This is done by focusing on the two core provisions of EU Competition Law, namely Articles 101 and 102 TFEU. Chapter 8 explains whether the scope of application of both provisions is opened which enables the Commission to conduct a potential competition law scrutiny. To verify whether this is indeed the case, the aim is to see whether the trade associations researched, their members and non-members, fulfil the legal boundary, which focuses on the concept of undertaking and satisfy some economic boundaries.

While it is likely that the scope of Articles 101 and 102 TFEU is opened, Chapter 9 takes a closer look at the question whether the participation of

23 The six trade associations researched operate on the markets for regulation and private ordering, whereas their members operate on adjacent second-tier commodities markets.

the trade associations researched, their members and – arguably – non-members, in the six nonlegal sanctions amounts to anticompetitive agreements under Article 101. This is done by determining whether each of the three group of actors – separately – satisfy the collusion agreement and whether their participation in the six types of nonlegal sanctions prevents, restricts or distorts competition by object of effect pursuant to Article 101(1) TFEU. Albeit that a justification is typically considered under Article 101(3) TFEU as soon as an illegality under the first tier of this provision is established, the existence of a rule-of-reason analysis under Article 101 (1) TFEU will also be discussed. This aims to contribute to the completeness of the research by delving into a plethora of concepts and promote knowledge-sharing.

Chapter 10 discusses whether the participation of the trade associations researched and their members in nonlegal sanctions which restrict Article 101(1) TFEU can be justified. To do so, the aim is to inspect two relevant block exemption regulations (BERs) and, in particular, to outline whether the exemption route laid down in Article 101(3) TFEU is applicable. Albeit that the former exemption possibilities are dealt swiftly, a more thorough analysis of the latter provision is conducted, which provides that Article 101(1) TFEU may be declared inapplicable when four cumulative conditions are satisfied. Although these requirements somehow mirror the rule-of-reason analysis under Section 1 of the Sherman Act, they are more rigid.

Following the discussion of whether the trade associations researched, their members and non-members violate Article 101 TFEU with regard to the six nonlegal sanctions, Chapter 11 assesses the existence of a violation of Article 102 TFEU by the former two group of actors because of these extrajudicial measures. This assessment is made by concentrating on the existence of a dominant position in the relevant market which impacts the EU territory and by putting emphasis on the existence of exclusionary abuses of such positions vis-à-vis refusals to grant access to an essential facility. Furthermore, to invigorate this discussion, objective justification defences are touched upon.

In Part IV (consisting of two Chapters) a succinct summary of the research, conclusions and best practice guidelines for trade associations and their members which orchestrate nonlegal sanctions to not transgress the bounds of US Antitrust Law and EU Competition Law will be given. Chapter 12 presents the results of the research in order to eschew extraneous findings and describe the most pertinent aspects as a means of stimulating reflection on the illegality of nonlegal sanctioning in PLSs under US Antitrust Law and EU Competition Law. This will be done by re-stating the key findings of every Chapter. Following this brief overview of the research, Chapter 13, first, answers the central research question concisely, clearly and specifically, which given the more broad but still succinct overview outlined in Chapter 12 is adequate and appropriate and, second, to develop best practice guidelines for trade associations and members on how to not exceed the bounds of US Antitrust Law and EU Competition Law when they orchestrate nonlegal sanctions against disloyal industry actors for not complying with an arbitral award stemming from specialized commercial arbitration. To do so, advice is given to both actors to adumbrate which of the six extrajudicial measures they should and should not use and, if appropriate, how they can structure nonlegal sanctions in a manner that complies with US Antitrust Law and EU Competition Law. Recommendations which require trade associations and members to be surreptitious even though a nonlegal sanction infringes one or both legal systems will not be included in the best practice guidelines. The intention is to develop a comprehensive set of recommendations proposals which do not promote illegal conduct to stay out off the radar of the responsible US and EU enforcement agencies. This discourages trade associations and their members to violate US Antitrust Law and EU Competition Law and subverts the fallacious belief of both actors that it is better to escape antitrust liability rather than to abide by both laws.

Part I:
Framework and Research Question

Chapter 1: Rise of Specialized Commercial Arbitration in Global Markets

A. An historical overview of PLSs

Incentives to comply with law are not always shaped by legal, but also by nonlegal sanctions stemming from private initiatives. Informal discipline, which emerges when the formal coercive apparatus is unable to provide sufficient deterrence in the sense that rational individuals with a reasonably degree of risk aversion are expected to deviate from the law, has been around since ancient times. [24] The oldest surviving accounts can be found in archaic Greece, especially with regard to classical Athens (*I*)[25] and the Roman Republic (*II*).

Likewise, but even more illustrative for the existence of early private self-regulation or a PLS, the special law for the merchant class (*stilus mercatorum, jus mercatorum, lex mercatoria*), which spread across Europe after the 11th century AD must be mentioned (*III*).[26] During the transition to new manufacturing processes from the 18th century to the 19th century in Europe, more commonly known as the Industrial Revolution, it came to describe a system in which troublemakers could be extrajudicially sanctioned (*IV*).[27]

---

24 S. Kube and C. Traxler, "The interaction of legal and social norm enforcement", *Journal of Public Economic Theory* 2010, p. 1.

25 A. Lanni, "*Law and Order in Ancient Athens*", New York: Cambridge University Press 2016, p. 1-27.

26 See, *inter alia*, G. Calliess, "Lex Mercatoria", *Zentra Working Papers in Transnational Studies No. 52 / 201* 2015, p. 1-15; G. Calliess, "Lex mercatoria", *Encyclopedia of Private International Law* 2017, p. 1119-1129; Although *Lex Mercatoria* translates as "law" of merchants, it would be more suitable to refer to it as the "legal system" of merchants. Despite its scholarly value, arguments in favour of this concept will not be discussed. In this research reference will only be made to the law of merchants.

27 K. E. Hendrickson, "*The Encyclopedia of the Industrial Revolution in World History*", Band 3, London: Rowmann & Littlefield 2015, p. 103.

I. Ancient Greece: "Self-regulation within the Oikos in classical Athens"

In the 4th and 5th centuries BC, Athens was a rather Stateless political community, without a well-functioning court system.[28] Vagueness of statutes prevented *ex ante* a predictable outcome of jury verdicts and ensuing enforcement was not always possible.[29] Nonlegal sanctions (*i.e.* informal discipline) such as a refusal to engage in reciprocal relations, unwillingness to share food or refusal to eat with offenders and the loss of reputation dictated everyday life.[30]

An absence of State interference is perhaps more obvious when looking at the private sphere of the household (*i.e.* Oikos).[31] In classical Athens, the secluded space for private life (or private domain) was seen as the foundation of economic, political and military life. It served as a cornerstone that needed to be protected from any form of state intrusion.[32]

In contrast with its contemporary understanding, albeit not globally agreed upon, it can best be described as an androcentric and patriarchal hierarchical model.[33] The masculine head of the household (*i.e.* the *kyrios* or master) enjoyed complete disciplinary control over his household, who typically lived in the same physical house[34] and operated – in this capacity – entirely apart from the formal legal system.[35] He could privately disci-

---

28 P. Cartledge, P. Millett, and S. v. Reden, "*Kosmos: Essays in Order, Conflict and Community in Classical Athens*", Cambridge/New York/Melbourne: Cambridge University Press 1998, p. 1.

29 A. Lanni, "*Law and Order in Ancient Athens*", New York: Cambridge University Press 2016, p. 4.

30 Ibid., p. 20, 25; Interestingly, classical Athens was not a close-knit society, as its citizens regularly traded with foreigners. Hence, according to *Lanni*, the deterrent effect of social sanctioning, in particular, reputational loss is not so convincing.

31 For a brief overview thereof, see C. Ando and J. Rüpke, "*Public and Private in Ancient Mediterranean Law and Religion*", Berlin/Munich/Boston: Walter de Gruyter GmbH 2015, p. 37-41.

32 S. U. Sörling et al., "*Studies presented to Pontus Hellström*", in: B. L. Sjöberg, "The Greek oikos: a space for interaction, revisited and reconsidered", Uppsala: S. U. Sörling et al. 2014, p. 315.

33 See, *inter alia*, U. Terlinden, "*City and Gender: Intercultural Discourse on Gender, Urbanism and Architecture*", Opladen: Leske + Budrich 2003, p. 43.

34 R. Parker, "*Polytheism and Society at Athens*", Oxford: Oxford University Press 2005, p. 9.

35 C. Ando and J. Rüpke, "*Public and Private in Ancient Mediterranean Law and Religion*", Berlin/Munich/Boston: Walter de Gruyter GmbH 2015, p. 40; The Oikos was not a legally defined entity in Athens. See R. Parker, "*Polytheism and Society at Athens*", Oxford: Oxford University Press 2005, p. 9.

pline (*e.g.* whipping, torture) his slaves for fleeing, stealing, lying and laziness with the exception that killing his slaves was not permitted.[36] Also, he could penalize his wife for non-capital offences.

II. The Roman Empire: "Flexibility & risk allocation with regard to lease contracts in the agriculture sector"

Especially in the last years of the Roman Republic, nonlegal sanctioning was used by politicians when they came to power to blacklist certain families that did not support them.[37] This, however, standing alone is not sufficient to establish that a PLS existed next to State-enforced law.

A much more convincing example relates to the allocation of risk with regard to lease contracts in the agriculture sector. In classical Roman law, a tenant bore all foreseeable risks concerning the price and size of the crops relating to agriculture (*i.e. vitia ex re*). Those persons only had the right to obtain a remission of rent in the event of an unforeseeable natural disaster, the invasion of an army or unusual infestation of the crops by infested birds.[38] In contrast, the landowner was to a great extent non-liable. In that time, such inflexibility was seen as a threat to the continuance of lease contracts, which in turn would hamper the economy of the ancient Roman Empire. Consequently, the Roman legislature allowed the parties who entered into a lease contract to go beyond the requirements laid down in law by, for example, decreasing the rent for a scarcity of crops.[39] Even though it established some basic rights and obligations, private ordering was allowed in order to reach a friendly settlement.[40] This led to the existence of a private initiative that even included informal disciplining in the agriculture sector that existed next to the public legal system. As some may consider such a freedom for the parties to a lease contract not sufficient to

36 A. Lanni, "*Law and Order in Ancient Athens*", New York: Cambridge University Press 2016, p. 34.

37 K. E. Hendrickson, "*The Encyclopedia of the Industrial Revolution in World History*", Band 3, London: Rowmann & Littlefield 2015, p. 103.

38 H. D. Baker and M. Jursa, "*Documentary Sources in Ancient Near Eastern and Greco-Roman Economic History*", Oxford/Philadelphia: Oxbow Books 2014, p. 147.

39 T. A. J. McGinn, "*Obligations in Roman Law: Past, Present, and Future*", Ann Arbor: University of Michigan Press 2012, p. 201.

40 D. P. Kehoe and T. McGinn, "*Ancient Law, Ancient Society*", Ann Arbor: University of Michigan Press 2017, p. 126.

prove the existence of a PLS, it at least illustrates that already some form of private initiative existed.

III. Medieval Times: "Lex Mercatoria"

To cope with the excessive demands of regulation in the context of an upcoming intensification in trade, a special law for merchants was developed in the Middle Ages.[41] Its aim was to create uniformity for merchants active in transnational trade without the mediation of the legislative powers of States.[42] Mainly through the communication and interchange of merchants as early as the 11th century AD in Italy, especially pertaining to Venice, Genoa and Florence[43], but also spreading to many market places in Europe, *Lex Mercatoria* codified the norms and procedural principles established by and for commerce.[44]

Despite it not being unanimously agreed that early *Lex Mercatoria* qualifies as a PLS, disputes were resolved through private merchant arbitration.[45] For *Goldman*[46] this was sufficient to evidence the presence of a PLS

41 H. G. Leser, "*Gesammelte Schriften*", Band 1, Tübingen: J.C.B. Mohr (Paul Siebeck) 1968, p. 11.

42 For an in-depth study, see F. Galgano, "*Lex mercatoria: storia del diritto commerciale*", Munich: Il Mulino 1993.

43 P. H. Vishny, "*Guide to International Commerce Law*", New York: McGraw-Hill Inc. 1984, p. 2.

44 G. Saputelli, "The European Union, the Member States, and the Lex Mercatoria", *Notre Dame Journal of International & Comparative Law: Vol. 8: Is. 2, Article 3* 2018, p. 3; R. Michaels, "The True Lex Mercatoria: Law Beyond the State", *Indiana Journal of Global Legal Studies 14* 2007, p. 448; L. A. DiMatteo, "*International Business Law and the Legal Environment: A Transactional Approach*", New York/London: Routledge 2017, p. 127.

45 *Elcin* defined *Lex Mercatoria* as "*the law of adjudication of the disputes arising from international commercial contracts on the basis of a few substantive and procedural principles, under which the reasonable expectations of the parties to a particular contract become the single source of their contractual rights, obligations and risk allocations*". See M. Elcin, "*Lex Mercatoria in International Arbitration Theory and Practice*", Vol. 1, Florence: Mert Elcin 2012, p. 5.

46 B. Goldman, "Frontières du Droit et Lex Mercatoria", *Arch. De Philosophie Du Droit* 1964, p. 177-192; Travaux du Comité français de droit international privé, "*Droit international privé:*", in: B. Goldman (ed), "La lex mercatoria dans les contrats et l'arbitrage internationaux: réalité et perspectives", Paris: Travaux du Comité français de droit international privé 1979, p. 221-270; C. Dominicé, "*Etudes de droit international en l'honneur de Pierre Lalive*", in: B. Goldman (ed),

that operated autonomously from the State. For others, such as, for example, *Schmitthoff*, the legal basis of *Lex Mercatoria* was anchored to the State system, since it was developed in respect of the State-guaranteed principle of party autonomy.[47] Whichever line of reasoning is followed is immaterial,[48] what matters is that some form of private initiative and informal disciplining also existed in the Middle Ages.[49]

IV. The Industrial Revolution

The cornerstone invention of steam power, the development of intermodal rail transport and the emergence of a factory system resulted in an unprecedented economic growth, which began in mid-18th century in England.[50] In a few years it spread throughout Europe. This period that later came to be known under the name Industrial Revolution continued for the remainder of the 19th century and shifted the economy from manual labour to artificial labour (*i.e.* labour supported by labour-replacing machines).[51]

In this period, many people became financially dependent on the jobs offered in those industries, mainly because of the continually rising de-

---

"Nouvelles Riflexions sur la Lex Mercatoria", Basel/Frankfurt am Main: Helbing Lichtenhahn Verlag 1993, p. 241-256.

47 C. M. Schmitthoff, "*The Unification of the Law of International Trade*", London: Sweet & Maxwell 1968; U. Stein, "*Lex mercatoria: Realität und Theorie*", Band 28, Frankfurt am Main: Vittorio Klostermann 1995 p. 188.

48 P. Mazzacano, "The Lex Mercatoria as Autonomous Law", *Comparative Research in Law & Political Economy Research Paper No.* 29 2008, p. 1. "*The lex mercatoria is at once both non-state law and state-based law. It is not created in the state; it is not created exclusively in commerce.*"

49 *Lex Mercatoria* is a topic that deserves extensive study, debate and argumentation. The aim of this Paragraph is merely to provide a short overview without going beyond that overview.

50 E. Crooks, "*The Unrelenting Machine: A Legacy of the Industrial Revolution*", Morrisville: Lulu 2012, p. 65.

51 *Marx* recognized two characteristics in relation to this economic change: first, the expropriation of nature. This entails that each individual worker loses any real degree of control over his labour process, since he has to adopt himself to the rhythm of machine production. Second, the expropriation of the product. This entails that the each worker is not the owner of the end-product. See K. Marx, "*Pre-Capitalist Economic Formations*", New York: International Publishers 1965, p. 37, 104 [edited version by E. J. Hobsbawm].

mand for industrial labour.[52] Given that there was no shortage of labourers, owners exploited their employees[53] by compelling them to perform under horrendous working conditions. Working hours were long, wages were low and working conditions and workers rights were not respected.[54] Wealthy industrialists could act how they wanted to and enforced a system of internal labour discipline. Blacklists were drawn up and shared between owners, which included the names of those workers who were seen as troublemakers.[55] Once on the list, a worker would have difficulties getting hired. Hence, labour activism was to a great extent curtailed.

In terms of its rationale, informal discipline and nonlegal sanctions were seen as necessary to guarantee a system of hierarchical division of work (*i.e.* owner-worker relationship), which was crucial to maintaining a well-functioning economy. [56] Therefore, the State only played a marginal role and allowed great freedom for industrialists (*i.e. laissez-faire* capitalism).[57] By promoting private initiative and by operating in the shadow of the public legal system, the existence of a PLS can be substantiated. Whether or not this is true largely depends on the arguments being used.

B. The theory on present-day PLSs

Throughout history formal legal rules that impose negative sanctions for violations (and positive sanctions for compliance) are only one side of the coin.[58] The other side concerns out-of-court private initiatives that overrule (, arguably, any form of) legal enforcement.

---

52 K. S. Madhavan, "*Business & Ethics - An Oxymoron?*", Bangalore: KS Madhavan, p. 40. Workers were needed to satisfy the demand for industrial products in society.

53 *Marx* refers to the distinction between the "industrialist" and "workers" as the "Proletariat" and the "Bourgeoisie". See K. Marx, "*Pre-Capitalist Economic Formations*", New York: International Publishers 1965, p. 30 [edited version by E. J. Hobsbawm].

54 M. Beggs-Humphreys, H. Gregor, and D. Humphreys, "*The Industrial Revolution*", Abingdon: Routledge 1959, p. 27.

55 K. E. Hendrickson, "*The Encyclopedia of the Industrial Revolution in World History*", Band 3, London: Rowmann & Littlefield 2015, p. 103.

56 J. Horn, L. N. Rosenband, and M. R. Smith, "*Reconceptualizing the Industrial Revolution*", Cambridge/London: The MIT Press 2010, p. 157.

57 G-H. Lévesque, "The Concrete Characteristics of Laissez-Faire Capitalism", *Relations industrielles / Industrial Relations, vol. 5, no. 5,* 1950, p. 41-42.

58 B. Bouckaert and G. de Geest, "*Encyclopedia of Law and Economics*", in: S. Panther (ed), "Non-Legal Sanctions", Aldershot: Edward Elgar 2000, p. 1000. According

Classifying present-day private initiatives as PLS is not straightforward. Certain characteristics confine its ambiguous wording (Paragraph I). Perhaps the most distinctive feature of a present-day PLS, which, in my opinion, substantiates that the membrane between private and public law enforcement is rather rigid, relates to its ability to guarantee self-enforcement. Whereas legal systems have rules to govern the behaviour of citizens, within PLSs reliance is on nonlegal sanctioning.[59] Examples can be found in some present-day industries that are described in Chapter 2 (Paragraph II).

After this typology of sanctions has been described, increased efficiency as the principle argument for rejecting State-enforced law is discussed (Paragraph III).[60] This will be done by comparing the costs of entering into legally enforceable contracts with the costs of becoming a party to unenforceable (*i.e.* extralegal) contracts.[61]

I. Present-day PLSs: General characteristics

1. Self-governance in reputation-based networks vs. governance of members by and through associations

When a State is dysfunctional,[62] unwilling to provide institutions, or is inefficient,[63] private modes of governance can take over the State's role to enforce contracts. Nowadays, such private ordering by self-governance mainly occurs in the following two scenarios. The first scenario takes place when in reputation-based networks behaviour is organized on the basis of

---

to *Panther*, legal scholars refer to sanctions as punishments, whereas sociologists refer to it as both punishments and rewards.

59 The terms "social sanctions" and "non-legal sanctions" are synonymous for the purpose of this research.

60 This Paragraph will only discuss the reasons for the existence of PLSs next to formal legal rules. How a PLS is established is only of marginal interest. For a detailed discussion of the (spontaneous) formation of PLSs, see A. Aviram, "The Paradox of Spontaneous Formation of Private Legal Systems", *John M. Olin Law & Economics Working Paper No. 192 (2D Series)* 2003, p. 1-72.

61 L. Bernstein, "Opting out of the Legal System: Extralegal Contractual Relations in the Diamond Industry", *The Journal of Legal Studies, Vol. 21, No. 1* 1992, p. 115.

62 J. McMillan and C. Woodruf, "Private Order under Dysfunctional Public Order", *Michigan Law Review, Vol. 98, No. 8* 2000, p. 2421.

63 A. K. Dixit, "*Lawlessness and Economics: Alternative Modes of Governance*", Princeton: Princeton University 2004, p. 4. Least efficient entails most costly.

self-governance. This manifests itself when actors all belong to the same homogenous market and State-enforced law is insufficient to guarantee observance (*i.e.* to punish a deviating actor).[64] Exemplary for such private ordering to discipline an actor's opportunistic behaviour relates to stand-up comedy.[65] Persons engaged in comedy performed on a stage cannot adequately protect their intellectual property rights (*e.g.* jokes) against unfair use and duplication by other comedians on the basis of copyright laws.[66] Instead, they rely on social norm-based sanctions. Badmouthing, refusals to work with disobedient stand-up comedians and (a threat of) physical violence are some examples of extralegal sanctions to guarantee observance.[67] Put differently, a career can be hampered by questioning one's reputation.

The second scenario in which private ordering takes places occurs when trade associations step into the role of the State and govern the behaviour of their members on the basis of tailormade privately-designed rules.[68] For the purpose of this research, this category will be of principal interest, even though at times arguments can find support in relation to the first possibility of private ordering.[69]

64 Homogenous market can best be defined as a marketplace where actors trade a particular type of commodities functionally identical with each unit traded.

65 D. Oliar, "There's No Free Laugh (anymore): The Emergence of Intellectual Property Norms and the Transformation of Stand-up Comedy", *Virginia Law Review, Vol. 94, No. 8* 2008.

66 Ibid., p. 1789. There is an absence of copyright lawsuits against stand-up comedians.

67 Ibid., p. 1791; According to *Dixit*, social-norm based sanctions are only effective, when three minimum conditions are met. First, deviating actors must be punished by willing parties. Second, in order to punish deviating actors in time and justly, infringements must be detected on a timely basis and must comply with some standards. Third, actors must have a continuous long-term relationship that exceeds the payoffs of opportunistic behaviour. See A. K. Dixit, "*Lawlessness and Economics: Alternative Modes of Governance*", Princeton: Princeton University 2004, p. 60-61.

68 S. Gomtsian, A. Balvert, B. Hock, and O. Kirman, "Between the Green Pitch and the Red Tape: The Private Legal Order of FIFA", *TILEC Discussion Paper* 2017, p. 8, 12.

69 This is because the second category of private ordering is more likely to transgress the bounds of EU Competition law and US Antitrust law. In other words, it is more suitable to research.

2. Market of trust

It does not come as a surprise that under multilateral and repeated transactions, members of an association need to be able to "trust" other members. Reputation[70] is often crucial for the selection of business partners, contractual terms, the structure of a transaction, as well as for determining its price.[71] To be regarded as a reliable and acceptable trading partner that obeys the rules and bylaws of the relevant trade association, membership of an association is a crucial indicator.

Failure to comply with privately designed rules stemming from the relevant association can negatively affect the overall faith bestowed on membership. Consequently, it can hamper the trust placed in that association. Preventing short-term opportunistic behaviour by wrongdoers is imperative. In a market of trust, private-order decision-making can be regarded as a form of governance that yields economic efficiency and lowers transaction costs that is preferable to public-order regimes.[72]

3. Naming and shaming through an information exchange

As explained above, members of a trade association are more likely to conduct business with honest and reliable members when they search for potential trading partners. To punish those members that cheat, within a present-day PLS, a trade association often includes an arbitration clause in its bylaws.[73] This empowers such an institution to impose nonlegal sanctions on a disloyal industry actor for non-payment of an arbitral award. The most common extrajudicial measure relates to the dissemination of the names of industry actors that default on standardized contracts in what

---

70 *Camerer* with respect to modern game theory explains that "*a player's reputation is crisply defined as the probability that she* […] *will take a certain action*". See C. F. Camerer, "*Behavioral Game Theory: Experiments in Strategic Interaction*", Princeton/ Woodstock: Princeton University Press 2003, p. 445.

71 L. Bernstein, "Private Commercial Law in the Cotton Industry: Creating Cooperation Through Rules, Norms, and Institutions", *Michigan Law Review* 2001, p. 7.

72 E. D. Katz, "Private Order and Public Institutions", *Michigan Law Review, Vol. 98, No. 8* 2000, p. 2482.

73 V. Gessner, "*Contractual Certainty in International Trade: Empirical Studies and Theoretical Debates on Institutional Support for Global Economic Exchanges*", in: W. Konradi (red), "The Role of Lex Mercatoria in Supporting Globalised Transactions", Oxford/Portland: Hart Publishing 2009, p. 67.

are known as blacklists and circulates them to other members.[74] Once being placed on a blacklist, wrongdoers that did not adhere to an arbitral award will have great difficulty in conducting trade with a non-blacklisted member. Sometimes even with non-members when the list has been made available to the general public.[75] Publishing the name of a recalcitrant party results in a forfeiture of its reputation. This not only ensures compliance with arbitral awards, it also can be seen as a necessary mechanism to safeguard the success of governance beyond the State-nation.[76] Nonetheless, due to institutional changes in culture, geopolitics and technology, the effectiveness of such a coordinated exchange of information may change.[77]

4. Market where a loss of social standing is important

In small, closed and homogenous markets, business and personal relations of members (*i.e.* natural persons) belonging to a trade association are intertwined.[78] Reputation thus is inherent to the social and business understanding that members have among themselves.[79] Non-conformity with an arbitral award stemming from specialized commercial arbitration not only damages the economic position of the trader, but also its social position and sometimes even the trader's family. Honouring one's agreement can, therefore, be seen as a moral obligation. Violating it will result in a loss of respect. When honest dealing is important in a privately organised market, this may be sufficient to deteriorate the standing of that member in the community altogether.[80]

74 W. Mattli and T. Dietz, "*International Arbitration & Global Governance: Contending Theories and Evidence*", Oxford: Oxford University Press 2014, p. 190.

75 An example is the ICA, which will be discussed in Part 1, Chapter 2, A.

76 W. H. van Boom, I. Giesen, and A. J. Verheij, "*Gedrag en privaatrecht: Over gedragspresumpties en gedragseffecten bij privaatrechtelijke leerstukken*", in: J. van Erp, "Naming en shaming in het contractenrecht? Het reputatie-effect van schadevergoedingen tussen ondernemingen", The Hague: Boom Juridische Uitgevers 2008, p. 166.

77 B. D. Richman, "An Autopsy of Cooperation: Diamond Dealers and the Limits of Trust-based Exchange", *Journal of Legal Analysis, Vol. 9, No. 2* 2017, p. 279.

78 A good example is the DDC, which will be described in Part I, Chapter 2, C.

79 R. C. Post, "The Social Foundations of Defamation Law: Reputation and the Constitution", *California Law Review, Vol. 74, No. 691* 1986, p. 692.

80 K. Binmore, "*Game Theory and the Social Contract: Playing Fair*", Cambridge/London: The MIT Press 1994, p. 112.

Although good faith, fair dealing, integrity and honesty are important for the formation of contracts and ultimately their impact on economic growth, it is debatable whether a loss of social standing also occurs when the members of a trade association are not natural persons but undertakings. This is because a legal entity does "*not possess [...] the capacity for intimate relationships*".[81] Fortunately, a thought-intensive discussion can be put to a halt. Undertakings are represented by natural persons who deal with representatives of other member undertakings. Social shaming in the event of non-conformity with arbitral awards is to a large extent similarly important when only legal persons are involved.

Yet, if a self-policing market is not confined by a homogenous composition of members (*i.e.* close-knit community), but rather by a globally dispersed and changing group of members, loss of social standing in the community is negligible. Wrongdoers, be they natural persons or representatives of undertakings, often do not have any personal relationship with other traders. This truism can be contradicted when parties to a transaction know each other privately. Then, not adhering to an arbitral award can affect both social and business relations.

II. Typology of nonlegal sanctions in present-day PLSs

By failing or refusing to perform an award stemming from specialized commercial arbitration within a present-day PLS, the credibility of the relevant business community is under jeopardy. To prevent this, besides disseminating the names of wrongdoers in a blacklist (Paragraph 1), five others types of nonlegal sanctions are imposed by modern trade associations which operate within present-day PLSs. These are withdrawing membership (Paragraph 2), denying membership for expelled members on the basis of an additional entry barrier (Paragraph 3), refusing to deal with an excluded member (Paragraph 4), entering the premises of wrongdoers without a warrant (Paragraph 5) and limiting adequate access to public courts prior to arbitral proceedings and after an award (Paragraph 6).[82] These

81 E. J. Imwinkelried and R. D. Friedman, "*The New Wigmore: A Treatise on Evidence: Evidentiary Privileges*", Aspen: Aspen Law & Business Publishers 2002, p. 763.

82 Given that the effect of social sanctions declines with the number of violations, it is necessary to guarantee an optimal deterrence. See A. M. Polinsky and S. Shavell, "*Handbook of Law and Economics: Volume 2*", Amsterdam: Elsevier 2007, p. 1604.

types of nonlegal sanctions are codified in the bylaws and rules of trade associations.

1. Blacklisting

A first type of nonlegal sanctioning concerns the practice of blacklisting or disseminating the names of recalcitrant industry actors. As explained above, the very real fear of being blacklisted often warrants compliance with arbitral awards. Damage of an industry actor's reputation as well as a loss of relation-specific advantages caused by being blacklisted are sufficient to draw this conclusion.[83] Not only is the actor's reputation damaged, it will also harm its future business. Repeated transactions with the same member (*i.e.* repeated deal) or other members; sometimes even nonmembers if a blacklist is made publicly available, are more difficult.

In theory and sometimes in practice, the targeted wrongdoer can respond to the increased risk of loss from future dealings. Concessions (*e.g.* offering a higher price) and/or reforms (*e.g.* terminating the employment contract of an individual who was responsible for not complying with an arbitral award) can offset reputational harm.[84] Whether this is true must be reviewed on a case-to-case basis after carefully examining all available information.[85]

---

83 *Charny* considers both types of nonlegal sanctions pertaining to a breach of a commitment. See D. Charny, "Nonlegal Sanctions in Commercial Relationships", *Harvard Law Review* 1993, p. 392-393.

84 Quantifying reputation loss from a breach is not an easy task, as it can be considered unduly speculative and can be skewed towards the future harm done to the blacklisted industry actors without sufficiently taking into account concessions or reforms. Put differently, according to Willis Towers Wadson, "Preserving Your Reputation", *Willis Alert, Issue 17* 2011, p. 3, albeit about the insurance industry, but not less weighty that "*there is no magic potion* [...] *that can repair a damaged reputation*." Figure 1 offers only a simplified view of how to calculate blacklisting-related reputational harm.

85 Combining the cost of lost business and the cost of reforms/concessions to avoid reputational harm can be seen as the "aggregate cost" of reputational damage.

Figure 1: Calculating blacklisting-related reputational harm

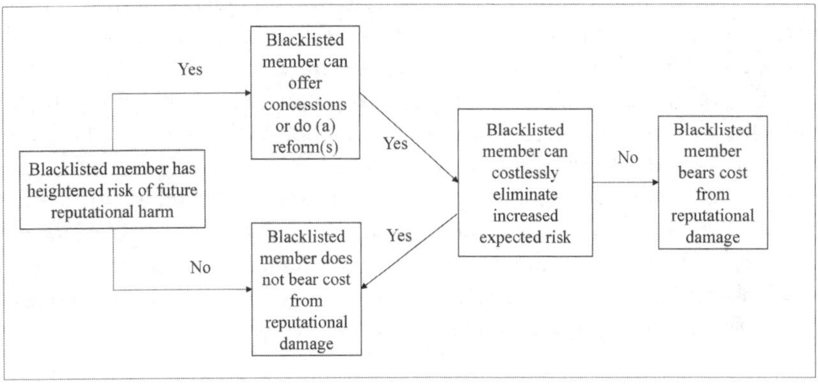

2. Withdrawing membership

A second type of nonlegal sanctioning relates to the termination, removal or withdrawal of membership from a relevant trade association. At first glance, threatening defectors with ostracism may seem like an extreme measure in order to enforce cooperation.[86] Yet, members cooperate because they want to avoid such an extreme punishment.[87] Alienation of an excluded member undertaking not only damages a member's commercial reputation, it also takes away relation-specific advantages for no longer belonging to the relevant trade association.

However, this basic assumption that suggests that withdrawing membership is analogous to business harm can occasionally be negated. Three variables can offset the devastating impact of this type of nonlegal sanctioning. First, the likelihood of survival of the member undertaking after having its membership withdrawn (*i.e.* the corporate longevity of the business). When a member is insolvent, over-indebted, close to bankruptcy or bankrupt and survival of a company is inconceivable in the short- and

86 J. Prüfer, "Business Associations and Private Ordering", *TILEC Discussion Paper* 2012, p. 4.

87 First written proof of social ostracism can be traced back to 500 BC, when Athenians determined whether a member of a community, regularly a former political leader, should be exiled from the city for a period of ten years. This was done by casting votes on shards of clay. See K. D. Williams, "Ostracism", *Annual Review of Psychology* 2007, p. 428.

long-term, being banished will not result in reputational harm.[88] Second, the probability that remaining member and non-member undertakings are willing to conduct business with a banished member (*i.e.* the alacrity or readiness of members and non-members). Third, homogeneity and social standing of the members within the association is a factor that affects reputational harm (*i.e.* the degree of reputational harm). In markets where the business and social lives of members are intertwined, being banished can have far-reaching repercussions. It can disrupt social life and business altogether. Similar to calculating the reputational harm of being blacklisted, measuring damage to reputation after membership has been withdrawn, albeit a more far-reaching coercive measure, must be assessed on a case-by-case basis evaluating all available information.[89]

Figure 2: Calculating withdrawal of membership-related reputational harm

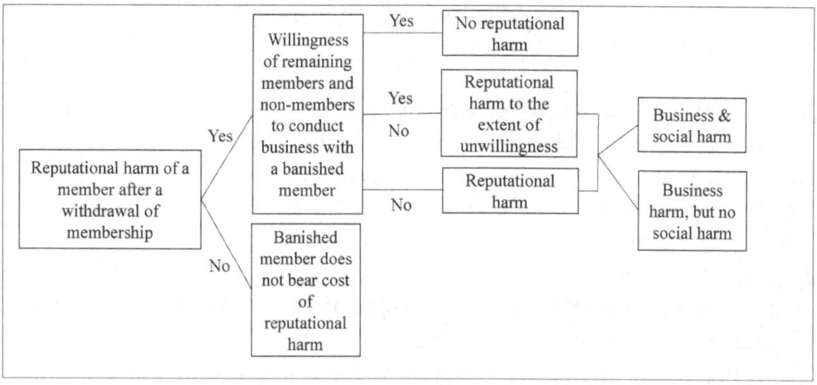

88 An insolvent, over-indebted, close to bankruptcy or bankrupt member undertaking can, when all the requirements in national law are fulfilled, continue to operate its business post-liquidation and post-bankruptcy. However, for the purpose of the first variable, it encompasses only the situation that a member company post-ostracism will not continue its business.

89 Figure 2 provides only a simplified overview of how to assess the extent of reputational harm for an excluded member belonging to a trade association.

3. Denying membership for expelled members on the basis of an additional entry barrier

A third type of nonlegal sanctioning concerns the situation in which an expelled member is denied being re-admitted to membership of a relevant trade association (which withdrew the membership) on the basis of an additional entry barrier. By denying access to the trade association, the industry actor is forestalled from obtaining access to the services of a trade association. Similar to withdrawing membership, denying membership results in alienating the industry actor, which damages its reputational and takes away relationship-specific advantages. Much will depend on calculating the amount of reputational damage on a case-by-case basis.

Figure 3: Calculating denial to reobtain membership-related reputational harm

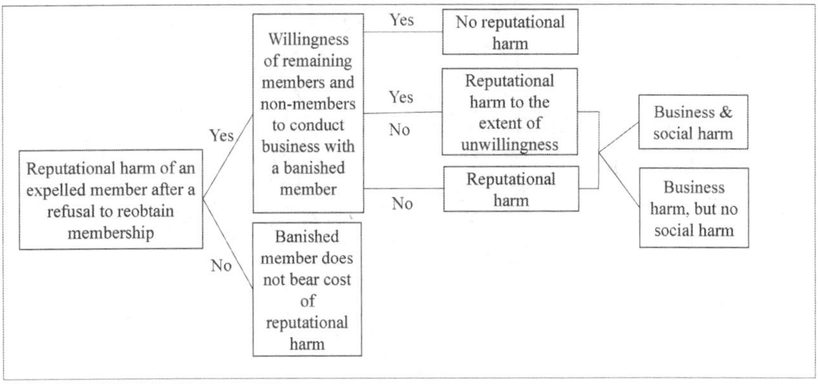

4. Refusing to deal with an expelled member

Sometimes within a legal regime driven predominantly by private legal enforcement, blacklisting and withdrawing membership cannot ensure sufficient deterrence to prevent non-compliance with arbitral awards stemming from specialized commercial arbitration. Alongside both nonlegal sanctions, a trade association can instruct its members to not conduct business with a banished former member.[90] In other words, the fourth type of non-

90 Interestingly, in G. Calliess and P. Zumbransen, "*Rough Consensus and Running Code: A Theory of Transnational Private Law*", Oxford/Portland: Hart Publishing 2010, p. 2110, the authors identify three types of non-enforcement mechanisms:

legal sanctioning can be referred to as refusing to deal with an expelled member.

At first glance it may appear like an extreme measure, perhaps even interchangeable with the term boycott. Notwithstanding this fear, it can serve as an important mechanism not to succumb to the situation in which blacklisting and ostracism appear ineffective. It not only increases the effect of deterrence for not complying with an arbitral award, it also - albeit not completely[91] - closes the gap. Mainly by completely damaging a targeted former member's commercial reputation and taking away all remaining relationship-specific advantages.

Figure 4: Addressing scenarios in which blacklisting and a withdrawal of membership do not achieve sufficient deterrence.

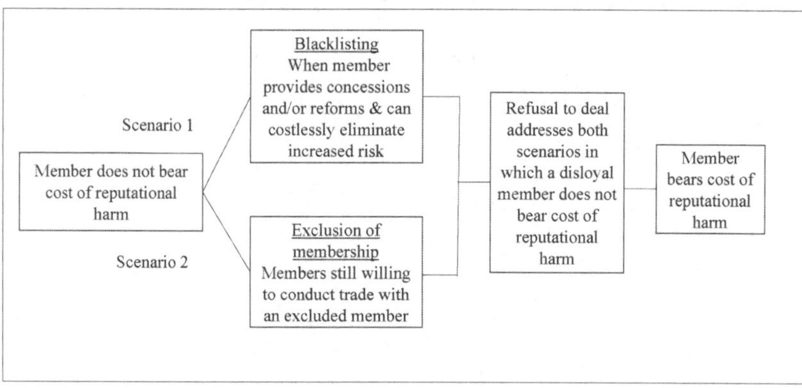

first, a reputation mechanism. Second, an exclusion mechanism. Third, private force or coercion. Whereas the last may refer to, in my opinion, a refusal to contract with an excluded member, the first two kinds of non-enforcement refer to blacklisting and withdrawing membership.

91 When a member is insolvent, over-indebted, close to bankruptcy or bankrupt and survival of a company is inconceivable in the short- and long-term, blacklisting, withdrawing membership and refusing to deal with an ostracized member will not result in reputational harm. However, if the company is active in a market where interpersonal relationships are important, nonlegal sanctioning can still harm the social standing of the persons belonging to the company.

5. Entering the premises of a recalcitrant industry actor

A fifth nonlegal sanction to punish disloyalty by industry actors to satisfy an arbitral award relates to the possibility of a trade association to enter the premises of such an individual or undertaking. Obviously, such a privacy-invasive measure has the potential to harm the industry actor's reputation when other industry actors active in the market become aware of such an activity. Yet, reputational damage is lower when compared to the previously discussed extrajudicial measures.

Figure 5: Calculating entry to the premises of a recalcitrant industry actor-related reputational harm

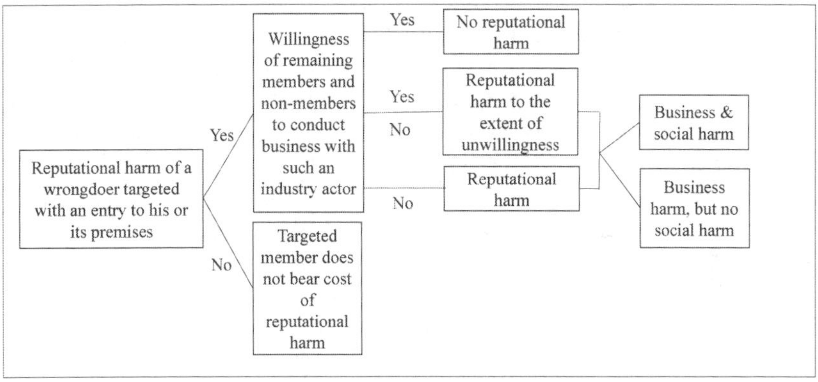

6. Limiting adequate access to public courts prior to arbitral proceedings and after an award

The sixth and final nonlegal sanctioning measure relates to the limiting adequate access to public courts prior to arbitral proceedings and after an award. While this measure is atypical with regard to the previously discussed extrajudicial measures for the reason that it does not inflict reputational harm on a wrongdoer, it produces negative repercussions for disloyal industry actors. Without the possibility of judicial review at a public court, members are coerced into referring a dispute to specialized commercial arbitration and to forego any other review than that provided by a relevant trade association. This has the risk of hampering the business interests of targeted industry actors.

C. Present-day PLSs vs. State-enforced contract law

Public law encompasses everyone and does not empower individuals/companies to choose whether they are bound by it or not. Put differently, law can be considered non-excludable.[92] Yet, in some markets where there is acceptance among participants, the operation of State-supplied law can be ousted.[93] Assessing the reasons under which this occurs is not straightforward and may differ in relation to each industry that relies on privately-tailored rules. Nonetheless, some general characteristics can be identified.

I. Inefficiency of the court system

Perhaps the main reason that explains the existence of present-day PLSs as a substitute for failing public institutions concerns the weaknesses of the court system. In some commercial markets protection against opportunistic behaviour of market participants that are members of a trade association is often so inefficient that compliance at low enforcement costs can only be achieved by resolving conflicts through extrajudicial arbitration.

More precisely, three reasons explain the suboptimal cost of *post facto* remedies offered by public courts: First, the pace of litigation. Because of the lengthy nature of many trials, sometimes caused by appeals that can go as far as putting a halt to or unnecessarily slowing down the decision-making process, for example, when they are frivolous and unavailing, the cost of judicial decision-making is high.[94] Attorneys' fees and expenses also bear

---

92 B. Chaplan, "The Economics of Non-State Legal Systems", *Libertarian Alliance* 1997, p. 13.

93 C. E. Mitchell, "*Contract Law and Contract Practice: Bridging the Gap between Legal Reasoning and Commercial Expectation*", Oxford/Portland: Hart Publishing 2013, p. 30; Under the two-dimensional taxonomy, where there are two types of enforcement strategies, including enforcement through State judicial institutions and private enforcement initiatives that takes place outside the realm of State-supplied law (*i.e.* the formal vs. informal divide), the non-excludability of law is to some extent renounced.

94 J. Dammann and H. Hansmann, "Globalizing Commercial Litigation", *Cornell Law Review, Vol. 94, No. 1* 2008, p. 1. The cost of judicial decision-making varies widely from country to country. "*In some jurisdictions, the courts resolve commercial disputes quickly, fairly, and economically, while in others, they are slow, inefficient, incompetent, biased, or corrupt.*"

evidence to the high cost of litigation.[95] In contrast, specialized commercial arbitration offers more flexible and speedy proceedings that prevent unnecessary delays.[96]

Second, judges of the court often lack the expertise to deal with disputes that arise from a specific industry under review. Put differently, judges often have difficulty in understanding and weighing the evidence and values of a conflict between market participants that are active in a specific industry.[97] As a result, the outcome of a judgment can be uncertain. This surprise effect can to some extent be offset when the relevant judge in the proceeding has specific industry experience and knowledge. Yet, an in-depth understanding of the *operatus modi* by such an individual is an exception rather than a refutation of the presumption that he lacks expertise and know-how.[98] In private dispute resolution, arbitrators are often selected from among market participants and understand the industry much better. Therefore, enforcement costs are more predictable and, as a rule, lower.

Third, even in the (unlikely) event that the result of legal proceedings is a satisfactory judgment, given that commercial trade is often global with market participants dispersed over different countries or regions, recognition of a foreign judgment ("RFJ") is not always possible and may prove costly. Some countries may be unwilling, whereas others make it almost impossible to recognize and enforce such a judgment.[99] Specialized commercial arbitration within a PLS to a large prevents added costs incurred

95 E. Sussman and J. Wilkinson, "Benefits Of Arbitration for Commercial Disputes", *Dispute Resolution Magazine* 2012; Administrative fees of arbitration can also be significant and, in theory and practice, can match those of normal courts. See A. Redfern, and M. Hunter, *"Law and Practice of International Commercial Arbitration"*, London: Sweet & Maxwell 2004, p. 24.

96 C. N. Candlin, *"Discourse and Practice in International Commercial Arbitration: Issues, Challenges, and Prospects"*, London/New York: Routledge 2016, p. 265. While *Candlin* does not talk about specialized commercial arbitration, he talks more generally about the advantages of arbitration in general. Yet, his arguments also have merit with regard to private dispute resolution.

97 Even though a judge can request an expert testimony, he still is responsible for deciding a case on the merits and quantifying the damages that have to be awarded to the claimant. Albeit helpful for the judge, such an expert testimony can increase the duration of the case and, thus, cause considerable delay.

98 Incidental expertise of the judge responsible for a case cannot be expected as a general rule.

99 For example, recognition and enforcement of foreign judgments in China is very limited. If not allowed in arrangements and treaties, the only legal basis for recognizing and enforcing a foreign judgment is when the principle of reciprocity is

from the RFJ beyond its jurisdiction. This is because arbitral awards stemming from such a private mode of dispute resolution do not need to be recognized and enforced by a foreign court when there is a cross-border dispute. Rather, nonlegal sanctions ensure compliance with arbitral awards.

Aside from cost-related reasons, the other main benefit of private enforcement over judicial proceedings and, thus, bearing testimony to the ineffectiveness of the court systems, concerns the confidentiality of arbitral awards stemming from specialized commercial arbitration.[100] Court's publish judgments that include the names of the parties to proceedings as well as the reasons for the conflict on, *inter alia*, the internet. It is possible that trade secrets and/or intellectual property may become publicly available after proceedings, which is harmful for both parties in a conflict. In contrast, in specialized commercial arbitration, parties have complete confidentiality. Hearings are secret, public records are absent and parties control which information may become publicly available. Trade secrets and intellectual property remain confidential.

II. Increased contractual security / Safeguarding the sanctity of contract

A second reason that clarifies the presence of present-day PLSs relates to the failure of formal law to guarantee optimal contractual security. In

---

upheld. See Article 281 of the Mainland CPL. This Article provides that "*After a people's court reviews an application or pleading for the recognition and enforcement of a legally effective judgment or ruling rendered by a foreign court according to the international treaties concludes or acceded to by the PRC or based on the principle of reciprocity, if the court considers that such a judgment or ruling does not contradict the basic principles of the laws of the PRC nor violates the national, social, and public interest of PRC, the court may render a ruling to recognize its force. Where the enforcement is necessary, the court may issue an order to enforce a foreign judgment according to the relevant provisions of this Law, if a legally effective judgment or ruling rendered by a foreign court contradicts the basic principles of the law of the PRC or the national, social, and public interest of PRC, the people's court shall reject the application for recognition and enforcement.*"; Yet, mainland courts have only sporadically used this principle to recognize a foreign judgment. See, *inter alia*, J. Huang "*Interregional Recognition and Enforcement of Civil and Commercial Judgments*", Oxford/Portland: Hart Publishing 2014, p. 58-59.

100 M. J. Block, "The Benefits of Alternate Dispute Resolution for International Commercial and Intellectual Property Disputes", *The Digital Journal of Rutgers School of Law, Vol. 44* 2016, p. 7-8. Albeit not specifically relating to specialized commercial arbitration, confidentiality plays a similar role.

global industries it is crucial that when market participants duly enter into a contract that they honour their obligations. Parties must not be able to escape their contractual obligations, but must keep their bargain (*i.e.* the principle of the sanctity of contract).[101] However, sometimes market participants have an incentive to deviate from or terminate a contract. This is first and foremost to be expected, when entering into a contract with another party brings more benefits (*e.g.* money) than the original contract and the threat of court damages does not offset those benefits.

A hypothetical example would be the market for cotton, in which weather conditions, insect damage, genetics and diseases influence the kilo price.[102] As a result, price fluctuations are not uncommon. When there is a bad cotton harvest, prices will be higher on the ground of scarcity and when there is a good season, prices will be lower due to an (over-)abundance of cotton. By taking into account this general awareness, imagine the scenario where a supplier enters into a futures contract with a distributor (*i.e.* Distributor A), in which the latter agrees to pay € 1,600,000 for 1,000 kilos of cotton that must be collected and paid six months later.[103] While providing a fixed price security for both parties, it is possible that six months later the availability of cotton is so limited owing to a specific disease that the supplier can sell 1,000 kilos of cotton to another distributor (*i.e.* Distributor B) for € 2,200,000 instead. If the expected cost of legal damages would only be € 200,000, the supplier has made a profit of € 400,000.[104]

In other words, in such a scenario public law would be unable to prevent contract deviations and safeguard the principle of the sanctity of contract. To overcome this, nonlegal sanctions made within a PLS would offer

101 P. Mäntysaari, "*The Law of Corporate Finance: General Principles and EU Law - Volume II: Contracts in General*", Berlin/Heidelberg: Springer 2010, p. 159. Generally, a contract is binding.

102 H. Adanacioglu, "The Futures Market in Agricultural Products and an Evaluation of the Attitude of Farmers: A Case Study of Cotton Producers in Aydin Province in Turkey", *New Medit, No. 2* 2011, 58.

103 J. B. Bittman, "*Trading and Hedging with Agricultural Futures and Options*", Hoboken: John Wiley & Sons 2013, p. 2. A futures contracts is a standardized contract between a buyer and a seller to exchange commodities for an agreed-upon price that is not the result of negotiations and is delivered on a specific delivery date.

104 Obviously, it is also possible that the wholesaler deviates from the contract, when the original futures contract with the supplier is less beneficial for him and expected legal damages are lower than conducting business with another supplier for the specific quantity of cotton.

a better protection against contract deviation.[105] Blacklisting, withdrawing membership and refusing to deal predominantly harm the reputation of such a disloyal supplier and are better deterrents. Where public law fails, private legal enforcement steps in.

III. Lower transaction costs

A third reason that rationalizes the setting aside of public law by present-day PLSs has to do with decreased transaction costs. According to *Coase*, in a perfect society without any transaction costs, contracting between participants active in a specific market is efficient and will be unaffected by legal rules.[106] Obviously, the presence of such a utopia can immediately be rebutted because we do not live in a perfect society and transaction costs are to be expected. This is particularly true with regard to obtaining legal redress in public courts. Judicial enforcement is more costly than nonlegal sanctioning, as it requires contractual parties to invest in three and sometimes four[107] different types of transaction costs. First, they must find reliable parties to limit the likelihood of disloyalty (*i.e.* contact costs).[108] Second, they must negotiate and draft a contract (*i.e.* contracting costs). Third, after an agreement enters into force they must *ex post* monitor compliance

---

105 Such a focus to change the strategic environment by inducing market participants to behave in a desired way, so that the resulting equilibrium behaviour is efficient is called "contract theory".

106 For a discussion of the Coase Theorem and its understanding by other authors, see B. Bouckaert and G. de Geest, "*Encyclopedia of Law and Economics, Volume I. The History and Methodology of Law and Economics*", in: S. G. Medema (ed), R. O. Zerbe, "The Coase Theorem", Cheltenham: Edward Elgar 2000, p. 837-838.

107 The fourth and last transaction cost concerns the resolution of a dispute after a breach of contract, which is not always necessary.

108 C. Kirchner and A. Picot, "Transaction Cost Analysis of Structural Changes in the Distribution System: Reflections on Institutional Developments in the Federal Republic of Germany", *Journal of Institutional and Theoretical Economics, Vol. 143* 1987, p. 64; For the interested reader: a categorization of transaction costs was first discussed by *Williamson*. He explained that transaction costs consist of *ex-ante* costs (*i.e.* the costs of negotiating and drafting a contract) and *ex-post* costs (*i.e.* the costs of policing and enforcing the contract after disloyalty). See O. E. Williamson, "*The Economic Institutions of Capitalism*", New York: Macmillan 1985, p. 20; S. Wengler, "*Key Account Management in Business-to-Business Markets: An Assessment of Its Economic Value*", Berlin: Deutscher Universitäts-Verlag 2006, p. 112. Yet, *Williamson* fails to give a clear definition of what can be understood under the term transaction costs.

with its terms (*i.e.* monitoring costs). Fourth, in the event of a breach of contract disputes must be resolved (*i.e.* resolution costs).

Despite these transaction costs within a PLS also being relevant, they are significantly lower. Because of nonlegal sanctioning market participants can more easily select business partners with a good reputation or standing belonging to the same trade association. Notwithstanding, they still bear the risk of disloyalty in the event they contract with parties that are not members of a trade association. With regard to *ex post* monitoring costs, the transaction costs within the public legal system and within a PLS are comparable. Resolution costs to resolve disputes, on the other hand, are more cost-efficient and expeditious in private commercial arbitration.

IV. Lower distribution costs

Lower prices for end-users in the wake of decreased distribution costs is a last reason to explain the manifestation and appearance of present-day PLSs. On the grounds that PLSs benefit market participants in certain commercial industries by offering a more efficient mechanism to resolve contract disputes, contractual security is higher and transaction costs are lower compared to the situation absent such a system. As a result, the costs incurred to deliver a product to end-users will decrease (*i.e.* distribution costs). Not only will those individuals benefit from lower prices, the market participants will also benefit more. This is because demand will be higher owing to lower prices.[109]

109 B. Atkinson and S. John, "*Studying Economics*", Basingstoke/New York: Palgrave Macmillan 2001, p. 9. This statement is rather a general assumption and can occasionally be rebutted. Under which this is possible will not be discussed, as it will require a long discussion by taking into account a comprehensive economic analysis, supported by algebraic calculations.

Chapter 2: Examples of Present-day PLSs in which Private-enforcement / Nonlegal Sanctioning Ensures Compliance

A. *Introduction*

In the current legal and political environment in some industries, State-supplied commercial law proves to be an insufficient deterrent. *Morgan* suggests that operational PLSs can be detected in over 50 industries.[110] Globally, but also domestically, private enforcement as a low-cost substitute for commercial laws promulgated by a State legislature can be found in the diamond, cotton, grain, feed, rice, peanut, rubber, hay, tea, burlap, printing and independent film industry. This is done by setting up trade associations in which trade rules (that apply to all members and even non-members when this code of behaviour is chosen to govern a contract) are defined and codified and enforced through specialized commercial tribunals.

As the success of such specialized commercial arbitration largely depends on nonlegal sanctions, this Chapter investigates how compliance with arbitral awards is guaranteed. To answer this question, six cases of successful commercial trade associations are presented: (i) the ICA (Paragraph B); (ii) the DDC (Paragraph C); (iii) GAFTA (Paragraph D); (iv) the FCC (Paragraph E); (v) the LME (Paragraph F); and (vi) FOSFA (Paragraph G). These cases were chosen because of the detailed insight they provide into six different industries. More specifically, three reasons can substantiate such a selection: first, the chosen trade associations operate in markets where nonlegal sanctioning is most obvious. Second, the trade rules provided by these trade associations form the basis of the usual business between industry actors in each relevant commodities industry. Third, the trade associations represent the largest number of members that are active within specific commodities industries as opposed to other trade associations.

---

110 J. Morgan, "*Contract Law Minimalism: A Formalist Restatement of Commercial Contract Law*", Cambridge/ New York: Cambridge University Press 2013, p. 208.

To understand how nonlegal sanctioning in each relevant trade association works, it is insufficient to merely give a brief taxonomy of private enforcement. This Chapter adopts the following structure: first, a detailed overview/characterization of the industry is given for each trade association (Paragraph B-H, I). Second, the types of nonlegal sanctions specific to each trade association in order to enforce arbitral contracts stemming from specialized commercial arbitration are described (Paragraph B-H, II). Third, the rationale of nonlegal sanctioning pertaining to each trade association is explained (Paragraph B-H, III).

B. The International Cotton Association

I. Background

1. History

Because raw cotton could not be grown in the British Isles, it needed to be imported from distant (semi-) tropical suppliers. This process of importation started in the late 18th and early 19th century, in particular in the seaport of Liverpool. [111] During this time, Liverpool became the largest cotton market as well the major port in which merchants sold this type of raw material to spinners.[112]

To safeguard the interests of traders and to regulate the market, bodies that represent the interests of these persons needed to be established. Consequently, the Liverpool Cotton Brokers Association was founded in 1841 despite some form of cooperation having already existed prior to this

111 Historic Society of Lancashire and Cheshire, "*Transactions of the Historic Society of Lancashire and Cheshire*", in: N. Hall (ed) "A 'Quaker Confederation'? The great Liverpool cotton speculation of 1825 reconsidered", Liverpool: Historic Society of Lancashire and Cheshire, Vol. 151 2002, p. 1.

112 Historic Society of Lancashire and Cheshire, "*Transactions of the Historic Society of Lancashire and Cheshire*", in: N. Hall (ed) "The Liverpool Cotton Market: Britain's First Futures Market", Liverpool: Historic Society of Lancashire and Cheshire, Vol. 149, 2000, p. 99; Yet, the manufacture of cotton stagnated in all of the UK as well as in Europe. For example, it took 67 years to double the annual amount of cotton used in clothes to 3.87 million pounds. In the USA, this was the daily amount supplied to spinners. See S. Beckert, "*Empire of Cotton: A Global History*", New York: Vintage Books 2014, p. 40.

date.[113] The initial success of the association was founded on two main reasons: first, it gave merchants who sought membership access to facilities and, second, it protected them against unfair competition. Unfortunately, despite these benefits, merchants faced three major inconveniences. First, due to the laying of the transatlantic telegraph cable, some brokers dealt directly with traders in the United States.[114] Second, all cotton needed to go through a clearinghouse, which caused delays. Third, merchants who wanted to important cotton needed to pay 1% commission to brokers when they wanted to hedge their trades. These disadvantages resulted in some quarrels between merchants and brokers which in 1881 led to the formation of a rival association, namely the Liverpool Cotton Exchange.[115] One year later, since having two separate associations was rather ineffective, both associations merged into the ICA.[116] Even though the ICA was closed from 1946 to 18 May 1954 and despite its shares being sold in 1963 and again in 1964, it took up residence in its current offices in Liverpool in 1967.

2. Legal form

Ever since February 1963 and under the current Companies Act 2006[117], the ICA is a "private limited company by guarantee" with membership open for individuals and limited companies that are engaged in the cotton

113 S. Alford, J. Barrow, and S. J. D. Nigel Hall, "*Northern History*", in: N. Hall (ed), "The governance of the Liverpool raw cotton market, c. 1840-1914", Abingdon: Taylor & Francis, Vol. 153, Is. 1, 2016, p. 98; Even though the date of establishment of the Liverpool Cotton Brokers Association is vague, it is generally accepted that it was formed in 1841. See T. Ellison, "*The Cotton Trade of Great Britain: including a history of the Liverpool cotton market and of the Liverpool Cotton Brokers' Association*", London: Effingham Wilson 1886, p. 181–182.

114 P. Norman, "*The Risk Controllers: Central Counterparty Clearing in Globalised Financial* Markets", Chichester: John Wiley & Sons 2011, p. 60.

115 W. O. Henderson, "*The Lancashire Cotton Famine 1861 - 65*", New York: Augustus M. Kelley 1969, p. 34.

116 J. A. Todd, "*The cotton world: a survey of the world's cotton supplies and consumption*", London: Sir I. Pitman & Sons 1927, p. 91.

117 Since 2006 the law to incorporate a limited company can be found in Part 2 of the Companies Act 2006 (to access: http://www.legislation.gov.uk/ukpga/2006/46/pdfs/ukpga_20060046_en.pdf).

trade.[118] This implies that the ICA has legal identity and that its members are protected against legal liability for the association.[119] However, even though full liability is excluded, in the course of liquidation each member is still liable for the nominal amount it has agreed to pay (*i.e.* the guarantee).[120] Other characteristics of the ICA as a "private limited company by guarantee" include the absence of a fixed number of members[121] and for the major reason that payment of the guarantee is postponed on the operation on a not-for-profit basis.[122]

3. Institutional structure

The ICA is divided into three branches: the legislative (*i.e.* the Annual General Meeting), the executive (*i.e.* the Board of Directors), and the judicial (*i.e.* the Arbitration Tribunal). The Annual General Meeting as stipulated in Bylaw 100(6) of the ICA Bylaws and Rules (2018) is a meeting of individual members to elect the ordinary directors belonging to the Board of Directors on a yearly basis (Bylaw 100(5) of the ICA Bylaws and Rules (2018)).[123] Their competence is to manage the ICA on a daily and active basis. In addition, the members choose the associate directors, whose main task is to represent the interests and concerns of all international members belonging to the ICA.[124]

After the Board of Directors is installed, the directors then elect the President as well as the First and the Second Vice President (Bylaw 100(5) of

---

118 J. Roche, "*The International Cotton Trade*", Cambridge: Woodhead Publishing 1994, p. 17.

119 J. Clarke, "*Managing Better: Becoming a Limited Company*", Dublin: Combat Poverty Agency 1996, p. 2.

120 Part 1, Article 3 (3) of the Companies Act 2006; Limited liability for the members of the ICA is established in Article 5 of the Articles of Association of the International Cotton Association (to access: https://www.ica-ltd.org/wp-content/uploads/2018/10/Articles_Nov2018.pdf).

121 Article 110 of the Articles of Association of the International Cotton Association.

122 J. Clarke, "*Managing Better: Becoming a Limited Company*", Dublin: Combat Poverty Agency 1996, p. 2; J. Law, "*A Dictionary of Law*", Oxford: Oxford University Press 2015, p. 371.

123 Bylaws and Rules of the International Cotton Association Limited of 2018 (to access: https://www.ica-ltd.org/media/layout/documents/rulebooks/2018-11-rulebook-en.pdf).

124 https://www.ica-ltd.org/about-ica/our-board/.

the ICA Bylaws and Rules (2018)) who have the same competences (Bylaw 104) and elect committees and their Chairmen (Bylaw 407 of the ICA Bylaws and Rules (2018)). These committees discuss various topics of importance in the transnational cotton industry. The third layer that completes the organizational governance within the ICA concerns the Arbitration Tribunal and can be found in Sections 3 and 4 of the ICA Bylaws and Rules (2018). This disciplinary procedure is thoroughly discussed in Paragraph 5.

Figure 6: Institutional structure within the ICA

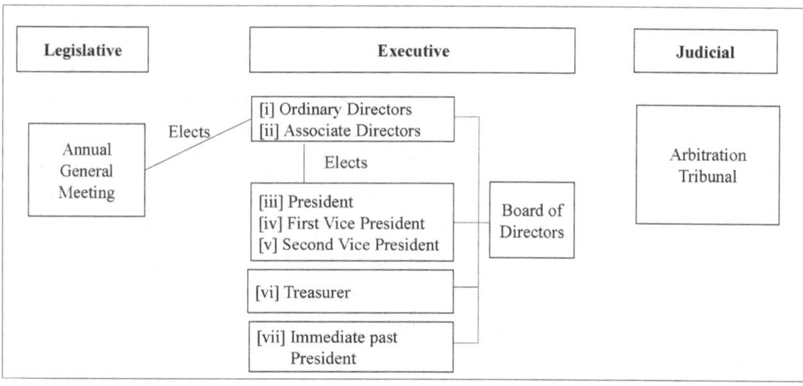

4. Membership

According to the website of the ICA, the association has more than 550 members internationally and perceives itself as the world's leading international trade organisation and arbitration provider in the international cotton trade.[125] As can also be seen on the association's website, members are divided into two classes.[126] The first class comprises private individual members or natural persons.[127] The second class includes member companies that, according to Bylaw 100(21) of the ICA Bylaws and Rules

125 https://www.ica-ltd.org/about-ica/.
126 See also Article 1 of the Articles of Associations of the International Cotton Association.
127 Currently there are 238 private individual members. See https://www.ica-ltd.org/safe-trading/member-search/.

(2018) fall within one of the following five categories.[128] The first category concerns a "principal firm", which includes firms that are merchants, producers or mills and are registered as such under the Bylaws (Bylaws 100(24) and 405(1) of the ICA Bylaws and Rules (2018)). The second category encompasses an "association member firm", which comprises producers or mills that are also members of an affiliated association related to the cotton industry that declared its support of the Bylaws and principles of the ICA (Bylaw 405(4) and (5) of the ICA Bylaws and Rules (2018)). The third category includes an "affiliate industry firm", which signifies a company or organisation that provides a service to the cotton trade and is registered as such under the Bylaws (Bylaws 100(17) and 405(2) of the ICA Bylaws and Rules (2018)). The fourth category entails an "agent firm" that brings a principal firm into contractual relationships with other parties and is registered as such under the Bylaws (Bylaws 100(18) and 405(3) of the ICA Bylaws and Rules (2018)). The last category is the company related to a principal firm or an affiliate firm (*i.e.* a "related firm") (Bylaw 100(29) of the ICA Bylaws and Rules (2018)).

Following this taxonomy, one can draw the conclusion that membership is open for almost all individual persons and firms that at least have some connection to the cotton industry. Yet, granting membership is not straightforward. Each firm seeking membership needs to comply with Articles 6 to 17 of the Articles of Association of the ICA and Bylaws 400 to 405 of the ICA Bylaws and Rules (2018). Following these rules, a potential member that has a connection with the cotton industry and that falls within the above described definition of membership needs to fulfil three additional requirements prior to being accepted.[129] First, the potential member must be proposed by two members of the ICA (Article 13.1 of the Articles

128 Currently there are 324 member firms. See https://www.ica-ltd.org/safe-trading/member-search/.

129 For historic reference only, at a meeting on 18 February 1841 *Messrs*, *Clare* and *Gill* proposed the following resolution that was accepted unanimously: "*no individual shall be admitted a member of the Association unless he shall have served an apprenticeship as a broker in an office where the cotton brokerage business is carried on, or have been in business at this port for three years at the least as a cotton broker, and unless such individual shall be proposed and seconded in the usual manner after one week's notice having been given, and the meeting generally by a majority thereof approves him as a member.* [...] *That in future no individual shall have a right of membership in consequence of his being taken into partnership by any existing member, and that those individuals only who have the management of the cotton department in concerns carrying business as general brokers, are eligible as members, being duly elected, or being already members of the Association*". See T. Ellison, "*The cot-*

of Association of the ICA) that are both resident in different countries (Article 13.3 of the Articles of Association of the ICA) without being a member within the same firm as the candidate (Article 13.2 of the Articles of Association of the ICA). If a potential member cannot find two members, the President of the ICA may second as a *locum tenens* (Article 13.4 of the Articles of Association of the ICA). An application requesting membership can be rejected when a member has filed objections to the application within a six-day deadline following the application for membership, unless directors overturn the disapproval (Articles 16 and 17 of the Articles of Association of the ICA). Second, the potential member firm must provide information to the directors of the ICA, including the constitution, capital and nature of the firm (Article 15 of the Articles of Association of the ICA). Third, the potential member must pay a registration fee (Bylaw 404(1) of the ICA Bylaws and Rules (2018) and Article 38.1 of the Articles of Association of the ICA).

5. Specialized commercial arbitration

a. A dichotomy of arbitration forms

In addition to maintaining trading rules, the ICA provides a well-organised system of specialized commercial arbitration after a dispute arises. In fact, it provides two forms of arbitration.[130] The first concerns "quality arbitration" for disputes arising from the manual examination of the quality of cotton and/or erroneous quality characteristics that can only be determined by "instrument testing" (Bylaw 300(1) of the ICA Bylaws and Rules (2018)). The second form pertains to "technical arbitration" and addresses all other non-quality disputes when the value of a dispute is above $75,000 (Bylaw 300(1) of the ICA Bylaws and Rules (2018)). In the event a disputes falls below this monetary sum, "small claims technical arbitration" is applicable (Bylaw 316(1) of the ICA Bylaws and Rules (2018)). Both forms of

---

ton trade of Great Britain: including a history of the Liverpool cotton market and of the Liverpool Cotton Brokers' Association", London: Effingham Wilson 1886, p. 184. This illustrates that already in the 19th century some extra requirement needed to be met by potential members in order to gain membership of the ICA.

130 https://www.ica-ltd.org/arbitration/.

arbitration are available to members of the ICA, but also to non-members that contracted under the ICA Bylaws and Rules (2018).[131]

b. Selection of arbitrators

i. Quality arbitration

The arbitration tribunal of the ICA with regard to quality arbitration is normally composed of two arbitrators (Bylaw 331(1) of the ICA Bylaws and Rules (2018)), one selected by the claimant and one by the defendant (Bylaw 332(3) of the ICA Bylaws and Rules (2018)), unless the parties to the conflict unanimously agree that one arbitrator is sufficient to offer redress (Bylaw 332(1) of the ICA Bylaws and Rules (2018)). More specifically, the claimant must propose an arbitrator to the defendant, either by informing the defendant that it wishes to have a sole arbitrator (Bylaw 332(1) of the ICA Bylaws and Rules (2018)) or not (Bylaw 333 of the ICA Bylaws and Rules (2018)).[132] In the event of choosing only one arbitrator, the defendant can within a timeframe of 14 days either accept (by acquiescence) the sole arbitrator or appoint a second arbitrator (Bylaws 332(1) and 334 of the ICA Bylaws and Rules (2018)). The selection of this person must then be accepted (by acquiescence) or rejected within a timeframe of seven days (Bylaws 332(2) and 335(1) of the ICA Bylaws and Rules (2018)). If the claimant does not ask the defendant to nominate a sole arbitrator, the defendant also has 14 days to nominate a second arbitrator and, following such selection, the claimant again has seven days to file reasoned objections (Bylaws 333 and 335(1) of the ICA Bylaws and Rules (2018)). Provided that a party fails to nominate or find a replacement, the President of the

131 In quality arbitration non-members must also apply for arbitration (Bylaw 330(1) of the ICA Bylaws and Rules (2018)). In relation to technical arbitration such requirement seems non-existent. However, it is likely that non-members must also register for arbitration (Bylaw 330(1) of the ICA Bylaws and Rules (2018) by analogy).

132 Choosing an arbitrator must be a well-contemplated choice, as arbitrators can adjudicate based on their political ideology and/or any other bias and may act in self-interest to further their career. See P. Nunnenkamp, "Short Note: Biased Arbitrators and Tribunal Decisions Against Developing Countries: Stylized Facts on Investor-state Dispute Settlement", *Journal of International Development* 2017, p. 851. Whereas *Nunnenkamp* makes these truisms with regard to international investment arbitration, in my opinion, they also apply to specialized commercial arbitration.

ICA can nominate a substitute arbitrator (Bylaw 335(2) of the ICA Bylaws and Rules (2018)). As a prerequisite, a period of 14 days following a notice of that intention must have elapsed (Bylaw 335(3) of the ICA Bylaws and Rules (2018)). However, either party can appeal this intention to the Board of Directors within seven days of that timeframe (Bylaw 336(4) of the ICA Bylaws and Rules (2018)).

After two arbitrators are confirmed and contingent upon disagreement, both parties have 21 days to appoint a referee to resolve the dispute (Bylaws 331(2) and 336(3) of the ICA Bylaws and Rules (2018) by analogy).[133] Interestingly, to be selected as a referee or an arbitrator, a person must be a member of the ICA (Bylaw 331(3) of the ICA Bylaws and Rules (2018)) who has successfully completed the basic level examination and advanced training that focuses on contract law and the Sales of Good Act 1979, arbitral issues and application of the Arbitration Act 1996 to the cotton market.[134] There is no prohibition on lawyers being selected as an arbitrator. For non-members of the ICA that contract under the Bylaws of the ICA with members of this association, this rule places them at a disadvantage, because they are often more unfamiliar with members that can offer arbitration as opposed to members of the ICA.

In appeal, the case is heard by a Quality Appeal Committee, consisting of two, but not more than four, members who are considered the most qualified (Bylaw 352(4) of the ICA Bylaws and Rules (2018)). These arbitrators are selected by the chairman and deputy chairman of the Quality Appeal Panel.

ii. Technical arbitration

Disputes, when contracting under the Bylaws of the ICA, that are of a non-quality nature are normally heard by an arbitration tribunal consisting of three arbitrators, unless both parties agree that a single arbitrator (*i.e.* qualified arbitrator) is sufficient to resolve the difference of opinions between the claimant and the defendant (Bylaw 303 of the ICA Bylaws and Rules

133 Bylaw 336(3) of the ICA Bylaws and Rules (2018) enables the President of the ICA to revoke an appointment and appoint an alternative arbitrator, when two arbitrators do not appoint a referee within 21 days after being appointed. In analogy to this rule, a referee must be selected within the 21-day timeframe following disagreement.

134 https://www.ica-ltd.org/advanced-level-arbitrator-training/; https://www.ica-ltd.org/basic-level-arbitrator-training/.

(2018)). In more detail, the claimant has the right to appoint an arbitrator or to propose a sole arbitrator and the defendant must then within a timeframe of 14 days either appoint a second arbitrator or agree to a sole arbitrator (Bylaw 304 (1)). Within seven days after selecting the second arbitrator, the ICA will appoint a third arbitrator who is selected from the members of the ICA Arbitration Strategy Committee (Bylaw 304(2) of the ICA Bylaws and Rules (2018)).[135] In the event that either party has failed to nominate an arbitrator or find a replacement, the ICA will select an arbitrator to fill the vacancy (Bylaw 304(7) of the ICA Bylaws and Rules (2018)). Similarly, as compared to quality arbitration, the arbitrators must be qualified members of the ICA under the standards set by the Board of Directors (Bylaw 304(4) of the ICA Bylaws and Rules (2018)). Also here, lawyers are not barred from acting as an arbitrator. Obviously, this raises a similar burden for non-members of the ICA that contract under the association's Bylaws as compared to quality arbitration, since they are often unfamiliar with the arbitrators. In appeal, the appeal committee is composed of a Chairman, who is selected from the ICA Arbitration Strategy Committee and four other arbitrators (Bylaw 314(4) of the ICA Bylaws and Rules (2018)).

c. Choice of tribunal and jurisdiction of arbitration tribunals

i. Quality arbitration

Quality arbitration is held at the place which the parties to the agreement contracting under the Bylaws of the ICA opted for (Bylaw 33(1) of the ICA Bylaws and Rules (2018)). When such consensus is absent, the arbitration tribunal will be held at the arbitration room of the ICA in Liverpool. Notwithstanding the place of arbitration, any arbitral awards rendered by a tribunal that is in conformity with the applicable procedural rules drafted in the Bylaws of the ICA is stamped and made effective in Liverpool (Bylaw 338(3) of the ICA Bylaws and Rules (2018)). Although a choice of

135 P. Šarčević, *"Essays on International Commercial Arbitration"*, London/Dordrecht/Boston: Graham & Trotman/Martinus Nijhoff 1989, p. 69. In technical arbitration the third arbitrator is not a referee. This is because in arbitration with a referee (such as in line with quality arbitration) two arbitrators try to reach a decision and only if they are deadlocked, may the tribunal be supplemented by a third arbitrator. This is different from a tribunal consisting of three arbitrators from the outset.

tribunal is not mentioned in the Bylaws of the ICA pertaining to instrument testing, the same rule applies regarding quality arbitration.

When ascertaining the jurisdiction of the quality arbitration tribunal to resolve conflicts deriving from agreements formed in connection with the Bylaws of the ICA, English law is applicable (Bylaw 200 of the ICA Bylaws and Rules (2018)). In more detail, the arbitrators (and when relevant the referee) may decide on jurisdiction of a case (Bylaw 340 of the ICA Bylaws and Rules (2018)).[136] The only condition is that there is a valid consensus *ad idem* between two parties to sign an agreement under the terms and conditions of the Bylaws.[137] Jurisdiction may only be denied if either party substantiates evidence that such an agreement does not refer to quality arbitration, but rather technical arbitration (Bylaw 341(1) of the ICA Bylaws and Rules (2018)). Subsequently, unless parties agree otherwise, arbitration will take the latter form.

ii. Technical arbitration

Unfortunately, the ICA does not include any provision that clarifies the place of arbitration with regard to technical arbitration. Yet, it seems apparent that this form of arbitration will be held at the place that both parties that entered into an agreement under the Bylaws of the ICA have agreed to (Bylaw 338(1) of the ICA Bylaws and Rules (2018) by analogy). In the absence of a common intention, technical arbitration is held in the arbitration room of the ICA in Liverpool (Bylaw 338(3) of the ICA Bylaws and Rules (2018) by analogy).

With regard to claiming jurisdiction, any technical arbitration tribunal constituted under the Bylaws of the ICA may claim authority to scrutinize whether an agreement is valid, what matters have been submitted and if the tribunal was correctly established (Bylaw 306 of the ICA Bylaws and Rules (2018)). As a condition, English law must be complied with (Bylaw 200 of the ICA Bylaws and Rules (2018)).

---

136 J. D. M. Lew, L. A. Mistelis, and S. M. Kröll, "*Comparative International Commercial Arbitration*", The Hague/London/New York: Kluwer Law International 2003, p. 332. Obviously, by including such a broad competence, recalcitrant parties are prevented from contesting the existence or validity or a choice of governing law, thereby forestalling considerable delays.

137 P. E. Nygh, "*Autonomy in International Contracts*", Oxford: Oxford University Press 1999, p. 92.

d. Procedure

i. Quality arbitration

Before quality arbitration can be commenced, it must, first, be established whether such a proceeding pertains to quality arbitration based on manual examination of cotton or instrument testing. The basis for ascertaining this is the inclusion of a clause in the agreement between the parties (Bylaw 222(3) of the ICA Bylaws and Rules (2018)). However, in the absence of an explicit insertion, quality arbitration "*will be conducted on the basis of samples and decided by manual examination for grade and staple, unless both parties agree in writing to accept instrument testing*" (Bylaw 339(1) of the ICA Bylaws and Rules (2018)). With regard to manual classification, it can be initiated when (i) an application is made to the ICA and is accepted by this association, unless an application is unnecessary; (ii) the requesting firm/person informs the receiving firm/person of its intention to start arbitration proceedings; and (iii) the requesting firm/person selects an arbitrator/sole arbitrator (Bylaw 329(1) of the ICA Bylaws and Rules (2018)). After fulfilling these formalities, the defendant must complete the tribunal by either accepting (by acquiescence) the sole arbitrator or name a second arbitrator.[138] Notwithstanding the number of arbitrators, the tribunal must then resolve the conflict on the basis of all evidence presented by the parties as well as their interpretation of the law and by taking into account the Bylaws of the ICA. Where a sole arbitrator rules in favour of either party, or two arbitrators reach a decision, or a referee decides in favour of either party after an arbitral deadlock, an arbitral award is rendered which is analogous to a court judgment (Bylaw 350 of the ICA Bylaws and Rules (2018)).[139]

For instrument testing, on the other hand, a conflict is decided solely on the basis of test reports (Bylaw 339(2) of the ICA Bylaws and Rules (2018)).[140] The reports are final, unless the parties: (i) disagree on the place

---

138 For a complete analysis of how the quality arbitration tribunal is formed, see Part I, Chapter 2, B, I, 5, b, i.

139 V. K. Bhatia, G. Garzone, and C. Degano, "*Arbitration Awards: Generic Features and Textual Realisations*", Newcastle upon Tyne: Cambridge Scholars Publishing 2012, p. 177. The outcome of an arbitration tribunal is an award even if the award is of a non-monetary nature and/or the tribunal decides in favour of or against the claims of the claimant.

140 Instrument testing is final once the steps laid down in Bylaws 224 and 233 of the ICA Bylaws and Rules (2018) are complied with.

of testing; (ii) have not negotiated to pay a fixed sum nor paid that amount within 14 days after the report has been issued; and/or (iii) disagree on the interpretation of the test report (Bylaw 339(2) of the ICA Bylaws and Rules (2018)). Then, the arbitrators will make an award in accordance with Bylaw 350. Normally, the award publicizes the names of the firms in the dispute, the names of the arbitrators and, when relevant, of the referee, unless both parties opt for anonymous quality arbitration (Bylaw 349 of the ICA Bylaws and Rules (2018)). Importantly, an award rendered in quality arbitration can be appealed before the Quality Appeal Committee.

ii. Technical arbitration

To initiate technical arbitration, the requesting firm/person must (i) send a written request to the ICA (Bylaw 302(1) of the ICA Bylaws and Rules (2018)); (ii) select an arbitrator or sole arbitrator (Bylaw 30 (2) of the ICA Bylaws and Rules (2018)); and (iii) wait for the ICA to send a copy of the written application to the defendant (Bylaw 302(3) of the ICA Bylaws and Rules (2018)). With that said, as an entry requirement, the total value of the dispute must exceed $75,000. If this fixed sum is not reached, small claims technical arbitration is available (Bylaw 316(1) of the ICA Bylaws and Rules (2018)). This entails that arbitration proceedings will be adjudicated by a sole arbitrator appointed by the ICA (Bylaw 316(2) of the ICA Bylaws and Rules (2018)).[141]

In contrast, when the threshold mentioned above is met the defendant must, *inter alia*, agree to the sole arbitrator proposed by the claimant, or name a second arbitrator followed by the selection of a third arbitrator by the ICA to complete the arbitration tribunal.[142] For the tribunal to reach a swift outcome, it is pivotal that the parties provide information regarding procedural and evidential matters expeditiously (Bylaw 307a(4) of the ICA Bylaws and Rules (2018)) and in the English language (Bylaw 307a(7) of the ICA Bylaws and Rules (2018)). When a tribunal reaches a decision, a technical arbitral award will be issued (Bylaw 309(1) of the ICA Bylaws

141 For the complete set of rules pertaining to small claims technical arbitration, see Bylaws 316 to 328 of the ICA Bylaws and Rules (2018). In my opinion, this form of arbitration is interesting, but will bring more unnecessary complexity to understanding the arbitration system of the ICA. Hence, it will not be thoroughly discussed in this Chapter.

142 For a complete analysis of how the quality arbitration tribunal is formed, see Part I, Chapter 2, B, I, 5, b, ii.

and Rules (2018)). This award can be appealed before an appeal committee (Bylaw 312(1) of the ICA Bylaws and Rules (2018)).

e. The finality of arbitration or the possibility of (some) legal redress in public courts according to the association

i. Quality arbitration

The outcome of quality arbitration is the issuance of an award in writing, which does not state the reasons why the potential dispute was dealt with in such manner (Bylaw 350(2) of the ICA Bylaws and Rules (2018)). An award stemming from this form of arbitration will be treated as having been made in England irrespective of where the proceedings took place, or where the award was sent, delivered, or signed (Bylaw 350(4) of the ICA Bylaws and Rules (2018)). Yet, five conditions have to be complied with: first, the award must be stamped by the ICA on the date of issuance (Bylaw 350(5) and (6) of the ICA Bylaws and Rules (2018)). Second, the parties must be notified post-stamping (Bylaw 350(7) of the ICA Bylaws and Rules (2018)). Third, any outstanding (stamping) fees, costs and expenses must be paid (Bylaw 350(8) of the ICA Bylaws and Rules (2018)). Fourth, each party must receive an original hardcopy version of the award and a PDF copy by email (Bylaw 350(9) of the ICA Bylaws and Rules (2018)). Five, the deadline for lodging an appeal as stated in the arbitral award has expired (Bylaw 352(1) of the ICA Bylaws and Rules (2018)) or involves a dispute over the cost of arbitration (Bylaw 352(3) of the ICA Bylaws and Rules (2018)).[143]

When all the conditions are fulfilled, the quality arbitration award becomes final and has *res judicata effect* (*i.e.* not open to arbitral appeal).[144] By accepting the Bylaws of the ICA, both parties in a dispute waive their right

143 Any appeal is heard by a Quality Appeal Committee consisting of a maximum of four but no less than two members selected by the chairman and deputy chairman of the Quality Appeal Panel (Bylaw 352(4) of the ICA Bylaws and Rules (2018)). The task of this panel is to install the Quality Appeal Committee annually. Importantly, the Quality Appeal Committee must give an opinion and re-assess the quality of the cotton and when relevant instrument testing (Bylaw 353(1) of the ICA Bylaws and Rules (2018)).

144 A. Redfern and M. Hunter, "*Law and Practice of International Commercial Arbitration*", London: Sweet & Maxwell 2004, p. 387. An arbitral award has three aspects of *res judicata*: first, it can put a halt to existing disputes between the par-

to lodge an appeal to the English High Court under Section 69 of the Arbitration Act 1996 for all questions arising out of fact and law.[145] Yet, an appeal to the English High Court seems possible for other matters (Bylaw 366(5) of the ICA Bylaws and Rules (2018)). Either party can also apply to the courts of England and Wales when the ICA has no further power to do what is required to obtain security for the demand of the claimant during arbitrational proceedings or an appeal (Bylaw 300(5) and (6) of the ICA Bylaws and Rules (2018)). In addition, members may apply to any court once quality arbitration proceedings are refused in the event that (i) the name of either of the parties was mentioned in the association's list of unfilled rewards part 1 at the time that the disputed contract was signed or once the contract predates a placement on this list; or (ii) when a member (or related firm) was suspended by the ICA at the time this party signed the disputed contract (Bylaws 300(7) and 330(1) of the ICA Bylaws and Rules (2018)).

ii. Technical arbitration

An award resulting from technical arbitration becomes effective once the requirements laid down in Bylaw 309 have been fulfilled. These completely mirror those of an award rendered following quality arbitration with the exception that parties must appeal an award within 28 days (Bylaw 309(7) of the ICA Bylaws and Rules (2018)) as opposed to within a deadline for appeal written on the award.

Similarly, technical arbitration awards are also final and cannot be appealed at the English High Court according to Section 69 of the Arbitration Act 1996 on matters of fact and law. When the ICA cannot guarantee

ties. Second, it has an effect on future disputes between the parties. Third, it can also have consequences for third parties.

145 The Arbitration Act 1996 of 17 June 1996; Mainly three arguments that are in support of setting aside Section 69 of the Arbitration Act 1996 can be given: first, arbitral awards are final and should not be able to be re-examined. Second, international commercial custom of the cotton industry is alien to English law. Third, parties that opt for contracting under the Bylaws of the ICA intend to exclude Section 69 of the Arbitration Act 1996. See N. Andrews, "*Arbitration and Contract Law*", Basel: Springer International Publishing 2016, p. 140; In my opinion, a fourth argument can be added. Parties that opt for specialized commercial arbitration do so out of reasons of privacy, as they do not want detailed and sensitive information becoming known to the public. This cannot be guaranteed by the English High Court.

security for a claimant's demand during arbitrational proceedings or an appeal, parties in a dispute may also find legal redress at the public courts in England and Wales. Importantly, the grounds of dismal for arbitrational proceedings as laid down in Bylaws 300(7) and 330(1) of the ICA Bylaws and Rules (2018)) do not apply to technical arbitration. Yet, if the ICA fails to copy a request for technical arbitration to the defendant, either party may apply for a remedy at any court (Bylaws 300(7) and 302(3) of the ICA Bylaws and Rules (2018)).

II. Nonlegal sanctioning

To guarantee that awards originating from the well-established two-tier arbitration system for both quality and technical disputes are adhered to, the Bylaws of the ICA provide four different types of nonlegal sanctions.

1. Blacklisting

When an arbitral award is not observed by the other party following a contractual dispute, the directors of the ICA are informed of this refusal (Bylaw 366(1) of the ICA Bylaws and Rules (2018)). On behalf of these persons, the Secretary of the ICA then notifies the non-compliant person or undertaking that its (company) name will be published and passed on to all members and member associations belonging to the International Co-operation between Cotton Associations ("CICCA"). [146] In addition, the Secretary of the ICA will display his/its name on a publicly accessible section of the website of the ICA known as the "ICA List of Unfulfilled Awards: Part 1" (the "default list") (Bylaw 366(2)-(4) of the ICA Bylaws and Rules (2018)).[147] To avoid being blacklisted, the defaulter can within a timeframe of 14 days convince the directors with compelling reasons not to do so (Bylaw 366(2) of the ICA Bylaws and Rules (2018)).

Besides the name of the defaulter being placed on the default list, the Secretary may circulate the name(s) of any other entity (*e.g.* subsidiary) related to the defaulter on a separate not publicly available default list (By-

146 http://www.cicca.info/. The CICCA is an umbrella organization consisting of the most important global trade associations (*e.g.* such as the ICA) involved in the cotton trade.

147 https://www.ica-ltd.org/safe-trading/loua-part-one/.

law 366(6) of the ICA Bylaws and Rules (2018)). This blacklist is referred to as the "ICA List of Unfulfilled Awards: Part 2".[148] Given that an inclusion has far-reaching consequences, a targeted entity can refute the existence of a link with the defaulter of an arbitral award within a timeframe of 14 days (Bylaw 366(7b) of the ICA Bylaws and Rules (2018)). This company must then provide accurate evidence to convince the Secretary of the opposite (Bylaw 366(9) of the ICA Bylaws and Rules (2018)).

2. Withdrawing membership

When a party fails, neglects or refuses to comply with an award issued by the two-tier arbitration tribunal within 14 days (Article 25.1.4/9 of the Articles of Association of the ICA), the directors must then appoint a disciplinary committee from the approved panel (Article 24 of the Articles of Association of the ICA) whose main task is to impose an equitable penalty for such conduct. Any member will be liable to a formal statement from the ICA that expresses severe disapproval (*i.e.* censure), a fine not exceeding £100,000 and/or a withdrawal of membership (Article 25.1 of the Articles of Association of the ICA).[149] Notice thereof will be sent to all registered members of the ICA and published on the website of this association once the decision of the disciplinary committee is final (Article 31.1 of the Articles of Association of the ICA).

In the event the committee decides to suspend or ostracize a member, all membership privileges will be (pending a suspension) forfeited (Article 31.2 of the Articles of Association of the ICA). This also applies to related companies of the targeted member. However, any disloyal former or suspended member is still liable for arbitration for any extraneous dispute arising from a contract entered into before a suspension or expulsion (Article 31.3 of the Articles of Association of the ICA). Whereas expelled members will have their rights immediately cancelled (Article 31.9 of the Articles of Association of the ICA), membership privileges of suspended members will be denied for the period of abeyance. This entails that suspended

148 The ICA List of Unfulfilled Awards: Part 2 is only available for ICA members and is not made publicly accessible.

149 Even though these sanctions are targeted towards disloyal members of the ICA, it is not unconceivable that defaulting non-members that contracted under the Bylaws of the ICA face being barred from using the arbitral services of the ICA on future occasions. Moreover, they can be denied membership of the ICA in the future. See, for example, Union Internationale Des

members will not be able to arbitrate on disputes arising out of contracts entered into during the suspension period (Article 31.4 of the Articles of Association of the ICA) and can no longer exercise entitlements such as attending ICA events, representing the ICA, serving as an arbitrator for non-ongoing disputes, participating in elections and proposing or recommending individuals or undertakings for membership of the ICA (Article 31.5 of the Articles of Association of the ICA). Yet, a suspended member is not entitled to voluntarily leave the ICA and must still pay the annual subscription fee (Article 31.6/7 of the Articles of Association of the ICA). However, a suspended member may ask the directors in writing to grant him a temporary restoration of all ICA membership privileges (Article 31.8 of the Articles of Association of the ICA). The directors can reject/accept such request, or can agree subject to limitations or conditions. In addition, the directors can change or rescind that resolution whenever they deem fit. Expelled members, on the other hand, cannot ask for a temporary restoration of membership.

3. Denying membership for expelled members on the basis of an additional entry condition

An expelled wrongdoer will be subject to two additional entry conditions to reobtain membership of the relevant trade association. First, a reapplication for membership is only possible after the lapse of a two-year time period (Article 31.10 of the Articles of Association of the ICA). Second, the Board of Directors must agree to a reinstatement of membership (Article 31.10 of the Articles of Association of the ICA). If a targeted wrongdoer is barred from reobtaining membership on either of these grounds, that wrongdoer is extrajudicially sanctioned.

4. Refusing to deal with expelled members

A member can also suffer censure, a fine not exceeding £100,000 and/or withdrawal of membership once that member enters into a contract with an individual or (related) firm mentioned on the ICA List of Unfulfilled Awards 1 and 2 (Article 25.1.1 of the Articles of Association of the ICA and Bylaw 415(1) of the ICA Bylaws and Rules (2018)), or contracts with a member that has been expelled from the ICA (Article 25.1.2 of the Articles of Association of the ICA). Such refusal to deal can only be circumvented when a member advises the directors in writing of an intention to contract with a blacklisted member and provides the directors within seven days after that contracts has been entered into "*with a copy of that contract or contracts showing the date, reference number and estimated date of fulfilment of that contract and the relevant settlement agreement, with any confidential information redacted as required*" (Article 25.2 of the Articles of Association of the ICA and Bylaw 415(2)).[150] In the event a member undertaking wishes to settle an award with a blacklisted member, or has an outstanding contract with such a member, the same proof must be substantiated to the directors within seven days (Bylaw 415(3) and (4) of the ICA Bylaws and Rules (2018)).

III. Rationale for private enforcement/nonlegal sanctioning

For individuals and undertakings active in the cotton trade, upholding a reputation of contractual trustworthiness is crucial for long-term cooperation. This is because a good reputation enhances future deals.[151] Given that deals are made on the telephone, even if worth millions of dollars and are only documented for tax or customs reasons, it is important that cotton is delivered on time, for an agreed amount and quality.[152]

It does not come as a surprise that this freedom can occasionally be exploited by suppliers and distributors of cotton when both parties enter into an agreement to buy or sell a quantity of cotton at a predetermined price and at a specified time in the future (*i.e.* futures contract).[153] This is because the price of cotton crops is extremely volatile (*e.g.* weather conditions, (insect) plagues and war) and can induce either party to deviate from this contract. If both parties negotiated the delivery of a quantity of cotton for an average price per kilo in the future and a few months later there was a scarcity of cotton in the market, the price of cotton will go up. This will induce the supplier to find another distributor to sell his cotton at a higher price per kilo when the expected surplus offsets any possible costs of court

150 Members cannot justify entering into a contract with an expelled former member.

151 J. van Erp, "Reputational Sanctions in Private and Public Regulation", *Erasmus Law Review, Vol. 1, Is. 5* 2009, p. 146.

152 T. Townsend, "*Cotton Trading Manual*", Cambridge: Woodhead Publishing Limited 2005, p. iii.

153 See Part I, Chapter 1, C, II for an example of how the cotton futures market works.

proceedings. Alternatively, when both parties again agreed a fixed amount of cotton for a price per kilo in the future and a few months later there is an abundance of cotton in the market, the price of cotton will decrease. Obviously, this could trigger the distributor to find another supplier when the expected surplus outweighs the cost of any court proceedings. In other words, equivalent to the syllogism in both scenarios, court proceedings would insufficiently deter wrongdoers and reward deviating from the contract by either the supplier or the distributor.

As a breach of the principle of sanctity of contract can be seen as hazardous for the cotton industry, specialized commercial arbitration offered by the ICA enforced by nonlegal sanctions more efficiently prevents a departure from an agreed arrangement between the supplier and the distributor. Apart from this reason, the necessity of nonlegal sanctions can also be explained by the lack of alternatives. Enforcement of an arbitral award is possible in a public court, but, often, such an enforcement decision needs to be recognized by another State in accordance with the United Nations Convention on the Recognition and Enforcement of Foreign Arbitral Awards (the "New York Convention").[154] This is because members of the ICA are globally dispersed and parties contracting under a standardized contract prepared by this trade association are usually not in one and the same State. Given that in such scenario two courts would need to recognize the arbitral award, enforceability is too slow in comparison with specialized commercial arbitration. In addition, recognition may also prove uncertain, as some States do not readily enforce arbitral awards even though they are members of the New York Convention (*e.g.* Thailand).

C. *The Diamond Dealers Club*

I. Background

1. History

The New York DDC was founded and incorporated in 1931 as a voluntary US-based association with bylaws and mandatory rules in order to realize a more amicable interplay between merchants active in the diamond indus-

154 United Nations Convention on the Recognition and Enforcement of Foreign Arbitral Awards of 1958.

try at a central and safe trading place in the midst of the Depression.[155] It modelled itself after Europe's older diamond bourses and consisted of 50 original members and 12 founding incorporators.[156] During the course of World War II the diamond industry in the German-occupied territories came to a stand-still.[157] As the majority of diamond merchants were of Jewish descent, many of them fled to New York. After the war, some returned to the now liberated European countries, whereas a large number of merchants remained in the US.[158]At the end of the 20th century, the DDC consisted of about 1,800 to 2,000 members.[159]

During this time (and arguably also from the outset), the DDC is a brokerage for diamonds and a social club for predominantly Jewish merchants.[160] It respects the Jewish Sabbath and other holy days and even has its own Torah and *Beith Midrash*.[161] Moreover, it offers an infrastructure to govern the diamond trade and provides an elaborate arbitration system to resolve disputes between merchants. Since 1941 the DDC is located in Manhattan's diamond district on 47th Street, New York.[162] Over the last 20 years DDC membership has dropped from 2,000 to 1,200 members. This can be explained by an unwillingness of merchants to be bound to mandatory arbitration and evidence of serious financial mismanagement within the DDC in the period from 2006 to 2009.[163]

---

155 B. D. Richman, "The Antitrust of Reputation Mechanisms: Institutional Economics and Concerted Refusals to Deal", *Virginia Law Review, Vol. 95:325* 2009, p. 332; R. S. Shield, "*Diamond Stories: Enduring Change on 47th Street*", London: Cornell University Press 2002, p. 92.

156 B. D. Richman, "*Stateless Commerce: The Diamond Network and the Persistence of Relational Exchange*", Cambridge/London: Harvard University Press 2017, p. 42.

157 R. Kobrin and A. Teller, "*Purchasing Power: The Economics of Modern Jewish History*", Philadelphia: University of Pennsylvania Press 2015, p. 201.

158 Ibid., p. 202. In 1945, 70% of all diamond merchants active in New York were from Antwerp.

159 B. D. Richman, "*Stateless Commerce: The Diamond Network and the Persistence of Relational Exchange*", Cambridge/London: Harvard University Press 2017, p. 42.

160 L. Lambert, "*Spirituality, Inc.: Religion in the American Workplace*", New York/London: New York University Press 2009, p. 73.

161 A *Beit Midrash* is a Jewish "study hall" located in communal buildings.

162 A. Oltuski, "*Precious Objects: A Story of Diamonds, Family, and a Way of Life*", New York: Scribner 2011, p. 76; https://www.nyddc.com/contact-us.html.

163 B. D. Richman et al, "*Journal of Legal Analysis, Vol. 9, Is. 2*", in: B. D. Richman (ed), "An Autopsy of Cooperation: Diamond Dealers and the Limits of Trust-based Exchange", Oxford: Oxford University Press 2017, p. 255-256; https://www.diamondintelligence.com/magazine/magazine.aspx?id=9862.

2. Legal form

The DDC is a not-for-profit "incorporated company" with membership open for individuals active in the diamond trade.[164] This entails that it is formed pursuant to the laws of the State of New York, is managed by a Board of Directors, has shareholders and is run on a daily basis by officers.[165] The reason for choosing this legal structure is that it shields members from liability of the DDC, even though members are still liable for the annual fees paid. According to the website of the DDC, "*the liability of the DDC and all of its affiliates and employees shall be limited to the membership or user fees paid to the DDC for the current year*".[166] Another benefit for having the DDC incorporated is that this legal form outlives any member.

3. Institutional structure

As the current bylaws and articles of association of the DDC are not publicly available for non-members[167] and whereas this association's website does not clarify its institutional structure, the latter contains some evidence of a corresponding organization compared to the ICA.[168] According to the membership section of the website of the DDC, membership is contingent upon approval by the Board of Directors and, once installed, every member has the right to attend general meetings and to serve on a committee.[169] Moreover, any dispute between members or a member and a

164 The procedure for incorporation can be found in Article 3 of the Companies Act (to access: http://www.oas.org/juridico/english/mesicic3_jam_companies.pdf).

165 International Business Publications, "*US: Importing into the Unites States Practical Guide*", Washington; International Business Publications 2008, p. 186.

166 https://www.nyddc.com/terms--conditions.html.

167 Due to the unwillingness of the DDC to allow access for non-members to the currently in place (and updated) Bylaws, in the subsequent Paragraphs reference will be made to the Diamond Dealers Club Bylaws from 1999 ("DDC Bylaws (1999)"). This is because this document is the last written information made available to both members and non-members. Even though some discrepancies are to be expected, it is unlikely that the internal rules for DDC members have changed much over time. Thereby it serves as an important reference in this research.

168 After repeated requests, the DDC refuses to give access to its Bylaws and Articles of Association.

169 https://www.nyddc.com/membership.html.

non-member which is governed by the Bylaws of the DDC will be resolved in arbitral proceedings.[170]

Put differently, the DDC is divided in three branches: the legislative (*i.e.* the annual general meeting), the executive (*i.e.* the Board of Directors[171]) and the judicial (*i.e.* the Arbitration Tribunal).

4. Membership

Only individuals are eligible for membership once they are 21 years old or more and have been employed in the diamond, jewellery or related fields for a minimum of two years.[172] Once these easy to meet requirements are fulfilled, a candidate must submit an application to the executive office, which must then be approved by the Board of Directors.[173] In addition, a candidate must post his picture on the trading floor wall for a period of ten days to give members of the DDC the opportunity to comment on his application (Art. 3 § 8 of the DDC Bylaws (1999)). According to *Richman*, this process of admitting new members is rigorous.[174] Even though membership, in theory, is open for all individuals that satisfy the seemingly easy to meet entry requirements mentioned above, the Board of Directors retains discretionary freedom to deny entry. This makes the process of obtaining membership unpredictable.[175] In addition, according to *Richman*, it appears that membership is subject to the constraints of the physical ca-

170 https://www.nyddc.com/arbitration.html; Section 1b of the Site Terms and Conditions of Use (to access: https://www.nyddc.com/terms--conditions.html).

171 The Board of Directors consists of 16 directors, one president, one vice president, one secretary and one treasurer. See https://www.wfdb.com/diamond-dealers-club; https://www.nyddc.com/officers.html.

172 https://www.nyddc.com/membership.html; Art. 3, § 1 of the DDC Bylaws (1999).

173 Ibid; For the application form, see http://www.nyddc.com/uploads/2/3/7/3/23730718/ddc_membership_application.pdf.

174 Art. 3 of the DDC Bylaws (1999); B. D. Richman, "The Antitrust of Reputation Mechanisms: Institutional Economics and Concerted Refusals to Deal", *Virginia Law Review, Vol. 95:325* 2009, p. 332.

175 It would appear that the Board of Directors could deny membership to an individual for, *inter alia*, immoral conduct (*e.g.* an individual in the past made racist remarks against Jews) and when it is clear that a potential member will be unharmed by social sanctioning for not complying with an arbitral award (*e.g.* if an individual does not belong to the close-knit group).

pacity of the headquarters of the DDC.[176] In contrast, for immediate relatives of current faithful and loyal DDC members, more lenient entry requirements have to be complied with (Art. 3 § 3a-b of the DDC Bylaws (1999)).[177]

Characteristically, nearly 85% to 90% of all the members belonging to the DDC are Jewish.[178] Given that people belonging to this religion tend to live in tightly knit insular communities,[179] being a member of the DDC is not only necessary for business, but also for maintaining social standing.[180] Club membership signals to other members that an individual is reliable and trustworthy (to conduct trade with).[181] A dealer who is a member of the DDC is also automatically a member of the World Federation of Diamond Bourses ("WFDB").[182] This entails that this member is also allowed to trade on all member bourses belonging to this umbrella federation.[183]

5. Specialized commercial arbitration

a. The single arbitration model

Any dispute between members is resolved through arbitration provided by the DDC. However, when there is a non-member involved in the dispute,

---

176 Ibid., p. 349.

177 *E.g.* according to Art. 3 § 3a of the DDC Bylaws (1999), any widow of a member is automatically accepted, without needing to pay an admission fee.

178 B. D. Richman, "How Community Institutions Create Economic Advantage: Jewish Diamond Merchants in New York", *Law & Social Inquiry, Vol. 31, Is. 2* 2006, p. 398. From the remaining non-Jewish members, approximately 10% are Indian.

179 R. S. Shield, "*Diamond Stories: Enduring Change on 47th Street*", London: Cornell University Press 2002, p. 12.

180 In the event of death, many members pass down their diamond business within the family. In other words, the influence of the Jewish culture within the DDC remains steady. See B. D. Richman et al, "*Journal of Legal Analysis, Vol. 9, Is. 2*", in: B. D. Richman (ed), "An Autopsy of Cooperation: Diamond Dealers and the Limits of Trust-based Exchange", Oxford: Oxford University Press 2017, p. 251.

181 R. A. Epstein, "*Contract - Freedom and Restraint: Liberty, Property, and the Law*", New York/Abingdon: Routledge 2000, p. 363-364.

182 https://www.wfdb.com/.

183 For a complete list of all trade associations belonging to the WFDB, see https://www.wfdb.com/wfdb-bourses.

arbitration is only possible when three requirements are fulfilled.[184] First, a member has sold, transferred or delivered goods to such an individual. Second, a member has invited a non-member to be a guest of the DDC (Art. 17 of the DDC Bylaws (1999)). Third, the non-member has agreed or signed an acceptable arbitration clause.[185]

When looking at the single arbitration model of the DDC from the outside, one can draw two conclusions. First, according to *Allen* and *Qian*, DDC arbitration is rather straightforward and rapid, often resulting in an outcome that estimated damages must be divided.[186] Second, notwithstanding the severity of the dispute, due to the DDC's aversion to outsiders and respect for privacy, arbitration hearings are typically secret, unless arbitral awards are not complied with.[187] Only highly publicized cases provide some evidence that a hearing took place, although they only identify the name of the wrongdoer and the amount to be paid.[188]

b. Selection of arbitrators

Prior to a selection of arbitrators, parties are required to resolve a dispute by entering into reconciliation proceedings. When successful, the chairman (who is part of a three-person conciliation panel) may return the mandatory arbitration fee (Art. 12 § 2 and 8 of the DDC Bylaws (1999)). If such voluntary negotiations fail, before arbitration may be initiated and arbitrators can be selected, the Floor Committee of the DDC must reach the

---

184 https://www.nyddc.com/arbitration.html. Watch the video on this website for an overview of the requirements.

185 Ibid. The arbitration clause can cover either "*the single transaction that the memo, invoice or letterhead refers to*", or "*all transactions where the member is the seller or transferor of the stone*". Importantly, once an arbitration clause covers a transaction, "*any claims about that transaction can be brought to arbitration by both the member and the non-member*".

186 J. J. Heckman, R. L. Nelson, and L. Cabatingan, "*Global Perspectives on the Rule of Law*", in: F. Allen and J. Qian, "Comparing Legal and Alternative Institutions in Finance and Commerce", Abingdon/New York: Routledge 2010, p. 128.

187 B. D. Richman, "Community Enforcement of Informal Contracts: Jewish Diamond Merchants in New York", *The Harvard John M. Olin Discussion Paper, No. 384* 2002, p. 17.

188 B. D. Richman, "*Stateless Commerce: The Diamond Network and the Persistence of Relational Exchange*", Cambridge: Harvard University Press 2017, p. 42-43.

decision that a material issue of fact exists.[189] If not, and when the panel advises to refer the case to arbitration, DDC arbitration may be commenced.

Three arbitrators (from whom one serves as chairman) are selected by the vice president of the DDC from a group of 40 arbitrators (that includes 16 chairmen), 14 of which are appointed by the Board of Directors and 26 of these who are elected by the members of the DDC every two years.[190] To be part of that group of arbitrators is insurmountable for those members who do not hold the highest esteem within the DDC.[191] Once belonging to the group of 40 arbitrators, any new arbitrator must attend three one-hour seminars at the premises of the DDC in New York City to learn how to comply with the Bylaws of the DDC and Chapter 8 of the Consolidated Laws of the State of New York (*i.e.* Civil Practice Law and Rules).[192] In addition, they are taught how to render standard arbitration awards. There is no explicit prohibition against lawyers qualifying as an arbitrator. Any award rendered by the first-tier arbitration panel may be appealed in second-tier arbitration. The arbitration panel then consists of five arbitrators (Art. 12 § 17 of the Bylaws of the DDC (1999)).

c. Choice of tribunal and jurisdiction of arbitration tribunals

The system of private law-making through the single arbitration model takes place at the premises of the DDC in New York.[193] When the Floor Committee refers a dispute to arbitration, by respecting the secrecy of its proceedings, this form of dispute resolution cannot take place outside the DDC building. This entails that individual DDC members and non-members who are bound by the Bylaws of the DDC cannot choose a different place of arbitration.

---

189 L. Bernstein, "Opting out of the Legal System: Extralegal Contractual Relations in the Diamond Industry", *The Journal of Legal Studies, Vol. 21, No. 1* 1992, p. 124.

190 R. S. Shield, "*Diamond Stories: Enduring Change on 47th Street*", Ithaca/London: Cornell University Press 2002, p. 191.

191 B. D. Richman, "*How Community Institutions Create Economic Advantage: Jewish Diamond Merchants in New York*", Law & Social Inquiry, Vol. 31, Is. 2 2006, p. 395.

192 Consolidated Laws of the State of New York of 1909.

193 https://www.nytimes.com/1979/05/06/archives/the-citys-most-exclusive-club.html.

With regard to the jurisdiction of the arbitration tribunal, in each dispute a three-person arbitration panel must decide a case on their own jurisdiction. As a requirement, a material issue of fact for arbitration to decide must exist and arbitration must be performed in conformity with Section 7501 of the Civil Practice Law and Rules (Art. 12 of the Bylaws of the DDC (1999)).[194] On the substance, arbitrators must base their findings in consideration of trade customs and usages and not on the law for damages and contract of the State of New York.[195] However, they must respect the laws and statutes of this State.[196] Even though *Bernstein* explains that DDC arbitrators do not take past decisions stemming from DDC arbitration into consideration,[197] *Mark & Weidemaier* disagree.[198] According to both authors, despite arbitral awards being secretive and not stating any reasons, the structured system of the DDC might to some extent influence arbitrators.[199]

d. Procedure

As explained above,[200] albeit in less detail, any dispute arising out of a breach of the Bylaws of the DDC between members or a member with a

---

194 According to Section 7501 of the Civil Practice Law and Rules, "*A judgment shall be entered upon the confirmation of an award* [...] *The judgment-roll consists of the original or a copy of the agreement and each written extension of time within which to make an award; the statement required by section 7508 where the award was by confession; the award; each paper submitted to the court and each order of the court upon an application under sections 7510 and 7511; and a copy of the judgment*".

195 L. Bernstein, "Opting out of the Legal System: Extralegal Contractual Relations in the Diamond Industry", *The Journal of Legal Studies, Vol. 21, No. 1* 1992, p. 126.

196 Section 19 of the Site Terms and Conditions of Use (to access: https://www.nyddc.com/terms--conditions.html).

197 L. Bernstein, "Opting out of the Legal System: Extralegal Contractual Relations in the Diamond Industry", *The Journal of Legal Studies, Vol. 21, No. 1* 1992, p. 126.

198 W. Mark, and C. Weidemaier, "Toward a Theory of Precedent in Arbitration", *William & Mary Law Review, Vol. 51, Is. 5* 2010, p. 1901.

199 In my opinion, for example, if an arbitrator is selected within a three-person arbitration panel to review a dispute between merchants, it is possible that this individual will take into consideration reasons and conclusions from former arbitral disputes, reasons in which he was also an arbitrator. In other words, some precedent is being generated within the DDC arbitration system.

200 See Part I, Chapter 2, C, I, 5, bb.

non-member should, but necessarily must be, resolved through voluntary pre-arbitration conciliation proceedings. Often resulting in a settlement agreement, it is estimated that around 85 percent of all disputes submitted for arbitration in 2015 were ironed out at such an early stage.[201] The reason for its success is two-fold. First, when successful, parties do not need to pay arbitration fees.[202] Second, after an arbitral award, the names of the parties are published, which can hamper their reputation and social standing.[203]

When conciliation is fruitless, one member can start arbitral proceedings by notifying the Managing Director of the DDC in writing.[204] Consequently, the Vice President of the DDC has the discretionary freedom to officially start arbitration by referring the dispute to the Floor Committee. This official dispute resolution body of the DDC is tasked with finding out whether a material issue of fact exists. This must be based on the evidentiary materials provided by both parties without ordering a hearing.[205] When according to Art. 8 § 7B of the Bylaws of the DDC (1999) a party fails to uphold his commercial obligations with another member and there is no material issue of fact involved, the Floor Committee can penalize this person. Typically, it can impose a final fine of up to $1,000 and/or ostracize such an individual for a period not exceeding 20 days. After reaching a decision, parties can appeal the decision of the Floor Committee by paying the mandatory $ 100 fee. Yet, if there is a material issue of fact, such a possibility is precluded. The Floor Committee then refers the dispute to arbitration within the DDC.

Once the three-person panel is established,[206] arbitrators must, within a period of ten days following a hearing, render an arbitral award in line with Section 7501 of the Civil Practice Law and Rules. This will be done by respecting the principle of majority voting. When an arbitrator with-

201 M. Bussani and A. J. Sebok, "*Comparative Tort Law: Global Perspectives*", Cheltenham/Northampton: Edward Elgar Publishing 2015, p. 18. Absent data, it is unlikely that this amount changed in 2019.

202 R. S. Shield, "*Diamond Stories: Enduring Change on 47th Street*", London: Cornell University Press 2002, p. 190.

203 M. Bussani and A. J. Sebok, "*Comparative Tort Law: Global Perspectives*", Cheltenham/Northampton: Edward Elgar Publishing 2015, p. 18.

204 R. S. Shield, "*Diamond Stories: Enduring Change on 47th Street*", London: Cornell University Press 2002, p. 191.

205 This is similar compared to obtaining a summary judgment in the USA. See S. Subrin, and M. Y. K. Woo, "*Litigating in America: Civil Procedure in Context*", New York: Aspen Publishers 2006, p. 165.

206 To understand how the selection of arbitrators works, see Part 1, Chapter 2, C, I, 5, bb.

holds his vote and the other two arbitrators within the panel are at an impasse, a new panel is formed.[207] The losing party of an arbitral award will be forced to pay the arbitration fee and any other expenses (Art. 12 § 2 of the Bylaws of the DDC (1999)). Although an arbitral award is final, following receipt of the award by either party, both individuals can within a period of ten days legitimately request an appeal by notifying the Board of Directors of the DDC. Unfortunately, this does not come without difficulties for the requesting party. This is because this individual must provide security (*e.g.* payment) to cover the costs of the dispute and he must deposit an arbitration fee three times the amount paid in first instance (Art. 12 § 15 of the Bylaws of the DDC (1999)).

e. The finality of arbitration or the possibility of (some) legal redress in public courts according to the association?

A party that disagrees with an arbitral award stemming from a DDC arbitrational appeal proceedings can appeal to the New York State courts under New York State law for relief when this individual can substantiate that procedural irregularities have occurred.[208] Examples of previous caselaw relate to an individual who was sympathetic to a Palestinian Liberation Organization[209] and an arbitrator engaged in private communications with the party who won the arbitral proceedings.[210] In other words, improper conduct of a discriminatory and biased arbitrator is grounds for a litigant to challenge an arbitral award at the State court.

When a party from the outset tries to seek relief at a public court for a matter that is covered by DDC arbitration, or litigates at the State court for other matters than irregularities of an award stemming from a DDC arbitrational appeal, such an individual can be fined and ostracized.[211]

---

207 R. S. Shield, "*Diamond Stories: Enduring Change on 47th Street*", London: Cornell University Press 2002, p. 192.

208 R. A. Epstein, "*Contract - Freedom and Restraint: Liberty, Property, and the Law*", New York/Abingdon: Routledge 2000, p. 369.

209 Rabinowitz v. Olewski, 473 N.Y.S. 2d 232, 234 (N.Y. App. Div. 1984).

210 Goldfinger v. Lisker, 500 N.E.2d 857, 858 (N.Y. App. Div. 1986).

211 B. D. Richman, "*Stateless Commerce: The Diamond Network and the Persistence of Relational Exchange*", Cambridge: Harvard University Press 2017, p. 42.

II. Nonlegal sanctioning

To safeguard the enforcement of DDC arbitral awards, the association imposes two types of nonlegal sanctions, which are discussed below. Although at first glance they may appear similar to the methods to guarantee compliance with arbitral awards provided in the ICA Bylaws, caution is required. According to *Richman*, the diamond industry is an unusual industry with certain specific characteristics that can only be found in a small number of other industries.[212]

1. Blacklisting

When an individual fails to pay an outstanding award within ten working days, his picture and a brief explanation of his disloyalty are published on the wall of the DDC's main trading hall (Art. 12 § 25 of the Bylaws of the DDC (1999)).[213] Moreover, his picture is also published on the walls of every major trading association belonging to the WFDB.[214] According to *Epstein*, in an industry where reputation is crucial to guaranteeing future trade, blacklisting has a high risk of putting a disloyal person out of business.[215] News spreads rapidly and makes future members and non-members resistant to conduct trade with a defaulter who (in their eyes) cannot be trusted. In other words, it signals to other members that he is not com-

---

212 B. D. Richman, "Community Enforcement of Informal Contracts: Jewish Diamond Merchants in New York", *The Harvard John M. Olin Discussion Paper, No. 384* 2002, p. 0 (abstract). According to *Richman*, "*The diamond industry is home to many unusual features: the predominance of an ethnically homogeneous community of merchants* [...] *the norm of intergenerational family businesses*"; *Konradi* confirms the idea of *Richman* that the diamond industry is different than most industries. See V. Gesner, "*Contractual Certainty in International Trade: Empirical Studies and Theoretical Debates on Institutional Support for Global Economic Exchanges*", in: W. Konradi (ed.), "The Role of *Lex Mercatoria* in Supporting Globalised Transactions: An Empirical Insight into the Governance Structure of the Timber Industry", Oxford/Portland: Hart Publishing 2009, p. 70.

213 B. D. Richman, "The Antitrust of Reputation Mechanisms: Institutional Economics and Concerted Refusals to Deal", *Virginia Law Review, Vol. 95:325* 2009, p. 333.

214 It is also possible that his picture will be published on the walls of other trade associations active in the diamond trade not belonging to the WFDB.

215 R. A. Epstein, "*Contract - Freedom and Restraint: Liberty, Property, and the Law*", New York/Abingdon: Routledge 2000, p. 393.

mitted to long-term cooperation.[216] In addition to harming one's business reputation, due to the unique structure of the diamond industry, as many merchants active in the DDC belong to a close-knit social group, having one's picture placed on the wall can even affect an individual's social standing. Social exclusion or isolation from the group of diamond merchants can cause a complete or near-complete loss of contact with those individuals whom he (not always, but often) feels so acquainted with. Therefore, preventing one's picture from ever reaching the wall is crucial.[217]

2. Withdrawing membership

The arbitration board of the DDC is also empowered to suspend or expel a member for failing to pay an arbitral award when such conduct "*reflects adversely upon the integrity of any member of the Organization*" (Art. 7 § 2 of the Bylaws of the DDC (1999)).[218] Such freedom of discretion can be perceived as arbitrary, as it gives the Board the possibility to go after certain defaulters, whereas others are not targeted. Pending a suspension or after an expulsion, wrongdoers are (i) not entitled to enter the DCC's club room, unless given explicit permission; (ii) unable to exercise their DDC membership voting rights[219]; (iii) prevented from maintaining access to the DDC Secure Online Trading Platform; and (iv) are forestalled from gaining access to the DDC arbitration system. Despite such a loss of rights, a (temporarily) ostracized member must fulfil all duties and obligations of a member in good standing relating to his transactions that were concluded in the period he was a member of the DDC.[220]

According to *Richman*, a (temporary) withdrawal of membership can impact the business (or commercial opportunities) of defaulters in two

216 C. Hawkins, "*Roman Artisans and the Urban Economy*", Cambridge: Cambridge University Press 2016, p. 120.

217 B. D. Richman, "Community Enforcement of Informal Contracts: Jewish Diamond Merchants in New York", *The Harvard John M. Olin Discussion Paper, No. 384* 2002, p. 102.

218 Abraham v. Diamond Dealers, 896 N.Y.S. 2d 848 (N.Y. App. Div. 2010). The only limitation to DDC membership is a suspension or expulsion. Other than that, DDC membership carries no expiration date.

219 Ibid. An immediate automatic suspension of the voting rights of DDC members for not complying with an arbitral award is illegitimate. The DDC must give reasonable notice.

220 Section 1b of the Site Terms and Conditions of Use.

ways. First, DDC members will most likely not conduct trade with ostracized individuals, as it would hamper their own reputation.[221] Second, any suspension and expulsion from the DDC entails an automatic suspension and expulsion from all 29 affiliated bourses belonging to the WFDB.[222] This would restrict trading for a defaulter on a global scale. It is self-evident that any form of ostracism will also affect the wrongdoer's social status in the diamond merchant society. Perhaps even more than when such a person is only blacklisted.[223]

III. Rationale for private enforcement/nonlegal sanctioning

The diamond industry faces unique difficulties, as diamonds are small in size and have an expensive value that is difficult to ascertain with the naked eye.[224] Disputes are not uncommon and often involve a substantial amount of money. The industry's reputation is fragile due to many difficulties in tracking down blood diamonds and stolen diamonds.[225] As a result, or as *Richman* defines it, in general, every diamond sale is "*an extreme instance of a hazardous transaction*".[226] To solve this issue, as the industry depends on trust and reputation, disputes are better dealt with within a PLS as opposed to a public legal system.

Mainly three arguments support the undesirableness of the latter system: first, whereas diamond disputes involve a lot of money, merchants do not

---

221 B. D. Richman, "The Antitrust of Reputation Mechanisms: Institutional Economics and Concerted Refusals to Deal", *Virginia Law Review, Vol. 95:325* 2009, p. 334. Collective refusals to deal cannot be found in the Bylaws of the DDC. Yet, the effect of ostracism can be seen as similar.

222 Ibid; Section 1a of the World Federation of Diamond Bourses By-laws and Inner Rules (2016).

223 Whether this is true largely depends on empiric evidence, which is currently not factored in.

224 S. Li, "*Managing International Business in Relation-Based versus Rule-Based Countries*", New York: Business Expert Press, LCC 2009, p. 49; An example of a situation where the value of a diamond cannot be detected with the naked eye involves laser treatment. When a diamond is treated to improve its colour, it often makes the stone less valuable. Unfortunately, such a treatment cannot be detected with the naked eye, but requires a complex laser examination.

225 E. Zirhlioglu, "The Diamond Industry and the Industry's Dispute Resolution Mechanisms", *Arizona Journal of International and Comparative Law* 2013, p. 4.

226 B. D. Richman, "*Stateless Commerce: The Diamond Network and the Persistence of Relational Exchange*", Cambridge: Harvard University Press 2017, p. 77.

want such an amount frozen pending a court outcome that can last for years.[227] Second, when a court reaches a decision, the outcome will become public. This can hamper the reputation of respectable diamond traders within the industry. Third, neither harmed diamond sellers can be satisfactorily compensated, nor can theft be sufficiently deterred by a court.[228] To overcome this, the DDC arbitration system was introduced, as it can resolve disputes cheaply, quickly and easily by taking into account the peculiarities of diamond trade practices.[229] As members of the DDC are part of a close-knit group that largely works together with one other, and because a bad reputation can hamper future business and social life, this "closure" enables the association to impose nonlegal sanctions that are binding on all members. By doing so, all members are motivated to ensure compliance with arbitral awards and safeguard the overall trust in the diamond industry. In turn, costs involved in finding a respectable buyer or seller are reduced.

D. The Grain and Feed Trade Association

I. Background

1. History

The origins of GAFTA can be traced back to 1878, the year that the London Corn Trade Association ("LCTA") was formed by some corn traders to facilitate the standardization of contract terms[230] for its members and to establish a system of arbitration to resolve disputes.[231] The association was

---

227 S. Li, "*Managing International Business in Relation-Based versus Rule-Based Countries*", New York: Business Expert Press, LCC 2009, p. 50.

228 B. D. Richman, "*Stateless Commerce: The Diamond Network and the Persistence of Relational Exchange*", Cambridge: Harvard University Press 2017, p. 77.

229 https://www.diamonds.net/News/NewsItem.aspx?ArticleID=49902&ArticleTitle=New+York+Adapting+to+Changing+Diamond+Market.

230 A. B. Bruce, "Bailliére's Encyclopædia of Scientific Agriculture", *Bailliér, Tindall and Cox* 1931, p. 520. An example of a standard term concerned the quality. Every contract of the LCTA contained one or multiple clauses indicating the quality standard of corn; J. Morgan, "*Great Debates in Contract Law*", London: Palgrave 2015, p. 88. Standard terms provided by the LCTA reduced the cost of doing business.

231 A. Lista, "*International Commercial Sales: The Sale of Goods on Shipment Terms*", Abingdon/New York: Routledge 2017, p. 4.

concerned with grading imported corn and did not develop formal grades for the domestic trade.[232] In most other industries it would serve as the standard model for private ordering.[233]

In 1906, some members who traded in vegetable proteins used as animal feedingstuffs, which were only three years before being introduced to the market, left the LCTA and established the London Cattle Food Trade Association ("LCFTA").[234] Decades later, in 1971, both associations amalgamated and formed GAFTA. This international organization represents 1,800 members in 95 countries consisting of traders, brokers, superintendents, analysts, fumigators[235], arbitrators, individuals, professionals and branches trading in grain, animal feedingstuffs, general produce, pulses[236] and rice.[237] By developing standard contracts and providing a well-respected international dispute resolution system in the form of mediation and arbitration, instead of relying on the public legal system, GAFTA functions within a PLS.[238]

2. Legal form

Similar to the ICA, GAFTA is a non-profit "private limited liability company by guarantee" under the current Companies Act 2006.[239] This alterna-

232 A. Velkar, "'Deep' integration of 19th century grain markets: coordination and standardisation in a global value chain", *London School of Economics* 2010, p. 24.

233 G. Mallard and J. Sgard, "*Contractual Knowledge: One Hundred Years of Legal Experimentation in Global Markets*", Cambridge: Cambridge University Press 2016, p. 157.

234 https://www.gafta.com/about.

235 Those individuals are tasked with removing harmful insects, bacteria and diseases from something or somewhere by using poisonous gas.

236 Pulses are the edible seeds of peas, beans, or lentils.

237 https://www.gafta.com/Membership.

238 A. Lista, "*International Commercial Sales: The Sale of Goods on Shipment Terms*", Abingdon/New York: Routledge 2017, p. 11. *Lista* explains that the standard contracts developed by GAFTA are more detailed than the Incoterms®. Whereas the Incoterms® are intended to clarify the risks, costs and tasks inherent to the international delivery of goods and transportation, standard contracts of GAFTA cover all aspects of the delivery of goods (*e.g.* quality standards).

239 F. Cafaggi, "*Enforcement of Transnational Regulation: Ensuring Compliance in a Global World*", Cheltenham/Northampton: Edward Elgar Publishing 2012, p. 218; https://www.gafta.com/. Below the webpage, in the contact section, the legal status of GAFTA is explained: "*The Grain and Feed Trade Association, 9 Lincoln's Inn Fields, London, WC2A 3BP Registered in England & Wales with liability*

tive type of corporation that is specifically used to accommodate not-for-profit trade associations has two benefits: first, it does not require a limit of a maximum number of members. Second, liability is limited to the nominal amount paid by the members.

3. Institutional structure

In line with the openness of GAFTA in terms of providing rules and guidelines concerning membership and arbitration, its institutional structure is well explained.[240] All the affairs of this association relating to the constitution of the association, domestic affairs as well as financing are managed by the Council that is composed of 22 people (Art. 3.1 of the General Rules of GAFTA (2017)).[241] These individuals are elected by the Annual General Meeting which is chaired by a President.[242] Day-to-day business is under the leadership of the Director General.[243] Members have the right to join committees that are tasked with rule-making; examples include the China Trade Committee and the Arbitration Committee.[244]

---

limited by guarantee under Company no. 1006456 VAT Registration No. GB 243 8967 24".

240 Although the task of the annual general meeting is not well explained, the Council's tasks are defined in The General Rules and Regulations Applicable to All Members of 2017 (hereinafter referred to as "the General Rules of GAFTA (2017)") (to access: https://www.gafta.com/write/MediaUploads/Membership/General_Rules_and_Regulations_Applicable_to_All_Members_2017.pdf); In addition, the judicial branch of GAFTA known as the two-tier arbitration system is very detailed. Examples include the General Rules and Regulations Applicable to all Member (to access: https://www.gafta.com/write/MediaUploads/Membership/General_Rules_and_Regulations_Applicable_to_All_Members_2017.pdf); Arbitration Rules No. 125 (to access: https://www.gafta.com/write/MediaUploads/Contracts/2018/125_2018.pdf); Gafta Rules - Mediation Rules & Agreement (to access: https://www.gafta.com/write/MediaUploads/Contracts/2014/128_2014.pdf).

241 https://www.gafta.com/Council; For all rules in order to become a member, President, Deputy President, or Vice President of the Council, see Art. 3.2 till 3.12 of the General Rules of GAFTA (2017)).

242 C. Tietje and A. Brouder, "*Handbook of Transnational Economic Governance Regimes*", Leiden/Boston: Martinus Nijhoff Publishers 2009, p. 657.

243 https://www.gafta.com/Staff/75508.

244 C. Tietje and A. Brouder, "*Handbook of Transnational Economic Governance Regimes*", Leiden/Boston: Martinus Nijhoff Publishers 2009, p. 657. Only two members from any single country can join a committee.

Once again, as can immediately be seen, when comparing this association with the ICA and the DDC, it consists of a legislative (*i.e.* the Annual General Meeting), executive (*i.e.* the Council) and judicial branch (*i.e.* the two-tier Arbitration Tribunal).

4. Membership

Currently, as stated above, GAFTA consists of 1,800 members. To be eligible, potential members must be categorized as a corporate body that is represented by a representative, an unincorporated body that is represented by a representative, or a natural person (Definitions, Art. 1.2 and 1.3 of the General Rules of GAFTA (2017)). Besides this qualification, any potential member must also be active in the grain and feed trade (Art. 1.1 of the General Rules of GAFTA (2017)).

When a potential member considers that it meets the entry requirements, an individual person or the representative of an (un)incorporated company can submit a written application to the Council to request membership (Art. 1.5 and 1.6 of the General Rules of GAFTA (2017)). In the application the applicant must, *inter alia*, explain which category of membership it falls under (Art. 1.7 and 1.12 of the General Rules of GAFTA (2017)).[245] After, the applicant must pay the entry fee determined by the Council as well as the subscription fee that is mandatory for the category of membership the applicant belongs to (Art. 1.8 of the General Rules of GAFTA (2017)).

245 According to Art. 1.12 of the General Rules of GAFTA (2017): "*There shall be the following categories of membership: (A) Trading principals in agricultural commodities and general produce (B) Brokers who do not trade as principals (C) Superintendent and Surveyor Members (D) Individual Qualified Arbitrator and Individual Qualified Mediator Members (E) Individuals engaged or who have been engaged in the trade (other than current category D members) (K) Trading principals in spices and general produce The following categories ((F), (G), (H), (I), (J), (L) and (M)) are Associate Members and do not have voting rights. (F) Laboratories on the Register of Approved Analysts (G) Professional Firms, Agro Supply and Service Companies who provide services to the Trade (H) Branches of Members (whose parent company is in the same country) (I) Qualified Arbitrators and Qualified Mediators employed by a Member of Gafta, acting with their employer's consent (J) Fumigant Operators (L) Students (M) Individuals not engaged in the trade*".

5. Specialized commercial arbitration

a. Tripartite arbitration

Disputes arising out of contracts in the grain and feedstock trade are resolved by specialized commercial arbitration provided by GAFTA.[246] Even though there is increasing attention to resolving any conflict with mediation, especially since parties can opt for this method of alternative dispute resolution, arbitration is the standard and consensual route.[247] According to *Rubino-Sammartano*, it can be seen as fast-track arbitration.[248]

When looking more closely, three different forms of arbitration can be detected. The most common form refers to the GAFTA Arbitration Rules No. 125. These standard arbitration rules are similar to those of the ICA, and divide arbitration into two types. The first type concerns disputes relating to the quality and condition of goods. The second type concerns arbitration relating to any other dispute resulting from standard contracts. However, unlike the ICA, both types are colloquially referred to as "technical arbitration", since uniform arbitration rules exist. The second form can be found in the GAFTA Simple Disputes Arbitration Rules No. 126 and is applicable to uncomplicated legal issues in which a quick and easy answer can be given in an award that does not fully provide reasons.[249] This form of arbitration is used in order to resolve a minor disagreement. The third and last form concerns the procedure for resolving conflicts stemming from the standard agreement for the carriage of goods between the charterer and the ship-owner (*i.e.* GAFTA Charter Party) as well as other forms of maritime transport. These rules can be found in the GAFTA Arbitration

---

246 C. Tietje and A. Brouder, "*Handbook of Transnational Economic Governance Regimes*", Leiden/Boston: Martinus Nijhoff Publishers 2009, p. 659. According to *Tietje* & *Brouder*, specialized commercial arbitration provided by GAFTA eclipses domestic court adjudication.

247 Food and Agriculture Organization of the United Nations, "*Proceedings of the FAO Rice Conference 2004: Rice in Global Markets*", Rome: Food and Agriculture Organization of the United Nations 2005, p. 56.

248 M. Rubino-Sammartano, "*International Arbitration: Law and Practice, Third Edition*", New York: JurisNet 2014, p. 1085-1086.

249 Simple Disputes Arbitration Rules No. 126 of 2010 (to access: https://www.gafta.com/write/MediaUploads/Contracts/2010/126.pdf). The scope of application can be found in Art. 8:2 of the Simple Disputes Arbitration Rules No. 126.

Rules for Charter Parties No. 127.[250] Even though the last two forms of arbitration cannot be underestimated, the focus in this Chapter will be on the GAFTA Arbitration Rules No. 125. This is because parties entering into a standard GAFTA contract automatically agree to arbitrate any potential dispute under these rules.[251]

b. Selection of arbitrators

As a general rule, the arbitration tribunal of GAFTA consists of three arbitrators. The first arbitrator is appointed by the claimant from the list of qualified arbitrators, or by GAFTA on its behalf (Art. 3.2 (a) of the GAFTA Arbitration Rules No. 125). The defendant or respondent must then appoint a second arbitrator from the list of qualified arbitrators, following which GAFTA completes the tribunal by selecting a third arbitrator (Art. 3.2 (b), (c) and (d) of the GAFTA Arbitration Rules No. 125). Optionally, both parties can also agree to refer the dispute to a sole arbitrator who is to be selected by GAFTA (Art. 3.1 of the GAFTA Arbitration Rules No. 125). In appeal, the board of arbitrators consists of three arbitrators when sole arbitration is agreed upon by the parties, or is composed of five arbitrators when an award is rendered by a tribunal of three arbitrators (Art. 11.1 of the GAFTA Arbitration Rules No. 125). In this instance, all arbitrators are selected by GAFTA without any influence of the parties.

Given the complexities of the grain and feed trade and its international magnitude, in order to be eligible to serve as an arbitrator only individuals who are sufficiently qualified may be selected (Art. 3.7 of the GAFTA Arbitration Rules No. 125).[252] Such a person must satisfy the general eligibility and qualification criteria, which are laid down in the Rules and Code of Conduct for Qualified Arbitrators & Qualified Mediators ("Rules for

---

250 Arbitration Rules No.127 For use with Charter Parties or Other Forms of Maritime Transport of 2014 (to access: https://www.gafta.com/write/MediaUploads/Contracts/2014/127_2014.pdf).

251 I. Polovets, M. Smith, and B. Terry, "GAFTA Arbitration as the Most Appropriate Forum for Disputes Resolution in Grain Trade", *Arizona Journal of International & Comparative Law*
Vol. 30, No. 3 2013, p. 572.

252 C. Tietje and A. Brouder, "*Handbook of Transnational Economic Governance Regimes*", Leiden/Boston: Martinus Nijhoff Publishers 2009, p. 659.

GAFTA Qualified Arbitrators")[253] (Art. 2 of the Guidelines for GAFTA Appointment of Arbitrators).[254] The entry requirements are two-fold: first, a potential arbitrator must be an individual member or an associate member of GAFTA (Art. 1.1 of the Rules of GAFTA Qualified Arbitrators).[255] Second, he or she must meet the association's criteria and the GAFTA Professional Development (GPD) programme (Art. 1.2 of the Rules of GAFTA Qualified Arbitrators). The programme requires potential arbitrators to attend all mandatory courses about trade foundation, commodities contracts, commodities shipping and commodities dispute resolution and to pass a final exam.[256] Alternatively, such a person can participate in the GAFTA Distance Learning Programme (DLP), which is an online course consisting of six modules and requires a potential arbitrator to pass all of the mandatory written assignments.[257] Upon completion of either course, when a candidate has at least ten years' experience in the grain and feed trade, one last exam must be successfully completed. This is the GAFTA Trade Diploma Examination.[258] Interestingly, members who are lawyers are not barred from participating in this exam and obtain the status of arbitrator upon successful completion. When officially having achieved this status, an individual must participate in ten hours of activities each year to maintain his professional standing.[259]

---

253 Rules and Code of Conduct for Qualified Arbitrators & Qualified Mediators (to access: https://www.gafta.com/Rules-and-Code-of-Conduct-for-Qualified-Arbitrators-Qualified-Mediators).

254 Guidelines for GAFTA Appointment of Arbitrators (to access: https://www.gafta.com/Guidelines-for-Gafta-Appointment-of-Arbitrators).

255 In-house lawyers working for GAFTA members can also be eligible to serve as a qualified arbitrator. See https://www.gafta.com/write/MediaUploads/Arbitration/Gafta_Qualified_Arbitrator_Status_2018.pdf.

256 https://www.gafta.com/Gafta-Professional-Development-GPD.

257 https://www.gafta.com/Distance-Learning-Programme. The six modules consist of an "*introduction to contracts, fulfilling contractual obligations, payment and risk, charterparties and international carriage regime, what to do in exceptional circumstances and problems and how to resolve them*".

258 https://www.gafta.com/Trade-Diploma.

259 https://www.gafta.com/Gafta-Qualified-Arbitrators-Annual-Continuing-Professional-Development-GPD-Policy. Examples of activities include giving presentations and attending seminars.

c. Choice of tribunal and jurisdiction of arbitration tribunals

According to Article 1.3 of the GAFTA Arbitration Rules No. 125, arbitration takes place at the premises of GAFTA in London, unless the parties in a dispute agree otherwise in writing. Then, arbitration can be held anywhere the parties wish. Once the arbitration tribunal has been installed, the sole arbitrator or three arbitrators – jointly - may rule on their own jurisdiction to decide matters, such as whether the tribunal is properly constituted and whether the arbitration agreement and matters relating to it are legitimate (Art. 8.1 of the GAFTA Arbitration Rules No. 125). Arbitrators must take English law into consideration, trade usage as well as all the rules and bylaws of GAFTA.[260]

d. Procedure

When parties conduct business on the basis of one of GAFTA's standard contracts, they are bound by the Bylaws and Rules of the association. When a conflict occurs, there is a growing tendency to, first, use mediation rather than arbitration, especially because disputants will be swayed into reaching a mutually acceptable commercial settlement with the help of a third party, rather than escalating the conflict to an *ad hoc* arbitration tribunal. Other characteristics of this procedure that can be found in the GAFTA Mediation Rules No. 128[261] pertain to its non-binding, confidential, informal and amicable nature without reaching a formal award.[262]

When reconciliation cannot be attained or is not preferred by the parties in a dispute and provided that the parties have traded on the basis of a GAFTA standard contract, which typically incorporates an arbitration clause, the dispute under consideration must be resolved through arbitration in line with GAFTA Arbitration Rules No. 125.[263] To start proceed-

---

260 Disputes arising out of GAFTA's standardized contracts are governed by English law. See https://www.gafta.com/about.

261 Mediation Rules No. 128 of 2012 (to access: https://www.gafta.com/write/MediaUploads/Contracts/2012/128.pdf).

262 I. Polovets, M. Smith, and B. Terry, "GAFTA Arbitration as the Most Appropriate Forum for Disputes Resolution in Grain Trade", *Arizona Journal of International & Comparative Law Vol. 30, No. 3* 2013, p. 571.

263 For an example of an arbitration clause within a GAFTA standard agreement, see Article 22 (a) of the Contract for the Delivery of Goods Central and Eastern Europe in Bulk or Bags No. 49 of 2018 (to access: https://www.gafta.com/write/

ings, the claimant must send a notice stating its intention to refer a dispute to arbitration as well as the name of its selected arbitrator to the defendant (Art. 2 of the GAFTA Arbitration Rules No. 125). The defendant must then name a second arbitrator or agree to sole arbitration. When two arbitrators are appointed, GAFTA selects a third arbitrator to complete the arbitration tribunal.[264] After, the claimant must present arguments for its case and pay the costs, fees and expenses of arbitration that GAFTA deems fit within a timeframe of 60 days (Art. 4.1 of the GAFTA Arbitration Rules No. 125). The defendant is then given the opportunity to present counter-arguments (Art. 4.2 of the GAFTA Arbitration Rules No. 125). Simultaneously, copies of all evidence must be sent to GAFTA in English (Art. 4.3 and 4.4 of the GAFTA Arbitration Rules No. 125). When the arbitration tribunal deems suitable, in order to prevent unnecessary delays and expenses, it can give both parties more time to present arguments (Art. 4.5 and 4.6 of the GAFTA Arbitration Rules No. 125). Oral hearings are optional and members of a three-person tribunal need not meet in person (Art. 4.8 and 4.9 of the GAFTA Arbitration Rules No. 125).[265]

When a sole arbitrator or the three-person arbitration panel have reached a decision, they render a final and binding award (Art. 6.4 and 9 of the GAFTA Arbitration Rules No. 125). Within a period of 30 days after such an award is made, either party then has the right to appeal the tribunal's decision (Art. 10.1(a) of the GAFTA Arbitration Rules No. 125).[266]

MediaUploads/Contracts/2018/49_2018.pdf). According to this clause: "*Any and all disputes arising out of or under this contract or any claim regarding the interpretation or execution of this contract shall be determined by arbitration in accordance with the GAFTA Arbitration Rules, No 125, in the edition current at the date of this contract; such Rules are incorporated into and form part of this Contract and both parties hereto shall be deemed to be fully cognisant of and to have expressly agreed to the application of such Rules*".

264 For a more detailed discussion of how the arbitration tribunal is formed, see Part I, Chapter 2, D, I, 5, b.

265 Discussing a case via email, telephone, etc. is sufficient between arbitrators in the arbitration tribunal.

266 For an explanation of the appeal procedure and the rendering of an award, see Art. 12 and 15 of the GAFTA Arbitration Rules No. 125.

e. The finality of arbitration or the possibility of (some) legal redress in public courts according to the association?

Given that GAFTA standard contracts contain an exclusive jurisdiction clause, it appears that the inclusion of exclusive jurisdiction prevents a claimant from seeking ancillary relief outside of the two-tier arbitration system of GAFTA for any dispute that must be dealt with in arbitration.[267] This is understandable as prolonged delays and enforcement problems in foreign jurisdictions of court decisions are to be expected. Despite these arguments in favour of arbitration and the fact that most GAFTA standard contracts contain a clause that instructs both parties to first refer a dispute to GAFTA arbitration before taking any court action (*i.e.* Scott v. Avery clause),[268] arbitral proceedings can be reviewed by English courts, unless the proceedings concern enforcement issues.[269]

II. Nonlegal sanctioning

When a recalcitrant party neglects or deliberately does not comply with an arbitral award decided in GAFTA first instance or second instance arbitration, nonlegal punishment takes the form of blacklisting. Expulsions and refusals to deal are not mentioned in the Bylaws and Rules of GAFTA.

---

267 GAFTA arbitration consists of two instances. It contains a first instance tribunal and the possibility to reconsider a case in full in a second instance appeal procedure.

268 For an example of such an arbitration clause within a GAFTA standard agreement, see Article 22 (b) of the Contract for the Delivery of Goods Central and Eastern Europe in Bulk or Bags No. 49 of 2018. According to this clause: "*Neither party hereto, nor any persons claiming under either of them shall bring any action or other legal proceedings against the other in respect of any such dispute, or claim until such dispute or claim shall first have been heard and determined by the arbitrator(s) or a board of appeal, as the case may be, in accordance with the Arbitration Rules and it is expressly agreed and declared that the obtaining of an award from the arbitrator(s) or board of appeal, as the case may be, shall be a condition precedent to the right of either party hereto or of any persons claiming under either of them to bring any action or other legal proceedings against the other of them in respect of any such dispute or claim*".

269 Ibid., see Art. 21.

1. Blacklisting

The method of ensuring compliance with arbitral awards can be found in Article 24.1 of the GAFTA Arbitration Rules No. 125. This provision empowers the Council of GAFTA to sanction a refusal to deal by posting the name of an individual or undertaking on its notice board, website and/or informing its members in any other way to ensure a similar effect.[270] To be taken off the list or have an individual's or company's good name restored, full payment must be made. Although no express provision is found in the Bylaws that instructs GAFTA to inform a defaulter of its intention to blacklist that defaulter, warnings are typically issued in order to induce compliance.[271]

III. Rationale for private enforcement/nonlegal sanctioning

Similar to the cotton market in which the ICA is an important trade association, the market for grain and feed trade can be classified as a market where derivative financial instruments (such as futures) play a pivotal role.[272] Moving GAFTA commodities from a seller to a buyer is risky primarily due to price swings.[273] To overcome this, despite many developing countries refusing to do so, futures are used to manage risks.[274] This entails that delivery is to be made at a future date and that prices are calculated on the basis of a predetermined method by referring to the exchange mar-

---

270 For the GAFTA default list from 2011 to 2018, see https://www.gafta.com/write/MediaUploads/Arbitration/Defaulters/Defaulters_on_Gafta_Awards_of_Arbitration_2011-present.pdf.

271 I. Polovets, M. Smith, and B. Terry, "GAFTA Arbitration as the Most Appropriate Forum for Disputes Resolution in Grain Trade", *Arizona Journal of International & Comparative Law Vol. 30, No. 3* 2013, p. 580; L. Boisson de Chazournes, M. Kohen, and J. E. Viñuales, "*Diplomatic and Judicial Means of Dispute Settlement*", Leiden/Boston: Koninklijke Brill NV 2013, p. 273. Blacklisting facilitates the efforts of creditors and objectifies their claims.

272 C. Tietje and A. Brouder, "*Handbook on Transnational Economic Governance Regimes*", Leiden/Boston: Martinus Nijhoff Publishers 2009, p. 656.

273 M. Atkin, "*The International Grain Trade*", Abington: Woodhead Publishing 1995, p. 113. Although *Atkin* explains that price variations apply to grain trade, the prices of other types of commodities which are traded under GAFTA contracts are also volatile.

274 Ibid., p. 111.

ket.[275] Obviously, this bears the risk that a seller would be induced to breach the contract in the event he can get a higher price for his commodities compared to the predetermined fixed price. Alternatively, the buyer will be persuaded to breach his contract with the seller if a different supplier can give him a better price. In other words, both scenarios instigate and reward contract deviation when the gains of either person offset any expected legal fees.

Instead of court adjudication, GAFTA arbitration, under the threat of nonlegal sanctioning (here: blacklisting) following non-compliance with an award, is a more effective method to guarantee sanctity of contract and strengthen its credibility. GAFTA's use of nonlegal sanctioning as a governing body to oversee trade and arbitration, without having a direct interest or bias, is essential for proper functioning of the market. A second reason for the introduction of nonlegal sanctions refers to the slow and uncertain enforcement and recognition procedure under the New York Convention. As members of GAFTA are dispersed globally, it is highly conceivable that parties contracting under standardized contracts of this association are not established in one and the same State. Hence, if arbitral awards were to be enforced in a public court, this would require the recognition of that enforcement judgment by a court established in another State. This procedure causes unnecessary delays. In addition, it is possible that the court tasked with the recognition may refuse to do so.

---

275 R. Duncan, "*Agricultural Futures and Options: A Guide to Using North American and European markets*", Abington: Woodhead Publishing 1992, p. 53-54, 109. Please be aware that farmers active in the grain trade prefer the options market over the market for futures. Options do not contain an obligation to purchase, but a right (or option) to buy a certain amount of commodities at a predetermined price within a fixed time period. As a condition, the seller must make an upfront premium payment, which cannot be reimbursed. Despite this observation, the present Paragraph rationalizes the existence of nonlegal sanctioning found in Article 24.1 of the GAFTA Arbitration Rules No. 125 by referring to the market for futures. This is because, notwithstanding that it provides a rather one-sided and simplistic explanation, futures are used by parties drafting under GAFTA contracts and provide a satisfactory argument to substantiate the existence and effectiveness of nonlegal sanctioning.

E. The Federation of Cocoa Commerce

I. Background

1. History

To meet the demands of the Western European market,[276] cocoa was imported from South and Middle America from as early as the 17th century.[277] This was risky for many merchants, as storms, corrupt harbour officials, piracy and other dangers could make the quantity of expected cocoa delivery unpredictable. To lower the financial risk of individual journeys, ship-owners started to sell their cargo at auctions or sometimes privately before the commodities arrived.[278] This strategy remained till the beginning of the 19th century, as it was sufficient to accommodate the needs of drinkable chocolate consumers in Western Europe. Decades later, things changed due to increased international trade contingent upon improved vessels and the emergence of large factories that required a steady, high quality and reliable supply of cocoa.[279] In other words, physical arrival of cocoa was almost certain and the risk of a loss of supply was minimal. This enabled merchants to sell cocoa before it even arrived on a fixed day in the future (*i.e.* the emergence of the futures market). As cocoa trade intensified in the subsequent century, also by virtue of the increase in African cocoa supply, merchants who wanted to conduct trade expeditiously favoured trading on standardized contracts. The benefit being that they were easily understood by both parties, without the need of having detailed discussions about the quality of the commodities, risks involved (*e.g. force majeure*) and the settlement of potential disputes.[280] At that time, most standardized contracts stemmed from two trade associations that catered for

---

276 M. Castleman, "*The New Healing Herbs: The Classic Guide to Nature's Best Medicines*", Emmaus: Rodale 2001, p. 140. Cocoa was particularly popular in Belgium, Switzerland, Holland and England as a beverage.

277 L. E. Grivetti and H. Shapiro, "*Chocolate: History, Culture, and Heritage*", in: J. H. Momsen and P. Richardson (ed), "Caribbean Cocoa: Planting and Production", Hoboken: John Wiley & Sons 2009, p. 481. In the mid-17th century, cocoa was also grown in the Spanish and French islands.

278 R. Dand, "*The International Cocoa Trade*", New York: Woodhead Publishing 1996, p. 82.

279 Ibid., p. 83.

280 R. Dand, "*The International Cocoa Trade*", Cambridge/Philadelphia/New Delhi: Woodhead Publishing 2011, p. 97.

the interests of cocoa merchants in Western Europe. The first association is the Cocoa Association of London (CAL) formed in 1928 and the second is the Association Française du Commerce (AFCC), founded in 1935. In 2002 both associations amalgamated to develop a single robust commercial framework for the cocoa market that became known under its current name, the FCC. Its headquarters are located in London.[281]

2. Legal form

Similar to the ICA and GAFTA, the FCC is a not-for profit limited liability company by guarantee.[282] Its goal is to regulate, promote and protect the international cocoa trade and to safeguard the interests of its members. The trade association has neither a fixed number of members, nor any shares or shareholders, but every member can be held liable for his nominal amount paid (Art. 7 and 8 of the FCC Articles of Association (2017)).

3. Institutional structure

The FCC gives members as well as non-members access to its Articles of Association in which its institutional structure is well defined. In detail, this association consists of four bodies that can be subsumed under the following three branches: the legislative (*i.e.* the General Meeting), the executive (*i.e.* the Council and the Board) and the judiciary (*i.e.* the *ad hoc* arbitration tribunal). The General Meeting takes place annually and is tasked with, *inter alia*, organising a poll to allow members to cast a vote to (re-)elect a member for the Council (Art. 32 and 92 of the FCC Articles of Association (2017)).[283] The Council consists of a maximum number of 18 individuals, 14 voting members who are elected in the General Meeting and four non-voting-members who are appointed by the councillors following the installation of the Council (Art. 29 till 34 of the FCC Articles of Association (2017)). The main duty and right of the Council is to appoint the FCC's Board, consisting of the chairman, the vice-chairman and the

281 30 Watling St, London EC4M 9BR, UK.

282 Prelude and Article 6 of the FCC Articles of Association (2017) (to access: https://www.cocoafederation.com/dashboard/documents/download/371).

283 For all rules pertaining to the General Meeting, see Articles 92 to 122 of the FCC Articles of Association (2017).

treasurer and is tasked with representing the association *ex-officio* (Art. 36 and 58 of the FCC Articles of Association (2017)).[284] In addition, the Council has many other tasks, including drafting or amending standardized contracts, organising arbitration, etc. (Art. 56 and 78a of the FCC Articles of Association (2017)).[285] The fourth body of the association is the arbitration tribunal, which is discussed below.[286]

4. Membership

The FCC, which represents over a 1,000 members in 84 countries[287], divides membership into five categories (Art. 10 to 15 inclusive of the FCC Articles of Association (2017)).[288] The first class is the voting member, which can be any individual, partnership, unincorporated association or any other legal entity or body corporate active in the cocoa trade with (capital) assets exceeding £500,000 (Art. 10 of the FCC Articles of Association (2017)). The second class consists of associate members who are individuals, body corporates or entities that cannot meet the capital requirement mentioned above, but have more than £100,000 and/or satisfy other requirements determined by the Council (Art. 11 of the FCC Articles of Association (2017)). The third category comprises individual non-voting members serving the cocoa trade, without being actively involved (Art. 12 of the FCC Articles of Association (2017)). The last two categories are made up of group members, who are composed of body corporates connected (*e.g.* shareholding) with a voting member/non-voting member (as

284 The Board also comprises of a secretary, although this individual does not have voting powers. See Article 58 of the FCC Articles of Association (2017).

285 The Council is tasked with "*(ii) issuing and amending forms of contracts, charter-parties, bills of lading, policies of insurance and other transactional documentation to be used in the course of the Trade as promoted by the Federation; (iii) settling and amending rules for the accurate sampling, analysis and examination of Cocoa Beans, Cocoa Products and related articles; (iv) arbitrating the settlement of disputes arising out of transactions in or relating to the Trade; (v) petitioning, making representations to or entering into any arrangement with any parliaments, governments, agencies or authorities, supreme, municipal, local or otherwise; (vi) the appointment and removal of the Secretary (and any joint, assistant or deputy secretary); and (vii) organising Members' events and education and training*".

286 For a more detailed discussion of how the arbitration tribunal is formed, see Part I, Chapter 2, E, I, 5.

287 https://www.cocoafederation.com/fcc/members.

288 https://www.cocoafederation.com/membership/categories-of-membership.

well as constituting a body corporate) active in or serving the cocoa trade (Art. 14 of the FCC Articles of Association (2017)) and honorary members (Art. 15 of the FCC Articles of Association (2017)). To become eligible, besides falling under one of the five categories of membership, a potential member of the FCC must also submit an application and pay a fee, unless he is an honorary member (Art. 18 till 22 of the FCC Articles of Association (2017)).

5. Specialized commercial arbitration

a. A dichotomy of arbitration forms

To promote the trade in cocoa, the FCC has developed a system of arbitration to resolve disputes between market participants trading on the basis of standardized contracts of the association. Despite having uniform arbitration rules, the FCC divides arbitration into two forms: first, quality and, second, other than quality arbitration. Whereas both proceedings have different time limits for submitting evidence in first instance and second instance appeal as well as for hearings in both instances, no further differences exist (Art. 2.11, 2.14, 3.1, 3.8 and 3.12 of the FCC Arbitration and Appeal Rules (2017)).[289] Therefore, this Chapter does not divide arbitration into two proceedings, but discusses both forms as if they were very similar, with some emphasis on the differences mentioned above.

b. Selection of arbitrators

Providing a remedy for the settlement of disputes is paramount for organising and maintaining a system of private ordering by the FCC. Once a conflict arises between two market participants in the wake of a coca sale and/or purchase contract, subject to and conditional upon an acceptance of FCC arbitration in a clause and an application to start arbitration by the claimant, the Secretary of the FCC appoints three qualified arbitrators (Art. 1.2, 1.11, 2.4 (a) of the FCC Arbitration and Appeal Rules (2017)). Only when the parties do not agree on the nomination, or when an arbi-

289 The FCC Arbitration and Appeal Rules of 2017 (to access: https://www.cocoafederation.com/dashboard/documents/freecontent/rules/arbitration-and-appeal/arbitration-appeal-rules/ENG).

trator dies, becomes ill or incapable, is the composition of the arbitration tribunal final (Art. 2.4 (d), 2.6 and 2.7 of the FCC Arbitration and Appeal Rules (2017)). To reach a decision on a dispute that is referred to them, the tribunal must render an arbitral award on the basis of the majority rule (Art. 2.8 of the FCC Arbitration and Appeal Rules (2017)). In the absence of a majority or unanimity, the chairman of the tribunal has the decisive vote. In appeal, the Secretary of the FCC nominates three arbitrators of the Panel to constitute a Board of Appeal (Art. 3.2 (a) of the FCC Arbitration and Appeal Rules (2017)).

In terms of eligibility, an individual voting and associate member of the FCC (irrespective of his job as a lawyer) is qualified to serve as an arbitrator when he is selected from a panel of experienced cocoa professionals who are approved by the Council.[290] In order to be placed on the list of qualified arbitrators, the procedure to become either a technical or a quality arbitrator must be successfully followed. With regard to the former, the Secretariat of the FCC proposes an individual who has passed all mandatory FCC arbitration training courses for initial review to the Council (Art. 3.1.1 of the Application Procedure to Join the FCC Arbitration and Appeal Panel).[291] If the Council agrees that an individual is suitable to serve as a technical arbitrator, the candidate will be considered officially a technical arbitrator (Art. 3.1.2 and 3.1.3 of the Application Procedure to Join the FCC Arbitration and Appeal Panel).

Albeit partly similar, the procedure to become a quality arbitrator appears to be more specific. Again the Secretary has to propose a candidate to the Council pending initial review (Art. 3.2 of the Application Procedure to Join the FCC Arbitration and Appeal Panel). Yet, to be officially installed, this individual must (i) attend a cocoa bean quality assessment; (ii) substantiate any evidence of his proficiency in quality assessment in accordance with the FCC Contract and Quality Rules (*e.g.* measuring broken beans); and (iii) effectuate a cut test that assesses his generic expertise of bean count and quality (Art. 3.2.3 to 3.2.5 inclusive of the Application Procedure to Join the FCC Arbitration and Appeal Panel).

290 https://www.cocoafederation.com/services/arbitration/arbitration; https://www.cocoafederation.com/dashboard/documents/download/211.

291 The Application Procedure to Join the FCC Arbitration and Appeal Panel of 2017 (to access: https://www.cocoafederation.com/dashboard/documents/download/382).

c. Choice of tribunal and jurisdiction of arbitration tribunals

Any dispute that is referred to FCC arbitration is governed by the legal jurisdiction of England and Wales (Art. 1.4 of the FCC Arbitration and Appeal Rules (2017)). In addition, the provisions of the Arbitration Act 1996 or any other replacement thereof apply to the proceedings. When an arbitration tribunal is installed, the arbitrators may rule on their own substantive jurisdiction, but only to establish whether there is a valid and properly constituted arbitration agreement and for all matters submitted to arbitration pursuant to an arbitration clause (Art. 4.1 of the FCC Arbitration and Appeal Rules (2017)). English law (*i.e.* the Arbitration Act 1996) must be complied with.[292]

d. Procedure

In the event of a contractual dispute, the claimant starts arbitral proceedings by submitting an application of arbitration to the Secretary of the FCC and notifying the other party within a timeframe of 56 days thereof (Art. 2.1 and 2.2 of the FCC Arbitration and Appeal Rules (2017)). After, a three-person arbitration tribunal is composed in line with the procedural rules found in Articles 2.4 to 2.9 inclusive of the FCC Arbitration and Appeal Rules (2017).[293] To make a good, accurate and complete decision, the parties in the arbitration proceedings must send all copies of evidence submitted to the other party to the tribunal (Art. 2.11 of the FCC Arbitration and Appeal Rules (2017)).[294] Typically, no hearing takes place, unless the

---

292 Dispute Resolution Service: A Guide to FCC Arbitration of 2015 (to access: https://www.google.de/url?sa=t&rct=j&q=&esrc=s&source=web&cd=2&ved=2ahUKEwjjrYja14HhAhWCyqQKHVmID60QFjABegQICRAC&url=https%3A%2F%2Fwww.cocoafederation.com%2Fdashboard%2Fdocuments%2Fdownload%2F211&usg=AOvVaw38QHl1n8pHknBUKlz_6uof).

293 For a more detailed discussion of how the arbitration tribunal is formed, see Part I, Chapter 2, E, I, 5, b.

294 It is important to emphasize that different timetables of submissions of evidence apply with regard to quality and other than quality arbitration. For the former, the claimant must submit his statement to the respondent at the time of his request for arbitration, followed by submission of a defence statement by the latter individual to the claimant no later than within 21 days (Art. 2.11.1 of the FCC Arbitration and Appeal Rules (2017)). With regard to other than quality arbitration, the claimant must send his statement of the case to the respondent within 21 days after his request to start arbitration proceeding (Art. 2.11.2 (i) of

arbitration tribunal or either party/both parties favour this (Art. 2.14 of the FCC Arbitration and Appeal Rules (2017)). Following contemplation of the dispute by the arbitration tribunal, the tribunal renders a final, conclusive and binding award (Art. 5.1 to 5.3 and 5.7 inclusive of the FCC Arbitration and Appeal Rules (2017)).

If either party disagrees with the findings of the arbitration tribunal in first instance, this individual can request a notice of appeal (Art. 3.2 (a) of the FCC Arbitration and Appeal Rules (2017)). Once the board is installed, except when the appeal concerns a jurisdictional dispute, it must render a final, conclusive and binding award on the basis of all copies of evidence sent to it that have also been sent by one party to the other party and vice versa (Art. 3.8 and 5.9 of the FCC Arbitration and Appeal Rules (2017)).[295]

e. The finality of arbitration or the possibility of (some) legal redress in public courts according to the association?

Judicial power is vested in the FCC two-tier arbitration system. The FCC Arbitration and Appeal Rules (2017) only explain that an award stemming from FCC specialized commercial arbitration is binding and final, without (in wording) excluding the possibility of legal redress at the courts. Whether or not this entails that compensation cannot be found outside the FCC is unclear. Fortunately, these rules contain some articles that specifically refer to the English High Court in conjunction with Section 105 of the Arbitration Act 1996 to revoke the authority of an arbitrator in first and in second instance (Art. 1.11 (h), 2.7 and 3.4 of the FCC Arbitration and Appeal Rules (2017)).

---

the FCC Arbitration and Appeal Rules (2017)). After, the respondent must within a period of 21 days submit his defence to the claimant. (Art. 2.11.2 (ii) of the FCC Arbitration and Appeal Rules (2017)). Subsequently, the claimant must within a timeframe of 21 days make a statement of his counter-claim to the respondent (Art. 2.11.2 (iii) of the FCC Arbitration and Appeal Rules (2017)).

295 The same time limits for the submission of evidence apply pertaining to FCC arbitration proceedings in first instance, with the exception that for quality arbitration the appellant must submit evidence to the respondent within 21 days following his request to start arbitral proceedings. See Art. 3.8 of the FCC Arbitration and Appeal Rules (2017).

II. Nonlegal sanctioning

The FCC provides two methods of punishing non-compliance with awards by disobedient parties following specialized commercial arbitration. As is explained below, a party can be blacklisted and/or excluded from the association.

1. Blacklisting

As stipulated by Article 5.16 of the FCC Arbitration and Appeal Rules (2017), once a party refuses to comply with a final and binding arbitral award stemming from the FCC two-tier arbitration system, the Council is empowered to publish the name of the offender on the website of this association.[296] In addition, the Council has complete freedom to disseminate this information to all members and organisations worldwide, without taking limitations into account.[297]

2. Withdrawing membership

At the absolute discretion of the Council of the FCC, membership can also be suspended or withdrawn in the event that a member does not comply with an arbitral award (Art. 25 of the FCC Articles of Association (2017)). That decision "may" be posted by the Board and, if decided by the Council, "shall" be published on the website of the FCC and/or sent to all members and/or organizations, without having regard to constraints (Art. 26 of the FCC Articles of Association (2017)).

296 For the FCC's complete default list, see https://www.cocoafederation.com/services/arbitration/defaulters.

297 FCC Dispute Resolution Service: A Guide to FCC Arbitration of 2015, p. 6 (to access: https://www.google.de/url?sa=t&rct=j&q=&esrc=s&source=web&cd=1&cad=rja&uact=8&ved=2ahUKEwjE0eqVpdngAhXDsHEKHSQ_DtQQFjAAegQIBBAC&url=https%3A%2F%2Fwww.cocoafederation.com%2Fdashboard%2Fdocuments%2Fdownload%2F211&usg=AOvVaw38QHl1n8pHknBUKlz_6uof).

III. Rationale for private enforcement/nonlegal sanctioning

As already partially explained in the historic overview of the formation of the FCC, due to the limited risks and certainty of the arrival of physical cocoa shipments, this commodity can be sold before it even enters the port of destination. Despite this benefit, the price of physical cocoa is highly volatile. To protect the buyer and the seller active in the trade against any risk, the FCC has developed standardized futures contracts. This entails that the buyer and the seller engage in forward sales by determining a fixed price to be paid to the seller at an agreed place and time in the future.[298] This is important, as it protects the buyer and the seller against uncertain future prices. If the price of cocoa goes up, the buyer can still purchase this commodity from the seller at the agreed price. Alternatively, if the price goes down, the buyer must pay the seller the agreed price. [299]

Much like the standardized contracts of the ICA and GAFTA, futures contracts bear the risk that either party can violate its duty to comply with contractual obligations. Disloyalty can be rewarding when the seller can get a higher price for the same quantity of cocoa, in the event this individual is delivering to another buyer rather than complying with the futures contract. Vice versa, the buyer can be triggered to buy cocoa from another merchant in lieu of adhering to the futures contract if the former party can buy cocoa at a decreased price. Either way, the principle of the sanctity of contract can be violated when expected legal fees do not offset the potential gains.

To prevent this, a system of FCC arbitration was introduced to safeguard the notion that once parties enter into a futures contract, they must honour their obligations under that contract. When a party is ordered by an FCC *ad hoc* arbitration tribunal to compensate the other party, there is still a risk that this decision is unenforceable in court. Fortunately, the FCC provides two types of nonlegal sanctions to ensure compliance, namely blacklisting and withdrawing membership. In other words, to ensure the success and effectiveness of futures contracts, nonlegal sanctioning plays a pivotal role.

---

298 J. Baffes, D. F. Larson, and P. Varangis, "*Commodities Market Reforms: Lessons of Two Decades*", Washington: The International Bank for Reconstruction 2001, p. 38.

299 P. Robbins, "*Stolen Fruit: The Tropical Commodities Disaster*", London/New York: Zed Books et al 2003, p. 167.

In addition to this explanation, nonlegal sanctions are necessary in the sense that enforcement of arbitral awards in public courts has proven to cause unnecessary problems. This is mainly because of the fact that parties of the standardized contracts provided by the FCC are often located in two different States. As a result, a public court in the State of registration must issue an enforcement judgment and another State's court must recognize this judgment. This is often not as straightforward as it may appear and causes unnecessary delays and uncertainty.

F. The London Metal Exchange

I. Background

1. History

The historical roots of the LME can be traced back all the way to the formation of the London-based Royal Exchange in 1571.[300] This bourse was the first futures commodities exchange of the world and was the meeting point for traders active in the metal trade.[301] Notwithstanding its historical importance, metal trading was rather underdeveloped in the 16th and 17th centuries. This changed during the course of the Industrial Revolution of the late 18th and the 19th century owing to a considerable increase in the demand for metals, which often required large investments to be made by merchants.[302] Not only had the volume of international trade expanded, but also its structure had changed.[303] To mitigate the high risks involved in importing metals by dint of sharply fluctuating prices, a futures market developed in which metals could be sold at a fixed price (negotiated at the trade date) for delivery at a future place and time.[304]

---

300 P. Bernholz and R. Vaubel, "*Explaining Monetary and Financial Innovation: A Historical Analysis*", Heidelberg/New York/Dordrecht/London: Springer International Publishing 2014, p. 267.

301 M. L. Huszar, "*Rohstoffe als Investmentklasse: Eine theoretische und empirische Analyse*", Hamburg: Diplomica Verlag GmbH 2008, p. 4-5.

302 N. Schoon, "*Modern Islamic Banking: Products and Processes in Practice*", Chichester: John Wiley & Sons 2016, p. 117.

303 M. Gorham and N. Singh, "*Electronic Exchanges: The Global Transformation from Pits to Bits*", London a.o.: Elsevier 2009, p. 4.

304 C. Hibbert, B. Weinreb, and J. Keay, "*The London Encyclopaedia (3rd Edition)*", London: Macmillan London Limited 1983, p. 505.

Against this background and on account of the increasing importance of the trade in non-ferrous metals, the LME was formed in London in 1877.[305] From the outset, this trade association had four functions: first, to provide a single-market place in which non-ferrous metals could be traded. Second, to publish standardized futures contracts. Third, to record the daily prices of non-ferrous metal. Fourth, to offer industry actors contracting under LME standardized rules a possibility to settle their disputes in specialized commercial arbitration.

2. Legal form

Since its formation in 1877 the LME operated as a member-owned mutual society. Although this corporate structure lasted for more than a century, in 1987 the LME exchange was converted into a "company limited by guarantee" under the Companies Act.[306] Once again, in the wake of the growing significance of technology, the members of the LME opted for a change of organization and corporate structure in 2000, resulting in the formation of a new holding company (*i.e.* the LME Holdings Ltd) in 2001.[307] Existing members were given shares in the holding company (or after a refusal, cash payments) to allow future capital raisings.[308] Despite its conversion of a mutual company owned by its members into a "private company limited by shares" (*i.e.* the process of demutualization), the LME is still operated on a not-for-profit basis.

3. Institutional structure

Full-disclosure is given by the LME with regard to its institutional structure. This association is composed of three main bodies, namely the Gener-

305 Non-ferrous metals are metals or alloys that do not contain iron (ferrite) in appreciable amounts.

306 E. Banks, "*Exchange-Traded Derivatives*", Chichester: John Wiley & Sons 2003, p. 105.

307 Ibid., p. 106; Article 1.1 of the London Metal Exchange Rules and Regulations of 2019 (to access: https://www.lme.com/LME-Clear/Rules-and-regulations).

308 Liability of the members of the LME is limited to the amount of their shares. See Article 3 of the LME Articles of Association of 2013 (to access: https://www.lme.com/-/media/Files/LME-Clear/Governance/Approved-LMEC-Articles-of-Association.pdf?la=en-GB).

al Meeting, the Board and, in the event of a dispute, an *ad hoc* arbitration tribunal. The General Meeting, which is convened by the Board with a notice period of a minimum of 14 days, takes place annually and is tasked with adopting new resolutions such as, *inter alia*, the removal of a director or auditor before the expiration date of his office in line with Section 282 of the Companies Act 2006 (Art. 2 (a), 45 (a), 57 (b) of the LME Articles of Association (2013)). The Board, on the other hand, consists of nine directors who are mandated to promote the success of the association as whole (Art. 6(a) and 22(a) of the LME Articles of Association (2013)). By taking decisions in line with the majority principle, this body which is responsible for representing the members on a day-to-day basis can be seen as the impetus of the association (Art. 9 of the LME Articles of Association (2013)). Although not instructed to resolve conflicts between parties who conducted business on the basis of one of the standardized rules of the LME, it supervises the installation of an *ad hoc* arbitration tribunal. Such a dispute resolution mechanism is formed on the basis of specific rules that are discussed below.[309]

4. Membership

The Board of the LME is empowered to grant membership when a potential candidate falls within one of the seven categories of membership, fulfils the applicable requirements (*e.g.* admission fee) and makes an application on the basis of Part 2, Article 5.1 of the LME Rulebook (2019).[310] Potential category 1 members comprise foreign undertakings or undertakings/managing members of undertakings which are foreign undertakings or body corporates incorporated in the UK[311] that have an exclusive right to trade LME contracts in the telephone market, by open outcry in the

309 For a more detailed discussion of how the arbitration tribunal is formed, see Part I, Chapter 2, F, I, 5.

310 The LME Rulebook of 2019 (to access: https://www.lme.com/-/media/Files/Regulation/Rulebook/Full-Rulebook/Rulebook-as-of-January-2019.pdf?la=en-GB).

311 These requirements for the legal nature of potential candidates apply to categories 1 to 5 of LME membership.

Ring[312] or on LMEselect (Part 2, Art. 2.2 of the LME Rulebook (2019)).[313] In addition, they are entitled to clear trade in the clearinghouse. A candidate of category 2 membership must fulfil similar conditions, but is not permitted to trade LME contracts by open outcry in the Ring (Part 2, Art. 2.3 of the LME Rulebook (2019)).[314]

More distinctly, potential category 3 candidates must be clearing members that are authorized to trade LME contracts on LMEselect and in the telephone market, without, unlike the first two categories of membership, being allowed to issue client contracts (Part 2, Art. 2.4 of the LME Rulebook (2019)). Category 4 membership requires candidates not to be clearing members, whilst having the competence to trade client contracts on LMEselect and in the telephone market (Part 2, Art. 2.5 of the LME Rulebook (2019)). Categories 5 mandates candidates to be a customer of a category 1 to 4 member of the LME or qualify as a physical market participant wishing to be associated with this association, whereas categories 6 and 7 concern individuals who desire to be near to the LME community and honorary members (Part 2, Art. 2.6 to 2.8 of the LME Rulebook (2019)).

5. Specialized commercial arbitration

a. The single arbitration model

To sustain an orderly market, with the purpose of resolving member-to-member disputes, without having to resort to public court decision-making, the LME provides a well-functioning specialized commercial arbitration system. Different from the ICA, GAFTA and the FCC, but similar to the DDC, this association caters for a single arbitration model, without differentiating between quality and technical dispute resolution.

---

312 Open outcry in the Ring is the trading of metal in sessions of five minutes on the LME exchange. See https://www.lme.com/en-GB/Trading/Trading-venues/Ring#tabIndex=0.

313 LMEselect is the electronic member of the member trading system that allows anonymous trading by respecting certain tradable hours. See https://www.lme.com/en-GB/Trading/Systems/LMEselect#tabIndex=0.

314 https://www.lme.com/en-GB/Trading/Access-the-market/Membership-categories#tabIndex=0.

b. Selection of arbitrators

Typically, all disputes arising out of contracts subject to the rules of the LME are referred to two arbitrators (Part 8, Art. 3.1 of the LME Rulebook (2019)). However, both parties can agree to sole arbitration or, at the request of either party and when at least one arbitrator deems this necessary, allow the Secretary of the LME to appoint a third arbitrator (Part 8, Art. 3.5 of the LME Rulebook (2019)). Alternatively, a third arbitrator who will be considered the chairman of the *ad hoc* arbitration tribunal can be appointed when two arbitrators cannot reach a decision and request the Secretary to nominate a third arbitrator (Part 8, Art. 3.6 and 12.2.1 of the LME Rulebook (2019)).

To become eligible to be selected as an LME arbitrator, panellists do not have to be members of the LME or have to be linked to the association, but need to demonstrate a broad knowledge owing to the individual's practical experience in trading metals.[315] What this entails is unclear, as any yardstick to measure the required amount of experience is not provided by the LME or explained in legal doctrine. In spite of this uncertainty, the associations names twenty-three arbitrators that may serve on *ad hoc* arbitration panels.[316] Being a lawyer is not a limitation to serve as an arbitrator.

c. Choice of tribunal and jurisdiction of arbitration tribunals

Any LME arbitration is held in England and Wales (*i.e.* the seat of arbitration) (Part 8, Art. 7.7 of the LME Rulebook (2019)). Whereas hearings are usually held at a venue in both countries, the parties can deviate from this general rule. Documents-only or telecommunication/video-linked arbitration is possible as well as hearings that take place outside both countries (Part 8, Art. 7.1, 7.3 and 7.4 of the LME Rulebook (2019)).

With regard to the jurisdiction of any formed LME arbitration tribunal, the appointed arbitrator or arbitrators of this tribunal must decide on their own jurisdiction in compliance with English law. This entails that the Arbitration Act 1996 must be adhered to or, where the arbitration regulation provides otherwise, the applicable alternative English law defined in that arbitration regulation.

---

315 https://www.lme.com/en-GB/About/Regulation/Arbitration#tabIndex=0.
316 https://www.lme.com/About/Regulation/Arbitration/Arbitration-panel.

d. Procedure

LME arbitration, which is not designed for mediation or conciliation commences when a claimant notifies the respondent of its intention to arbitrate a dispute (Part 8, Art. 2.1 of the LME Rulebook (2019)). Concurrently, the claimant must provide a copy of this notification to the Secretary of the LME as well as a duplicate of the registration fee paid and deposit that indicates the date of payment (Part 8, Art. 2.3 of the LME Rulebook (2019)). After this notification, the arbitration tribunal will be formed, which can be composed of a sole arbitrator, two arbitrators or three arbitrators.[317] Within a timeframe of 21 days following the installation of the tribunal, the claimant must then provide the respondent and the tribunal of all evidence to substantiate its claim (Part 8, Art. 6.2 of the LME Rulebook (2019)). Subsequently, within 21 days the respondent must send the claimant and the tribunal its written defence (Part 8, Art. 6.4 of the LME Rulebook (2019)). Following receipt of the respondent's written defence, the claimant may make a counterclaim within 21 days, which must be forwarded to the respondent and the tribunal (Part 8, Art. 6.5 of the LME Rulebook (2019)). In complete freedom, the respondent may then submit a counterclaim to the claimant and the tribunal within 21 days (Part 8, Art. 6.6 of the LME Rulebook (2019)).

Following an economic, expeditious and just assessment of the dispute, the arbitration tribunal then makes an award in writing (Part 8, Art. 4 and 12.1 of the LME Rulebook (2019)). This decision is final and binding on the parties and may not be appealed within the LME (Art. 12.8 of the LME Rulebook (2019)).

e. The finality of arbitration or the possibility of (some) legal redress in public courts according to the association?

Any LME arbitration tribunal has the exclusive competence to resolve disputes arising out of the completion, validity or existence of this association's standardized rules (Part 8, Art. 10.1 and 11.3 of the LME Rulebook (2019)).

317 For a more detailed discussion of how the arbitration tribunal is formed, see Part I, Chapter 2, F, I, 5, b.

In addition, unless the parties agree otherwise, contesting an award at any public court is prohibited (Part 8, Art. 12.8 of the LME Rulebook (2019)).

II. Nonlegal sanctioning

Once the time for payment of an arbitral award has elapsed, as is discussed below, the LME can punish a defaulter by entering the defaulter's premises to search for information, publishing the defaulter's name on a default list and suspending or withdrawing the defaulter's membership.[318] Even though the LME does not instruct members to abstain from trading with an expelled member, the LME has far-reaching powers to ensure compliance with any award stemming from this association's arbitration.

1. The power to enter premises

The LME has the authority to enter the premises belonging to the defaulter to seize any records and extracts concerning the defaulter's trading and accounting activities with the aim to determine (i) other unsettled contracts; (ii) the names and addresses of counterparties; (iii) information of warrants and money held (to pay other counterparties); (iv) records of other property; and (iv) all information the LME may deem necessary or expedient to carry out its duties under the Default Regulation (Part 9, Art. 5.1 of the LME Rulebook (2019)).[319] To help prevent this invasion of privacy from further affecting its reputation, since news spreads quickly, any defaulter must cooperate with the power to enter its premises (Part 9, Art. 5.2

---

318 Only when a category 1 to 4 member is declared a defaulter for not adhering to an award made in LME arbitration, is the Default Regulation as laid down in Part 9 of the LME Rulebook (2019) be applicable. Category 5, 6 or 7 members are not bound by this regulation, unless they entered into an LME contract (Art. 2.1 of the LME Rulebook (2019)). Any defaulter as well as the other party have 14 days to submit a confirmation of payment to the Secretary following the sending of a notice of application (*i.e.* non-payment has occurred) to the Secretary (Part 8, Art. 12.12 and 12.14 of the LME Rulebook (2019)). See also https://www.lme.com/About/Regulation/Arbitration#tabIndex=1).

319 Much like the power of the EU Commission to enter the premises of suspected competition law offenders in line with Article 20 of Regulation 1/2003, the LME has similar competences to inspect.

and 5.3 of the LME Rulebook (2019)). Counterparties are also invited to provide information about unsettled contracts

2. Blacklisting

Following the LME establishing that a party is considered a defaulter under the Default Regulation, the exchange is obligated to post a notice of this finding in the exchange and inform, where appropriate, other persons and counterparties of unsettled contracts with the defaulter (Part 9, Art. 4.1 of the LME Rulebook (2019)). This notice may also be circulated to other exchanges and clearinghouses approved under Part VII of the Companies Act 1989,[320] the Secretary of State, the Treasury, recognized investment exchanges or regulatory bodies, applicable office holders, and any authority or body associated with the defaulter under the arbitrated contract (Part 9, Art. 10 of the LME Rulebook (2019)).

3. Withdrawing membership

When a disloyal member is considered a defaulter within the meaning of the Default Regulation, the Directors may also immediately suspend or withdraw membership (Part 2, Art. 15.1, 15.2.3 and 15.2.4 of the LME Rulebook (2019)). For a suspension to be considered legitimate, this method must be unavoidable to ensure an orderly market and alternative methods to ensure compliance with statutory obligations must be absent (Part 2, Art. 15.3 of the LME Rulebook (2019)). As such nonlegal sanction can seriously harm members, a targeted individual/company has the right to ask for a reassessment of the facts of the case (*i.e.* lodge an appeal) at the LME Appeal Committee (Part 9, Art. 15.4 of the LME Rulebook (2019)).

With regard to an expulsion, the Directors have complete discretion to effectuate this form of nonlegal sanctioning, without having to comply with any or similar yardstick vis-à-vis a suspension (Part 9, Art. 15.5 of the LME Rulebook (2019)). Although any targeted member may appeal at the LME Appeal Committee, that member's membership is suspended pending the outcome of the appeal. After the committee confirms that the decision of the arbitrator to expel a member is justified, that member's mem-

320 The Companies Act of 1989 (to access: http://www.legislation.gov.uk/ukpga/1989/40/contents).

bership will be withdrawn. As a result, the defaulter forfeits all privileges of being a member of the LME (e.g. right to entry to the exchange), without being entitled to be reimbursed for subscription or fees already paid (Part 2, Art. 16.1 and 16.2 of the LME Rulebook (2019)).

III. Rationale for private enforcement/nonlegal sanctioning

The LME is a designated futures exchange for aluminium, copper, tin, lead, zinc and silver.[321] To hedge price fluctuations concerning these commodities, the exchange provides standardized rules for its members to exchange an underlying security at an agreed price for future delivery.[322] Under the contract, the buyer is obligated to purchase the underlying asset for the predetermined price and the seller is duty-bound to deliver the contract for this monetary sum.

Although prices are calculated on the basis of the world's demand and supply as well as on the price of the British Pound sterling and the US Dollar, there is a clear risk that both buyers and sellers conducting trade on the basis of futures are induced to deviate from agreed contracts, especially when entering into another contract with a different buyer/seller brings more profit for the seller/buyer and contingent upon the estimation that future legal compensation pertaining to court adjudication is lower than the gains. The LME's setting up its own system of arbitration, and ensuring compliance with its awards by nonlegal sanctions, eliminates this risk of parties deviating from their futures contracts. Access to the LME is important to trade in the metals market, and being blacklisted, expelled as well as having one's premises being searched can hamper a member's reputation. In other words, nonlegal sanctions to guarantee compliance with LME arbitral awards is crucial to safeguarding the system of standardized futures contracts and greatly curtails disloyalty.

Similar to the ICA, FOSFA and the FCC, a second reason for the use of nonlegal sanctions concerns the inadequacy of public court enforcement of arbitral awards as an efficient alternative to nonlegal sanctioning. Given

321 A. E. Branch, "*International Purchasing and Management*", London: Thomson 2000, p. 63; D. H. Chew, "*Corporate Risk Management*", New York: Columbia University Press 2008, p. 28. Future contracts on copper have already been introduced by the LME in 1883

322 B. A. Goss, "*Futures Markets (Routledge Revivals): Their Establishment and Performance*", in: B. A. Goss (ed.), "The Forward Pricing Function of the London Metal Exchange", London/Sydney: Croom Helm 1986, p. 157.

that LME members are scattered throughout the world and, therefore, parties contracting under an LME standardized rules are located in different States, if public court enforcement had been chosen, the court in the State of registration would need to issue an enforcement judgment of the arbitral award, which then would need to be recognized by a court in another State. This procedure as laid down in the New York Convention causes unnecessary delays and sometimes even more severe problems, such as an unwillingness of a court to recognize an enforcement judgment. Put differently, nonlegal sanctioning completely removes these risks and provides a much better alternative.

G. *The Federation of Oils, Seeds and Fats Association*

I. Background

1. History

The use of edible oils, seeds and fats has its origin in the late 19th and early 20th century with the discovery of the process of hydrogenation, which concerns the transformation of inexpensive liquid unsaturated fats into solid fats by adding hydrogen.[323] As a result, as whale and fish oils could now be made edible and to meet the UK's increase in demand, many plants were erected in this country to execute this process.[324] To develop, *inter alia*, a standard for the purchase of linseed, as early as in 1861 the oil crushers founded the non-profit and impartial Incorporated Oil Seeds Association (IOSA).[325] With the purpose of creating a stronger association, the IOSA merged with three other associations in 1971, including the London Oil and Tallow Trades Association (LOTTA) established in 1910, the London Copra Association (LCA) incorporated in 1913, and the Seed, Oil, Cake, and General Produce Association (SOCGPA) founded in 1935. This international association that is tasked with, *inter alia*, issuing standardized rules to regulate the sale and purchase of oils, seeds and fats and to main-

323 A. S. Villegas and A. Sanchez-Taínta, "*The Prevention of Cardiovascular Disease through the Mediterranean Diet*", London/San Diego/Cambridge/Oxford: Elsevier 2018, p. 49.

324 G. Hoffmann, "*The Chemistry and Technology of Edible Oils and Fats and Their High Fat Products*", London/San Diego: Academic Press 1989, p. 201.

325 J. Mark, R. Strange, and J. Burns, "*The Food Industries, Vol. XXVIII*", London: Chapman & Hall 1993, p. 236.

tain a system of specialized commercial arbitration for the settlement of disputes became known as FOSFA.[326]

2. Legal form

FOSFA is a not-for-profit[327] private company limited by guarantee without share capital.[328] Hence, members are shielded by the "corporate veil" from unlimited liability, even though they are still liable for the amount they have pledged to pay in the event of liquidation of the association.

3. Institutional structure

Comparable to the trade associations already discussed, FOSFA consists of three bodies: the General Meeting, the Council and the *ad hoc* established arbitration tribunals. The General Meeting takes place annually and is tasked with, *inter alia*, despite some vagueness in the FOSFA Rules and Regulations (2018), electing new council members.[329] The Council, on the other hand, which consists of nine directors,[330] has the power to approve new members, publish rules concerning the conduct and procedure of the two-tier arbitration system of FOSFA, to install an appeal board, delegate tasks to specialist/sub committees and ask them to comment on proposals

---

326 T. H. Applewhite, "*Proceedings of the World Conference on Lauric Oils: Sources, Processing, and Application*", Champaign: AOCS Press 1994, p. 29.

327 F. Cafaggi, "*Enforcement of Transnational Regulation: Ensuring Compliance in a Global World*", Cheltenham/Northampton: Edward Elgar 2012, p. 218.

328 https://uk.globaldatabase.com/company/federation-of-oils-seeds-and-fats-associations-limited; http://www.datalog.co.uk/browse/detail.php/CompanyNumber/00926329/CompanyName/FEDERATION+OF+OILS+SEEDS+AND+FATS+ASSOCIATIONS+LIMITED.

329 FOSFA Rules and Regulations of 2018 (to access: https://www.fosfa.org/about-us/rules-and-regulations/).

330 See Article 25 of the FOSFA Rules and Regulations (2018). The Council consists of (i) the President; (ii) the Deputy President; (ii)] the Immediate Past President; (iv) the Chairman of the Oilseeds Section Committee; (v) the Vice Chairman of the Oilseeds Section Committee; (vi) the Chairman of the Oils and Fats Section Committee; (vii) Vice Chairman of the Oils and Fats Section Committee; (viii) the Chairman of the Contracts Committee; and (ix) a NOFOTA representative in an ex-officio (non-voting) capacity; For the current officers of the federation, see https://www.fosfa.org/about-us/officers-of-the-federation/.

(Art. 14 and 34 to 37 of the FOSFA Rules and Regulations (2018)). If there is a conflict between industry actors arising out of one of FOSFA's standardized rules, an *ad hoc* arbitration tribunal may be formed when the claimant requests this.[331]

4. Membership

FOSFA is an international contract-issuing association with over 1,000 members in 84 countries worldwide.[332] Qualifying for membership requires two rules to be complied with. First, an application must be completed, which contains an explanation of which category of FOSFA membership the candidate falls under and whether the candidate is active in the oilseeds and/or oils and fats trade (Art. 4 and 6 of the FOSFA Rules and Regulations (2018)). Second, after acceptance by the Council of the candidate's membership request, payment of the appropriate subscription fee contingent upon the relevant category of membership must be made (Art. 7 of the FOSFA Rules and Regulations (2018)).

With reference to the categories of membership, candidates can fall under the following six groups of members (Art. 4 of the FOSFA Rules and Regulations (2018)). First, normal trading members consisting of companies, sole trader organizations or others conducting trade as principals concerning the commodities of FOSFA. Second, full or associate broker members composed of undertakings, sole traders, organizations or others not acting as principals pertaining to FOSFA contracts that receive commission from the relevant contracting principal(s). Third, full or associate non-trading members, such as organizations, or market participants that do not qualify under any other membership category from time to time. Fourth, FOSFA accredited and recognized analyst members (*i.e.* laboratories or analysts) associated with an undertaking, or organization active in the trade in this association's commodities, without falling under another category of membership. Fifth, FOSFA recognized independent superintendents with the aim of superintending under this association's contracts, without being a member of another category of membership.

331 For a more detailed discussion of how the arbitration tribunal is formed, see Part I, Chapter 2, G, I, 5.

332 https://www.fosfa.org/membership/categories-of-membership/; A. Lista, "*International Commercial Sales: The Sale of Goods on Shipment Terms*", Abingdon/New York: Informa Law from Routledge 2017, p. 10.

5. Specialized commercial arbitration

a. Tripartite arbitration

Disputes arising out of GAFTA contracts are typically solved in compliance with the "internal" arbitration proceedings as laid down in the FOSFA Rules of Arbitration and Appeal (2018)).[333] As this document gives specific information about the arbitration procedure, the composition of the arbitration board as well as measures taken in the event of default with an arbitral award, despite it being only available for members and non-members who pay a fee of £15, it is a key reference in the following Paragraphs.[334] In addition to the standard arbitration procedure, FOSFA governs two other types of dispute resolution, which can be found in the FOSFA Rules for Small Claims Single Tier (2018)[335] and the FOSFA Rules for Brokerage Commissions and Interest (2018).[336] In spite of the fact that both procedures merit discussion, these will not be explained here.[337]

333 FOSFA Rules of Arbitration and Appeal of 2018 (to access: https://www.fosfa.org/document-library/rules-of-arbitration-and-appeal-april-2018/).

334 While FOSFA bans the author's attaching the FOSFA Rules of Arbitration and Appeal (2018) to this research, in the following Paragraphs more quotations are given for the purpose of clarity.

335 https://www.fosfa.org/document-library/rules-for-small-claims-single-tier-april-2018/. This procedure, which can only be chosen when both parties agreed to it in writing is fast-track arbitration proceedings, where a dispute is resolved by a sole arbitrator and where no right of appeal exists (*i.e.* one-tier arbitration system). Unfortunately, it is only available for members and for non-members who pay a fee of £15.

336 https://www.fosfa.org/document-library/rules-for-brokerage-commissions-and-interest-april-2018/. This procedure is applicable in the event of non-payment or late payment of (interest payable on) commission of the brokers in conjunction with FOSFA Contract No. 95. Similar to the other two arbitration proceedings, the FOSFA Rules of Brokerage Commission and Interest (2018) are only accessibly for members and non-members who pay a fee of £15.

337 In my opinion, to discuss these two specialist arbitration proceedings alongside the one laid down in the FOSFA Rules of Arbitration and Appeal (2018) would only increase the complexity of the research, even though they are not common procedure.

b. Selection of arbitrators

Either party in FOSFA specialized commercial arbitration has the right to appoint one arbitrator, unless both parties agree on sole arbitration (Art. 2(a) of the FOSFA Rules of Arbitration and Appeal (2018)). When two arbitrators are appointed or where FOSFA appoints a second arbitrator in the event the respondent fails to nominate such an individual, the association selects a third arbitrator (Art. 2(b) and (e) of the FOSFA Rules of Arbitration and Appeal (2018)). In appeal, the arbitration panel consists of five arbitrators who are appointed by FOSFA (Art. 8(a) of the FOSFA Rules of Arbitration and Appeal (2018)).

To be eligible for such a selection, "*only Trading, Full Broker and Full Non-Trading Members or their nominated representative/s to the Federation shall have the right to act as arbitrators subject to retirement at age 75, if still active in the trade, or two years after retirement, whichever comes first*" (Art. 2(b) of the FOSFA Rules of Arbitration and Appeal (2018)). In addition, candidate arbitrators need to demonstrate a minimum of ten year's experience in the trade, successful completion of periodic training, and a willingness to abide by the Code of Practice for Arbitrators.[338] Individuals who are wholly or principally engaged in private legal practice are not barred from serving as an arbitrator.[339]

c. Choice of tribunal and jurisdiction of arbitration tribunals

To resolve conflicts between parties arising out of FOSFA contracts or questions of law in connection with FOSFA contracts, arbitration takes place in London (Preamble of the FOSFA Rules of Arbitration and Appeal (2018)). Pursuant to Section 3 of the Arbitration Act 1996, the judicial seat of arbitration is therefore England.

Once an *ad hoc* arbitration board is formed, the arbitrator(s) may rule on their own jurisdiction to establish whether a valid agreement exists (Art. 5 (a) of the FOSFA Rules of Arbitration and Appeal (2018)). However, the

338 https://www.fosfa.org/arbitration/directory-of-fosfa-arbitrators/; FOSFA Code of Practice for Arbitrators of 2018 (to access: https://www.fosfa.org/content/uploads/2018/03/Code-of-Practice-for-Arbitrators-and-Time-Sheet-April-2018.pdf).

339 An express prohibition cannot be found in either the FOSFA Rules of Arbitration and Appeal (2018), or in any other document.

construction, validity and performance of any contract is governed by English law.[340]

d. Procedure

To start arbitral proceedings, the claimant must, in writing, send this application to the respondent as well as deliver copies to the appointed arbitrator and to FOSFA (Art. 4 (a) (i) of the FOSFA Rules of Arbitration and Appeal (2018)). If the respondent decides to respond to the claimant's submission, the respondent must also send a copy to FOSFA and a copy to the claimant's arbitrator as well as to the arbitrator it has selected, unless the respondent agrees to sole arbitration (Art. 4. (a) (ii) of the FOSFA Rules of Arbitration and Appeal (2018)). At this stage, in line with the rules on formation described above, the *ad hoc* arbitration tribunal must be formed.[341]

After making a well-contemplated decision on the basis of the documents provided by both parties, the tribunal renders an arbitral award (Art. 4 (c) and (d) and 6 (a) of the FOSFA Rules of Arbitration and Appeal (2018)). Notice of the award is given to both parties (Art. 6 (b) of the FOSFA Rules of Arbitration and Appeal (2018)). Upon receipt, the unsuccessful party has 42 days to pay the award, following which it has an opportunity to lodge an appeal under Article 7 of the FOSFA Rules of Arbitration and Appeal (2018). As a condition, an application for appeal must be made "*not later than 12.00 hours London Time on the 28th consecutive day after the day on which the award is sent to the parties*" (Art. 7 (a) of the FOSFA Rules of Arbitration and Appeal (2018)). Upon the composition of the five-person Board of Appeal and the possibility of both parties having the case heard orally and in writing, the Board issues a binding award (Art. 7 (b) of the FOSFA Rules of Arbitration and Appeal (2018)).

340 FOSFA Guide to Arbitrations and Appeals of 2018 (to access: https://www.fosfa.org/content/uploads/2018/03/FOSFA-Guide-to-Arbitrations-and-Appeals-April-2018.pdf).

341 For a more detailed discussion of how the arbitration tribunal is formed, see Part I, Chapter 2, G, I, 5, b.

e. The finality of arbitration or the possibility of (some) legal redress in public courts according to the association?

An award stemming from specialized commercial arbitration is final and binding (Art. 7 (b) of the FOSFA Rules of Arbitration and Appeal (2018)). Obtaining legal redress at public courts prior to commencing arbitration proceedings and after the rendering of an award is not clarified by FOSFA in any of its rules. The association only explains that a party in whose favour an award has been made has the right to seek enforcement at the English High Court and in other signatory States of the Geneva Convention of 1927 and the New York Convention (FOSFA Guide to Arbitrations and Appeals (2018)).

II. Nonlegal sanctioning

If any party post arbitral proceedings neglects or refuses to carry out or abide by an award of arbitrators or board of appeal, the Council of FOSFA is tasked with putting two types of nonlegal sanctions into effect to punish that party's disloyalty. The first method pertains to blacklisting and the second to withdrawing membership. Both are explained below.

1. Blacklisting

Following non-compliance with an arbitral award, whether stemming from first-tier or second-tier arbitration, the claimant and the respondent must within a period of 28 consecutive days after the date of issuance take up the award (Art. 11(c) of the FOSFA Rules of Arbitration and Appeal (2018)). If this time limit has lapsed, the Council of FOSFA must notify both parties of such disloyalty. When this call is again not heeded, the Council is empowered to post on FOSFA's notice board and/or disseminate this information to its members in any way it considers effective (Art. 11(c) and (d) of the FOSFA Rules of Arbitration and Appeal (2018)).[342] Whether the Council is also empowered to give information concerning defaulters to other associations/exchanges and non-members

342 Dissemination of the names of defaulters is done by means of a circular. The list of companies posted is published on a yearly basis, but remains only accessible for FOSFA members. See https://www.fosfa.org/arbitration/posted-companies/.

remains unclear. As it stands, the rules of FOSFA do not contain a provision that neither permits nor prohibits this.

2. Withdrawing membership

After a member has been blacklisted by the Council of FOSFA, that member's membership is automatically terminated, if a majority of Directors support withdrawing membership (Art. 18 of the FOSFA Rules and Regulations (2018)). However, at least three-quarters of the Council must be present to take away the membership of an undertaking, organization, sole trader or others. This entails that they lose access to FOSFA as well as, *inter alia*, voting rights in the general meeting. In addition, targeted members are placed at a disadvantage in three other ways. First, they do not have the right to lodge an appeal. Second, they are not awarded a refund of subscription fees already paid. Third, they will not be notified of the reasons for termination.

III. Rationale for private enforcement/nonlegal sanctioning

Unlike the previously discussed UK-based trade associations that provide members with standardized futures contracts in which participants purchase and sell a stipulated quantity of commodities for delivery on a specified future date at a predetermined price (*i.e.* the ICA, GAFTA, the FCC and the LME), FOSFA issues standard rules for the physical transfer of oils, seeds and fats.[343] In other words, this association is a rule-generating system for market participants active in the cash or spot markets in which prices are determined instantly as opposed to on the basis of forward prices.[344] Characteristic for the trade in such markets is that contracting parties do not enter into complete standardized contracts, but incorporate all or some of the relevant trading rules provided by, in this instance, FOS-

---

343 D. R. Erickson, "*Practical Handbook of Soybean Processing and Utilization*", Urbana: AOCS Press 1995, p. 50.

344 N. N. Chatnani, "*Commodities Markets: Operations, Instruments, and Applications*", New Delhi: Tata McGraw Hill 2010, p. 4.

FA.[345] As a result of this cherry-picking, each sales agreement may vary in terms of its delivery terms, quality and quantity.

Whereas trading partners conducting trade under the terms of FOSFA are often unfamiliar with one another, especially given the global dimension of the trade in oils, seeds and fats, disputes are not uncommon. Owing to the inefficiency of the public court system as well as a lack of know-how and experience of judges in public courts with regard to these commodities, and to address contractual unfaithfulness, FOSFA has put a two-tier arbitration system in place. By operating in the shadow of the law, even though arbitral awards may be enforced in public courts, a party in whose favour such a decision is made is protected by dint of nonlegal sanctions.[346] Given that blacklisting and withdrawing membership are harmful to the reputation of market participants and even have a foreclosure effect, FOSFA arbitral awards are typically complied with.

A second reason for the use of nonlegal sanctions by FOSFA relates to the enforcement and recognition of judgments pursuant to the New York Convention. This is problematic in the hypothetical situation that two parties contracting under a standardized agreement of this trade association on the cash or spot markets can only seek enforcement in a public court. Given that such parties are often globally dispersed, it would require the enforcement of an arbitral award in one State and the recognition of a different court in another State. For this reason, which results in a slow procedure and owing to an uncertainty whether the latter court will recognize this award, the procedure is considered less efficient. FOSFA arbitration functions properly under the threat of nonlegal sanctions, because it addresses both problems and provides a necessary alternative form of dispute resolution.

345 A. R. Baldwin, "*World Conference on Emerging Technologies in the Fats and Oils Industry*", in: E.C. Campbell (ed.), "Trade Association Rules - Impact on International Trade", Urbana: American Oil Chemists' Society 1986, p. 24.

346 According to the FOSFA Guide to Arbitrations and Appeals (2018), only if nonlegal sanctions are insufficient to induce a party to pay an award, is enforcement in the public legal system advised.

Chapter 3: A comparative view of the Present-Day PLSs and their respective enforcement mechanisms

A. *Introduction*

Based on the discussed transnational trade associations active in a wide spectrum of the commodities trade, whether providing standardized futures contracts or trade rules for the cash or spot markets, all have set up an arbitration system and have introduced nonlegal sanctions to punish disloyalty with its awards. By generating rules and resolving industry-specific conflicts, the trade associations as well as their members and – arguably – non-members operate PLSs as substitutes for the public court system.

In my opinion, drawing such a conclusion is not contentious. However, additional emphasis must be given to establish in what way and to what extent the trade associations differ and coincide with regard to (a) legal form; (b) access to membership; (c) structure and composition of an arbitration tribunal; (d) place of arbitration and applicable law; (e) right to appeal to public courts before and after an arbitration award; (f) types of nonlegal sanctions; and (g) rationale for nonlegal sanctioning. As a result, the goal of this Paragraph is to carry out a well-balanced review of these aspects with the purpose of describing the trade associations in more general terms, without – although occasionally required – specifically referring to them. Particular importance is given to the possibility to appeal at public courts, since UK law (*i.e.* the Arbitration Act 1996), which underlays standardized contracts/rules for five out of the six trade associations researched does not in every aspect correspond with the right of appeal rules of these associations before arbitral proceedings and after an award.[347] Also, standardized DDC contracts, which are underlaid by US law and New York State law might not be in harmony with the two laws.

347 These five associations are the ICA, GAFTA, the FCC, the LME and FOSFA.

B. Legal form

Five of the trade associations researched are UK-based, whereas one is established in New York.[348] With reference to these five trade associations, four of the five are incorporated as a "private limited liability company by guarantee" under the Companies Act 2006.[349] This implies that members are shielded from full liability, with the exception of their nominal amount paid (*e.g.* subscription fee). The sixth trade association is registered as a "private company limited by shares" under the Companies Act 2006, which entails that liability is limited to the shares members hold in the organization.[350] Apart from this (in my opinion, minor) legal distinction, all five trade associations operate on a not-for-profit basis. Similar to a "private limited liability company by guarantee", the New York-based trade association holds members accountable for annual fees paid. Also here, this association, which is registered as an "incorporated company" is not operated with the intention to raise money.

In sum, one can draw the conclusion that rule-generating/dispute-resolving trade associations active in a wide array of commodities trading have two things in common: first, they offer their services on a not-for-profit basis. Second, they limit the liability of their members to the amount paid or the outstanding shares held.

C. Access to membership

All trade associations researched have three entry requirements to obtain membership. First, candidates need to be able to substantiate some sort of connection to/experience in the commodities traded in the relevant industry. Second, candidates must file an application for membership, including an explanation under which membership category they fall.[351] Third, candidates must pay an entry/registration fee.

Apart from these general requirements, two trade associations use additional and more far-reaching requirements that must be complied with.

348 The DDC is located in New York City.

349 The ICA, GAFTA, the FCC and FOSFA are private limited companies by guarantee.

350 The LME is a private limited company by shares.

351 All six trade associations have different forms of membership. For a thorough analysis, see Part I, Chapter 2, B/C/D/E/F/G, I, 4.

The first association is the ICA, which requires that all candidates be proposed by at least two members of the association. In addition, candidates are obligated to comply with the requirement of dissemination. This entails that they must present the directors with all information concerning the constitution, capital and nature of the company. The second trade association that has introduced more stringent requirements is the DDC. It requires that candidates for membership demonstrate a minimum of two years' experience in the diamond trade and that they successfully convince the Board of Directors. With regard to the latter requirement, every candidate must post his picture on the trading floor wall of the DDC for a period of ten days, during which members of this association can make comments. Despite this influence of members, the Board of Directors retains full freedom of discretion to either grant or deny membership.

D. Structure and composition of the arbitration tribunal

The resolution of disputes is a principal goal of all the trade associations researched. To this extent, all have introduced a specialized system of arbitration which aims to resolve conflicts arising out of standardized contracts/rules made by these associations. Apart from the DDC, which favours mediation over arbitration in the sense that arbitration may only be commenced when reaching an amicable settlement is not possible, the other trade associations prioritize arbitration.

I. First-tier arbitration

To select the arbitrators of an arbitration tribunal, the associations can be divided into two groups. The first group consists of the DDC and the FCC that are solely responsible for appointing the arbitration panel. To this extent, both associations nominate three qualified arbitrators. The second group is composed of the ICA, GAFTA, the LME and FOSFA and allows each party to name an arbitrator, or to agree to sole arbitration. Yet, some differences can be detected concerning the selection of a third person when the latter form of arbitration is not chosen. The ICA pertaining to technical arbitration and GAFTA are tasked with appointing a third arbitrator, whereas the LME can only do so (here: the Secretary) when the claimant and/or the respondent request(s) this and where at least one arbitrator deems this necessary. Another difference relates to quality arbitration offered by the ICA, following which the parties can nominate a referee in case of a disagreement, without permitting the selection of a third arbitrator.

II. Second-tier arbitration/internal appeal

Another interesting aspect of the specialized commercial arbitration system provided by the trade associations relates to possibility of internal appeal. Except for the LME, the other five associations maintain a two-tier arbitration system which allows awards rendered in first-tier arbitration to be reviewed/re-assessed by a special appeal committee. Nonetheless, the number of arbitrators who make up these committees varies. FOSFA, the DDC and the ICA concerning technical arbitration require five arbitrators[352], whereas the FCC requires an appeal committee to be composed of three arbitrators. GAFTA takes a middle position in the sense that when an award is rendered by a sole arbitrator, the committee is composed of three arbitrators and whenever an award is rendered by a tribunal consisting of three arbitrators, the appeal committee is composed of five arbitrators. In another way, the ICA pertaining to quality arbitration has a more flexible understanding of the number of arbitrators. An appeal committee must be composed of between two and four arbitrators who are deemed most qualified to arbitrate the relevant dispute.

III. Qualification criteria for candidate arbitrators

In general, candidates need to comply with three requirements to become a qualified arbitrator. First, irrespective of being employed as a legal representative or as a lawyer, candidates must be members of the relevant trade association. An exception is the LME, which also permits non-members to serve as an arbitrator. Second, candidates need to demonstrate some practical experience in the industry. With the exception of GAFTA and FOSFA that require a period of time of ten years to be complied with, the other trade associations remain vague. Although the LME explains that candidate arbitrators need to demonstrate a broad knowledge indicative of their

352 The ICA pertaining to technical arbitration requires that an appeal committee consist of five individuals. Four of whom serve as normal arbitrators and one as chairman.

practical experience in metals trading, it seems that individuals who want to become an arbitrator in the ICA, the DDC and the FCC will only be selected, in practice, if they can demonstrate some experience in the relevant commodities industry. Third, candidate arbitrators need to successfully complete specific examinations that are laid down in the standards set by the association. Typically, the standards require individuals to display (arguably basic) knowledge of the applicable laws and the functioning of the relevant commodities trade and arbitration.

E. The place of arbitration and applicable law

The place of arbitration is an important concept that pertains to arbitration proceedings. With regard to the LME and the FCC, arbitration is held in England and Wales, unless otherwise agreed by both parties. Whereas the same contractual deviation applies to GAFTA arbitration, which is held at the association's premises in London, FOSFA arbitration can only take place in London. A similar rule, even though the location differs, applies to DDC arbitration, which can only be conducted at the premises of the association in New York City. In contrast, ICA arbitration may take place wherever the parties in a dispute opt for. In the absence of a consensus, arbitration will be held at the arbitration room of the ICA in Liverpool.

Logically, the place of arbitration determines the applicable law that governs the arbitration proceedings. Concerning the five UK-based trade associations, each arbitration panel is entitled to decide a case on their own jurisdiction with regard to the validity, performance and construction of any contract stemming from the relevant trade association. As a condition, English law must be complied with. To this extent, the most important law is the Arbitration Act 1996. With reference to the DDC, any arbitration panel must decide a dispute on its own jurisdiction in conformity with trade usages and customs, without determining the law for damages and contract of the State of New York. Notwithstanding, all other statutes and laws of this State must be adhered to.

F. The finality of arbitration or the possibility of (some) legal redress in public courts

The objective of specialized commercial arbitration is to issue final and binding arbitral awards, thereby limiting the possibility that parties in arbitral proceedings seek legal redress at any public court for matters of fact and law. Be that as it may, the trade associations researched must be divided into three groups. This is because of some differences between them. The first group consists of the LME and the ICA in quality and technical arbitration in the sense that they strictly prohibit parties of a contract to lodge an appeal at a public court to set aside an arbitral award.[353] The second group consists of FOSFA and the FCC that to a large extent remain silent as to whether parties can seek legal redress at public courts.[354] The third and last group is composed of GAFTA and the DDC that are seemingly more open to allowing some form of judicial review. Whereas GAFTA explains that parties can have an arbitration award reviewed at an English court for issues other than enforcement issues, the DDC empowers either party in arbitral proceedings to lodge an appeal at the New York State Courts when procedural irregularities have occurred.[355] Despite these self-claimed rules pertaining to the permissibility of judicial review by public courts offered by the trade associations researched, they may be contrary to the Arbitration Act 1996, which applies to the five UK-based associations and Article 75 of the New York Civil Practice Law and Rules ("CPLR") and the Federal Arbitration Act ("FAA") pertaining to the DDC. This conformity or lack of conformity is explained below. To make a thor-

353 However, some reservation must be made. The ICA allows parties to seek legal redress at any public court, when they opt this, whereas the LME authorized this, when security of an award cannot be attained in specialized commercial arbitration offered by this association.

354 While this is largely true, both associations allow some form of review by public courts. FOSFA explains that the enforcement of an award can be achieved at the English High Court and in any other signatory State of the Geneva Convention of 1928 and the New York Convention, whereas the FCC empowers parties in arbitral proceedings to ask English courts for revocation of an arbitrator in first- or second-tier arbitration.
However, when a party to DDC arbitral proceedings requests a judicial review for matters of fact and law covered by these proceedings, he may be held liable to pay a fine and can be subject to termination of membership.

355 However, when a party to DDC arbitral proceedings requests a judicial review for matters of fact and law covered by this procedure, he may be held liable to pay a fine and can be subject to termination of membership.

ough analysis, the possibility to obtain legal redress before arbitral proceedings have commenced as well as after an arbitral award has been rendered merits separate analysis.

I. The English Arbitration Act 1996

1. Judicial review at a public court prior to arbitral proceedings

a. Stay of proceedings pursuant to Section 9 of the Arbitration Act 1996

If two market participants have a conflict concerning a matter which is covered by a standardized contract provided by one of the UK-based trade associations, they are bound by *ad hoc* arbitration. This is because the standardized contracts include exclusive arbitration clauses, which bar both parties access from judicial review in public court. When a party, contrary to such an exclusive jurisdiction clause, initiates court proceedings, the defendant is entitled to stop the judicial proceedings (Section 9(i) of the Arbitration Act 1996).[356] To realize this, the defendant must successfully demonstrate to the court that (i) the counterparty exclusively started the judicial proceedings; (ii) an arbitration agreement exists that covers the dispute; and (iii) the parties are the same as the parties to the agreement.

However, when the court is sufficiently satisfied that the arbitration agreement is null and void, inoperative, or incapable of being performed, the court may carry out a substantive review of the case (Section 9(iv) of the Arbitration Act 1996). Unfortunately, convincing the court is not an easy task. The burden of proof, which is shifted from the defendant to the claimant is high. In the case of *Joint Stock Company "Aeroflot Russian Airlines" v. Berezovsky et al* it was decided that only when the court reaches a "clear conclusion" that one of the defences applies, without any shred of

356 For an example, see Ust-Kamenogorsk Hydropower Plant JSC (Appellant) v. AES Ust-Kamenogorsk Hydropower Plant LLP (Respondent), [2011] EWCA Civ 647; This approach is equivalent to the German arbitral estoppel as laid down in § 1032 (i) ZPO. See J. Frohloff, "*Verletzung von Schiedsvereinbarungen: Eine Untersuchung des deutschen Schiedsverfahrensrechts zu den Pflichten der Schiedsparteien und den Rechtsfolgen ihrer Verletzung*", Tübingen: Mohr Siebeck 2017, p. 50; In Lombard North Central plc et al v. GATX Corporation [2012] EWHC 1067 (Comm), para. 21 the court also has the freedom of discretion to put a halt to its proceedings and refer to arbitration.

evidence to the contrary the court proceedings will continue.[357] This is does not come without its problems for the relevant court, as the defences are open for interpretation. These are explained below.

i. "Null and void" defence

The first defence relates to the situation in which there is no arbitration agreement between the parties, or, but also more exceptionally to the situation in which the parties have not entered into a contract that is connected with the arbitration agreement. With regard to the former situation, three possible methods have been given by UK courts to explain when arbitration is void. First, when the arbitration agreement infringes the right to a fair trial under Article 6 ECHR.[358] Second, as the court in *Albon v. Naza Motor Trading SBD BHD (No 3)* explained, when the arbitration agreement entirely lacks legal effect.[359] In this judgment, Justice *Lightman* referred to the US judgment in *Rhone Mediterranee v. Achille Lauro*, in which the 3rd Circuit Court of Appeals ruled that a "null and void" defence can be employed by the claimant when fundamental policies of the enforcing State are contravened, or in the event of duress, a mistake, fraud or a waiver.[360] Third, albeit unclear whether it specifically concerns the "null and void" defence, or (one of) the other defences, public policy (*e.g.* the exclusion of statutory remedies) is another ground for declaring an arbitration agreement void.[361]

By keeping this in mind, with regard to the UK-based trade associations, it must be determined on a case-by-case basis whether these three scenarios justify a "null and void" defence for the claimant. This is irrespective of whether an arbitration agreement exists at all.[362] One reason is that the

357 Joint Stock Company "Aeroflot Russian Airlines" v. Berezovsky et al [2012] EWHC 1610 (Ch), par. 73.

358 Stretford v. The Football Association Ltd et al (CA) [2007] EWCA Civ 238, para. 38, 67; The UK has a dualistic system and, therefore, Art. 6 ECHR is incorporated in the Human Rights Act 1988.

359 Albon v. Naza Motor Trading Sdn Bhd (No 3) [2007] Lloyd's Rep. L.

360 Rhone Mediterranee v. Achille Lauro [1983] 712 F. 2d 50.

361 Assaubayev et al v. Michael Wilson and Partners Ltd, [2014] EWCA Civ 1491.

362 As it would be redundant to explain the invalidity of the arbitration agreements pertaining to the UK-based trade associations both in this and in the next Paragraph, it would be more suitable to discuss it in the latter Paragraph. To this extent, the requirements to have a valid arbitration agreement under normal circumstances, the special category where an agreement includes an arbitration

standardized contracts/rules originating from these trade associations merely include an arbitration agreement "by reference". However, this does not necessarily invalidate the arbitration agreement according to Sections 5(3) and 6(2) of the Arbitration Act 1996 if the reference is specific enough to satisfy established UK case law.

ii. "Inoperative" defence

Unlike the "null and void" defence, in which an arbitration agreement has never been entered into from the outset, the "inoperative" defence pertains to validly completed arbitration agreements that have ceased to have legal effect. Examples of these are given by UK courts. An arbitration agreement is inoperative, when (i) the underlying agreement is terminated[363]; (ii) the identities of the parties are unclear; and (iii) the dispute is not covered by the arbitration clause.[364]

Against this backdrop, regarding the UK-based trade associations, it cannot be established in general that this defence is applicable for the claimant to justify public court proceedings. This must be reviewed on a case-by-case basis.

iii. "Incapable of being performed" defence

The "incapable of being performed" defence is enforceable where the claimant is prevented from performing its duties under the disputed contract owing to an external cause. A good example of this defence relates to capacity. When a consumer has entered into an arbitration agreement, the consumer will generally not be subject to arbitration proceedings (Section 89 of the Arbitration Act 1996). This is because any arbitration agreement

---

agreement "by reference" as well as the likely reaction of the trade associations in the event its members declare an arbitration agreement invalid for a lack of reference, will be discussed.

363 Downing v. Al Tameer Establishment [2002] EWCA Civ 721. In this case, a repudiatory breach of the underlying contract was a ground for terminating that contract.

364 Fulham Football Club (1987) Ltd v. Richards [2011] EWCA Civ 855. In this case, despite there not being (an implied) arbitration agreement, arbitration could be initiated.

with a consumer is not enforceable. It is unlikely that this defence can be used by the claimant to legitimize a review by a public court.

b. Application to the court for preliminary ruling on jurisdiction

Either party in arbitral proceedings provided by one of the five UK-based trade associations has a limited right to apply to any court in order to challenge the substantive jurisdiction of this tribunal (Section 32 of the Arbitration Act 1996). As a condition, one of the following two situations must be met. First, both parties apply to the relevant court in writing to consider a preliminary ruling on jurisdiction (Section 32(2)(a) of the Arbitration Act 1996). Second, one party applies to the court with the permission of the tribunal and also sufficiently satisfies the court "*(i) that the determination of the question is likely to produce substantial savings in costs; (ii) that the application was made without delay; and (iii) that there is a good reason why the matter should be decided by the court*" (Section 32(2)(b) of the Arbitration Act 1996).

Importantly, according to the Queen's Bench Division in *Vale do Rio Doce Navegacos SA*, an application to the court for a preliminary ruling on jurisdiction must only be seen as an exception.[365] Contesting the substantive jurisdiction of an arbitration tribunal is usually done by the arbitrators of this tribunal themselves pursuant to Section 30 of the Arbitration Act 1996. Nonetheless, a Section 32 application against the general rule is more appropriate when it would save considerable time and costs[366] if the defendant in arbitration is refusing to clear the substantive jurisdiction and when the tribunal cannot completely solve all questions relating to jurisdiction.[367]

Once all the requirements of Section 32 of the Arbitration Act 1996 are fulfilled and the relevant court has determined the substantive jurisdiction, it issues a declaration.[368] Be that as it may, restricting arbitral proceedings

---

365 Vale Do Rio Doce Navegacao SA & Anor v Shanghai Bao Steel Ocean Shipping Co Ltd. [2000] EWHC 205 (Comm), para. 45.

366 Azov Shipping co. v. Baltic Shipping co. [1999] 1 Lloyd's Rep. 68, para. 5 and 31; Toyota Tsusho Sugar Trading Ltd v. Prolat S.R.L [2014] EWHC 3649 (Comm), para. 2.

367 Esso Exploration and Production UK Ltd v. Electricity Supply Board [2004] EWHC 787 (Comm).

368 It is not always necessary that all the requirements pursuant to Section 32 of the Arbitration Act 1996 be fulfilled for the relevant court to issue a declaration.

by making an injunction is not possible according to *Welex AG v Rosa Maritime Ltd.*[369] Whether or not a Section 32 application will be permissible for the claimant of a dispute that arose out of a standardized contract/rules originating from one of the five UK-based trade associations depends on various factors. The defendant may be unwilling to go to the court, the arbitration tribunal might disagree, or the court might be insufficiently satisfied, amongst other factors.

2. Judicial review at a public court after an arbitral award has been rendered

Once an arbitral award, which characteristically awards damages against a party, has been rendered by one of the five UK-based trade associations, public courts have jurisdiction to correct/review/re-assess such an award in certain circumstances. These are discussed below.

a. Insufficient reference made to a broader arbitration agreement within an arbitration clause included in a standardized agreement

Section 5(1) of the Arbitration Act 1996 requires that an arbitration agreement be made in writing. While this is rather ambiguous, Section 5(2) of the Arbitration Act 1996 considers three types of categories that fulfil this criterion. First, written documents that are (un)signed. Second, an exchange of communication in writing (*e.g.* e-mails, faxes or records).[370] Third, agreements that do not themselves embody, but evidence the agreement in writing, including oral agreements that evidence written terms pursuant to Section 5(3) of the Arbitration Act 1996.[371]

Against this background, given that standardized contracts stemming from the UK-based trade associations contain arbitration clauses that refer to a broader arbitration agreement, the first two categories of the "in writ-

---

See, for example, Mackley & Co Ltd v Gosport Marina Ltd [2002] EWHC 1315, para. 20, 22, 39. Despite its importance, this case must be seen as an exception.

369 Welex AG v. Rosa Maritime Ltd [2003] EWCA Civ 938.

370 B. Harris, R. Planterose, and J. Tecks, "*The Arbitration Act 1996: A Commentary*", Oxford/Malden/Melbourne: Blackwell Publishing 2007, p. 47.

371 R. Merkin and L. Flannery, "Arbitration Act 1996", Oxon: Informa Law 2014, p. 24. This category functions as a safety net and entails that any shred of evidence can prove the existence of an arbitration agreement.

ing" requirement are of no interest. This is because the parties that contract under one of the standardized contracts do not specifically concur on the relevant arbitration agreement, but are nevertheless bound by this document. To put it differently, by incorporating an arbitration clause in a standardized contract, which refers to a broader arbitration agreement, the UK trade associations obligate the parties to adhere to the latter agreement.[372] Therefore, in my opinion, such a link between two documents is akin to the third category of the "in writing" requirement laid down in Section 5(1) and (2) of the Arbitration Act 1996.[373] However, as already briefly discussed above,[374] it is questionable whether the arbitration clauses that can be found in the standardized contracts "sufficiently refer" to the relevant arbitration agreements. Section 6(2) of the Arbitration Act 1996, legal doctrine and case law of the UK courts provide some guidance.

i. "Sufficient reference" to arbitration agreements within the standardized agreements provided by the UK-based trade associations

To determine whether market participants that enter into standardized contracts/rules provided by the UK-based trade associations are bound by an external arbitration agreement that is linked to the former document, Section 6(2) of the Arbitration Act 1996 must first be mentioned. This provision stipulates that "*The reference in an agreement to a written form of arbitration clause or to a document containing an arbitration clause constitutes an arbitration agreement if the reference is such as to make that clause part of the agreement*". In other words, this definition explains that both the standardized contract and the arbitration agreement need to be connected. However, it does not explain how much reference is needed.

To address this vagueness, the following question needs to be answered: Is a general reference sufficient, or should the arbitration clause incorporated in the standardized agreement in great detail link both documents? In my opinion, this is not a trivial question because an uncertain link bears the risk that the arbitration agreements are invalid. Fortunately, according

372 See, for example, Article 27 of the GAFTA Contract No. 1 – General Contract for Shipment of Feeding Stuffs in Bags Tale Quale – CIF/CIFFO/C&F/C&FFO Terms of 2018. (to access: https://www.gafta.com/write/MediaUploads/Contracts/2018/1_2018.pdf).

373 Importantly, oral agreements that evidence written terms (Section 5(3) of the Arbitration Act 1996) are outside the scope of this research.

374 See Part I, Chapter 2, H, V, 1, a, i.

to *Merkin* & *Flannery*, English case law gives guidance to understand the scope of the required intensity of referral needed for incorporation of the arbitration agreement to the standardized contracts.[375] Nonetheless, both authors explain that the English courts have only discussed an incorporation by reference with regard to two distinctive categories: first, in cases where there is only a single contract, but the communication between the parties refers to the standard terms and conditions in which the arbitration agreement is laid down. Second, in the event that one party enters into two contracts with two different parties (*e.g.* A enters into a contract with B, but A also with C), in which one of the contracts contains an arbitration agreement (*e.g.* the contract between A and B) and the other contract does not (*e.g.* the contract between A and C), but the latter contract incorporates the arbitration agreement contained in the former contract "by reference" (*e.g.* the contract between A and C refers to the arbitration agreement contained in the contract between A and B by reference).

Within the bounds of both categories which English case law is focused on, one can draw the conclusion that neither category fits the situation in which an arbitration clause that is included in a standardized contract refers to a broader arbitration agreement. Yet, in my opinion, unlike the second category,[376] the first category bears more similarities. This is because in both situations reference is made to a broader arbitration agreement, even though it is made within a standardized contract as opposed to a communication. As a result, it seems (to a certain extent) justified to use English case law concerning a category one referral, which explains that no explicit, but a general reference is satisfactory "*when the terms are readily available and the question arises in the context of dealings between established players in a well-known market*".[377] If, however, an English court in potential proceedings deems a category two standard more adequate, a stricter standard has to be used.[378] General language will then be insufficient and

375 R. Merkin, L. Flannery, "*Arbitration Act 1996*", Oxon: Informa Law 2014, p. 32-33.

376 The second category is very different as the English Courts focus is on the corporation of charterparties terms and conditions (including arbitration clauses) into the bill of lading. See, for example, Federal Bulk Carriers v C Itoh & Co default [1989] 1 Lloyd's Rep 103.

377 Sea Trade Maritime Corporation v. Hellenic Mutual War Risks Association (Bermuda) Ltd (The "Athena") (No 2), [2007] 1 Lloyd's Rep. 280, para. 65.

378 Ibid, par. 64.

an "express reference" must be made.[379] In the absence of an express reference, the intention to incorporate the arbitration agreement must be unequivocal.[380]

ii. Examples of arbitration clauses within standardized contracts provided by the UK-based trade associations that refer to a broader arbitration agreement

The UK-based trade associations have drafted hundreds of standardized contracts/rules. Owing to the level of similarity as well as by virtue of time constraints, it would be redundant to assess all those arbitration clauses that refer to broader arbitration agreements. Henceforth, as illustrated in the following table, one standardized agreement which includes an arbitration clause is selected for each of the five UK-based trade associations[381] to scrutinize whether these fulfil the "by reference" yardstick as laid down in English case law appropriate to category one and/or two.

Trade Association	**Example of a standardized contract**	**The relevant arbitration clause that refers to a broader arbitration agreement**
The ICA	The ICA International Shipment Contract Form 1 (2004)[382]	Art. 15. All disputes relating to this contract will be resolved through arbitration in accordance with the bylaws of the International Cotton Association Limited. This agreement incorporates the bylaws which set out the Association's arbitration procedure.

379 Aughton Limited (formerly Aughton Group Limited) v. M.F. Kent Services Limited, [1991] 57 BLR 1. This case was about incorporating an arbitration agreement from one subcontract in another subcontract, which is distinctive as opposed to standardized contracts which include arbitration clauses that refer to broader arbitration agreements. Therein, Judge Sir John Megaw explained that only an express reference in contrast with general language can be considered as a suitable reference.

380 Trygg Hansa Insurance Co. Ltd. v. Equitas Ltd, [1998] 2 Lloyd's Rep. 439. Unlike the typical category two cases, this judgment concerns insurances. Notwithstanding, it appears to be of general application to this category.

381 An exception is the LME, as will be explained in the table below.

382 https://www.ica-ltd.org/media/layout/documents/publications/lca_econtract.pdf.

GAFTA	GAFTA Contract No. 1 – General Contract for Shipment of Feeding Stuffs in Bags Tale Quale CIF/CIFFO/C&F/ C&FFO Terms (2018)[383]	Art. 27 (a). Any and all disputes arising out of or under this contract or any claim regarding the interpretation or execution of this contract shall be determined by arbitration in accordance with the GAFTA Arbitration Rules, No 125, in the edition current at the date of this contract; such Rules are incorporated into and form part of this Contract and both parties hereto shall be deemed to be fully cognisant of and to have expressly agreed to the application of such Rules.
The FCC	The FCC Contract Rules for Cocoa Beans (2017)[384]	Art. 19.2. If the Parties cannot agree upon the terms at which to settle the close out then the dispute shall be referred to arbitration subject to the FCC Arbitration and Appeal Rules. If the Arbitrators decide that a default has occurred they shall declare the contract to be closed out and determine the market price at the date of default.
The LME	The LME does provide standardized contracts, but does not automatically include an arbitration clause. One example is the LMEprecious Contract Specifications.[385] The LME advises parties who wish to make use of the arbitration service in order to resolve any dispute arising out of or in connection with such a contract to incorporate the following model arbitration clause.[386]	Any dispute arising out of or in connection with this agreement, including any question regarding its existence, validity or termination, shall be referred to and finally resolved by arbitration under the Arbitration Regulations of The London Metal Exchange.
FOSFA	FOSFA Contract For European Oilseeds CIF Terms (2015)[387]	Art. 30. Any dispute arising out of this contract, including any question of law arising in connection therewith, shall be referred to arbitration in London (or elsewhere if so agreed) in accordance with the Rules of Arbitration and Appeal of the Federation of Oils, Seeds and Fats Associations Limited, in force at the date of this contract and of which both parties hereto shall be deemed to be cognizant

383 https://www.gafta.com/write/MediaUploads/Contracts/2018/1_2018.pdf.

384 https://www.cocoafederation.com/dashboard/documents/freecontent/rules/cocoa-beans/contract-rules-for-cocoa-beans/ENG.

385 https://www.lme.com/-/media/Files/Metals/Precious-Metals/LMEprecious/LMEprecious-Contract-Specifications.pdf.

386 https://www.lme.com/en-GB/About/Regulation/Arbitration#tabIndex=2.

387 http://www.rheinische-warenboerse.de/upload/Contract_No_26_2822.pdf.

The arbitration clauses included in the preceding table that contain a reference to broader arbitration agreements vary in terms of explicitness. Some are more general, whereas others are more explicit. While it is a bit confusing to explain in words how the clauses compare, it is more suitable to insert the following table to illustrate the differences.

Trade Association	1. Number of disputes		2. The scope of the dispute				
	All disputes	The dispute	Relating to this contract	Arising out of or under this contract/arising out of or in connection with this agreement	Regarding the interpretation or execution of this contract	Including any question regarding its existence, validity or termination	Including any question of law arising in connection therewith
The ICA	✓		✓				
GAFTA	✓			✓	✓		
The FCC		✓					
The LME	✓			✓		✓	
FOSFA	✓			✓			✓

Trade Association	3. Reference to arbitration rules			4. Agreement's incorporation of the arbitration rules		
	In accordance with the bylaws of a specific arbitration rule	Referred to arbitration in London	In the version current at the date of this contract	This agreement incorporates the bylaws	Both parties hereto shall be deemed to be fully cognisant	Both parties have expressly agreed to the application of such Rules
The ICA	✓			✓		
GAFTA	✓		✓	✓	✓	✓
The FCC	✓					
The LME	✓					
FOSFA	✓	✓	✓	✓	✓	

Based on this table, one can draw immediate conclusions. The arbitration clause provided by GAFTA is unmistakeably the most specific, because it contains detailed information about the number of disputes, the scope of the dispute, reference to the arbitration rules as well as to the standardized agreement incorporating the arbitration rules. FOSFA's and the ICA's arbitration clause have a similar coverage, but are less detailed. However, the FOSFA's arbitration clause is a bit more specific. The model clause provided by the LME that can, but not necessarily must, be included in a standardized agreement if both parties want to make reference to the LME's arbitration rules, does not explain that (i) the standardized agreement incorporates the bylaws; (ii) the parties are cognisant; and (iii) the parties have expressly agreed to be bound by these rules.[388] Reference is made to the arbitration regulations of the LME in general words, but it remains vague where to find these. Along the same lines, the FCC arbitration clause is nebulous. Despite it containing a reference to the FCC Arbitration and Appeal Rules, it does not state, *inter alia*, that the agreement incorporates the arbitration rules. In other words, it is written in a very general manner.

Consistent with the reasoning above, it is not easy to determine whether the arbitration clauses fulfil the "by reference" yardstick developed in English case law. Much will depend on whether English courts require a general reference or a more explicit reference. As this justifies a much broader debate, it almost impossible to give a well-balanced conclusion here. In my opinion, all five arbitration clauses found above have sufficient reference to arbitration where general wording suffices. This is mainly because the arbitration rules are readily available. Yet, it becomes problematic when English courts require a more specific reference. Whereas GAFTA's, FOSFA's and the ICA's arbitration clause are more detailed and, thus, may, but not necessarily will, satisfy the more stringent requirement, the model arbitration clause of the LME and the arbitration clause of the FCC have a clear risk of falling below the required threshold. This is because these clauses include a general reference to the relevant arbitration rules of both trade associations. If indeed an English court draws the conclusion that there is insufficient reference, the broader arbitration agreement will become invalid. This will have the effect that an award stemming from specialized commercial arbitration offered by these trade associations will be null and void.

388 Parties are free to incorporate such a model clause in an LME standardized contract. However, they can also decide to include an arbitration clause with a more detailed reference to the LME's Rules and Regulations, in particular parts 8 and 9.

iii. The trade association and its members joint reprisal against members who/that seek redress at a public court to invalidate an arbitration agreement for the reason that the arbitration clause within a standardized agreement has "insufficient reference" to the former agreement

While contesting the legality of an arbitration clause is possible at a public court in order to strike down this clause, members of the UK-based trade associations can be faced with a dilemma. Once a member fails to comply with an arbitration award and asks for legal redress at a public court, that member goes against the rules of the relevant association, thereby running the risk that this association will impose nonlegal sanctions. Put differently, when a member seeks the invalidity of an arbitration agreement at a public court based on "insufficient reference" made within the arbitration clause included in the relevant standardized agreement, that member can be fined and sometimes even ostracized.

b. Lack of substantive jurisdiction of an arbitrator or arbitrators

The second method for a public court to *ex post facto* re-assess an arbitration award relates to Section 67 of the Arbitration 1996. This provision enables a party to arbitral proceedings to challenge an award at a public court where that party believes that the arbitrator(s) did not have substantive jurisdiction. However, before this provision can be used, the routes for obtaining relief must be exhausted.[389] This entails that the tribunal must be given the chance to clarify or correct the award within a period of 28 days beginning on the date of the award at a party's request (Sections 52(5) and 70(3) of the Arbitration Act 1996).[390] Put differently, internal arbitral appeal and the related 28-day period must have lapsed.

389 N. Andrews, "*Arbitration and Contract Law: Common Law Perspectives*", Cambridge: Springer 2016, p. 130.

390 The arbitrator has the competence to set a specific date of the award (Section 54(1) of the Arbitration Act 1996); When the arbitrator or arbitrators did not fix this, the date will be that on which the arbitrator or the last arbitrator [in the event of multiple arbitrators] has signed the award (Section 54(2) of the Arbitration Act 1996); According to Section 79(1) of the Arbitration Act 1996, the relevant public court can extend the initial period of 28 days by another 28 days, when it deems fit.

After this deadline has lapsed and no sufficient corrections and/or clarification is provided by the arbitration tribunal, the challenging party can ask the relevant public court to review the substantive jurisdiction of the arbitrators. However, when neither party has challenged an award on jurisdiction before the main award has been made (Section 73(2) of the Arbitration Act 1996), or when either party has not objected to an assertion of jurisdiction in the arbitral proceeding (Section 73(1) of the Arbitration Act 1996) that party loses the right to apply to any public court. When a party is not debarred and requests the court to challenge (an) arbitrator(s) substantive jurisdiction, this court may on its own initiative allow the challenging party to present its case orally.[391] This can amount to a full re-hearing. When the court reaches a decision, it can either affirm the award (Section 67(3)(a) of the Arbitration Act 1996), vary the award (Section 67(3)(b) of the Arbitration Act 1996), or set aside the award in whole or in part (Section 67(3)(c) of the Arbitration Act 1996).

c. Unfair proceedings

The third method that allows a public court to review an arbitral award can be found in Section 68 of the Arbitration Act 1996. According to this provision, which may be invoked when all internal appeal procedures have been exhausted, a party may challenge an arbitral award on the grounds of "serious irregularities" in the arbitral proceedings, or on a point of law. Examples of this method are narrowly defined and listed in Section 68(2) of the Arbitration Act 1996.[392] To prevent a somewhat exhaustive enumeration of a myriad of factors to illustrate when serious irregularities lead to substantial injustice for an applicant, the following table provides a more lucid summary.[393]

391 B. Harris, R. Planterose, and J. Tecks, "*The Arbitration Act 1996: A Commentary – fourth edition*", Blackwell Publishing 2007, p. 309.

392 R. Jänig, "*Commercial Law: Selected Essays on the Law of Obligation, Insolvency and Arbitration*", Göttingen: Universitätsverlag Göttingen 2012, p. 125. The examples included in Section 68(2) of the Arbitration Act 1996 are mandatory and may not be ignored by the parties. Put differently, party autonomy is not permissible.

393 Albeit its significance cannot be understated, the following table does not contain a broader analysis of each example. In my opinion, a superficial summary of what falls within the scope of "serious irregularities" is sufficient to under-

List of conduct that leads to serious irregularities and causes substantial injustice to an applicant	
A.	A failure of the arbitration tribunal to act fairly and impartially, not giving the party a reasonable opportunity to explain his case and not adopting a suitable procedure, which causes unnecessary delays or expenses (Section 33 of the Arbitration Act 1996).
B.	Different from a Section 67 of the Arbitration Act 1996 challenge, when the arbitration tribunal exceeds its powers.
C.	A failure by the arbitration tribunal to carry out the proceedings in line with the procedure agreed by the parties.
D.	An omission of the arbitral tribunal to deal with all the issues that were put to it by the parties.
E.	A sole arbitrator/ multiple arbitrators who exceed its/their powers.
F.	An uncertain or ambiguous effect of the award.
G.	A fraudulent award, or an award contrary to public policy
H.	An award that does not observe the mandatory form.
I.	Irregularities with regard to the conduct of the proceedings, the award admitted by the arbitration tribunal, or the arbitration tribunal itself.

d. Review on the merits

The last possibility to challenge an arbitral award in a public court can be found in Section 69 of the Arbitration Act 1996 and is referred to as a "legal error appeal".[394] This provision opens the possibility for a public court to do a full review on the merits of the dispute decided in, *inter alia*, specialized commercial arbitration.[395] However, according to *Gharavi* & *Liebscher*, this provision is only of limited importance due to four reasons.[396] First, the internal arbitral procedure deadline or proceedings must be finished (Section 70(2) and (3) of the Arbitration Act 1996). Second, parties have contractual freedom to deviate from the rule that a party can request a public court to conduct a review on the merits after an award has been rendered (Section 69(1) of the Arbitration Act 1996). Albeit that an express waiver in the arbitration agreement is sufficient, the situation is a bit more

stand the basics. Overly complicating these grounds for rebuttal purposes is unnecessary.

394 See, for example, E. E. Sutherland, "*Law Making and the Scottish Parliament*", Edinburgh: Edinburgh University Press 2011, p. 314.

395 The Arbitration Act 1996 is unique in the world pertaining to the possibility of a public court to re-consider an arbitral award on the facts and law.

396 H. Gharavi and C. Liebscher, "*The International Effectiveness of the Annulment of an Arbitral Award*", The Hague: Kluwer law International 2002, p. 34.

complex. It is uncertain whether the arbitration clauses laid down in the standardized agreements/rules stemming from the UK-based trade associations incorporate the broader arbitration agreements. This is crucial, because in the absence of "sufficient reference" there is not a valid waiver of a review on the merits. Notwithstanding this discussion, it is also questionable whether the broader arbitration agreements stemming from some UK-based trade associations exclude a review on the merits by a public court. Whereas the LME and the ICA explicitly prohibit this,[397] FOSFA and the FCC remain silent and GAFTA in its standardized agreements even allows an appeal for matters other than enforcement. As a result of this, it is difficult to ascertain whether parties contracting under the standardized agreement provided by the latter three trade associations have validly excluded a possibility of appeal to a public court for a full review of the merits. Fortunately, this debate does not have to be answered, as it is likely that the trade associations will not accept a party of specialized commercial arbitration to allow such a reconsideration. If such an individual/company disregards this warning, it is possible that member will be fined or ostracized.

Third, a public court can only conduct a review on the merits of the case in relation to arbitral awards subject to English law. With regard to arbitration agreements, this limitation is complied with because all the arbitration agreements attributed to the UK-based trade associations are governed by English law. Fourth, the public court must be convinced "*(a) that the determination of the question will substantially affect the rights of one or more of the parties, (b) that the question is one which the tribunal was asked to determine, (c) that, on the basis of the findings of fact in the award— (i) the decision of the tribunal on the question is obviously wrong, or (ii) the question is one of general public importance and the decision of the tribunal is at least open to serious doubt, and(d) that, despite the agreement of the parties to resolve the matter by arbitration, it is just and proper in all the circumstances for the court to deter-*

397 In Sukuman Ltd v. Commonwealth Secretariat [2007] EWCA Civ 243, para. 36 a somewhat comparable clause constituted an express waiver of a review on the merits by a public court. This clause is worded as follows: "*The judgment of the tribunal shall be final and binding on the parties and shall not be subject to appeal. This constitution shall constitute an 'exclusion agreement' within the meaning of the laws of any country requiring arbitration or as those provisions may be amended or replaced*". Whereas the latter sentence cannot be found in the arbitration agreements of the LME and the ICA, in my opinion, one can still draw the conclusion that the first sentence, which is comparable to the clause contained in the arbitration agreements of both associations is sufficient to speak of a waiver.

mine the question" (Section 69(3) of the Arbitration Act 1996). Whether or not the parties contracting under standard contracts provided by the UK-based trade associations can convince the court depends on a case-by-case basis review. Hence, it is impossible to give a final conclusion.

In sum, despite the risk that market participants contracting under the standard agreements of GAFTA, FOSFA and the FCC can potentially appeal an arbitral award for a full review on the facts at a public court, these trade associations will punish them for doing so. Put differently, nonlegal sanctions will most likely deter such parties from obtaining this type of legal redress.

II. Article 75 of the New York Civil Practice Law and Rules and the US Federal Arbitration Act

1. Judicial review at a public court prior to arbitral proceedings

a. Stay of proceedings pursuant to Article 75, Section 7503 of the New York Civil Practice Law and Rules

When both parties are active within the same State or in different States[398] and one party [the challenging party] seeks legal redress for a dispute that arose under an agreement that is made subject to DDC arbitration at the State Court of New York,[399] then the other party [the defendant] may re-

398 DDC arbitration is covered by the CPLR, the UNCITRAL Model Law, the New York Convention and the FAA. In more detail, the former Act is applicable when the parties of a DDC standardized agreement are both active within the same state, whereas the other laws apply to the situation in which two parties are operating from different states (*i.e.* international arbitration). See T. Lörcher, G. Pendell, and W. Lowery, "CMS Guide to Arbitration, Vol. 1", *CMS Legal Services EEIG* 2012, p. 521; J. H. Carter, J. Fellas, "*International Commercial Arbitration in New York*", New York: Oxford University Press 2010, p. 16. Importantly, the FAA's scope is very broad and covers almost every significant business transaction in the USA.

399 E. Brunet, E. J. Brunet, R. E. Speidel, J. E. Sternlight, S. H. Ware, and S. J. Ware, "*Arbitration Law in America: A Critical Assessment*", New York: Cambridge University Press 2006, p. 124. Even if the FAA were applicable, parties must go to a New York State court rather than a federal court. This is because the FAA does not create federal jurisdiction; Moses H. Cone Mem'l Hosp. v Mercury Constr. Corp., 460 U.S. 1, 24-27 (1983) and Southland Corp. v. Keating, 465 U.S. 1, para. 12 (1984). However, this statement appears to be incorrect. According to

quest that court to stop the judicial proceeding (*i.e.* stay of proceedings). This is laid down in Article 75, Section 7503 of the CPLR and in the FAA, 9 U.S.C. § 3.[400] However, with regard to the former provision, a request to postpone judicial proceedings indefinitely must be made within 20 days (Article 75, Section 7502(c) of the CPLR).[401] If this time limit has lapsed, the defendant may still request the arbitration tribunal of the DDC to commence arbitral proceedings. Contingent upon the tribunal's full discretion, the arbitrator(s) may then render a decision to continue arbitral proceedings.

Irrespective of the possibility to include a much broader debate about such competence of a State court, an extensive analysis is redundant. The reasons for this are threefold. First, albeit subject to differences, Section 9 of the Arbitration Act 1996, which has been discussed in great detail, contains the same competence for the court. It would be unnecessary to do a full analysis in this Paragraph again. Second, a cursory explanation is sufficient to understand the basic functionality of the "stay of proceedings" competence. Third, defences that function as a safety net for the challenging party to continue judicial proceedings at a State court are more limited.

b. Application to the court for preliminary ruling on jurisdiction

Although Article 75 of the CPLR and the FAA[402] do not contain any provision that enables a party to a standardized agreement of the DCC to challenge the substantive jurisdiction of the arbitral tribunal prior to the com-

---

both cases, the FAA creates a body of substantive law that is both applicable in a federal and in a state court; Buckeye Check Cashing, Inc. v. Cardegna, 546 U.S. (2006) [J. Thomas, dissenting].Yet, the FAA should not be invoked in state court proceedings.

400 Despite being of interest, the UNCITRAL Arbitration Rules and the New York Convention will not be discussed. This is mainly because a discussion of both would overcomplicate and unnecessarily prolong this Paragraph.

401 The 20-day time limit is treated by the courts as a statute of limitations. See Aetna Life & Casualty Co. v. Slekardis, 34 N.Y.2d 182 (N.Y. App. Div. 1974); Although there the 20-day time period does not need to be upheld where the parties "never agreed to arbitrate", the parties subject to DDC contracts cannot invoke this exception. This is because each standardized contract stemming from this association includes an arbitration clause. See Matarasso v. Continental Casualty Co., 56 N.Y.2d 264 (N.Y. App. Div. 1982).

402 The UNCITRAL Model Law and the New York Convention are not researched.

mencement and during arbitral proceedings, US courts have ruled on the possibility of interlocutory objections concerning jurisdictional competence by interpreting the FAA. In *Buckeye Check Cashing, Inc. v. Cardegna* the Supreme Court held that "*regardless of whether the challenge is brought in federal or state court, a challenge to the validity of the contract as a whole, and not specifically to the arbitration clause, must go to the arbitrator*".[403] Put differently, the arbitration tribunal must rule on its own jurisdiction when the contract and the arbitration clause jointly (*i.e.* the entire agreement), or the underlying contract is invalid. This has been confirmed by, *inter alia*, the 5th District Court in *Brown v. Pacific Life Ins. Co.*[404] and the 9th Circuit Court in *Nagrampa v. MailCoups, Inc.*[405] Obviously, this line of reasoning also entails [by drawing an *argumentum e contrario*] that US courts have the competence to review the substantive jurisdiction of an arbitration tribunal when an arbitration clause is "specifically" invalid, void or terminated.

2. Judicial review at a public court after an arbitral award has been rendered

Ex post facto judicial review of a binding DDC arbitral award by a State court of New York is possible (with some reservations) in accordance with the scenarios explained below. From the outset it is worth mentioning that they are similar to the ones discussed under the Arbitration Act 1996, with two important exceptions. First, the DDC does not provide standardized agreements containing arbitration clauses that refer to a broader arbitration agreement, but allows members to put an arbitration clause in place in their memos, invoices and letterheads.[406] As a result, the question

---

403 Buckeye Check Cashing, Inc. v. Cardegna, 546 U.S. (2006), para. 8.

404 Brown v. Pacific Life Ins. Co., 462 F.3d 384, 396 (5th Cir. 2006). The Court held that "*Where claims of error, fraud, or unconscionability do not specifically address the arbitration agreement itself, they are properly addressed by the arbitrator, not a federal court*".

405 Nagrampa v. MailCoups, Inc., 469 F.3d 1257 (9th Cir. 2006), para. 43. The court ruled that if "*after examining the crux of the complaint, the district court concludes that the challenge is not to the arbitration provision itself but, rather, to the validity of the entire contract, then the issue of the contract's validity should be considered by an arbitrator in the first instance*".

406 https://www.wfdb.com/media-news-press/news-headlines/370-ddc-announces-new-initiative-to-safeguard-diamond-transactions.

whether the arbitration agreement is invalid owing to insufficient reference made to a broader arbitration agreement does not play a role. Second, a review on the merits is not possible by a public court under the CPLR, the FAA and the case law of the US courts.[407]

a. Lack of substantive jurisdiction of an arbitrator or arbitrators

Judicial scrutiny by a public court concerning whether the arbitration tribunal had substantive jurisdiction is also available for this court after a binding DDC award is rendered in accordance with the FAA. As a requirement, both parties must be active in different States. If the parties in an arbitral proceeding of this association are active in the same State, the substantive jurisdiction of the arbitration tribunal *ex post facto* cannot be scrutinized by a public court. This is because Article 75 CPLR, Section 7511 only permits an award to be vacated at the request of a party "*who neither participated in the arbitration nor was served with a notice of intention to arbitrate*".

In more detail, with regard to the FAA, public courts have the competence to review the substantive jurisdiction of an arbitration tribunal after an award has been rendered, when (i) a claim was not covered by an arbitration agreement, or (ii) when there is no arbitration agreement from the outset.[408] This follows from the case law of the US courts by interpreting the FAA, 9 U.S.C. § 203, which contains the (rather general) possibility for district courts to claim jurisdiction. Whereas the first requirement is rather clear-cut, especially given that the 2nd District Court in the 2nd Circuit judgment in *Smith/Enron Cogeneration Ltd. P'ship. v. Smith Cogeneration Int'l Inc.* ruled that there is a presumption that the arbitration clause (also in the event of doubt) covers the relevant claim, concluding that an arbitration agreement is invalid requires more emphasis.[409] According to the

407 Also here, the UNCITRAL Model Law and the New York Convention will not be discussed.

408 P. Sherwin, J. D. Roesser, P. L. Miller, and V. Loughery, "Proskauer on International Litigation and Arbitration: Managing, Resolving, and Avoiding Cross-Border Business or Regulatory Disputes", *Proskauer Rose LLP* 2007, chapter 21.

409 Smith/Enron Cogeneration Ltd. P'ship. v. Smith Cogeneration Int'l Inc., 198 F.3d 88 (2d Cir. 1999), para. 49. The 2nd District Court reiterates the 2nd District judgment in Worldcrisa Corp. v. Armstrong, 129 F.3d 71 (2d Cir. 1997), para. 74, in which the court ruled that "*the existence of a broad agreement to arbitrate creates a presumption of arbitrability which is only overcome if it may be said with*

New York District Court in *Antco Shipping Co., Ltd. v. Sidermar S. p. A.* it requires "*the party resisting enforcement of the agreement [to prove] that the essence of the obligation or remedy is prohibited by a pertinent statute or other declaration of public policy*".[410] To this extent, examples of disputes that are not covered by arbitration relate to criminal offences and insolvency and bankruptcy conflicts.

b. Unfair proceedings

Another possibility for a US public court to review a DDC arbitral award after the award has been delivered to both parties can be invoked by the court when arbitral proceedings were unfair pursuant to Article 75, Section 7511 of the CPLR and the FAA, 9 U.S.C. §§ 10 and 11. Given that both laws contain many examples of situations to reach such a conclusion, the following table structures these grounds that empower a public court to vacate or modify an award.

positive assurance that the arbitration clause is not susceptible of an interpretation that covers the asserted dispute. Doubts should be resolved in favor of coverage".

410 Antco Shipping Co., Ltd. v. Sidermar S. p. A., 417 F. Supp. 207 (S.D.N.Y. 1976), para. 215.

	Article 75, Section 7511 of the CPLR = intrastate arbitration	**The FAA, 9 U.S.C. §§ 10 and 11 = interstate/international arbitration**
Grounds to vacate an award	*(b)(i) corruption, fraud or misconduct in procuring the award; or*	*10(a)(1) Where the award was procured by corruption, fraud, or undue means*
	(ii) partiality of an arbitrator appointed as a neutral, except where the award was by confession; or	*(2) Where there was evident partiality or corruption in the arbitrators, or either of them.*
	(iii) an arbitrator, or agency or person making the award exceeded his power or so imperfectly executed it that a final and definite award upon the subject matter submitted was not made; or	*(3) Where the arbitrators were guilty of misconduct in refusing to postpone the hearing, upon sufficient cause shown, or in refusing to hear evidence pertinent and material to the controversy; or of any other misbehavior by which the rights of any party have been prejudiced.*
	(iv) failure to follow the procedure of this article, unless the party applying to vacate the award continued with the arbitration with notice of the defect and without objection" the arbitral award can be vacated.	*(4) Where the arbitrators exceeded their powers, or so imperfectly executed them that a mutual, final, and definite award upon the subject matter submitted was not made.*
		(5) Where an award is vacated and the time within which the agreement required the award to be made has not expired the court may, in its discretion, direct a rehearing by the arbitrators.
Grounds to modify an award	*(c)1. there was a miscalculation of figures or a mistake in the description of any person, thing or property referred to in the award; or*	*11(a) Where there was an evident material miscalculation of figures or an evident material mistake in the description of any person, thing, or property referred to in the award.*
	2. the arbitrators have awarded upon a matter not submitted to them and the award may be corrected without affecting the merits of the decision upon the issues submitted; or	*(b) Where the arbitrators have awarded upon a matter not submitted to them, unless it is a matter not affecting the merits of the decision upon the matter submitted.*
	3. the award is imperfect in a matter of form, not affecting the merits of the controversy.	*(c) Where the award is imperfect in matter of form not affecting the merits of the controversy.*

III. Statement about the conformity of the trade associations and their members' joint limitation to seek legal redress at a public court with the English Arbitration Act 1996, Article 75 of the CPLR and the FAA

All six trade associations researched have in their bylaws and rules limited the possibility to obtain legal redress before and after an arbitral award is rendered. To this extent, the ICA and the LME are the most restrictive. Whereas the ICA allows for judicial review by a public court when consensus between the parties is reached, the LME only allows this judicial review to obtain security of an arbitral award. Apart from this, arbitral awards are final and binding and may not be appealed. This prohibition imposed on actors that contract under standardized agreements provided by both associations runs counter to the Arbitration Act 1996. This Act allows a broader basis to seek legal redress at a public court both prior to the commencement of arbitral proceedings (*i.e.* when a defence to negate a stay of proceedings is justifiable and when the arbitration tribunal has no substantive jurisdiction) and after an arbitral award is provided (*i.e.* when there is a lack of substantive jurisdiction of the arbitration tribunal, when proceedings were unfair and –arguably – if the arbitration clause within the standardized agreements insufficiently refers to a broader arbitration agreement and when a full review of the arbitrator's factual and legal determinations is permissible).

For FOSFA and the FCC it is more difficult to ascertain whether their rules contravene the Arbitration Act 1996. This is because these trade associations remain silent about the possibility of parties seeking redress at a public court that are involved in a dispute arising out of a standardized contract stemming from both associations. Nevertheless, they explicitly permit a review by public courts to ensure the enforcement of an award at the English High Court (*i.e.* FOSFA) and to replace an arbitrator in first- or second-tier arbitration at English courts (*i.e.* the FCC). It is unsure whether this entails that all other methods to obtain legal redress at a public court as mentioned in the Arbitration Act 1996 are barred. If yes, the "recourse to a public court" rules of both associations contradict this overarching statutory instrument and, when no these rules are valid, even though they do not explain all the possibilities to go to a public court prior to arbitral proceedings and after the rendering of an arbitral award.

GAFTA's rules "on the recourse to a public court" are clearly in agreement with the Arbitration Act 1996, as they allow parties to obtain judicial recourse by English courts for matters other than enforcement issues. Furthermore, in my opinion, this broad statement seems to even go beyond that law. Along the same lines, but referring to a different trade association, namely the DDC, which is not bound by Arbitration Act 1996, but by Article 75 of the CPLR and the FAA, a somewhat similar conclusion can be drawn. This DDC explicitly allows the possibility for a public court to review an arbitral award stemming from this association's arbitration on the grounds of unfair proceedings. Apart from that, it explains that a review on the merits of a case by a public court after an award has been rendered is punishable with a fine and/or a termination of membership. When meticulously reading both Article 75 of the CPLR and the FAA, this seems to be in complete conformity. Yet, both laws also allow for a judicial review prior to and during arbitral proceedings and after an award is rendered concerning the substantive competence of the arbitration tribunal. This possibility is not included in the rules of the DDC. Whether this means that this trade association bars such review is unclear. Much will depend on the reaction of the DDC once a party opts for this legal option.

In sum, there is a clear risk that the six trade associations are not compliant with the relevant applicable laws. Some do this explicitly, others do not portray the full legal possibilities for parties bound by the associations' arbitration tribunals to ask for legal redress at a public court. Even though a party could disregard the "recourse to public courts" prohibition set by trade associations and invoke applicable statutory law, there is a risk that party could be liable to a penalty or even ostracized from the relevant association. This is because that party would be violating the association's rules.

G. A typology of nonlegal sanctions

To ensure that a system of specialized commercial arbitration is successful, arbitral awards must be adhered to. Guaranteeing their enforcement by any public court runs counter to this aim. Market participants contracting under a standardized contract provided by the six trade associations researched are internationally dispersed and, as a result, are dependent on whether a public court renders an enforcement judgment and if another country's court recognizes this decision. It does not come as a surprise that this has proven to be a very uncertain, time-consuming and cost-intensive method, because not all courts located in specific States recognize foreign arbitral awards. Put differently, some States are not member to the Convention on the Recognition and Enforcement of Foreign Arbitral Awards, whereas others – despite being members – are simply unwilling to consider recognition. To negate such unwanted inefficiency, the trade associations combined (although differences exist) impose the following types of nonlegal sanctions to punish recalcitrant parties for not paying their arbitral awards.

I. Blacklisting

The most common nonlegal sanction that is used by all six trade associations researched to guarantee compliance with arbitral awards concerns the practice of blacklisting. In general, one can say that this extrajudicial measure enables the publishing/sharing of the names of disobedient non-paying parties with other members. However, two main differences among the trade associations can be detected, as is illustrated in the following table.

Trade Association	**1. The method of publishing and its scope**
ICA	Dissemination of the names of all disloyal members in a publicly available list (*i.e.* the list of unfulfilled awards: part 1) and the names of all related entities in a non-public list (*i.e.* list of unfulfilled awards: part 2).
DDC	Posting of the name and the picture of a recalcitrant party on the wall of the trading hall of the DDC as well as on the wall of the trading hall of any trade association belonging to the WFDB with a caption that details of that party's failure to comply with the arbitration panel's ruling.
GAFTA	Posting the name of a non-compliant individual or undertaking on its notice board, a section on its website which is publicly available and/or informing its members in any other way to ensure a similar effect.
The FCC	Publishing the name of a recalcitrant party on a publicly available section on the website of this association and disseminating this information to all members of the FCC and any other organisation worldwide (without any restriction).
The LME	Publishing the name of a defaulter in the exchange and inform where appropriate other persons and counterparties of unsettled contracts with the defaulter. In addition, information of blacklisting can also be published to other exchanges and clearing houses, the Secretary of State, the Treasury, recognized investment exchanges or regulatory bodies, applicable office holders and any authority of body associated with the default.
FOSFA	Posting the name of a disloyal party on FOSFA's notice board, which is only accessible to members and in any other way it considers effective. It is unclear whether this information may be exchanged to associations/exchanges or non-members.
Trade Association	**2. Responsible institution within the trade association and the obligation to blacklist**
ICA	After being informed of non-compliance, the directors of the ICA "instruct" this association's secretary to blacklist the name of a disloyal party. However, with regard to related companies belonging to a blacklisted party, the secretary "may" blacklist this individual/company.
DDC	The DDC "must" publish the picture, name as well as the reason for blacklisting an individual.
GAFTA	The Council of GAFTA in its full discretion "may" blacklist a disloyal individual/company.
The FCC	The Council of the FCC in its full discretion "may" blacklist a disloyal individual/company.

The LME	The exchange is obligated to blacklist the name of a defaulter in the exchange as well as disseminate this information to his/this companies other parties and counter parties. For all other possibilities mentioned above, the FCC "may" do so.
FOSFA	The Council of FOSFA, after sending a notification to both parties, "may" black-list

II. Withdrawing membership

It is largely self-explanatory that the second method of nonlegal sanctioning, namely withdrawing membership, be it temporary or permanent, has more far-reaching consequences than blacklisting. Taking away membership causes a significant loss of credibility in the relevant market, which membership of a trade association signals and a loss of access to the services of this association, including its arbitration facilities. As a result, five out of the six trade associations (with the exclusion of GAFTA) use this measure to punish non-compliance with arbitral awards in order to ensure a smooth running and effective arbitration system. Notwithstanding their use of suspension and termination of membership, three differences can be detected. These are illustrated in the following table.

Trade Association	**1. Responsible institution within the trade association and the obligation to withdraw membership**
ICA	The directors "must" after 14 days of non-compliance with an arbitral award appoint a disciplinary committee from an approved panel, whose task is to impose an equitable penalization (*i.e.* a withdrawal of membership).
DDC	The arbitration board of the DDC "*may*" suspend or expel a member for non-compliance with an arbitral award, when such conduct "reflects adversely upon the integrity of any member of the Organization".
The FCC	The Council of the FCC "may" suspend or terminate the membership of a member, when that individual/company does not adhere to an arbitral award.
The LME	The directors of the LME "may" suspend membership, when this method is unavoidable to ensure an orderly market and alternative methods to ensure compliance with statutory obligations are absent. In addition, the directors "may" also terminate the membership of a member, without having to comply with any condition.
FOSFA	After a member has been blacklisted by the Council of FOSFA, his membership "shall" automatically be terminated, if a majority of directors [and when at least three-quarters of the Council is present] support such a withdrawal
Trade Association	**2. Publication of the withdrawal of membership decision**
ICA	Notice of the disciplinary committee's decision to withdraw membership will be published on the website of the ICA and provided to all registered members of this association.

DDC	The withdrawal of membership decision will not be published.
The FCC	The withdrawal of membership decision may be posted by the Board and, if decided by the Council of the FCC must be published on the website of this association and send to all members/organisations.
The LME	The withdrawal of membership decision will not be published.
FOSFA	The withdrawal of membership decision will not be published.
Trade Association	**3. Possibility of appeal against a withdrawal of membership**
ICA	Whereas an appeal is not possible against a complete withdrawal of membership, a suspended member can ask the directors in writing to grant a temporary restoration of membership. The directors can accept this, require alterations, or deny such a request at any time they deem fit. Expelled members do not have this right.
DDC	A possibility of appeal against a withdrawal of membership decision is not expounded.
The FCC	A possibility of appeal against a withdrawal of membership decision is not expounded.
The LME	Members can lodge an appeal against a temporary or final withdrawal of membership at the LME Appeal Committee.
FOSFA	Members of FOSFA do not have a right to lodge an appeal against a withdrawal of membership.

III. Denying membership for expelled members on the basis of an additional entry barrier

The third nonlegal sanction concerns denying membership of an expelled member on the basis of an additional entry barrier. This extrajudicial measure, which aims to make withdrawing membership a stronger deterrent and prolongs the reputational harm and inability to access the services of the association, is only used by one of the trade associations researched, namely the ICA. This is illustrated in the following table.

Trade Association	Additional entry barriers for expelled members to regain membership
ICA	Expelled members only have the right to re-apply for membership after a period of two years, following which the directors "may" grant membership.
DDC	A restoration of membership is not expounded.
The FCC	A possibility of appeal against a withdrawal of membership decision or a restoration of membership is not expounded.
The LME	A restoration of membership after a longer period has elapsed is not expounded.
FOSFA	A restoration of membership is not expounded.

IV. Refusing to deal with an expelled member

Arguably an even more severe measure that a trade association can impose on its members concerns refusing to deal with an expelled member, which entails that members cannot conduct trade with an expelled member. This has the result - in practice - that the expelled member will lose all access to the relevant market in which that member operates. This is because all important market players are often members of such a trade association and trade with them is crucial to remain solvent. Based on the examination on whether the six trade associations researched enforce a refusal to deal prohibition, only the ICA punishes recalcitrant parties that did not adhere to arbitral awards in such a way. This being said, to target a member it is necessary that the member must have been included on the ICA List of Unfiled Awards 1 or 2, or that the member's membership must have been withdrawn. No deviation will be allowed in any case, except when a targeted member asks permission from the directors of the ICA and the directors allow this.

V. Entering the premises of a recalcitrant industry actor

The LME (being the only one of the six trade associations researched) has decided to go one step further. This association permits entry without a warrant to the premises of a defaulting party that did not comply with an arbitral award. This is done in order to determine if there are other unsettled awards, whether this party has money to satisfy the arbitral award, if this party has other property and to find other necessary information to carry out its duties to ensure compliance. Obviously, in a digitalized world news spread rapidly and can have serious negative effects for a targeted member of this trade association. When an officer breaks down a door, or even uses more excessive force to conduct the search, this information can potentially reach all other members and even non-members. In this way, they might be persuaded not to enter into a contract with such a member.

VI. Limiting adequate access to public courts prior to arbitral proceedings and after an award.

The last nonlegal sanction, which – of course – does not fit within this term, but is treated as such throughout this research, pertains to limiting adequate access to public courts prior to arbitral proceedings and after an award. As seen above, in Part I, Chapter 3, F, III two trade associations clearly use this practice (*i.e.* the ICA and the LME), whereas two remain silent (*i.e.* FOSFA and the FCC), and two do not (*i.e.* GAFTA and the DDC).

H. Reasons for nonlegal sanctioning

To understand the rationale behind nonlegal sanctioning to facilitate and guarantee compliance with awards rendered by arbitration tribunals formed under the rules of the six trade associations researched, one must divide these organizations into two groups. The first group consists of the ICA, GAFTA, the FCC, the LME and FOSFA in which futures play a significant role. The second group comprises the DDC, which does not provide such futures, but concentrates on safeguarding non-deviation with contracts that underlays an even more high-risk, capital-intensive trade as compared with the first group. Put differently, it is about a market in which trust plays an even more important role.

I. Markets in which futures play a crucial role

The ICA, GAFTA, the FCC, the LME and FOSFA have one thing in common: the commodities that they represent are subject to extreme price fluctuations. To hedge this risk of price volatility, these associations provide standardized contracts/terms for their members (and sometimes even non-members) to exchange a specific quantity of commodities at a predetermined price and specified time in the future. In other words, by providing futures contracts, the buyer is obligated to buy the commodities and the seller is duty-bound to perform the contract for the agreed sum in the future. While good in theory, however, in practice either party is often triggered to deviate from its contractual duties to comply with the award depending on the circumstances. If the buyer and the seller were to negotiate an average price and in the future owing to scarcity of the commodities the former person were to gain more profit by selling to another buyer, when – of course – expected legal fees do not offset this monetary advance, contract deviation cannot be excluded. Similarly, if both persons were to negotiate an average price and in the future there is an abundance of commodities that is to be traded, the buyer may be induced not to fulfil its contractual obligations and buy the commodities at a lower price. Once again, the surplus must then outweigh the cost of any court proceedings.

Against this backdrop, it becomes immediately clear that court proceedings are not always sufficient to deter contract deviations by either the buyer or a seller. Awards stemming from specialized commercial arbitration enforced by nonlegal sanctions provide a much better alternative. The threat of being blacklisted, or sometimes even being ostracized or being targeted by a refusal to deal from remaining members of a trade association has even more far-reaching consequences. This is because the reputation of targeted individuals/companies, which is essential for an individual/company to operate in a market in which a specific commodity is traded, is challenged and to some extent even ruined. Other market participants would be less likely to conduct (long-term) trade with such a targeted actor and are to some extent prevented from engaging in future deals.

Notwithstanding the explanation why nonlegal sanctions are necessary to ensure compliance with future contracts, a second reason for the imposition of such sanctions relates to the New York Convention. Given that market participants contracting under standardized (futures) contracts are often located in different States, if an award must be enforced in public court and after a different court in another State has to recognize the former court's enforcement decision under the New York Convention, this bears the risk of two problems. First, this procedure could take too long. Second, the court tasked with recognizing the enforcement decision can decide not to do so. Put differently, public court enforcement can, when two market participants are located in different countries, be seen as a lengthy and uncertain procedure. Nonlegal sanctioning to guarantee compliance with arbitral awards provides a far more effective alternative method, since it puts an end to both risks.

II. A market in which trust plays a crucial role

From all the six trade associations researched, the DDC can be seen as the most peculiar. To substantiate this, three arguments can be given. First, unlike the other five trade associations, this association does not issue standardized (future) contracts/terms for the trade in diamonds, but only provides arbitration and imposes nonlegal sanctions on wrongdoers after a wrongdoer does not comply with an arbitral award. Second, having a good reputation is arguably even more important as compared with the other five trade associations, because diamonds are small, worth a large amount of money and can easily be duplicated. In other words, there is a higher risk involved in trading this material and, hence, having a good standing is crucial in order to be seen as a reliable trader. Third, diamond traders who are members of the DDC are part of a close-knit group that have social relationships with one another. In contrast, the members of the other trade associations are often unfamiliar with each another.

By taking this into account, given that the diamond industry must operate as efficiently and swiftly as possible by having as many trustworthy traders as possible, choosing public court adjudication instead of DDC arbitration, or enforcing DDC arbitral awards in court is undesirable. Courts are slow, non-flexible and often ill-equipped to safeguard the reputation of traders active in the diamond industry. Specialized commercial arbitration enforced by nonlegal sanctioning is a better alternative, because compliance with arbitral awards can be achieved more efficiently. The reason for this is that such sanctions specifically target a trader's reputation as well as his social standing.

Chapter 4: The Limits of Nonlegal Sanctioning

A. *The boundaries of nonlegal sanctioning*

By deviating from the general rule that a dispute is to be adjudicated and enforced in a public court, as was already mentioned before, nonlegal sanctioning through a trade association has a far greater impact for targeted individuals or companies. Being blacklisted, ostracized, and unable to conduct trade with members of a trade association ruins commercial reputations and/or causes social estrangement. Consequently, given the importance of the trade associations, it can lead to a partial or complete loss of access to the relevant commodities market.

In this way, the punishment of foreclosing market entry gives rise to overdeterrence and a complete distortion of the reasoning proper to any legal system, where limitations to market access infringe competition law. Protection of competitors, as one of the major goals that this type of law safeguards, can be infringed. Due to the existence of many competition laws around the world,[411] in my opinion, it is necessary to limit this research to the two largest and most influential systems of competition regulation globally that apply to the situation of the six trade associations researched.[412] The first is US Antitrust Law and the second is EU Competition Law.

I. US Antitrust Law: Sections 1 and 2 of the Sherman Act

The main antitrust law of the USA can be found in Sections 1 and 2 of the Sherman Act.[413] Whereas Section 1 outlaws, *inter alia*, every contract in restraint of trade or commerce among US states or foreign nations, the Section 2 prohibits attempts to monopolize, conspiracies with any other per-

---

411 It is estimated that more than 100 countries worldwide have some form of competition law in place. See J. Duns, A. Duke, and B. Sweeney, "*Comparative Competition Law*", Cheltenham/Northampton: Edward Elgar Publishing 2015, p. 172.

412 R. Mansell, "*The International Encyclopedia of Digital Communication and Society, 3 Volume Set, Volume 1*", Hoboken: Wiley-Blackwell 2015, p. 79.

413 Sherman Antitrust Act of 1890.

son(s) and behaviour to monopolize any part of the trade or commerce among US states or foreign nations. On its face, both definitions are very broad and have, in my opinion, a seemingly unlimited scope. Yet, legal commentary and case law of the US judiciary, in the field of antitrust, address and clarify most ambiguities.

II. EU Competition Law: Articles 101 and 102 TFEU

The most relevant provisions of EU Competition Law that could apply to the practice of nonlegal sanctioning are laid down in Articles 101 and 102 TFEU. The Article 101 prohibits anti-competitive agreements, whereas Article102 strikes down any abuse of a dominant position. Even though both provisions are an emulation of Sections 1 and 2 of the Sherman Act, one cannot say that researching EU Competition Law is redundant. This is because of three reasons. First, the provisions in both laws are worded differently. Second, interpretation by enforcement agencies and courts dealing with EU Competition Law and US Antitrust Law differs. Third, the approach of competition law is different in both legal regimes.

B. Prisoner's dilemma type of function analogy

The prisoner's dilemma type of function analogy concerns the situation in which two individuals by acting in their own self-interest do not reach the best outcome because either person is triggered to cheat.[414] An illustration of such a situation was given by *Aviram*.[415] He explains that if two individuals were caught for robbing a bank, without being able to talk to one another prior to a criminal court's decision and both individuals were given two options, namely to betray the other person or not to talk at all, either party will choose the option that minimalizes his risk to go to prison, even though this would go against the common interest. *Aviram* exemplifies this by using the following three options that can, but do not necessarily, result in a prison sentence.[416]

---

414 R. P. Malloy, "*Law in a Market Context: An Introduction to Market Concepts in Legal Reasoning*", Cambridge: Cambridge University Press 2004, p. 132.

415 A. Aviram, "The Paradox of Spontaneous Formation of Private Legal Systems", *John M. Olin Law & Economics Working Paper No. 192* 2003, p. 39-41.

416 Ibid., p. 39-40.

Option	Years in Prison
1. One individual confesses that the other person is guilty, whereas the other person remains silent	Betrayed individual goes to prison for 15 years, whereas the other person is exculpated
2. Both individuals betray one another	Both persons must serve 10 years in prison
3. Both individuals do not betray one another	Both parties must serve 3 years in prison

From a mutual cooperation point of view, the best outcome would be that both remain silent, because then both parties would only go to prison for 6 years. If only one party betrays the other party, this would result in a combined 15 years' prison sentence. The worst case scenario would be when both parties betray one another (*i.e.* mutual default), as then both individuals would go to prison for a combined 20 years. Yet, despite this seeming truism, either individual will most likely (for selfish reasons) want to obtain the best possible outcome for himself. As a result, it is highly conceivable that both persons would betray the other person in order to not go to prison.[417]

Obviously, this illustration cannot be completely transposed to the situation of nonlegal sanctioning by the six trade associations researched. Especially because both situations are not comparable. Be that as it may, an analogy appears permissible. In the absence of nonlegal sanctions to enforce arbitral awards, losing parties have no incentive to comply with such determinations on the merits of a dispute. This is because enforcement in any public court has proven to be problematic, especially when parties in specialized commercial arbitration proceedings (which is not uncommon) are established in different States. Such an award must then be enforced in two States, namely the State of registration and the State of recognition. This often results in serious delays and insecurities. In more detail, the following table lays down the two options that a losing party in arbitration has as well as the results of each decision.

417 For a more extensive discussion of the prisoner's dilemma, see, *inter alia*, J. Cirace, "*Law, Economics, and Game Theory*", London: The Rowman & Littlefield Publishing Group 2018, p. 113-119.

Option	Result
1. Comply with the arbitration award	Pay the monetary sum stipulated in the award and, hence, contribute to a well-functioning and reliable arbitration system, in which awards are respected.
2. Not comply with the arbitration award	Insecure whether the monetary sum stipulated in the award must be paid in the future, in particular, in the event a second court does not recognize the enforcement decision rendered by the first court. By not complying with an award, the relevant arbitration system may become untrustworthy.

To achieve mutual cooperation, the first option is the best possible outcome. Especially since it secures the success of the arbitration system. However, in line with the above illustration of the prisoner's dilemma type of function, albeit only by analogy, non-compliance with an arbitral award gives a losing party a possible reward after cheating. The losing party then has a chance that the monetary sum stipulated in the arbitral award will not need to be paid. As a result, some market participants will most likely prefer the second option, which in turn can seriously hamper the functionality of the arbitration system. To overcome this problem of opportunistic behaviour and to have measures in place that ensure low enforcement costs, nonlegal sanctioning is the best possible choice. It sufficiently deters or coerces deviating from arbitral awards as efficiently as possible to imagine.[418] Put differently, nonlegal sanctioning is a good method to resolve the prisoner's dilemma of the adverse impact of opportunistic behaviour. Despite such coercive measures having an unmistakeably positive effect for the arbitration systems provided by the six trade associations researched, there is a risk that solving this type of game impedes market access for targeted parties under US Antitrust Law and EU Competition Law.

C. *The actors involved in nonlegal sanctioning*

Before conducting a thorough and extensive research of whether nonlegal sanctions infringe US Antitrust Law and EU Competition Law, it is necessary to identify the actors that take part in such extrajudicial measures and, on the other hand, are the recipients of such coercive measures.

418 A. Aviram, "The Paradox of Spontaneous Formation of Private Legal Systems", *John M. Olin Law & Economics Working Paper No. 192* 2003, p. 41.

I. Actors that take part in nonlegal sanctioning

Only three actors can be detected that take part in nonlegal sanctioning. The first group of actors concerns the "trade associations", also known as industry trade groups, which are tasked with imposing nonlegal sanctions on disloyal industry actors for not complying with arbitral awards stemming from specialized commercial arbitration. The second group of actors encompasses the members of a trade association which have a role in the execution of nonlegal sanctions following this institution's imposition of nonlegal sanctions. The third and last group of actors comprises individuals/companies other than the members of a trade association which (albeit less obviously) have a role in the execution of nonlegal sanctions following this institution's imposition of nonlegal sanctions.

1. Trade associations

The role of a trade association is to promote the common interests of its members (who/that are almost always competitors in a market) as good as possible.[419] For the reason of achieving this objective, such an institution provides rules for the formation of an arbitration tribunal in the event a contractual dispute between members and occasionally between a member and a non-member occurs. Furthermore, it imposes nonlegal sanctions on wrongdoers for not complying with an arbitral award.

2. Members of a trade association

It is debatable whether an association can be seen as the (sole) instigator of extrajudicial coercive measures. To this extent, it is necessary to answer the following question: Is a trade association responsible for nonlegal sanctioning, or do its members have a role to play in nonlegal sanctioning to punish a disloyal industry actor? Answering this question is not easy, because it is uncertain whether a trade association must only be seen as a vehicle through which members organise themselves. If yes, members would be

419 C. S. Mack, "*The Executive's Handbook of Trade and Business Associations: How They Work-and How to Make them Work Effectively for You*", New York/Westport/Connecticut/London: Quorum Books 1991, p. 14.

the sole instigators of nonlegal sanctioning by making use of the rules provided by a trade association.

From my point of view, both the association as well as its members are collectively the driving force of nonlegal sanctioning. The association as the actor responsible for imposing extrajudicial measures and the members as the actor in charge of executing such measures. Hence, it is crucial to distinguish between both actors when discussing a potential liability under US Antitrust Law and EU Competition Law due to their respective role in nonlegal sanctioning.

3. Non-members of a trade association

The last actor concerns market participants that do not belong to the relevant trade association, but are involved in a contractual dispute with one of its members. If this institution were to impose a nonlegal sanction on the member, the non-member would also have a role to play in the execution of this extrajudicial measure. This is because this non-member agrees to abide by the standardized rules which refer to a broader arbitration agreement in which nonlegal sanctions are included. With regard to other non-members, they will often refrain from entering into future contracts with an extrajudicially sanctioned industry actor. Even though express consent is lacking, they might tacitly agree to this type of enforcement and have a role to play in its execution.

II. Recipients of nonlegal sanctioning

There are two types of recipients of nonlegal sanctions. First, the disloyal members of a trade association that do not comply with an arbitral award. Second, non-members that enter into a standardized contract which is linked to a broader arbitration agreement in which nonlegal sanctions are included with a member and do not comply with an award stemming from specialized commercial arbitration. Other non-members cannot be disciplined with nonlegal sanctions.

D. Research Question

Nonlegal sanctioning appears a good method to ensure compliance with arbitral awards stemming from the specialized arbitration systems provided by the six trade associations researched. However, this form of extrajudicial disciplining has a risk of driving out market participants and sometimes of even completely foreclosing market access for such an individual or company. It has long been recognized by some authors that such coercive measures can substantiate a restriction of competition law, namely under Sections 1 and 2 of the Sherman Act and Articles 101 and 102 TFEU.

To date, nonlegal sanctioning imposed by a trade association and executed by its members and non-members has not been considered by the relevant competition enforcement agencies, has never been scrutinized in case law and has not been mentioned in US or EU legislation. Despite this omission, be it justified or not, one cannot draw the conclusion that nonlegal sanctioning is permissible. The compatibility with the antitrust laws of both legal systems must be carefully explained by using a plethora of arguments, legislation, decisional practice and similar cases. Conclusively, the research question is formulated as follows: "*Do the trade associations researched, their members and non-members, for their role in the imposition and execution of nonlegal sanctions, infringe US Antitrust Law and EU Competition Law and, if yes, can they justify these extrajudicial measures?*"

Chapter 5: Research Design and Research Methods

A. *Case studies*

Before the research question can be answered by delving into US Antitrust Law and EU Competition Law, it was necessary to determine in which PLSs and to what extent nonlegal sanctioning occurs. Although some authors have only mentioned a single PLS in which this type of extrajudicial enforcement occurs, such as *Bernstein* with regard to the ICA,[420] *Musmann* with reference to the Bremen Cotton Exchange,[421] and *Richman* pertaining to the DDC,[422] no legal scholar has conducted full-fledged and extensive research by comparing multiple trade associations which operate within PLSs. In my opinion, by only considering a single PLS in which nonlegal sanctioning occurs, it is neither possible to depict a complete picture of what this method of enforcement entails, nor is it feasible to understand other characteristics, such as (i) the options available for internal and judicial appeal against an award; (ii) the possibility of regaining membership after membership has been withdrawn; and (iii) the rationale of nonlegal sanctioning.[423] These characteristics are important in order to contemplate the illegality and possible justification grounds with regard to the involvement of all three actors in extrajudicial enforcement pursuant to Sections 1 and 2 of the Sherman Act and Articles 101 and 102 TFEU. To provide an as good as possible framework against which to conduct a competition law study, this research has, therefore, discussed six cases (which operate within PLSs) in which extrajudicial enforcement occurs. These cases are the ICA, the DDC, GAFTA, the FCC, the LME and FOSFA.[424]

For some, this selection of cases may still appear inadequate to portray the complete picture of nonlegal sanctioning within a PLS. This is because

420 L. Bernstein, "Opting out of the Legal System: Extralegal Contractual Relations in the Diamond Industry", *The Journal of Legal Studies, Vol. 21, No. 1* 1992.

421 A. C. Musmann, "*Recht und soziale Sanktionen: Eine Untersuchung am Beispiel des grenzüberschreitenden Baumwollhandels*", Baden-Baden: Nomos 2018.

422 B. D. Richman, "The Antitrust of Reputation Mechanisms: Institutional Economics and Concerted Refusals to Deal", *Virginia Law Review, Vol. 95:325* 2009.

423 The fact that such research has not been carried out is not because it is unsuitable for empirical research.

424 These six trade associations are discussed in Part I, Chapters 2 and 3.

there are many more PLSs in which similar extrajudicial enforcement methods are proscribed. The Bremen Cotton Exchange and BIMCO are the first ones that immediately come to mind.[425] To address this, it is necessary to answer the following question: Why are the six cases suitable to forming the foundation of competition law scrutiny? To answer this question, two arguments in support of the researched cases must be mentioned.[426] These are mentioned below.

I. Unnecessary redundancy exploratory research methodology

Research must not only be accurate and thorough, it should also be as efficient and as economical as possible.[427] Investigating all PLSs in which nonlegal sanctioning occurs is not expedient. It would not only cause unnecessary redundancy, but it would also deviate from the core of this research, namely to explore the compatibility of trade associations, their members and non-members for their role in extrajudicial enforcement with US Antitrust Law and EU Competition Law.

II. Methodological adequacy

The six cases which have been chosen consist of large trade associations that represent global market players operating in different commodities markets. Because nonlegal sanctioning can foreclose market access of competitors that operate in a different State, this not only can trigger the applicability of both laws, it can also infringe their core provisions. Smaller trade associations, such as the Bremen Cotton Exchange, most likely do

425 The Baltic International Maritime Council (BIMCO) is considered one of the largest international shipping associations that represents ship owners. In line with its policy of restricting public access, only members are granted access to the bylaws and rules of this association. It is, therefore, not possible to understand the arbitration system and the nonlegal sanctions provided by this association. Notwithstanding, various experts active in the maritime industry, who have indicated they wish to remain anonymous, have corroborated the existence of extrajudicial enforcement rules.

426 No author should ever be absolved from the duty to spell out the methodological reasons for the selection of a specific case or cases.

427 J. Barton and R. H. Smith, "*The Handbook for the New Legal Writer*", New York: Wolters Kluwer 2019, p. 345.

not fall within the ambit of US Antitrust Law or EU Competition Law, because they represent fewer market participants in the relevant commodities market and have a smaller impact on US or EU competition. Hence, they are not suitable for research.

B. Delimitation

This research deals with the potential liability of the trade associations researched, their members and non-members for their participation in nonlegal sanctioning, which takes place within a PLS with US Antitrust Law as well as EU Competition Law. More specifically, the focus is to establish whether the most relevant prohibitions under both laws, which can be found in Sections 1 and 2 of the Sherman Act and Articles 101 and 102 TFEU, are infringed and/or possibly justified. Since these legal norms are very vast, especially given that they are interpreted repeatedly by antitrust enforcement agencies, courts as well as the literature, the research must be limited in some ways so as to be able to answer the overarching central research question.

I. US Antitrust Law

First of all, the analysis of US Antitrust Law does not contain an explanation of whether the Sherman Act is applicable and does not factor in various concepts, such as the existence of a standardization agreement. The anti-competitiveness of nonlegal sanctioning is discussed only against the yardsticks laid down in legislation, case law of US courts and legal doctrine. Rendering a detailed explanation is not the author's main objective, as a succinct discussion of the issue whether the researched trade associations, their members and non-members with regard to nonlegal sanctioning violate US Antitrust Law is sufficient. Reasons for this are threefold.

First, five of the six trade associations researched have a closer connection to EU Competition Law. Only the DDC, as a US-based trade association appears more strongly connected to US Antitrust Law. As a result, a more thorough analysis is required with regard to EU Competition Law rather than US Antirust Law. Irrespective of this, such an observation might be refuted if the Federal Trade Commission ("FTC") were to claim competence to scrutinize the liability of the trade associations researched, their members and non-members for their involvement in nonlegal sanctioning under US Antitrust Law. Despite this possibility, because such extraterritorial application would probably upset, *inter alia*, the EU Commission and politicians, it is an unlikely course of events.

Second, my considerable expertise in EU Competition Law justifies a broader analysis with regard to this law rather than US Antitrust Law. Third, whereas *Richman* already in 2009 thoroughly discussed the lawfulness of nonlegal sanctioning against US Antitrust Law,[428] such a detailed discussion about the compatibility of such measures under EU Competition Law has not been carried out to date. Despite *Musmann* in 2018 analyzing the lawfulness of blacklisting and withdrawing membership against Articles 101 and 102 TFEU, her research gives a broad overview only of the main case law and legislation without delving into the specifics.[429] In addition, her focus is – arguably - more on the illegality of nonlegal sanctioning with German Competition Law, namely the Law Against Constraints of Competition (GWB)[430] and the Law Against Unfair Competition (UWG).[431] It is for these reasons that a more thorough and extensive discussion on the lawfulness of nonlegal sanctioning under Articles 101 and 102 TFEU is necessary.

To carry out a concise review of US Antitrust Law, as was already described before, the emphasis should be on two provisions, namely Sections 1 and 2 of the Sherman Act. With regard to Section 1, the research revolves around the question whether (i) the dissemination of the names of recalcitrant industry actors in a blacklist; (ii) withdrawals of membership; (iii) refusals to re-admit expelled members based on an additional entry condition; (iv) refusal to deal with expelled members; (v) entering the premises of a wrongdoer without a warrant; and (vi) limiting adequate access to public courts prior to arbitral proceedings and after an award constitute agreements in restraint of trade. Section 2 of the Sherman Act considers the liability of the trade associations researched and their members for these measures, although the focal is on the denial of access to an essential

428 See B. D. Richman, "The Antitrust of Reputation Mechanisms: Institutional Economics and Concerted Refusals to Deal", *Virginia Law Review, Vol. 95:325* 2009.

429 A. C. Musmann, "*Recht und soziale Sanktionen: Eine Untersuchung am Beispiel des grenzüberschreitenden Baumwollhandels*", Baden-Baden: Nomos 2018.

430 Gesetz gegen Wettbewerbsbeschränkungen of 2017.

431 Gesetz gegen den unlauteren Wettbewerb of 2019.

facility against the concept of anti-competitive (attempted) monopolization or a conspiracy to monopolize.[432]

II. EU Competition Law

The second limitation of this research is in reference to EU Competition Law. More specifically, it concerns the question whether the trade associations researched, their members and non-members, for their participation in nonlegal sanctioning, infringe Articles 101 and 102 TFEU. With regard to both Articles, corresponding with the delimitation of US Antitrust Law explained above, the focus is to analyze whether (i) the dissemination of the names of recalcitrant industry actors in a blacklist; (ii) withdrawals of membership; (iii) refusal to re-admit expelled members on the basis of an additional entry condition; (iv) refusal to deal with expelled members; (v) entering the premises of a wrongdoer without a warrant; and (vi) limiting adequate access to public courts prior to arbitral proceedings and after an award constitute anti-competitive agreements and/or refusals of access to an essential facility through monopolization.[433] Here, the research is much broader. This is because of two reasons: First, different from the analysis under US Antitrust Law, the scope of application of EU Competition Law is discussed. Second, every relevant decision of the Commission, case law of the CJEU as well as legislation will be taken into consideration. With regard to US Antitrust Law, only the most crucial and relevant decisions are discussed.

III. Type of reasoning

Answering the central research question will be done by deductive legal reasoning by occasionally borrowing concepts found in philosophy and economics. This is necessary to prevent a tunnel vision analysis. Yet, applying economic insights to support legal arguments is to a large extent beyond the scope of this research. Not only would this unnecessarily increase

432 Importantly, the potential single dominance of a member of one of the trade associations researched is not discussed. This is because it is unlikely.

433 Importantly, the potential single firm dominance of a member of one of the trade associations researched is not discussed. This is because it is unlikely.

the complexity of the research, it would also carry the risk of debunking legal arguments without having the required personal expertise to do so.

C. Reflection on the research question

The central research question put forward above will be answered in two steps. First, the illegality of the researched trade associations, their members and – arguably – non-members for their participation in nonlegal sanctioning will be examined under US Antitrust Law. Second, potential anti-competitiveness of all three actors for this practice will be discussed pursuant to EU Competition Law. In more detail, the analysis will be divided into eight Chapters (starting with Chapter 6), each of which contribute to answering this question.

- In Chapter 6, a review of all relevant legislation, case law and literature is conducted to determine whether the trade associations researched, their members and non-members violate Section 1 of the Sherman Act for their participation in nonlegal sanctioning. This is done in six Paragraphs. In the first Paragraph (A), a broad introduction is given. In the second Paragraph (B) examines whether the actors involved in nonlegal sanctioning qualify as a corporation or individual and, hence, fall within the ambit of Section 1 of the Sherman Act. The third Paragraph (C) establishes whether there is a concurrence of wills. The fourth Paragraph (D) scrutinizes whether the practice of blacklisting, withdrawing membership, denying membership for expelled members on the basis of an additional entry condition, refusing to deal with an expelled member, entering the premises of wrongdoers without a warrant, and limiting adequate access to public courts prior to arbitral proceedings and after an award constitute restraints of trade. The fourth Paragraph (E) pursues a rule-of-reason analysis to assess whether each of these measures are permissible. The fifth Paragraph (F) provides the key findings.
- In Chapter 7, a review of relevant legislation, case law and literature is again conducted to determine whether the trade associations researched and their members violate Section 2 of the Sherman Act for their participation in nonlegal sanctioning. This is done in five Paragraphs. A brief overview is given in the first Paragraph (A), followed by a discussion in the second Paragraph (B) of whether the trade associations actually monopolize any part of the trade or commerce among the several States, or with foreign nations. The third Paragraph (C), de-

bates whether any of these institutions attempt to monopolize any part of the trade or commerce among the several States, or with foreign nations. This includes a balancing exercise between the anti-competitiveness of conduct and their pro-competitive benefits. The fourth Paragraph (D) examines whether the role of the members of the trade associations when executing extrajudicial enforcement is contrary to Section 2 of the Sherman Act. The last Paragraph (E) presents the key findings.

- In Chapter 8, a review is conducted of relevant legislation, case law and literature to establish whether the trade associations researched, their members and non-members satisfy the scope of application of EU Competition Law for their participation in nonlegal sanctioning. This is done in five Paragraphs. The first Paragraph (A) provides a brief overview of the objectives, responsible enforcement agencies and the absence of precedents to determine nonlegal sanctioning as a restriction of Articles 101 and 102 TFEU. A discussion in the second Paragraph (B) highlights the necessity of fulfilling the scope of application of EU Competition Law with regard to both Articles. The third Paragraph (C) examines fulfillment of the legal boundary (or undertaking concept) while the fourth Paragraph (D) discusses compliance with the economic boundaries (or the effect on trade between member states concept). This requires, from the beginning of this Paragraph, describing the threshold as interpreted by the CJEU and the Commission and, subsequently, establishing whether the practice of nonlegal sanctioning by the trade associations researched, their members and non-members meet the economic boundaries. The fifth Paragraph (E) presents the key findings.
- Chapter 9 examines the unlawfulness of the trade associations researched, their members and non-members for their role in nonlegal sanctioning pursuant to Article 101(1) TFEU by reviewing relevant legislation, enforcement practice of the Commission, case law, and the literature. This is done in five Paragraphs. The first Paragraph (A) provides a broad introduction to the subject. The second Paragraph (B) focuses on the concept of collusion or a concurrence of wills. An explanation is given in the third Paragraph (C) as to whether the trade associations researched, their members and non-members because of their participation in nonlegal sanctions breach Article 101(1) TFEU by object or effect. The fourth Paragraph (D) explores whether these actors can justify nonlegal sanctioning under the first arm of Article 101 TFEU in light of the fact that the existence of such a rule of reason ana-

lysis is debatable. The fifth and last Paragraph (E) summarizes the key findings.

- In Chapter 10, possible justifications for the trade associations researched and their members to escape antitrust liability under Article 101(1) TFEU for their role in nonlegal sanctioning are discussed by analyzing two BERs and Article 101(3) TFEU. The following four Paragraphs examine these issues. The first Paragraph (A) provides a short introduction. The second Paragraph (B) discusses the applicability of two block exemption regulations, namely the Research and Development BER and the Specialization Agreements BER. Both legal documents can debar nonlegal sanctioning from an infringement of Article 101(1) TFEU in a relatively easy and uncomplicated manner. The third Paragraph (C) weighs the participation of the trade associations researched and their members pertaining to nonlegal sanctioning which is contrary to the first arm of Article 101 TFEU against the four exemption conditions laid down in Article 101(3) TFEU. The key findings are provided in the fourth Paragraph (D).
- In Chapter 11, the anti-competitiveness of the trade associations researched for their role in the imposition of nonlegal sanctions are examined against the existence of an abuse of a dominant position pursuant to Article 102 TFEU. This is done by reviewing all legislation, enforcement practice of the Commission, case law and the literature. The review is divided into the following four Paragraphs. The first Paragraph (A) provides a broad introduction to the topic. The second Paragraph (B) examines the existence of a dominant position in the EU markets for regulation and private ordering in which the trade associations operate. The third Paragraph (C) reviews the existence of an abuse of a dominant position in the secondary commodities markets on which their members operate. In Paragraph C, the focus is on the concept of an exclusionary abuse, the essential facility doctrine, the existence of a causal connection between market power of the trade associations on the primary EU markets for regulation and private ordering and an abuse on the second-tier commodities markets on which their members operate and possible justifications. The fourth and last Paragraph (D) summarizes the most important key findings.
- In Chapter 12, the research is summarized in order to understand whether the trade associations researched, their members and nonmembers which have a role in the imposition and execution of nonlegal sanctions within present-day PLSs infringe US Antitrust Law and EU Competition Law and, if yes, if these actors can justify these extraju-

dicial measures. This is done in the following nine Paragraphs. The first Paragraph (A) discusses the peculiarities of present-day PLSs; the second Paragraph (B) discusses the similarities and differences between the six trade associations, which are the most important actors within present-day PLSs. In the third Paragraph (C), an explanation is provided of the antitrust limits of nonlegal sanctioning, which is a salient feature of these trade associations. The fourth Paragraph (D) examines whether the trade associations researched, their members and non-members for their role in nonlegal sanctioning are in restraint of trade or commerce pursuant to Section 1 of the Sherman Act. The fifth Paragraph (E) discusses whether the trade associations researched and their members for their role in nonlegal sanctioning violate Section 2 of the Sherman Act. In the sixth Paragraph (F), an explanation of the applicability of Articles 101 and 102 TFEU is provided. The seventh Paragraph (G) furthers the discussion on whether the trade associations researched, their members and non-members for their role in nonlegal sanctioning infringe Article 101(1) TFEU. In the eighth Paragraph (H), examines justifications for an infringement of this provision by focusing on two BERs and Article 101(3) TFEU. And the last Paragraph (I) further examines whether the trade associations researched and their members for their role in nonlegal sanctioning violate Article 102 TFEU.
- In Chapter 13, the research question is answered and best practice guidelines are developed for trade associations and their members in order for them to escape liability under US Antitrust Law and EU Competition when the former group of actors impose nonlegal sanctions and the latter group of actors execute such measures. This is done in four Paragraphs. The first Paragraph (A) succinctly answers the central research question. The second Paragraph (B) provides introductory comments to draft best practice guidelines for compliance with US Antitrust Law and EU Competition Law, while the third Paragraph (C) provides best practice guidelines for trade associations. The fourth Paragraph (D) concludes with presenting best practice guidelines for members of trade associations.

D. *Objectives of this research*

This research is the most comprehensive study to date that describes the liability of trade associations, their members and non-members (that function within PLSs) with regard to competition law. The reason being that it considers the two most important competition law jurisdictions in the world, namely US Antitrust Law and EU Competition Law. Given that, to date, no study has ever been carried out that analyses extrajudicial enforcement under both laws, answering the main research question will clearly contribute to the general understanding of whether trade associations, their members and non-members involved in this disciplinary method should fear infringing competition law. If the FTC with regard to US Antitrust Law and/or the Commission with regard to EU Competition Law were to reasonably perceive nonlegal sanctioning as an infringement of either law, this could endanger the whole system of specialized commercial arbitration within present-day PLSs. This is because extrajudicial enforcement of arbitral awards would suffer from the threat of invalidity. In turn, judicial enforcement of these awards would remain the only alternative, even though this has proven to be a less efficient option due to issues of unreliability and expected delays. In my opinion, preventing any risk that could impact the functionality (or even the survival) of present-day trade associations which represent industry actors active in the commodities industries should, therefore, be seen as crucial. To do so, the objective of this research is threefold. First, to provide guidance to the trade associations researched, their members and non-members if their participation in nonlegal sanctioning complies with both competition law regimes. Second, to promote transparency for the trade associations researched, their members and non-members concerning a potential US or EU competition law infringement vis-à-vis nonlegal sanctions. Third, to draft or promulgate guidelines for trade associations and their members to ensure that nonlegal sanctioning does not exceed the bounds of US Antitrust Law and EU Competition Law.

I. Guidance for compliance with competition law

Surveying the potential liability of trade associations, their members and non-members for their participation in anti-competitiveness of nonlegal sanctions which are imposed and enforced within PLSs offers much needed clarity on a complex and not widely discussed subject. It is for this reason that guidance for compliance with competition law is provided in Parts II, III and IV of this research. Given that this research is broad and extensive, Chapter 12 summarizes the most important findings, and Chapter 13 provides a succinct conclusion.

II. Promoting transparency for trade associations, their members and non-members

By discussing the potential non-conformity of the trade associations researched, their members and non-members for their role in nonlegal sanctioning with the competition laws of the US and the EU, all actors involved in this type of extrajudicial enforcement may be warned against the possibility of either the FTC, with regard to US Antitrust Law, and the Commission, with regard to EU Competition Law, might one day hold them accountable for antitrust violations.[434] This contributes to increasing the antitrust liability transparency of these actors with regard to orchestrating nonlegal sanctions.

III. Promulgating best practice guidelines for actors that infringe US Antitrust Law and EU Competition Law

On the basis of this research on the liability of the trade associations researched, their members and non-members under US Antitrust Law and EU Competition Law, as is thoroughly explained in Chapters 6 to 13, the ultimate goal of this research is to formulate best practice guidelines for the actors that infringe US Antirust Law and EU Competition Law and to make recommendations on what to do to avoid, or minimalize, the risk of antitrust liability under both legal regimes for the actors' involvement in nonlegal sanctioning. This research also provides words of warning about taking steps to avoid contravening US Antitrust Law and EU Competition Law.

These best practice guidelines have been drafted with taking the following four intersecting key functions into account. First, the guidelines identify the risks that actors face and provide advice (*i.e.* the identification function). Second, the guidelines include warnings about protecting actors from antitrust liability (*i.e.* the prevention function). Third, the guidelines resolve any difficulty with compliance (*i.e.* the resolution function). Fourth, the guidelines state the most effective measures that ought to be taken to ensure compliance with US Antitrust Law and EU Competition Law (*i.e.* the efficacy function).

434 The concept of transparency is subject to much debate in the literature. This debate will not be discussed here.

Figure 7: The intersecting functions of establishing best practice guidelines for trade associations and their members

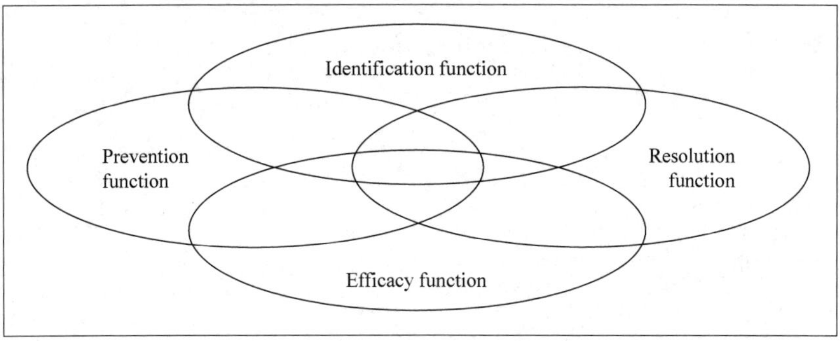

Part II:
Study of US Antitrust Law

Chapter 6: Restraint of Trade or Commerce under Section 1 of the Sherman Act

A. *Introduction*

The trade associations researched are empowered to impose nonlegal sanctions on disloyal industry actors for not complying with an arbitral award, insofar as these measures are included in the bylaws and rules of these associations. If they do so, their members and non-members have a role in the execution of such extrajudicial measures.[435] These measures are carried out by blacklisting, expelling a member, denying membership for an ostracized member on the basis of an additional entry condition, refusing to deal with an expelled member, entering the premises of a wrongdoer without a warrant, and limiting adequate access to public courts prior to arbitral proceedings and after an award. Even if these measures are necessary to maintaining an effective alternative to judicial enforcement in public courts, they may run afoul of Section 1 of the Sherman Act.

According to this provision, "*Every contract, combination in the form of trust or otherwise, or conspiracy, in restraint of trade or commerce among the several States, or with foreign nations, is declared to be illegal*". This requires that an agreement (contract, combination, or conspiracy) exists that unjustifiably has the effect of reducing competition in a relevant market place,

---

435 For the reasons stated in Part I, Chapter 5, B, I, the scope of application will not be mentioned in this Chapter (with the exception of Part II, Chapter 6, B). The focus will be on analysing whether the trade associations researched, their members and non-members can be held accountable for their participation in the practice of nonlegal sanctioning under Section 1 of the Sherman Act. Although the industry actors active in the diamond industry which the DDC represents have a closer connection to the US and, hence, will more readily fall within the scope of US Antitrust Law, this is more difficult to establish with regard to the industry actors active in the commodities industries represented by the five UK-based trade associations. Especially because EU Competition Law has a closer connection to this group of members. Despite this convergence, it will be presumed that all six trade associations researched, their members and non-members satisfy the scope of application of US Antitrust Law. The main reason being that a potential illegality of all three actors with regard to nonlegal sanctioning pursuant to Section 1 of the Sherman Act can be better scrutinized rather than by focusing on one industry.

which has been entered into by more than one individual or corporation.[436] To reach the conclusion that the nonlegal sanctions provided by the trade associations researched and executed by their members and nonmembers violate Section 1 of the Sherman Act, first, the actors involved in nonlegal sanctioning must qualify as a corporation or individual (Paragraph B). Second, a concurrence of wills must be present (Paragraph C). Third, the involvement of the three actors in the six types of nonlegal sanctioning must constitute a restraint of trade (Paragraph D). Fourth and last, in the event Section 1 of the Sherman Act is violated, possible justification grounds must not outweigh the restriction of competition (Paragraph E). At the end of this Chapter, the conclusions of the first three Paragraphs are summarized and critically discussed (Paragraph F).

B. *The actors involved in nonlegal sanctioning*

An important jurisdictional element to open the scope of Section 1 of the Sherman Act requires that either individuals or legal entities are engaged in anticompetitive conduct.

I. Individual members, member undertakings and non-members

For individual members of a trade association who execute nonlegal sanctions on the basis of the rules of this association, this does not require much emphasis. The word person can be understood readily and is unmistakably fulfilled. The same can be said for the undertakings engaged in executing extrajudicial enforcement. They are corporations within the mean-

436 Albeit that Section 1 of the Sherman Act only refers to persons, according to Section 7 of the Sherman Act, "*The word "person", or "persons", wherever used in sections 1 to 7 of this title shall be deemed to include corporations and associations existing under or authorized by the laws of either the United States, the laws of any of the Territories, the laws of any State, or the laws of any foreign country*"; E. G. Perle, M. A. Fischer, and J. T. Williams, "*Perle and Williams on Publishing Law*", Austin/Boston/Chicago/New York: Wolters Kluwer Law & Business 2009, p. 10-11. An undertaking acting alone or a single individual cannot infringe Section 1 of the Sherman Act. A plurality of actors is required; See also American Bar Association, "*Jury Instructions in Criminal Antitrust Cases, 1976-1980: A Compilation of Instructions Given by United States District Courts*", Chicago: American Bar Association 1982, p. 311.

ing of Sections 1 and 7 of the Sherman Act. Non-members also satisfy the jurisdictional threshold, as they comprise corporations and individuals. They are also involved in nonlegal sanctioning in the sense that they tacitly agree with the extrajudicial punishment of recalcitrant market participants for not complying with an award rendered in specialized commercial arbitration. Sometimes they also expressly agree with this conduct when they are a party to a standardized agreement with a member of a trade association and this agreement made reference to this association's bylaws in which the nonlegal sanctions are included. Whether this is sufficient to justify antitrust scrutiny does not play a role here. This is examined in the following Paragraphs.

II. Trade associations

For a trade association, as being the driving force of imposing nonlegal sanctions, this is less obvious. Especially because such an organization structure is not synonymous with the word corporation. After careful reading of Sections 1 and 7 of the Sherman Act, it is unclear whether a trade association, which comprises many member undertakings can be held liable for an infringement of the former provision. It was left to US courts to decide whether an association could be held accountable for antitrust purposes.[437]

In 1984, the Supreme Court initiated this discussion in *Copperweld Corp. v. Independence Tube Corp* by introducing the concept of a "single entity".[438] Albeit relating to the observation that Section 1 of the Sherman Act is applicable to a parent and its wholly-owned subsidiary, especially because both constituted a single entity in the sense that they pursued a common goal and had the same economic objective, these arguments can, in my opinion, also be used to confirm that the trade associations researched, which comprise a plurality of member undertakings, amount to a single entity. Both actors have the same goal, namely to punish disloyalty with arbitral awards. In addition, they have the same economic interest to reduce transaction and distribution costs.

437 P. van Cleynenbreugel, "Single Entity Tests in US Antitrust and EU Competition Law",
Orbi 2011, p. 6; Obviously, a trade association cannot be referred to as a private person.

438 Copperweld v. Independence Tube, 467 U.S. 752 (1984), para. III.

More than two decades later, in 2006, the 10th Circuit Court also used the second benchmark for determining whether a trade association classifies as a legal entity. This was done in *Gregory v. Port Bridger Rendezvous Association*.[439] On the merits of this legal dispute, both the board of the Fur Breeders Agricultural Cooperative and its member undertakings were engaged in unilateral conduct, because the latter group of actors had a direct economic interest in reducing the number of members and non-members that were entitled to sell goods on the basis of a policy that was introduced by the former actor.[440] Likewise, the members of the trade associations as well as their members are both engaged in unilateral conduct, namely to extrajudicially sanction recalcitrant industry actors to achieve a more thriving industry. As a result, they classify as a "legal entity" within the meaning of Section 1 of the Sherman Act. This entails that such actors can be held liable for violation of this provision when – of course – the other conditions are fulfilled.

C. *Collusion: "a concurrence of wills"*

Before being able to discuss the anti-competitiveness of nonlegal sanctioning, at least one of the three forms of collusion needs to be present. These forms of collusion include a contract, a combination, or a conspiracy. Given that each of them has a different meaning, it must be discussed whether the participation of the trade associations researched, their members and non-members, when engaged in nonlegal sanctioning, amounts to an agreement within the meaning of Section 1 of the Sherman Act.[441]

I. Contract

The existence of a contract requires an explicit consensus between at least two actors in writing. This is laid down in the 9th Circuit Court's judgment in *County of Tuolumne v. Sonora Cmty. Hosp.*[442] According to the

---

439 Gregory v. Fort Bridger Rendezvous Ass'n, 448 F.3d 1195 (10th Cir. 2006).

440 Gregory v. Fort Bridger Rendezvous Ass'n, 448 F.3d 1195, 1201 (10th Cir. 2006).

441 K. N. Hylton, "*Antitrust Law and Economics*", Cheltenham: Edward Elgar Publishing 2010, p. 24. The collective term agreement comprises a contract, a combination and a conspiracy.

442 County of Tuolumne v. Sonora Cmty. Hosp., 236 F.3d 1148, 1155 (9th Cir. 2001), para. IV, A, I.

Supreme Court in *Monsanto Co. v. Spray-Rite Serv. Corp.*, this requires that conspirators "*had a conscious commitment to a common scheme designed to achieve an unlawful objective*".[443] Not only must there be a common design and understanding, a meeting of minds in an unlawful arrangement is also required.[444]

To answer the question whether nonlegal sanctioning amounts to a contract, the role of the members of the trade associations researched and – arguably –non-members in executing nonlegal sanctions needs to be discussed. With regard to the members, at the time of obtaining membership, these industry actors have agreed to uphold and respect the bylaws and rules of the relevant trade association. As a result, they have expressly agreed to execute extrajudicial enforcement on the basis of the rules included in these documents. Jointly, along with all other members, they have thus entered into a contract. The internal pressure from within associations to compel members to execute nonlegal sanctions under the threat of being sanctioned themselves does not change the outcome of this legal assessment. This is because they have agreed to execute such sanctions from the moment they accepted the bylaws and rules of the relevant trade association. In addition, when a member contracts with a member (or non-member) on the basis of a standardized contract offered by the relevant trade association, they consent to the execution of nonlegal sanctions. Especially because standardized contracts refer to a broader arbitration agreement, in which clauses exist that empower the relevant trade association to impose extrajudicial measures on disloyal industry actors. The argument that members are not expected to read all the rules drafted in the bylaws and rules when acquiring membership is not convincing. The operation of specialized commercial arbitration enforced by nonlegal sanctions should be clear for all applicants for membership.

This assessment is different for non-members. This group of actors only tacitly agrees to the execution of nonlegal sanction and does not enter into a written contract. An exception is possible when an individual market participant has entered into a standardized contract with a member of a trade association and this document refers to the bylaws of this association which contains a clause proscribing non-compliance with an arbitral award under the threat of nonlegal sanctioning. In this way, a written contract can be substantiated.

443 Monsanto Co. v. Spray-Rite Serv. Corp., 465 U.S. 752, 764 (1984).
444 American Tobacco Co. v. U.S., 328 U.S. 781, 809f, 66 S.Ct. 1125, 90 L.Ed. 1575 (1946), para. III.

II. Combination in the form of trust or otherwise

A combination in the form of a trust pertains to a monopoly type of organization structure which is created by shareholders of companies by transferring a controlling number of their shares (*i.e.* the majority) to a single board of trustees in return for trust certificates.[445] As a result, the companies retain their legal identity, but are controlled by a business policy of the trust combination.

When looking at the situation of the researched trade association, it does not need much explanation to draw the conclusion that they do not classify as a combination in the form of a trust. This is because their members have not transferred shares to the associations with the goal of forming a trust.[446] The trade associations researched were not established to control the business policy of their members. There main task is to represent the interests of their members on a not-for-profit basis by providing certain services (*e.g.* standardized contracts). Notwithstanding, this does not mean that no combination can be detected. According to the Antitrust Guide provided by the Association of Legal Administrators, trade associations typically qualify as a combination pursuant to Section 1 of the Sherman Act.[447] The word combination serves as a catch-all provision. Hence, collusion in the form of a combination can be established. For members and non-members it would require thought-provoking reasoning to explain that they collude in this manner. A combination is perfectly suited to establish whether the trade associations researched can be held accountable for their role in imposing nonlegal sanctions.

445 K. Chander, "*Encyclopaedic Dictionary of Commerce: Volume 3*", New Delhi: Sarup & Sons 1999, p. 780.

446 Even though the members of the LME transferred shares, this association was formed as a "private limited company by shares" and not as a trust.

447 Association of Legal Administrators, "Antitrust Guide: For Members of the Association of Legal Administrators", *Association of Legal Administrators* 2019, p. 1; The standard case used to establish the existence of a combination refers to the Supreme Court judgment in American Tobacco Co. v. United States, 3278 U.S. 781 (1946). In that case, the big three tobacco manufacturers purchased large quantities of cheap tobacco leaves so that other manufacturers had to buy more expensive tobacco. This evidenced a combination.

III. Conspiracy

A conspiracy is a concerted action between at least two actors to achieve an unlawful purpose[448], or as the Oxford English Dictionary defines it, "*a combination of persons* [here: actors] *for an evil or unlawful purpose; an agreement between two or more to do something criminal, illegal or reprehensible; a plot*".[449] An agreement does not necessarily have to be written, Section 1 of the Sherman Act also includes tacit agreements.[450] According to the Supreme Court in *Interstate Circuit, Inc. v. United States*, this requires at a minimum that there must be evidence that competitors have agreed, without having a previous agreement in place, to an invitation to participate in a plan that results in a restraint of interstate commerce.[451]

By ascertaining whether trade associations, their members and non-members fall within this definition, one must make a distinction between two situations. First, for members that execute nonlegal sanctions that are drafted/initiated by the relevant trade association to which they belong, even though their co-action satisfies this rule, there is evidence of a written contract. As a result, nonlegal sanctioning by both actors can be placed better under the collusion category of a contract. Second, for non-members that have not contracted with a member of a trade association, there is no direct evidence of a written contract between this actor and the relevant trade association. Even more, there can be a tacit agreement when this actor, following the situation when a member (or non-member) is extrajudicially sanctioned, also executes this decision. Given that non-members will most likely not conduct further trade with an extrajudicially sanctioned industry actor, the role of non-members can also be relevant for antitrust purposes.

When applying the *Interstate* doctrine, it is unsure whether the rule established in *Interstate* is clear enough to determine whether non-members that are not contracting under a standardized agreement drafted by a trade association have conspired. Also, the Supreme Court's judgments in *Monsanto Co. v. Spray-Rite Service Corp*[452] and *Matsushita Electric Industrial Co. v. Zenith Radio Corp.* that require a "*conscious commitment to a common*

---

448 Aspen Publishers, "*Antitrust*", New York: Aspen Publishers 2004, p. 38.

449 Oxford Corpus, "*Shorter Oxford English Dictionary: Sixth Edition*", Oxford: Oxford University Press 2007.

450 See, *inter alia*, American Tobacco v. United States, 328 U.S. 781, 809 (1946).

451 Interstate Circuit, Inc. v. United States, 306 U.S. 208, 227 (1939).

452 Monsanto Co. v. Spray-Rite Svc. Corp., 465 U.S. 752, 768 (1984). This case concerns vertical constraints.

scheme" is rather vague.[453] Fortunately, later case law has defined what is to be understood as a conscious commitment. In *United States v. Cont'Group* the Third Circuit Court requires that any market participant must knowingly or intentionally have entered into an agreement to effectuate the objective of the conspiracy,[454] unless, according to the Model Jury Instructions in Criminal Antitrust Cases, there is a deliberate blindness to be part of that conspiracy.[455] On the basis of this annotation, in my opinion, one cannot with absolute guarantee make the argument that non-members have consciously participated in the enforcement of nonlegal sanctions. Their role in the execution seems to be more of an indirect nature. To prevent non-members from escaping antitrust scrutiny at this early stage, it would be unwise to conclude that they have not conspired. Despite not willingly, although this is open for debate and largely depends on the arguments being used, it is at least conceivable that such market participants have colluded on a deliberately unaware basis. This means that for non-members that did not conduct trade on the basis of a standardized contract with a member of a relevant trade association, to some extent evidence of a conspiracy can be found.

D. *An unreasonable restraint on competition: The existence of an illegal horizontal agreement and collective boycott*

Regulatory sanctioning for not complying with arbitral awards, which are drafted/initiated by the trade associations and executed by their members and non-members can have serious consequences for targeted market participants. Not only is there an elevated risk that targeted industry actors are driven out of the second-tier commodities markets, but their social standing can also be jeopardized. Any antitrust lawyer could build a good and solid defence for these wrongdoers, especially because the involvement of the three actors in nonlegal sanctioning amounts to a horizontal agreement that, depending on the measure being imposed and executed, can infringe various antitrust doctrines. The most important are discussed in this

453 Matsushita v. Zenith Radio Corp., 475 U.S. 574 (1986); American Bar Association, "*Proof of Conspiracy under Federal Antitrust Laws*", Chicago: American Bar Association 2010, p. 24. The Supreme Court transposes the Monsanto rule to horizontal agreements.

454 United States v. Cont'Group 603 f.2d 444, 463 (5th Cir. 1979).

455 American Bar Association, "*Model Jury Instructions in Criminal Antitrust Cases*", Chicago: American Bar Association 2009, p. 71-75.

part and relate to the collection and dissemination of market information, membership rules and barriers for market access, collective refusal to deal, entering the premises of a recalcitrant industry actor without a warrant, and limiting adequate access to public courts prior to arbitral proceedings and after an award.

I. Collection and dissemination of market information

All of the trade associations researched have one thing in common: they collect and disseminate the names of wrongdoers that deviate from their obligations in blacklists. Although this method is initiated by a trade association itself, its council, or its board of directors, depending on the relevant trade association, its execution is only effective if a sufficient number of members and – arguably – non-members commit to ruling out trading with recalcitrant market participants on the second-tier commodities market.[456] If the latter two actors were to refuse to do so and were to continue to conduct trade with a blacklisted member, this type of extrajudicial enforcement would be ineffective in deterring non-compliance with arbitral awards. In other words, the collection and dissemination of the names of wrongdoers requires a co-action between at least the relevant trade association and its members, but – arguably – also with non-members.

By foreclosing market access, all three actors (to the extent of their respective role) run the risk of being complicit in a horizontal collective boycott, which substantiates an unreasonable restraint on competition under Section 1 of the Sherman Act. The severity of this restraint should not be underestimated, as the Supreme Court in various judgments held that a collective boycott is prohibited.[457] This is because it has a pernicious effect on competition and lacks any redeeming virtue. According to the United States Court of Appeals for the District of Columbia Circuit in *Fed. Maritime Comm'n v. Aktiebolaget Svenska Amerika Linien*, any horizontal agree-

456 B. D. Richman, "The Antitrust of Reputation Mechanisms: Institutional Economics and Concerted Refusals to Deal", *Virginia Law Review, Vol. 95:325* 2009, p. 340.

457 See, *inter alia*, Eastern States Lumber Assn. v. United States, 234 U. S. 600 (1914); Fashion Originators' Guild v. Federal Trade Comm'n, 312 U. S. 457, 465 (1941); Kiefer-Stewart Co. v. Seagram & Sons, 340 U. S. 211, 214 (1951); Times-Picayune Publishing Co. v. United States, 345 U. S. 594, 625 (1953); Northern Pacific R. Go. v. United States, 356 U. S. 1, 5 (1958); Klor's, Inc. v. Broadway-Hale Stores, Inc., 359 U.S. 207, 212 (1959).

ment to collectively boycott competitors should even be seen as illegal per se.[458] This entails that a court will not consider possible justifications. Whether the practice of blacklisting is indeed designed to multilaterally eliminate competitors and can be seen as inherently illegal is unclear. To date, no US case law or legislation has ever touched upon the illegality of blacklisting within a PLS. To address this uncertainty, the most closely related non-statutory law will be thoroughly discussed with regard to all three actors.

1. Blacklists by trade associations

As discussed throughout this research, trade associations are tasked with drafting rules concerning the collection and dissemination of market participants and imposing this type of nonlegal sanctioning when a market participant does not comply with an arbitral award. To draw the conclusion that there is an unreasonable restraint on trade, a mere facilitation of an anticompetitive agreement might be sufficient. The Supreme Court ruled that this is particularly true when a trade association exchanges information on sales, delivery charges and prices.[459] Such conduct amounts to an illegal facilitation contrary to Section 1 of the Sherman Act. For blacklisting, this is much more difficult to say. This is because US courts have never considered such a nonlegal sanction which is imposed by a trade association. However, the legal rule derived from the Supreme Court's judgment in *Eastern States Retail Lumber Dealers' Ass'n. v. United States* provides some guidance.[460] In this case, lumber associations consisting of retailers collected complaints from their members about wholesalers that sold lumber directly to consumers.[461] The names of such disloyal wholesalers were then drafted in a blacklist, which was sent by these associations to its members.[462] Following dissemination of the blacklist, in practice, the members

458 Fed. Maritime Comm'n v. Aktiebolaget Svenska Amerika Linien, 390 U.S. 238, 250 (1968).

459 American Column & Lumber Co. v. United States, 257 U.S. 377 (1921); United States v. American Linseed Oil Co., 262 U.S. 371 (1923).

460 Eastern States Retail Lumber Dealers' Ass'n. v. United States, 234 U.S. 600 (1914).

461 Eastern States Retail Lumber Dealers' Ass'n. v. United States, 234 U.S. 600, 605 (1914).

462 Eastern States Retail Lumber Dealers' Ass'n. v. United States, 234 U.S. 600, 608 (1914).

then refused to deal with wrongdoers included on that list. The Court found that this clearly hindered or impeded the trade of wholesalers and constituted a violation of Section 1 of the Sherman Act by the trade associations.[463] According to *Hylton*, the Supreme Court had not decided that a horizontal agreement was illegal because of its effects, but had drawn the more stringent conclusion that inducing the members to refuse to deal with a blacklisted wholesaler amounted to a *per se* outlawed group boycott.[464] No justifications were determined on the merits of the case that could redeem the associations.

Similarly, and perhaps even more akin to the collection and dissemination of wrongdoers initiated by the trade associations researched, in *Fashion Originators Guild of America (FOGA)* the Supreme Court found a *per se* violation within the meaning of Section 1 of the Sherman Act with regard to the blacklisting practice pertaining to a trade association of designers, manufacturers, distributers and retailers ("FOGA").[465] In this case, FOGA had blacklisted the names of all retailers who sold pirated garments, despite it having a pro-competitive purpose, namely to protect all members against "*the evils growing from the pirating of original designs*".[466] The main argument used by the Court was that even if copying garments was illegal in all states of the US, self-help in the form of blacklisting is a restraint on interstate commerce in violation of Section 1 of the Sherman Act.[467] For the trade association researched, this case has far-reaching implications. Their enforcement activity by initiating the practice of blacklisting directed at industry actors that did not comply with an arbitral award can easily be seen as a self-policing attempt to guarantee compliance. Despite the District Court in *NYNEX Corp. v. Discon, Inc.* to some extent mitigating this outcome, especially because it ruled that the *per se* rule is not applicable when an agreement generates a pro-competitive effect, in my opinion, there is a clear risk that participating in a collective boycott for the main ground of self-policing violates Section 1 of the Sherman Act.[468] The gravity of the illegality can even be worse when the relevant trade association

463 Eastern States Retail Lumber Dealers' Ass'n. v. United States, 234 U.S. 600, 614 (1914).
464 K. N. Hylton, "*Antitrust Law and Economics*", Cheltenham: Edward Elgar Publishing 2010, p. 33.
465 Fashion Originators' Guild of America v. FTC, 312 U.S. 457, 468 (1941).
466 Fashion Originators' Guild of America v. FTC, 312 U.S. 457, 458 (1941).
467 Fashion Originators' Guild of America v. FTC, 312 U.S. 457, 468 (1941).
468 NYNEX Corp. v. Discon, Inc., 525 U.S. 128, 134 (1998). Importantly, this case involves a vertical agreement and not a horizontal agreement and is not com-

has published the name of a wrongdoer in a publicly accessible blacklist. By doing so, not only would members be induced to participate in the collective refusal to deal, but also non-members that had not even conducted trade with a targeted member.

If the FTC and, in appeal, a US court were to indeed reach the conclusion that self-policing in the form of a blacklist constitutes a *per se* violation of Section 1 of the Sherman Act, this could endanger the existence of present-day PLSs. In my opinion, given the efficiencies created by operating in the shadow of the law, this is an unwanted outcome. The anti-competitiveness of blacklisting which has been facilitated by a trade association should at least be balanced against possible justification grounds in a rule-of-reason analysis. This raises the ensuing question: How can a trade association escape the *per se* illegality pursuant to Section 1 of the Sherman Act? Providing an answer is perhaps more straightforward than it might appear at first glance. If the trade associations researched classify as joint ventures, the *per se* rule is not always appropriate. For example, in *Broadcast Music, Inc. v. CBS, Inc.* the Supreme Court ruled that "*joint ventures and other cooperative arrangements are* […] *not usually unlawful*".[469] However, according to *Cross & Miller*, this does not mean that they are not subject to antitrust scrutiny pursuant to Section 1 of the Sherman Act.[470] When a joint venture fixes prices and/or divides territories or customers, a *per se* violation of this provision is likely. If not, notwithstanding an illegality, a rule-of-reason analysis is possible.

For the trade associations researched, it is clear that they do not participate in a horizontal agreement to fix prices or divide markets. They exclusively target wrongdoers for not complying with an arbitral award. Put differently, the collection and dissemination of market participants in blacklists does not constitute a *per se* violation if the trade associations qualified as joint ventures. Even though they facilitate an anticompetitive collective group boycott, they will then have the possibility of a rule-of-reason defence to escape a violation of Section 1 of the Sherman Act. There is only one problem: the trade associations researched would need to qualify as joint ventures. Under the rules of US Antitrust Law, the term joint venture

---

pletely suitable to discover the necessity of a rule-of-reason defence over a finding of *per se* illegality.

469 Broadcast Music, Inc. v. CBS, Inc., 441 U.S. 1 (1979), para. E.

470 F. B. Cross, R. L. Miller, "*The Legal Environment of Business: Text and Cases – Tenth Edition*", Boston: Cengage Learning 2018, p. 571.

does not have a single meaning.[471] It encompasses any collaborate activity,[472] or, as the District Court of Kentucky put it in *McElhinney v. Medical Protective*, *"the term 'joint venture' denotes a group of independent economic actors who have joined together, in part, to provide a common product or service"*.[473] Despite some authors preferring a narrower conceptualization, in my opinion, the trade associations researched are joint ventures.[474] The reasons are two-fold. First, comparable with the broad definition, market participants have established trade associations with the purpose of a common overall aim, namely to represent and provide arbitration services to them. Second, given the procompetitive benefits that a system of specialized commercial arbitration under the threat of the collection and dissemination of the names of market participants in blacklists generates, it would be unwise to exclude the possibility to balance such an efficiency against a violation of Section 1 of the Sherman Act. If the trade associations researched do not qualify as a joint venture, any rule-of-reason analysis could not be considered.

In sum, by facilitating the collection and dissemination of market participants in blacklists, the trade associations researched violate Section 1 of the Sherman Act. This is because such practice amounts to a collective group boycott. Owing to the efficiencies this practice generates, establishing the existence of a *per se* violation is not preferred. The most sensible way to escape this conclusion is to consider the trade associations as joint ventures. In that way, a rule-of-reason analysis can be conducted.

---

471 J. M. Jacobson, "*Antitrust Law Developments (sixth)*", Chicago: American Bar Association, Vol. 1, 2007, p. 433.

472 P. J. Welch, G. F. Welch, "*Economics: Theory and Practice – Ninth Edition*", Hoboken: John Wiley & Sons 2010, p. 408.

473 McElhinney v. Medical Protective Co., 549 F. Supp. 121, 132 (E.D. Ky. 1982)

474 A narrower definition of what defines a joint venture was, for example, given in J. F. Brodley, "Antitrust Analysis of Joint Ventures: An Overview", *American Bar Association, Vol. 66, No. 3,* 1998, p. 1526. Following this journal, a joint venture must fulfil the following four conditions. First, the enterprise must be under the joint control of parent companies (which are not under related control). Second, every single parent has to give a substantial contribution to the enterprise. Third, the parents and the enterprise are separate business entities. Fourth, the enterprise must generate new technology, productive quality, create a new product, or commence in a new market. For the trade associations researched it is unlikely that they can be considered as joint venture on the basis of this four-step test. Especially because the trade associations do not achieve the goals under the fourth condition.

2. Execution of blacklists by members of trade associations

The role of the trade associations researched in blacklisting the names of market participants for not complying with an arbitral award is clear: they produce and impose this type of sanction. Despite blacklisting facilitating an illegal collective boycott, the effectiveness of this practice would remain fruitless if the members of the trade associations researched were to decide not to execute such measure. In other words, a wrongdoer can only be punished when both a trade association and its members work together to blacklist this individual or company.

Whereas the trade associations researched violate Section 1 of the Sherman Act, it is not implausible that a similar conclusion can be drawn concerning their members to the extent they execute the practice of blacklisting. This is because restricting the business opportunities of market participants is so severe that it has an exclusionary effect.[475] The best example of a case that illustrates the culpability of the members of the trade associations researched again refers to the Supreme Court's judgment in *Eastern States Retail Lumber Dealers' Ass'n. v. United States.* In that case, the dissemination of a blacklist was only effective because the members of the association acted upon that information and refused to deal with wrongdoers.[476] This constituted a *per se* violation for them. Although some companies did not agree to this outcome, two arguments can be made in favour of establishing a restraint of trade for the role that members play in blacklisting market participants.[477] First, without the members of a relevant trade association executing that measure, the purpose of the blacklist, namely to collectively boycott competitors from that market, cannot be achieved. Second, the members of the trade associations researched are capable of adjusting the policy of the latter actors to blacklist wrongdoers. A trade association is merely a combination of market participants that wish to be represented by an overarching institution in order to obtain certain benefits. Members could change the bylaws of the trade associations and delete the relevant

475 J. F. Ponsoldt, "The Application of the Sherman Act Antiboycott law to Industry Self-Regulation: An Analysis Integrating Nonboyocott Sherman Act Principles", *Bepress* 1981, p. 13.

476 It even follows from H. Hovenkamp, "*The Antitrust Enterprise: Principle and Execution*", Cambridge/London: Harvard University Press 2005, p. 2 that the members of the lumber associations destroyed the wholesale business of blacklisted market participants.

477 B. D. Shaffer, "*In Restraint of Trade*", Cranbury/London/Mississauga: Associated University Presses 1997, p. 64.

clauses which empower the trade association to blacklist recalcitrant market participants. If they refuse to do so, members are just as responsible for the imposition of this type of nonlegal sanction on other market participants as the trade associations to which they belong.

Despite one being able to make an argument that the complicity of the members of the trade associations researched in blacklisting wrongdoers can also amount to a *per se* violation of Section 1 of the Sherman Act, the qualification of the trade associations as joint ventures would also excuse the former actors from such finding that prohibits any form of justification. This is because members are the foundation on which a trade association is built and without them would merely be an empty vehicle. Notwithstanding, the concerted action of members to execute the collection and dissemination of market participants in blacklists is sufficient to constitute a violation of Section 1 of the Sherman Act. This is irrespective of the fact that the severity of any violation of this provision depends on the economic harm done to a wrongdoer. Determining the exact degree is not an easy task. Much depends on the combined total shares that the members have on the second-tier market and how essential it is to be a member of the relevant trade association.[478]

The precise harm inflicted upon a wrongdoer is difficult to ascertain. Empirical evidence relating to the market shares that members of the trade associations have is missing. Fortunately, logical reasoning provides some lucidity. All of the trade associations researched are the most important institutions that represent individuals and/or companies in a specific commodities market. Given the services and benefits that these associations offer, membership is crucial to survive in each relevant market. As a result, many market participants will choose to be closely connected with the relevant trade association. When a member or non-member is blacklisted, it not only negatively affects a market participant's business reputation, but also inflicts economic harm. This is especially true when a trade association not only disseminates this information to its members, but also circulates it to every other trade association representing members in the same commodities market. In addition, when such list becomes public, the harm inflicted upon wrongdoers intensifies.[479]

---

478 C. C. Bird, "Sherman Act Limitations on Noncommercial Concerted Refusals to Deal", *Duke Law Journal, Vol. 1970, No. 2* 1970, p. 253-254.

479 For a comparable observation, albeit referring to Section 6 of the Clayton Act, the United States v. King, 229 F. 275 (D. Mass. 1915) case deserves emphasis. In that judgment, Judge Morton held that when the association in this case circu-

In sum, despite there being only a single judgment that has ever ruled on the illegality of executing blacklists, members of the trade associations researched violate Section 1 of the Sherman Act. Their complicity in this type of nonlegal sanction amounts to a collective boycott. Yet, the gravity of restrictiveness is debatable, as much depends on determining the harm done to wrongdoers on a case-by-case basis. Owing to the procompetitive efficiencies created by the operation of specialized commercial arbitration, and its enforcement of awards usually being complied with due to the threat of blacklisting, it would be unwise to exclude the possibility of justification grounds at this stage. Members of the trade associations researched are the founders of these joint ventures and their conduct must be subject to a rule-of-reason analysis, even though their involvement amounts to a collective boycott.

3. Execution of blacklists by non-members

The complicity of non-members in an illegal collective boycott by executing a blacklist initiated by one of the trade associations researched merits being considered with regard to two situations. The first concerns the circumstance that a non-member has entered into a standardized agreement with a member of a trade association which agreement is linked to a broader arbitration agreement in which the practice of blacklisting is laid down and that trade association blacklists the latter individual or undertaking. Then, not only do all its members execute that extrajudicial measure, but also that specific non-member. Whether or not the complicity of such a non-member violates Section 1 of the Sherman Act is uncertain. To date, no statutory law or case law has ever touched on this subject. Irrespective of this unavailability, in my opinion, non-members that contract on the basis of a standardized contract cannot be held accountable for a violation of Section 1 of the Sherman Act owing to two reasons. First, these individuals and or undertakings do not have the competence to rescind a clause permitting this institution to blacklist a wrongdoer. Second, non-

lated a blacklist to non-members and instructed them to refuse to deal with members on the list, also the members were engaged in a proscribed restraint on trade; For an analysis of this case, see D. A. Frederick, "*Antitrust status of Farmer Cooperatives: The Story of the Capper-Volstead Act*", Washington DC: United States Department of Agriculture 2002, p. 84.

members are often unaware that a standardized contract is linked to a broader arbitration agreement which includes a blacklisting clause.

The second situation to determine the complicity of non-members in a prohibited group boycott which is initiated by one of the trade associations researched refers to the scenario in which this group of actors has not entered into a standardized agreement with a member of this institution. When there is no connection between a trade association and market participants, it is unlikely that the latter group of non-members is sufficiently involved in the practice of blacklisting to reasonably prove participation in an illegal collective boycott. The fact that these non-members act upon the information provided in the blacklist by (completely or to some extent) refraining from dealing with a targeted market participant, contingent upon the public accessibility of this list, does not change this observation. Such a broadening of the scope of Section 1 of the Sherman Act has the risk of punishing every individual and company operating in the relevant commodities market. This would be an injudicious development resulting in over-punishment over rationale.

II. Membership rules and barriers for market access

If the practice of blacklisting was already tantamount to a group boycott for the trade associations researched, their members and occasionally non-members, it is not unlikely that withdrawing membership, be it temporary or permanent, can also give rise to a violation of Section 1 of the Sherman Act by all three actors. Punishing a bad industry participant by terminating a market participant's membership not only sends a signal to other industry actors that this individual or company is unreliable, it also takes away association-specific benefits and services. As severe as this may appear, the following Paragraph (Paragraph 1) explains whether indeed case law substantiates the existence of a violation of Section 1 of the Sherman Act. Subsequently, it will be examined on the basis of relevant case law of the US courts whether denying membership for an expelled member on the basis of an additional entry condition violates this provision (Paragraph 2).

1. Withdrawal of membership of a trade association

Membership of the trade associations researched is vital to being competitive on each relevant commodities market for market participants. Owing to the competitive importance and strength of these trade associations, withdrawing access to its facilities and services places such recalcitrant member at a serious competitive disadvantage.[480] As is discussed below, trade associations, their members, but also non-members can violate Section 1 of the Sherman Act.

a. Withdrawal by a trade association

All of the trade associations researched have included the possibility to expel wrongdoers following non-compliance with an arbitral award in their bylaws. When such conduct occurs, depending on the relevant trade association, a Board of Directors, Council, Disciplinary Committee or arbitration board "may" with full discretionary freedom initiate this nonlegal sanction. Even though there is no obligation to do so, this Paragraph examines whether Section 1 of the Sherman Act is violated once a market participant has its membership temporarily or permanently terminated.

A good place to start a discussion of the anti-competitiveness of withdrawing membership by a trade association is the Supreme Court's judgment in *American Medical Assn. v. United States*.[481] In that case, the Court found that expelling physicians from the American Medical Association when accepting employment under Group Health, a nonprofit health maintenance organization, constituted a restraint of trade.[482] Although this case exclusively related to a permanent loss of membership, three decades later the US District Court for the Northern District of Georgia in *Blalock v. Ladies Professional Golf Association* held that also a one-year suspension of membership from the golf association violated Section 1 of the

480 T. V. Vakerics, "*Antitrust Basics*", New York: Law Journal Press 2006, p. 6-40.

481 American Medical Assn. v. United States, 317 U.S. 519 (1943).

482 American Medical Assn. v. United States, 317 U.S. 519, 535-536 (1943). The American Medical Association violated Section 3 of the Sherman Act. This Section extends the scope of the provision of Section 1 by including the District of Colombia; For the differences and similarities between Sections 1 and 3, see H. I. Saferstein and J. C. Everett, "*State Antitrust Practice and Statutes (Fourth)*", Chicago: American Bar Association 2009, p. 10-3, 10-4.

Sherman Act.[483] The Court held that such punishment for illegally moving a golf ball excluded this person's access to the entire market, because she could not compete in other tournaments. The suspension initiated by the golf association constituted a *per se* unlawful boycott.[484] Whether or not the Court would have reached this conclusion without the influence of members to convince the golf association to carry out a suspension is difficult to ascertain. The fact remains that the golf association imposed the boycott.[485]

For the trade associations researched, the precedent of US courts showcases that their promulgation of permanent withdrawals of membership corresponds to a *per se* violation of Section 1 of the Sherman Act. This is particularly true because this type of extrajudicial enforcement has the effect of ostracizing a targeted industry actor from the market. Without membership, a former member not only loses access to a trade association's facilities, but also suffers enormous reputational harm. With regard to a suspension, the establishment of a *per se* violation is not so obvious. Even though a suspended market participants loses access to the facilities of a trade association and suffers reputational damage, unlike the Court's reasoning in *Blalock v. Ladies Professional Golf Association* following which no tournament could be competed in, such an individual or company can still deal with any other member of the trade association, or with non-members.[486]

In later case law, such as in the Supreme Court's judgment delivered in *NW Wholesale Stationers v. Pac. Stationery*, the severity of such type of extrajudicial enforcement that amounted to a collective boycott was mitigated.[487] Following this case, an expulsion of a member from a cooperative is generally subject to rule-of-reason analysis under Section 1 of the Sherman

483 Blalock v. Ladies Professional Golf Association, 359 F. Supp. 1260 (N.D. Ga. 1973).

484 Blalock v. Ladies Professional Golf Association, 359 F. Supp. 1260, 1265-1266 (N.D. Ga. 1973).

485 See also Deesen v. Professional Golfers' Association of America, 358 F. 2d 165 (9th Cir. 1966) involving a similar expulsion for poor performance. In its judgment, the Federal Appellate Court did not find a restraint of trade pursuant to Section 1 of the Sherman Act, because the targeted individual could take some steps in order to play golf tournaments; K. N. Hylton, "*Antitrust Law and Economics*", Cheltenham: Edward Elgar, Vol. 4 2010, p. 50.

486 If a US court were to examine the illegality of a suspension initiated by one of the trade associations, it is possible that this institution would reach a different conclusion.

487 NW Wholesale Stationers v. Pac. Stationery, 472 U.S. 284 (1985).

Act when such collaboration was designed to make the market more competitive and increase efficiency without manifesting predominant anticompetitive effects.[488] To achieve this, the cooperative must establish and enforce reasonable rules.[489] Only if the cooperative has market power, or has exclusive access to an essential facility that is necessary for an expelled member to compete, a *per se* treatment might be more appropriate.[490] Whether or not the trade associations researched fall under this rule is debatable. A cooperative and a trade association are two different things, since in the first the members have an equity interest, because all of them own a portion of the cooperative, whereas in a trade association the members have a non-equity position.[491] In my opinion, transposing the legal rules derived from *NW Wholesale Stationers v. Pac. Stationery* to determine the anti-competitiveness of the trade associations researched seems appropriate.[492] Not only because of the efficiency gains that were being created by these legal entities, but also since an expulsion could be a reasonable method to dissuade the members of these associations from not complying with an arbitral award and thereby maintaining the functionality and operability of present-day PLSs. Despite the clear foreclosure effect for targeted market participants following a suspension or termination of membership, especially because the trade associations are essential for industry actors to compete in a relevant commodities market, a *per se* treatment would present the trade associations with the opportunity to at least justify their rationale for expulsion.[493] Another argument in support of this view is the qualification of the trade associations researched as joint ventures. Such collaboration typically does not give rise to *per se* violation.

The argument that only members of trade associations can be targeted with expulsion does not change the outcome that such type of extrajudicial

488 NW Wholesale Stationers v. Pac. Stationery, 472 U.S. 284, 295 (1985).

489 NW Wholesale Stationers v. Pac. Stationery, 472 U.S. 284, 296 (1985).

490 Ibid.

491 www2.ef.jcu.cz/~sulista/pages/kdfp/BUEN1-1.pdf.

492 T. J. Waters and R. H. Morse, "*Antitrust & Trade Associations: How Trade Regulation Laws Apply to Trade and Professional Associations*", Chicago: American Bar Association 1996, p. 58. The legal rules described in NW Wholesale Stationers v. Pac. Stationery apply to both a cooperative and a trade association. Put differently, both legal entities can be used interchangeably.

493 American Bar Association, "*Joint Ventures: Antitrust Analysis of Collaborations Among Competitors*", Chicago: American Bar Association 2006, p. 102. A court will usually consider the following two criteria to assess membership restrictions: first, the level of necessity that access has on effective competition, and second, the nature and scope of the infringement.

enforcement violates Section 1 of the Sherman Act. Ostracizing disloyal members amounts to a collective boycott. The severity of the boycott – arguably – increases when a trade association publishes its withdrawal of membership in a publicly accessible section of the website of this association just as two out of five of the trade associations researched have done.[494] This depends on whether (the responsible institution within) a trade association already circulated the name of a wrongdoer in a blacklist.[495] If not, the expulsion will bring additional reputational harm.

Offering ostracized recalcitrant members with the possibility to obtain an internal appeal against a withdrawal of membership decision to some degree negates the exclusionary effect of this measure.[496] However, according to the Supreme Court in *NW Wholesale Stationers v. Pac. Stationery*, the presence of procedural safeguards (*i.e.* possibility of internal appeal) does not change the conclusion that Section 1 of the Sherman Act is violated.[497] Procedural protection in itself does not justify a conclusive presumption of a predominantly anticompetitive effect of a membership being withdrawn.[498] The American Bar Association confirms this conclusion and establishes that the lack of procedural safeguards for suspending or expelling a member does not create an antitrust violation.[499] However, post-*NW Wholesale stationers v. Pac. Stationery*, the US District Court for the District of Vermont in *Charleton v. Vt. Dairy Herd Improvement Ass'n*[500] and the US District Court for the District of Kansas in *Pretz v. Holstein Friesian Ass'n*[501]

494 See Part I, Chapter 3, G, III.

495 If the FTC decides to make an antitrust case pursuant to Section 1 of the Sherman Act against one of the trade associations researched, the existence of a blacklist as well as the dissemination of an expulsion decision would need to be established on a case-by-case basis.

496 Only the ICA and the LME discuss the possibility of an internal appeal against a withdrawal of membership. The DDC and the FCC do not expound on this possibility. Members of FOSFA do not have a right to lodge an appeal against a withdrawal of membership.

497 NW Wholesale Stationers v. Pac. Stationery, 472 U.S. 284, 293 (1985).

498 American Bar Association, "*Joint Ventures: Antitrust Analysis of Collaborations Among Competitors*", Chicago: American Bar Association 2006, p. 102.

499 American Bar Association, "*Antitrust & Trade Associations: How Trade Regulation Laws Apply to Trade and Professional Associations*", Chicago: American Bar Association 1996, p. 62; Silver v. New York Stock Exch. 373 U.S. 341 (1963). A lack of notice on the reasons for suspension or expulsion by itself also does not infringe Section 1 of the Sherman Act.

500 Charleton v. Vt. Dairy Herd Improvement Ass'n, 782 F. Supp. 926, 932 (D. Vt. 1991).

501 Pretz v. Holstein Friesian Ass'n, 698 F. Supp. 1531, 1539 (D. Kans. 1988).

ruled that an absence of due process in withdrawing membership may be considered in a rule-of-reason analysis as evidence of the intent of the restriction pursuant to Section 1 of the Sherman Act.[502]

b. Execution of the withdrawal of membership by members of a trade association

There is a preponderance of evidence that the members of the trade associations researched, when these associations initiate a withdrawal of membership, also violate Section 1 of the Sherman Act. This is because these market participants have the competence to abide by and execute this non-legal sanction, or to use their power to overturn a withdrawal of membership, or can remove such a measure in the bylaws and rules of a relevant trade association. Put differently, members have a guiding role in boycotting a specific market participant. This raises the ensuing question: If the trade associations researched violate Section 1 of the Sherman Act, then why do their members not?

Answering this question on the basis of case law is difficult, as neither the FTC nor any US court has ever ruled that members specifically, or as a group, violate Section 1 of the Sherman Act for their complicity in expelling a member from a trade association. In line with the Supreme Court's decision in *NW Wholesale Stationers v. Pac. Stationery*, an answer can be given to some extent. In this case, although the cooperative initiated an exclusion of membership and committed an illegal horizontal agreement, without the concerted action of its members this would not have resulted in a termination of membership of the disloyal undertaking. This is particularly true because the members of the cooperative were the ones who voted to expel this market participant.[503]

In my opinion, because of the role that members play in orchestrating an expulsion, it may very well be possible that the FTC and/or US courts would find a similar degree of accountability for a violation of Section 1 of the Sherman Act. Much will depend on the analysis of either or both institutions in determining whether targeted members are placed at a severe competitive disadvantage following their membership being withdrawn.

---

502 These are lower court judgments and are in contrast with the Supreme Court's judgment in *NW Wholesale Stationers v. Pac. Stationery.*

503 NW Wholesale Stationers v. Pac. Stationery, 472 U.S. 284, 287 (1985).

c. Execution of the withdrawal of membership by non-members

Whether industry actors that are not members of a relevant trade association also partake in expelling a wrongdoer and violate Section 1 of the Sherman Act must be assessed on the basis of two scenarios. The first pertains to the situation that a non-member has entered into a standardized agreement with a member of a trade association that is linked to a broader arbitration agreement in which there is a clause that permits the relevant trade association to withdraw the membership of a wrongdoer and that wrongdoer is expelled. In this scenario, members as well as the relevant non-member have a role in the execution of that extrajudicial measure. Despite no statutory law or non-statutory law having ever explained whether the non-member violates Section 1 of the Sherman Act, in my opinion, liability should be refused on account of two reasons. First, non-members often have no knowledge that a standardized agreement is linked to a broader arbitration agreement which includes an expulsion clause. Second, these individuals and or undertakings do not have the competence to rescind an expulsion clause laid down in the bylaws and rules of a trade association.

The second scenario concerns non-members that are in no way connected to a trade association but, after becoming aware of a withdrawal of membership, discontinue trade with a targeted industry actor. By doing so, added reputational harm inflicted upon an expelled wrongdoer cannot be excluded. Whether or not a withdrawal decision is published or not is irrelevant. It is highly unlikely that the Commission will pursue non-members for placing additional reputational harm on ostracized members of a trade association. This is especially true because it is impossible to require non-members not to conduct business with a suspended or expelled member of a trade association. Any market participant has its reasons for selecting potential business partners. If a person's or a company's reputation is questionable, market participants cannot be forced to enter into a contract with a wrongdoer under the threat of antitrust illegality pursuant to Section 1 of the Sherman Act. Using competition law infringements proactively, as a "sword" would not only hamper the professional freedom of non-members, but it would also result in penalization beyond the aim of this provision.

2. Denial of membership for an expelled member on the basis of an additional entry requirement

In the event a member temporarily or indefinitely loses its membership status of one of the trade associations researched, on the ground that this status is crucial to operating on a relevant secondary commodities market, an expelled market participant has a compelling interest to become a member again. A limitation of regaining membership might seem to a certain extent justified, but once, in my opinion, an ostracized member again fulfils the entry requirement of the relevant trade association and after a certain period of time has elapsed, membership should be reinstated. To assess whether such a denial complies with Section 1 of the Sherman Act, the focus will be again on the three actors.

a. Access restrictions by a trade association

With regard to a refusal to regain membership of a trade association following a suspension or expulsion, discussing the anti-competitiveness of this refusal is not so straightforward. This is particularly true because only one out of the six trade associations researched makes restoration of membership subject to additional requirements besides the normal entry conditions, namely the lapse of a period of two years and acceptance by a Board of Directors of a reinstatement of membership.[504] This raises the ensuing question: In line with the observation that four out of six of the trade associations researched do not impose (similar) entry requirements, does this entail that discussing the anti-competitiveness of access restrictions pursuant to Section 1 of the Sherman Act is pointless? This question must be answered in the negative for three reasons. First, the trade associations researched are only a selection of many other institutions that punish disloyalty of members for not complying with arbitral awards by using nonlegal sanctions. It is very well possible that they also put access restrictions in place after withdrawing membership. Second, even though four out of the six trade associations researched do not impose written rules with regard to difficulties to regain membership after being ostracized, these institutions

504 Only the ICA imposes additional entry barriers for ostracized members to regain membership. The DDC, the FCC, the LME and FOSFA do not impose rules with regard to additional re-entry requirements for ostracized members.

can still refuse re-admission on the basis of non-written grounds.[505] Third, discussing the antitrust boundaries of access restrictions would provide guidance as completely as possible as to when and to what extent Section 1 of the Sherman Act is violated.

It follows from these reasons that considering the illegality of access restrictions pursuant to Section 1 of the Sherman Act is necessary. A good start relates to the Supreme Court's judgment in *NW Stationers v. Pac. Stationary & Printing Co.*, in which the Court ruled that trade associations "*must establish and enforce reasonable rules in order to function effectively*".[506] This requires that membership access requirements must be fair, non-discriminative and appropriate. Obviously, such a standard immediately raises the following question: Are the standard entry requirements and additional prerequisites for regaining membership after an expulsion demanded by the trade associations researched reasonable within the meaning of Section 1 of the Sherman Act?

When discussing the anti-competitiveness of the normal entry requirements for industry actors under Section 1 of the Sherman Act, the following table which does not go in-depth, but merely provides a short overview, is guiding.[507]

Standard entry requirements that all trade associations have in common	**Violation of Section 1 of the Sherman Act?**
1. Connection with the secondary commodities market which the trade association represents	No. Industry restrictions are legitimate under Section 1 of the Sherman according to the first Circuit Court's judgment in *Clamp-All Corp. v. Cast Iron Soil Pipe Institute.*[508]
2. An application for membership.	No. Without an application, obtaining membership is impossible.

505 Whether or not this occurs remains vague, since no information is available in the literature, etc.

506 NW Stationers v. Pac. Stationary & Printing Co., 472 U.S. 284, 297 (1985).

507 An in-depth analysis will be conducted with regard to the additional access barriers following a withdrawal of membership. This is because normal entry barriers apply not only to ostracized members, but to every new applicant. They are seemingly less discriminatory, even though they can still violate Section 1 of the Sherman Act.

508 Clamp-All Corp. v. Cast Iron Soil Pipe Institute, 851 F.2d 478, 490, 492 (11th Cir. 1988).

3. Entry fee	No. In *United States v. Realty Multi-List* Inc. the Fifth Circuit Court of Appeal ruled that an entry fee "*which bears no relation to cost factors [...] may not only create a significant barrier to new entry into the association, but may create "a strong inference that the amount has been set up as a barrier against" new applications*".[509] The entry fees required by the trade associations researched most likely satisfy this rule because the fee are needed to operate these institutions and are not unreasonably restrictive of competition.[510]
Standard entry requirements that not all trade associations have in common	**Violation of Section 1 of the Sherman Act?**
1. Support by at least two members of the relevant trade association	Maybe. This rule could prevent new market entrants from competing in the relevant commodities industry. This is because without access to one of the trade associations researched, it is not possible to be on equal footing with its members.[511]
2. Minimum duration of experience in the relevant commodities market	Maybe. This rule could prevent new market entrants from competing in the relevant commodities industry. This is because without access to one of the trade associations researched, it is not possible to be on equal footing with its members.[512]
3. Satisfy the Board of Directors and post a picture on the main trading wall for other members to comment on	Yes. This rule enables the Board of Directors to deny any potential candidate for membership for any reason. Because access to one of the trade associations researched is necessary to compete on a relevant commodities market, it raises high entry barriers for market participants.[513]

Several lessons can be drawn from this comparative analysis of the antitrust limits of the normal entry requirements for market participants to

509 United States v. Realty Multi-List Inc., 629 F.2d 1351 (5th Cir. 1980), para. 107. In this case an entry fee of $1000 infringed Section 1 of the Sherman Act.

510 Although this is true, the FTC and/or any US court can always reach a different conclusion.

511 A broader discussion to assess the illegality of such a rule pursuant to Section 1 of the Sherman Act is required. Yet, such research will not be carried out because it applies to all potential candidates for membership and not exclusively to (temporarily) expelled members that re-apply for membership.

512 Ibid. However, in Deesen v. Professional Golfers Assn of America, 358 F.2d 165 (9th Cir. 1966) the Ninth Circuit Court of Appeals argued that the requirement that a sufficient number of years of experience for members is justified. It is not inconceivable that this ruling can be applied to argue that a minimum duration of experience in a commodities market is an acceptable membership requirement.

513 The anti-competitiveness of this rule will be discussed in more depth with regard to the additional access barriers following a withdrawal of membership.

obtain membership of one of the trade associations researched. First, once an applicant for membership is refused by one of the trade associations researched on the basis of standard entry requirements that all of these trade associations have in common, it is unlikely that this institution violates Section 1 of the Sherman Act. A connection with a specific adjacent commodities market that a trade association represents, an application for membership and a reasonable membership fee are within the bounds of this provision. Second, once a trade association refuses access of an applicant to obtain membership on the basis of entry requirements that not all the trade associations researched have in common, with the exception of the requirement to satisfy a Board of Directors, since it violates Section 1 of the Sherman Act beyond a reasonable doubt, it is possible that this provision is also infringed. Not only because it raises high market barriers for market entrants, but it also weakens the ability of established undertakings and/or individuals to compete. Despite this observation, neither the FTC nor a US court has ever ruled on the illegality of such rules. Whether this entails that more restrictive rules for membership are permissible within the meaning of Section 1 of the Sherman Act must be rejected. Silence is not synonymous with permissibility.

With regard to additional requirements to regain membership after membership is withdrawn, a broader discussion is required. This is because restrictive membership policies have a clear risk of infringing Section 1 of the Sherman Act and must be necessary to the existence and the effective functioning of a trade association.[514] Whether indeed the lapse of a period of two years following a withdrawal of membership and the discretionary freedom by a Board of Directors of a relevant trade association to decline re-admission constitute prohibited entry requirements and impose market barriers for ostracized industry actors, the guidelines provided by the American Bar Association in its Antitrust and Association Handbook and the case law of US courts on the restraints on non-member access to association services play a central role. With regard to the Handbook, all membership requirements must be objective and have a legitimate function in the sense that they cannot be applied discriminatorily by a relevant trade association and serve competitive reasons for limiting access.[515] In addition, they must be consistently and objectively applied to

514 American Bar Association, "*Antitrust and Associations Handbook*", Chicago: American Bar Association 2009, p. 64.

515 Ibid., p. 68.

both membership applicants and current members.[516] To this extent, subjective judgments are only permissible if they are necessary, proportionate and can be applied in a nondiscriminatory manner.[517] If not, subjective judgments would raise red flags for the FTC and US courts.

It follows from these guidelines that additional requirements to regain membership after membership is withdrawn issued by a trade association are not compatible with Section 1 of the Sherman Act. This is particularly true because they only apply to targeted disloyal industry actors and not to all members. Such rules can be seen as discriminatory. Empowering the Board of Directors of a trade association to deny an ostracized member's request for membership is even more restrictive. Such broad competence enables this body to completely put a halt to restoration of membership. In my opinion, this can be seen as an arbitrary method. It is well possible that directors abuse their position and deny membership to market participants they dislike and accept re-admission when they favour an industry actor. This causes problems, as the risk of a complete denial of membership effectively drives such industry actor out the market. Without this status, it is significantly more difficult to send a signal of trustworthiness to other market participants and obtain access to the many services provided by a relevant trade association. Section 1 of the Sherman Act is undoubtedly infringed.

Restraints on access to market essential services for non-members is also a topic that has been extensively discussed by US courts. A good starting point is the Supreme Court's judgment in *United States v. Terminal Railroad Association*. In this judgment, the Court ruled that equal treatment to facilities is required.[518] According to the Supreme Court in *Associated Press v. United States,* this entails that when membership is necessary to compete, a trade association cannot block new applicants from obtaining this status and limit access to its facilities.[519] Such a policy by a trade association typically results in an infringement of Section 1 of the Sherman Act, which is subject to a rule-of- reason analysis.[520] However, one important requirement exists. Access to the benefits of membership of a trade association

516 Ibid.

517 Ibid., p. 69.

518 United States v. Terminal R.R. Ass'n, 224 U.S. 383 (1912).

519 Associated Press v. United States, 326 U.S. 1, 23 (1945).

520 NW Wholesale Stationers v. Pac. Stationery, 472 U.S. 284, 295-297 (1985). The rule of reason has become the primary mode to assess restrictions to obtain association membership.

must be considered essential[521] without the existence of other viable alternatives.[522]

When following these precedents derived from the case law of US courts, to the extent a trade association imposes additional entry barriers to acquire membership for (temporarily) excluded former members, such practice is contrary to Section 1 of the Sherman Act. Given that an ostracized industry actor no longer has access to the services of one of the trade associations researched following a temporary or unlimited revocation of membership, a denial of the request of an ostracized member to re-obtain membership by a relevant trade association on the basis of an additional access barrier must be seen as an unduly restrictive practice. By taking into account that US courts are reluctant to apply a *per se* violation for limitations on access to services, a rule-of-reason analysis can justify such stifling of competition. This is done in Part II, Chapter 6, E of this research.

b. Access restrictions by members of a trade association

Obviously, when a trade association refuses to re-admit an expelled member as a member of the association on the basis of access restrictions, it is, in practice, the members of that association that acting in concert refuse to deal with a competitor. This is because members belonging to a trade association have the ultimate authority to amend and delete membership requirements laid down in the bylaws and rules of that association. Hence, in my opinion, one can say that the members are responsible when this association refuses a reapplication for membership on the basis of such barriers. A denial of membership restricts access to competitively valuable association services and violates Section 1 of the Sherman Act. Whether indeed the FTC and/or the US courts pursue members is unlikely. To date, case law has focused on trade associations as the recipients of antitrust scrutiny

521 T. J. Waters and R. H. Morse, "*Antitrust & Trade Associations: How Trade Regulation Laws Apply to Trade and Professional Associations*", Chicago: American Bar Association 1996, p. 65; One example refers to the US District Court for the Western District of Pennsylvania judgment in United States v. Western Winter Sports Representatives Ass'n, Inc., 1962, Trade Cas. (CCH) 74,263 (W.D. Penn. 1973). In this case, a refusal of access to a trade association's trade show for non-members is not permissible when this restricts the right and ability to compete in the relevant market.

522 Thompson v. Metro. Multi-List, Inc. 934 F.2d 1566, 1582 (11th Cir. 1991).

rather than its members. Whether this prevents future antitrust scrutiny remains to be seen.

c. Access restrictions by non-members

Non-members have no competence to prevent a trade association from denying a reapplication for membership by an expelled member on the basis of entry restrictions. It is also unlikely that this group of actors places reputational harm on such an individual or undertaking. For these reasons, an absence of guidance by the FTC, legal doctrine and US courts, and the fact that non-members comprise a large group of industry actors that are often not even aware of any barriers to re-application for membership, they comply with Section 1 of the Sherman Act.

When a non-member conducts trade with a member of a trade association on the basis of this association's standardized agreement which is linked to a broader arbitration agreement in which additional re-entry requirements are laid down and an expelled member is barred from re-obtaining membership because of those grounds, both types of actors have a role in the execution of this barrier to membership. However, in an absence of statutory and case law, a violation of Section 1 of the Sherman Act cannot be attributed to such a non-member. This is because that non-member is often unaware that a standardized contract is linked to a broader arbitration agreement which empowers the relevant trade association to impose additional barriers to access.

III. Refusal to deal with an expelled member

An instruction of a trade association to its members to refuse to deal with an ostracized member can be used as an economic weapon to curtail the commercial activities of such an industry actor.[523] According to *Haddock*, this has serious competitive effect and involves a *per se* violation.[524] To what degree this is true for the complicity of the trade associations researched, their members and non-members is reviewed below.

523 C. F. Barber, "Refusals to Deal under the Federal Antitrust Laws", *University of Pennsylvania Law Review, Vol. 103, No. 7* 1955, p. 847.

524 G. B. Haddock, "The Right of Trade Associations to Deny Membership and to Expel Members", *Antitrust Bulletin 13 Antitrust Bull.* 1968, p. 555-556.

1. Refusal to deal with an expelled member by a trade association

Section 1 of the Sherman Act was designed to foster, protect and encourage competition.[525] Initiating a refusal to deal by instructing members of a trade association not to conduct business with an ostracized industry actor contravenes this objective. Not only because it can be seen as an illegal boycott against targeted individuals and/or undertakings, but also by virtue of its ability to seriously curb a former member's commercial standing. In early US case law, the Supreme Court ruled that an association's refusal to deal with non-members is sufficient to violate Section 1 of the Sherman Act. The first noteworthy example refers to the Supreme Court's judgment in *Montague & Co. v. Lowry*.[526] In this case an association of manufacturers and dealers in tiles instructed its members, under threat of being expelled from the trade association, not to buy materials from non-members.[527] This conduct has the aim of excluding such an industry actor from the relevant market[528] and is proscribed by Section 1 of the Sherman Act.[529] In subsequent cases, the Supreme Court followed its stance on refusals to deal with non-members. In *Fashion Originators' Guild of America, Inc. v. FTC*, it ruled that a boycott program that forced member textile manufacturers to not sell goods to dress manufactures which sold pirated goods to stores and coerced member garment manufacturers not to sell to stores which sold pirated garments infringed Section 1 of the Sherman Act.[530] In *Associated Press v. United States*, the Supreme Court argued that a trade association's bylaw was contrary to Section 1 of the Sherman Act, because it prohibited members from supplying spontaneous news to non-members.[531]

Although the Supreme Court in these cases failed to clarify whether a *per se*, or a rule-of-reason standard was more appropriate and despite the

525 A. S. Zito Jr., "Refusals to Deal: The Sherman Antitrust Act and the Right to Customer Selection", *The John Marshall Law Review, Vol. 14, Is. 2* 1981, p. 357.

526 Montague & Co. v. Lowry, 193 U.S. 38 (1904).

527 Montague & Co. v. Lowry, 193 U.S. 38, 44 (1904).

528 J. W. Meisel, ""Now" or Never: Is There Antitrust Liability for Noncommercial Boycotts?", *Columbia Law Review, Vol. 80, No. 6* 1980, p. 1317.

529 Another case which affirmed the anti-competitiveness of a refusal to deal with non-members concerns the Supreme Court's judgment in United States v. United States v. Colgate & Co., 250 U.S. 300 (1919). However, this case concerns a vertical refusal to deal which is different than that of the trade associations researched.

530 Fashion Originators' Guild of America v. FTC, 312 U.S. 457, 465 (1941).

531 Associated Press v. United States, 326 U.S. 1, 2 (1945).

Supreme Court in *NW Stationers v. Pac. Stationary & Printing Co.* stating that "*there is more confusion about the scope and operation of the per se rule against group boycotts than in reference to any other aspect of the per se doctrine*,"[532] it is not inconceivable that the FTC and/or US courts favour the more rigid *per se* violation. Mainly two arguments rationalize the applicability of this test: first, a refusal to deal places additional reputational harm on ostracized industry actors and can completely remove them from the market. Second, a refusal to deal does not have a pro-competitive justification, but has nothing but anti-competitive aspects.[533] This is because in the event non-compliance with an arbitral award is punished by withdrawal of membership, an auxiliary attached instruction to members to refuse to deal with an ostracized industry actor results in overdeterrence.

Admitting that it is very well possible that a *per se* violation could be favoured in a potential antitrust case under Section 1 of the Sherman Act, an alternative view that supports a rule-of-reason analysis is also comprehensible. A rebuttal can find support in the structure of a trade association as a joint venture and the existence of procompetitive benefits that could outweigh anticompetitive harm. As a result, the necessity and proportionality of a refusal to deal is better considered in a separate rule-of-reason analysis.

In sum, there are two diverging possibilities to determine how the role of a trade association in instructing its members not to do business with an ostracized industry actor should be perceived. In my opinion, neither possibility is sufficiently convincing and arguments can be made for each. Whether a *per se* standard or a rule-of-reason standard is to be chosen will largely depend on the FTC and/or US courts. Notwithstanding this absence of clarity, Part II, Chapter 6, E considers the anticompetitive effects of a refusal to deal against its procompetitive benefits to operate an effective PLS in a rule-of-reason analysis.

---

532 NW Stationers v. Pac. Stationary & Printing Co., 472 U.S. 284, 294 (1985); See also CHA-Car, Inc. v. Calder Race Source, Inc., 752 F.2D 609, 613 (11th Cir. 1985). Therein, the 11th Circuit Court of Appeals ruled that even though a *per se* standard for a concerted refusal to deal is customary, case law in this area is unsettled and a confusing array of qualifications and exceptions continues to develop; The United States District Court for the Eastern District of New York and the Second Circuit Court of Appeals have confirmed such a source of confusion in Bennett v. Cardinal Health Marmac Distribs., 2003-2 Trade Cas. (CCH) 74, 137 (E.D.N.Y. 2003) and Bogan v. Hodgkins, 166 F.3D 509, 515 (2d Cir. 1999).

533 https://thebusinessprofessor.com/knowledge-base/the-sherman-act-antitrust-law/.

2. Execution of the refusal to deal with an expelled member by members of a trade association

If a trade association instructs its members to no longer do business with an expelled member under the threat of being punished, these members would most likely consent by acquiescence or by agreement to this type of nonlegal sanction. This is not only understandable from a commercial motive, as not abiding by an association's instruction to forfeit trade with an ostracized market participant can make such a member subject to nonlegal sanctions that lead to commercial reprisals and reputational harm, but is also evident from the coercive nature of the obligation, since members will in all likelihood abide by the rules of the relevant trade association when put under pressure. In spite of the fact that these arguments will most likely be used by some members to escape from a finding of illegality pursuant to Section 1 of the Sherman Act if the FTC decides to pursue these industry actors, it is unlikely that these arguments would hold any merit. Members have the competence to adapt or delete a clause in the bylaws and rules of a relevant trade association which empowers this association to prohibit its members from continuing to trade with an ostracized industry actor. Hence, in my opinion, they are engaged in an illegal group boycott under Section 1 of the Sherman Act.

Albeit not relating to the same circumstances compared with a refusal to deal initiated by one of the trade associations researched after a (temporary) termination of membership, the Supreme Court holds that it is not only a trade association that can infringe the first provision of the Sherman Act, but also its members. In *Eastern States Retail Lumber Dealers' Association v. United States*, the Court ruled that because a group of retailers that were united in a trade association agreed not to purchase lumber from a non-member supplier, they participated in an illegal boycott on the ground that their concerted refusal to deal excluded competing wholesalers from the retail market.[534] Hence, the Court held that this agreement was a *per se* violation.[535] While this case provides the best analogy to understand the extent members of a trade association can be subject to illegality under Section 1 of the Sherman Act for their concerted behavior in discontinuing trade with a non-member of a trade association following a with-

534 Eastern States Retail Lumber Dealers' Ass'n. v. United States, 234 U.S. 600, 601, 614 (1914).

535 K. L. Hall, "*Oxford Companion to the Supreme Court of the United States, Second Edition*", Oxford: Oxford University Press 2005, p. 145.

drawal of membership, albeit more tenuous, two other judgments are worth mentioning. The first concerns the Supreme Court's judgment in *Radiant Burners, Inc. v. Peoples Gas Light & Coke Co.*[536] In its judgment, the Court reviewed the illegality of a trade association which ensures the safe use of natural gas and its members comprising gas utilities companies, manufacturers and gas pipeline companies under Section 1 of the Sherman Act.[537] The Court argued that arbitrarily denying a seal of approval by both actors which targeted a non-member classified as an unlawful concerted refusal to deal which is treated as a *per se* violation.[538] The second case pertains to the Supreme Court's judgment in *Klor's, Inc. v. Broadway-Hale Stores, Inc.*, in which a retailer of appliances disliked the price-cutting techniques of a competing retailer and demanded manufacturers supplying to both parties to stop selling to this undertaking, unless at excessively high prices.[539] The Court concluded that the retailer as well as the manufacturers were involved in a concerted refusal to deal resulting in a *per se* violation under Section 1 of the Sherman Act.[540]

Whereas all three cases date back from a time in which the executors of a refusal to deal initiated by another company or trade association were held accountable under the rigid *per se* doctrine and the second and third cases are not very comparable,[541] it is not sure whether the FTC and/or US courts would use this standard or allow a more lenient rule of reason when dealing with a potential case in which the members of one of the trade associations researched participate in a concerted refusal to deal with an ostracized industry actor. Regardless of both possibilities, Part II, Chapter 6, E will determine the complicity of the members of a trade association in a rule-of-reason analysis.

536 Radiant Burners, Inc. v. Peoples Gas Co., 364 U.S. 656 (1961).

537 Ibid.

538 Radiant Burners, Inc. v. Peoples Gas Co., 364 U.S. 656, 659 (1961).

539 Klor's, Inc. v. Broadway-Hale Stores, Inc., 359 U.S. 207 (1959).

540 Klor's, Inc. v. Broadway-Hale Stores, Inc., 359 U.S. 207, 212-213 (1959).

541 In Radiant Burners, Inc. v. Peoples Gas Light & Coke Co the relevant trade association did not instruct its members to put a halt to all contact with a non-member. In addition, in Klor's, Inc. v. Broadway-Hale Stores, Inc. there was no trade association involved, but the case concerned a retailer that instructed manufacturers to stop selling to its competitor.

3. Execution of the refusal to deal with an expelled member by non-members

In the event a trade association obligates its members to refuse to conduct business with an ostracized former member, non-members cannot be held accountable for a violation of Section 1 of the Sherman Act. The reasons are three-fold: first, non-members do not have the competence to change the bylaws and rules of a trade association in which the possibility to extralegally punish a recalcitrant member by refusing to deal is incorporated. Second, the group of non-members is undefined, so it is not possible to hold all of these industry actors accountable. Third, most non-members will most likely never hear about a trade association imposing a refusal to deal on its members, because none of the trade associations researched has published this decision. As a result, additional reputational harm inflicted on a targeted market participant due to a refusal to deal by non-members is debatable.

Also, when a non-member has entered into a standardized agreement with a member of a trade association which is linked to a broader arbitration agreement in which a refusal to deal with an expelled member is laid down and that association imposes this extrajudicial measure on an expelled member, that non-member does not violate Section 1 of the Sherman Act. Even though there is no statutory and/or case law on this issue, two reasons justify the role of non-members in the execution of a refusal to deal with an ostracized member. First, non-members are often unaware that a standardized contract is linked to a broader arbitration agreement which includes a clause on blacklisting. Second, these non-members cannot annul such a clause in the bylaws and rules of the relevant trade association.

IV. Entering the premises of a recalcitrant industry actor without a warrant

When a defaulter does not pay the monetary fee ordered in an arbitral award, one of the trade associations researched enables its officials to conduct a full-fledged research by entering the premises belonging to the defaulter. Obviously, as was discussed before,[542] barging into the premises of

542 See Part I, Chapter 2, II, 1.

the defaulter without being invited can result in a non-neglectable breach of privacy and – arguably – reputational harm.

Although invasion of privacy is not covered by Section 1 of the Sherman Act, any horizontal agreement that can negatively impact the competitiveness of a market participant could fall within the ambit of this provision. Whether indeed entering the premises of a defaulter at the instruction of a trade association is in restraint of trade and, hence, violates this provision is unlikely. Despite much depending on the willingness of the FTC to consider the anti-competitiveness of such conduct under Section 1 of the Sherman Act, in my opinion, three reasons contradict a finding of illegality. First, neither the FTC nor any US court has considered the unlawfulness of an extensive right to enter premises under this provision. Second, not Section 1 of the Sherman Act, but criminal law is the more appropriate legal statute to challenge an uninvited entry of premises. Third, it is almost impossible to determine the degree of reputational harm inflicted upon a targeted industry actor. This is particularly true since no decision of any investigation will be published. A restraint of trade is doubtful. Consequently, a thorough analysis pertaining to the role that a trade association, its members and non-members play in invasive investigations in market participants' properties is unnecessary.

V. Limiting adequate access to public courts prior to arbitral proceedings and after an award

As was described in Part I, Chapter 3, F, II, there is a risk that US-based trade associations representing market participants in specific commodities markets do not comply with Article 75 of the CPLR and the FAA. This is because the bylaws of the association researched, the DDC, allow industry actors less redress to a public court than both laws. This raises the following question: Does this mean that a trade association as well as its members that draft these rules can be held liable for a violation of Section 1 of the Sherman Act for limiting the possibilities of a judicial review at a public court? In the absence of any FTC decision or case law stemming from US courts, this is difficult to answer. In my opinion, a parallel can be drawn between insufficient possibilities of redress to judicial review in the bylaws of a trade association and the Supreme Court's judgment in *NW Wholesale Stationers v. Pac. Stationery* in which a trade association, its members and non-members did not provide procedural safeguards following a withdrawal of membership. As the latter situation did not violate Section 1 of the Sherman Act, it is far-fetched to assume that inadequate access to public courts would violate this provision. A violation of the CPLR and the FAA is more appropriate.[543]

Be that as it may, when a trade association extrajudicially punishes a member for seeking legal redress at a public court on the ground that there is, for example, insufficient referral to a broader arbitration agreement, a different conclusion could be drawn. Then, depending on the nonlegal sanction chosen, Section 1 of the Sherman Act could be violated by the responsible trade association and its members.

E. A rule-of-reason analysis under Section 1 of the Sherman Act

Since the Supreme Court's judgment in *Standard Oil Co. of New Jersey* v. *United States* and *United States. v. American Tabaco Co.*, defendants of antitrust scrutiny under Section 1 of the Sherman Act can, as an exception to this indiscriminatory prohibition, raise a rule of reason defence focusing on the effect and conduct of the measure.[544] This entails two elements: first, a rule of reason justification is not a separate defence that may be produced after a finding of illegality under Section 1 of the Sherman Act.[545] In fact, it is something that is considered at the stage of illegality on the basis of all the arguments provided by defendants from the outset.[546] Second, once a finding of a *per se* violation is not applicable, not only will the

543 In Mitsubishi Motors Corp. v. Soler Chrysler-Plymouth, Inc., 473 U.S. 614 (1985) the Supreme Court ruled that once a party decides to arbitrate a statutory claim (*e.g.* antitrust issue) an arbitration agreement should be generously construed and must offer this individual or undertaking access to all substantive rights afforded by statute. In my opinion, this ruling must be interpreted to signify that the bylaws of a trade association should also afford all legal methods to obtain judicial redress in a public court. Limiting access to public courts in the bylaws of a trade association contradicts the CPLR and the FAA.

544 Standard Oil Co. of New Jersey v. United States, 221 U.S. 1 (1911); United States v. American Tobacco Company, 221 U.S. 106 (1911).

545 This defence is not similar to EU Competition Law, namely Article 101 (3) TFEU, which can be commenced at the request of a defendant after a finding of anti-competitiveness pursuant to Article 101 (1) TFEU.

546 K. Rißmann, "*Die kartellrechtliche Beurteilung der Markenabgrenzung*", Munich: Herbert Utz Verlag 2008, p. 108. This limits the broad scope of application of Section 1 of the Sherman Act at the stage of illegality.

harmfulness of a specific conduct be considered, but also its beneficial effects or procompetitive justification grounds.[547]

Whether indeed the trade associations researched and their members can justify their complicity in ousting an industry actor from the market by dint of blacklists, withdrawals of membership, refusals to allow expelled member to reobtain membership on the basis of an additional entry condition and refusals to deal is a matter of interpretation. Even though there is general consensus about the two-stage structure of a rule-of-reason defence,[548] what constitutes a valid justification is unclear and surprisingly underexplored.[549]

I. First step of the rule-of-reason defence: The existence of visibly plausible procompetitive benefits

The first step of a procompetitive justification concerns the determination of US courts to consider whether the rule-of-reason standard or the more severe conclusive presumption of net anticompetitive effects is applicable (*i.e. per se* illegality standard).[550] Drawing the boundary between both doctrines is not easy. Yet, the Supreme Court's judgment in *Broadcast Music, Inc. v. CBS, Inc.*, provides much needed clarity.[551] When a restraint of trade probably has on its face procompetitive attributes even if a conclusive rule-of-reason analysis is not appropriate, then a *per se* illegality is more fitting.[552]

As discussed in Part II, Chapter 6, D, I, II and III, the anticompetitive harm inflicted upon disloyal members that did not comply with arbitral awards by the use of blacklists, withdrawals of membership, refusals to deal with expelled members on the basis of an additional entry condition

547 R. H. Allensworth, "The Commensurability Myth in Antitrust", *Vanderbilt Law Review, Vol. 69, No. 1* 2016, p. 5 (citation 7).

548 An exception to this clarity refers to the observation of the Supreme Court's judgment in California Dental Ass'n v. Federal Trade Commission, 526 U.S. 756, 780 (1999). In its judgment, the Court explains that the quality of proof required depends on the circumstances.

549 J. M. Newman, "Procompetitive Justifications in Antitrust Law", *Social Science Research Network* 2017, p. 7.

550 California Dental Ass'n v. Federal Trade Commission, 526 U.S. 756, 763 (1999).

551 Broadcast Music, Inc. v. CBS, Inc., 441 U.S. 1 (1979).

552 See also R. A. Givens, "*Antitrust: An Economic Approach*", New York: Law Journal Press 2005, p. 4-48.28.

and refusals to deal initiated by the trade associations researched and executed by their members should be weighed against the procompetitive benefits of specialized commercial arbitration. This is because in the absence of these nonlegal sanctions,[553] specialized commercial arbitration would prove ineffective which could jeopardize the complete operability of PLSs.

II. Second step of the rule-of-reason defence: Illustration that the visibly plausible efficiency or benefit cannot exist without the anticompetitive risk

After the establishment that blacklisting, withdrawing membership, refusing to deal with an expelled member on the basis of an additional entry condition and refusing to deal with an ostracized member have visible plausible effects, the likelihood and magnitude of recognizable efficiencies must be considered against the overall effect on competition in the relevant market.[554] Furthermore, it must be established whether these efficiencies are sufficient to offset the market foreclosure of targeted industry actors.

Before we can go into this analysis, it must be established in more depth what the specific efficiencies which are being realized by dint of nonlegal sanctions in specialized commercial arbitration are. While this might appear difficult to ascertain, reference should be made to the rationale of present-day PLSs as were described in Part I, Chapter 1, C of this research. Following this discussion, it was explained that a present-day PLS can emerge when such private initiative increases contractual security and significantly lowers distribution and transaction costs when compared to State-enforced contract law. In more detail, with regard to commodities industries in which industry actors have formed trade associations, these arguments play a pivotal role. By establishing a system of specialized commercial arbitration to resolve conflicts between the members of a relevant trade association, relying on out of court settlements for these industry actors has proven to be a more efficient alternative to cumbersome, time-in-

553 It is not sure whether refusals to deal are necessarily beneficial or merely inflict unnecessary additional harm on a targeted industry actor. For the sake of argument, this conduct will be considered against the rule-of-reason yardstick.

554 K. Mathis, "*Law and Economics in Europe: Foundations and Applications*", Dordrecht: Springer 2014, p. 374.

tensive and costly judicial redress in court. Given that blacklisting, withdrawing membership, refusing to deal with an expelled member on the basis of an additional entry condition and refusing to deal with an ostracized member are the only means to ensure the success of this system, these nonlegal sanctions also have a pivotal role in ensuring the same efficiencies a PLS tends to create.

Despite these obvious benefits, it requires a study of US case law to determine whether the four types of nonlegal sanctions (i) qualify as permissible pro-competitive grounds for a rule-of-reason analysis pursuant to Section 1 of the Sherman Act; and (ii) whether they can justify the harmful and anticompetitive effect placed on targeted members.[555]

1. Efficiency defence: Consumer or total welfare justification

To determine whether increased transactional security and lowered distribution and transaction costs are justified as procompetitive benefits under Section 1 of the Sherman Act, it is necessary to understand the objective that antitrust laws should promote. Perhaps the best definition of the early objective was laid down in a Report of the Attorney General's National Committee to Study the Antitrust Laws.[556] In this Report, it was explained that antitrust law should promote competition in open markets and must

---

555 The Court's ultimate goal is to balance the procompetitive and anticompetitive effects of potential unlawful conduct. See Craftsmen Limousine v. Ford Motor Co., 491 F.3d 380, 389 (8th Cir. 2007); Stop & Shop Supermarket Co. v. Blue Cross & Blue Shield of R.I., 373 F.3d 57, 61 (1st Cir. 2004); Fraser v. Major League Soccer, 284 F.3d 47, 59 (1st Cir. 2002); The competitive conditions in the market before and after the restraint must be compared with the restraint's history, nature, purpose, economic impact as well as the availability of a less restrictive alternative. See N. A. Armstrong, Jr., J. D. Carroll, and C. C. Yook, "Sherman Act Section 1 Fundamentals", *LexisNexis* 2019, p. 3; It is sufficient to establish that a specific conduct's procompetitive benefits outweigh its anticompetitive harm. See American Bar Association, "*Antitrust Health Care Handbook, Fourth Edition*", Chicago: American Bar Association 2010, p. 50-51. It is sufficient to establish that a specific conduct's procompetitive benefits outweigh its anticompetitive harm.

556 Attorney General's National Committee to Study the Antitrust Laws, "Report of the Attorney General's National Committee to Study the Antitrust Laws", *Attorney General's National Committee to Study the Antitrust Laws* 1955; This is a 400-page document that describes almost all facets of antitrust doctrine and enforcement. For more information, see T. E. Kauper, "The Report of the Attorney

be seen as a policy "*against undue limitations on competitive conditions*".[557] Although this objective was seen as uncontroversial by a variety of authors, including, *inter alia*, *Hofstadter*[558], *Kahn*[559]*and Kaysen* and *Turner*[560], in 1979 this changed when the Supreme Court in *Reiter v. Sonotone Corp.* accepted the consumer welfare standard.[561] In this case the US acting as amici curiae supported the petitioners and took the position that the "*primary purpose of the Sherman Act was consumer protection*".[562]

Nowadays, according to *Blair & Sokol*, the main goal of the Sherman Act is to protect not only consumer welfare but also total welfare.[563] Strikingly, no goal is necessarily dominant over the other, especially since there is a lot of confusion about what the appropriate objective of the Sherman Act is and what should serve as the yardstick for a rule-of-reason defence.[564] Throughout its case law, the Supreme Court does not provide any clarity and seems to apply either justification ground arbitrarily.[565] Fortunately, with regard to the nonlegal sanctions initiated by the trade associations researched and executed by their members, choosing between both grounds is redundant. Extrajudicial enforcement benefits both consumer welfare,

---

General's National Committee to Study the Antitrust Laws: A Retrospective", *Michigan Law Review*
Vol. 100, No. 7 2002, p. 1867.

557 Attorney General's National Committee to Study the Antitrust Laws, "Report of the Attorney General's National Committee to Study the Antitrust Laws", *Attorney General's National Committee to Study the Antitrust Laws* 1955, p. 1, 3.

558 R. Hofstadter, "*The Paranoid Style in American Politics and Other Essays*", Cambridge: Harvard University Press 1965. Hofstadter was a supporter of the enactment of the Sherman Act.

559 A. E. Kahn, "Market Power and Economic Growth: Guides to Public Policy", *Antitrust Bulletin, Vol. 8* 1963.

560 C. Kaysen and D. F. Turner, "*Antitrust Policy: An Economic and Legal Analysis*", Cambridge: Harvard University Press 1959.

561 Reiter v. Sonotone Corp., 442 U.S. 330 (1979).

562 Brief for the United States As Amici Curiae Supporting Petitioners, Reiter, 442 U.S. 330 (1979) (No. 78-690), 1979 WL 213494, para. 12.

563 R. D. Blair, D. D. Sokol, "The Rule of Reason and the Goals of Antitrust: An Economic Approach", *UF Law Scholarship Repository* 2012, p. 476.

564 Ibid; See, for example, R. H. Bork, "Legislative Intent and the Policy of the Sherman Act", *The Journal of Law and Economics, Vol. 9* 1966. Blair and Sokol argue that Judge Bork confusingly considers total welfare as synonymous with consumer welfare in many of his judgments; An example is the Supreme Court's decision in Leegin Creative Leather Prods., Inc. v. PSKS, Inc., 551 U.S. 877 (2007).

565 R. D. Blair and D. D. Sokol, "The Rule of Reason and the Goals of Antitrust: An Economic Approach", *UF Law Scholarship Repository* 2012, p. 480.

which entails the equivalent to consumer surplus and total welfare, which implies the equivalent to consumer plus producer surplus and economic efficiency.[566] This is particularly true because a system of specialized commercial arbitration in which arbitral awards are guaranteed under the threat of nonlegal sanctions significantly reduces transaction costs for the members of the trade associations researched when compared to its public court system alternative. It is clear that this benefits the economic position of these individuals and/or undertakings. In addition, it lowers the costs of end-users of commodities products. Subsequently, nonlegal sanctions positively impact the two most important goals of the Sherman Act, namely consumer welfare and total welfare. Given the willingness of US courts to consider these objectives in a rule-of-reason analysis under Section 1 of the Sherman Act, a defence should spotlight both antitrust aims.

2. Total welfare and consumer welfare vs. collective boycotts of targeted industry actors

It is true that specialized commercial arbitration provided by the trade associations researched enhances total welfare and consumer welfare. But does this mean that increased efficiency justifies the collective boycotting of industry actors that do not comply with arbitral awards? This question will be answered by focusing on each of the four relevant types of extrajudicial enforcement. In this framework, the role of the trade associations researched and their members will be discussed together.

a. Blacklisting

The main aim of blacklisting is to hamper the reputation of a wrongdoer and thwarts its business opportunities in the relevant commodities market. Whereas the extent of the gravity of this anticompetitive act depends on whether a blacklist is available only to its members or to any third party as well, one thing is sure: having a bad standing can give rise to a serious foreclosure effect for a blacklisted member of one of the trade associations researched on the relevant second-tier commodities market. This raises the following question: Is the practice of blacklisting reasonably necessary to

566 K. Heyer, "Consumer Welfare and the Legacy of Robert Bork", *The University of Chicago Press* 2014, p. 20.

achieve an increase in total welfare and consumer welfare that outweigh the anticompetitive effects?[567]

In my opinion, present-day PLSs exist because State-enforced law has failed to provide an efficient solution for industry actors active in specific commodities markets. In these markets, market participants have organized themselves in trade associations which represent their interests. Specialized commercial arbitration in the event of a conflict between members has proven to be crucial to obtaining a fast, cost-friendly and anonymous decision. For this system to be effective, on the ground that enforcement of awards would often require a lengthy and insecure procedure involving at least the court of enforcement and the court of recognition under the framework of the New York Convention, and since parties are often globally dispersed, the threat of being blacklisted would appear reasonably necessary to realize the procompetitive benefits. Less severe alternatives such as a hefty fine or a reprimand are ineffective.[568] It is only when an industry actor's reputation is at peril, is payment of arbitral awards feasible.

Unfortunately, case law of US courts does not help in determining how a rule-of-reason analysis under Section 1 of the Sherman Act should be conducted with regard to the practice of blacklisting. The reasons are twofold: first, decisions that focused on an illegal exchange of information, such as the Supreme Court's judgments in *Eastern States Retail Lumber Dealers' Ass'n v. United States* and *Fashion Originators Guild of America (FOGA)* with regard to trade associations and in *Eastern States Retail Lumber Dealers' Ass'n v. United States* where the members of a trade association originate from a time before the introduction of a rule-of-reason standard. Second, case law to determine the illegality of an information exchange/ blacklisting after the introduction of such a defence is non-existent.

As a result of this lack of clarity owing to an absence of case law, it is difficult to forecast whether the FTC and US courts would be willing to accept a rule-of-reason defence pertaining to the blacklisting of disloyal

567 N. Shemtov, "*Beyond the Code: Protection of Non-Textual Features of Software*", Oxford: Oxford University Press 2017, p. 65.

568 There is clear risk that a hefty fine or a reprimand do not trigger a recalcitrant losing party in arbitral proceedings to pay an award. If confronted with an additional monetary sum following non-payment of an arbitral award, such an industry actor will most likely not be swayed to pay the penalty. Punishing bad behaviour with a reprimand would be equally ineffective. Such a sanction is not severe enough to ensure that a system of specialized commercial arbitration functions.

members of a trade association. The following table states the main arguments for and against its permissibility that both institutions should balance.

Arguments that justify a legality of blacklisting pursuant to Section 1 of the Sherman Act	Arguments against a legality of blacklisting pursuant to Section 1 of the Sherman Act
1. Blacklisting is the least severe effective measure to guarantee that a system of conflict resolution through specialized commercial arbitration can operate.	1. Blacklisting can result in market foreclosure for a targeted member of a trade association.
2. Blacklisting is necessary to maintain a system of specialized commercial arbitration that benefits total welfare and consumer welfare.	2. Non-payment of an award should not result in market foreclosure. It is disproportionate to the principles of proportionality and subsidiarity. Blacklisting is a too severe sanction.
3. In most markets, being blacklisted does not have social ramifications. Members of a trade association are often globally dispersed and alien to one another.	3. In some markets, being blacklisted can also have social ramifications. It can disrupt interpersonal relationships within close-knit groups.
4. When a wrongdoer's (company) name is published in a blacklist which is only accessible for members of the relevant trade association, market foreclosure is limited.	4. When a wrongdoer's (company) name is published in a publicly accessible list, the likelihood of market foreclosure increases.
5. Many industry actors that are placed on a blacklist are already bankrupt and are often non-members. It is unlikely that additional reputational harm will be inflicted upon them.[569] The foreclosure effect should be mitigated.	5. Even though many industry actors that are blacklisted are bankrupt and/or classify as non-members, the foreclosure effect of this type of extrajudicial enforcement on liquid members is still severe.

On the basis of this table one can draw the conclusion that for every argument in support of permissibility under Section 1 of the Sherman Act there is also a counter-argument. Yet, blacklisting is the least severe measure to operate specialized commercial arbitration that fosters total welfare and consumer welfare due to efficiency gains. Even though blacklisted market participants bear reputational harm and can be ousted from the relevant commodities market, this type of extrajudicial enforcement is reasonably necessary to achieve the two most prominent goals of the Sherman Act. Inclusion on a blacklist is to be reasonably expected following non-payment of an arbitral award, and disloyal industry actors still have the possibility to ask a public court to strike down this measure. However, a

569 See, for example, ICA List of Unfulfilled Awards: Part 1 (https://www.ica-ltd.org/safe-trading/loua-part-one/). When delving into the liquidity status of market participants included in this list, many are bankrupt.

trade association and its members can still be held accountable for a violation of Section 1 of the Sherman Act when the dissemination of the name of a wrongdoer is not structured in the least restrictive manner. In particular, five requirements must be complied with to meet this provision. First, blacklists should not be made publicly available, but accessible for members only. Second, it would be better to allow a third party to collect, handle and disseminate the names of a wrongdoer in a blacklist, instead of a trade association which is often biased. Third, the dissemination of the names of disloyal industry actors in a blacklist should only occur after clear deadlines have lapsed and a final warning. Fourth, when the effect of blacklisting also targets an industry actor's social standing, more reluctance should be shown. Fifth, every blacklisted member should be given the opportunity to ask for an internal appeal to object to such a decision. Currently, as it stands, the trade associations researched and their members can be held accountable for a violation of Section 1 of the Sherman Act. This is because the practice of blacklisting is not structured in the least restrictive form. If both groups of actors were to introduce these changes, total welfare and consumer welfare benefits would outweigh the boycotting of wrongdoers vis-à-vis the dissemination of the names of wrongdoers in blacklists. Subsequently, Section 1 of the Sherman Act would not be violated.

b. Membership rules and barriers for market access

It does not require much emphasis to determine that a withdrawal of membership has more far-reaching consequences for a targeted member belonging to a relevant trade association. Without access to the facilities of one of the trade associations researched, not only will crucial services such as specialized commercial arbitration, networking events and the possibility to contract under standardized contracts be unavailable, it is not uncommon that a disloyal industry actor's reputation deteriorates beyond repair. An expulsion, be it temporary or indefinite, signals untrustworthiness and an unwillingness to fulfill obligations. Consequently, a disloyal market participant's market presence, financial strength and profitability, and track record of compliance with financial and legal obligations are at jeopardy.[570] This seriously affects the financial liquidity of targeted industry ac-

570 B. Bossone, "The Role of Trust in Financial Sector Development", *Policy Research Working Paper 2200* 1999, p. 18. Although factors that affect the reputa-

tors and may in some cases even result in bankruptcy. The imposition of additional entry requirements following a withdrawal of membership compared to the those imposed on normal membership applicants exacerbate the exclusionary effects

Regardless of the total welfare and consumer welfare benefits of having a system of specialized commercial arbitration for the members of the trade associations researched in place, similar to the practice of blacklisting it is essential to answer the following question: Is a withdrawal of membership and difficulties to regain membership following such an imposition reasonably necessary to achieve an increase in total welfare and consumer welfare that outweigh the anticompetitive effects? Answering this question should focus on both stages: the actual suspension and termination of membership and the denial of membership of an expelled member on the basis of an additional entry barrier. This question is answered in the following two Paragraphs.

i. Withdrawal of membership

As the Supreme Court affirmed in *NW Wholesale Stationers v. Pac. Stationery*, a withdrawal of membership is permissible when it is considered a reasonable rule that makes a particular market more competitive and is efficiency-enhancing without having predominant exclusionary effects. The Court went on to argue that when an association has market power and access to its services can be perceived as an essential facility, it would be difficult to conclude that a trade association can impose a withdrawal of membership.

Applying this logic to suspension and termination of membership initiated by the trade associations researched is not straightforward. It necessitates that the services provided by these associations classify as essential facilities and that the associations have market power. Before discussing whether ostracized market participants lose access to an essential facility, it must first be discussed if the essential facility doctrine can be applied within the scope of Section 1 of the Sherman Act, or if Section 2 of the Sherman Act is more appropriate. Without conducting an in-depth examina-

---

tion capital were discussed with regard to financial intermediaries, these variables are useful to determine the extent of reputational harm following a withdrawal of membership from one of the trade associations researched.

tion, *Enaux* explains this doctrine can be applied under both provisions,[571] but that that it may only be applied to the first provision when a monopolistic alliance of competition jointly controls an essential facility and prevents competition.[572]

The co-action between the trade associations researched – acting as joint ventures – and their members fall under this rule. This is because the members have a direct influence on the policy of each relevant trade association and jointly control the services provided by the associations. But does this mean that the services are essential? The Court of Appeals of the District of Columbia Circuit in *Hecht v. Pro-Football, Inc.* answered this question by providing the following definition: "*To be "essential" a facility need not be indispensable; it is sufficient if duplication of the facility would be economically infeasible and if denial of its use inflicts a severe handicap on potential market entrants.*"[573] When applying this definition to the situation of punishing recalcitrant members of the trade associations researched that did not adhere to an arbitral award, access to the services provided by these associations is equivalent to an essential facility. The reasons are two-fold: first, there are no feasible alternatives when access to one of these associations is suspended or terminated.[574] Second, denial of services would place wrongdoers at an enormous competitive handicap.

Regardless of the anticompetitive effects that a denial of the services of one of the relevant trade associations researched produces, in my opinion, a withdrawal of membership in some cases can be viewed as a feasible method to punish disobedient industry actors that are insufficiently deterred after the dissemination of that actor's name in a blacklist. For some industry actors that were already close to a bankruptcy, reputational harm is not always important. This is because once a member has sufficient

---

571 American Bar Association, "*Model Jury Instructions in Civil Antitrust Cases*", Chicago: American Bar Association 2005, p. C-35.

572 C. Enaux, "*Effiziente Marktregulierung in der Telekommunikation: Möglichkeiten und Grenzen der Ruckführung sektorspezifischer Sonderregulierung in das allgemeine Wettbewerbsrecht*", Münster: Lit Verlag 2004, p. 148.

573 Hecht v. Pro-Football, Inc., 570 F.2d 982, 992 (D.C. Cir. 1977). For a more in-depth discussion pertaining to the essential facility doctrine, Part 2, Chapter 7 of this research discusses this doctrine with regard to Section 2 of the Sherman Act. This is because Section 2 of the Sherman Act is the more appropriate legal basis to apply this concept; A specific case in which the essential facility doctrine was discussed under Section 1 of the Sherman Act refers to the judgment of the District Court of Minnesota in United States v. Otter Tail Power Co., 331 F. Supp. 54, 61 (D. Minn. 1971). In appeal, this approach was not mentioned.

574 For this reason some may even argue that access to the facilities is indispensable.

monetary funds, this individual or company can request to be taken off the list by paying the arbitral award and any related penalties. In addition, such an unreliable and disloyal industry actor continues to have access to all the services provided by the trade association. To guarantee the successful operation of a system of specialized commercial arbitration, a suspension or withdrawal of membership would function as an additional safeguard in situations in which a threat of being blacklisted is inept at ensuring compliance with arbitral awards. Whether this type of extrajudicial enforcement is reasonably necessary to offset the anticompetitive harm inflicted upon targeted members is questionable. Much will depend on the considerations of the FTC and/or US courts. In the following table the most important arguments in support of and against ostracism are presented.

Arguments that justify a legality of a withdrawal of membership pursuant to Section 1 of the Sherman Act	**Arguments against a legality of a withdrawal of membership pursuant to Section 1 of the Sherman Act**
1. Withdrawals of membership provide a successful measure to ensure compliance with arbitral awards when blacklisting is ineffective (*e.g.* bankruptcy).	1. Besides the reputational harm, cancelling all services provided by a relevant trade association carries a risk of completely ousting a member from the second-tier relevant commodities market. Taking away an essential facility is unlawful.
2. Withdrawals of membership are necessary to maintain a system of specialized commercial arbitration that benefits total welfare and consumer welfare.	2. Non-payment of an award should not result in a withdrawal of membership. It is disproportionate to the principles of proportionality and subsidiarity. Withdrawing membership is a too severe sanction.
3. In most markets, having one's membership suspended or terminated does not result in social ramifications. Members of a trade association are often globally dispersed and alien to one another.	3. In some markets, having one's membership suspended or terminated can also have social ramifications. It can disrupt interpersonal relationships within close-knit groups.
4. Often, a withdrawal of membership decision is not published. Added reputational harm is not to be expected, because industry actors are globally active and may be unaware of the suspension or termination.	4. When a trade association publishes the decision that it has suspended or terminated membership, all members and sometimes even non-members will not likely conduct trade with such a market participant. Reputational harm inflicted upon a targeted individual or company is not unlikely.
5. Many industry actors that have their membership suspended or terminated are bankrupt. It is only a symbolic measure that chiefly contributes to the overall compliance with arbitral awards.	5. Having one's membership suspended or terminated takes away the chance that a member subject to a withdrawal of membership decision becomes financially sound midst such a withdrawal of membership.

6. Historically, individuals have been ostracized.[575] This measure is not exclusively reserved for the commodities trade. It would be unwise to prohibit withdrawals of membership.	6. Historical examples do not justify the anticompetitive harm inflicted upon targeted members.

There is no easy answer to establish that the procompetitive benefits of a withdrawal of membership outweigh its anticompetitive consequences. From my point of view, a withdrawal of membership is a measure that is reasonably necessary to ensure the success of specialized commercial arbitration. This is particularly true if including the name of a market participant on a blacklist is unsuccessful in guaranteeing compliance and avoiding an evasion of the principle pertaining to the sanctity of contracts. It is of paramount importance to close any loophole that can impair the operability of a PLS. Total welfare and consumer welfare arguments should outweigh the anticompetitive harm done to disloyal members. Only when there is a threat of ostracism will compliance with arbitral awards increase. However, owing to the importance of being a member of one of the trade associations researched, any withdrawal of membership can eliminate a rival from the market. The trade associations researched and their members are both subject to a potential antitrust scrutiny pursuant to Section 1 of the Sherman Act and should not take a legality of a suspension or termination for granted. The FTC and US courts will on a case-by-case basis take into consideration the impact of an expulsion from the market and the necessity of that expulsion in a concrete situation.

To ensure that a withdrawal of membership falls outside of the antitrust radar, in my view, four steps should be considered. First, a withdrawal of membership should not be an automatic consequence of non-payment of an arbitral award, but should only be applied when blacklisting is ineffective in a concrete case.[576] Second, it must be researched on a case-by-case basis whether another less intrusive measure can ensure enforcement of an arbitral award.[577] If yes, this measure should be preferred. Third, possibili-

575 For an historical example of a banishment, see Part I, Chapter 2, B, II.

576 It would be recommended to task a committee of specifically selected, impartial and unbiased members with deciding whether a withdrawal of membership is just in a specific situation.

577 An example would be to debar a wrongdoer from using a standardized contract of or derived from a relevant trade association, attending its networking events and using its arbitral services in another case when such an industry actor does not pay an additional monetary sum each time.

ties for internal appeal against an arbitral award should be put in place.[578] Fourth, as is the focus in the next Paragraph, when membership is indefinitely terminated re-application for membership should not be made too difficult. Put differently, a withdrawal of membership procedure based on clearly defined, transparent, non-discriminatory reviewable criteria that allows for cumulative penalties enforceable in national courts, with a final threat of a suspension, or in the worst case scenario when non-compliance is combined with other misconduct, an indefinite expulsion would be justifiable provided that the trade association has objective, reasonable and legitimate reasons for doing so and the rules and criteria are fair and neutral (*i.e.* do not favour certain members over others). Furthermore, expelled members should be given the chance to request recourse in public courts.

ii. Denial of membership for expelled members on the basis of an additional entry condition

An expulsion is a severe measure that can oust a market participant from the market. Any targeted industry actor should be given the chance to ask for re-admission to membership when that actor again fulfils all membership requirements and a reasonable period time has elapsed. Allowing a Board of Directors to decide whether an ostracized industry actor can be re-admitted to the trade association is highly arbitrary. This measure as well as not accepting member applications for a period of two years contributes to stifling competition for targeted individuals and/or companies. Membership rules should be equal, fair, non-discriminatory and legitimate.[579] Denying reapplication for membership of expelled members on the basis of an additional entry condition seems to go beyond this aim.

Be that as it may, members of a trade association can have a valid interest in not accepting a wrongdoer back in their midst. For an expulsion to be a sufficient deterrent, regaining membership should not be made too easy. Therefore, also here, it is necessary to balance the procompetitive benefits of denying a reapplication for membership of an expelled member

578 While an absence of due process is permissible under Section 1 of the Sherman Act, in my opinion, the possibility of an internal appeal against an arbitral award would decrease the chance that membership of a wrongdoer is suspended or terminated. It would be wise to include this possibility in the bylaws of a trade association.

579 See Part II, Chapter 6, D, II, 2, a.

on the basis of an additional entry barrier against the anticompetitive consequences for ostracized former members. To succeed, the task of navigating this difficult legal, regulatory and subjective balancing exercise requires clear guidance. The following two tables present the arguments for and against an illegality under Section 1 of the Sherman Act of the two additional entry barriers imposed by the trade associations researched, namely (i) the lapse of a period of two years following an expulsion; and (ii) the approval of a Board of Directors.

Arguments that justify imposing a lapse of a two-year time period following an expulsion in order to reapply for membership under Section 1 of the Sherman Act	**Arguments against the imposition of a lapse of a two-year time period following an expulsion in order to reapply for membership under Section 1 of the Sherman Act**
1. The imposition of a two-year period to reapply for membership is reasonably necessary to make an expulsion effective. If targeted wrongdoers were able to immediately reapply for membership, the functionality of this type of extrajudicial enforcement would be rendered (to some degree) ineffective.	1. If an expelled member again complies with all the membership requirements, pays the arbitral award and any related penalties, it would not be reasonably necessary to impose a two-year waiting period. This would unduly harm the financial standing of a terminated former member.
2. Because a two-year waiting period is necessary to ensure the effect of an expulsion, the enforcement of awards of specialized commercial arbitration is better guaranteed. This enhances total welfare and consumer welfare.	2. Albeit that specialized commercial arbitration enhances total welfare and consumer welfare, once an expelled former member qualifies as a member, it would be unreasonable to oust him from the market for a long period.
3. A two-year period is proportionate and a reduced period would not contribute to the deterrent effect of an expulsion.	3. A two-year period is excessively long. It would be better to either abolish a period altogether, or reduce it to, for example, six months.[580] By doing so, the foreclosure effect of expelled former members is reduced.
4. It is reasonably necessary to make an exception to the rule that membership rules should be equal and non-discriminatory. Without such a rule, an expulsion is insufficiently deterring and would be rendered ineffective. This can undermine the enforcement of arbitral awards of specialized commercial arbitration. In addition, it can induce members not to pay an arbitral award.	4. Given that membership rules should be equal for all applicants and must not discriminate, imposing a two-year period which only applies to expelled former members is contrary to this rule. This follows from the Supreme Court's judgment in *NW Wholesale Stationers v. Pac. Stationery.*

580 A period of six months would still guarantee the effect of an expulsion and would give an expelled former member the possibility to demonstrate that it is a reliable business partner.

Arguments that justify the necessity of an approval of a readmission of membership by the relevant Board of Director after an expulsion under Section 1 of the Sherman Act	**Arguments against the necessity of an approval of a readmission of membership by the relevant Board of Director after an expulsion under Section 1 of the Sherman Act**
1. When a member is expelled from a trade association, tasking the Board of Directors with assessing whether a reinstatement of membership is fair and just is not only necessary, but also democratically sound. Arbitrators are the legal representatives of trade associations and should be given the right to approve re-admission to membership. This would increase the severity of an expulsion and strengthen the enforcement with arbitral awards. In addition, it would enhance total welfare and consumer welfare.	1. Allowing the Board of Directors to deny an expelled former member from reobtaining membership, even though such an industry actor satisfies all membership requirements and pays the arbitral award and any related penalties, is discriminatory and unfair. These individuals can arbitrarily oust an industry actor from the market.
2. A trade association should be selective in allowing industry actors to become members. This is especially true in the event a member has proven to be unreliable and unwilling to pay an arbitral award. The relevant Board of Directors should critically review a reapplication for membership to protect the reliability of specialized commercial arbitration.	2. There is a risk that the relevant Board of Directors tasked with approving re-admission to membership of an expelled former member are motivated by personal resentment against a former member, capricious decision-making and the mood of the directors on a given day. It would be unwise to give such body the possibility to deny membership to such an industry actor, as it can result in market foreclosure.
3. To ensure that an expulsion sufficiently deters members from not complying with an arbitral award, allowing the relevant Board of Directors to approve a re-admission to membership is reasonably necessary. There must be an exception to the legal rule provided by the Supreme Court's judgment in *NW Wholesale Stationers v. Pac. Stationery.*	3. Given that membership rules should equal for all applicants and must not discriminate, allowing the relevant Board of Directors to strike down a membership reapplication of an expelled member is contrary to this rule. This follows from the Supreme Court's judgment in *NW Wholesale Stationers v. Pac. Stationery.*

Imposing additional entry barriers on expelled members to re-obtain membership should be approached with reservation. It has an increased risk of over-punishing a former member subject to an expulsion and foreclosing market access. Anticompetitive harm is especially to be expected when a Board of Directors is able to arbitrarily and capriciously deny a re-admission to membership. In my opinion, such a freedom of discretion violates Section 1 of the Sherman Act and can even entail that an expelled former member will never be able to become a member again. This is not only disproportionate, but also an unreasonable method to ensure the successful operation of specialized commercial system, which contributes to the enhancement of total welfare and consumer welfare. Instead of allowing a Board of Directors to deny a reapplication for membership, an independent third-party panel (not connected with the relevant trade association) should be tasked with doing this by taking clearly defined, equally applicable, transparent, non-discriminatory criteria into account, such as (i) the current liquidity status of the former member; (ii) an unwillingness to pay the fine for non-compliance with the arbitral award; and (iii) evidence of probable disloyalty in the future.

With regard to the two-year period following an expulsion, a violation of Section 1 of the Sherman Act is not so clear-cut. Without an interim period following the enforcement of this measure and a reapplication for membership, expulsions would be rendered inefficient and would not deter wrongdoers. A targeted industry actor can then immediately following an expulsion satisfy all membership requirements, pay the arbitral award and any related penalties and be re-admitted. Yet, in my opinion, a two-year period is too long and should be reduced given the consequence that an expelled former member loses access to an essential facility. An alternative would be to impose a six-month timeframe for non-payment of an award and if this is combined with previous other misconduct a time period of one year.[581] All things considered, it is possible to make a successful rule-of-reason defence by a relevant trade association and its members and both actors can justify the imposition of a time period if the length of that period is more proportionate to the gravity of a denial of an essential facility.

c. Refusal to deal with an expelled member

The instruction of a trade association to its members not to conduct business with an expelled member is a far-reaching measure. Its effect on targeted former members is even more severe than an expulsion.[582] An impossibility to conduct business with any member of one of the trade associations researched eradicates the financial standing of a targeted industry actor. This results in market elimination altogether. Despite the anticompetitive nature of a refusal to deal, it must be assessed whether this mea-

581 Examples refer to situations in which an expelled member had already in the past been warned for not paying the yearly fee, committed theft or fraud, intentionally damaged property of members belonging to a relevant trade association, and has threatened others.

582 This is because a refusal to deal with members follows a withdrawal of membership. So it is an additional nonlegal sanction.

sure is merely an instrument for suppressing competition, or if it is reasonably necessary to enhance total welfare and consumer welfare.

The importance of a balancing-exercise that is not only indissociable from, but truly embedded in, antitrust analysis is the most obvious method to compare whether procompetitive benefits outweigh the anticompetitive effects of a refusal to deal with an ostracized member. The following table presents the arguments for and against an illegality under Section 1 of the Sherman Act of this type of extrajudicial enforcement.

Arguments that justify the imposition of a refusal to deal with ostracized members of a trade association imposed upon its members under Section 1 of the Sherman Act	**Arguments against the imposition of a refusal to deal with ostracized members of a trade association imposed upon its members under Section 1 of the Sherman Act**
1. Following a withdrawal of membership, targeted industry actors can still conduct business with the members of a trade association. To punish those that have broken the most essential rule of a trade association, namely to pay an outstanding award, expulsion is not always a sufficient deterrent. It is when an industry actor can no longer conduct trade with the member of a trade association, the best possible compliance with arbitral awards of specialized commercial arbitration can be expected. Hence, it is reasonably necessary to enforce this type of nonlegal sanction.	1. The imposition of a refusal to deal with ostracized members is too severe and unnecessarily reduces the competitive status of targeted industry actors. An expulsion which fulfils all the appropriate safeguards is already a sufficient deterrent. Why add unnecessary financial and reputational harm? The assumption that more preclusive measures such as a refusal to deal are reasonably necessary can be rebutted.
2. Because a refusal to deal with an ostracized industry actor is necessary to guarantee maximum compliance, the enforcement of awards of specialized commercial arbitration is better guaranteed. This enhances total welfare and consumer welfare.	2. Albeit that a refusal to deal with ostracized members will increase the threat of non-compliance with an arbitral award, thereby benefiting the operability of specialized commercial arbitration which enhances total welfare and consumer welfare, the financial harm placed upon expelled market participants chiefly outweighs a contentious rise in the compliance with arbitral awards.

3. US courts dance around the topic of whether to treat a refusal to deal as a *per se* violation or allow a rule-of-reason analysis. Its unbalanced treatment of *stare decisis* adds to the vagueness of how to perceive a refusal to deal under Section 1 of the Sherman Act.[583] It would be better to draw a clear-cut yardstick. To this extent, a good example would be to establish that any refusal to deal is tolerable when it was clear before the wrongful act what triggered this type of extrajudicial enforcement and that at least some procompetitive benefits such as improved total welfare and consumer welfare are being produced. In light of this necessary guidance, any member of a trade association which has included the possibility of a refusal to deal after a withdrawal of membership is well aware that both types of nonlegal sanctions can be expected. In addition, increased compliance with arbitral awards enhances consumer welfare and total welfare. It is not illogical to exculpate any trade association and its members for their role in executing a refusal to deal.	3. Absent guidance by the FTC and US courts it is not easy to formulate a clear-cut yardstick of how to assess a refusal to deal with an ostracized member. A definition should be as restrictive as possible, because of the harmful effects of a refusal to deal on targeted industry actors, which are clearly not pernicious. Only when absent a refusal to deal is increased total welfare and consumer welfare unlikely[584], a rule rule-of-reason analysis can successfully exculpate a trade association and its members. It does not need much clarification that this is not the case for a refusal to deal with ostracized members. The dissemination of the name of a wrongdoer in a blacklist or withdrawing its membership already guarantees compliance with arbitral awards and, thus, enhances total welfare and consumer welfare. Albeit that a refusal to deal – arguably – to some degree increases the operability of specialized commercial arbitration, this is disproportionate to the anticompetitive effect on targeted industry actors.

Contrary to the arguments in favour of illegality of a refusal to deal with ostracized members under Section 1 of the Sherman Act, one cannot deny the negative and restrictive effects for targeted industry actors. Not only is their financial standing worse compared with merely an expulsion, also the reputational damage inflicted upon them is more severe. Under antitrust doctrine this should be enough evidence to not legitimize a refusal to deal with an ostracized member. This type of extrajudicial enforcement is unnecessarily injurious to an ostracized member and in no way should be seen as proportionate to the wrong of not complying with an arbitral award. Alternative sanctions which provide less severe consequences for wrongdoers are available and have a comparable positive impact on consumer welfare and total welfare. Subsequently, a refusal to deal with ostracized members is not reasonably necessary to enhance both procompetitive benefits.

583 H. J. Hovenkamp, "The Rule of Reason", *Penn Law: Legal Scholarship Repository* 2018, p. 96.

584 There must be an essential causality between the refusal to deal and an increase in total welfare and consumer welfare.

F. Key findings

All of the six trade associations researched operate a system of specialized commercial arbitration in which awards are enforced by use of nonlegal sanctions.[585] Although there are some differences between these associations in which modes of extrajudicial enforcement are available, the following six nonlegal sanctions are discernible. First, the dissemination of the name of a wrongdoer in a blacklist. Second, a withdrawal of membership. Third, a refusal to allow an expelled member to reobtain membership on the basis of an additional entry condition. Fourth, a refusal to deal with an ostracized member. Fifth, entering the premises of a wrongdoer without being invited and without a warrant. Sixth, albeit not a legal sanction, but treated as such for reasons of structure, limiting adequate access to public courts prior to arbitral proceedings and after an award. Without being affected by the observation that from the outset neither the FTC nor US courts have ever considered the illegality of these measures under Section 1 of the Sherman Act, this Chapter has aimed to shed some light on a potential unlawfulness under this provision which prohibits all contracts, combinations, and conspiracies in restraint of trade.[586] This was done by focusing on four steps: first, to determine whether the actors involved in initiating and executing the nonlegal sanctions qualify as a corporation or individual. Second, to establish whether there is a necessary concurrence of wills. Third, to assess whether the trade associations researched, their members and non-members, for their participating in the six types of nonlegal sanctions, can be held liable for a violation of Section 1 of the Sherman Act. Fourth, to discuss whether their participation in each anticompetitive measure realizes procompetitive benefits which outweigh the anticompetitive harm for targeted wrongdoers.

---

585 See Part II, Chapter 6, A.

586 On the ground that only *Richman* has ever considered the anti-competitiveness of blacklisting following non-compliance with an arbitral award under Section 1 of the Sherman Act, the research is still embryonic. Neither the FTC and US courts nor legal doctrine has ever explored the lawfulness of the other types of extrajudicial enforcement typically available.

I. Qualification as member or undertaking

It does not require any elaborate analysis to classify the members and non-members as individuals or undertakings.[587] For a trade association this is perhaps a bit more difficult.[588] A qualification as an undertaking requires, according to the Tenth Circuit Court of Appeals in *Gregory v. Port Bridger Rendezvous Association*, that this actor as well as its members are engaged in unilateral conduct. When applying this legal rule to the conduct of the trade associations researched, given that both actors have a role in imposing and enforcing nonlegal sanctions, it is unmistakable that such institutions are undertakings within the meaning of Section 1 of the Sherman Act.

II. Collusion: "a concurrence of wills"

Section 1 of the Sherman Act also requires that there is either a contract, a combination in the form of trust or otherwise, or a conspiracy.[589] The execution of nonlegal sanctions by members of the trade associations researched amounts to a contract, because they have agreed to the bylaws and rules of these associations when obtaining membership.[590] This is especially true when members conduct trade under a standardized contract which refers to these bylaws and rules which include nonlegal sanctions. A non-member can also enter into a contract, but only to the extent this industry actor conducts trade on the basis of a standardized contract provided by a relevant trade association with one of its members.

A combination in the form of trust or otherwise, at first glance, is not suitable to define a necessary collusion. Yet, the word combination serves as a catch-all provision and can be used to classify the role of the trade associations researched in the imposition of nonlegal sanctions.[591] The main reason being that a trade association protects the interests of its members on a not-for-profit basis by providing services. For non-members such argumentation is not plausible.

---

587 See Part II, Chapter 6, B, I.
588 See Part II, Chapter 6, B, II.
589 See Part II, Chapter 6, C.
590 See Part II, Chapter 6, C, I.
591 See Part II, Chapter 6, C, II.

With regard to the third form of collusion, namely the existence of a conspiracy, the former two forms of collusion are more suitable to define the cooperation between the trade associations researched and their members in imposing and executing nonlegal sanctions.[592] Non-members also do not typically fall within the constraints of this concept, absent a lack of intent. Nevertheless, for the purpose of this research, they have conspired.

III. The anti-competitiveness of nonlegal sanctions

Nonlegal sanctions have a clear risk of violating Section 1 of the Sherman Act.[593] This is especially true with regard to the practice of blacklisting,[594] withdrawals of membership,[595] refusals for expelled members to regain membership on the basis of an additional entry condition,[596] and refusals to deal with ostracized members.[597] These measures stifle the financial standing of a targeted industry actor and cause reputational harm. Due to the high risk of market foreclosure and limited possibilities to undo reputational harm, one might draw the conclusion that this is sufficient evidence to establish that unlike non-members, both the trade associations researched as well as their members engage in collective boycotts which are inherently illegal.

However, three arguments rebut this assumption in favour of a more lenient approach, namely a rule-of-reason analysis. First, a trade association and its members classify as a joint venture, which is typically subject to a rule-of-reason defence. Second, there has been a paradigm shift in how to treat a collective boycott. Whereas in the past the more stringent *per se* violation approach was favoured, the focus is now on the more lenient rule-of-reason analysis. Third, nonlegal sanctions appear necessary to operate a system of specialized commercial arbitration as efficiently as possible, which lowers transaction and distribution costs. For refusals to deal with ostracized members, it is more doubtful whether this practice is inherently prohibited or whether procompetitive benefits may be balanced against its anticompetitive effects. The existence of less grave alternatives and its haz-

---

592 See Part II, Chapter 6, C, III.
593 See Part II, Chapter 6, D.
594 See Part II, Chapter 6, D, I.
595 See Part II, Chapter 6, D, II, 1.
596 See Part II, Chapter 6, D, II, 2
597 See Part II, Chapter 6, D, III.

ardous effect on targeted industry actors may be sufficient to favour the former approach. Regardless, this type of extrajudicial enforcement was discussed in a rule-of-reason analysis. The reason being that in the event of doubt it is better to understand the full picture and assess whether its pro-competitive benefits outweigh the anticompetitive harm placed upon targeted market participants. In contrast, entering the premises of a recalcitrant member of a trade association without a warrant is insufficient to violate Section 1 of the Sherman Act. In addition, even if not a nonlegal sanction, limiting adequate access to public courts prior to arbitral proceedings and after an award does not violate this provision.

IV. Rule-of-reason defence

Section 1 of the Sherman Act ought to be deployed, not to subvert measures that are reasonably necessary to operate a system that enhances total welfare and consumer welfare, but to bust colluding quislings with sinecures in perpetuity.[598] This truism is the foundation on which to assess the proportionality of the practice of blacklisting, withdrawals of membership and subsequent refusals to re-admit expelled members to membership on the basis of an additional entry barrier and refusals to deal with ostracized member. Considering that specialized commercial arbitration lowers transaction and distribution costs,[599] which clearly benefits total welfare and consumer welfare[600] and by reason that judicial enforcement has proven to be inefficient and less severe measures imposed by a trade association are insufficient to guarantee compliance with awards, nonlegal sanctions appear reasonably necessary.[601] While this is true for the dissemination of the names of wrongdoers in non-public blacklists[602] and withdrawals of membership[603] when both extrajudicial measures are structured in the least restrictive manner, refusing to re-admit ostracized members to membership because a two-year period has not yet elapsed and a Board of Directors is unconvinced, is either too long or too arbitrary and capricious.[604] Such re-admission conditions are not reasonably necessary to en-

598 See Part II, Chapter 6, E.
599 See Part II, Chapter 6, E, II.
600 See Part II, Chapter 6, E, II, 1.
601 See Part II, Chapter 6, E, II, 2.
602 See Part II, Chapter 6, E, II, 2, a.
603 See Part II, Chapter 6, E, II, 2, b, i.
604 See Part II, Chapter 6, E, II, 2, b, ii.

sure compliance with arbitral awards of specialized commercial arbitration. They primarily result in market foreclosure for targeted industry actors and cannot be offset by the procompetitive benefits realized by such a system. Similarly, but even more obvious, obligating members of a trade association to refuse to deal with ostracized members is too rigid and severe.[605] Targeted wrongdoers not only lose all access to the facilities of a trade association, but also can no longer conduct trade with other members of that association, which encompasses the most important commodities traders in a specific industry. As a result, these individuals and/or undertakings are subject to a dramatic reduction in the loss of market access. Attributable to an exacerbated market foreclosure when compared with the other nonlegal sanctions, the principle of proportionality is infringed.

605 See Part II, Chapter 6, E, II, 2, c.

Chapter 7: Monopolization of any Part of the Trade or Commerce under Section 2 of the Sherman Act

A. *Introduction*

The conduct of the trade associations researched and their members in excluding industry actors by imposing and executing nonlegal sanctions may also violate Section 2 of the Sherman Act. At its core, this provision is a mosaic of three offences. The first is "monopolization", applicable when an undertaking has accumulated sufficient market shares to exclude competition.[606] The second is "attempted monopolization", which is fitting when a single entity in furtherance of its monopoly status acts with a dangerous probability of success.[607] The final unilateral conduct which is deemed illegal by Section 2 of the Sherman Act is a "conspiracy to monopolize", applicable when at least two participants have a specific intent to achieve a monopoly through concerted action.[608]

For the purpose of this research, the first two offences are of principal importance to assess the illegality of imposing nonlegal sanctions by the trade associations researched when boycotting industry actors on adjacent second-tier commodities markets. The third offence is suitable to determine misconduct of their members when executing nonlegal sanctions. To conduct such research, it will, first, be discussed whether the trade associations researched actually monopolize any part of the trade or commerce among the several states, or with foreign nations (Paragraph B).[609] Second,

---

606 R. Miller and G. Jentz, "*Cengage Advantage Books: Business Law Today: The Essentials*", Mason: Thomson West 2008, p. 674.

607 D. Woods, "Hybrid Single Entities and the Market Power Requirement for Conspiracies to Monopolize Following Fraser: Are Courts Putting Form over Substance?", *University of Illinois Law Review* 2004, p. 1262.

608 W. F. Adkinson, Jr., K. L. Grimm, and C. N. Bryan, "Enforcement of Section 2 of the Sherman Act: Theory and Practice", *FTC Working Paper* 2008, p. 4.

609 The trade associations researched and their members are undertakings and persons within the meaning Section 1 of the Sherman Act. See Part II, Chapter 6, B, I, II. This entails that both actors are also subject to Section 2 of the Sherman Act. An additional discussion is not required; Similarly, a concurrence of wills is not a component of the first two offences of Section 2 of the Sherman Act analysis and will not be discussed. With regard to a conspiracy to monopolize, the concept of an agreement will be touched upon; non-members do not fit within

it will be debated if these institutions attempt to monopolize any part of the trade or commerce among the several states, or with foreign nations (Paragraph C). Third, it will be pointed out whether the role of the members of the trade associations in executing judicial enforcement is contrary to Section 2 of the Sherman Act (Paragraph D). Fourth, the statements made and the arguments used in the previous Paragraphs will be summarized by presenting the most important key findings (Paragraph E).

B. *Unlawful monopolization by the trade associations researched*

At its core, Section 2 of the Sherman Act prohibits any undertaking or person to acquire or maintain monopoly power illegally.[610] Interpretation of this definition was provided by the Supreme Court in *United States v. Grinnell Corp.*, following which monopolization consists of two elements: "*(1) the possession of monopoly power in the relevant market and (2) the willful acquisition or maintenance of that power as distinguished from growth or development as a consequence of a superior product, business acumen, or historic accident*".[611]

The imposition of nonlegal sanctions by the trade associations researched must be analysed against this yardstick. Be that as it may, the fact that such extrajudicial enforcement does not have an effect on the market for regulation and private ordering on which these associations operate, but has an effect on targeted industry actors on a second-tier adjacent commodities market renders a difficult non-equivocal analytical challenge to a review.

I. The possession of monopoly power in the relevant market

According to the above mentioned definition provided by the Supreme Court in *United States v. Grinnell Corp.*, but also in its decision in *Verizon Commc'ns Inc. v. Law Offices of Curtis V. Trinko, LLP*, monopolization re-

---

the description of Section 2 of the Sherman Act and are outside of the scope of this Chapter.

610 U.S. Department of Justice, "Competition and Monopoly: Single-firm Conduct under Section 2 of the Sherman Act", *U.S. Department of Justice* 2008, p. 5.

611 United States v. Grinnell Corp., 384 U.S. 563, 570 (1966).

quires "*the possession of monopoly power in the relevant market*".[612] The most common way to determine this is first to define the relevant market and then analyse whether the trade association has monopoly power within that market.[613] Unfortunately, two problems prevent applying this approach easily. First, nonlegal sanctions are imposed by the trade associations which are active in the market for regulation and private ordering, but have an impact on disloyal industry actors active in adjacent second-tier commodities markets. Hence, it is unsure in which market the trade associations researched should possess a monopoly: in the first-tier market for regulation and private ordering or the second-tier commodities market.[614] Second, setting a specific percentage as the required market share is controversial.

1. Market definition: Monopoly leveraging

Typically, to fall within the ambit of Section 2 of the Sherman Act, unilateral action (*e.g.* nonlegal sanctions) should be imposed and felt within one and the same market. With regard to the trade associations researched, the situation is different. They use one market to be dominant in order to punish bad behaviour of their members in adjacent second-tier commodities markets. This raises the ensuing question whether the trade associations researched must also possess market power in the other market? If the answer to this question is affirmative, it would require a difficult and thought-provoking calculation of the market shares of their members in each relevant commodities market. To prevent this, the concept of "monopoly leveraging" provides a more straightforward solution. In consonance with this theory, monopoly leveraging is the use of monopoly power in one market in order to obtain a competitive advantage in another market by means of anticompetitive conduct.[615] Even though establishing anti-competitiveness pursuant to Section 2 of the Sherman Act is not

612 Verizon Commc'ns Inc. v. Law Offices of Curtis V. Trinko, LLP, 540 U.S. 398, 407 (2004).

613 N. F. Diebold, "*Non-Discrimination in International Trade in Services: 'Likeness' in WTO/GATS*", Cambridge: Cambridge University Press 2010, p. 277.

614 Trade associations are active on the market for regulation and private ordering and their members on relevant commodities markets. While an oversimplified observation, it is correct.

615 J. H. Bogart, "*Circuit Conflicts in Antitrust Litigation*", Chicago: American Bar Association 2009, p. 34.

the aim under the first requirement of monopolization, this concept illustrates that it is sufficient for the trade associations researched to have a monopoly status in their respective markets for regulation and private ordering.

2. Market shares in the market for regulation and private ordering

Calculating the market shares for each of the trade associations researched is contentious, as it largely depends on each trade association's own indication of this amount and sometimes the literature. Absent other reliable sources, this is briefly discussed below for each of them.

a. The International Cotton Association

By taking a cursory glance at the "activity" or "about" section, it is unmistakable that the ICA sees itself as the world's leading association to help regulate the sale and purchase of raw cotton on the basis of a set of bylaws and rules, including, but not limited to, providing arbitration services on the market for regulation and private ordering.[616] As this may be an over-exaggeration to attract more potential member undertakings, especially since it appears that countries with a large economy have similar trade associations,[617] reference should be made to the ICA membership directory of 2010.[618] In that directory, the ICA explains that today 60% of the world's cotton is still traded using these rules.[619] It would be wise to define the market of regulation and private ordering in the cotton industry in which the ICA is active, globally. While information is lacking about the amount of market shares the ICA has in the territory of the US, which is required to establish the existence of monopoly power under Section 2 of the Sherman Act, it is not unlikely that a similar amount of market shares

616 http://www.ica-ltd.org/about-ica/.

617 Important trade associations include: the Association Cotonnière Africaine (http://www.africotton.org/aca/en/), the China Cotton Association (http://english.china-cotton.org/) and the American Cotton Shippers Association (http://acsa-cotton.org/). For a full list of the trade associations that are members of the CICCA, see http://www.cicca.info/member_associations.php.

618 ICA, ICA membership directory, incorporating annual review, P. 12.

619 See also http://www.liverpoolmuseums.org.uk/maritime/exhibitions/cotton/traders/trading-rules.aspx.

can be detected when the market is defined regionally in the territory of the US.

b. The Diamond Dealers Club

With regard to the US-based DDC, the mission statement (as can be found on its website) suggests that this association is the largest diamond trade organization in the United Stated and one of the leading diamond exchanges in the world.[620] In 1985, the DDC handled roughly 80% of all diamonds coming into the United States, with a worldwide purchase that amounted to $22 billion (*i.e.* 36% of the world market).[621] However, DDC membership has declined over the past two decades, from 2,000 to 1,200 undertakings.[622] Given the secrecy of this association, no recent information concerning market capitalization is available. Such lack of empirical data renders it difficult to measure market shares. However, one thing is sure: the DDC remains the largest operator on the market for regulation and private ordering in diamonds when the market is defined regionally in the territory of the US.[623]

620 https://www.nyddc.com/about-the-ddc.html.

621 http://articles.latimes.com/1985-08-18/business/fi-1708_1_diamond-prices; In 1979 also 80% of all diamonds were traded through the DDC in the US.

622 B. D. Richman et al, "*Journal of Legal Analysis, Vol. 9, Is. 2*", in: B. D. Richman (ed), "An Autopsy of Cooperation: Diamond Dealers and the Limits of Trust-based Exchange", Oxford: Oxford University Press 2017, p. 256.

623 When the market is defined globally, DDC market shares are significantly less. Given the competition of the Federation of Belgium Diamond Bourses (the "FBDB"), which holds 84% shares for the market for regulation and private ordering in rough diamonds and 50% market shares in polished diamonds globally, monopolization is not to be expected when the market is defined globally; SBD, "De Belgische Diamentnijverheid", *Algemene vergadering van SBD* 2014, p. 7; In 2012, the percentage of worldwide rough diamond that went through Antwerp amounted to 80%. See Antwerp World Diamond Centre, "Antwerp Diamond Masterplan – Diamonds love Antwerp 2020", *Antwerp World Diamond Centre* 2012, p. 5, 69, 148, 154. In the exchange of rough diamonds, Antwerp is the world leader; The Heritage Diamond Group (http://www.heritagediamonds.net/antwerp-diamond-bourse/) explains on its website that 85% of the world's rough and more than 65% of polished diamonds are exchanged in Antwerp; The Auction House of the Russian Federation (AHRF) explains that Antwerp is the most important centre for the diamond business is Antwerp. Approximately 80% of all diamonds that are processed and sold in the world are traded in this city. See https://www.auction-house.ru/en/news_analytics/rynok-almazov-mira/;

c. The Grain and Feed Trade Association

In my view, GAFTA is active on the global market for regulation and private ordering in agricultural commodities, spices and general produce because it perceives itself as an international organization that promotes trading for more than 1,700 international members that are located in 90 countries worldwide.[624] Even though it does not appraise its own market share, a rough calculation is redundant. This is because of the paucity of international competing trade associations that are active on the market for regulation and private ordering with regard to the grain and feed trade industry. When the market is defined regionally to the territory of the US, it is almost certain that similar levels of market power are held by GAFTA on the market for regulation and private ordering.

d. Federation of Cocoa Commerce

Although calculating market shares involves an exorbitant empirical-intensive enquiry, the literature agrees that virtually all international business in tangible cacao is conducted on the basis of standardized contracts for sales that were developed by the FCC and the Cocoa Merchants' Association of America (CMAA).[625] Subsequently, the FCC is active on the global market for regulation & private ordering in the cocoa trade. When the market is

---

The market capitalization of the FBDB has not changed over the last 15 years. Richman explains that "*Eight out of ten of the world's uncut diamonds and one in two polished diamonds pass through Antwerp, generating $36 billion in exports in 2004.*" See B. D. Richman, "How Community Institutions Create Economic Advantage: Jewish Diamond Merchants in New York", *Law & Social Inquiry* 383 2006, p. 18.

624 https://www.gafta.com/Membership.

625 S. T. Beckett, "*Industrial Chocolate Manufacture and Use – Fourth Edition*", Hoboken: Blackwell Publishing 2009, p. 25; S. T. Beckett, M. S. Fowler, and G. R. Ziegler, "*Beckett's Industrial Chocolate Manufacture and Use – Fifth Edition*", Hoboken: Wiley-Blackwell 2017, p. 28; https://www.icco.org/about-cocoa/trading-a-shipping.html. Also the International Cocoa Organisation (ICCO) supports the view that the FCC and the CMAA are the main international cocoa trade associations; R. Dand, "*The International Cocoa Trade*", Cambridge/Philadelphia/New Delhi: Woodhead Publishing Limited 2011, p. 97-98. The market influence of the FCC and the CMAA may change in the future due to the recently formed Cocoa Association of China (CAC). Despite its aim to publish contract terms, it has till now failed to do so.

defined regionally to the territory of the US, owing to an absence of US competing trade associations, it is also plausible that the majority of cocoa contracts affecting US trade are based on the standardized contracts of the FCC.

e. London Metal Exchange

Schofield explains that the majority of global transactions are made on the basis of the contractual terms of the LME.[626] In addition, in 2018 *Revuelta* explains that more than 80% of global non-ferrous business is transacted through the LME, with an annual aggregate trading of about $10 trillion.[627] Hence, the LME is active on the global market for regulation and private ordering in the metal trade. When the market is defined regionally to the territory of the US, a similar market share amount can be expected.

f. Federation of Oils, Seeds and Fats Association

Following only a cursory glance at the opening page of its website, FOSFA defines itself as "*a professional international contract issuing and arbitral body concerned exclusively with the world trade in oilseeds, oils and fats with 1,123 members in 90 countries*". [628] Its dominance can especially be confirmed by looking at the fact that an estimated 85% of all international trade in oilseeds, oils and fats are conducted using FOSFA contracts.[629] As a result,

---

626 N. C. Schofield, "*Commodities Derivatives: Markets and Applications*", Hoboken: John Wiley & Sons 2007, p. 75; See also F. A. Lees, "*Financial Exchanges: A Comparative Approach*", New York/Abingdon: Routledge 2012, p. 164; R. King, "*Jehovah Himself Has Become King*", Bloomington: AuthorHouse 2010, p. 252. The LME is the world's leading trade association active in non-ferrous metals. It facilitates on a busy day contracts worth more than $10 billion.

627 M. B. Revuelta, "*Mineral Resources: From Exploration to Sustainability Assessment*", Cham: Springer International Publishing AG 2018, p. 44; A similar empirical outcome relates to The London Metal Exchange, "A Guide to the LME", *The London Metal Exchange* 2013, p. 1; Other support for *Revuelta's* statement can be found in The London Metal Exchange, "A Guide to Trading LME", The London Metal Exchange 2016, p. 1.

628 https://www.fosfa.org/.

629 A. Lista, "*International Commercial Sales: The Sale of Goods on Shipment Terms*", Abingdon/New York: Routledge 2017, p. 10; Food and Agriculture Organization of the United Nations and World Health Organization in collaboration

FOSFA is active on the global market for regulation and private ordering in oilseeds, oils and fats. Also here, when the market is defined regionally to the territory of the US, it is likely that a large majority of US trade in oils, seeds and fats is conducted on the basis of standardized contracts provided by FOSFA.

3. Monopolization in the market for regulation and private ordering

To date, US courts differ on the market share required for monopoly power. The 6th Circuit Court of Appeals in *Spirit Airlines v. Northwest Airlines* and the 5th Circuit Court of Appeals in *Heattransfer Corp. v. Volkswagenwerk, A.G.* argued that holding more than 70% market share creates a *prima facie* showing of such a position.[630] Conversely, in *Blue Cross & Blue Shield v. Marshfield Clinic.*, the 7th Circuit Court of Appeals argued that "*Fifty percent is below any accepted benchmark for inferring monopoly power from market share*".[631] High entry barriers is a factor that affects this analysis as well.

With that said, all of the six trade associations researched are the most important players when the market of regulation and private ordering is defined regionally to the territory of the US. Two of them hold probably more than 70% market shares when the market is defined regionally,[632]

---

with the National Institute for Public Health and the Environment (Netherlands), "*Development of Criteria for Acceptable Previous Cargoes for Fats and Oils*", Food and Agriculture Organization of the United Nations and World Health Organization in collaboration with the National Institute for Public Health and the Environment (Netherlands) 2007, p. 20; J. R. Pritchard, "Oilseed quality requirements for processing", *Journal of the American Oil Chemists' Society* 1983, p. 322. In 1983, 80% of all international trade on oilseeds, oils and fats was conducted on the basis of FOSFA contracts; A. Baldwin, "*World Conference on Emerging Technologies in the Fats and Oils Industry*", In: E.C. Campbell (red.), "Trade Association Rules - Impact on International Trade", Urbana: American Oil Chemists' Society 1986, p. 24. In 1986, FOSFA contracts amounted to a market share of around 80% in the international trade of oilseeds, oils and fats.

630 Spirit Airlines v. Northwest Airlines, 431 F.3d 917, 935-936 (6th Cir. 2005); Heattransfer Corp. v. Volkswagenwerk, A.G., 553 F.2d 964, 981 (5th Cir. 1977).

631 Blue Cross & Blue Shield v. Marshfield Clinic, 65 F.3d 1406, 1411 (7th Cir. 1995); This has been reiterated by the 11th Circuit Court of Appeals in Bailey v. Allgas, Inc., 284 F.3d 1237, 1250 (11th Cir. 2002). In its judgment, the Court argued that "*A market share at or less than 50 percent is inadequate as a matter of law to constitute monopoly power*".

632 This is true for the LME and FOSFA.

whereas the other four have either 60% market share,[633] are without serious competitors,[634] or its members trade almost exclusively on the basis of the association's standardized contracts.[635] These observations in combination with market foreclosure effects when an industry actor is targeted by nonlegal sanctions is enough evidence to conclude that these trade associations researched hold monopoly power in the markets for regulation and private ordering concerning the US territory.

II. Anticompetitive conduct

Following the Opinion of Justice Scalia in the Supreme Court's judgment in *Verizon Commc'ns Inc. v. Law Offices of Curtis V. Trinko, LLP*, "*the possession of monopoly power will not be found unlawful unless it is accompanied by an element of anticompetitive conduct*".[636] This entails that the rather difficult wording provided by the Supreme Court in *United States v. Grinnell Corp.*, which requires "*the willful acquisition or maintenance of that power as distinguished from growth or development as a consequence of a superior product, business acumen, or historic accident*", should be interpreted to mean that Section 2 of the Sherman Act is violated when a monopolist's conduct results in anticompetitive effects by harming the competitive process.[637] There is only one problem: no consensus exists on what is considered anticompetitive.[638] Four theories are available to measure such harm. First, the effects balancing test which focuses on the overall impact of unilateral conduct on consumers or net effects on consumer welfare, and whether this is

633 The ICA.
634 GAFTA and the DDC.
635 FCC.
636 Verizon Commc'ns Inc. v. Law Offices of Curtis V. Trinko, LLP, 540 U.S. 398, 407 (2004); R. L. Miller, "*Cengage Advantage Books: Business Law Today, The Essentials: Text and Summarized Cases – 11th Edition*", Boston: Cengage Learning 2015, p. 617. The main reason being that it would be unwise to punish any company that is efficient and well managed and, hence, has a strong financial position.
637 Aspen Publishers, "*Antitrust: Keyed to Pitofsky, Goldschmid, and Wood's Trade Regulation: Cases and Materials Fifth Edition*", New York: Aspen Publishers 2004, p. 71.
638 U.S. Department of Justice, "Competition and Monopoly: Single-firm Conduct under Section 2 of the Sherman Act", *U.S. Department of Justice* 2008, p. 34.

sufficient to offset any potential adverse effects.[639] Second, the profit-sacrifice and no-economic-sense tests which draw the thin line between merely aggressive competition and prohibited conduct that damages the competitive process in the sense that both theories ask the question whether there are less restrictive alternatives available and if the non-exclusionary profits are greater than the harm.[640] Third, the equally efficient competitor test in which one party must prove that unilateral conduct is likely to exclude an equal or more efficient competitor from the market, whereas the other party must provide evidence that procompetitive benefits outweigh anticompetitive harm.[641] Fourth, the disproportionality test which determines whether anticompetitive harm is disproportionate to economic and consumer benefits.[642]

Fortunately, choosing one theory to assess the illegality of nonlegal sanctions imposed by the trade associations researched is immaterial. All of them contain a rule-of-reason analysis by balancing the generated procompetitive benefits against anticompetitive harm.[643] Before explaining each of the four forms of extrajudicial enforcement as to whether the bounds of Section 2 are contravened, it is first necessary to refer back to the concept of monopoly leveraging. This is because the unilateral actions of the trade associations researched do not have an impact on actors operating on the same market for regulation and private ordering, but on targeted industry operators active on the adjacent second-tier commodities markets.

639 S. C. Salop, "Exclusionary Conduct, Effect on Consumers, and the Flawed Profit-Sacrifice Standard", *73 Antitrust L. J.* 2006, p. 330.

640 U.S. Department of Justice, "Competition and Monopoly: Single-firm Conduct under Section 2 of the Sherman Act", *U.S. Department of Justice* 2008, p. 39. It is possible to approach the profit-sacrifice and no-economic-sense test as two separate tests. Here, however, owing to its similarities both have been discussed together.

641 R. A. Posner, "*Antitrust Law, Second Edition*", Chicago: University of Chicago Press 2001, p. 194-195.

642 Amicus Curiae Briefs in Verizon Commc'ns Inc. v. Law Offices of Curtis V. Trinko, LLP, 540 U.S. 398 (2004). See https://www.justice.gov/atr/case-document/brief-united-states-and-federal-trade-commission-amici-curiae-supporting-0.

643 This is to some degree similar to the approach in Section 1 of the Sherman Act. The defendant must provide all information regarding procompetitive benefits. Yet, in this Chapter the chosen structure differs. The anti-competitiveness of nonlegal sanctions will be discussed at the same time with a balancing of its procompetitive benefits generated. This is because there is no discussion if monopolization is subject to a *per se* or rule-of-reason standard under Section 2 of the Sherman Act. A rule-of-reason standard is the norm under this provision.

1. Monopoly leveraging doctrine: Attributing liability for a violation of Section 2 of the Sherman Act to the trade associations researched for utilizing a monopoly position in one market to punish wrongdoers operating on a different market

As already briefly touched upon in the monopolization requirement as discussed above,[644] the theory of monopoly leveraging provides the best yardstick to measure unilateral conduct that has an effect on actors operating on another market. From a historical perspective, the doctrine was first introduced by the Supreme Court in *United States v. Griffith*.[645] In its judgment, the Court affirmed that having a monopoly in one market cannot be used to foreclose competition, or to destroy a competitor in another market.[646] While this created a legal hiatus as to whether the two requirements of monopolization need to be present, or if the theory of monopoly leveraging creates a stand-alone prohibition, the Eastern District of Louisiana District Court *In re Educ. Testing Serv.*,[647] the District of Columbia Court of Appeals in *Covad Communications Company v. Bell Atlantic Corp.*,[648] and the 11th Circuit Court of Appeals in *Morris Communications Corp. v. PGA Tour*[649] ruled that a single entity can only be held liable for monopoly leveraging when both monopolization requirements are fulfilled.

Against this background, due to the fact that the unilateral conduct of the trade associations researched falls within the ambit of the doctrine of monopoly leveraging as elaborated by US courts, the two-tier test of monopolization must be fulfilled to hold these associations liable for violation of Section 2 of the Sherman Act. Whereas the existence of monopoly power is confirmed, the next Paragraph focuses on the unlawfulness of nonlegal sanctioning as imposed by the trade associations researched by applying the four theories of anti-competitiveness for each restriction. In addition, the overarching legal rule provided by US courts is introduced.

644 See Part II, Chapter 7, B I, 1.
645 United States v. Griffith, 334 U.S. 100 (1948).
646 United States v. Griffith, 334 U.S. 100, 107-108 (1948).
647 In re Educ. Testing Serv. Litig., 429 F. Supp. 2d 752, 759 (E.D. La. 2005).
648 Covad Communications Company v. Bell Atlantic Corp., 398 F.3d 666, 672 (D.C. Cir. 2005).
649 Morris Communications Corp. v. PGA Tour, 364 F.3d 1288, 1294 (11th Cir. 2004).

2. The anti-competitiveness of nonlegal sanctioning attributable to the trade associations researched and the existence of a rule-of-reason defence

An analysis of the anti-competitiveness of nonlegal sanctioning and the availability of a rule-of-reason defence will bear many similarities with the discussion pertaining to their unlawfulness pursuant to Section 1 of the Sherman Act. This is because for both provisions balancing procompetitive benefits against the anti-competitiveness harm placed upon targeted wrongdoers plays a central role.[650] However, there is one important difference: the standard of determining whether unilateral conduct is or is not permissible under Section 2 of the Sherman Act is more clearly defined.[651] In this regard, the 8th Circuit Court of Appeals in *Trace X Chemical, Inc. v. Canadian Industries* must be mentioned.[652] In its judgment, the Court ex-

650 A rule-of-reason analysis cannot only be used to justify the anti-competitiveness of certain nonlegal sanctions pursuant to Section 1 of the Sherman Act, it also governs most monopolization claims under Section 2 of the Sherman Act. See United States v. Microsoft Corp., 253 F.3d 34, 59 (D.C. Cir. 2001); See also Standard Oil Co. of New Jersey v. United States, 221 U.S. 1, 62 (1911). The Court ruled that "*when the second section [of the Sherman Act] is thus harmonized with and made as it was intended to be the complement of the first, it becomes obvious that the criteria to be resorted to in any given case for the purpose of ascertaining whether violations of the section have been committed is the rule of reason, guided by the established law*"; See also R. M. Hilty, A. Früh, "Lizenzkartellrecht: Schweizer Recht. gespiegelt am US-amerikanischen und europäischen Recht", Bern: Stämpfli Verlag AG 2017, p. 64; According to Fifth Circuit Court of Appeals in Mid-Texas Communications v. Am. Tel. Tel., 615 F.2d 1372, 1389 n. 13 (5th Cir. 1980), this entails that a similar rule-of-reason analysis must be carried out under both provisions.

651 This is merely an assumption that can be rebutted. Regardless of this uncertainty, in my opinion, the yardstick with regard to Section 2 of the Sherman Act is more precise by virtue of two reasons: first, a monopoly is not necessarily bad for competition, whereas an agreement between competitors usually is. As a result, drafting a legal rule to assess an infringement of Section 2 of the Sherman Act is more straightforward, as the focus should be on normal business conduct or not. For the establishment of illegality under Section 1 of the Sherman Act such a rule does not exist. There are many legal rules on how to approach an infringement pursuant to Section 1 of the Sherman Act. Second, there is more antitrust case law pertaining to a Section 1 of the Sherman Act violation than a Section 2 of the Sherman Act infringement. Hence, it is logical than there is more divergence in terms of having a clear-cut legal rule with regard to the former provision than the latter provision.

652 Trace X Chemical v. Canadian Industries, 738 F.2d 261 (8th Cir. 1984).

plained that anticompetitive conduct is conduct without a legitimate business purpose, which is not an ordinary business practice typically used in a competitive market.[653] In addition, the Court ruled that anticompetitive intent is insufficient to reach the conclusion that conduct contravenes Section 2 of the Sherman Act,[654] unless according to the 7th Circuit Court of Appeals in *Ball Memorial Hospital, Inc. v. Mutual Hospital Insurance, Inc.*, unilateral conduct is also rational for a non-dominant company.[655] Put differently, in line with the reasoning of the 6th Circuit Court of Appeals in *MCI Communications Corp. v. AT&T*, when a non-monopolist finds unilateral conduct of a monopolist beneficial then it is - arguably - legitimate.[656]

Against this background, for each of the types of nonlegal sanctions described in this research, it will be argued whether they are considered ordinary business practices of the trade associations researched or atypical harmful anticompetitive conduct. As Part II, Chapter 6 of this research outlines, there are many arguments that must be balanced against each other. To prevent a discussion that mirrors and overlaps with that in the previous Chapter, the analysis of whether the role of the trade associations researched in initiating the practice of blacklisting, withdrawing membership, denying membership for expelled members on the basis of an additional entry condition, refusing to deal with an ostracized member and entering the premises of a wrongdoer to collect evidence violates Section 2 of the Sherman Act, will be less thorough.[657]

a. Blacklisting

Each of the six trade associations researched includes the names of wrongdoers for not complying with an arbitral award in a blacklist. Does this mean that it is standard business practice and thereby permissible under Section 2 of the Sherman Act? In my opinion, providing an answer can best be done by approaching this question from the perspective of two groups. The first group comprises those individuals who advocate unimpeded competition (*i.e.* the liberalists). Subsequently, the practice of black-

653 Trace X Chemical v. Canadian Industries, 738 F.2d 261, 266 (8th Cir. 1984).
654 Trace X Chemical v. Canadian Industries, 738 F.2d 261, 268 (8th Cir. 1984).
655 Ball Memorial Hospital, Inc. v. Mutual Hospital Insurance, Inc., 784 F.2d 1325, 1338-1339 (7th Cir. 1986).
656 MCI Communications Corp. v. AT&T, 708 F.2d 1081, 1113 (7th Cir. 1982).
657 United States v. Microsoft Corp., 253 F.3d 34, 59 (D.C. Cir. 2001).

listing should be considered as unilateral conduct of a trade association to ensure the enforcement of arbitral awards of specialized commercial arbitration. It is not convincing that any non-monopolist company (here: targeted wrongdoer) would disagree with such an observation because without this method of extrajudicial enforcement, the whole arbitration system is at risk of being ineffective.

The second group (*i.e.* the institutionalists) consists of individuals who apply the four theories of anti-competitiveness to conduct more comprehensive research in order to address the overgeneralization and superficial reasoning of the first group. In view of this, blacklisting is the least restrictive measure to ensure the success of specialized commercial arbitration, which in turn enhances total welfare and consumer welfare (*i.e.* the profit-sacrifice and no-economic-sense tests). Both procompetitive benefits offset the adverse effects placed upon blacklisted wrongdoers, even though this type of unilateral conduct can exclude such a competitor from the other members of a relevant trade association from an adjacent second-tier commodities market (*i.e.* the effects-balancing test and the equally efficient competitor test). The anticompetitive harm is proportionate to realize economic and consumer benefits (*i.e.* the disproportionality test).

Whichever group is chosen matters. The second group undertakes a far more detailed research and must be preferred, whereas the first group is not useful here. Albeit that blacklisting is indeed the least restrictive of all the extrajudicial measures, how it is structured by the trade associations researched is not. Five recommendations must be made in order to escape antitrust liability under Section 2 of the Sherman Act. First, blacklists should not be made publicly available, but accessible for members only. Second, it would be better to allow a third party to collect, handle and disseminate the names of a wrongdoer in a blacklist, instead of a trade association which is often biased. Third, the dissemination of the names of disloyal industry actors in a blacklist should only occur after clearly defined deadlines have lapsed and a final warning. Fourth, when the effect of blacklisting also targets an industry actor's social standing, more reluctance should be shown. Fifth, every blacklisted member should be given the opportunity to ask for an internal appeal to object to such decision.

b. Membership rules and barriers for market access

With regard to membership rules and barriers for market access, the following two Paragraphs focus on whether a withdrawal of membership and difficulties in being re-admitted to membership after such an expulsion are considered anticompetitive within the meaning of Section 2 of the Sherman Act.

i. Withdrawal of membership

The majority of the trade associations researched have included the possibility to ostracize a wrongdoer in their bylaws and rules.[658] As a result, a targeted industry actor has a substantial risk of being ousted from the relevant adjacent second-tier commodities market. Considering that Section 2 of the Sherman Act is primarily aimed at preventing harm done to competition by excluding market participants, the restrictiveness of an expulsion must not be underestimated.[659] Whereas the liberalists' view is in favour of exculpating any of the trade associations researched that engage in ostracizing a member, the reasons being that expulsions are common in many commodities industries and are well within the competences of these associations to organize a model of extrajudicial enforcement that is as effective as possible to punish disobedient industry actors (*i.e.* freedom of association), the institutionalists would not reach such a conclusion prematurely. Instead, they would apply the four theories of anti-competitiveness as a yardstick to consider a violation of Section 2 of the Sherman Act.

Before conducing such a balancing exercise, the extent of the anti-competitiveness must be encapsulated. To do so, the essential facility doctrine plays a pivotal role. This theory is applicable when a denial of access to an essential facility enables a monopolist to extend its monopoly in an adjacent market.[660] In establishing liability under this doctrine for the trade associations which impose a withdrawal of membership on a recalcitrant member, the 7th Circuit Court of Appeals in *MCI Communications Corp. v. ATCT* reiterated US case law and summarized previous mandatory aspects developed in the judgments of US courts in a test consisting of four

658 GAFTA does not engage in suspending or terminating membership, unlike the other trade associations researched.

659 W. F. Adkinson, Jr., K. L. Grimm, and C. N. Bryan, "Enforcement of Section 2 of the Sherman Act: Theory and Practice", *Working Paper* 2008, p. 3.

660 D. Gabel and D. F. Weiman, "*Opening Networks to Competition: The Regulation and Pricing of Access*", New York: Springer Science+Business Media 1998, p. 190.

prongs.[661] Subsequently, to assess when a refusal of access to an essential facility constitutes actionable monopolization, this test requires the "*(1) control of the facility by the monopolist; (2) a competitor's inability to reasonably duplicate the facility; (3) the monopolist's denial of the facility's use to the competitor; and (4) the feasibility of providing access to the facility*".[662]

Whereas in Part II, Chapter 6, II, b, i all of the four requirements were discussed in a concise review, given that the essential facility doctrine is more appropriate with regard to Section 2 of the Sherman Act, a more detailed discussion is required. Unfortunately, this is a rather arbitrary and difficult task. None of the prongs of the four-step essential facility doctrine test are sufficiently clear to give practical guidance.[663] What constitutes "essential", "reasonable duplication", "denial" and "feasibility" are ill-defined and can vary from case to case. In my opinion, *Lao* provides the best way to interpret whether a monopolist refuses access to an essential facility.[664] *Lao* summarizes the four prongs in three prongs, namely in terms of essentiality: a denial of access, "non- rivalrousness", and feasibility.[665] With regard to the first requirement, a facility is essential when control of it has the potential to eliminate competition and when duplication of the facility is not reasonably possible.[666] This follows also from the previously discussed judgment of the Court of Appeals of the District of Columbia Cir-

661 MCI Communications Corp. v. ATCT, 708 F.2d 1081 (7th Cir. 1983); The judgment serves as a clarification. See S. M. Colino, "*Competition Law of the EU and UK*", Oxford: Oxford University Press 2019, p. 393.

662 MCI Communications Corp. v. ATCT, 708 F.2d 1081, 1132 (7th Cir. 1983); The test was developed as an obiter dictum. See C. Enaux, "*Effiziente Marktregulierung in der Telekommunikation: Möglichkeiten und Grenzen der Rückführung sektorspezifischer Sonderregulierung in das allgemeine Wettbewerbsrecht*", Münster: Lit Verlag 2004, p. 156; Subsequent US court judgements have reiterated this test. See, for example, Intergraph Corp. v. Intel Corp., 195 F.3d 1346, 1356, 1357 (Fed. Dis. 1999); City of Anaheim v. S. Cal. Edison Co., 955 F.2d 1373, 1380 (9th Cir. 1992); City of Malden v. Union Elec. Co., 887 F.2d 157, 160 (8th Cir. 1989); Ferguson v. Greater Pocatello Chamber of Commerce, Inc., 848 F.2d 976, 983 (9th Cir. 1988).

663 E. Hope, "*Competition and Trade Policies: Coherence or Conflict*", London/New York: Routledge 2005, p. 61.

664 M. Lao, "Search, Essential Facilities, and the Antitrust Duty to Deal", *Northwest Journal of Technology and Intellectual Property, Vol. 11, Is. 5* 2013, p. 298-304.

665 Ibid., p. 301. *Lao* considers the first two requirements under the four-step essential facility doctrine under the concept of "essentiality". He does this by arguing that the infeasibility of duplication requirement is "*almost inextricable from the essentiality concept*".

666 Ibid., p. 298.

cuit in *Hecht v. Pro-football, Inc.* When applying this definition to assess whether the services provided by the trade associations researched are essential, two arguments corroborate such finding. First, there are no feasible alternatives following a withdrawal of membership for a targeted industry actor. Second, it is clear that access to the services is vital to being competitive within the relevant adjacent second-tier commodities market for such a wrongdoer.

The second requirement of the essential facility doctrine, namely the denial of access, does not normally give rise to misinterpretation by US courts.[667] This entails that a withdrawal of membership can be seen as a denial of access to the services of a relevant trade association. Pertaining to the feasibility requirement, the 9th Circuit Court of Appeals in *City of Anaheim et al v. Southern California Edison* ruled that it should be interpreted to mean that the monopolist has "no valid business reason" for denying access to the facility.[668] This entails that such unilateral conduct must be balanced against efficiency justifications, or the four theories of anti-competitiveness. While approaching each of them separately is appropriate, a succinct discussion is satisfactory. A withdrawal of membership addresses the loophole in enforcement when blacklisting alone is not sufficient to ensure compliance with an arbitral award. Subsequently, it has a positive impact on maintaining an efficient and successful system of specialized commercial arbitration. This enhances total welfare and consumer welfare. Adverse effects for targeted industry actors do not outweigh these positive effects *(i.e.* the effects-balancing test) if there are procedural safeguards in place comparable to those described in Part II, Chapter 6, E II, 2 b, i.[669] There are also no alternative methods of extrajudicial enforcement available when blacklisting is ineffective and the exclusionary profits for a relevant commodities market are greater than the harm inflicted upon a targeted wrongdoer (*i.e.* the profit-sacrifice and no-economic-sense test). Expulsions are likely to exclude a targeted recalcitrant member from the market, but the procompetitive benefits offset such harm (*i.e.* the equally efficient competitor test). Put differently, the anticompetitive harm is propor-

667 Ibid., p. 301. Only in the case of search, this requirement is not that easy to fulfil (*e.g.* Google search inquiry, etc.).

668 City of Anaheim et al v. Southern California Edison 995, F2d 1373, 1380 (1992).

669 These are (i) the imposition of a withdrawal of membership only when blacklisting is ineffective; (ii) a case-by-case imposition; (iii) an imposition of a withdrawal of membership only when internal appeal possibilities are exhausted; and (iv) regaining membership following an expulsion is not made too difficult.

tionate to the economic and consumer benefits generated (*i.e.* the disproportionality test).

However, the manner in which withdrawals of membership are structured by the trade associations researched does not take the least restrictive form. Instead, a withdrawal of membership procedure should be based on clearly defined, transparent, non-discriminatory reviewable criteria that allow for cumulative penalties enforceable in national courts, with a final threat of a suspension, or in the worst case scenario when non-compliance is combined with other misconduct, an indefinite expulsion provided that the trade association has objective, reasonable and legitimate reasons for doing so which are based on fair and neutral criteria (*e.g.* do not favour certain members over others). In addition, expelled members should be given the chance to request an internal appeal tribunal to review such a decision and must be advised of the possibility to ask for recourse in public courts. If these recommendations are adhered to, it is unlikely that the trade associations researched violate Section 2 of the Sherman Act.

ii. Denial of membership for expelled members on the basis of an additional entry condition

When it is made more difficult for an ostracized member to regain membership and, as a result, access to an essential facility is unnecessarily denied, this can be incongruous with Section 2 of the Sherman Act. Any trade association should not impose overly burdensome and gratuitous entry requirements for wrongdoers.[670] The lapse of a period of two years following an expulsion and the approval by a Board of Directors tend to bar disloyal former members from easily re-obtaining membership. Whereas both measures are restrictive, it is the latter entry condition that can be seen as the most harmful. It carries the risk of refusing access to an essential facility without explanation, valid grounds and is based on arbitrary decision-making. Regardless of the fact that it renders an expulsion a better deterrent, as regaining membership may be indefinitely excluded once an arbitral board is satisfied, serious anticompetitive effects are inevitable for

670 For the reason that only two of the trade associations researched impose additional re-entry barriers following a withdrawal of membership, the liberalists' approach is not applicable. Such an imposition is not standard business practice. Subsequently, the focus is on the institutionalists' approach by applying the four theories of anti-competitiveness.

targeted industry actors. It is unreasonable and disproportionate to guarantee a well-functioning system of specialized commercial arbitration, which enhances total welfare and consumer welfare (*i.e.* the disproportionality test). Adverse effects for ostracized former members that are arbitrarily denied re-obtaining membership outweigh both efficiency gains (*i.e.* the effects-balancing test). Arbitrarily denying re-admission to membership for an expelled member is also likely to exclude this wrongdoer from the market (*i.e.* the equally efficient competitor test). This is because of the necessity to have access to the services/essential facility of a relevant trade association. Less restrictive measures are also available to guarantee the effectiveness of a withdrawal of membership (*i.e.* the post-sacrifice and no-economic-sense test). Instead of allowing a Board of Directors to deny a reapplication for membership, an independent third-party panel (not connected with the relevant trade association) should be tasked with doing this by taking clearly defined, equally applicable, transparent, non-discriminatory criteria into account, such as (i) the current liquidity status of the former member; (ii) an unwillingness to pay the fine for non-compliance with the arbitral award; and (iii) evidence of probable disloyalty in the future.

Concerning the lapse of a two-year waiting period in order to re-apply for membership following an expulsion, one must again conduct a balancing exercise by applying the four theories of anti-competitiveness. Absent any waiting period, any expulsion would be rendered ineffective. Once an ostracized member satisfies the entry requirements, readmission to membership is possible. This raises the ensuing question: Why not allow the trade associations researched to impose a waiting period before an expelled member can reapply for membership? In my opinion, it is not unfair to give a trade association the possibility to enforce a waiting period on wrongdoers, but its duration makes it anticompetitive (*i.e.* the disproportionality test). It would be better to impose a less restrictive alternative by imposing a six-month timeframe for non-payment of an award or, if this is combined with previous other misconduct, a time period of one year (*i.e.* the profit-sacrifice and no-economic-sense test). This ensures the success of a withdrawal of membership which in turn ensures a successful operational system of specialized commercial arbitration that enhances total welfare and consumer welfare. Both benefits offset the adverse effects caused by a denial of regaining membership/access to an essential facility during the waiting period (*i.e.* the effects-balancing test and the equally efficient competitor test).

c. Refusal to deal with an expelled member

Only one of the trade associations researched instructs its members not to conduct business with an expelled member. As a result, one can conclude that it is not a typical business practice in the commodities trade. The liberalists' view must not be followed. Instead, the anti-competitiveness of such unilateral conduct must be assessed against the four theories as employed by the institutionalists. Reaching a different conclusion when compared with Section 1 of the Sherman Act is unlikely.[671] The anticompetitive impact for targeted industry actors is significant. But more so, it is not necessary to guarantee the success of specialized commercial arbitration. The practice of blacklisting and expulsions are sufficient to do so and constitute less restrictive alternatives (*i.e.* the profit-sacrifice and no-economic-sense test). The overall impact of a refusal to deal with an ostracized member is so severe that it clearly cannot be justified by total welfare and consumer welfare benefits as generated by specialized commercial arbitration (*i.e.* the effects-balancing test). Such harm is also disproportionate to attain both benefits (*i.e.* the disproportionality test) and excludes an industry competitor from the market without sufficiently generating these benefits (*i.e.* the equally efficient competitor test). No structural changes can exempt trade associations which orchestrate such a measure from antitrust liability pursuant to Section 2 of the Sherman Act.

d. Entering the premises of a recalcitrant industry actor without a warrant

Similar to Section 1 of the Sherman Act, despite some reputational harm not being unlikely when other industry actors hear about the premises of a recalcitrant industry actor being entered without a warrant, it is difficult to quantify the level of business harm for a targeted wrongdoer. Such conduct does not fit within the anti-competitiveness standard pursuant to Section 2 of the Sherman Act. Neither is it standard business practice of the trade association researched, nor are the four theories of anti-competitiveness applicable.

671 See Part II, Chapter 6, E, II, 2, c for the reasons why a refusal to deal with an ostracized member violates Section 1 of the Sherman Act.

III. Interim conclusion

All of the six trade associations researched are engaged in anticompetitive "monopolization" to the extent they disseminate the names of wrongdoers in blacklists, withdraw membership, refuse a reapplication for membership of an expelled member on the basis of a denial by a Board of Directors, or because a two-year period has not elapsed, and refuse to deal with an ostracized member. Besides the last measure which cannot be justified, if the first three extrajudicial measures are not structured in the least restrictive manner, the responsible trade association violates Section 2 of the Sherman Act.

C. *The functioning of the concept of illegal attempted monopolization as a safety net when one or more of the trade associations researched does not hold sufficient market power to establish monopolization*

In the event the FTC and/or US courts reach a different decision with regard to the existence of monopoly power held by one or more of the trade associations in the market for regulation and private ordering concerning the US territory, these institutions can still be held accountable under Section 2 of the Sherman Act when they participate in an anticompetitive attempt to monopolize.[672] For the purpose of this Chapter, these trade associations are referred to as "residual trade associations". However, to violate this provision different requirements must be fulfilled. According to the Supreme Court in *Spectrum Sports, Inc. v. McQuillan,* these necessitate that (i) there is a specific intent to monopolize; (ii) a dangerous probability of achieving monopoly power exists; and (iii) the defendant has participated in anticompetitive conduct.[673]

I. Specific intent to monopolize

With regard to the first requirement, "the specific intent to monopolize", there must not be proof of actual monopolization, but instead whether

---

672 Both concepts do not require bilateral action. See United States v. American Airlines, Inc., 743 F.2D, 1114, 1116-1117 (5th Cir. 1984).

673 Spectrum Sports, Inc. v. McQuillan, 506 U.S. 447, 456 (1993).

there is a specific intent to produce monopoly power.[674] However, neither a mere possession of market power is synonymous with a specific intent,[675] nor is an intent to prevail over one's competitor[676], or engaging in vigorous competition[677] sufficient to satisfy this element. There are two ways to prove whether the "specific intent to monopolize" requirement is complied with: first, by looking at the nature of the unilateral conduct imposed by the relevant residual trade association. According to this method, there must be evidence that the intention of the conduct is to restrain competition unreasonably.[678] Absent such exclusionary or anticompetitive conduct, it is not possible to support a finding of specific intent.[679] Second, specific intent may also be corroborated by looking in the business documents of an offender. Even though documents made by lower level officials without authority do not bear sufficient evidence to establish a specific intent[680] and regardless of the fact that isolated documents produced by a company's official are inadequate to prove a specific intent,[681] coherent documents made by officials of a relevant trade association provide good indicators.

That being said, with reference to residual trade associations, it is not only necessary to establish whether they have a specific intent to monopolize in relevant markets for regulation and private ordering, but also in the relevant adjacent second-tier commodities markets. This follows from the theory of monopoly leveraging, as was discussed in Part II, Chapter 7, B, I, 1 by virtue of illegal "monopolization". Unfortunately, establishing whether this element is fulfilled is rather difficult. Very few judgments of US courts have confirmed the presence of this element.[682] With reference to the regionally-defined relevant markets for regulation and private ordering, if residual trade associations do not have sufficient market power to speak of monopolization, in the event these institutions impose any anti-

---

674 General Industries Corp., 810 F.2d 795, 801 (8th Cir. 1987).
675 Hunt-Wesson Foods, Inc. v. Ragu Foods, Inc., 627 F.2d 919 (9th Cir. 1989).
676 General Industries Corp., 810 F.2d 795, 801 (8th Cir. 1987).
677 Adjusters Replace-A-Car, Inc. v. Agency Rent-A-Car, Inc., 735 F.2d 884, 887-888 (5th Cir. 1984).
678 General Industries Corp., 810 F.2d 795, 801 (8th Cir. 1987).
679 Satellite Television & Associated Resources, Inc. v. Continental Cablevision, 714 F.2d 351, 358 (4th Cir. 1983).
680 MCI Communications Corp. v. AT&T, 708 F.2d 1081, 1143 (7th Cir. 1982).
681 Conoco, Inc. v. Inman Oil Company, Inc. 774 F.2d 895, 905 (8th Cir. 1985).
682 R. D. Blair and D. D. Sokol, "*The Oxford Handbook of International Antitrust Economics – Vol. 2*", Oxford: Oxford University Press 2015, p. 156.

competitive nonlegal sanction on wrongdoers that are active on relevant adjacent second-tier commodities markets, a specific intent to monopolize can be established in the first and also the second market.[683] Because the relevant residual trade association can only ensure compliance with its arbitral awards when (i) it holds a near monopoly type of position in the relevant market for regulation and private ordering; and (ii) a sufficiently large group of industry actors are deterred from being subjected to any type of nonlegal sanction on the relevant adjacent second-tier commodities market, a specific intent to monopolize exists on both markets. Documents made by officials, such as, with regard to the DDC a letter published by its managing director, indicating the impact of this trade association and discussing this association's current and long-term objective can be used to establish the presence of specific intent on the relevant market for regulation and private ordering.[684] With respect to the relevant adjacent second-tier commodities market, such a letter by one of the other trade associations' officials can also not be excluded.

II. Dangerous probability of achieving monopoly power

Under the second element of "attempted monopolization", the FTC and/or US courts must determine whether there is a dangerous probability that the attempt to monopolize will be successful. This is necessary to distinguish aggressive conduct, which may produce procompetitive benefits, from anticompetitive behavior, which does not.[685] As a requirement, a residual trade association must possess to some degree market power[686] (i)

683 Of course, any US court can reach a different outcome.

684 https://www.nyddc.com/ddc-news--events/rapaport-qa-with-david-lasher-managing-director-of-the-new-york-diamond-dealers-club. This is merely an example as it is unlikely that the DDC does not hold a monopoly position in the market for regulation and private ordering on the US territory.

685 P. H. LaRue, H. M. Applebaum, T. Calvani, W. D. Collins, J. T. Halverson, T. W. Johnston, J. A. Jones, J. F. Rill, W. M. Sayre, L. Schlitt, and R. A. Whiting, "*The Robinson-Patman Act: Policy and Law – Vol. 1*", Chicago: American Bar Association 1989, p. 25.

686 M. Dolmans, "*The Dominance and Monopolies Review*", London: Law Business Research Ltd 2014, p. 368. The required amount of a dangerous probability of achieving monopoly power is less than the standard of market power with reference to monopolization; See also McGahee v. N. Propane Gas Co., 858 F.2d 1487, 1505 (11th Cir. 1988).

from the time an anticompetitive nonlegal sanction is imposed;[687](ii) which is sufficient to illustrate a serious threat of monopolization;[688] and (iii) if it is held in a market which is susceptible for monopolization and not highly competitive.[689]

Against this background, even if one of the trade associations researched does not hold a monopoly position in the market for regulation and private ordering on the US territory, it is likely that such an association still has a dangerous probability of achieving market power in that market. This is because the market for regulation and private ordering concerning the US territory for all of the trade associations researched is not highly competitive and the degree of market power possessed by them can be seen as constituting a serious threat of monopolization. There is, however, one peculiarity: the nonlegal sanctions imposed by such an association do not target industry actors in the same market, but instead punish industry actors active in a relevant adjacent second-tier commodities market. According to the theory of monopoly leveraging, this doctrine is applicable when the near monopoly position in one market helps create a dangerous probability of a monopoly in the second market.[690] This raises the ensuing question: Do the industry actors that conduct business on the basis of the rules and bylaws of the relevant remaining trade association possess such a near monopoly position in the latter market? In my opinion, without access to such an association which provides a plurality of (facilitating) services, it is difficult to be competitive on the second-tier market. Most industry actors would prefer to contract under these rules. Despite the existence of other trade associations offering similar services, it may very well be possible that a near monopoly position can be established. If so, there is a dangerous probability of achieving monopoly power.

---

687 P. E. Areeda and H. Hovenkamp, "*Antitrust Law –Vol. 3*", New York: Aspen Publishers 2008, p. 446.

688 R. L. Miller, "*Business Law Today, Comprehensive: Text and Cases: Diverse, Ethical, Online, and Global Environment – 10th Edition*", Stamford: Cengage Learning 2015, p. 886.

689 United States v. Empire Gas Corp., 537 F.2d 296 (8th Cir. 1976). This is a price-fixing judgment and not comparable to nonlegal sanctions. Yet, the logic of this case can be transposed to the situation of the imposition of nonlegal sanctioning by the relevant remaining researched trade association.

690 M. Dolmans, "*The Dominance and Monopolies Review*", London: Law Business Research Ltd 2014, p. 373.

III. Anticompetitive conduct (and rule-of-reason)

With regard to the requirement that residual trade associations must have participated in anticompetitive conduct, the same logic must be applied as in the study of anti-competitiveness within the concept of monopolization.[691] The focus is again on exclusionary conduct absent a legitimate business purpose under the theory of monopoly leveraging.[692] Subsequently, a trade association engaged in the dissemination of the names of wrongdoers in publicly available blacklists, withdrawals of membership, denial of a reapplication for membership of an expelled member on the basis of a denial by a Board of Directors, or because a two-year period has not elapsed is engaged in anticompetitive conduct when these measures are not structured in the least restrictive manner. When a trade association instructs its members to refuse to deal with an ostracized member, this is even more clearly evident. Establishing anticompetitive conduct cannot be avoided.

IV. Interim conclusion

With regard to residual trade associations for which in the unlikely event no monopolization can be established in the markets for regulation and private ordering concerning the US territory, the existence of an unlawful attempt to monopolize serves as a catch-all provision. Whereas anticompetitive conduct and a specific intent to monopolize are not contentious, the same cannot be said for the third and last element, namely the dangerous probability of achieving monopoly power. Whereas a near monopoly position in the markets for regulation and private ordering concerning the US territory can be established, in the relevant adjacent second-tier commodities markets reaching such a decision is debatable. Whichever line of reasoning is followed, it impacts the outcome of whether residual trade associations violate Section 2 of the Sherman Act by undertaking an unlawful attempt to monopolize.

---

691 See Part II, Chapter 7, B, II.

692 E. T. Sullivan, "*Nonprice Predation under Section 2 of the Sherman Act*", Chicago: American Bar Association 1991, p. 55.

D. *Unlawful conspiracy to monopolize by members of the trade associations researched*

Section 2 of the Sherman Act is principally aimed at unilateral action, which is reflected in the concept of "monopolization" and "attempted monopolization". The reason being that anticompetitive concerted action is usually prosecuted under Section 1 of the Sherman Act.[693] There is, however, an important exception to this rule: when individuals and/or undertakings engage in anticompetitive concerted action which is directed at the acquisition of monopoly power, Section 2 of the Sherman Act is equally applicable.[694] This is referred to as "conspiracy to monopolize". While this concept is of no importance to determine whether the trade associations researched can be held accountable for their role in the imposition of non-legal sanctions under Section 2 of the Sherman Act, it is a good method to determine potential unlawfulness of their members in the execution of these extrajudicial measures under this provision.

According to the 2nd Circuit Court of Appeals in *Volvo North America Corp. v. Men's Int'l Prof'l Tennis Council* and the 9th Circuit Court of Appeals in *Hunt-Wesson Foods, Inc. v. Ragu Foods, Inc.*, three conjunctive elements must then be fulfilled.[695] First, the existence of an agreement between two or more parties.[696] Second, a specific intent to monopolize. Third, at least one overt act in furtherance of the agreement. Whereas the 7th Circuit Court of Appeals in *Great Escape, Inc. v. Union City Body* and the 10th Circuit Court of Appeals in *Olsen v. Progressive Music Supply, Inc.* even require the fulfilment of a fourth element, namely that there must be an "effect upon a substantial amount of interstate commerce",[697] this last element will not be discussed concerning the members of the trade associations researched. The reasons for this are two-fold: first, it is inconsistent with the rule developed by the Supreme Court's judgment in *American To-*

---

693 L. J. Oswald, "*The Law of Marketing – 2th Edition*", Mason: South-Western Cengage Learning 2010, p. 112.

694 U.S. Department of Justice, "Competition and Monopoly: Single-firm Conduct under Section 2 of the Sherman Act", *U.S. Department of Justice* 2008, p. 5.

695 Volvo North America Corp. v. Men's Int'l Prof'l Tennis Council, 857 F.2d 55, 74 (2d Cir. 1988); Hunt-Wesson Foods, Inc. v. Ragu Foods, Inc., 627 F.2d 919, 926 (9th Cir. 1980).

696 See also The Yale Law Journal Company, "Intra-Enterprise Conspiracy under the Sherman Act", *The Yale Law Journal Company, Vol. 63, No.* 3 1954, p. 372.

697 Great Escape, Inc. v. Union City Body., 791 F.2d 532, 540-541 (7th Cir. 1986); Olsen v. Progressive Music Supply, Inc., 703 F.2d 432, 438 (10th Cir. 1983).

bacco Co. v. United States which does not necessitate the establishment of an "*actual exclusion of competitors*".[698] Second, only two judgments have supported the existence of an additional requirement, whereas the majority of US court decisions have not.

By taking this into account, the following Paragraphs discuss the three elements which are necessary to determine if the role the members of the trade associations researched in executing nonlegal sanctions constitutes an illegal "conspiracy to monopolize" under Section 2 of the Sherman Act. Determining the degree of market power, establishing a dangerous probability of success, or creating a market definition is unnecessary.[699]

I. The existence of an agreement between two or more parties

The evidence required to prove an agreement in a claim of conspiracy to monopolize is similar to that of Section 1 of the Sherman Act, since a written contract, a combination, or a conspiracy fulfils this requirement.[700] As was described in Part II, Chapter 6, B, I, II and III, the members of the trade associations researched have entered into a written contract to execute nonlegal sanctions imposed by a trade association. This is true because these industry actors have agreed to adhere to the bylaws and rules of a relevant trade association in which such extralegal measures are incorporated when becoming a member. But even more so when members contract on

698 American Tobacco Co. v. United States, 328 U.S. 781, 809 (1946); Conversely, in my opinion, the judgment of the United States District Court of California in Standfacts Credit Services, Inc. v. Experian Information, 405 F.Supp.2d 1141 (Standfacts Credit Services, Inc. v. Experian Information, 405 F.Supp.2d 1141 (C.D. Cal. 2005) is an important exception to this observation. The Court requires a "causal antitrust injury" as a fourth requirement; This legal rule is a reiteration from the 9th Circuit Court of Appeals judgment in Paladin Assoc., Inc. v. Mont. Power Co., 328 F.3d 1145, 1158 (2003).

699 See United States v. Consolidated laundries Corp., 291 F.2d 563, 573 (2d Cir. 1961) [emphasis]; However, the uselessness of conducting a market definition is debatable. See, for example, J. L. Harwell, "The Relevant Market Concept in Conspiracy to Monopolize Cases under Section 2 of the Sherman Act", *The University of Chicago Law Review* 1977, p. 808-812.

700 T. V. Vakerics, "*Antitrust Basics*", New York: Law Journal Press 2006, p. 5-3; See also, Nova Designs, Inc. v. Scuba Retailers Association, 202 F.3d 1088, 1092 (9th Cir. 2000). Therein, the 9th Circuit Court of Appeals ruled that when no agreement under Section 1 of the Sherman Act exists, then there is also no agreement under Section 2 of the Sherman Act.

the basis of standardized contracts which refer to a broader arbitration agreement that includes nonlegal sanctions.

II. Specific intent to monopolize

The Eastern District of Illinois District Court in its judgment in *Choiceparts, LLC v. General Motors Corp.* explained that "*concerted action by knowing participants who have a specific intent to achieve a monopoly*" is required to prove a specific intent to monopolize under a conspiracy to monopolize claim.[701] Alternatively, the District Court for the Western District of Missouri in *United States v. Kansas City Star Company* argued that a specific intent signifies "*that the defendants must have done certain things in monopoly as their objective, which, if successfully performed, could result in actual monopolization*".[702] In my opinion, both definitions provide insufficient guidance on the necessary degree of intent which is required. While one could argue that a specific intent is similar to a claim of "attempted monopolization", as was mentioned above, should not a different threshold be applicable to measure the required amount when it involves a single actor as opposed to market participants acting in concert?[703] Unfortunately, neither legal doctrine nor US courts have provided much needed elucidation. It appears that again the restrictiveness of unilateral conduct and documentary evidence must be used to analyse whether a specific intent to monopolize exists. Even though the latter option can be used to prove fulfilment of this element, the former option is more obvious. This is because the 7th Circuit Court of Appeals in *Great Escape, Inc.* provided well-articulated guidance to measure when restrictive conduct is synonymous with a specific intent to monopolize. Following this judgment, this is the case when conduct "*has no legitimate business justification other than to destroy or to damage competition,*"[704] or violates Section 1 of the Sherman Act.[705]

---

701 Choiceparts v. General Motors Corporation, No. 01 C 0067 (N.D. Ill. 2005), para. 12. The specific intent to monopolize requirement is considered as an element of heightened intent.

702 United States v. Kansas City Star Company, No. 18444 (D. Kans. 1953).

703 D. T. Hibner, Jr., "Litigation as an Overt Act in Furtherance of an Attempt to Monopolize", *Ohio State Law Journal, Vol. 38, Nr. 2* 1977, p. 246.

704 Great Escape v. Union City Body Co., Inc., 791 F.2d 532, 541 (7th Cir. 1986). This is called predatory conduct.

705 E. T. Sullivan, "*Nonprice Predation under Section 2 of the Sherman Act*", Chicago: American Bar Association 1991, p. 58.

In consideration of the foregoing, the members of the trade associations researched execute nonlegal sanctions imposed by these institutions. As a result, these members engage in a concerted action to drive disloyal industry actors out of the market and even out of business.[706] This is true with regard to the dissemination of the names of wrongdoers in publicly available blacklists, withdrawals of membership, denials of membership for expelled members on the basis of a denial by a Board of Directors, or because a two-year waiting period has not elapsed, if not structured in the least restrictive manner. Furthermore, this is also true pertaining to refusals to deal with expelled members. These measures do not have a legitimate business justification other than to destroy or to damage competition. On the ground that they violated Section 1 of the Sherman Act, a specific intent to monopolize is established. Members that execute these extrajudicial measures do so with a specific intent to achieve a monopoly.

III. Overt act in furtherance of the agreement

The last argument which is required to establish whether the members of the trade associations researched can be held accountable for a conspiracy to monopolize for their role in executing anticompetitive nonlegal sanctions requires "*the commission of at least some overt act in furtherance of the conspiracy*".[707] Even this formulation might appear vague, the Supreme Court in *Yates v. United States* explained that this should be interpreted to mean that that the conspiracy is simply at work.[708] Further proof in support of this was given in *Lafave & Scott*.[709] According to both actors, "*if the agreement has been established but the object has not been attained, virtually any act will satisfy the overt act* [in furtherance of the agreement] *requirement*".[710] This is because its form which derives from the agreement is not important.

As it appears that both US case law and legal doctrine interpret the "overt act in furtherance of the agreement" requirement as a symbolic

706 A good illustration of this can be found in United States v. Consolidated Laundries Corp., 291 F.2d 563, 572-573.

707 Key Enterprises of Delaware v. Venice Hosp, 919 F.2d 1550, 1564 (11th Cir. 1990).

708 Yates v. United States 354 U.S. 298, 334 (1957).

709 W. R. Lafave and A.W. Scott, Jr., "*Substantive Criminal Law - 2nd Edition*", St. Paul: West Publishing Company 1986.

710 Ibid., p. 549.

catch-all element, the participation of the members of a trade association in executing anticompetitive nonlegal sanctions which arise from any relevant agreement is sufficient to satisfy the third element of a conspiracy to monopolize. Albeit that some might argue that the use of such a general observation is inappropriate, in my opinion, using a more in-depth form of argumentation is redundant.

IV. Interim conclusion

Members of the trade associations researched can be held accountable for their role in executing nonlegal sanctions directed at disloyal industry actors under Section 2 of the Sherman Act. In the event a wrongdoer is extrajudicially punished by a relevant trade association, to the extent such measure or measures are anticompetitive and cannot be offset by procompetitive benefits, that trade associations' members engage in concerted action with the aim to acquire monopoly power. This is because their role in the execution of the measure or measures satisfies the three-element conjunctive test which is required to establish an illegal "conspiracy to monopolize". They have entered into a written agreement, have a specific intent to monopolize by executing anticompetitive nonlegal sanctions, and are engaged in overt acts in furtherance of the agreement.

E. Key findings

Apart from the possibility to prosecute the trade associations researched and their members under Section 1 of the Sherman Act when they impose and execute anticompetitive nonlegal sanctions to discipline recalcitrant industry actors, Section 2 of the Sherman Act provides an alternative legal basis to hold both actors accountable with regard to antitrust law. As a requirement, the trade associations researched must have unlawfully "monopolized" or have "attempted to monopolize" and their members should have committed an illegal "conspiracy to monopolize".[711]

On the basis of the theory of monopoly leveraging, it is likely that all of the six trade associations researched have engaged in an illegal monopoly by disseminating the names of wrongdoers in publicly available blacklists, withdrawing membership without precautions and due process, arbitrarily

711 See Part II, Chapter 7, A.

denying, or requiring excessively long waiting period for reapplication for membership and instructing their members to refuse to deal with an ostracized member.[712] However, in the unlikely event that at least one of the trade associations researched does not hold a monopoly position, any anticompetitive attempt to monopolize is also illegal under Section 2 of the Sherman Act.[713] This concept serves as a safety net when the required amount of monopoly power is not reached. When such a residual trade association imposes nonlegal sanctions on wrongdoers, an attribution of liability under this provision requires the fulfilment of three conjunctive elements. Whereas the first two requirements are undeniably met, which consist of the existence of anticompetitive conduct[714] and a specific intent to monopolize,[715] the same cannot be said with regard to the dangerous probability of achieving monopoly power.[716] This is because even though it is presumed that any residual trade association has a near monopoly position in the relevant market for regulation and private ordering concerning the US territory, when this institution imposes anticompetitive nonlegal sanctions, its effects are not felt within the same market, but by disloyal industry actors operating on an adjacent second-tier relevant commodities market. This is where the theory of monopoly leveraging plays a central role. This theory requires that in such situation, the near monopoly position in the first market must create a dangerous probability of a monopoly in the second market. Unfortunately, it is unsure whether such a position is held on the latter market. Much depends on arguing whether their members are dependent on the services of a relevant residual trade association to speak of a near monopoly position. If this is confirmed, the element of dangerous probability of achieving monopoly power is satisfied and the residual trade association can be held accountable for an illegal attempt to monopolize when imposing anticompetitive nonlegal sanctions.

This is more obvious to attribute an infringement of Section 2 of the Sherman Act when the members of the trade associations researched execute anticompetitive nonlegal sanctions.[717] In such scenario they conspire to monopolize, because they fulfil the three-part test. Not only have they entered into a written agreement[718] and have a specific intent to monopo-

712 See Part II, Chapter 7, B.
713 See Part II, Chapter 7, C.
714 See Part II, Chapter 7, C, I.
715 See Part II, Chapter 7, C, II.
716 See Part II, Chapter 7, C, III.
717 See Part II, Chapter 7, D.
718 See Part II, Chapter 7, D, I.

lize,[719] but they also took part in overt acts in furtherance of the agreement.[720]

A rule-of-reason analysis to allow the trade associations researched and their members to escape antitrust illegality under Section 2 of the Sherman Act is available. Whereas refusals to deal with expelled members can never be justified, this is not true by virtue of the other three nonlegal sanctions which restrict Section 2 of the Sherman Act. When these measures are structured in the least restrictive manner, it is unlikely that both actors can be held accountable for a violation of this provision. With reference to the dissemination of the names of wrongdoers in a blacklist, such a list should not be made publicly available, but accessible for members only. Furthermore, a third party should be tasked with the collection, handling and dissemination of the names of a wrongdoer in a blacklist after clearly defined deadlines have lapsed, and a final warning. Lastly, the possibility of internal appeal against such a decision should be introduced and more reluctance should be shown when an industry actor's social standing would be affected.

With regard to withdrawals of membership, such a procedure should be based on clearly defined, transparent, non-discriminatory reviewable criteria that allow for cumulative fines enforceable in national courts, with a final threat of a suspension, or in the worst case scenario when non-compliance is combined with other misconduct, or an indefinite expulsion provided the trade association has objective, reasonable and legitimate reasons for doing so which are based on fair and neutral criteria (*e.g.* do not favour certain members over others). Moreover, ostracized members should be given the chance to request an internal appeal tribunal to review such a decision and must be advised of the possibility to request recourse in public courts.

Regarding a refusal to allow an expelled member to reobtain membership, because a period of two years following a withdrawal of membership has not elapsed, or a Board of Directors declines this re-application, a two-year period should be changed to a six-month standstill (or if this is combined with other misconduct a one-year) period. In addition, an independent third-party panel (not connected with the relevant trade association) should be tasked with considering a reapplication for membership for expelled members on the basis of clearly defined, equally applicable, transparent, non-discriminatory criteria, such as (i) the current liquidity status

719 See Part II, Chapter 7, D, II.

720 See Part II, Chapter 7, D, III.

of the former member; (ii) an unwillingness to pay the penalty for non-compliance with the arbitral award; and (iii) evidence of probable disloyalty in the future.

In sum, depending on how egregious the impact of nonlegal sanctions and a reasonable necessity to enhance total welfare and consumer welfare, it is not impossible that the trade associations researched and their members will be faced with liability under Section 2 of the Sherman Act. Comparable to Section 1 of the Sherman Act, much will depend on the willingness of the FTC and/or US courts to do so. Both actors could favour a more capacious, or develop a much more constrictive, yardstick to attribute a violation of this provision. However, even though all four nonlegal sanctions violate Section 2 of the Sherman Act based on how they are currently structured, when the dissemination of the names of wrongdoers in a blacklist, withdrawals of membership and denials to re-admit ostracized members on the basis of an additional entry are structured in the least restrictive form, antitrust liability under this provision is precluded. This is not true pertaining to refusals to deal with expelled members.

Part III:
Study of EU Competition Law

Chapter 8: The Scope of Application of European Competition Law

A. *The nucleus of European Competition Law: a brief overview*

Only a few areas of law garner as much press exposure as EU Competition Law.[721] This evolution bears testimony to its rise as a critical issue throughout Europe. Today, the constraints imposed by EU Competition Law have become imperative for the good functioning of the internal (or single) market and are instrumental in furthering efficiency and consumer welfare.[722] The EU substantive rules dealing with cartels and abuse of a dominant position[723] have ensured, in the past decades, unity in the application of comparable laws in European States. Yet, much of the success of these provisions of EU Competition Law depends on practical enforcement.[724]

Article 105(1) TFEU entrusts the Directorate General for Competition of the European Commission (the "Commission") with "the application of the principles laid down in Articles 101 and 102 [TFEU]". This entails that the Commission is given a pivotal role in the enforcement of EU Competition Law.[725] Unlike civil courts, the task of which is to safeguard the individual rights of private individuals, the Commission is the administrative authority the main objective of which is to act in the public interest (*i.e.* to

721 D. Geradin, A. Layne-Farrar, and N. Petit, "*EU Competition Law and Economics*", Oxford: Oxford University Press 2012, p. 1.

722 According to Article 3(3) TEU, European Competition Law must guarantee a system of undistorted competition, in order to promote the single market objective. This single market imperative is, as described by the EU Commission, one of the "EU's biggest assets". See R. Whish, D. Bailey, "*Competition Law: Eight Edition*", Oxford: Oxford University Press 2015, p. 54.

723 Also State aid has led to harmonization pertaining to the application of competition law among EU Member States. This area of competition law will not be elaborated on in this research.

724 A. Looijestijn-Clearie, C. S. Rusu, and M. Veenbrink, "*Boosting the Enforcement of EU Competition Law at the Domestic Level*", Newcastle upon Tyne: Cambridge Scholars Publishing 2017, p. 2.

725 M. Lorenz, "*An Introducion To EU Competition Law*", Cambridge: Cambridge University Press 2013, p. 45.

protect competition from restrictions in the interest of consumers and welfare).[726]

It has various competences, including acting in sensitive and high profile antitrust cases, issuing notices[727] and guidelines, drafting block exemptions,[728] and submitting legislative proposals to the Parliament and the Council for the adoption of Directives and Regulations.[729] Interestingly, it has a margin of discretion to set priorities in its enforcement activity.[730]

On a national level, National Competition Authorities ("NCAs") are the hands and feet of the Commission.[731] This is because NCAs must apply EU Competition Law as soon as it is applicable in a given case (*i.e.* if there is an effect on trade between Member States). According to Article 3(1) of Regulation 1/2003, such an obligation cannot be invalidated when NCAs apply national law as well.[732]

It does not come as a surprise that the EU Commission and NCAs are responsible for the great majority of competition cases throughout Europe. However, this co-action gives rise to some questions. First, who ensures that they use the powers granted to them to protect us appropriately, justly and fairly. Second, who can certify that we never need to be protected

---

726 A. Jones and B. E. Sufrin, "*EU Competition Law: Text, Cases, and Materials*", Oxford: Oxford University Press 2014, p. 1073.

727 See P. L. Landolt, "*Modernised EC Competition Law in International Arbitration*", The Hague: Kluwer Law International 2006, p. 237. Commission Notices do not have binding effect (i.e. are non-mandatory), but are, in practice, taken seriously by undertakings. Undertakings normally heed the Commission's interpretation of the application of EU competition law given its immense experience. Also, because it is the principal enforcer of this area of law.

728 C. Ehlermann, I. Atanasiu, "*European Competition Law Annual 2002: Constructing the EU Network of Competition Authorities*", Oxford/Portland: Hart Publishing 2004, p. 261.

729 This must be in accordance with the ordinary legislative proposal as laid down in Article 294 TEU. For an overview of the ordinary legislative procedure, see T. Dubowski, "*Białystok Law Books 2 Constitutional Law Of The European Union*", Bialystok: Temida 2 2011, p. 116-120.

730 See CFI 27 September 2006, Case T-204/03 (Haladjian Frères v Commission), [2006], ECR II-03779, para. 28; GC 23 November 2011, case T-320/07 (Jones et al v. Commission), [2011], ECR II-00417, para. 115; Commission Decision of 19 June 2015 relating to a proceeding under Articles 101 and 102 TFEU, Case No AT.39864 (BASF), para. 26.

731 W. Sauter, "*Coherence in EU Competition Law*", Oxford: Oxford University Press 2016, p. 256.

732 Council Regulation (EC) No 1/2003 of 16 December 2002 on the implementation of the rules on competition laid down in Articles 81 and 82 of the Treaty [now Article 101 and 102 TFEU] [OJ 2003, No L 001], p. 0001-0025.

from them?[733] To solve both issues, the Court of Justice of the European Union (the "CJEU") was established. This judicial arm comprises the General Court ("GC") and the European Court of Justice (the "ECJ"). Together they have various competences, including imposing fines, interpreting and annulling decisions adopted by the Commission in conjunction with Article 263 TFEU.[734]

Since the main players are now identified and described, it is imperative to analyse whether the trade associations researched, their members and non-members can attract the attention of the EU Commission and, ultimately, the CJEU. This is the case when their participation in regulated behaviour violates Articles 101 and 102 TFEU. Given that there are no reported precedents in which either or both Articles have been employed to bar trade associations from using such behaviour, this is not an easy task. In other words, it is relatively uncertain whether the three actors for their role in the six nonlegal sanctions can be held liable for a group boycott and/or an abuse of a dominant position. Much will depend on comparing and analysing decisional practice and guidance given by the Commission and scrutinizing case law of the CJEU.

B. *Introduction*

To ponder the idea of how and to what extent the "core" antitrust rules (*i.e.* Articles 101 and 102 TFEU) can be used to determine whether the trade associations researched for their role in the imposition of nonlegal sanctioning and their members and non-members for their role in the execution of those sanctions can be held accountable, it must first be examined whether these three actors and their extrajudicial measures fall within the *ratione personae* of EU Competition Law.[735] Therefore, it is necessary to examine the boundaries of this area of law. Perhaps the best approach to

---

733 The Roman poet Juvenal described this fundamental issue of what law seeks to address as "Quis custodiet ipsos custodes?" (Who will guard the guards themselves?). See L. Watson and P. Watson, "*Juvenal: Satire 6*", Cambridge: Cambridge University Press 2014, 196. This book provides a (literal) translation from Latin into English.

734 For an overview of how the appellate system of the CJEU works, see M. Lorenz, "*An Introduction to EU Competition Law*", Cambridge: Cambridge University Press 2013, p. 51-52.

735 To avoid excessive repetition of the term competition law/rules, reference to the expression "antitrust law/rules" will be made intermittently. The expression is

conduct such an examination requires that these actors be beyond the scope of competition law from the outset, unless they fulfil two boundaries. The first is referred to as the legal boundary (Paragraph C), which necessitates that the trade associations researched, their members and non-members must be defined as an undertaking. The second boundary comprises economically quantifiably thresholds developed by the Commission and the CJEU (*i.e.* effect on trade between Member States) (Paragraphs D & E).[736]

C. *Legal boundary*

Before the application of EU competition law takes effect, one must examine whether the trade associations researched, their members and non-members exceed the legal boundaries of Articles 101 and 102 TFEU. A crucial delimitation concerns the concept of "undertaking". This means that the Commission can only claim competence when the three actors qualify either as undertakings or as an association of undertakings pursuant to Article 101 TFEU. In contrast, when this cannot be established, the Commission has no authority to conduct a review.

I. Members of the trade associations researched and non-members

To establish whether the members and non-members of the trade associations researched are considered undertakings within the meaning of Articles 101 and 102 TFEU, they must fall under the legal rule provided by the ECJ in *Klaus Höfner*.[737] According to this case, an undertaking means "*any entity engaged in an economic activity, regardless of its legal status and the*

---

borrowed from US law, where it is generally referred to as antitrust law – even if, *stricto sensu* and *lato sensu* one cannot compare both legal systems.

736 W. Sauter, "*Coherence in EU Competition Law*", Oxford: Oxford University Press 2016, p. 75-87.

737 A. Jones, "The Boundaries of an Undertaking in EU Competition Law", *European Competition Journal* 2015, p. 302. Peculiarly, regardless of the centrality of the concept of undertaking in EU Competition Law, its actual definition was omitted from the lexicon of the TFEU. Rather, the meaning of the term has been left for elucidation by the CJEU.

way in which it is financed".[738] While this wording is easy to comprehend, in my opinion, it can be refined around two excessively broad elements: first, an "entity", which includes commercial bodies, civil companies, or public institutions[739] and, second, the carrying out of an "economic activity" by offering goods and services on a given market.[740] That being said, it is beyond a reasonable doubt that the members of the trade associations researched and non-members fulfil both elements insofar as they are not private individuals.[741] Not only are they commercial bodies, but they also operate on commodities markets with the main aim to maximize profit (*i.e.* economic activity). Subsequently, such members of the trade associations researched and non-members are considered undertakings within the meaning of Articles 101 and 102 TFEU.

---

738 ECJ 23 April 1991, Case C-41/90 (Klaus Höfner and Fritz Elser v. Macrotron GmbH), [1991] ECR I-1979, para. 21; ECJ 16 November 1995, Case C-244/94 (Federation Française des Sociétés d'Assurance, Société Paternelle Vie, Union des Assurances de Paris-Vie, Caisse d'Assurance et de Prévoyance Mutuelle des Agriculteurs and Ministère de l'Agriculture et de la Pêche), [1995] ECR I-4013, para. 14; ECJ 11 December 1997, Case C-55/96 (Job Centre coop. arl.), [1997] ECR I-7119, para. 21; ECJ 19 February 2002, Case C-309/99 (J. C. J. Wouters, J. W. Savelbergh and Price Waterhouse Belastingadviseurs BV v. Algemene Raad van de Nederlandse Orde van Advocaten, intervener: Raad van de Balies van de Europese Gemeenschap), [2002] ECR I-1577, para. 46; ECJ 11 July 2006, Case C-205/03P (Federación Española de Empresas de Tecnología Sanitaria (FENIN) v. Commission of the European Communities, [2006] ECR I-6295, para. 25; ECJ 10 September 2009, Case C-97/08P (Akzo Nobel NV et al v. Commission of the European Communities), [2009] I-08237, para. 54.

739 D. Geradin, A. Layne-Farrar, and N. Petit, "*EU Competition Law and Economics*", Oxford: Oxford University Press 2012, para. 1-134.

740 ECJ 16 June 1987, Case 118/85 (Commission of the European Communities v. Italian Republic), [1987] ECR 2599, para. 7; ECJ 18 June 1998, Case C-35/96 (Commission of the European Communities v. Italian Republic), [1998] ECR I-3851, para. 36; ECJ 11 July 2006, case C-205/03P (Federación Española de Empresas de Tecnología Sanitaria (FENIN) v. Commission of the European Communities), [2006] ECR I-6295, para. 25; CFI 12 December 2006, Case T-155/04 (SELEX Sistemi Integrati SpA v. Commission of the European Communities), [2006] ECR II-04797, para. 50.

741 Unlike US Antitrust Law (*i.e.* Section 1 of the Sherman Act), EU Competition Law cannot be used to assess the anti-competitiveness of conduct produced by merely private individuals.

II. Trade associations

Establishing whether the legal boundary is fulfilled for the trade associations researched, the approach pertaining to Article 101 and to Article 102 TFEU differs. With regard to Article 101, this requires evidence that these associations bring together a group of undertakings. The mere fact that an association brings together a group of individuals is not enough. By focusing on the trade associations researched and their members, it is clear that the associations can be considered associations of undertakings. Their members operate under the umbrella of these associations.

To establish whether the trade associations researched fulfil the legal boundary to invoke Article 102 TFEU is a more difficult task. The main reason being that this provision does not apply to associations of undertakings, but requires that these associations – standing alone – are considered undertakings. Unfortunately, two issues prevent an easy qualification under this concept: first, because the trade associations researched operate on a not-for-profit basis, one can say that they do not engage in an independent economic activity. Second, even if the trade associations researched could be classified as undertakings within the meaning of Article 102 TFEU, do their services not fall within the public authority exemption?[742] These associations offer public services in a now privatized market.

In my opinion, the first issue can be rebutted by looking at the ECJ judgment in *Van Landewyck v. Commission*. In that judgment, the Court explained that a pursuit of profit is not required to prove that an entity is engaged in an economic activity. On the ground that a trade association is an entity,[743] even though the trade associations researched do not have profit maximization as their main objective, given their role in supplying services to industry actors operating on an adjacent second-tier commodities markets, they are undertakings. With regard to the second issue, it may very well be possible that the public authority exemption is applicable. This entails that regardless of the classification as an undertaking, the services provided by the trade associations researched which includes nonlegal sanctions are excluded from the scope of Article 102 TFEU because they fall within the essential prerogatives of the State (*i.e.* essential function of the

742 ECJ 29 October 1980, joined cases 209 to 215 and 218/78 (Heintz van Landewyck SARL et al v. Commission of the European Communities), [1980] ECR 3125, para. 88.

743 The legal structure of an entity is not important. Trade associations are also considered entities.

State).[744] On the one hand, as said above, all of the trade associations researched carry out services which were are necessary for the general public in former State-run commodities markets. Due to inefficiency, overstaffing and a drain on public budget, these markets were privatized. As a result, whereas the trade associations researched only exist with the permission of States, they still perform essential State functions. Put differently, the trade associations researched are public undertakings and should be excluded from antitrust scrutiny under Article 102 TFEU. On the other hand, in my opinion, the trade associations researched provide their services (including nonlegal sanctioning to ensure the operability of specialized commercial arbitration) across countries. They were established to accommodate the needs of globally dispersed industry actors. They do not fit within the typical function of the State and are to a large degree detached from the State. Their operability within a PLS is sufficient proof of this. Moreover, as the study of US Antitrust Law has demonstrated, the effect of nonlegal sanctioning on targeted wrongdoers can result in market foreclosure. It would be unwise to not classify the trade associations researched as non-public undertakings. Any other conclusion would prevent the Commission and/or the ECJ from scrutinizing the potential hazardous impact of extra-judicial enforcement at such an early stage. This is contrary to the goal to take the competitive interest of every industry operating on a relevant market into account.

In sum, the trade associations researched are associations of undertakings within the meaning of Article 101 TFEU and undertakings within the meaning of Article 102 TFEU. The legal boundary is complied with.

D. Economic boundaries: the effect on trade between Member States

As a final step before being able to assess whether the trade associations researched, their members and non-members can be held accountable for

744 ECJ 18 March 1997, Case C-343/95 (Cali e Figli), [1997] ECR I-1547, para. 22-23. In this judgment, the Court ruled that an entity exercises public powers where the activity "*is a task in the public interest which forms part of the essential functions of the State*" and where the activity "*is connected by its nature, its aim and the rules to which it is subject with the exercise of powers* [...] *which are typically those of a public authority*"; See also I. E. Wendt, "*EU Competition Law and Liberal Professions: an Uneasy Relationship?*", Leiden: Koninklijke Brill NV 2013, p. 220; G. Monti, "*EC Competition Law*", Cambridge: Cambridge University Press 2007, p. 486.

their respective roles in imposing and executing nonlegal sanctions under Articles 101 and 102 TFEU, some economic boundaries must be complied with. The next two Paragraphs (Paragraphs I and II) describe the approach adopted by the Commission and by the Commission. Subsequently, it will be established (Paragraph III) whether the trade associations researched, their members and non-members have an effect on trade between Member States by applying both approaches to these actors.

I. Interpretation by the Court of Justice of the European Union

An economic boundary that needs elaboration concerns the more jurisdictional in nature concept of "effect on trade between Member States". Ever since the CJEU's judgment in *Consten and Grundig*, "inter-state trade effect" has been applied as an autonomous and separate criterion in EU Competition Law.[745] While the criterion is elusive in all Treaty provisions concerning substantive competition rules, it is most commonly used pertaining to Articles 101 and 102 TFEU.[746]

In later judgments, the Court of Justice developed a yardstick to define when an effect on trade is present. According to the Court, "[…] *it must be possible to foresee with a sufficient degree of probability on the basis of a set of objective factors of law or fact that it may have an influence, direct or indirect, actual or potential, on the pattern of trade between Member States, such as might prejudice the realization of the aim of a single market in all the Member*

---

745 R. Wesseling, "*The Modernisation of EC Antitrust Law*", Oxford/Portland: Hart Publishing 2000, p. 116-117. In *Consten and Grundig* the Court with regard to the effect on trade in the context of Article 81 EC (currently Article 101 TFEU) determined "*whether the agreement is capable of constituting a threat, either direct or indirect, actual or potential, to freedom of trade between Member States in a manner which might harm the attainment of the objectives of a single market between States*". See ECJ 13 July 1966, joined cases 56 and 58-64 (Établissements Consten S.à.R.L. and Grundig-Verkaufs-GmbH v. Commission of the European Economic Community), [1966] ECR 429, p. 341. This definition was meant to establish when the competition law of the EU or Member States is applicable. See J. B. Cruz, "*Between Competition and Free Movement*", Oxford/Portland: Hart Publishing 2002, p. 89.

746 The test for effect on trade is more commonly used in relation to Article 101 TFEU, but it has also been applied under Article 102 TFEU. For an example of a case pertaining to Article 102, see Commission Decision of 18 July 1988 relating to a proceeding under Article 86 of the EEC Treaty, Case No IV/30.178 (Napier Brown - British Sugar).

States".[747] At first glance, one may come to the conclusion that this definition might seem ambiguous, as it can entail that intra Union trade must be affected negatively (*i.e.* reduced or restricted) or positively. Fortunately, in *Ferriere Nord SpA*, the ECJ in a moment of lucidity provided much-needed clarity.[748] The Court explained that it is not required that trade between Member States is actually affected, but it is sufficient that the practice is capable of having that effect.[749] Moreover, the Court in *Consten and Grundig* decided that an effect on trade can also be established when an agreement or practice causes an increase in trade.[750]

Apropos the case studies discussed, it can immediately be seen that it is unclear where to draw a clear and unequivocal line concerning what constitutes an appreciable effect on interstate trade. The Court of Justice in *Völk v. S.P.R.L. Ets J. Vervaecke* attempted to close this legal gap by introducing the doctrine of appreciability in relation to Article 101(1) TFEU.[751] On the merits of the case, the Court developed a "de minimis standard" or "safe harbour" by explaining that an agreement falls outside the prohibition of Article 101(1) TFEU when it only has an insignificant effect on the internal market.[752]

---

747 ECJ 11 July 1985, Case 42/84 (Remia BV et al v. Commission of the European Communities), [1985] *ECR* 2566, para. 22; ECJ 25 January 2007, Case C-407/04P (Dalmine SpA v. Commission of the European Communities), [2007] ECR I-829, para. 90.

748 ECJ 17 July 1997, Case C-219/95P (Ferriere Nord SpA v. Commission of the European Communities), [1997] ECR I-04411, para. 19.

749 Ibid; This was later confirmed in ECJ 21 January 1999, Case C-216/96 (Carlo Bagnasco et al v. Banca Popolare di Novara soc. coop. arl. (BNP) et al), [1999] ECR I-135, para. 48; ECJ 23 November 2006, Case C-238/05 (Asnef-Equifax, Servicios de Información sobre Solvencia y Crédito, SL, Administración del Estado v. Asociación de Usuarios de Servicios Bancarios (Ausbanc)), [2006] ECR I-11125, para. 43.

750 ECJ 13 July 1966, joined cases 56 and 58-64 (Établissements Consten S.à.R.L. and Grundig-Verkaufs-GmbH v. Commission of the European Economic Community), [1966] ECR 429, p. 341.

751 ECJ 9 July 1969, case 5-69 (Franz Völk v S.P.R.L. Ets J. Vervaecke), [1969] ECR 295.

752 Ibid., para. 5-7.

II. Interpretation by the Commission

Even though the Court's reasoning is perspicuous, it neither quantified the required level nor did it provide clarity whether it applies to Article 102 TFEU.[753] This among other reasons is why the Commission published Guidelines on the effect on trade concept contained in Articles [101 and 102 TFEU] ("Guidelines on Inter-State Trade").[754] The Guidelines provide guidance in common situations and set out the methodology on the effect on trade concept by referring to case law of the EU courts.[755] Although non-binding and non-exhaustive, they further converge and harmonize the effect on trade concept throughout the European Union. Importantly, they state that the doctrine of effect on trade applies to Articles 101 and 102 TFEU, where a minimum level of cross-border effects within the EU is established.[756]

For determining when the doctrine is applicable, three aspects are of importance.[757] First, "*there must be an impact on cross-border activity involving at least two EU countries*" (trade between EU countries).[758] Second, "*it must be possible to foresee with a sufficient degree of probability on the basis of a set of objective factors of law or fact that the agreement or practice may have an influence, direct or indirect, actual or potential, on the pattern of trade between EU countries*".[759] This is the notion of "may affect". Last, the concept of appreciability must be fulfilled. Parameters to corroborate such finding include (i) the position and the importance of the relevant undertaking on the market for the products concerned; (ii) the nature of the agreement and practice; (iii) the nature of the products covered; and (iv) the market position of the undertakings concerned.[760]

---

753 E. Berry, M. J. Homewood, and B. Bogusz, "*Complete EU Law: Text, Cases, and Materials*", Oxford: Oxford University Press 2017, p. 610.

754 Commission Notice — Guidelines on the effect on trade concept contained in Articles 81 and 82 of the Treaty (now Articles 101 and 102 TFEU) of 27 April 2004, [OJ 2004, No. C 101/07].

755 N. Foster, "*Blackstone's EU Treaties and Legislation 2014-2015*", Oxford: Oxford University Press 2014, p. 609.

756 Commission Notice — Guidelines on the effect on trade concept contained in Articles 81 and 82 of the Treaty (now Articles 101 and 102 TFEU) of 27 April 2004, [OJ 2004, No. C 101/07], para. 6-7.

757 Ibid., para. 18.

758 Ibid., para. 21.

759 Ibid., para. 23.

760 Ibid., para. 44-45.

1. Commission Recommendation on SMEs and the positive and negative rebuttable presumption of non-appreciability

While it is true that the Guidelines on inter-state trade do not provide quantitative rules on when trade is appreciably affected, they do provide examples of situations where trade is normally not capable of being appreciably affected pursuant to Article 101 TFEU. First, as defined in the Commission Recommendation concerning the definition of micro, small and medium-sized enterprises or any future recommendation replacing it ("Commission Recommendation on SMEs"), agreements between small and medium-sized undertakings do not affect trade between Member States.[761]

Second, the Guidelines set out a negative rebuttable presumption of non-appreciability.[762] This arises where the (1) aggregate market share of the parties on any relevant market within the EU affected by the agreements does not exceed 5 percent; and (2) the parties' aggregate annual Community turnover is below 40 million.[763] The presumption continues to apply where the turnover threshold is exceeded during two successive calendar years by no more than 10 percent and the market share threshold by no more than 2 percent.

The Guidelines also set out a positive rebuttable presumption of appreciability in the case of agreements that by their very nature (*i.e.* by object) are capable of affecting trade between Member States. This arises in the event both thresholds are exceeded. However, this positive rebuttable presumption is no longer true, as the ECJ in *Expedia* stated that agreements, which restrict competition by object, "always" have an appreciable effect on competition.[764]

---

761 Ibid., para. 50; Commission Recommendation concerning the definition of micro, small and medium-sized enterprises or any future recommendation replacing it of 20 May 2003, [OJ 2003, No. L 124], p. 36.

762 Commission Notice — Guidelines on the effect on trade concept contained in Articles 81 and 82 of the Treaty (now Articles 101 and 102 TFEU) of 27 April 2004, [OJ 2004, No. C 101/07], para. 50.

763 Ibid., para. 52.

764 ECJ 13 December 2012, Case C-226/11 (Expedia Inc. v. Autorité de la concurrence et al), [2012] ECR I-795, para. 16-17, 35-37. In this judgment, the ECJ explained that the "effect on trade" requirement is fulfilled, in the event of "restrictions by object". In other words, the availability of the de minimis safe harbour was narrowed-down in terms of its application and impact.

2. The De Minimis Notice

In June 2014, the Commission, in an attempt to clarify the scope of the "effect on trade" doctrine, published a revised notice, namely the Commission Notice on Agreements of Minor Importance which do not Appreciably Restrict Competition under Article 101(1) TFEU (the "De Minimis Notice").[765] In its Notice, the Commission follows the reasoning of the ECJ in *Expedia* and stated that object restrictions are always deemed appreciable,[766] whereas effect restrictions below an aggregated market share of 10% in horizontal cases are not deemed appreciable.[767] Conversely, the de minimis doctrine does not apply in relation to Article 102 TFEU.[768] While providing a clear statement that the Commission will apply these principles in its own decisions, the De Minimis Notice is not treated as legally binding on the Community judiciary.[769]

III. Do the extrajudicial measures imposed by the trade associations researched and executed by their members and non-members have an effect on Community trade?

By keeping in mind the framework of the economic boundaries as outlined by the CJEU and the Commission, it must be examined whether the trade associations researched, their members and non-members, when imposing and executing nonlegal sanctions, have an appreciable effect on trade and, hence, trigger the scope of application of Articles 101 and 102 TFEU. While all actors prefer non-interference by dint of laissez-faire or

765 Commission Notice on Agreements of Minor Importance which do not Appreciably Restrict Competition under Article 101(1) TFEU (de minimis) of 30 August 2014 [OJ 2014, No. C 291/1].

766 Ibid., para. 2.

767 Ibid., para. 8 (a). See also A. Gideon, "*Higher Education Institutions in the EU: Between Competition and Public Service*", Liverpool/Singapore: T.M.C. Asser Press 2017, p. 74.

768 In ECJ 6 October 2015, Case C-23/14 (Post Danmark A/S v. Konkurrencerådet), [2015] 651, p. 70-73 the ECJ found that the setting of an appreciability (de minimis) threshold for the purposes of determining whether there is an abuse of a dominant position is not justified. Although pertaining to rebates, in my opinion, the Court's observation conforms to the line of established and controversial case law.

769 P. J. Slot and M. Farley, "*An Introduction to Competition Law*", Oxford/London/Portland: Hart Publishing 2017, p. 56.

tacit acquiescence of the EU Commission, their roles in nonlegal sanctioning can constitute an effect on trade between Member States. Therefore, to fall within the reach of the effect on trade doctrine, the following three elements must be fulfilled which can be distilled from Articles 101 and 102 TFEU, the case law of the CJEU and the Notice on Inter-State Trade.[770]

1. The concept of trade

This requirement is met, because all of the six trade associations researched, their members and even non-members engage in cross-border activities.

2. The presence of "may affect"

When imposing nonlegal sanctions on wrongdoers, the trade associations researched are "most likely" capable of having a direct or indirect, actual or potential, influence on the pattern of trade between Member States. This view receives support from the fact that little evidence needs to be adduced by the Commission to satisfy this requirement.[771] The same can be said for their members when executing nonlegal sanctions. For non-members this is more difficult to establish. Their role in the execution of extrajudicial measures is more dubious. Yet, their role in executing nonlegal sanctions at least may have an influence, direct or indirect, actual or potential, on the pattern of trade between EU countries. This is especially true when these actors are aware if an industry actor is extrajudicially sanctioned and, as a result, not conduct business with that company.

---

770 See also van Bael & Bellis (firm), "*Competition Law of the European Community*", The Hague: Kluwer Law Internationaal 2005, p. 101.

771 Only in ECJ 26 November 1975, Case 73-74 (Groupement des fabricants de papiers peints de Belgique et al v. Commission of the European Communities), [1975] ECR 1491, para. 32 was this requirement not fulfilled. The ECJ ruled that the Commission's definition of inter-state trade was defined insufficiently precisely.

3. The concept of appreciability

The trade associations researched, their members and non-members fulfil this requirement in relation to Article 101 TFEU when their role in the imposition and execution of nonlegal sanctions has as their object the prevention, restriction or distortion of competition. Although an onerous task, the following Chapter contains an in-depth examination of whether a restriction of competition by object can be established.[772] Conversely, if their practices restrict competition by effect pursuant to Article 101 TFEU,[773] it must be established *argumentum e contrario* that the trade associations researched, their members and non-members satisfy two requirements. First, that their aggregate Community market share exceeds 10 percent (*i.e.* de minimis) and, second, that their annual Community turnover exceeds 40 million euro.[774] Such a two-fold test is omitted in relation to Article 102

---

772 See Part III, Chapter 9, C.

773 This will be analysed in the following Chapters.

774 The two-tier test to prove the existence of appreciability typically requires proof of shares and turnover. Unfortunately, this is a rather complicated and daunting task. This is because the Commission will be required to examine whether both indicators are met by defining the relevant market. See M. M. Dabbah, "*International and Comparative Competition Law*", Cambridge: Cambridge University Press 2010, p. 71; usually, it is necessary to define the relevant market in order to appraise whether an agreement is caught by Article 101(1) TFEU. See Slaughter and May, "An overview of the EU competition rules – A general overview of the European Competition rules applicable to cartels, abuse of dominance, forms of commercial cooperation, merger control and State aid", *Slaughter and May* 2016, p. 8, 14; With regard to the three actors, a much more simplified overview will be given to see whether the two appreciability requirements are met by them separately; For further information on how to conduct a proper market analysis and important observations, see ECJ 14 February 1978, Case 27/76 (United Brands Company and United Brands Continental BV v. Commission of the European Communities), [1978] ECR 207, para. 10; Commission Notice on the definition of relevant market for the purposes of Community competition law of 9 December 1997 [OJ 1997, No. C 372/5]. Market definition requires an examination of the product and geographical market; A. Ezrachi, "*EU Competition Law: An Analytical Guide to the Leading Cases*", Oxford/Portland: Hart Publishing 2014, p. 33. Market definition is important to identify the boundaries of competition and to provide a framework in which effects may be determined; Commission Notice on the definition of relevant market for the purposes of Community competition law of 9 December 1997 [OJ 1997, No. C 372/5], para. 7; Competition Appeal Tribunal 19 March 2002, Case 1005/1/101 (Aberdeen Journals Limited v. Director General of Fair Trading), [2002] CAT 4, para. 96-97. The product market is defined as one which "*comprises all those products and/or services which are regarded as interchangeable or substitutable by the consumer,*

TFEU. In line with this provision, market shares are only relevant in the material examination of what amounts to dominance as opposed to the scope of application.[775]

a. Nonlegal sanctions as effect restrictions

An agreement between competitors usually falls outside the scope of Article 101(1) TFEU where the joint market share of them falls below 10% and where their joint annual Community turnover does not exceed 40 million euro. When the members of the trade associations researched execute nonlegal sanctions to punish wrongdoers that operate on the same commodities markets as they do, it is likely that both thresholds are met (except in the EU diamond market in which the members of the DDC operate).[776] This is because these industry actors are members of the most important globally active trade associations which represent their interests and many

by reason of the product' characteristics, their prices and their intended use"; Commission Notice on the definition of relevant market for the purposes of Community competition law of 9 December 1997 [OJ 1997, No. C 372/5], para. 8. A geographic market concerns the geographical area in which undertakings are involved with the supply and demand of products and services in which the same conditions of competition apply and which can be distinguished from neighbouring areas; Commission Notice on the definition of relevant market for the purposes of Community competition law of 9 December 1997 [OJ 1997, No. C 372/5], para. 6. Even though the Commission's Notice on market definition is guiding, it is important to note that the understanding of market definition by the Commission may differ from the practice of the CJEU. This is because European courts are not bound by the Notice. The Commission has a crucial role in defining the relevant market. In particular, because it involves a complex economic assessment. In appeal, the CJEU only has limited review possibilities. However, it can assess whether economic data is accurate, reliable and coherent. See CFI 9 September 2009, Case T-301/04 (Clearstream Banking AG and Clearstream International SA v. Commission of the European Communities), [2009] ECR II-3155, para. 47. In this case reference is made to CFI 17 September 2007, case T-201/04 (Microsoft Corp. v. Commission of the European Communities), [2007] ECR II-3601, para. 482.

775 See Part II, Chapter 8, B, I.

776 90 percent of the members of the DDC live in the tristate area of New York, New Jersey and Connecticut. See https://www.nyddc.com/ddc-news—events. Hence, in my opinion, it is unlikely that the market share threshold by the members of the DDC is met in the territory of the EU; The presence of an agreement for the members of the trade associations researched is discussed in Part III, Chapter 9, B, I.

of them prefer to receive their services.[777] Non-members also satisfy the two-tier requirement when they have entered into an agreement. It is without doubt that not all of the market participants are members of the trade associations researched, because some may prefer to not belong to a specific group, whereas others are members of competing trade associations active in some of the commodities markets researched.[778]

Establishing whether the trade associations researched satisfy the two appreciability requirements when they impose nonlegal sanctions on wrongdoers is far more contentious. This is because the trade associations researched operate on the market for regulation and private ordering concerning specific commodities industries on EU territory, whereas extrajudicial measures have an impact on targeted industry actors operating on adjacent second-tier commodities markets on EU territory. Obviously, this raises a problem: appreciability typically requires that the instigator of conduct has an effect on an industry actor that is active in the same market. The trade associations researched do not possess market power in the commodities markets, but satisfy the market share threshold in the markets for regulation and private ordering concerning specific commodities on EU territory.[779] In my opinion, this alone cannot be an obstacle to absolving the trade associations researched when they impose nonlegal sanctions. Their involvement in imposing extrajudicial measures has an appreciable impact on targeted wrongdoers and, hence, has an appreciable effect on the commodities markets researched when these markets are defined regionally to the territory of the EU. Subsequently, unilateral conduct of the trade associations researched meets the appreciability requirement insofar as its conduct can be defined as an agreement. This is explained in the next Chapter.[780]

777 See Part II, Chapter 7, B, I, 2.

778 It would require arduous research to calculate the market shares of non-members in comparison to those of members in each of the commodities industries researched. Therefore, non-members are deemed to possess more than 10% market shares and have more than an annual Community turnover of 40 million euro. The presence of an agreement for the members of the trade associations researched is discussed in Part III, Chapter 9, B, I and III.

779 Although EU-wide shares are unaccounted for, global empirical percentages and statements indicate the crucial role of these associations in international trade. Accordingly, establishing Community market shares can be considered extraneous and superfluous. It is also likely that the fairly low Community threshold is met, despite the trade associations researched operating on a not-for-profit basis.

780 See Part III, Chapter 9, B, II.

E. Key findings

Safeguarding the EU internal market against unacceptable conduct is quintessential for the EU Member States.[781] Upon a belief that an undistorted free market economy will further economic growth and benefit consumers, potential anti-competitive nonlegal sanctions imposed by the trade associations researched and executed by their members and non-members can infringe two core prohibitions of EU Competition Law: first, Article 101 TFEU and, second, Article 102 TFEU. Before going into a substantive analysis of whether indeed both provisions are infringed upon, the framework of the scope of application of both Articles must be extended. To claim authority as to whether this is the case, the Commission – being the principal enforcer of EU Competition Law – must provide evidence that, first, the legal boundary and, second, economic boundaries are fulfilled.[782]

The legal boundary, on the one hand, is exceeded by the members of the trade associations researched and non-members pursuant to Articles 101 and 102 TFEU.[783] Industry actors belonging to both groups of actors are undertakings within the meaning of both provisions because they engage in economic activities. This is not true when they are not entities, but are private individuals. Then, the legal boundary is not met. Determining whether the trade associations researched go beyond the legal boundary requires a more arduous reasoning.[784] Whereas these trade associations are associations of undertakings within the meaning of Article 101 TFEU and thus exceed the legal boundary, this concept does not exist under Article 102 TFEU. Put differently, to fall within the legal bounds of Article 102, the trade associations must be classified as undertakings. Given their functioning as umbrella organizations for different undertakings, such a qualification is not problematic. An absence of profit maximization as an underlying motive when providing services to their members also does not change this outcome. Whereas one could argue that services provided by the trade associations researched which include nonlegal sanctions are excluded from the scope of Article 102 TFEU because they fall within the essential prerogatives of the State (*i.e.* essential function of the State), in my opinion, they do not. The trade associations researched were formed to ac-

781 See Part III, Chapter 8, A.
782 See Part III, Chapter 8, B.
783 See Part III, Chapter 8, C, I.
784 See Part III, Chapter 8, C, II.

commodate the needs of globally active industry actors that operate in specific commodities markets. Hence, the trade associations are detached from the State and operate within a PLS. Moreover, due to the harmful effects for targeted wrongdoers, it would be imprudent to treat the trade associations researched as public undertakings. This would prevent an antitrust review on the merits. Consequently, the trade associations researched are undertakings within the meaning of Article 102 TFEU.

Exceeding the economic boundaries (*i.e.* the concept of the effect on inter-state trade), on the other hand, requires a more burdensome task for the Commission.[785] This is because the Commission must take the interpretation of this concept given by the CJEU into account which is profoundly less specific with regard to the appreciability standard.[786] In line with the CJEU's reasoning, the Commission must explain that the nonlegal sanctions imposed by the trade associations researched and executed by their members and non-members are capable of having the effect of hindering trade.[787] Whereas the definition used by the CJEU consists of overtly vague norms that need clarification through their application, the Commission needs to fulfil three elements before it can assess conduct under Articles 101 and 102 TFEU. These prerequisites can be found in the Guidelines on Inter-State Trade.

First, the Commission must establish that the three groups of actors are engaged in cross-border activity.[788] It deserves no further explanation that this requirement is fulfilled. Second, nonlegal sanctioning must be capable of having a direct or indirect, actual or potential, influence on the pattern of trade between Member States.[789] Given that little evidence is needed to satisfy this requirement and only once in the history of the CJEU has this requirement not been fulfilled, nonlegal sanctioning by the trade associations researched, their members and non-members can potentially influence Community trade. Obviously, when a member undertaking of a trade association gets punished for disloyal behaviour, market access and, thus, inter-state trade can be impeded. In turn, member undertakings of the trade associations researched have increased security when contracting and lower transaction and distribution costs. This also has an influence on Community trade.

785 See Part III, Chapter 8, D.
786 See Part III, Chapter 8, D, I.
787 See Part III, Chapter 8, D, II.
788 See Part III, Chapter 8, D, III, 1.
789 See Part III, Chapter 8, D, III, 2.

Third, the last concept to fall within the reach of the effects on interstate trade doctrine necessitates that the trade associations researched, their members and non-members fulfil the "appreciability" (*i.e.* de minimis) requirement.[790] Pursuant to Article 102 TFEU such an examination is redundant, in particular, due to the fact that the Commission must consider this criterion under the dominance requirement. Conversely, in relation to Article 101 TFEU, for the Commission to have authority to assess the potential anti-competitiveness of nonlegal sanctioning, the concept of appreciability is crucial. In this regard, the De Minimis Notice is guiding. Importantly, to understand when nonlegal sanctions which are imposed by the trade associations researched and executed by their members and nonmembers fulfil this criterion, it is at times difficult to make a distinction between restrictions by object and by effect.[791]

When the conduct of these undertakings can be classified as restrictions by object, in line with the judgment in *Expedia*, which forms the basis of the Commission's stance in its De Minimis Notice, the appreciability requirement is automatically fulfilled. However, where a nonlegal sanction has an effect on trade, this is not so obvious. The Commission must then undertake an assessment of whether self-regulatory sanctioning has an appreciable effect on trade. This requires evidence that the members of the trade associations researched possess – jointly – more than 10% market shares in each relevant EU commodities market. In addition, they must generate more than 40 million euro in annual turnover on that market. Despite an absence of clear data, the members of the trade associations researched satisfy both requirements (except the members of the DDC). This is because the majority of industry actors prefer to belong to the most important trade association which ensures efficiency gains to them. Nonmembers also fulfil both requirements when they have entered into an agreement. In some commodities markets, there are competing trade associations and some industry actors may prefer to not belong to a specific association. With regard to the trade associations researched, despite their operating on the markets for regulation and private ordering concerning specific commodities on EU territory and not on the second-tier adjacent commodities markets within which their extrajudicial measures take effect, these associations of undertakings meet the appreciability requirement. It would be unwise to exclude the possibility of antitrust scrutiny

790 See Part III, Chapter 8, D, III, 3.
791 See Part III, Chapter 8, D, III, 3, a.

under Article 101 TFEU when such unilateral conduct has an appreciable effect on targeted wrongdoers.

In sum, nonlegal sanctioning methods imposed by the trade associations researched and executed by their members and non-members falls within the scope of EU Competition Law. More specifically, conformity with Articles 101 and 102 TFEU can be examined by the Commission (and in appeal, the CJEU). This is because the legislative Community framework consisting of legal and economic boundaries is "unequivocally" applicable. In other words, the Commission is empowered to carry out its task of ensuring that both Articles vis-à-vis guaranteeing market freedom and benefitting consumers are complied with. This substantive analysis is the focus of the next Chapter.

Chapter 9: Anticompetitive Agreements under Article 101(1) TFEU

A. Introduction

Article 101 (1) TFEU regulates the culpability of undertakings that participate in agreements harmful to the functioning of the internal market. In other words, this provision prohibits agreements between undertakings, which have the restriction of competition as their object or effect. To scrutinize whether the trade associations researched, their members and non-members violated this prohibition for their participation in extrajudicially sanctioning a disloyal industry actor, it is, first, essential to answer the question whether they colluded (Paragraph B) and, second, whether their agreements restrict competition (Paragraphs C-H).[792]

B. *Collusion: "a concurrence of wills"*

Collusion plays a central role under Article 101(1) TFEU because it focuses on prohibiting any form of cooperation between undertakings that leads to prevention, restriction or distortion of competition within the internal market. While this might appear a broad catch-all provision, a concurrence of wills must take one of the three different forms described in Article 101(1) TFEU. These are (i) an "agreement between undertakings"; (ii) a "decision by an association of undertakings"; and (iii) a "concerted practice".[793]

---

792 A similar approach was followed in C. Barnard and S. Peers, "*European Union Law*", Oxford: Oxford University Press 2017, p. 521.

793 ECJ 8 July 1999, Case C-49/92P (Commission of the European Communities v. Anic Partecipazioni SpA), [1999] ECR I-4125, para. 112, 132, 133. In this case the ECJ held that "*whilst the concepts of an agreement and of a concerted practice have particularly different elements, they are not mutually incompatible* [...] *the [General Court] did not therefore have to require the Commission to categorise either as an agreement or as a concerted practice each form of conduct found but was right to hold that the Commission has been entitled to characterise some of those forms of conduct as principally "agreements" and others as "concerted practices* [...] *it must be pointed out that that this interpretation is not incompatible with the restrictive nature*

In practice, however, there is no need to identify whether a particular behaviour falls within one of these categories considered in Article 101(1) TFEU.[794] This is because the EU Commission tends to make a general distinction between independent conduct and collusion only.[795] Regardless of this approach, to assess whether the trade associations researched, their members and non-members have cooperated when extralegally punishing a recalcitrant industry actor, it is better to establish for each of these actors which form of collusion can be established within the meaning of Article 101 (1) TFEU.

I. Agreement between undertakings

The concept of "agreement between undertakings" is not legally defined in European law, but it has been extensively interpreted by the CJEU. According to the CFI, an agreement encompasses anything which encapsulates the "*faithful expression of the joint intention of the parties*"[796], irrespec-

---

of the prohibition laid down in [Article 101 TFEU] [...] *Far from creating a new form of infringement, the arrival at that interpretation merely entails acceptance of the fact that, in the case of an infringement involving different forms of conduct, they meet different definitions whilst being caught by the same provision and being all equally prohibited*". Moreover, the Commission in Commission Decision of 5 December 2001, Case No IV/37.614/F3 PO (Interbrew and Alken-Maes), para. 223 noted that "The concepts of "agreement" and "concerted practice" are variable and may overlap. Realistically, it may even be impossible to make such a distinction, since an infringement may simultaneously have the characteristics of both forms of prohibited behaviour, whereas taken separately, some of its elements may correctly be regarded as one rather than the other form. It would also be artificial from an analytical point of view to split what is clearly a continuous, collective enterprise with a single objective into several forms of infringement. A cartel may for instance constitute an agreement and a concerted practice at the same time.

794 See ECJ 23 November 2006, Case C-238/05 (Asnef-Equifax v. Ausbanc), [2006] ECR I-11125, para. 32. In this case the ECJ ruled that "*a precise characterisation of the nature of the cooperation at issue is not liable to alter the legal analysis to be carried out under Article [101 TFEU]*".

795 M. Lorenz, "*An Introduction to EU Competition Law*", Cambridge: Cambridge University Press 2013, p. 76.

796 CFI 6 April 1995, Case T-141/89 (Tréfileurope Sales SARL v. Commission of the European Communities), [1995] ECR II-791, para. 96.

tive of its form[797]. In other words, it is not only confined to binding or oral contracts of whatever kind, but also includes tacit collusion (acceptance) or acquiescence of unilateral policies. In many ways it is comparable to the existence of a contract under Section 1 of the Sherman Act.[798] As a result, the same logic can be applied. When one of the trade associations researched imposes any type of nonlegal sanction on a recalcitrant industry actor, it is in fact their members that execute such measure or measures. The reason for this is the members have expressly agreed to respect the by-laws and rules of the relevant trade association at the time of obtaining membership in which nonlegal sanctions are included. Moreover, when members conduct business with other members (or non-members) on the basis of a standardized contract from a relevant trade association, this is perhaps even more obvious. Such a document typically refers to a broader arbitration agreement which includes nonlegal sanctions. That being said, albeit that one can make an argument that new members are not expected to understand all the membership rules upon admittance and could argue that they have no knowledge of extrajudicial sanctioning, such logic should be rebutted. Members ought to be aware of the methods to punish disloyal market participants for not complying with an arbitral award.[799] Hence, the members of the trade associations researched entered into an agreement between undertakings.

Establishing an agreement for non-members is more difficult. Such market participants are not members of a trade association and have not

797 ECJ 6 January 2004, joined cases C-2/01 P and C-3/01P (Bayer v. Commission), [2004] ECR I-23, para. 101-102. In this case the ECJ ruled that a unilateral policy can constitute an agreement pursuant to Article 101 TFEU. Therefore, "*it is necessary that the manifestation of the wish of one of the contracting parties to achieve an anti-competitive goal constitute an invitation to the other party, whether express or implied to fulfil that goal jointly*". In other words, an unilateral invitation may constitute an agreement when it is expressly or tacitly accepted by the other party. It occurs when the conduct of the addressee reveals support to the unilateral course of conduct. An *argumentum e contrario* drawn from this definition entails that, in the event the other party reacts against an unilateral course of conduct, no agreement can be deemed to be constituted. See also M. Horspool and M. Humphreys, "*European Union Law*", Oxford: Oxford University Press 2012, p. 438, 439

798 See Part II, Chapter 6, C, I.

799 This is to some degree similar as ECJ 12 July 1979, joined cases 32/78, 36/78 to 82/78 (BMW Belgium SA et al v. Commission of the European Communities), [1979] ECR 2435, para. 36. Following this case, BMW Belgium instructed its dealers to refrain from dealing with non-approved dealers. Despite some pressure from BMW Belgium, its dealers could refuse to enter into this agreement.

agreed to abide by its rules and rules, which include extrajudicial sanctions. Only when a non-members enters into an agreement with a member of a relevant trade association on the basis of a standardized contract of this association which refers to a broader arbitration agreement that includes nonlegal sanctions, is there sufficient evidence of an agreement between undertakings within the meaning of Article 101(1) TFEU.

II. Decisions by associations of undertakings

The second category of collusion envisaged in Article 101(1) TFEU does not aim to cover direct forms of coordination (*e.g.* agreements or concerted practices) by undertakings, but institutionalized forms (*i.e.* acting through collective structures) of coordination. Whereas this description is not useful to define the behaviour of members and non-member undertakings in executing nonlegal sanctions, it is perfectly suitable to describe the cooperation of the trade associations researched when they impose any type of nonlegal sanction on an industry actor.[800] This is on the grounds that the imposition of nonlegal sanctions (i) originates from the governing body of a trade association;[801] (ii) the decisions are formal or informal;[802] and (iii) the trade associations researched are able to dictate a certain market economic behaviour applicable to their members.[803]

---

800 See Part II, Chapter 6, C, II. Albeit more obvious with regard to Article 101 TFEU, a decision by an association of undertakings is to a large degree similar to a combination in the form of trust or otherwise which is appropriate to describe the form of collusion by the trade associations researched under Section 1 of the Sherman Act.

801 Trade associations have sometimes been used as a vehicle by companies to collude. See M. M. Dabbah, "*EC and UK Competition Law: Commentary, Cases and Materials*", Cambridge: Cambridge University Press 2004, p. 69; The membership rules of trade associations have the effect of regulating standards and behaviour. See E. Berry, M. J. Homewood, and B. Bogusz, "*Complete EU Law: Text, Cases, and Materials*", Oxford: Oxford University Press 2017, p. 596.

802 D. Cahill, V. Power, and N. Connery, "*European Law*", New York: Oxford University Press 2011, p. 164.

803 C. Cucu, "Agreements, Decisions and Concerted Practices: Key Concepts in the Analysis of Anti-competitive Agreements", *Lex ET Scientia International Journal, Vol. 20, Issue* 1 2013 p. 222. A decision must be interpreted broadly; When one of the trade associations researched imposes a nonlegal sanction on a wrongdoer, the economic behaviour of its members towards such an industry actor is influenced. Typically, such members are less likely to conduct trade with a targeted undertaking.

III. Concerted practices

When the trade associations researched and their members orchestrate nonlegal sanctions, such conduct is defined as decisions by associations of undertakings with regard to the relevant trade association and agreements between undertakings pertaining to its members. There is no need to assess whether they have engaged in a concerted practice. This is different, however, for non-members that did not conduct trade on the basis of a standardized contract with a member of one of the trade associations researched. Applying the two forms of cooperation mentioned above is unsatisfactory. Much more can they have engaged in a concerted practice by discontinuing or avoiding trade with a targeted extrajudicially sanctioned industry actor. Whether such a change in commercial behaviour by non-members is sufficient to amount to a concerted practice depends on the various methods of interpretation communicated by the CJEU and in legal doctrine.

To start this discussion, the concept of concerted practice should be defined as a catch-all provision[804] to situations where parties without any formal agreement "*knowingly substitute practical cooperation for the risks of competition*".[805] In other words, it aims to forestall the possibility of undertakings evading the application of Article 101 TFEU by colluding in a manner falling short of an agreement. Strictly etymologically, the concept of concerted practice entails the conscious and deliberate cooperation of undertakings with a certain market behaviour. Albeit that this is rather vague and difficult to evidence, the CJEU developed a fathomable definition. In *Dyestuff* the ECJ defined the term concerted practice as "*a form of coordination between undertakings, which without having reached the stage where an agreement properly so-called has been concluded, knowingly substitutes practical cooperation for the risks of competition*".[806] One year later, in the *Sugar Cartel*

804 W. Frenz, "*Handbook of EU Competition Law*", Berlin/Heidelberg: Springer Verlag Berlin Heidelberg 2016, p. 270.

805 See ECJ 14 July 1972, Case 48/69 (Imperial Chemical Industries Ltd. v. Commission of the European Communities), [1972] ECR 619, para. 64; There are a lot of similarities with the concept of conspiracy pertaining to Section 1 of the Sherman Act. See Part II, Chapter 6, C, III.

806 ECJ 14 July 1972, Case 48-69 (Imperial Chemical Industries Ltd. v. Commission of the European Communities), [1972] ECR 619, para. 64.

case the CJEU revisited this concept and gave a more detailed definition.[807] The ECJ explained that there must be a form of coordination or practical cooperation between undertakings and that such collusion must be achieved through a direct or indirect contact between the undertakings concerned.[808] Absent a preponderance of evidence, the standard of proof that the Commission has to meet can be considered as "not very high".[809] Moreover, the Commission does need to show that the concerted practice has anti-competitive effects on the market.[810]

---

807 ECJ 16 December 1975, joined cases 40 to 48, 50, 54 to 56, 111, 113 and 114-73 (Coöperatieve Vereniging "Suiker Unie" UA et al v. Commission of the European Communities), [1975] ECR 1663.

808 Ibid., para. 174. The ECJ ruled that "*it does however strictly preclude any direct or indirect contact between* [...] *operators, the object or effect whereof is either to influence the conduct on the market of an actual or potential competitor or to disclose to such a competitor the course of conduct which they themselves have decided to adopt or contemplate adopting on the market*". This definition was understood in literature as consisting of three separate requirements that need to be fulfilled. See van Bael & Bellis (firm), "*Competition Law of the European Community*", The Hague: Kluwer Law Internationaal 2005, p. 52.

809 With regard to the standard of proof, the Court in ECJ 7 January 2004, joined cases C-204/00 P, C-205/00 P, C-211/00 P, C-213/00 P, C-217/00 P and C-219/00 P, (Aalborg Portland et al v. Commission of the European Communities), [2004] ECR I-123, para. 81 ruled that according to settled case law, "*It is sufficient for the Commission to show that the undertaking concerned participated in meetings at which anti-competitive agreements were concluded, without manifestly opposing them, to prove to the requisite standard that the undertaking participated in the cartel. Where participation in such meetings has been established, it is for that undertaking to put forward evidence to establish that its participation in those meetings was without any anti-competitive intention by demonstrating that it had indicated to its competitors that it was participating in those meetings in a spirit that was different from theirs*".

810 ECJ 8 July 1999, Case C-199/92P (Hüls AG v. Commisson of the European Communities), [1999] ECR I-4287, para. 163-166. The ECJ stated that a concerted practice falls under Article 101 TFEU, "*even in the absence of anti-competitive effects on the market*". In this regard, the Court used three arguments. "*First, it follows from the actual text of that provision that, as in the case of agreements between undertakings and decisions by associations of undertakings, concerted practices are prohibited, regardless of their effect, when they have an anti-competitive object. Next, although the very concept of a concerted practice presupposes conduct by the participating undertakings on the market, it does not necessarily mean that that conduct should produce the specific effect of restricting, preventing or distorting competition. Lastly, that interpretation is not incompatible with the restrictive nature of the prohibition laid down in Article 81(1) EC* [now Article 101(1) TFEU] [...] *since, far from extending its scope, it corresponds to the literal meaning of the terms used in that provision*".

Against this background, defining the conduct of non-members that did not contract on the basis of a standardized contract with a member of a relevant trade association as a concerted practice within the meaning of Article 101(1) TFEU is rather contentious. If an (unintentional) joint adjustment of a market strategy by non-members is already considered a concerted practice, this runs the risk that every seemingly small shred of evidence substantiating a common market adjustment is enough to substantiate collusion within the meaning of Article 101(1) TFEU. In spite of this observation, if one would allow non-members to escape antitrust scrutiny at this early stage by denying the presence of a concerted practice, it would immunise them and prevent the Commission and the CJEU from delving into an antitrust analysis for the participation of non-members in the execution of nonlegal sanctions. Accordingly, non-members that did not contract with a member of a trade association on the basis of the trade association's standardized contract have colluded in the form of a concerted practice.

C. Prevention, restriction or distortion of competition: The existence of an illegal horizontal agreement and collective boycott

Nonlegal sanctioning has the potential to oust an industry actor from any relevant commodities market and in some markets even harms social relationships within a close-knit society. This alone is sufficient to justify a thorough analysis of whether nonlegal sanctioning is considered anticompetitive. To provide a comprehensive analysis comparable to Section 1 of the Sherman Act[811], the focus will be on the collection and dissemination of the names of wrongdoers in blacklists, withdrawing membership, denying membership for expelled members on the basis of an additional entry condition, refusing to deal with ostracized members, entering the premises of recalcitrant industry actors without a warrant, and limiting adequate access to public courts prior to arbitral proceedings and after an award.

I. Restrictions by object or effect

Before researching whether the trade associations researched, their members and non-members violate Article 101 (1) TFEU, it is necessary to un-

811 See Part II, Chapter 6, D.

derstand the difference between restrictions by object and effect. In this regard, the ECJ in *Société Technique Minière (L.T.M.) v. Maschinenbau Ulm GmbH (M.B.U.)* must be mentioned.[812] In its judgment, the Court ruled that a restriction by object is given when an agreement or concerted practice is so deleterious to competition that negative effects on the internal market are assumed, whereas a restriction by effect is established when the anticompetitive effects of specific conduct on the market are proven.[813] These non-cumulate, but alternative requirements[814] - arguably - bear similarities to the *per se* rule and effects rule applied by the FTC and US courts when dealing with a claim relating to Section 1 of the Sherman Act.

When assessing whether conduct violates Article 101(1) TFEU by object or effect, the Commission and in appeal the CJEU must first consider the former rule before applying the second rule. This is because "*there is no need to take account of the concrete effects of an agreement once it appears that it has as its object the prevention, restriction or distortion of competition*".[815] To determine whether an "object" restriction exists, the purpose of the agreement must be examined in light of the legal and economic context,[816] the wording of the provision of the agreements concerned and the objectives they are intended to attain,[817] without taking into account the actual and

812 ECJ 30 June 1966, Case 56/65 (Société Technique Minière (L.T.M.) v. Maschinenbau Ulm GmbH (M.B.U.)), [1966] ECR 235.

813 Ibid., p. 249.

814 Ibid. The ECJ ruled that "*these are not cumulative but alternative requirements, indicated by the conjunction 'or', leads first to the need to consider the precise purpose of the agreement, in the economic context in which it is to be applied*". See also Communication from the Commission – Notice – Guidelines on the application of Article 81(3) of the Treaty [now Article 101 (3) TFEU] of 27 April 2004, [OJ 2004, No. C 101/97], para. 20.

815 ECJ 13 July 1966, joined cases 56 and 58-64 (Établissements Consten S.à.R.L. and Grundig-Verkaufs-GmbH v. Commission of the European Economic Community) [1966] ECR 299, p. 342.

816 ECJ 28 March 1984, joined cases 29 and 30/83 (Compagnie Royale Asturienne des Mines SA and Rheinzink GmbH v. Commission of the European Communities), [1984] ECR 1979, para. 26; ECJ 4 June 2009, Case C-8/08 (T-Mobile Netherlands BV, KPN Mobile NV, Orange Nederland NV and Vodafone Libertel NV v. Raad van Bestuur van de Nederlandse Mededingingsautoriteit), [2009] ECR I-4529, para. 27.

817 ECJ 20 November 2008, Case C-209/07 (Competition Authority v. Beef Industry Development Society Ltd and Barry Brothers (Carrigmore) Meats Ltd.), [2008] ECR I-8637, para. 21. Importantly, the ECJ ruled that "*an agreement may be regarded as having a restrictive object even though it does not have the restriction of com-*

concrete effects of the agreements.[818] To elaborate on this, non-exhaustive guidance on what constitutes a restriction by object can be found in Commission block exemptions, guidelines and notices.[819]

If conduct does not have the object of harming competition, the consequences of the agreements should then be considered. For it to be caught by Article 101 TFEU, it is then necessary to show that "*competition has in fact been prevented or restricted or distorted to an appreciable extent*".[820] To determine the effects on competition, both actual and potential effects must

---

petition as its sole aim but also pursues other legitimate objectives [...] *It is only in connection with Article 81(3) EC [now Article 101(3) TFEU] that matters* [...], *if appropriate, be taken into consideration for the purposes of obtaining an exemption from the prohibition laid down in Article 81(1) EC [now Article 101(1) TFEU]*".

818 ECJ 30 January 1985, Case 123/83 (Bureau national interprofessionnel du cognac v. Guy Clair), [1985] ECR 391, para. 22; ECJ 28 June 2005, joined cases C-189, 202, 205-208 and 213/02P (Dansk Rørindustri A/S et al v. Commission of the European Communities), [2005] ECR I-5425, para. 145; ECJ 7 February 2013, Case C-68/12 (Protimonopolný úrad Slovenskej republiky v. Slovenská sporiteľňa a.s), ECLI:EU:C:2013:71, para. 17.

819 See, in particular, the Communication from the Commission – Notice – Guidelines on the application of Article 81(3) of the Treaty [now Article 101(1) TFEU] of 27 April 2004, [OJ 2004, No. C 101/97], para. 21-22. In this Notice the Commission summarizes case law and gives some policy statements by explaining that "*Restrictions of competition by object are those that by their very nature have the potential of restricting competition. These are restrictions which in light of the objectives pursued by the Community competition rules have such a high potential of negative effects on competition that it is unnecessary for the purposes of applying Article [101](1) to demonstrate any actual effects on the market. This presumption is based on the serious nature of the restriction and on experience showing that restrictions of competition by object are likely to produce negative effects on the market and to jeopardise the objectives pursued by the Community competition rules. The assessment of whether or not an agreement has as its object the restriction of competition is based on a number of factors. These factors include, in particular, the content of the agreement and the objective aims pursued by it. It may also be necessary to consider the context in which it is (to be) applied and the actual conduct and behaviour of the parties on the market. In other words, an examination of the facts underlying the agreement and the specific circumstances in which it operates may be required before it can be concluded whether a particular restriction constitutes a restriction of competition by object. The way in which an agreement is actually implemented may reveal a restriction by object even where the formal agreement does not contain an express provision to that effect. Evidence of subjective intent on the part of the parties to restrict competition is a relevant factor but not a necessary condition*"; See also the Guidelines on the applicability of Article 101 of the Treaty on the Functioning of the European Union to horizontal co-operation agreements of 14 January 2011, [OJ 2011, No. C 11/01].

820 ECJ 30 June 1966, Case 56/65 (Société Technique Minière (L.T.M.) v. Maschinenbau Ulm GmbH (M.B.U.)), [1966] ECR 235, p. 249.

be taken into account[821] in the context in which they occur, in light of the situation which would have existed in the absence of the agreement[822] with special emphasis on the economic and legal context of such agreements.[823] In addition, the CFI ruled that in examining the restrictive effects "*the nature of the products or services concerned, as well as the real operating conditions and the structure of the market concerned*" should be thoroughly assessed.[824] It is therefore necessary to examine, first, what the competition would have been in the absence of the agreement and, second, whether the impact of the agreement on competition can be sufficiently substantiated.[825]

II. Collection and dissemination of market information

It is clear that in a market where operators disseminate detailed and (potentially) commercially sensitive information, sharing data can facilitate collusion, or even lead to an agreement in violation of Article 101(1) TFEU.[826] But can the same conclusion be drawn when one of the trade

---

821 ECJ 28 May 1998, Case C-7/95P (John Deere Ltd v. Commission of the European Communities), [1998] ECR I-311, para. 77; Guidelines on the applicability of Article 101 of the Treaty on the Functioning of the European Union to horizontal co-operation agreements of 14 January 2011, [OJ 2011, No. C 11/01], para. 26.

822 ECJ 25 November 1971, Case 22-71 (Béguelin Import Co. v. S.A.G.L. Import Export), [1971] ECR 949, para. 17. See, in particular, CFI 2 May 2006, Case T-328/03 (O2 (Germany) GmbH & Co. OHG v. Commission of the European Communities), [2006] ECR II-1231, para. 69. In this case the CFI ruled that the analysis of "*taking into account of the competition situation that would exist in the absence of the agreement, does not amount to carrying out an assessment of the pro- and anti-competitive effects of the agreement and thus to applying a rule of reason, which the Community judicature has not deemed to have its place under Article [101(1) TFEU]*".

823 ECJ 12 December 1967, Case C-23/67 (SA Brasserie de Haecht v. Consorts Wilkin-Janssen), [1967] ECR 525, p. 415.

824 GC 24 May 2012, Case T-111/08 (MasterCard, Inc. et al v. European Commission), [2012] ECR II-000, para. 87; CFI 2 May 2006, Case T-328/03 (O2 (Germany) GmbH & Co. OHG v. Commission of the European Communities), [2006] ECR II-1231, para. 66.

825 CFI 2 May 2006, Case T-328/03 (O2 (Germany) GmbH & Co. OHG v. Commission of the European Communities), [2006] ECR II-1231, para. 73.

826 J. Drexl and F. Di Porto, "*Competition Law as Regulation*", Chelthenham/ Northampton: Edward Elgar Publishing 2015, p. 296; A. Jones and B. E. Sufrin,

associations researched places a recalcitrant industry actor on a blacklist? Though a great deal of case law reflects on the difficult relationship between an illicit exchange of information and this provision, the Commission, NCAs and the CJEU have not dealt with the blacklisting of member undertakings for not complying with arbitral awards, which blacklisting is imposed by trade associations and executed by its members and non-members.[827] To address this, the focus in this Paragraph is to discuss (relatively) comparable case law where the exchange of information through (regulatory) circulars constituted an infringement of Article 101(1) TFEU and more fitting cases, where the publication of default lists for non-adhering to bylaws/regulatory terms by trade associations either violated or did not violate this provision. A potential antitrust infringement attributable to the trade associations researched, their members and non-members for their respective roles in the dissemination of market information through a blacklist will be discussed separately.

"*EU Competition Law: Text, Cases, and Materials*", Oxford: Oxford University Press 2016, p. 163.

827 Generally, exchanges of information are about prices, production and sales, costs, investments and capacities. See, *inter alia*, ECJ 16 December 1975, joined cases 40 to 48, 50, 54 to 56, 111, 113 and 114-73 (Coöperatieve Vereniging "Suiker Unie" UA et al v. Commission of the European Communities), [1975] ECR 1663; ECJ 31 March 1993, joined cases C-89/85, C-104/85, C-114/85, C-116/85, C-117/85, C-125/85, C-126/85, C-127/85, C-128/85 and C-129/85 (Ahlström Osakeyhtiö et al v. Commission), [1993] ECR I-01307; Commission Decision of 13 July 1994 relating to a proceeding under Article 85 of the EC Treaty [now Article 101 TFEU], Case No IV/C/33.833 (Cartonboard); Commission Decision of 30 November 1994 relating to a proceeding under Article 85 of the EC Treaty [now Article 101 TFEU], Case No IV/33.126 and 33.322 (Cement); ECJ 28 May 1998 (John Deere Limited v. Commission of the European Communities), [1998] ECR I-3111; ECJ 8 July 1999, Case C-49/92P (Commission of the European Communities v. Anic Partecipazioni SpA), [1999] ECR I-4125; CFI 15 March 2000, joined cases T-25/95, T-26/95, T-30/95, T-31/95, T-32/95, T-34/95, T-35/95, T-36/95, T-37/95, T-38/95, T-39/95, T-42/95, T-43/95, T-44/95, T-45/95, T 46/95, T-48/95, T-50/95, T-51/95, T-52/95, T-53/95, T-54/95, T-55/95, T-56/95, T-57/95, T-58/95, T-59/95, T-60/95, T-61/95, T-62/95, T-63/95, T-64/95, T-65/95, T-68/95, T-69/95, T-70/95, T-71/95, T-87/95, T-88/95, T-103/95 and T-104/95 (Cimenteries CBR et al v. Commission), [2000] ECR II-491; ECJ 2 October 2003, Case C-194/99P (Thyssen Stahl AG v. Commission of the European Communities), [2003] ECR I-10821.

1. Blacklists by trade associations

In the bylaws of all of the trade associations researched there is a clause included that either obligates, or empowers, these associations to blacklist recalcitrant industry actors when such undertakings do not satisfy arbitral awards from specialized commercial arbitration. When a nonlegal sanction is imposed, there is a clear risk that a relevant trade association violates Article 101(1). The reasons are two-fold. First, the Commission in its guidelines on the applicability of Article 101 of the Treaty on the Functioning of the European Union to horizontal co-operation agreements ("Guidelines on Horizontal Cooperation Agreements") referred to the exchange of information as one of the six most common types of horizontal restraints incompatible with the provisions of Article 101.[828] Second, the dissemination of market information through a blacklist has raised antitrust concerns such as in the ECJ's judgment in *Asnef-Equifax/Ausbanc*[829] and the Commission's, CFI's and ECJ's judgments in *Compagnie Maritime Belge*.[830]

---

828 Guidelines on the applicability of Article 101 of the Treaty on the Functioning of the European Union to horizontal co-operation agreements of 14 January 2011, [OJ 2011, No. C 11/01], para. 5; See also A. Fatur, "*EU Competition Law and the Information and Communication Technology Network Industries*", Oxford: Hart Publishing 2012, p. 112; Regardless of the fact that the Commission in its Guidelines on horizontal cooperation agreements refers to exchange of information as part of the activities of a cartel, this document is not very useful other than stating that an exchange of information is a common type that infringes Article 101(1) TFEU. This is mainly engendered by two reasons: first, the Guidelines do not contain a definition of what constitutes a cartel. Second, whereas the Guidelines speak of qualification as a restriction by object or effect, there is no reference made to a situation comparable to the practice of blacklisting by the trade associations researched. Support given by the Guidelines on applicability of Article 101 of the Treaty on the Functioning of the European Union to horizontal co-operation agreements of 14 January 2011 [OJ 2011, No. C 11/01], para. 72-94 to determine under which category of restriction the practice of blacklisting falls is ill-matched. A qualification as a restriction by either object or effect is impossible without considering the decisional practice of the Commission and the case law of the CJEU.

829 ECJ 23 November 2006, Case C-238/05 (Asnef-Equifax, Servicios de Información sobre Solvencia y Crédito, SL and Administración del Estado v. Asociación de Usuarios de Servicios Bancarios (Ausbanc)), [2006] ECR I-11125.

830 Commission Decision of 23 December 1992 relating to a proceeding pursuant to Articles 85 [now Article 101 TFEU], Case No IV/32.448 and IV/32.450 (Cewal, Cowac and Ukwal) and 86 [now Article 102 TFEU], Case No IV/32.448 and IV/32.450 (Cewal) of the EEC Treaty; CFI 8 October 1996, joined cases T-24/93, T-25/93, T-26/93 and T-28/93 (Compagnie Maritime Belge Transports SA and

Before delving into the legal reasoning of both cases, it should be mentioned that already an exchange of information through a circular gives rise to competition law concerns. A good illustration of this is the French NCA's decision in *Lucie-Ilec* (autorité de la concurrence).[831] In that decision, the NCA ruled that sharing information concerning views of an association with members on the potential unlawful anti-competitive behaviour of a specific non-member is contrary to EU Competition Law, insofar as a concerted action is recommended.[832] Even though this decision provides some general guidance on how to deal with an information exchange, it is rather far removed from the factual situation that an association blacklists an industry actor operating on a second-tier commodities market. Therefore, the next two Paragraph thoroughly discuss the more closely (but not entirely) related ECJ judgment in *Asnef-Equifax/Ausbanc* and the Commission's decisional practice and CJEU's line of reasoning in *Compagnie Maritime Belge*.

Compagnie Maritime Belge SA v. Commission of the European Communities), [1996] ECR 11-1201; ECJ 16 March 2000, joined cases C-395/96P, C-396/96P (Compagnie Maritime Belge Transports SA et al v. Commission of the European Communities), [2000] ECR I-1365; Commission Decision of 30 April 2004 relating to a proceeding under Article 82 of the EC Treaty [now Article 102 TFEU], Case No COMP/D/32.448 and 32/450 (Compagnie Maritime Belge); CFI 1 July 2008, Case T-276/04 (Compagnie Maritime Belge SA v. Commission of the European Communities), [2008] ECR II-1277.

831 Decision N° 05-D-33 of 27 June 2005 on practices implemented by Ilec.

832 Ibid., p. 6. The French NCA ruled that this does not dissuade member undertakings from entering into a contract with the reported undertaking (Lucie) and can, therefore, not be classified as a boycott; The NCA ruled that the dissemination of information is permissible when it aims to help members to perform their activity. See also Décision N° 98-D-73 of 25 November 1998 on a referral and a request for interim measures submitted by the National Employers' Union of dental technicians; To a lesser degree of importance, see the Opinion of the Advocate-General Poiares Maduro of 23 May 2007, Case C-438/05 (International Transport Workers' Federation v. Viking Line ABP et al), [2008] IRLR 143, para. 7. In that Opinion, the Advocate-General stated that the exchange of information through a circular by the International Transport Workers' Federation (ITF) to persuade other trade unions not to enter into negotiations with one of its members (Viking Line) effectively precluded – pertaining to the principle of solidarity – any possibility of this company to deal with another trade union. While infringements of EU Competition Law were not discussed, this opinion provides an explanatory description of an information exchange, which could potentially be of interest to establish a violation of Article 101(1) TFEU.

a. Asnef-Equifax/Ausbanc

In *Asnef-Equifax/Ausbanc*, the ECJ considered an online register of the Spanish association of financial institutions (ASNEF) that set up an electronic register of credit information that disclosed the history of potential customers.[833] The effect was that each bank was aware of each potential client's credit history and took this into account when negotiating further loans. It is common ground that this system makes relevant information about existing or potential borrowers available to credit providers and has the ability to blacklist bad customers.[834]

While the ECJ stressed that such registers do not have, by their very nature, the object of restricting or distorting EU Competition Law within the meaning of Article 101(1) TFEU, a doctrine was introduced to establish when they do "not" have the effect of doing so.[835] In other words, the ECJ ruled that an information exchange of credit agencies is permissible when (i) relevant markets are not highly concentrated;[836] (ii) the identity of lenders is not disclosed, directly or indirectly;[837] and (iii) the conditions of access to the registry are non-discriminatory for all operators on the market, in law or in fact.[838] Following this line of reasoning, the ECJ explained that it cannot be inferred solely from the existence of an information exchange that such conduct classifies as a collective boycott prohibited under Article 101(1) TFEU.[839] This is also because the Court found that clients may check and, where necessary, correct or delete harmful information concerning them.[840]

Whereas the ECJ shed light on the fine line between anti-competitive behaviour and genuine business in the exchange of clients' financial information, it is doubtful how the exchange of information in a blacklist which is imposed by the trade associations researched must be assessed against this background. To adumbrate how the EU Commission and the

833 ECJ 23 November 2006, Case C-238/05 (Asnef-Equifax, Servicios de Información sobre Solvencia y Crédito, SL and Administración del Estado v. Asociación de Usuarios de Servicios Bancarios (Ausbanc)), [2006] ECR I-11125, para. 7.
834 Ibid., para. 46.
835 Ibid., para. 47-48.
836 Ibid., par. 58. See also ECJ 2 October 2003, Case C-194/99P (Thyssen Stahl AG v. Commission of the European Communities), [2003] ECR I-10821, para. 84.
837 Ibid., para. 59.
838 Ibid., para. 60.
839 Ibid., para. 62.
840 Ibid., para. 63.

CJEU would assess the imposition of such a measure is uncertain and even obscure. The reason being that even though the dissemination of the names of wrongdoers in blacklists which is initiated by the trade associations researched reduces costs, as members can select faithful contracting parties, such a measure differs from the exchange of information in *Asnef-Equifax/Ausbanc*. This is because the banks disseminated information about the solvency and creditworthiness of clients (*i.e.* non-members) as opposed to the names of members. However, one should not disregard the legal ruling from *Asnef-Equifax/Ausbanc* altogether.

When trying to look through the lens of the decision-maker in this judgment, in an attempt to transpose this ruling to fit the situation of that of the trade associations researched, their involvement in blacklisting appears illegitimate pursuant to Article 101(1) TFEU by effect. The reasons are three-fold: first, disseminating the names of wrongdoers in blacklists has the potential to oust targeted industry actors from the market. Second, the trade associations researched possess high levels of market concentration on the market for regulation and private ordering concerning EU territory.[841] Because many industry actors that operate on relevant adjacent second-tier commodities markets are members of these associations, the exclusionary effect for targeted member undertakings is exacerbated. Third, albeit depending on the availability of a blacklist to the general public or limited only to members, when undertakings are blacklisted in publicly accessible lists (*e.g.* the ICA) this is more harmful than when they are placed on a secret list, because it would allow non-member undertakings as well as any other third party to be informed about the reliability of conducting trade with a blacklisted company instead of only the members.

b. Compagnie Maritime Belge

Perhaps having an even closer connection to the dissemination of the names of undertakings in a blacklist by the trade associations researched concerns the two different, but similar, proceedings in *Compagnie Maritime Belge*. In these cases, the Associated Central West Africa Lines (CEWAL) shipping conference, which at the material time had more than 90% percent of the market operated, *inter alia*, "fighting ships" schemes pursuant to which it offered liner services at special rates different from their normal rates. These rates were lower than that of its main competitor

841 See part III, Chapter 8, D, III, 3, a.

Grimaldi & Cobelfret (G&C).[842] The purpose of this regulatory strategy was to deter shippers and consignees from using (at least occasionally) the services of other independent lines.[843] If a shipper still used the services of another line which was not a member of CEWAL, that shipper would be blacklisted.

It follows from the decisions of the Commission and the CFI that, *inter alia*, due to the exclusionary nature of blacklisting, an abuse of a dominant position was found.[844] Regardless of the fact that it is evident that when a trade association has considerable market share, both the Commission and the CFI favour the establishment of an infringement pursuant to Article 102 TFEU, some remarks can be made with regard to this line of reasoning. This is because the suggestion of CEWAL to its members, both directly and indirectly, which has as an effect to prevent members from doing business with third parties can also be considered as an anti-competitive agreement in violation of Article 101(1) TFEU. Therefore, the reasoning in *Compagnie Maritime Belge* is tantamount to discuss whether the trade associations researched violate Article 101(1) TFEU when they disseminate the names of recalcitrant market participants in a blacklist.[845] This is important not only because such undertakings can no longer compete under the

842 D. Geradin and N. Petit, "Price Discrimination under EC Law: The Need for a Case-by-Case Approach", *Coleurope* 2005, p. 15. For a background of this Article, see K. Czaprack, "*Intellectual Property and the Limits of Antitrust: A Comparative Study of US and EU Approaches*", Chelthenham/Northampton: Edward Elgar Publishing 2009, p. 32. Cewal members operated liner services between Zaire (the current name is the "Republic of Congo"), Angola and other European ports in the North Sea. CEWAL had implemented a cooperation agreement with Ogefrem (the Zairian shipping authority), which had as its effect that all goods shipped between Cewal ports were exclusively carried out by Cewal members.

843 CFI 8 October 1996, joined cases T-24/93, T-25/93, T-26/93 and T-28/93 (Compagnie Maritime Beige Transports SA and Compagnie Maritime Belge SA v. Commission of the European Communities), [1996] ECR 11-1201, para. 170.

844 Commission Decision of 23 December 1992 relating to a proceeding pursuant to Articles 85 [now Article 101 TFEU], Case No IV/32.448 and IV/32.450 (Cewal, Cowac and Ukwal) and 86 [now Article 102 TFEU], Case No IV/32.448 and IV/32.450 (Cewal) of the EEC Treaty, para. 86; CFI 8 October 1996, joined cases T-24/93, T-25/93, T-26/93 and T-28/93 (Compagnie Maritime Beige Transports SA and Compagnie Maritime Belge SA v. Commission of the European Communities), [1996] ECR 11-1201, para. 172, 182-183.

845 Another interesting judicial decision that concerned the practice of blacklisting concerns CFI 27 September 2006, Case T-204/03 (Haladjian Frères SA v. Commission of the European Communities), [2006] ECR 11-3779, para. 34, 36. This case involved Caterpillar, a US company which designs, develops, engineers,

same conditions with other industry actors that operate on the same relevant commodities market, but also because it has clear exclusionary effects. This hints at a violation of Article 101(1) TFEU by effect. Differences such as the fact that in *Compagnie Maritime Belge* not industry actors which operate on the same market, but third parties got blacklisted and the different reason for such a measure should be disregarded.

c. Statement

The practice of blacklisting with reference to the legal proceedings in *Asnef-Equifax/Ausbanc* and *Compagnie Maritime Belge* is different from the situation of the trade associations researched. Yet, the effect of blacklisting is similar, namely to punish bad behaviour and to warn actors (*i.e.* banks, shippers/consignees or other industry actors) not to deal with disloyal individuals and/or undertakings. As the Commission and the CJEU have not, to date, defined the practice of blacklisting as a restriction by object, it is not unlikely that both institutions in the future will classify the dissemination of the names of industry actors, as is done by any of the trade associations, as a restriction by effect. Any different outcome would prevent a full-fledged analysis of justification grounds under Article 101(3) TFEU, even though there are benefits to total welfare and consumer welfare which are generated by an effective system of specialized commercial arbitration in which awards are typically complied with under the threat of blacklisting. Whether this measure occurs in public or private lists is not important at this stage. Both manifestations of blacklists infringe Article 101(1) TFEU by effect.

---

manufactures, markets and sells among others construction machines via a worldwide dealer network. This included the United States, the EU/EFTA area and Africa. While prices varied between these geographic zones, it induced a number of resellers to take advantage of the differences from one zone to another. To prevent this, Caterpillar sent its dealers a blacklist (*i.e.* the list of inter-zone sellers), which was updated at intervals, of resellers involved in inter-zone sales. It should be noted that this case was assessed in relation to a vertical relationship and will inevitably differ from one in relation to a horizontal agreement. Therefore, the merits of the case only give an illustrative example of blacklisting pertaining to the trade associations researched.

2. Execution of blacklists by members of trade associations

The practice of blacklisting is initiated by the trade associations researched, but is only successful when their members execute such measure. Without their members, these trade associations are merely empty vehicles that cannot efficaciously blacklist recalcitrant industry actors for not complying with arbitrational awards. The reason for this is that in this scenario it is unlikely that industry actors would change their commercial (and sometimes social) behaviour towards a targeted wrongdoer. In addition, members have the power to change the bylaws of any of the trade associations researched and strike down clauses which permit/obligate these institutions to blacklist disloyal undertakings. Subsequently, member undertakings have a crucial role to play in the effectiveness of blacklisting. It is for this reason that members participate in an anti-competitiveness agreement between undertakings every time a trade association blacklists a wrongdoer. Even though the decisional practice of the Commission and case law of the CJEU do not clarify whether members infringe Article 101(1) TFEU when they execute the dissemination of the name of a wrongdoer in a blacklist, they participate in a collective boycott in violation of Article 101(1) TFEU. This is true when the names of recalcitrant industry actors are placed in private and public blacklists.

3. Execution of blacklists by non-members

Comparable to the analysis of Section 1 of the Sherman Act when considering the illegality of non-members for their role in the execution of blacklisting, two situations must be discussed.[846] The first pertains to the situation in which a member of one of the trade associations researched conducts trade with a non-member on the basis of such an association's standardized contract which is linked to a broader arbitration agreement in which there is a clause on blacklisting and the former actor gets blacklisted. Whereas a non-member has no possibility to rescind a blacklisting clause and owing to the situation that such an undertaking is often not aware that a standardized contract is linked to an arbitration agreement which includes a blacklisting clause, Article 101(1) TFEU is not infringed upon.

---

846 See Part II, Chapter 6, D, I, 3.

The same conclusion can be drawn with regard to non-members that in no way are connected to a relevant trade association which disseminates the names of disloyal industry actors in a blacklist and merely act upon that information. Albeit that an aversion to conduct trade with such an industry actor is likely, this is not enough to violate Article 101(1) TFEU. It would preposterously broaden the scope of Article 101(1) TFEU and carries the risk that any industry actor, no matter what its involvement, could violate this Article 101(1).

III. Membership rules and barriers for market access

Having outlined the first competition law concern in the face of all-capturing, ever applicable competition rules, a withdrawal of membership and a refusal of an expelled member to reobtain membership on the basis of an additional entry condition are discussed in this Paragraph. This is because the trade associations researched, their members and non-members could infringe Article 101(1) TFEU.

1. Withdrawal from a trade association

a. Withdrawal by a trade association

Trade associations must be able to put an end to the privileges of members that in a serious way fail to comply with its bylaws and rules. Expelling those undertakings that are no longer *bona fide* members of the industry, or ostracizing those undertakings the activities of which harm or are likely to harm the interests of the association must not necessarily infringe Article 101(1) TFEU.[847] It is insufficient to identify conduct as an illegal anticompetitive collusion when the bylaws and rules of a trade association solely, without further tendency to reduce or discourage competition, allow for the expulsion of members that contravene the association's "gener-

847 An example of this can be found in Paragraph 3(5)(b) of the Statutes of Verband der Sachversicherer. This provision *"provides for the expulsion of a member for serious or repeated failure to comply with the statutes or conduct which is grossly contrary to the interests of the Association"*. See the Opinion of the Advocate-General Darmon of 20 November 1986, case 45/85 (Verband der Sachversicherer v. Commission of the European Communities), [1987] ECR 405, p. 438.

al policy".[848] However, expelling a member from a trade association may also be seen as harmful. An example is when rules provide the possibility to withdraw membership for vague "disloyal behaviour".[849]

To assess whether the trade associations researched infringe Article 101(1) TFEU, it is necessary to consider the objective criteria of membership established by the Commission in nine cases concerning London commodities markets.[850] The Commission established three requirements that must be complied when a trade association withdraws the member-

848 Order of the President of the CFI of 21 January 2004, case T-245/03R (Fédération Nationale des Syndicats d'Exploitants Agricoles (FNSEA) et al v. Commission of the European Communities), [1996] ECR I-4971, para. 45. This is in line with settled case law. See Order of the President of the CFI of 14 December 2000, case T-5/00 R (Nederlandse Federatieve Vereniging voor de Groothandel op Elektrotechnisch Gebied v. Commission of the European Communities), [2000] ECR II-4121, para. 56, 64. In that case, "*members were bound to abide strictly by the provisions of the articles of association, the internal rules and the decisions of the Board of Directors and meetings*". Both orders have been confirmed in the Order of the President of the CFI of 21 January 2004, case T-217/03R (Federation nationale de la coopération bétail v. Commission of the European Communities), [2004] ECR II-241, para. 52-54.

849 In Danish Competition Council of 30 January 2008, (Lokale Pengeinstitutter (the Association of Local Banks, Savings Banks and Coopertive Banks in Denmark; the Association) the trade association's bylaws stipulated that its Board could withdraw membership for demonstrating "*a lack of collegial behaviour*". See H. Peyt and N. Nørager, "Current Developments in Member States", *European Competition Journal 4* 2008, p. 332.

850 Commission Decision of 13 December 1985 relating to a proceeding under Article 85 of the EEC Treaty [now Article 101 TFEU], Case No IV/27.590 (London Sugar Futures Market Limited); Commission Decision of 13 December 1985 relating to a proceeding under Article 85 of the EEC Treaty [now Article 101 TFEU], Case No IV/27.591 (London Cocoa Terminal Market Association Limited); Commission Decision of 13 December 1985 relating to a proceeding under Article 85 of the EEC Treaty [now Article 101 TFEU], Case No IV/27.592 (Coffee Terminal Market Association of London Limited); Commission Decision of 13 December 1985 relating to a proceeding under Article 85 of the EEC Treaty [now Article 101 TFEU], Case No IV/27.593 (London Rubber Terminal Market Association Limited); Commission Decision of 10 December 1986 relating to a proceeding under Article 85 of the EEC Treaty [now Article 101 TFEU], Case No IV/29.688 (The London Grain Futures Market); Commission Decision of 10 December 1986 relating to a proceeding under Article 85 of the EEC Treaty [now Article 101 TFEU], Case No IV/30.176 (The London Potato Futures Association Limited); Commission Decision of 10 December 1986 relating to a proceeding under Article 85 of the EEC Treaty [now Article 101 TFEU], Case No IV/31.614 (The London Meat Futures Exchange Limited); Commission Decision of 10 December 1986 relating to a proceeding under Article 85 of the EEC

ship of an industry actor in order not to violate Article 101(1) TFEU.[851] First, a trade association can only propose an expulsion when it is accompanied by the reasons for such action. Second, any withdrawal of membership must be accompanied by the reasons for such action.[852] Third, a trade association must provide appropriate possibilities of representation after an expulsion (*e.g.* reconsideration of this decision).[853] Fourth, a trade association must establish an appropriate appeal procedure and, depending upon the facts, recourse to the courts.[854] In addition to these requirements, the Commission in *Ship classification* required two additional conditions that a trade association must comply with following the withdrawal of membership of a disloyal industry actor.[855] These are setting clear deadlines for the revocation of membership and the independent appeal board following a withdrawal formation of an.[856] Moreover, in the *International Dental Exhibition* the Commission ruled that the withdrawal of membership after a single infringement must be abolished from the bylaws of a trade association if this association wishes not to contravene the aim of Article 101(1) TFEU, namely to bolster competition within the internal market.[857]

Against this background, since the clauses of the trade associations researched permit these associations to ostracize members for not complying with arbitral awards, it is not unlikely that imposing a withdrawal of membership infringes Article 101(1) TFEU by effect. An expulsion amounts to an illegal coordinated group boycott, because it prevents market access and

---

Treaty [now Article 101 TFEU], Case No IV/29.036 (The GAFTA Soya Bean Meal Futures Association); Commission Decision of 4 December 1986 relating to a proceeding under Article 85 of the EEC Treaty [now Article 101 TFEU], Case No IV/30.439 (Petroleum Exchange of London Limited).

851 See, for example, Commission Decision of 10 December 1986 relating to a proceeding under Article 85 of the EEC Treaty [now Article 101 TFEU], Case No IV/31.614 (The London Meat Futures Exchange Limited).

852 Ibid., para. 12.

853 Ibid.

854 Ibid., para. 18. See also the Commission Decision of 2 December 1977 relating to a proceeding under Article 85 of the EEC Treaty [now Article 101 TFEU], Case No IV/147 (Centraal Bureau voor de Rijwielhandel), para. 28.

855 Commission Decision of 14 October 2009 relating to a proceeding under Article 81 of the EC Treaty [now Article 101 TFEU] and Article 53 of the EEA Agreement, Case No COMP/39.416 (Ship classification).

856 Ibid., para. 3(f)-(g).

857 Notice pursuant to Article 19(3) of Council Regulation No 17 (Î) of 9 January 1999 concerning Case No IV/F-1/36.160 (International Dental Exhibition), para. 8.

forecloses future commerce through the signalling of untrustworthiness to other merchants.[858] To make things worse, the majority of the trade associations researched provide insufficient guarantees following a withdrawal of membership. Only two (and arguably three when considering the ICA) out of six of the trade associations researched allow an internal appeal following a withdrawal of membership.[859] In addition, it can be argued that a life-time ban after a single infringement is contrary to the aim of Article 101(1) TFEU by effect.

b. Execution of the withdrawal of membership by members of a trade association

All of the trade associations researched can (and sometimes must) impose withdrawal of membership on a recalcitrant member following non-compliance with an arbitral award. Yet, the competence to impose this extrajudicial measure can easily be taken away from a trade association when its members jointly agree to abolish a clause in the bylaws and rules which permits such conduct. This raises the ensuing question: Is this observation sufficient to conclude that members can also be held accountable for a violation of Article 101(1) TFEU by effect in the event one of the trade associations researched imposes withdrawal of membership?

Whereas decisional practice of the Commission and case law of the CJEU focus on the conduct of a trade association and are silent on the liability of its members, this question must be answered in the affirmative. Members of a trade association have a crucial role to play in orchestrating withdrawals of membership. Regardless of the act that they are not standing directly behind a smoking gun, their indirect influence in boycotting a targeted member of a trade association should not be underestimated. Whether the Commission and/or CJEU will reach a similar conclusion has yet to be seen. Much will depend on whether they are willing to pursue individual members of a trade association following an expulsion.

858 B. D. Richman, "*Stateless Commerce: The Diamond Network and the Persistence of Relational Exchange*", Cambridge: Harvard University Press 2017, p. 14.

859 See Part I, Chapter 3, G, II.

c. Execution of the withdrawal of membership by non-members

Non-members are neither directly involved in the imposition of a withdrawal of membership nor do they have a role in its enforcement comparable with the members of a relevant trade association. Only if this group of industry actors is aware of a decision to withdraw membership and individual undertakings adjust their business policy against the interests of an expelled member, is there a risk that additional reputational harm is placed upon such an undertaking. This is particularly the case because it would isolate targeted wrongdoers even more than absent such behaviour. Despite some of the trade associations researched publishing a decision to withdraw membership,[860]it would be unwise to say that every non-member violates Article 101(1) TFEU by effect. Not only because it would broaden the scope of this Article well beyond its coverage in the sense that market-adjusting strategy of undertakings, which is a normal feature in every market, would now be seen as anticompetitive, but also because every non-member could infringe Article 101(1) TFEU by effect.

When a non-member conducts trade with a member of a trade association on the basis of a standardized contract which is linked to a broader arbitration agreement in which a withdrawal of membership is laid down and the member undertaking is expelled, some might draw the conclusion that Article 101(1) TFEU is violated. Yet, in my opinion, this can be rebutted on the basis of two arguments. First, non-members are often not aware that a standardized contract is linked to a broader arbitration agreement in which the measure of expulsion is included. Second, non-members cannot annul an expulsion clause which is incorporated in the bylaws and rules of a trade association.

2. Denial of membership for an expelled member on the basis of an additional entry requirement

a. Access restrictions by a trade association

In the event an undertaking is denied re-admittance as a member of a trade association after its membership was withdrawn for not complying with an arbitral award from that trade association's system of specialized commercial arbitration, Article 101(1) TFEU could be infringed. This applies

860 See Part I, Chapter 3, G, II.

in particular when membership of a trade association is necessary to compete in the specific market in which this undertaking operates.[861] While this is the case with regard to all of the trade associations researched, denying readmission for expelled members must underlie all of the membership conditions which apply to normal applicants insofar as they are (i) voluntary;[862] based on (ii) clear; (iii) objective;[863] and (iv) qualitative crite-

---

861 See Commission Decision of 2 December 1977 relating to a proceeding under Article 85 of the EEC Treaty [now Article 101 TFEU], Case No IV/28.948 (Cauliflowers), para. II (4). In this case membership of a trade association of dealers in vegetable products was necessary in order to gain access to an auction in France. The effect was to prevent new dealers from obtaining market access. See also van Bael & Bellis (firm), "*Competition Law of the European Community*", The Hague: Kluwer Law Internationaal 2005, p. 438.

862 Commission Decision of 10 July 1985 relating to a proceeding under Article 2 of Council Regulation (EEC) No 1017/68 applying rules of competition to transport by rail, road and inland waterway, Case No IV/31.029 (French inland waterway charter traffic: EATE levy), para. 51; In appeal, see ECJ 20 May 1987, Case 272/85 (Association nationale des travailleurs indépendants de la batellerie (ANTIB) v. Commission of the European Communities), [1987] ECR 2201, para. 25, 27-38; See also Pharmaceutische Handelsconventie' (PHC), Eighth Report on Competition Policy 1978, p. 73. In this case PHC's rules contained a provision that forced non-members that want to trade with PHC members, manufacturers, dealers and importers to become members of PHC. In conjunction they must accept the obligations of this trade association. Understandably, this raised barriers to competition, as membership was not voluntary.

863 CFI 21 March 2001, Case T-206/99 (Métropole Television SA v. Commission of the European Communities), [2001] ECR II-1057, para. 37. In this case the Court stated that membership rules must be "*objective and sufficiently determinate so as to enable them to be applied uniformly and in a non-discriminatory manner vis-à-vis all potential active members*"; This definition was based on settled case law. See ECJ 25 October 1977, Case 26-76 (Metro SB-Großmärkte GmbH & Co. KG v. Commission of the European Communities), [1977] ECR 1875, para. 20; Also, but not pertaining to access to a trade association, the Commission in Commission Decision of 31 July 2001 relating to a proceeding under Article 81 of the EC Treaty [now Article 101 TFEU] and Article 53 of the EEA Agreement, Case No COMP/37.462 (Identrus), para. 46 found no infringement of Article 101(1) TFEU. This is because access to Identrus infrastructures is open to all, provided that they meet the objective criteria; Moreover, this has been confirmed in the literature. See, for example, C. Ehlermann and L. Gosling, "*European Competition Law Annual 1998: Regulating Communications Markets*", Portland: Hart Publishing 2000, p. 476.

ria; (v) without being restrictive;[864] and (vi) are easily discernible.[865] In addition, the trade associations are obliged to provide written justification for denying re-admittance to membership with the possibility to be subject to an independent process review.[866]

That being said, the lapse of a period of two years following a withdrawal of membership and the freedom of discretion by a Board of Directors of a trade association to decline re-admission apply, which are only imposed by some of the trade associations researched on those industry actors that have been subject to a withdrawal of membership, does not correspond with these rules.[867] Imposing a two-year time period to be re-admitted as a

864 Commission, Competition in a media sector, press releases RAPID "Antitrust: Commission welcomes steps taken by collective rights management bodies in Hungary and Romania to improve competition" (to access: http://europa.eu/rapid/pressReleasesAction.do?reference=IP/11/284&format=HTML&aged=0&language=EN). In that press release, the Commission explained that the international association of national performers' collective management organization (SCAPR) had adopted certain membership clauses that would be restrictive of competition; Another example of a restrictive membership clause concerns the refusal of a trade association to grant access to undertakings that are members of competing associations. See, by analogy, *inter alia*, GC 12 April 2013, case T-442/08 (International Confederation of Societies of Authors and Composers (CISAC) et al v. European Commission), [2013] 5 CMLR, para. 12, 20. In this case the Court ruled that a membership clause that prevented collecting societies from not accepting as a member an author affiliated with another collecting society, was contrary to Article 101(1) TFEU; See also Commission Decision of 16 July 2008 relating to a proceeding under Article 81 of the EC Treaty [now Article 101 TFEU] and Article 53 of the EEA Agreement, Case No COMP/C2/38.698 (CISAC), para. 18, 125. In this case, the Commission decided that a provision that prevented members of another contracting society from becoming a member of the International Confederation of Societies of Authors and Composers (CISAC) was in violation of Article 101(1) TFEU.

865 Organisation for Economic Co-operation and Development, "Latin American Competition Forum", *DAF/COMP/LACF* 2011, p. 21.

866 National British Cattle and Sheep Breeders' Association, Twenty-second Report on Competition Policy 1992, Annex III, p. 416. In this case, the Commission achieved non-discriminatory access for undertakings of the British National Sheep Breeders' Association and the British National Cattle Breeders' Association to the activities of 200 affiliated breeders' societies. The two associations ensured that reasons for a rejection of any application would be given and that such restrictions would be subject to appeal on a non-discriminatory basis; See also Commission Decision of 2 December 1977 relating to a proceeding under Article 85 of the EEC Treaty [now Article 101 TFEU], Case No IV/147 (Centraal Bureau voor de Rijwielhandel), para. 28.

867 See Part II, Chapter 3, G, II.

member is discriminatory vis-à-vis all first-time membership applicants and is too restrictive. It infringes Article 101(1) TFEU by effect. The same arguments can be made when the Board of Directors of a trade association declines to readmit an expelled member. However, such a rule is also not clear, not objective, not easily discernible and is not based on qualitative criteria. It enables such a body to grant and refuse a reapplication for membership arbitrarily. This clearly is in violation of Article 101 TFEU by effect and perhaps even by object. Despite both types of restrictions being possible, not hindering a determination of the procompetitive benefits of a capricious denial of membership against its anticompetitive foreclosure effects, the former option is preferred. With regard to the obligation that trade associations must explain in writing why they refuse a reapplication for membership and the possibility of an appeal, none of them grant these rights to their former members that were expelled. This is further evidence that mitigating the risk of market foreclosure pertaining to targeted industry actors is not the aim of these associations.

In addition to these additional re-entry requirements, some of the standard entry requirements which apply to all applicants also do not correspond with the membership rules. The following table explains which of these entry requirements are in violation of Article 101(1) TFEU by effect.

Standard entry requirements that all trade associations have in common	**Violation of Article 101(1) TFEU?**
1. Connection with the secondary commodities market which the trade association represents	No. Decisional practice of the Commission and case law of the CJEU remain silent on whether this is illegal. In my opinion, it can be seen as a clear, objective and qualitative criteria that is not too restrictive and is easily discernible. This is also in line with the judgment of the ECJ in *Ordem dos Técnicos Oficiais de Contas v. Autoridade da Concorrência*.[868]
2. An application for membership.	No. Without an application, obtaining membership is impossible.

868 ECJ 28 February 2013, Case C-1/12 (Ordem dos Técnicos Oficiais de Contas v. Autoridade da Concorrência), [2013] 4 CMLR 20, para. 99.

3. Entry fee	No. Only when an entry fee is charged, which is so high that it can be seen as too restrictive and bears no relation to the normal cost of membership, is Article 101(1) TFEU is infringed. This is not the case with regard to the trade associations researched. Their entry fees are not unreasonably restrictive of competition.[869]
Standard entry requirements that not all trade associations have in common	**Violation of Article 101(1) TFEU?**
1. Support by at least two members of the relevant trade association	Maybe. This rule could obstruct new members from competing in the relevant commodities market.
2. Minimum duration of experience in the relevant commodities market	Maybe. This rule could obstruct new members from competing in the relevant commodities market.
3. Satisfy the Board of Directors and a post a picture on the main trading wall for other members to comment on	Yes. This rule enables the Board of Directors to deny any potential candidate for membership for any reason. As a result, it forecloses market access for membership applicants.

In sum, the trade associations researched can be held accountable for a violation of Article 101(1) TFEU by effect to the extent they impose additional entry barriers for re-admittance following a withdrawal of membership without providing reasons for a denial and not allowing for an appeal against such a decision. Furthermore, any other membership rule that makes admission for certain types of membership applicants more difficult than for others might also distort market access and result in a violation of Article 101(1) TFEU by effect. Yet, owing to this uncertainty, such rules will not be considered in an analysis under Article 101(3) TFEU.

b. Access restrictions by members of a trade association

Members of the trade associations researched can change the bylaws and rules of these associations. Therefore, they can also abolish rules allowing a trade association to impose additional re-entry barriers on ostracized former members. In the event one of the trade associations researched denies a reinstatement of membership while either a period of two years has not elapsed following an expulsion, or when a Board of Directors does not favour reinstatement, the members also violate Article 101(1) TFEU by ef-

869 Although this is true, the Commission and/or the CJEU can always reach a different conclusion.

fect. This is regardless of the fact that to date decisional practice of the Commission and case law of the CJEU are focused on trade associations as the recipients of antitrust liability for restrictive access to membership rather than their members. The future will tell whether this is sufficient to excuse this group of actors.

c. Access restrictions by non-members

When one of the trade associations researched denies a re-application for membership because an additional entry barrier has not been complied with, non-members cannot be held accountable for a violation of Article 101(1) TFEU by effect. The reasons are two-fold: first, the Commission and the CJEU have never contemplated an illegality of non-members with regard to a comparable situation. Second, non-members are often not aware of a denial of a re-application for membership caused by additional entry barriers.

In the event a non-member enters into a standardized contract with a member of a trade association and this document is linked to a broader arbitration agreement that enables this association to impose additional re-entry barriers and the former member is denied re-admittance to the trade association for any of these grounds, the role of the non-member undertaking in the execution of such measure also does not violate Article 101(1) TFEU by effect. This is because, first, it is often unclear for non-members that a standardized contract is linked to a broader arbitration agreement which includes such a measure and, second, such undertakings cannot rescind clauses which permit a trade association to impose additional re-entry barriers.

IV. Refusal to deal with an expelled member

1. Refusal to deal by a trade association

It appears from the language of Article 101(1) TFEU that its prohibition also includes an instruction from one of the trade associations researched to its member undertakings to not conduct trade with an ostracized member. This is particularly true when analysing the Commission's decision in

Centraal Bureau voor de Rijwielhandel.[870] In that decision, a regulatory clause was struck down that prevented the members of a trade association of bicycle traders from trading in bicycles and related goods with a non-recognized firms.[871] This was seen as forming a closed and cohesive system, which had an appreciable restrictive effect on competition.[872] As a result, the trade association of bicycle traders violated Article 101(1) TFEU by object.[873]

By analogy to the reasoning of the Commission in this decision, it is likely that a regulatory clause by one of the trade associations researched that coerces members into not dealing with disfavoured ostracized member undertakings amounts to an anticompetitive decision of an association of undertakings which is in breach of Article 101(1) TFEU by object.[874] This *de facto* conclusion can be supported by looking at the decisional practice of the Commission and the case law of the CJEU. In line with the judicial decisions of both institutions, in my opinion, even less obvious, but to some extent similar, infringements contravened Article 101(1) TFEU. Examples include (i) a no-competition clause that appreciably impeded access for non-member undertakings;[875] (ii) the prevention of non-members from

870 Commission Decision of 2 December 1977 relating to a proceeding under Article 85 of the EEC Treaty [now Article 101 TFEU], Case No IV/147 (Centraal Bureau voor de Rijwielhandel).

871 Ibid., para. 6.

872 Ibid., para. 29.

873 Ibid., para. 36. The Commission ruled that "*The collective arrangements set up by the CBR system eliminate[s] competition in respect of a substantial part of the goods supplied on the Dutch market, since by far the majority of all the dealers, manufacturers, importers and agents in the bicycle industry are members of the CBR. Accordingly, the application for a declaration of exemption for the Algemeen Reglement under Article 85(3) of the EEC Treaty [now Article 101(3) TFEU] must be rejected*". Based on this legal rule, in my opinion, the Commission seems to classify a refusal to deal with a non-recognized company as a restriction by object.

874 For similarities with the *Centraal Bureau voor de Rijwielhandel* (supra), see Commission Decision of 21 November 1975 relating to a proceeding under Article 85 of the EEC Treaty [now Article 101 TFEU], Case No IV/256 (Bomée-Stichting), para. II. While this case pertains to vertical restraints, the Commission ruled that the practice of the trade association of perfumes, toiletries and cosmetics that obligated its members (manufacturers) to sell only to wholesalers and retailers accepting the association's sale conditions amounted to a restrictive market protection system, which has as its object and effect the restriction of competition pursuant to Article 101(1) TFEU.

875 Commission Decision of 28 October 1988 relating to a proceeding pursuant to Article 85 of the EEC Treaty [now Article 101 TFEU], Case No IV/B-2/31.424,

trading in the auctions of a specific Member State;[876] and (iii) the method of ensuring loyalty, in particular, by prohibiting members from joining competing cooperatives[877] and by exclusively dealing with members only.[878]

Hudson's Bay-Dansk Pelsdyravlerforening, para. 1 (a), 9, 10, 11; In appeal, see CFI 2 July 1992, case T-61/89 (Dansk Pelsdyravlerforening v. Commission of the European Communities), [1992] ECR II-1931, para. 64, 78. As regards this legal proceeding, the Commission and the CFI emphasized, *inter alia*, that a no-competition clause that in particular prohibited members from acting as collecting agents for competitors enforced by the association of Danish fur breeders made it very difficult for third parties to enter the Danish market.

876 Commission, Competition in a media sector, press releases RAPID "Dutch fishermen allowed to land and auction catches in foreign ports following Commission action" (to access: http://europa.eu/rapid/press-release_IP-01-84_en.htm?locale=EN). The Commission investigated the internal rules of a group of private associations (which represent the great majority of fishermen in the Netherlands) that forced fishermen to "sell all catches" to be auctioned through the Dutch fish auctions and excluded harbours, auctions and other service providers in other Member States from competing for Dutch catches. While this gave rise to competition concerns under Article 101(1) TFEU, the groups have amended their rules.

877 ECJ 15 December 1994, case C-250/92 (Gøttrup-Klim Grovvareforening et al v. Dansk Landbrugs Grovvareselskab AmbA (DLG)), [1994] ECR I-5641, para. 35. In this case a provision of a cooperative purchasing association restricted the opportunity for members to join competing cooperatives. Therefore, they were discouraged from obtaining supplies elsewhere. The ECJ ruled that this might have adverse effects on competition.

878 Joined Opinion of the Advocate-General Tesauro of 12 September 1995, joined cases C-319/93, C-40/94, C-224/94, and C-399/93 (Dijkstra v Friesland (Frico Domo) Coöperatie BA and Cornelis van Roessel et al v. De coöperatieve vereniging Zuivelcoöperatie Campina Melkunie VA and Willem de Bie et al v. De Coöperatieve Zuivelcoöperatie Campina Melkunie BA), [1995] ECR I-4515, para. 10, 31; ECJ 12 December 1995, Case C-399/93 (H. G. Oude Luttikhuis et al v. Verenigde Coöperatieve Melkindustrie Coberco BA), [1995] ECR I-4515, para. 3. This case revolved around a fee payable to a milk association (Coberco) after withdrawal or expulsion. This amounted to a violation of Article 101(1) TFEU, since it infringed the doctrine as developed in Gøttrup-Klim (see ECJ 15 December 1994, Case C-250/92 (Gøttrup-Klim Grovvareforening et al v. Dansk Landbrugs Grovvareselskab AmbA (DLG)), [1994] ECR I-5641, para. 14). This doctrine entailed that "*the restrictions imposed on members by the statutes of cooperative associations intended to secure their loyalty must be limited to what is necessary to ensure that the cooperative functions properly and in particular to ensure that it has a sufficiently wide commercial base and a certain stability in its membership*"; A reiteration of this wording can be found in the Opinion of the Advocate-General Jacobs of 28 January 1999, joined cases C-115/97, C-116/97 and C-117/97 and case

2. Execution of the refusal to deal by members of a trade association

When one of the trade associations researched instructs its members not to conduct business with an expelled member, these undertakings typically agree to comply with this rather severe measure under the threat of being extrajudicially punished themselves. As a result, a refusal to deal is only effective in the event members play a role in its execution. Albeit that decisional practice of the Commission and case law of the CJEU have not focused on the accountability of this group of actors, three reasons make their conduct unlawful under Article 101(1) TFEU by object. First, the members of the trade associations researched can rescind any clause that permits the trade association to which they belong from obligating these undertakings to not conduct trade with an expelled former member. Second, individual members can disregard the imposition of a refusal to deal with an ostracized former member irrespective of the threat of being extrajudicially sanctioned as well. Third, the execution of a refusal to deal with an expelled former member can be seen as an anticompetitive agreement between undertakings.

3. Execution of the refusal to deal by non-members

Non-members are not involved in the execution of a refusal to deal with an expelled member when one of the trade associations researched instructs its members to execute this measure. This is because this group of actors does not have the competence to abolish a clause in the bylaws and rules which permits the relevant trade association to impose such a measure, and non-members are often unaware of a refusal to deal with an ostracized member decision. The trade associations researched do not publish this type of extrajudicial sanctioning. Hence, it would be unwise to hold all non-members accountable for a violation of Article 101(1) TFEU for a potential discontinuation of or future stop on entering into commercial activities with a former member that can no longer trade with other members of that trade association.

If a non-member conducts trade with a member of a trade association on the basis of a standardized contract which is linked to a broader arbitration agreement which includes a refusal to deal with an expelled member

---

C-219/97 (Albany International BV v. Stichting Bedrijfspensioenfonds Textielindustrie), [1999] ECR I-5751, para. 272.

and the expelled member is extrajudicially sanctioned vis-à-vis this measure, a breach of Article 101(1) TFEU is unlikely. This is unlikely not only because a non-member is often unaware that a standardized contract is linked to a broader arbitration agreement which incorporates a refusal to deal with an expelled member measure, but also since such an undertaking has no competence to change a refusal to deal clause.

V. Entering the premises of a recalcitrant industry actor without a warrant

In the event one of the trade associations researched orders its officers to enter the premises belonging to a recalcitrant industry actor to find evidence why this undertaking did not comply with an arbitral award, this results in a loss of privacy. Furthermore, when other members and non-members become aware of such conduct, it adds reputational harm in the sense that both groups of actors might not conduct future trade with a wrongdoer.

Similar to Section 1 of the Sherman Act,[879] privacy issues are not covered by Article 101(1) TFEU. With regard to added reputational harm, it is also unlikely this Article is infringed by the trade associations researched, their members and non-members. There is no decisional practice of the Commission and case law of the CJEU that consider anti-competitiveness when officers of a trade association enter the premises of a member without a warrant. Moreover, it is difficult to measure the degree of reputational harm, and criminal law is more suitable to challenging entering an undertaking's premises without an invitation.

VI. Limiting adequate access to public courts prior to arbitral proceedings and after an award

It is safe to say that much of the success of modern day PLSs can be attributed to a well-functioning system of specialized commercial arbitration provided by the trade associations researched. However, even though arbitration is a standard tool for resolving commercial disputes between member undertakings, a restricting access to ordinary courts can be seen as a

879 See Part II, Chapter 6, D, IV.

ground to substantiate an infringement of Article 101(1) TFEU.[880] This was clarified by the Commission in its notice on the *FIA* case,[881] and its guidance on FIFA,[882] following which arbitration must be voluntary with the possibility of recourse to national courts.[883]

1. Voluntary nature of specialized commercial arbitration

Most members of a trade association conduct trade with other members (and sometimes non-members) on the basis of standardized contracts provided by a relevant trade association. These contracts typically contain a clause which explains that any dispute between parties will be resolved in specialized commercial arbitration. As a result, some could argue that the voluntary nature of this type of arbitration is a fallacy. Whether this is true depends on the arguments used. Others might disagree and explain that parties are free to enter into a standardized agreement which is linked to a broader arbitration agreement. In my opinion, it is difficult to ascertain whether arbitration is sufficiently voluntary. The reason for this is that the Commission and the CJEU have not explained how the voluntary nature

880 According to the ECJs judgement in ECJ 1 June 1999, Case 126/97 (Eco Swiss China Time Ltd v. Benetton International NV), [1999] ECR I-3055, para 37, a Member State court system must ensure that arbitral awards comply with EU Competition Law (and in particular Article 101(1) TFEU). This is because an arbitral award inconsistent with the competition rules of the European Union is to be regarded as contrary to national rules of public policy.

881 Notice published pursuant to Article 19(3) of Council Regulation No 17 of 13 June 2001 concerning Case No COMP/35.163 (Notification of FIA Regulations), Case No COMP/36.638 (Notification by FIA/FOA of agreements relating to the FIA Formula One World Championship), and Case No COMP/36.776 (GTR/FIA), sect. 6.

882 Commission, Competition in a media sector, press releases RAPID "Commission closes investigations into FIFA regulations on international football transfers" (to access: http://europa.eu/rapid/press-release_IP-02-824_en.htm?locale=EN); Commission, concerning „Case IV / 36 583-SETCA-FGTB / FIFA" (to access: http://ec.europa.eu/competition/antitrust/cases/dec_docs/36583/36583_54_3.pdf).

883 A. Duval and B. v. Rompuy, "*The Legacy of Bosman: Revisiting the Relationship Between EU Law and Sport*", in: K. Pijetlovic (ed.), "EU Competition Law and Organisational Rules", T.M.C. Asser Press 2016, p. 148; Yet, it is not clear from both proceedings whether a denial of access to public courts (standing alone) is sufficient to violate Article 101(1) TFEU. A combination with other anticompetitive conduct might be required.

of arbitration should be interpreted. It might very well be possible that a violation of Article 101(1) TFEU by effect would be established (if combined with other anticompetitive conduct). If so, it is not only the trade associations researched, but also their members which can be held accountable for an infringement of this Article. This group of actors is able to change the standardized contracts by deleting a clause that is linked to a broader arbitration agreement. Non-members, however, are not able to change the standardized contracts which may be linked to a broader arbitration agreement with a member of a trade association, and, hence, do not breach Article 101(1) TFEU by effect.

2. Recourse to national courts

Some of the trade associations researched are very restrictive in the sense that they only allow judicial review at a public court when both parties in arbitral proceedings agree,[884] or in order to obtain security for an award.[885] This can be seen as providing insufficient recourse to national courts, as this policy violates the standards on recourse to public courts laid down in the Arbitration Act 1996. Other trade associations remain either silent[886] or provide an even better recourse to public courts than this legal document.[887] Put differently, whether a trade association sufficiently guarantees recourse to public courts prior to and after an arbitral award depends on whether the bylaws and rules do not limit the rights guaranteed in the Arbitration Act 1996. If yes, such a trade association can be held accountable for a violation of Article 101(1) TFEU by effect (if combined with other anticompetitive conduct). Members, on the one hand, also infringe Article 101(1) TFEU because they have the competence to change the bylaws and rules of a trade association. Non-members, on the other hand, (even though when a specific non-member enters into a standardized agreement which is linked to a broader arbitration agreement with a member of a trade association) cannot breach Article 101(1) TFEU since they do not have the competence to change the bylaws and rules of a trade association.

---

884 The ICA.
885 The LME.
886 FOSFA and the FCC.
887 GAFTA.

D. Rule-of-reason analysis under Article 101(1) TFEU

The trade associations researched and their members violate Article 101(1) TFEU when the trade associations (i) include the names of wrongdoers in blacklists; (ii) withdraw their membership, (iii) deny a subsequent reapplication for membership on the basis of an additional entry condition; (iv) instruct their members not to conduct trade with an ostracized member; and (iv) limit adequate access to public courts prior to arbitral proceedings and after an award. However, this observation might differ when benefits unrelated to competition, such as public or social policy (*i.e.* balancing of pro-competitive effects) can be taken into account prior to establishing an infringement by object or effect.[888] Despite some form of weighting pros and cons of anti-competitive collusion being allowed to determine the effects on competition,[889] it is unclear whether a rule-of-reason analysis must be conducted under Article 101(1) TFEU.

As can be traced back to US antitrust law, where the idea arose to mitigate the pervasive ascendency of Section 1 of the Sherman Act, especially by weighting pros and cons of anti-competitive behaviour, the existence of a balancing exercise under Article 101(1) TFEU is contentious.[890] *Prima facie*, a reconciliation of such a rule-of-reason analysis does not seem possible. This is particularly true when one looks at the works of *Goyder*,[891]

---

888 L. Nistor, "*Public Services and the European Union: Healthcare, Health Insurance and Education Services*", The Hague: T.M.C. Asser Press 2011, p. 183.

889 ECJ 12 December 1967, Case C-23/67 (SA Brasserie de Haecht v. Consorts Wilkin-Janssen), [1967] ECR 525, p. 415. The ECJ takes into account the economic and legal context, when considering the effects of an agreement.

890 The first ground-breaking fundamental comparative study between Section 1 of the Sherman Act and Article 101 TFEU was given by *René Joliet* in 1967. See R. Joliet, "*The Rule of Reason in Antitrust Law*", The Hague: Martinus Nijhof 1967, p. xx-198. In my opinion, this study provides a lucid, classic analysis of the transposition of the US rule-of-reason analysis under Article 85(1) of the Rome Treaty (now Article 101(1) TFEU).

891 D. G. Goyder, "*EC Competition Law, 3th Edition*", Oxford: Oxford University Press 1998, p. 145. In this book Goyder states that "*The United States Courts may take into account all the positive and negative features of the restraint, as well as the context in which it is applied, remaining as free from statutory restrictions as the courts of common law in assessing the local validity of contractual restraints between vendor and purchaser or employer and employee. By comparison, the Commission must operate within a rigid conceptual framework which allows less freedom of manoeuvre and requires the restriction to pass, not one single balancing test, but a cumulative series of four separate tests*".

Blanco,[892] *Stucke,*[893] and *Colino*.[894] Other authors, however, endorsed the inclusion of a rule-of-reason analysis for reasons of fairness and exception.[895] Interestingly, this fragmentation of viewpoints is addressed in the case law of the CJEU and in the Commission's White Paper on Modernisation of the Rules implementing Articles 85 and 86 of the EC Treaty (now Articles 101 and 102 TFEU) (the 1999 White Paper), which is described below.[896]

---

892 The criticism of *Goyder* has been reiterated in L. O. Blanco, "*Market Power in EU Antitrust Law*", Oxford/Portland: Hart Publishing 2011, p. 22. Weighting pros and cons under Article 101(1) TFEU would make Article 101(3) TFEU redundant.

893 For criticism raised against the rule-of-reason analysis under Section 1 of the Sherman Act, see M. E. Stucke, "Does the Rule of Reason Violate the Rule of Law?", *U.C. Davis Law Review, Vol. 42* 2009, p. 1422. His main critique concerns the absence of clear criteria that makes a case-by-case examination necessary. This gives rise to legal uncertainty. In my opinion, such an assessment also applies to the inclusion of a rule-of-reason analysis under Article 101(1) TFEU, as this provision does not contain clear criteria antithetical to Article 101(3) TFEU. Given the bifurcated structure of Article 101 TFEU, both provisions must be seen as fundamentally different.

894 S. M. Colino, "*Cartels and Anti-Competitive Agreements, Volume 1*", in: C. Callery (ed), "Should the European Union Embrace or Exorcise Leegin's "Rule of Reason"?", Abingdon/New York: Routledge 2012, p. 101. *Colino* states that this would conflate Art. 101 (1) and (3) into one provision akin to Section 1 of the Sherman Act.

895 See I. E. Wendt, "*EU Competition Law and Liberal Professions: an Uneasy Relationship?*", Leiden: Koninklijke Brill NV 2013, p. 269. The argument in favour of transposition of a rule-of-reason analysis under Article 101(1) TFEU pertains to the issue that this provision has been applied too broadly. In essence it catches all agreements, not excluding those beneficial to competition. In line with this reasoning, weighting pros and cons under Article 101(1) TFEU is imperative for a fairer assessment of anti-competitive collusion; See also T. Ackermann, "*Art. 85 Abs. 1 EGV und die rule of reason - Zur Konzeption der Verhinderung, Einschränkung oder Verfälschung des Wettbewerbs*", Cologne/Berlin/Bonn/Munich: Heymanns 1997, p. 2ff, 211ff. He proposes a three-step or four-step test. This requires that (i) an anti-competitive effect (ii) may be exempted from the prohibition of Article 101(1) TFEU in the event of benefits to competition, (iii) when the impairment is reasonably necessary for the purpose of achieving that objective. However, (iv) only as a consistency test and to correct absolutely intolerable results, weighting advantages and disadvantages is permissible. In line with his doctrine, a rule-of-reason analysis under Article 101(1) TFEU is only lawful to prevent extreme results.

896 Commission, "White Paper on Modernisation of the Rules implementing Article 85 and 86 of the EC Treaty [now Articles 101 and 102 TFEU]" of 28 April 1999, [OJ 1999, No. C 132/01].

I. Court of Justice of the European Union

With the start of the modernization process of EU Competition Law, the ECJ adopted a "more economic approach".[897] Consequently, but also to address the time-consuming and burdensome notification procedure of the Commission,[898] the two-tier structure of Article 101 TFEU (first applying Article 101(1) and then Article 101(3) TFEU) was "partially" undermined by the ECJ. This was done by introducing some form of balancing pro- and anti-competitive effects under Article 101(1) TFEU. In particular, the ECJ approved several agreements that, notwithstanding their restrictiveness, were pro-competitive under Article 101(1) TFEU.[899]

897 K. K. Patel and H. Schweitzer, "*The Historical Foundations of EU Competition Law*", Oxford: Oxford University Press 2013, p. 209. The ECJ has paid more attention to the effects of competition on a specific market, following the debate on introducing a "more economic approach".

898 A. Kaczorowska, "*European Union Law*", Abingdon/New York: Routledge-Cavendish 2008, p. 774.

899 ECJ 30 June 1966, Case 56/65 (Société Technique Minière (L.T.M.) v. Maschinenbau Ulm GmbH (M.B.U.)), [1966] ECR 235, p. 249. To determine the effects of an exclusive distribution agreement under Article 101(1) TFEU, the precise purpose of the agreement in the economic context in which it was applied had been taken into account; ECJ 28 January 1986, Case 161/84 (Pronuptia de Paris GmbH v. Pronuptia de Paris Irmgard Schillgallis), [1986] ECR 353. The ECJ took into account the pro-competitiveness of restraints related to franchising under Article 101 (1) TFEU; ECJ 8 June 1982, Case 258/78 (L.C. Nungesser KG and Kurt Eisele v. Commission of the European Communities), [1982] ECR 2015. The Court endorsed the benefits of an exclusive licence under Article 101(1) TFEU; ECJ 11 July 1985, case 42/84 (Remia BV et al v. Commission of the European Communities), [1977] ECR 1875. The Court ruled that a non-compete obligation connected to the sale of a business was declared pro-competitive and thus, permissible under Article 101(1) TFEU; The ECJ also implicitly applied the rule-of-reason analysis under Article 101(1) TFEU in ECJ 15 December 1994, Case C-250/92 (Gøttrup-Klim Grovvareforening et al v. Dansk Landbrugs Grovvareselskab AmbA (DLG)), [1994] ECR I-5641. In that judgment, the Court held that the membership clause of an association that proscribed members joining another association that competed in the same industry had beneficial effects on competition; See also CFI 15 September 1998, joined cases T-374/94, T-375/94, T-384/94 and T-388/94 (European Night Services Ltd (ENS) et al v. Commission of the European Communities), [1998] ECR II-1533. Some balancing of benefits and harm was allowed concerning a cooperative joint venture.

However, even though a rule-of-reason analysis was partially allowed by the ECJ with reference to these cases,[900] the ECJ rejected the balancing of benefits under Article 101(1) TFEU in *Metropole*.[901] The Court ruled that Article 101(3) TFEU would lose much of its effectiveness if such an examination had to be carried out under Article 101(1) TFEU. Therefore, weighing pro-competitive and anti-competitive efficiencies must occur exclusively under the third limb of Article 101 TFEU.[902] This line of reasoning was more recently reiterated in *van den Bergh*[903] and *O2*.[904] However, the CFI reaffirmed that (i) legal and economic factors;[905] (ii) the impact of an agreement on existing and potential competition; and (iii) the competition situation in the absence of that agreement must be taken into account.[906]

Further contradictions with the CFI's decision in *Metropole* and to some extent eroding and overruling the balancing-exclusivity given to Article 101(3) TFEU, the ECJ in *Wouters* ruled that public policy/interest benefits for a Member State must be contemplated under Article 101(1) TFEU.[907] Moreover, the Court ruled that for the purpose of the latter provision, "*account must first of all be taken of the overall context in which the decision of the association of undertakings was taken or produces its effects. More particu-*

---

900 Interestingly, albeit not relating to competition law, in ECJ 20 February 1979, Case C-120/78 (Rewe Zentrale v. Bundesmonopolverwaltung für Branntwein), [1979] ECR 649 (popularly referred to as the *Cassis de Dijon* case) the ECJ introduced a rule-of-reason analysis concerning the free movement of goods pursuant to Article 34 TFEU, in connection with Article 36 TFEU. This legal rule illustrates that a rule-of-reason analysis is not something new for the CJEU.

901 CFI 18 September 2001, Case T-112/99 (Métropole télévision (M6) et al v. Commission of the European Communities), [2001] ECR II-2459, para. 76.

902 Ibid., para. 74.

903 CFI 23 October 2003, Case T-65/98 (Van den Bergh Foods Ltd v. Commission of the European Communities), [2003] ECR II-4653, para. 107.

904 CFI 2 May 2006, Case T-328/03 (O2 (Germany) GmbH & Co, OHG v. Commission of the European Communities), [2006] ECR 1231, para. 69.

905 CFI 23 October 2003, Case T-65/98 (Van den Bergh Foods Ltd v. Commission of the European Communities), [2003] ECR II-4653, para. 84.

906 CFI 2 May 2006, Case T-328/03 (O2 (Germany) GmbH & Co, OHG v. Commission of the European Communities), [2006] ECR 1231, para. 71.

907 ECJ 19 February 2002, Case C-309/99 (J. C. J. Wouters, J. W. Savelbergh and Price Waterhouse Belastingadviseurs BV v. Algemene Raad van de Nederlandse Orde van Advocaten), [2002] ECR I-1577, para. 110. The Court decided that "*a national regulation* [...] *adopted by a body such as the Bar of the Netherlands does not infringe Article 85 (1) of the Treaty* [now Article 101 (1) TFEU], *since that body could reasonably have considered that that regulation, despite the effects restrictive of competition that are inherent in it, is necessary for the proper practice of the legal profession, as organised in the Member State concerned*".

larly, account must be taken of its objectives [...] *It has then to be considered whether the consequential effects restrictive of competition are inherent in the pursuit of those objectives*".[908] In the more recent *Meca Medina*, in a similar way Community goals were balanced under Article 101(1) TFEU.[909] However, this case differs from *Wouters*, as the Court did not balance pro- and anti-competitive effects, but justified the restraint on the ground of economic freedom.[910]

Against this background, since the CJEU has never officially annulled the CFI's decision in *Metropole*, it is unclear whether a rule-of-reason analysis must be conducted pursuant to Article 101(1) TFEU. However, it is clear that some weighing of pro- and anti-competitive effects is permissible under this Article. Interestingly, and giving rise to more legal uncertainty, the CFI in *Braserie Nationale* explained that the transposition of the US rule of reason to Article 101(1) TFEU concerning agreements that "by object" constitute a restriction of competition must be rejected.[911] It is yet to be seen whether this case establishes a legal precedent (*i.e. stare decisis*) for the weighting of benefits and harm, when collusion "by effect" restricts competition within the internal market.

II. Commission

In order to promote the decentralization of the application of Article 101 TFEU by allowing more competences for the NCAs and Member State courts, the Commission launched the process of modernization in its 1999

908 Ibid., para. 97; This is reiterated in ECJ 18 July 2006, Case C-519/04P (David Meca-Medina and Igor Majcen v. Commission of the European Communities), [2006] ECR I-6991, para. 42.

909 C. Townley, "*Article 81 EC and Public Policy*", Portland: Hart Publishing 2009, p. 64; ECJ 18 July 2006, Case C-519/04P (David Meca-Medina and Igor Majcen v. Commission of the European Communities), [2006] ECR I-6991, para. 45. The Court ruled that anti-doping rules by the International Olympic Committee were compatible with Article 101 (1) TFEU, "*since they are justified by a legitimate objective*". Such a limitation is necessary to ensure healthy rivalry between athletes and to guarantee the competitiveness of sport.

910 T. Heremans, "*Professional Services in the EU Internal Market: Quality Regulation and Self-Regulation*", Oxford: Hart Publishing 2012, p. 327.

911 CFI 27 July 2005, joined cases T-49/02 to T-51/02 85 (Brasserie nationale SA (formerly Brasseries Funck-Bricher and Bofferding) et al v. Commission of the European Communities), [2005] ECR II-3033, para. 85.

White Paper.[912] Therein, the Commission supported the establishment of a bifurcated system of the current Article 101 TFEU. The first limb of this Article contains an assessment of whether collusion can be seen as anti-competitive, whereas the third limb allows for *ex post* supervision or exemption of a restrictive practice.[913] Even though this structure clearly rules out a rule-of-reason analysis under Article 101(1) TFEU for the reason that Article 101(3) TFEU must not be evaded, balancing under Article 101(1) can be carried out in line with the "limited" case law of the CJEU. In particular, anent the ECJ'S decisions in *Nungesser* and *Pronuptia.*[914] It is clear that this way to interpret Article 101(1) TFEU creates confusion because it adds to the confusion of whether a rule-of-reason analysis is allowed under the first limb. This worsened when the Commission issued its Guidelines on the Application of Article 81(3) [now Article 101(3) TFEU]. In those Guidelines, this Commission stated that balancing pro-competitive and anti-competitive effects must be conducted "exclusively" pursuant to Article 101(3) TFEU.[915]

III. Summary evaluation

It follows from the CJEU's approach in *Metropole* and the policy statement of the Commission that a rule-of-reason analysis under Article 101(1) TFEU must be strongly rejected. There are, however, two exemptions: first, economic and legal factors may be taken into account. Second, public policy/interests may be considered. These grounds are of particular importance to assess the anti-competitiveness of nonlegal sanctioning committed by the trade associations researched and their members.

In sum, an extensive rule-of-reason analysis under the first limb of Article 101 TFEU must not be contemplated. This is because there is a risk that a party under scrutiny can more easily escape the application of Article 101

912 C. Ehlermann and I. Atanasiu, "European Competition Law Annual 2000: The Modernisation of EC Antitrust Policy", Portland: Hart Publishing 2000, p. 141.

913 A. Albors-Llorens, "*EC Competition Law and Policy*", Abingdon: Routledge 2002, p. 152.

914 Commission, "White Paper on Modernisation of the Rules implementing Articles 85 and 86 of the EC Treaty [now Articles 101 and 102 TFEU]" of 28 April 1999, [OJ 1999, No. C 132/01], para. 57.

915 Communication from the Commission – Notice – Guidelines on the application of Article 81(3) of the Treaty [now Articles 101(1) TFEU] of 27 April 2004, [OJ 2004, No. C 101/97], para. 11.

TFEU compared to the more stringent test in Article 101(3) TFEU. In particular, since the Article 101(3) requires two positive and two negative cumulative conditions to be fulfilled.[916] Owing to the limited guidance offered by the CJEU and the Commission, for the purpose of this research, balancing pros and cons will be done exclusively under the third limb of Article 101(3) TFEU. This provision is tailored to measure the efficiencies that collusion generates through the use of four cumulative conditions that are lucid, clear and sound.

E. Key findings

When trade associations impose nonlegal sanctions on disloyal industry actors for not complying with an arbitral award, it is not impossible that these associations as well as their members and non-members can be held accountable for a violation of Article 101(1) TFEU. This is true when such measures have the "object" or "effect" of preventing, restricting or distorting competition within the internal market. To date, neither the Commission nor the CJEU has ever ruled on the eligibility of extrajudicial measures after a member undertaking of a trade association failed to comply with an award of specialized commercial arbitration. Fortunately, many parallels can be drawn between this situation and prior decisional practice and guidance given by the Commission and the CJEU. To exceed the bounds of Article 101(1) TFEU, two conditions must be fulfilled: first, the trade associations researched, their members and non-members must have colluded. Second, a lack of redeeming virtue must be substantiated by establishing an infringement of Article 101(1) TFEU by object or effect.[917]

With regard to the collusion requirement, which can be seen as a preliminary constituent, anytime one of the trade associations researched imposes a nonlegal sanction on a wrongdoer that operates in a specific commodities market, this conduct is sufficient to qualify as a decision by an association of undertakings within the meaning of Article 101(1) TFEU.[918] The reason for this is that regulatory measures (i) come from the governing bodies of the trade associations researched; (ii) are formal (*i.e.* the bylaws);

---

916 C. Ehlermann and I. Atanasiu, "*European Competition Law Annual 2004: The Relationship Between Competition Law and the (Liberal) Professions*", Portland: Hart Publishing 2006, p. 454.

917 See Part III, Chapter 9, A.

918 See Part III, Chapter 9, B, II.

and (iii) impose a certain market economic behaviour on their members. Also, its members and non-members that conduct trade with a member on the basis of a standardized agreement that is linked to a broader arbitration agreement, which includes nonlegal sanctions, have then cooperated owing to their role in the enforcement. This qualifies as an agreement between undertakings, because there is a faithful expression of the joint intention of parties in writing.[919] Furthermore, to ensure that non-members which did conduct trade with a member of a trade association that imposed a nonlegal sanction on a wrongdoer escape antitrust scrutiny at an early stage, their role in the execution, which is mostly of an indirect nature by breaking (all) commercial ties with a recalcitrant industry actor qualifies as a concerted practice within the meaning of Article 101(1) TFEU.[920] This is because there is some form of collaboration, without having reached the stage than an agreement has been concluded. Put differently, all of the three actors have satisfied the collusion requirement.

Next, given that the mere existence of an agreement or decision is insufficient to establish an infringement of Article 101(1) TFEU, the second requirement requires scrutiny of whether the participation of the three actors in each specific type of nonlegal sanction violates Article 101(1) by object or effect.[921] The importance of this dichotomy should not be underestimated, as the former type of restriction, on the one hand, in contradiction to the effect of restricting competition, is much more severe and cannot be justified pursuant to Article 101(3) TFEU. This concerns when an agreement, by its nature and all readily ascertainable surrounding circumstances, is apt to seek effect.[922] An effect restriction, on the other hand, focuses on the effects of specific conduct and can be justified when the four-tier requirements laid down in Article 101(3) TFEU are fulfilled. Whether the nonlegal sanctions constitute an infringement of one, or both types is not easily discernible, as neither the Commission nor the CJEU has declared such conduct in violation of Article 101 TFEU. However, one thing is sure: they have a clear risk of exceeding the scope of what may be considered permissible conduct under the first limb of this Article. While this statement is too broad, the anti-competitiveness of the trade associations

919 See Part III, Chapter 9, B, I.

920 See Part III, Chapter 9, B, III.

921 See Part III, Chapter 9, C.

922 See Part III, Chapter 9, C, I; See also P. L. Landolt, "*Modernised EC Competition Law in International Arbitration*", The Hague: Kluwer Law International 2006, p. 46.

researched, their members and non-members with regard to each nonlegal sanction was meticulously discussed against analogous decisional practice of the Commission and case law of the CJEU.

The first measure that was reviewed pertains to the inclusion of the names of recalcitrant industry actors in blacklists.[923] Whereas any exchange of information was seen as one of the six most common types of horizontal restraints incompatible with Article 101(1) TFEU according to the guidelines on horizontal cooperation agreements, the ECJ judgment in *Asnef-Equifax/Ausbanc* and the decisions of the Commission and the CFI's and ECJ's judgments relating to *Compagnie Maritime Belge* provide good guidance to assess the liability of the trade associations researched under Article 101(1) TFEU when they disseminate the names of a wrongdoer in a blacklist for not complying with an award from specialized commercial arbitration. Even though both cases are not similar to such an exchange of information, the effect of such a measure is similar.[924] This is to punish bad behaviour and to warn industry actors against conducting trade with disloyal actors. In more detail, when one of the trade associations researched disseminates the names of a wrongdoer in a members-only, or public, blacklist, this constitutes a restriction by effect, because in line with the ECJ judgment in *Asnef-Equifax/Ausbanc* these associations possess high levels of market power in the market for regulation and private ordering concerning the EU territory and can oust a targeted industry actor from the relevant second-tier adjacent commodities market.[925] Furthermore, in keeping with *Compagnie Maritime Belge*, the practice of blacklisting has exclusionary effects and ensures that targeted wrongdoers can no longer compete with other industry actors active on that market.[926] Following the imposition of the practice of blacklisting, the members of the relevant trade association can also be held accountable for a violation of Article 101(1) TFEU by effect.[927] This group of actors has the competence to change the bylaws of this associations and can amend or abolish a clause which permits the trade association to blacklist a wrongdoer. When they do not, they participate in an illegal collective boycott. For non-members an attribution of liability under Article 101(1) TFEU by effect must be denied when this group of actors has not entered into a standardized contract with members of a

923 See Part III, Chapter 9, C, II, 1.
924 See Part III, Chapter 9, C, II, 1, c.
925 See Part III, Chapter 9, C, II, 1, a.
926 See Part III, Chapter 9, C, II, I, b.
927 See Part III, Chapter 9, C, II, 2.

trade association.[928] Similarly, when a specific non-member has conducted business on the basis of a standardized contract with a member of the relevant trade association and this association included the name of that member in a blacklist, a breach of Article 101(1) is also not established.

The second nonlegal sanction is the withdrawal of membership, thus expelling a member from the association.[929] Any withdrawal of membership imposed by one of the trade associations researched amounts to an illegal coordinated group boycott, because it prevents market access and forecloses future commerce through the signalling of untrustworthiness of other merchants.[930] Moreover, the majority of the trade associations researched insufficiently guarantee public recourse to courts following expelling a member and do not have an internal appeal procedure in place to re-assess such a measure. This, in combination with the restrictiveness of an expulsion, is sufficient to determine that any expulsion imposed by one of the trade associations researched violates Article 101(1) TFEU by effect. Members can also be held liable under Article 101(1) for their role in executing an expulsion.[931] Their ability to change a clause in the bylaws of a trade association that permits an expulsion substantiates their participation in a collective boycott which restricts Article 101(1) TFEU by effect. Non-members have no role in the execution of an expulsion of a member from one of the trade associations researched, except when an undertaking that falls under this group conducts trade on the basis of a standardized contract which is linked to a broader arbitration agreement that includes such a measure and the other party (the former member) is expelled.[932] Yet, even then such an undertaking does not enter into an illegal agreement between undertakings in violation of Article 101(1) TFEU.

With reference to the third nonlegal sanction, namely denying membership for expelled members on the basis of an additional entry barrier, decisional practice and guidance of the Commission and case law of the CJEU require that the rules relating to the admission of members must be easily discernible and voluntary based on clear, objective and qualitative criteria, without being too restrictive to not infringe Article 101(1) TFEU by effect.[933] To the extent the trade associations researched impose additional

928 See Part III, Chapter 9, C, II, 3.
929 See Part III, Chapter 9, C, III.
930 See Part III, Chapter 9, C, III, 1, a.
931 See Part III, Chapter 9, C, III, 1, b.
932 See Part III, Chapter 9, C, III, 1, c.
933 See Part III, Chapter 9, C, III, 2, a.

barriers for re-entry following a withdrawal of membership, such as a lapse of a period of two years following expulsion and an arbitrary denial for readmission to membership by a Board of Directors, this rule is not complied with. Furthermore, the trade associations researched do not provide reasons for a denial and do not provide for an internal appeal against a refusal. As a result, they can be held accountable for a violation of Article 101(1) TFEU by effect. Similarly, their members can also be held accountable for a violation for Article 101(1).[934] This group of actors can amend or abolish clauses in the bylaws of a trade association that allow the association to impose additional re-entry barriers. This amounts to an illegal group boycott in violation of Article 101(1) TFEU by effect. Typically, non-members do not violate Article 101(1), unless an undertaking belonging to this group has conducted trade on the basis of a standardized contract which is linked to a broader arbitration agreement that includes additional entry measures following withdrawal of membership and the other party (the former member) is targeted.[935] However, in such a scenario, a non-member has also not participated in an illegal agreement between undertakings in breach of Article 101(1) TFEU.

The fourth extrajudicial measure that was reviewed concerns the instruction of a trade association to its members not to conduct business with an ostracized member.[936] In line with the Commission's decision in *Centraal Bureau voor de Rijwielhandel* this instruction from this institution infringes Article 101(1) TFEU by object. A violation of Article 101(1) can also be attributed to the members of such a trade association.[937] This is because they can amend or abolish any clause that permits such an association to impose a refusal to deal with an expelled member on them, or disregard this extrajudicial measure and continue trade despite the risk of being sanctioned. If not, they participate in an illegal agreement between undertakings in breach of Article 101(1) TFEU by object. A non-member that conducted trade with a member on the basis of standardized contract which is linked to a broader arbitration agreement in which a refusal to deal with an ostracized member is laid down does not breach this provision insofar as this party is targeted with such a measure.[938] The same is true with regard to all other non-members.

934 See Part III, Chapter 9, C, III, 2, b.
935 See Part III, Chapter 9, C, III, 2, c.
936 See Part III, Chapter 9, C, IV, 1.
937 See Part III, Chapter 9, C, IV, 2.
938 See Part III, Chapter 9, C, IV, 3.

The fifth nonlegal sanction that was described pertains to entering the premises of a recalcitrant industry actor without a warrant.[939] While it can hamper the reputation of such a wrongdoer, it falls outside the scope of Article 101(1) TFEU. As a result, the trade associations researched, their members and non-members are compliant with Article 101(1).

The sixth type of conduct that was discussed is not a nonlegal sanction, but can also infringe Article 101(1) TFEU by effect and refers to limiting adequate access to public courts prior to arbitral proceedings and after an award.[940] In this regard, the Commission in its notice on the *FIA* case and its guidance on FIFA explained that arbitration must be voluntary with the possibility of recourse to national courts in order not to breach this provision. Whereas the voluntary nature of arbitration is doubtful, recourse to public courts is not provided by all of the trade associations researched. Two trade associations are clearly in violation of this rule, two trade associations remain silent and one trade association is compliant. Members can also be held accountable for limiting sufficient recourse to public courts because they have the competence to change the bylaws of a trade association. Non-members clearly do not have this competence.

Although five out of the six of the types of conduct described above are in violation of Article 101(1) TFEU, would this be different if some sort of balancing exercise had been permitted in this Paragraph with regard to restrictions by effect?[941] It must be said that weighing pro-competitive efficiencies and anti-competitive conduct is rather contentious at this stage. When reading the wording of Article 101(1), it is immediately clear that such a rule-of-reason analysis should be rejected. Article 101(1) TFEU does not contain grounds for exemption. Moreover, the Commission in its 1999 White Paper explains that Article 101(1) TFEU should be interpreted grammatically and does not leave room for any form of balancing.[942] The aim of the legislature was to create a bifurcated architecture that entitled parties, after a finding of anticompetitive collusion, the competence to seek impunity under the third limb of Article 101 TFEU. The CJEU, in *Metropole, van den Bergh* and *O2*, supported this stance.[943] In spite of neither the Commission nor the CJEU having officially renounced this viewpoint, they permitted some limited form of balancing in order to nullify

---

939 See Part III, Chapter 9, C, V.
940 See Part III, Chapter 9, C, VI.
941 See Part III, Chapter 9, D.
942 See Part III, Chapter 9, D, II.
943 See Part III, Chapter 9, D, I.

the effects repugnant to free competition. An example of this flexible approach can be found in *Wouters* and *Meca Medina*. Following both cases, the ECJ argued that legal and economic factors must be taken into account when an agreement restricts competition "by effect". This requires a determination of existing and potential competition as well as the situation prior and after the conclusion of an agreement. This must be done by focusing on the objectives of an agreement and by contemplating its overall context. While true, the following Chapter will exclusively consider whether the "by effect" restrictions discussed, including disseminating the names of wrongdoers in a blacklist, withdrawing membership and subsequently denying membership for expelled members on the basis of an additional entry barrier, and limiting adequate access to public courts prior to arbitral proceedings and after an award can be justified under Article 101(3) TFEU.

Chapter 10: Exemption under Article 101(3) TFEU

A. *Introduction*

Article 101(2) TFEU provides for the nullity of agreements that are found to be contrary to Article 101(1) TFEU. However, regardless of the fact that the Article 101(2) has an absolute character[944] and whereas the effects of a nullification have *ipso jure* a clear *erga omnes* effect,[945] the trade associations researched and their members can justify their anticompetitive participation in blacklisting, withdrawing membership, denying a reapplication for membership for expelled members on the basis of an additional entry condition, and limiting adequate access to public courts prior to arbitral proceedings and after an award which clearly violates Article 101(1) TFEU by effect, if the requirements laid down in either of the following two exemption routes are fulfilled. The first route exonerates such illegal collusion if it falls within the scope of the Block Exemption Regulation ("BER") (Paragraph B). The second route necessitates the fulfilment of four cumulative conditions which are laid down in Article 101(3) TFEU (Paragraph C).

B. *BER: Research and Development and Specialization Agreements*

EU law revolves around two well-established types of BERs with regard to horizontal cooperation which are currently in force under Regulation 2821/71,[946] namely (i) the research and development BER ("RDBER");[947]

---

944 ECJ 25 November 1971, Case 22-71 (Béguelin Import Co. v. S.A.G.L. Import Export), [1971] ECR 949, par. 29. The Court stated that "*an agreement which is null and void by virtue of this provision has no effect as between the contracting parties and cannot be set up against third parties*".

945 A. Komninos, "*EC Private Antitrust Enforcement: Decentralised Application of EC Competition Law by National Courts*", Portland: Hart Publishing 2008, p. 151.

946 Council Regulation (EEC) No 2821/71 of the Council of 20 December 1971 on application of Article 85(3) of the Treaty [now Article 101(3) TFEU] to categories of agreements, decisions and concerted practices, [OJ 1971, No. L 285].

947 Commission Regulation (EU) No 1217/2010 of 14 December 2010 on the application of Article 101(3) of the Treaty on the Functioning of the European Union to certain categories of research and development, [OJ 2010, No. L 335/36].

and (ii) the specialization agreements BER ("SABER").[948] Both documents were introduced to ameliorate the administrative burdens of companies that operate in the EU. In addition, they curtail the workload of the Commission.[949]

Worth mentioning here is the involvement of the trade associations researched and their members in the imposition and execution of nonlegal sanctions does not qualify under either block exemption. In detail, as can be seen in Article 1(1)(a) of the RDBER, in conjunction with Article 1(1)(m) of the RDBER, the imposition and execution of nonlegal sanctions cannot be classified as research and development agreements. This is because the trade associations researched and their members did not agree to carry out joint research and development, but merely disciplined unwanted behaviour of industry actors.[950] Furthermore, the extrajudicial measures of both actors also do not fall within the scope of the SABER. Article 1(1) of the SABER applies only to unilateral specialization agreements,[951] reciprocal specialization agreements,[952] or joint production agreements[953] regarding the production and distribution of goods.

948 Commission Regulation (EU) No 1218/2010 of 14 December 2010 on the application of Article 101(3) of the Treaty on the Functioning of the European Union to certain categories of specialisation agreements, [OJ 2010, No. L 335/43].

949 L. A. DiMatteo, "*International Business Law and the Legal Environment: A Transactional Approach*", Abingdon: Routledge 2016, p. 251.

950 Commission Regulation (EU) No 1217/2010 of 14 December 2010 on the application of Article 101(3) of the Treaty on the Functioning of the European Union to certain categories of research and development, [OJ 2010, No. L 335/36], Article 1(1)(m) (emphasis added).

951 Commission Regulation (EU) No 1218/2010 of 14 December 2010 on the application of Article 101(3) of the Treaty on the Functioning of the European Union to certain categories of specialisation agreements, [OJ 2010, No. L 335/43], Article 2(1)(a). This entails that "*one party agrees to fully or partly refrain from producing certain products and to purchase them from the other party*".

952 Ibid., Article 2(1)(b) of the SABER. This necessitates that "*two or more parties on a reciprocal basis agree to fully or partly refrain from producing certain but different products and to purchase them from the other parties*".

953 Ibid., Article 2(1)(c) of the SABER. This requires that "*two or more parties agree to produce certain products jointly*".

C. *Assessment of pro- and anti-competitive effects under Article 101(3) TFEU*

As seen above, anti-competitive nonlegal sanctions imposed by the trade associations researched and executed by their members cannot be exempted under the BERs mentioned above. However, Article 101(3) TFEU can also declare Article 101(1) TFEU inadmissible when pro-competitive benefits of extrajudicial measures which restrict Article 101(1) by effect outweigh the anticompetitive effects.[954] As a requirement, four cumulative conditions must be met. First, the agreement must contribute to improving the production or distribution of goods (or services), or to promoting technical or economic progress. Second, consumers must be allowed a fair share of the resulting benefits. Third, any restrictions imposed must be indispensable to attain the preceding objectives. Fourth, the agreement must not be capable of eliminating competition in relation to a substantial part of the products in question.

Unfortunately, all four requirements are imprecise without further regulatory and judicial interpretation. This is particularly true when focusing on the two main ways of how to interpret the four-tier test laid down in Article 101(3) TFEU with great assiduity.[955] On the one hand, the literature explains that the point of departure is a broad and generic test that allows a multitude of other policies, as opposed to purely economic ones to be taken into account.[956] On the other hand, the Commission in its Guidelines on the Application of Article 81(3) [now Article 101(3) TFEU] prefers

954 See Council Regulation (EC) No 1/2003 of 16 December 2002 on the implementation of the rules on competition laid down in Articles 81 and 82 of the Treaty [now Articles 101 and 102 TFEU] [OJ 2003, No L 001], Article 1(2); Before 2003, the Commission had the sole power to declare Article 101(1) TFEU inapplicable. See Council Regulation No 17/62, First Regulation Implementing Articles 85 and 86 of the Treaty [now Articles 101 and 102 TFEU], [OJ 1962, No 87 28], Art. 4; J. Stuyck, H. Gilliams, and E. Ballon, "*Modernisation of European Competition Law: The Commission's Proposal for a New Regulation Implementing Articles 81 and 82 EC*", Antwerp/Oxford/New York: Intersentia 2002, p. 108 (For a reiteration in the literature); However, as from 2003 the Council Regulation (EC) No 1/2003 of 16 December 2002 on the implementation of the rules on competition laid down in Articles 81 and 82 of the Treaty [now Articles 101 and 102 TFEU] [OJ 2003, No L 001], Article 3 (2) also bestowed this competence on national courts and NCAs (*i.e.* the decentralization of competition law).

955 U. Neergaard, E. Szyszczak, J. W. van de Gronden, and M. Krajewski, "*Social Services of General Interest in the EU*", The Hague: T.M.C. Asser Press 2013, p. 280.

956 Some examples of important policies include: consumer protection, industrial policy, public safety, culture, fair trading and environmental protection.

"a more economic approach" that was influenced by the Harvard School of thought.[957] Following this line of reasoning, an effects-based approach must be followed. This entails that only the economic goal of consumer welfare should be taken into account. Put differently, only agreements that yield economic benefits can take advantage of the escape route laid down in Article 101(3) TFEU.[958]

While it is impossible to conclude that the role of the trade associations researched and their members in the imposition and execution of nonlegal sanctions which is in violation of Article 101(1) TFEU by effect can be justified on the basis of such a general observation pursuant to Article 101(3) TFEU, it must be discussed whether the requirements of Article 101(3) are fulfilled for each anticompetitive conduct. Here, the decisional practice and guidance given by the Commission and case law of the CJEU is guiding.[959]

Two remarks must be made before going into an in-depth analysis of whether both actors can evade *ipso jure* nullity after a violation of Article

957 A. S. Papadopoulos, "*The International Dimension of EU Competition Law and Policy*", Cambridge: Cambridge University Press 2010, p. 272. The Harvard School was the first to propose that the use of data to determine the conduct of companies and the performance on the market are crucial indicators to make a distinction between perfect competition and a monopoly (*i.e.* the static model). The major focus of this US theory was on high entry barriers and concentrated markets; U. Neergaard, E. Szyszczak, J. W. van de Gronden, and M. Krajewski, "*Social Services of General Interest in the EU*", The Hague: T.M.C. Asser Press 2013, p. 280. For a good EU example of "the more economic approach", see the Guidelines on the Application of Article 81(3) [now Article 101(3) TFEU].

958 J. Basedow and W. Wurmnest, "*Structure and Effects in EU Competition Law: Studies on Exclusionary Conduct and State Aid*", Alphen aan den Rijn: Kluwer Law International 2011, p. 15. This was an important step in helping to empower NCAs and national courts to apply Article 101(3) TFEU (*i.e.* to facilitate the decentralization process). When determining exclusively the effects on a given market, these institutions to not have to make a trade-off between different policy goals; A. Al-Ameen, "*Antitrust: The Person-centred Approach*", Heidelberg/New York/Dordrecht/London: Springer International Publishing Switzerland 2014, p. 73. To improve antitrust enforcement, the Council Regulation (EC) No 1/2003 of 16 December 2002 on the implementation of the rules on competition laid down in Articles 81 and 82 of the Treaty [now Articles 101 and 102 TFEU] [OJ 2003, No L 001] was introduced. This functional structure was called "Modernisation".

959 This view is supported by *Christopher Townley* in C. Townley, "*Article 81 EC and Public Policy*", Portland: Hart Publishing 2009; For a reiteration of this theory, see A. Gideon, "*Higher Education Institutions in the EU: Between Competition and Public Service*", The Hague: T.M.C. Asser Press 2017, p. 75 (note 159).

101(1) TFEU by effect with regard to the extrajudicial measures discussed. First, the defendant in legal proceedings must invoke the third limb of Article 101 TFEU as a defence.[960] Consequently, this party must convince the Commission that there is a preponderance of evidence to allow for a justification[961] and that all four cumulative criteria are met.[962] Second, while every type of collusion may in principle benefit from Article 101(3) TFEU,[963] the Guidelines on the Application of Article 81(3) [now Article 101(3) TFEU] elucidate that anti-competitive agreements that have as their "object" the restriction of competition "*are likely to produce negative effects on the market and to jeopardise the objectives pursued by the Community com-*

960 D. Hildebrand, "*The Role of Economic Analysis in the EC Competition Rules*", Alphen aan den Rijn: Kluwer Law International 2009, p. 301. Undertakings are required to undertake a self-assessment of whether their restrictive agreement that infringed Article 101(1) TFEU might benefit from an exemption under Article 101(3) TFEU.

961 See, in particular, ECJ 7 January 2004, joined cases C-204/00 P, C-205/00 P, C-211/00 P, C-213/00 P, C-217/00 P and C-219/00 P, (Aalborg Portland et al v. Commission of the European Communities), [2004] ECR I-123, para. 78. In its judgment, the Court stated that "*it should be for the undertaking or association of undertakings invoking the benefit of a defense against a finding of an infringement to demonstrate that the conditions for applying such defense are satisfied, so that the authority will then have to resort to other evidence*"; For a more detailed definition, see ECJ 17 January 1984, joined cases 43/82 and 63/82 (Vereniging ter Bevordering van het Vlaamse Boekwezen, VBVB, and Vereniging ter Bevordering van de Belangen des Boekhandels, VBBB, v. Commission of the European Communities), [1984] ECR 19, para. 52. The Court ruled that "*it is in the first place for the undertaking concerned to present to the Commission the evidence intended to establish the economic justification for an exception, and if the Commission has objections to raise, to submit alternatives to it*".

962 CFI 27 November 1998, Case T-290/94 (Fort James France, formerly Kaysersberg SA v. Commission of the European Communities), [1997] ECR II-2137, para. 178–179. This case is illustrative of the implication that applicants must provide more evidence than merely contesting the Commission's findings. Even though this is, in my opinion, also true with regard to Article 101(3) TFEU, this case relates to Article 102 TFEU.

963 CFI 15 July 1994, Case T-17/93 (Matra Hachette SA v. Commission of the European Communities), [1994] ECR II-595, para. 85. The Court stated that an agreement "*which is anticompetitive in intent or has an anti-competitive effect on a given market*" can both be exempted under Article 101 (3) TFEU; For a reiteration of this legal rule, see Commission Decision of 8 July 2009 relating to a proceeding under Article 81 of the EC Treaty [now Article 101 TFEU], Case No 39.401 (E.ON/GDF), para. 265.

petition rules".[964] Accordingly, it is rather axiomatic that the four-stage test laid down in the third limb of Article 101 TFEU is not fulfilled. This is particularly true when collusion harms consumers. [965] As a consequence, the Commission can refrain from conducting a full-fledged investigation of the competitive impact with regard to the refusal to deal with ostracized members when imposed by one of the trade associations researched and executed by its members.[966]

I. First condition: efficiency gains

The first condition that must be fulfilled by the trade associations researched and their members in order to benefit from the exemption of Article 101(3) TFEU, insofar as they disseminate the names of wrongdoers in blacklists, withdraw membership, deny reapplications for membership for expelled members on the basis of an additional entry condition, and limit adequate access to public courts prior to arbitral proceedings and after an award, requires that any of these measures improves the production or distribution of goods (or services),[967] or ameliorates technical or economic progress. In other words, there must be some efficiency gains flowing from the restrictive practice/agreement.[968] This can be demonstrated when an agreement reduces costs (i) resulting from the introduction of new produc-

---

964 Communication from the Commission – Notice – Guidelines on the application of Article 81(3) of the Treaty [now Article 101(3) TFEU] of 27 April 2004, [OJ 2004, No. C 101/97], para. 21; D. Gerard, "Effects-based enforcement of Article 101 TFEU: the "object paradox"", Kluwer Competition Law Blog 2012, p. 1. Even though object restrictions are open to justification under Article 101(3) TFEU, such exemption has never been granted.

965 I. Kokkoris and I. Lianos, "*The Reform of EC Competition Law: New Challenges*", Alphen aan den Rijn: Kluwer Law International 2010, p. 402-403.

966 J. Bourgeois and D. Waelbroeck, "*Ten years of effects-based approach in EU competition law - State of play and perspectives*", in: H. Zenger and M. Walker (ed) "Theories of Harm in European Competition Law: A Progress Report", Brussels: Groupe de Boeck 2013, p. 195.

967 The first limb of Article 101(3) TFEU applies by analogy to services. See the Communication from the Commission – Notice – Guidelines on the application of Article 81(3) of the Treaty [now Article 101(3) TFEU] of 27 April 2004, [OJ 2004, No. C 101/97], para. 21

968 The Commission refers to the first condition as "efficiency gains". See the Communication from the Commission – Notice – Guidelines on the application of Article 81(3) of the Treaty [now Article 101(1) TFEU] of 27 April 2004, [OJ 2004, No. C 101/97], para. 50-51.

tion technologies and methods;[969] (ii) through the creation of synergies by means of integrating existing assets;[970] (iii) by dint of developing economies of scale[971] and/or economies of scope,[972] (iv) when collusion allows for better planning or production;[973] and (v) by method of joint purchasing of materials and joint distribution.[974] In addition, those efficiency gains may also be established by substantiating evidence of improved quality or innovations.[975]

Regardless of the focus on a strict economic approach, as demonstrated in the Guidelines on the Application of Article 81(3) [now Article 101(3) TFEU],[976] other non-economic benefits which are created or fostered through an agreement are only peripheral to the principle that competitive restrictions can only be justified by efficiency gains.[977] Examples include the environment, public health, development and assistance of the third world and employment. A minor role in contemplating non-economic

969 Ibid., para. 64.

970 Ibid., para. 65.

971 Ibid., para. 66.

972 Ibid., para. 67.

973 Ibid., para. 68. This increases capacity utilization and reduces the need to hold expensive inventory.

974 Commission Decision of 11 June 1993 relating a proceeding pursuant to Article 85 of the EEC Treaty [now Article 101 TFEU], Case No IV/32.150 (EBU/Eurovision System), para. 59-67.

975 T. Ottervanger, "Socially Responsible Competition: Competition law in a changing society", *Markt & Mededinging* 2010, p. 9.

976 See in detail the Communication from the Commission – Notice – Guidelines on the application of Article 81(3) of the Treaty [now Article 101(3) TFEU] of 27 April 2004, [OJ 2004, No. C 101/97], para. 11, 33 and 50. Paragraph 11 pertains to determining the pro-competitive benefits produced by an agreement and assessing whether pro-competitive effects outweigh the anti-competitive effects. Paragraph 33 explains that "*efficiencies may create additional value by lowering the cost of producing an output, improving the quality of the product or creating a new product. When the pro-competitive effects of an agreement outweigh its anti-competitive effects the agreement is on balance pro-competitive and compatible with the objectives of the Community competition rules*". Paragraph 50 stipulates that the purpose of the first condition of Article 101(3) TFEU "*is to define the types of efficiency gains that can be taken into account*".

977 Ibid., para. 42. The Commission only intended to include non-economic goals when they supplement the economic benefits of an agreement. It did so by defining that "*goals pursued by other Treaty provisions can be taken into account to the extent that they can be subsumed under the four conditions of Article 81(3)* [now Article 101(3) TFEU]" (emphasis added).

benefits can best be explained by the dearth of decisional practice of the Commission and case law of the CJEU.[978]

To prevent the first condition under Article 101(3) TFEU from becoming superfluous, the Commission, indirectly, offered concise and preponderant guidance by requiring that any party wishing to fulfil this provision must explain (a) the nature of the efficiencies claimed; (b) the link between the agreement and the efficiencies; (c) the likelihood and magnitude of each efficiency claimed; and (d) how and when each efficiency would be achieved.[979]. To discuss whether the trade associations researched and their members satisfy this evidential barrier for their role in the imposition and execution of nonlegal sanctions, this Chapter proceeds along the following lines: first, it discusses the nature of the efficiency claimed (*i.e.* (a)). Second, it describes the subsequent "inextricably linked" criteria (*i.e.* (b), (c) and (d)) in one Paragraph.

1. The nature of the efficiencies claimed

To qualitatively assess whether nonlegal sanctions imposed by the trade associations researched and executed by their members satisfy the first limb of the evidential test, both actors must show – separately – that these measures have "*appreciably objective advantages*" as opposed to the disadvantages owing to its impact on competition.[980] Put differently, both actors

978 An example of a case where the Commission ascribed weight to a non-economic objective (*i.e.* promoting a collective environmental benefit) accruing from an agreement when assessing the first condition under Article 101(3) TFEU concerns the Commission Decision of 24 January 1999 relating to a proceeding under Article 81 of the EC Treaty [Article 101 TFEU] and Article 53 of the EEA Agreement, Case No IV.F.1/36.718 (CECED), para. 55-57.

979 Communication from the Commission – Notice – Guidelines on the application of Article 81(3) of the Treaty [now Article 101(3) TFEU] of 27 April 2004, [OJ 2004, No. C 101/97], para. 51.

980 ECJ 13 July 1966, joined cases 56 and 58-64 (Établissements Consten S.à.R.L. and Grundig-Verkaufs-GmbH v. Commission of the European Economic Community), [1966] ECR 429, p. 348; This has, *inter alia*, been reiterated in ECJ 6 October 2009, joined cases C-501/06P (GlaxoSmithKline Services Unlimited v. Commission of the European Communities), C-513/06P (and Commission of the European Communities v. GlaxoSmithKline Services Unlimited), C-515/06P (European Association of Euro Pharmaceutical Companies (EAEPC) v. Commission of the European Communities), and C-519/06P (Asociación de exportadores españoles de productos farmacéuticos (Aseprofar) v. Commission of the European Communities), [2009] ECR I-09291, para. 7.

must demonstrate that nonlegal sanctions actually and sufficiently outweigh negative consequences or inconveniences that nonlegal sanctions may cause (*i.e.* appreciability).[981] Furthermore, these associations and members must explain that they are not the only ones to benefit from the extrajudicial measures (*i.e.* subjective advantages),[982] but the Community as a whole (*i.e.* objective advantages).[983]

That being said, although nonlegal sanctions often result in market foreclosure for targeted wrongdoers, they also can generate significant benefits (or efficiencies). In particular, they guarantee an optimal allocation and distribution of goods. This is realized by reducing transaction costs by having a reliable and efficient system of specialized commercial arbitration in place in which arbitral awards are protected by means of extrajudicial measures. By allowing an effective alternative as opposed to cumbersome, time-consuming and expensive litigation in court (*i.e.* by addressing externalities) to some degree Pareto efficiency is achieved.[984] Subsequently, it is

---

981 ECJ 29 October 1980, joined cases 209 to 215 and 218/78 (Heintz van Landewyck SARL et al v. Commission of the European Communities), [1980] ECR 3125, para. 185. The standard that was introduced in this case entails that benefits "*are likely sufficiently to compensate for the stringent restrictions which it imposes on competition*".

982 This follows as an *argumentum e contrario* from ECJ 13 July 1966, joined cases 56 and 58-64 (Établissements Consten S.à.R.L. and Grundig-Verkaufs-GmbH v. Commission of the European Economic Community), [1966] ECR 429, p. 348; L. O. Blanco, "*Market Power in EU Antitrust Law*", Oxford/Portland: Hart Publishing 2011, p. 104.

983 Ibid; Commission Decision of 11 March 1998 relating to a proceeding under Articles 85 and 86 of the EC Treaty [now Articles 101 and 102 TFEU], Case No IV/34.073, IV/34.395 and IV/35.436 (Van den Bergh Foods Limited), para. 224; Communication from the Commission – Notice – Guidelines on the application of Article 81(3) of the Treaty [now Article 101(3) TFEU] of 27 April 2004, [OJ 2004, No. C 101/97], para. 49 (emphasis added).

984 V. Pareto, "*Manual of Political Economy*", New York: Kelley 1906. Pareto optimality, made famous by the Italian economist *Vilfredo Pareto*, entails that "*an outcome is pareto efficient if it is not possible to make someone better off without making someone else worse off*"; B. Nguyen and A. Wait, "*Essentials of Microeconomics*", Abingdon/New York: Routledge 2016, p. 77. While this theory only allows for the balancing of efficiencies, without weighing up efficiency against other socially desirable objectives, it is perhaps not the most equitable, fair, or best market outcome; Furthermore, full Pareto efficiency is not achieved. Any regulatory sanctioned industry actor is deprived of obtaining access to a relevant commodities market. Consequently, given that at least someone is worse off is contrary to the idea of Pareto efficiency, which necessitates that not a single person or undertaking may be harmed.

not wrong to argue that nonlegal sanctions achieve appreciable objective advantages and benefit the Community as a whole within the meaning of the first requirement of Article 101(3) TFEU. Under the third requirement, which focuses on the concept of indispensability, a closer investigation may reach a different conclusion.

2. Sufficient link and likelihood and magnitude of the efficiency

While it is clear that the nonlegal sanctions which restrict Article 101(1) TFEU by effect are important to ensure that any losing party complies with awards issued by specialized commercial arbitration and, hence, reduce transaction costs, the trade associations researched and their members must – separately – explain that the extrajudicial measures have a sufficient[985] and direct[986] causal link with these efficiencies. Moreover, both actors must demonstrate the likelihood and magnitude of each efficiency claimed and explain how and when each efficiency would be achieved.[987]

In consideration of the foregoing, the trade associations researched and their members will have no problem substantiating this. All of the anti-competitive measures researched which restrict Article 101(1) TFEU by effect have a sufficient and direct causal link with these efficiencies. Specialized commercial arbitration is inoperative without the threat of being blacklisted, having membership withdrawn, being denied re-admission to membership on the basis of an additional entry condition and/or having adequate access to public courts limited prior to arbitral proceedings and after an arbitral award. As a result, lowered transaction costs are not realized. It is also likely that the extrajudicial measures discussed generate

985 Communication from the Commission – Notice – Guidelines on the application of Article 81(3) of the Treaty [now Article 101(3) TFEU] of 27 April 2004, [OJ 2004, No. C 101/97], par. 53.

986 Ibid., para. 54.

987 Ibid., para. 55. Both evidential barriers "*allow the decision-maker to verify the value of the claimed efficiencies, which in the context of the third condition of Article 81(3)* [now Article 101(3) TFEU] *must be balanced against the anti-competitive effects of the agreement* […]*. Given that Article 81(1)* [now Article 101(1) TFEU] *only applies in cases where the agreement has likely negative effects on competition and consumers (in the case of hard-core restrictions such effects are presumed) efficiency claims must be substantiated so that they can be verified*".

these rather significant efficiencies.[988] In this regard, the restrictive nature of these measures is of no importance. This follows from the decision of the Commission and the judgment of the ECJ in *FEDETAB*,[989] following which anticompetitive measures/agreements that seriously restrict competition, but allow for "*a more effective distribution*", fulfil the first requirement of Article 101(1) TFEU.[990]

II. Second condition: consumer pass-on

The protection of consumer interest is seen by the EU competition authorities as the most important driver for competition policy. This has, *inter alia*, been reflected by the former Commissioner for Competition Policy, *Mario Monti*. He explained that "*the goal of competition policy in all its aspects is to protect consumer welfare*".[991] This goal also finds its genesis in the

988 Ibid., para. 55. Both evidential barriers "*allow the decision-maker to verify the value of the claimed efficiencies, which in the context of the third condition of Article 81(3)* [now Article 101(3) TFEU] *must be balanced against the anti-competitive effects of the agreement* […]. *Given that Article 81(1)* [now Article 101(1) TFEU] *only applies in cases where the agreement has likely negative effects on competition and consumers (in the case of hard-core restrictions such effects are presumed) efficiency claims must be substantiated so that they can be verified*".

989 Commission Decision of 20 July 1978 relating to a proceeding under Article 85 of the EEC Treaty [now Article 101(1) TFEU], Case No IV/28.852 (GB-Inno-BM/Fedetab), Case No IV/29.127 (Mestdagh-Huyghebaert/Fedetab), Case No IV/29.149 (Fedetab Recommendation); ECJ 29 October 1980, joined cases 209 to 215 and 218/78 (Heintz van Landewyck SARL et al v. Commission of the European Communities), [1980] ECR 3125.

990 Commission Decision of 20 July 1978 relating to a proceeding under Article 85 of the EEC Treaty [now Article 101(1) TFEU], Case No IV/28.852 (GB-Inno-BM/Fedetab), Case No IV/29.127 (Mestdagh-Huyghebaert/Fedetab), Case No IV/29.149 (Fedetab Recommendation), par. 123; ECJ 29 October 1980, joined cases 209 to 215 and 218/78 (Heintz van Landewyck SARL et al v. Commission of the European Communities), [1980] ECR 3125, para. 183; This deduction was given by L. O. Blanco, "*Market Power in EU Antitrust Law*", Oxford/Portland: Hart Publishing 2011, p. 104.

991 M. Monti, EC Commissioner for Competition, "*The Future for Competition Policy in the European Union*", Speech, 9 July 2001, p. 2 (europa.eu/rapid/press-release_SPEECH-01-340_en.pdf); See also N. Kroes, EC Commissioner for Competition, "*European Competition Policy – Delivering Better Markets and Better Choices*", Speech, 15 September 2005, p. 2 (http://europa.eu/rapid/press-release_SPEECH-05-512_en.htm). She explained that "*consumer welfare is now well established as the standard the [European] Commission applies when assessing* […] *in-*

Americanization of the Commission's policy. By focusing on the US Chicago School developed formula of consumer protection, EU competition authorities embrace the essential role of this concept.[992] An illustration can be found in the second condition of Article 101(3) TFEU. This Article provides that agreements, practices or conditions which aspire to the exception must provide consumers a fair share of the resulting benefit.[993] In other words, when one of the trade associations researched and its members seeks to fulfil the second requirement laid down in Article 101(3) TFEU, they must prove that nonlegal sanctions pass on efficiencies to consumers (*i.e.* consumers receive a fair share of the resulting benefit).[994] Establishing whether this is true depends on two factors: first, there must be consumers. Second, the consumers must receive a fair share of these efficiencies.

---

fringements of the Treaty rules on cartels and monopolies"; The pivotal role of consumer protection in EU Competition law has also been reiterated, in the literature, by, for example, Philip Lowe. See P. Lowe, "The design of competition policy institutions for the 21st century — the experience of the European Commission and DG Competition", *Competition Policy Newsletter No. 3* 2008, p. 6. He mentioned that the promotion of consumer welfare, in the Commission's view, is the ultimate objective in the area of competition law.

992 A. Weitbrecht, "From Freiburg to Chicago and Beyond—the First 50 Years of European Competition Law", *European Competition Law Review* 2008, p. 85. This paradigm shift was never subject to public debate by the Commission and occurred without interference by the legislature.

993 A. Jones and B. E. Sufrin, "*EU Competition Law: Text, Cases, and Materials*", Oxford: Oxford University Press 2016, p. 247; Communication from the Commission – Notice – Guidelines on the application of Article 81(3) of the Treaty [now Article 101(1) TFEU] of 27 April 2004, [OJ 2004, No. C 101/97], para. 39. While the Guidelines on the Application of Article 81 (3) [now Article 101(3) TFEU] clearly indicate that the second condition (*i.e.* fair share for consumers) must only be considered after it has been determined that the restrictions incorporated in an agreement are indispensable (i.e. the third condition), this research follows the structure of Article 101(3) TFEU.

994 Communication from the Commission – Notice – Guidelines on the application of Article 81(3) of the Treaty [now Article 101(1) TFEU] of 27 April 2004, [OJ 2004, No. C 101/97], para. 83-104.

1. The scope of the term "consumers"

The concept of "consumers" is interpreted broadly to include final consumers[995] and occasionally intermediate consumers (*e.g.* wholesalers[996] and retailers[997]).[998] Such an extensive definition is justified by the axiom pursued by EU Competition law, namely to safeguard market participants against deleterious agreements.[999] While a broad scope of the term "consumers" is provided by the CJEU in its case law, a more detailed definition can be found in the Guidelines on the Application of Article 81(3) [now Article 101(3) TFEU]. In those Guidelines, by reflecting on the overarching consumer welfare goal,[1000] consumers are defined as legal or natural persons acting in a professional or private capacity.[1001] In other words, consumers can be defined as those who purchase or obtain a good or service from an actor that is located higher up the economic chain.[1002] When read-

995 CFI 22 April 1993, Case T-9/92 (Automobiles Peugeot SA and Peugeot SA v. Commission of the European Communities), [1993] ECR II-493, para. 27. The Commission generally refers to "final consumers" when dealing with the second condition of Article 101(3) TFEU.

996 Wholesalers are parties that sell in bulk quantities.

997 Retailers are parties that sell in small quantities.

998 See, *inter alia*, Commission Decision of 18 July 1975 relating to a proceeding under Article 85 of the EEC Treaty [now Article 101 TFEU], Case No IV/21.353 (Kabelmetal-Luchaire), para. 11; Commission Decision of 9 July 1980 relating to a proceeding under Article 85 of the EEC Treaty [now Article 101 TFEU], Case No IV/27.958 (National Sulphuric Acid Association), para. 47.

999 G. Monti, "*EC Competition Law*", Cambridge: Cambridge University Press 2007, p. 99.

1000 D. Leczykiewicz and S. Weatherill, "*The Images of the Consumer in EU Law: Legislation, Free Movement and Competition Law*", Oxford/Portland: Hart Publishing 2016, p. 70.

1001 Communication from the Commission – Notice – Guidelines on the application of Article 81(3) of the Treaty [now Article 101(1) TFEU] of 27 April 2004, [OJ 2004, No. C 101/97], para. 84. "*The concept of "consumers" encompasses all direct or indirect users of the products covered by the agreement, including producers that use the products as an input, wholesalers, retailers and final consumers, i.e. natural persons who are acting for purposes which can be regarded as outside their trade or profession. In other words, consumers within the meaning of Article 81(3)* [now Article 101(3) TFEU] *are the customers of the parties to the agreement and subsequent purchasers. These customers can be undertakings as in the case of buyers of industrial machinery or an input for further processing or final consumers as for instance in the case of buyers of impulse ice-cream or bicycles*".

1002 J. Drexl, W. S. Grimes, and C. A. Jones, "*More Common Ground for International Competition Law?*", Chelthenham/Northampton: Edward Elgar Publishing 2011, p. 52.

ing the Commission's wording, it seems incontrovertible that almost every user[1003] qualifies as a consumer apart from the parties to a deleterious agreement.[1004] However, the meaning of this concept is not always straightforward and confusion remains. This is particularly true for decisions from the CJEU,[1005] as well as for legal critics.[1006] Notwithstanding

---

1003 L. O. Blanco, "*Market Power in EU Antitrust Law*", Oxford/Portland: Hart Publishing 2011, p. 106. The concepts of "user" and "consumer" are interchangeable, even though in the competition laws of some Member States the former word is chosen (*e.g.* in Spain "usarios", in France "utilisateurs"), whereas in other Member States the latter word is used (*e.g.* in Germany "Verbraucher").

1004 However, this truisms can be rebutted. See Commission Decision of 5 December 1979 relating to a proceeding under Article 85 of the EEC Treaty [now Article 101 TFEU], Case No IV/29.011 (Rennet), para. 30. In that Decision, the Commission gave a description of when parties and consumers (users) are synonymous. In detail, it explained that "*purchasers of rennet and colouring agents for cheese, who may or may not be members of the Cooperative, and purchasers of cheese produced by members of the Cooperative, have had a fair share of the benefit resulting from the agreement*".

1005 An example is the Opinion of the Advocate General of 19 February 2009, Case C-8/08 (T-Mobile Netherlands BV et al v. Raad van bestuur van de Nederlandse Mededingingsautoriteit) [2009], ECR I-04529, para. 55. In that Opinion, AG *Kokott* described that the Dutch Court (College van Beroep voor het bedrijfsleven) by submitting a referral for a preliminary ruling and the defendants (KPN and Vodafone) made the argument that the exchange of information and concerted practice to determine the remuneration of dealers had no impact on final consumers. Accordingly, their agreement did not infringe Article 101(1) TFEU; This defence was not followed by the Court. See ECJ 4 June 2009, Case C-8/08 (T-Mobile Netherlands BV et al v. Raad van bestuur van de Nederlandse Mededingingsautoriteit) [2009] ECR I-04529, para. 36. The Court explicitly ruled that "*it is not possible on the basis of the wording of Article 81(1) EC* [now Article 101(1) TFEU] *to conclude that only concerted practices which have a direct effect on the prices paid by end users are prohibited*".

1006 An interesting discussion relates to the absence of a distinction between customers and consumers under Article 101(3) and the competition policy of the Commission. See P. Akman, ""Consumer" versus "Customer": the Devil in the Detail", *ESRC Centre for Competition Policy Working Paper No. 08-34* 2008, p. 8. While both only talk about consumers, this term encompasses final consumers (or customers). Moreover, it also includes intermediate consumers. This creates confusion, as two different concepts refer to the same term; See also P. Akman, "*The Concept of Abuse in EU Competition Law: Law and Economic Approaches*", Oxford/Portland: Hart Publishing 2012, p. 127. The Commission generally does not make the distinction between final users and intermediate users, but refers to "consumers". This is problematic, as the goal of the former is about the broad notion of satisfaction, whereas the goal of the latter concerns the maximisation of profits.

the opaque wording chosen by both institutions, in accordance with this research, one thing is clear: defining the concept of consumers so widely to encompass the public interest, or the general interest should be avoided.[1007] Stretching the concept of consumer so widely would unhinge, *inter alia*, the Commission, the CJEU and parties in antitrust proceedings. The reason being that it would be unclear for them how to differentiate between the first and second conditions of Article 101(3) TFEU.

Another notable trend that paved the way for greater clarity and a more coherent application of the rules is the ECJ's judgment in *Asnef-Equifax/Ausbanc*. Before this case it was unclear whether individual consumers, or the total number of consumers (*i.e.* the society as a whole) in a relevant market needed to obtain benefits from an agreement.[1008] Fortunately, the Court provided much needed guidance and stipulated that "*it is the beneficial nature of the effect on all consumers in the relevant markets that must be taken into consideration, not the effect on each member of that category of consumers*".[1009] In other words, emphasis is placed on the benefits that consumers, in general, obtain from an agreement.[1010] Although it is clear that benefits must be felt by consumers in the same market that the deleterious agreement affects, the ECJ in *Mastercard* explained that consumers in other markets can also be affected.[1011] This is particularly relevant when there is an undisputed interaction between both markets (*i.e.* when both markets are intertwined).[1012]

1007 L. O. Blanco, "*Market Power in EU Antitrust Law*", Oxford/Portland: Hart Publishing 2011, p. 107.

1008 A. Jones and B. E. Sufrin, "*EU Competition Law: Text, Cases, and Materials*", Oxford: Oxford University Press 2014, p. 259.

1009 ECJ 23 November 2006, Case C-238/05 (Asnef-Equifax, Servicios de Información sobre Solvencia y Crédito, SL, Administración del Estado v. Asociación de Usuarios de Servicios Bancarios (Ausbanc)), [2006] ECR I-11125, para. 70 (emphasis added).

1010 Note the difference between this standard and the "average" consumer standard, which was developed in EU free movement law. An example of the latter concerns ECJ 23 March 2010, joined cases C-236/08 to C-238/08 (Google Inc. v. Louis Vuitton Malletier SA et al), [2010] ECR I-02417, para. 3.

1011 ECJ 11 September 2014, Case C-382/12P (MasterCard Inc. et al v. European Commission), [2014] ECLI:EU:C:2014:2201.

1012 Ibid., para. 242.

2. Pass-on benefits (the concept of "fair share")

To assess whether benefits flowing from a deleterious agreement/measure can be passed on to consumers, the notion of "fair share" plays a central role. According to the Commission, by applying a narrow-cost-benefit analysis[1013], "*the pass-on benefits must at least compensate consumers for any actual or likely negative impact caused to them by the restriction of competition found under Article 101 (3) TFEU*".[1014] In this context, the final result after the negative and positive impact on consumers (*i.e.* the net effect) must "at least" be equal from the affected consumers' point of view.[1015] If they are below this equal position, the second condition cannot be accomplished.[1016] This is also reiterated in the ECJ's landmark decision in *Consten and Grundig*. In its judgment, the Court held that the benefits of competition must "*show appreciable objective advantages of such a character as to compensate for the disadvantages which they cause in the field of competition*".[1017]

Although the ECJ in *JCB Service* explained that not all benefits of an agreement must reach consumers,[1018] for, *inter alia*, undertakings such an evidential threshold may prove to be an onerous task.[1019] This is because it is difficult to accurately calculate the consumer pass-on rate without hav-

1013 L. Ankersmit, "*Green Trade and Fair Trade in and with the EU: Process-based Measures within the EU Legal Order*", Cambridge: Cambridge University Press 2017, p. 208.

1014 Communication from the Commission – Notice – Guidelines on the application of Article 81(3) of the Treaty [now Article 101(1) TFEU] of 27 April 2004, [OJ 2004, No. C 101/97], para. 85.

1015 Ibid.

1016 *Nicolaides* explains that the second condition in Article 101(3) TFEU is a filter, eliminating all agreements "*that fail to provide sufficient benefits to consumers*". See P. Nicolaides, "The Balancing Myth: The Economics of Article 81(1) & (3)", *Legal Issues of Economic Integration* 2005, p. 134-143.

1017 ECJ 13 July 1966, joined cases 56 and 58-64 (Établissements Consten S.à.R.L. and Grundig-Verkaufs-GmbH v. Commission of the European Economic Community), [1966] ECR 429, p. 348; For a reiteration of this wording, see CFI 23 October 2003, Case T-65/98 (Van den Bergh Foods Ltd v. Commission of the European Communities), [2003] ECR II-4653, para. 139.

1018 ECJ 21 September 2006, Case C-167/04P (JCB Service v. Commission of the European Communities), [2006] ECR I-8935, para. 162-163.

1019 Before the modernization of EU Competition Law, the evidential standard which was required to interpret the pass-on rate pertaining to the second condition of Article 101(3) TFEU was much lower. Hence, it was more easily satisfied. See M. Ioannidou, "*Consumer Involvement in Private EU Competition Law*

ing to rely on advanced economic calculations. To solve this, the Commission explained that "*Undertakings are only required to substantiate their claims by providing estimates and other data to the extent reasonably possible, taking account of the circumstances of the individual case*".[1020] Moreover, the Commission went on to explain that when the other three conditions of Article 101(3) TFEU are met, a full-fledged analysis of the second condition of Article 101(3) is superfluous for undertakings.[1021]

Insofar as an agreement is not likely to increase prices for consumers, in assessing whether a "fair share" is passed on, the Commission uses a sliding-scale approach. This necessitates the following rule: "*the greater the restriction of competition found under Article [101(3)] the greater must be the efficiencies and the pass-on to consumers*".[1022] In other words, consumers will suffer more when the impact of an agreement on competition is significant.[1023] The passing-on requirement must also occur within a reasonable time; the longer it takes for the gains to be passed on, the less likely they will be taken into account.[1024]

Also worth mentioning, the analytical framework that the Commission uses to analyse a pass-on to consumers differs between cost efficiencies and qualitative efficiencies. With regard to the former, the Commission takes into account (i) the characteristics and structure of the market; (ii) the nature and magnitude of the efficiency gains; (iii) the elasticity of demand, and (iv) the magnitude of the restriction of competition.[1025] For qualitative efficiencies, on the other hand, the Commission evaluates the compensa-

---

Enforcement", Oxford: Oxford University Press 2015, p. 34; For an example of this "relatively" low threshold in the case-law of the ECJ, see ECJ 25 October 1977, case 26-76 (Metro SB-Großmärkte GmbH & Co. KG v. Commission of the European Communities), [1977] ECR 1875, para. 47. In this case, the Court ruled that the mere improvement in supply was sufficient to satisfy the second condition of Article 101(3) TFEU.

1020 Communication from the Commission – Notice – Guidelines on the application of Article 81(3) of the Treaty [now Article 101(1) TFEU] of 27 April 2004, [OJ 2004, No. C 101/97], para. 94.

1021 Ibid., para. 90.

1022 Ibid; for a reiteration of this rule, see the Guidelines on the applicability of Article 101 of the Treaty on the Functioning of the European Union to horizontal co-operation agreements of 14 January 2011, [OJ 2011, No. C 11/01], par. 103.

1023 Communication from the Commission – Notice – Guidelines on the application of Article 81(3) of the Treaty [now Article 101(1) TFEU] of 27 April 2004, [OJ 2004, No. C 101/97], para. 92.

1024 Ibid., para. 87.

1025 Ibid., para. 96.

tion for consumers caused by the anti-competitive effects of an agreement either (a) by means of sufficiently creating value, or (b) by introducing new products or achieving a higher quality of products.[1026]

3. An efficient allocation of resources to countervail the negative effects of nonlegal sanctions imposed by the trade associations researched and executed by their members

Efficient competition is imperative for consumers, since it enables them to benefit from greater innovation, higher quality of products and services and lower prices.[1027] As a result, the aim of an efficient spectrum policy in the EU is to accommodate the benefits of consumers by "*enhancing consumer welfare and by ensuring an efficient allocation of resources*".[1028] The trade associations researched and their members have a crucial role in the promotion of these objectives.[1029] By offsetting high costs of monitoring compliance for undertakings that a system of specialized commercial arbitration in which awards are enforced by imposing nonlegal sanctions achieves, member undertakings of these associations do not have to resort to cumbersome, time- consuming and expensive litigation in court. This significantly reduces transaction costs for these companies. But does this mean that also these efficiencies are passed on to consumers?

If member undertakings of the trade associations researched have to resort to litigation in court rather than specialized commercial arbitration, the cost of doing business is higher and less economical. This would harm final consumers, because these members will most likely pass on losses to them. As a result, distribution costs will increase. To analyse such pass-on

1026 Ibid., para. 102.

1027 ICN Advocacy Working Group, "Explaining the Benefits of Competition to the General Public", *International Competition Network* 2017, p. 3.

1028 Communication from the Commission – Notice – Guidelines on the application of Article 81(3) of the Treaty [now Article 101(1) TFEU] of 27 April 2004, [OJ 2004, No. C 101/97], par. 13; *Hawk* assumes that consumer welfare and achieving an efficient allocation of goods are two sides of the same coin. See B. E. Hawk, "*International Antitrust Law & Policy: Fordham Corporate Law 2003*", Huntington: Juris Publishing 2004, p. 423.

1029 For an overview of benefits that are generated by trade associations, see TradeAssociationForum, "The Benefits of Trade Associations", *TradeAssociationForum* 2009, p. 2, 4.

costs, it is important to explain the game theory provided by *Cirace*.[1030] He demonstrated that "*if all firms in a competitive industry have higher costs, and the industry sells products that consumers greatly desire, the quantity purchased will be little changed after a price rise* [...], *so the higher costs will be totally passed on to consumers*".[1031] Absent extrajudicial measures, this theory is applicable by virtue of three reasons: first, members of these associations will incur higher costs. Second, these members sell products that final consumers desire. Third, there is no proof that the quantity of products will change after an increase in price. As a result of falling within the description of this three-tier test, final consumers have to deal with higher prices for industry products when a system of specialized commercial arbitration is not safeguarded under the threat of nonlegal sanctions. Vice versa, if awards are extrajudicially enforced within a system of specialized commercial arbitration, lower prices are passed on to final consumers.[1032] This lowers distribution costs. These measures guarantee appreciable objective advantages for these individuals. Notwithstanding the anticompetitive harm placed on recalcitrant industry actors, this is sufficient to establish that the trade associations researched and their members fulfil the second requirement of Article 101(3) TFEU. In this situation, a general conclusion is sufficient and there is no need to establish for each extrajudicial measure whether it results in a pass-on for consumers. With regard to the next requirement, this approach will differ.

III. Third condition: Indispensability - without restriction, elimination or significant reduction of efficiencies

After making a detailed assessment of the efficiency claim and before the issue of pass-on to consumers,[1033] the third condition under Article 101(3)

1030 J. Cirace, "*Law, Economics, and Game Theory*", Lanmore: The Rowman & Littlefield Publishing Group, Inc. 2018, p. 238.

1031 Ibid.

1032 With regard to "prices", *Jones & Pickering* explain that "*the lower the price, all other things being equal, the greater the consumer benefit*". See T. T. Jones, J. F. Pickering, "The Consumer's Interest in Competition Policy", *Journal of Consumer Studies and Home Economics* 1979, p. 98.

1033 For the purpose of the Guidelines on the Application of Article 81(3) [now Article 101(3) TFEU] it is considered appropriate to invert the order of the third (*i.e.* indispensability) and second condition (*i.e.* pass-on to consumers) of Article 101(3) TFEU.

TFEU requires that the anticompetitive extrajudicial measures imposed by the trade associations researched and executed by their member must be "indispensable"[1034] to achieve the efficiency gains claimed.[1035] To apply this concept, the Guidelines on Article 81(3) EC [now Article 101(3) TFEU] require that the trade associations researched and their members provide evidence, for each extrajudicial measure which they impose and execute on a wrongdoer, that this restriction of Article 101(1) TFEU by effect is indispensable to achieve the efficiencies referred to first condition in Article 101(3) TFEU.[1036] Put differently, according to the Commission's decision in *Telefónica/Portugal Telecom*, "*the question when analysing indispensability under Article 101 (3) of the Treaty is* [...] *whether the restriction is indispensable to attain the efficiencies in question*".[1037]

To apply this test, the trade associations researched and their members must substantiate that each extrajudicial measure which they impose and execute on a recalcitrant industry actor is the least restrictive option.[1038]

1034 Before the introduction of the Guidelines on Article 81(3) [now Article 101(3) TFEU], "indispensability" was interpreted by the GC as synonymous with "strictly necessary". See CFI 23 February 1994, joined cases T-39/92 and T-40/92 (Groupement des Cartes Bancaires "CB" and Europay International SA v. Commission of the European Communities), [1994] ECR II-49113, para. 114; The EU Commission only referred to "necessary" with regard to interpreting indispensability. See CFI 15 September 1998, joined cases T-374/94, T-375/94, T-384/94 and T-388/94 (European Night Services Ltd (ENS) et al v. Commission of the European Communities), [1998] ECR II-1533, para. 203.

1035 Indispensability is an important balancing threshold. See C. Townley, "*Article 81 EC and Public Policy*", Portland: Hart Publishing 2009, p. 273.

1036 Communication from the Commission – Notice – Guidelines on the application of Article 81(3) of the Treaty [now Article 101(1) TFEU] of 27 April 2004, [OJ 2004, No. C 101/97], para. 73.

1037 Ibid; Commission Decision of 23 January 2013 relating to a proceeding under Article 101 of the Treaty on the Functioning of the European Union, Case No COMP/39.839 (Telefónica/Portugal Telecom), para. 444.

1038 This is a proportionality test. The term "proportionality" was introduced by the Court in CFI 15 July 1994, Case T-17/93 (Matra Hachette SA v. Commission of the European Communities), [1994] ECR II-595, para. 135. The Court stated that "*any adverse effects on competition* [...] *are proportionate to the contribution made by it to economic or technical progress*"; A clearer reiteration can be found in the Opinion of the Advocate-General Kirschner of 21 February 1990, Case T-51/89 (Tetra Pak Rausing SA v. Commission of the European Communities), [1990] ECR II-309, para. 72; This approach has been reiterated in the literature. See, for example, S. Kingston, "*Greening EU Competition Law and Policy*", Cambridge: Cambridge University Press 2012, p. 280. *Kingston* explains that indispensability involves the principle of proportionality.

Blanco call this the "less restrictive alternatives test".[1039] While a vague concept, the Commission provides guidance in two ways: first, it equates "indispensability" with "reasonably necessary".[1040] Second, it explains in its Guidelines on the application of Article 81(3) of the Treaty [now Article 101(1) TFEU] that a party that invokes Article 101(3) TFEU must by looking from the perspective of "*any rational undertaking*"[1041] clarify that there are no economically practicable and less restrictive means of achieving the claimed efficiencies.[1042] Albeit that this definition is still too broad, inextirpable and vague, the Commission provided further guidance. It explicated that "*It will only intervene where it is reasonably clear that there are realistic and attainable alternatives.* [As a result,] *The parties must only explain and demonstrate why such seemingly realistic and significantly less restrictive alternatives to the agreement would be significantly less efficient.*"[1043]

That being said, it must be established with regard to the dissemination of the names of wrongdoers in a blacklist, withdrawals of membership, denials of readmission to membership for expelled members on the basis of an additional entry condition and limiting adequate access prior to arbitral proceedings and after an award, which clearly restrict Article 101(1) TFEU

1039 L. O. Blanco, "*Shipping Conferences under EC Antitrust Law: Criticism of a Legal Paradox*", Portland: Hart Publishing 2007, p. 375; *Lianos* & *Geradin* call this the requirement of "less restrictive alternatives". See I. Lianos and D. Geradin, "*Handbook on European Competition Law: Substantive Aspects*", Cheltenham/ Northampton: Edward Elgar Publishing 2013, p. 160.

1040 Communication from the Commission – Notice – Guidelines on the application of Article 81(3) of the Treaty [now Article 101(1) TFEU] of 27 April 2004, [OJ 2004, No. C 101/97], para. 78; See also American Bar Association, "*Federal antitrust guidelines for the licensing of intellectual property*", Chicago: American Bar Association 2010, p. 71. The Commission takes a pragmatic point of view when interpreting indispensability.

1041 The Commission does not focus on the parties to an agreement, but uses the yardstick of "*any rational undertaking in a similar situation*".

1042 Communication from the Commission – Notice – Guidelines on the application of Article 81(3) of the Treaty [now Article 101(1) TFEU] of 27 April 2004, [OJ 2004, No. C 101/97], para. 75.

1043 Ibid; The objectives achieved by a deleterious agreement must first be recalled. See Commission Decision of 12 December 1988 relating to a proceeding under Article 85 of the EEC Treaty [now Article 101 TFEU], Case No IV/27.393 and IV/27.394 (Publishers Association - Net Book Agreements), para. 73; In appeal, the AG of the ECJ reiterated that the concept of indispensability "*can be properly assessed only if there is clarity as to the objectives of the agreement in question*". See the Opinion of the Advocate-General Lenz of 16 June 1994, Case C-360/92P (The Publishers Association v. Commission of the European Communities), [1995] ECR I-23, para. 43.

by effect when directed at an industry actor, that these measures – separately - are reasonably necessary to achieve lowered transaction costs. Put differently, the focus is on whether there are less restrictive alternatives and whether, absent its imposition and execution, these efficiencies are eliminated or significantly reduced.[1044] The following Paragraphs explain for each of the extrajudicial measures whether they are indispensable within the meaning of the third requirement of Article 101(3) TFEU. The role of the trade associations researched and their members will not be separately discussed. Importantly, to avoid a duplicative discussion, many arguments will be borrowed from the previous discussion pertaining to the rule-of-reason analysis pursuant to Section 1 of the Sherman Act.[1045]

1. Blacklisting

On the one hand, disseminating the names of recalcitrant industry actors in a blacklist has debilitating effects on such wrongdoers. Above all, their future business decisions and competitive freedom are negatively influenced.[1046] On the other hand, blacklisting wrongdoers is unavoidable to have an efficient system of specialized commercial arbitration which lowers transaction and distribution costs. This raises the ensuing question: Is the practice of blacklisting wrongdoers reasonably necessary to achieve these efficiency gains, or is there a less restrictive alternative? It is difficult to draw a line between pro-competitive and anticompetitive exchanges of information.[1047] Hence, it is a daunting task to reason[1048] when dissemina-

---

1044 Ibid., para. 79; Here, the Commission applies a sliding scale approach: the more restrictive the restraint, the stricter the indispensability test.

1045 See Part II, Chapter 6, E, II, 2. However, refusals to deal with an expelled member will not be discussed. Unlike with regard to Section 1 of the Sherman Act, this nonlegal sanction violates Article 101(1) TFEU by object and cannot be justified under Article 101(3) TFEU.

1046 I. E. Wendt, "*EU Competition Law and Liberal Professions: an Uneasy Relationship?*", Leiden: Koninklijke Brill NV 2013, p. 512.

1047 L. Ritter and W. D. Braun, "*European Competition Law: A Practitioner's Guide*", The Hague: Kluwer Law International 2005, p. 249; The problem is that such a value-laden balancing exercise would compare incommensurable factors. See I. Lianos and D. Geradin, "*Handbook on European Competition Law: Substantive Aspects*", Cheltenham/Northampton: Edward Elgar Publishing 2013, p. 160.

1048 Reasoning is synonymous with arguing. It means to justify, to give reasons pro and con, to criticize, to verify, to demonstrate and to deliberate. See C. Perel-

tion of the names of a wrongdoer in a blacklist is legitimate.[1049] This is because less severe alternatives such as a reprimand or a penalty are too soft and do not ensure that industry actors comply with arbitral awards of specialized commercial arbitration. Only when an industry actor's commercial reputation is at risk, conformity with arbitral awards is probable. To make things clearer, it is necessary to weigh arguments for and against the indispensability of blacklisting under the third requirement of Article 101(3) TFEU. Here, the same arguments can be used which were presented with regard to the rule-of-reason analysis of blacklisting under Section 1 of the Sherman Act.[1050]

Arguments that confirm the indispensable nature of blacklisting pursuant to Article 101(3) TFEU.	**Arguments against the indispensable nature of blacklisting pursuant to Article 101(3) TFEU.**
1. Blacklisting is the least severe effective measure to guarantee that a system of conflict resolution through specialized commercial arbitration can operate.	1. Blacklisting can result in market foreclosure for a targeted member of a trade association.
2. Blacklisting is necessary to maintain a system of specialized commercial arbitration that benefits total welfare and consumer welfare.	2. Non-payment of an award should not result in market foreclosure. It is disproportionate to the principles of proportionality and subsidiarity. Blacklisting is too severe a sanction.
3. In most markets, being blacklisted does not result in social ramifications. Members of a trade association are often globally dispersed and alien to one another.	3. In some markets, being blacklisted can also have social ramifications. It can disrupt interpersonal relationships within close-knit groups.
4. When a wrongdoer's (company) name is published in a blacklist which is only accessible for members of the relevant trade association, market foreclosure is limited.	4. When a wrongdoer's (company) name is published in a publicly accessible list, the likelihood of market foreclosure increases.
5. Many industry actors that are placed on the blacklist are already bankrupt and are often non-members. It is unlikely that additional reputational harm will be inflicted on them. The foreclosure effect should be mitigated.	5. Even though many industry actors that are blacklisted are bankrupt and/or classify as non-members, the foreclosure effect of this type of extrajudicial enforcement on liquid members is still severe.

man, "*Justice, Law, and Argument: Essays on Moral and Legal Reasoning*", Dordrecht: D. Reidel Publishing Company 1980, p. 59.

1049 F. Ferretti, "*EU Competition Law, the Consumer Interest and Data Protection: The Exchange Consumer Information in the Retail Financial Sector*", Heidelberg/New York/Dordrecht/London: Springer 2014, p. 47.

1050 See Part II, Chapter 6, E, II, 2, a; The arguments presented in the table with regard to Section 1 of the Sherman Act are reproduced verbatim in this table.

Despite there being a counterargument against every argument, as seen in this table, there is no less severe alternative measure to ensure that awards from specialized commercial arbitration are complied with. Disseminating the names of wrongdoers in closed, non-public blacklists is reasonably necessary to lower transaction costs. However, when the trade associations researched and their members include the names of wrongdoers in publicly available list, this is not the least restrictive alternative. The reason is that it is difficult (or impossible) to delete freely circulating information which would not only be available for the members of the associations, but also for every private person and public undertaking on a global scale.[1051] Even though a blacklisted industry actor may get taken off the list, "the internet never forgets".[1052] Future consumers and undertakings that want to deal with a formerly blacklisted company can change their commercial strategy on the basis of such information (*e.g.* by breaking off contract negotiations).[1053]

Support of the indispensable nature of blacklisting by comparing it with online review forums must be declined. This will be the focus in the next Paragraph, even though it could have also been discussed with regard to the legality of blacklisting under Section 1 of the Sherman Act.

1051 S. van der Hof, B. van den Berg, and B. Schermer, "*Minding Minors Wandering the Web: Regulating Online Child Safety*", The Hague: T.M.C. Asser Press 2014, p. 136.

1052 C. Molenaar, "*E-Marketing: Applications of information technology and the internet within marketing*", Abingdon: Routledge 2012, p. 105.

1053 This is not as straightforward, when looking at what may happen in the future. Much depends on how the internet advances. It is possible that internet will open up more for consumers, thereby enabling them to access information on blacklisted industry actors more readily (*e.g.* one easy search query). Accordingly, blacklisting can be even more restrictive than how it is now. See J. P. Martínez, "*Net Neutrality: Contributions to the Debate*", Madrid: Fundación Telefónica 2011, p. 139; On the contrary, it is also very well possible that legislation pertaining to online privacy protection will play a more pivotal and mature role in the nearby future. This could "potentially" lead to less restrictive effects for blacklisted industry actors. In particular, because information of those mentioned in such lists will not be so readily available. See K. Chen, A. Fadlalla, "*Online Consumer Protection: Theories of Human Relativism: Theories of Human Relativism*", New York: IGI Global 2009, p. 278.

a. The juxtaposition with online evaluation forums

Traditionally, consumers shared information about products and services among themselves on an informal basis (*i.e.* word-of-mouth information).[1054] This produced regulatory effects, especially when the information consisted of negative feedback. Yet, companies did not often suffer reputational harm, because word-of-mouth information did not easily extend across the society (or indeed the world). This changed in the computer-mediated era, because new media allows consumers to obtain information about goods and services from a vast, geographically dispersed group of people besides from the people they know.[1055] Particularly, by engaging in online forums and review sites, consumers share their opinions and write down their thoughts on products and services, be they positive or negative, anonymous or not.[1056] Such a popular[1057] form of consumer interaction with one another through virtual communities does not only increase the value of companies, but also has detrimental effects on a compa-

1054 I. Nee, "*Managing Negative Word-of-Mouth on Social Media Platforms: The Effect of Hotel Management Responses on Observers' Purchase Intention*", Bremen: Springer Fachmedien Wiesbaden 2016, p. 2.

1055 C. M. K. Cheung and M. K. O. Lee, "Online Consumer Reviews: Does Negative Electronic Word-of-Mouth Hurt More?", *Association for Information Systems* 2008, p. 2; T. Hennig-Thurau, K. P. Gwinner, G. Walsh, and D. D. Gremler, "Electronic Word-of-mouth via Consumer-Opinion Platforms: What Motivates Consumers to Articulate Themselves on the Internet", *Wiley Periodicals* 2004, p. 39. In their article, the authors explain that an electronic word of mouth circulation of information encompasses "*any positive or negative statement made by potential, actual or formers customers about a product or company which is made available to multitude of the people and institutes via the internet*"; This is the most widespread definition of electronic word of mouth information according to *Trenz and Berger*. See M. Trenz and B. Berger, "Analyzing Online Customer Reviews – An Interdisciplinary Literature Review and Research Agenda", *ECIS* 2013, p. 2.

1056 Examples, *inter alia*, include purchase and review sites (*e.g.* Amazon), strict review sites (*e.g.* Tripadvisor/Yelp), social sharing sites (*e.g.* Youtube/Flickr) and blogging sites (*e.g.* Facebook/Twitter). See L. Robinson, Jr. "*Marketing Dynamism & Sustainability: Things Change, Things Stay the Same*", Heidelberg/ Dordrecht/New York/London: Springer 2012, p. 304.

1057 Two reasons explain the success of electronic word of mouth information: first, increased popularity by consumers to read online reviews of other consumers. Second, consumers more than ever like to disseminate information. See Anonymous, "*How to Deal with Negative Electronic Word-Of-Mouth?*", Norderstedt: GRIN Verlag 2011, p. 4.

ny's standing.[1058] In other words, it may act as an online reputation mechanism.[1059] Whereas positive information may encourage consumers to buy a product or service, negative electronic word-of-mouth (eWOM) information may discourage consumers from buying products.[1060] Evidence of such an effect can be supported by an empirical questionnaire that illustrated that 61% of consumers check online forums before making a purchase decision.[1061]

Against this background, it is clear that one cannot neglect the resemblance between this method of virtual sanctioning with the blacklisting of defaulting industry actors by the trade associations researched and their members. Both measures impede market accessibility of undertakings and regulate the behaviour of market recipients. At first glance, a comparison between both forms of regulatory sanctioning mechanisms may seem useful and appropriate. However, in my opinion, it can be seen as an oversimplification, mainly because this view does not take the full spectrum into account. Four differences prevent an unequivocal, scientifically true comparison.[1062] First, whereas through online valuation forums "consumers" can do reputational damage to undertakings, the trade associations researched and their members blacklist industry actors active in the same commodities market as the latter group of actors (*i.e.* the consumer-industry actor fallacy). Second, given the anonymity of consumers who dissemi-

1058 W. Currie, "*Value Creation from E-Business Models*", in: N. Madeja and D. Schoder, "Value creation from Corporate websites: how different features contribute to success in e-Business", Oxford: Elsevier 2004, p. 216.

1059 M. D. Lytras, E. Damiani, J. M. Carroll, D. Avison, R. D. Tennyson, A. Dale, A. Naeve, P. Lefrere, F. Tan, J. Sipior, and G. Vossen, "*Visioning and Engineering the Knowledge Society - A Web Science Perspective*", Berlin/Heidelberg: Springer-Verlag 2009, p. 501.

1060 I. Lee, "*Encyclopedia of E-Commerce Development, Implementation, and Management, Band 1*", Hershey: IGI Global 2016, p. 1985.

1061 T. Jung and M. C. tom Dieck, "*Augmented Reality and Virtual Reality: Empowering Human, Place and Business*", Cham: Springer International Publishing AG 2018, p. 148.

1062 Similar reticence is required with regard to the German system that prevents over-indebtedness from consumers. This is called the Protective Society for General Credit Assurance (SCHUFA) and rates the ability of those individuals to pay. Once registered in the personal information system, it will be more difficult for consumers to get, *inter alia*, bank loans. Accordingly, this credit system can be seen as a form of regulating behaviour. Despite being of interest, it will not be scrutinized in more detail. For an overview, see N. Jentzsch, "*Financial Privacy: An International Comparison of Credit Reporting Systems*", Berlin/Heidelberg: Springer-Verlag 2006, p. 89-94.

nate information via online valuation forums, it is more difficult to determine the credibility of their information as compared to the blacklisting of industry actors (*i.e.* the anonymity of the sender fallacy).[1063] Third, consumers active on online valuation forums encompass an indefinite number of persons who are spatially separated and scattered worldwide, whereas the trade associations researched and their members belong to a closed group (*i.e.* the open-closed group fallacy). Fourth, consumers give positive and negative information about products and services via online valuation forums, whereas the dissemination of the names of recalcitrant industry actors in blacklist only follows after non-compliance with an arbitral award (*i.e.* the institutional discrepancy fallacy).

2. Membership rules and barriers for market access

a. Withdrawal of membership

Withdrawal of membership is a severe measure that can oust a targeted member of a trade association from the relevant second-tier commodities market. It is not easy to establish whether this conduct is indispensable to lower transaction costs. To provide guidance, comparable to the legality of withdrawals of membership pursuant to Section 1 of the Sherman Act,[1064] the following table presents the most important arguments for and against the indispensable nature of a withdrawal of membership.[1065]

1063 R. Sumangla and A. Panwar, "*Capturing, Analyzing, and Managing Word-of-Mouth in the Digital Marketplace*", Hershey: IGI Global 2016, p. 172.

1064 See Part II, Chapter 6, E, II, 2, b, i.

1065 Differences with regard to the table which includes the arguments for and against the legality of expulsions under Section 1 of the Sherman Act are twofold. First, with regard to indispensable nature pursuant to Article 101(3) TFEU, the goal is not to increase total welfare and consumer welfare, but to reduce transaction costs (see the second requirement). Second, the seventh argument is not included with regard to Section 1 of the Sherman Act.

Arguments that prove the indispensable nature of a withdrawal of membership pursuant to the third requirement of Article 101(3) TFEU.	**Arguments against the indispensable nature of a withdrawal of membership pursuant to the third requirement of Article 101(3) TFEU**
1. Withdrawals of membership provide a successful measure to ensure compliance with an arbitral award when blacklisting is ineffective (*e.g.* bankruptcy).	1. Besides the reputational harm, cancelling all services provided by a relevant trade association carries a risk of completely ousting a member from the second-tier relevant commodities market. Taking away an essential facility is unlawful.
2. Withdrawals of membership are necessary to maintain a system of specialized commercial arbitration that lowers transaction costs	2. Non-payment of an award should not result in a withdrawal of membership. It is disproportionate to the principles of proportionality and subsidiarity. Withdrawing membership is too severe a sanction.
3. In most markets, having one's membership suspended or terminated does not result in social ramifications. Members of a trade association are often globally dispersed and alien to one another.	3. In some markets, having one's membership suspended or terminated can also have social ramifications. It can disrupt interpersonal relationships within close-knit groups.
4. Often, a withdrawal of membership decision is not published. Added reputational harm is not to be expected, because industry actors are globally active and may be unaware of the suspension or termination.	4. When a trade association publishes the decision that it has suspended or terminated membership, all members and sometimes even non-members will not likely conduct trade with such a market participant. Reputational harm inflicted upon a targeted individual or company is not unlikely.
5. Many industry actors that have their membership suspended or terminated are bankrupt. It is only a symbolic measure that chiefly contributes to overall compliance with arbitral awards.	5. Having one's membership suspended or terminated takes away the chance that a member subject to a withdrawal of membership decision becomes financially sound amidst a withdrawal of membership.
6. Throughout history individuals have been ostracized.[1066] This measure is not exclusively reserved for the commodities trade. It would be unwise to prohibit withdrawals of membership.	6. Historical examples do not justify the anti-competitive harm inflicted upon targeted members.
7. The mere absence of procedural safeguards does not entail that withdrawals of membership are not indispensable to lower transaction costs. Any targeted industry actor can challenge an expulsion at public court, even though the relevant trade association does not enable this former member to do so.	7. The majority of the trade associations researched offer insufficient guarantees following a withdrawal of membership. In detail, recourse to public courts and the possibility of an internal appeal are not offered/explained following an expulsion.

On the basis of this table, the arguments in support of a withdrawal of membership are more convincing. Expulsions are reasonably necessary to lower transaction costs. This is because enforcement of arbitral awards from specialized commercial arbitration is better safeguarded, which in

1066 For an historical example of a banishment, see Part 1, Chapter 2, B, II.

turn enables the specialized commercial arbitration system to function more efficiently. However, as it stands, the trade associations researched and their members do not structure the dissemination of the names of wrongdoers in the least restrictive manner. In my opinion, there is a less restrictive option: a procedure based on clearly defined, transparent, non-discriminatory reviewable criteria that allows for cumulative penalties enforceable in national courts, with a final threat of a suspension, or in the worst case scenario when non-compliance is combined with other misconduct, an indefinite expulsion, provided the trade association has objective, reasonable and legitimate reasons for doing so which are based on fair and neutral criteria (*e.g.* do not favour certain members over others). In addition, expelled members should be given the chance to ask an internal appeal tribunal to review such a decision and be advised of the possibility to seek recourse in public courts. If these changes are introduced, blacklisting is indispensable to lower transaction costs and satisfies the third requirement under Article 101(3) TFEU.

b. Denial of readmission to membership

A denial of a reapplication for membership following an expulsion must be based on voluntary, clear, objective and qualitative criteria which are easily discernible and not too restrictive.[1067] Furthermore, when denied, the relevant industry actor must be able to ask for an independent process review to reconsider the membership reapplication. To understand whether denials of reapplication for membership, such as, a lapse of a two-year period following an expulsion and the necessity to obtain an approval from a Board of Directors of a trade association, are indispensable to lower transaction costs, the arguments for and against both additional entry barriers must be laid down. This is done in the following two tables, which bear a great degree of similarity to the discussion on the legality of both barriers pursuant to Section 1 of the Sherman Act.[1068]

1067 See Part III, Chapter 9, C, III, 2, a.

1068 See Part II, Chapter 6, E, II, 2, b, ii. However, there are some differences: First, the second argument with regard to the lapse of a two-year period following an expulsion focuses on a decrease of transaction costs under Article 101(3) TFEU rather than an increase of total welfare and consumer welfare under Section 1 of the Sherman Act. Second, the fourth argument against the permissibility of a lapse of a two-year period does not refer to the US case of NW Wholesale Stationers v. Pac. Stationery. Instead, it does not link to any EU

Arguments that justify the indispensable nature of a lapse of a two-year time period following an expulsion in order to reapply for membership to lower transaction costs under the third requirement pursuant to Article 101(3) TFEU.	**Arguments against the imposition of a lapse of a two-year time period following an expulsion in order to reapply for membership to lower transaction costs under the third requirement pursuant to Article 101(3) TFEU**
1. The imposition of a two-year period to reapply for membership is reasonably necessary to make an expulsion effective. If targeted wrongdoers were able to immediately reapply for membership, the functionality of this type of extrajudicial enforcement would be rendered (to some degree) ineffective.	1. If an expelled member again complies with all membership requirements, pays the arbitral award and any related penalties for non-compliance, it would be reasonably unnecessary to impose a two-year waiting period. This would unduly harm the financial standing of a ostracized former member.
2. Because a two-year waiting period is necessary to ensure the effect of an expulsion, the enforcement of awards from specialized commercial arbitration is better guaranteed. This lowers transaction costs.	2. Albeit that specialized commercial arbitration lowers transaction costs, once an expelled former member qualifies as a member, it would be unreasonable to oust that member from the market for a long period.
3. A two-year period is proportionate and a reduced period would not contribute to the deterrent effect of an expulsion.	3. A two-year period is excessively long. It would be better to either abolish a period altogether, or reduce it to, for example, six months.[1069] By doing so, the foreclosure effect of expelled former members is reduced.
4. It is reasonably necessary to make an exception to the rule that membership rules should be the same for all members and non-discriminatory. Without such a rule, an expulsion is an insufficient deterrent and would be rendered ineffective. This could undermine the enforcement of arbitral awards from specialized commercial arbitration. In addition, it can induce members not to pay an arbitral award.	4. Given that membership rules should the same for all applicants and must not discriminate, imposing a two-year period which only applies to expelled former members is contrary to this rule.

case. Third, the third argument with regard to an approval of readmission to membership by the relevant Board of Directors, unlike Section 1 of the Sherman Act, does not refer to NW Wholesale Stationers v. Pac. Stationery.

1069 A period of six months would still guarantee the effect of an expulsion and would give an expelled former member the possibility to demonstrate that it is a reliable business partner.

Arguments in support of the indispensable nature of an approval of readmission to membership by the Board of Directors after an expulsion to lower transaction costs under the third requirement pursuant to Article 101(3) TFEU.	Arguments against the indispensable nature of an approval of readmission to membership by the board of director after an expulsion to lower transaction costs under the third requirement pursuant to Article 101(3) TFEU.
1. When a member is expelled from a trade association, tasking the Board of Directors with assessing whether a reinstatement of membership is fair and just is not only necessary, but also democratically sound. Arbitrators are the legal representatives of a trade associations and should be given the right to approve a re-admission to membership. This will increase the severity of an expulsion and strengthen enforcement of arbitral awards. In addition, it will enhance total welfare and consumer welfare.	1. Allowing the Board of Directors to deny an expelled former member from being re-admitted to membership, even though such an industry actor satisfies all membership requirements and pays the arbitral award and any related penalties, is discriminatory and unfair. These individuals can arbitrarily oust an industry actor from the market.
2. A trade association should be selective in allowing industry actors to become members. This is especially true in the event a member has proven to be unreliable and unwilling to pay an arbitral award. A Board of Directors should critically review a reapplication for membership to protect the reliability of specialized commercial arbitration.	2. There is a risk that the Board of Directors tasked with approving a re-admission to membership of an expelled former member is motivated by personal resentment against a former member, capricious decision-making and the mood of the directors on a given day. It would be unwise to give such a body the possibility to deny membership to such an industry actor, as it can result in market foreclosure.
3. To ensure that an expulsion sufficiently deters members from not complying with an arbitral award, allowing a Board of Directors to approve a re-admission to membership is reasonably necessary.	3. Given that membership rules should be the same for all applicants and must not discriminate, allowing a Board of Directors to deny a membership application of an expelled member is contrary to this rule.

Whereas both tables illustrate that many arguments can be made in support of or against the indispensable nature of a lapse of a two-year period following an expulsion and the necessity of a Board of Directors to approve reapplication, both barriers are not the least restrictive methods. This is particularly true when, on the one hand, a Board of Directors can arbitrarily and capriciously deny a re-admission to membership. This could even mean that when a Board of Directors dislikes an expelled former member, this individual or undertaking can never become a member again, with all the related anticompetitive consequences. It would be better to exclusively allow an independent third-party panel (not connected with the relevant trade association) to deny a reapplication for membership on the basis of clearly defined, equally applicable, transparent, non-discriminatory criteria, such as (i) the current liquidity status of the former member; (ii) an unwillingness to pay the penalty for non-compliance with the arbitral award; and (iii) evidence of probable disloyalty in the future.[1070] Furthermore, preliminary approval pending a full examination would reduce the harmful effects for expelled former members of a trade association. A waiting period, on the other hand, to reapply for membership may perhaps be seen as reasonably necessary to ensure the success of an expulsion and, thereby, to safeguard a system of specialized commercial arbitration which lowers transaction costs. However, a denial of access for two years is overly excessive. A least restrictive barrier would be to impose a six-month standstill period following non-payment of an award, or if this is combined with other misconduct, a one-year period.

If trade associations and their members were to impose and execute both entry barriers without structuring it the same way as above, it is unlikely that the Commission or the CJEU would support their indispensable nature to lower transaction costs. If yes, the third requirement of Article 101(3) TFEU is fulfilled.

3. Limiting adequate access to public courts prior to arbitral proceedings and after an award

Specialized commercial arbitration must be voluntary and not limit recourse to public courts. However, the trade associations researched and their members do not respect this legal rule. The reasons are two-fold: first, the majority of trade between members of the trade associations researched (and sometimes with a member and non-member) is done on the basis of standardized contracts that are linked to broader arbitration agreements which stipulate that any dispute must be decided in arbitration. Second, only two of the six trade associations researched offer an equivalent recourse to public courts prior to arbitral proceedings and after an award compared with the Arbitration Act 1996, whereas the other four associations either remain silent or offer less judicial protection. While – arguably – sufficient to violate Article 101(1) TFEU by effect, this raises the ensuing question: Is limited access to public courts prior to arbitral proceedings and after an award indispensable to lower transaction costs? A

1070 See ECJ 28 February 2013, Case C-1/12 (Ordem dos Técnicos Oficiais de Contas v. Autoridade da Concorrência), ECLI:EU:C:2013:127, para. 99. The ECJ stated that "*as regards the conditions for access to the market of compulsory training for chartered accountants, the objective of guaranteeing the quality of the services offered by them could be achieved by putting into place a monitoring system organised on the basis of clearly defined, transparent, non-discriminatory, reviewable criteria likely to ensure training bodies equal access to the market in question*".

PLS is an efficient alternative to State adjudication when a trade association acting in that State establishes a system of specialized commercial arbitration to resolve member vs. member and member vs. non-member conflicts. This lowers transaction costs. If any party to a dispute were allowed to seek recourse at a public court prior to arbitral proceedings and after an award, specialized commercial arbitration would become ineffective. In such a scenario, any party could go to a public court before commencement of arbitral proceedings and could contest arbitral awards. To overcome this, limiting access to State courts is important. Only when a trade association exclusively limits recourse to public courts when both parties in proceedings agree, or in order to obtain security for an award, are such rules not indispensable to lower transaction costs. A justification of an arguable violation of Article 101(1) TFEU by effect is not possible. When a trade association and its members at least offer a similar protection of recourse to public courts comparable with the Arbitration Act 1996, the third requirement laid down in Article 101(3) TFEU is fulfilled.

IV. Fourth condition: no elimination of competition

The last condition of Article 101(3) TFEU requires that the extrajudicial measures imposed by the trade associations researched and executed by their members must not be able to substantially eliminate competition between parties.[1071] This entails that if both actors are able to eliminate competition in a substantial part of the market in question, an exemption does not appear warranted.[1072] While the criterion may appear vague, its goal is to ensure that effective competition remains in the relevant market. To overcome this lack of clarity, guidance is offered with regard to four concrete benchmarks. These are presented in the following table:

1071 Communication from the Commission – Notice – Guidelines on the application of Article 81(3) of the Treaty [now Article 101(1) TFEU] of 27 April 2004, [OJ 2004, No. C 101/97], para. 105.

1072 M. M. Dabbah, "*EC and UK Competition Law: Commentary, Cases and Materials*", Cambridge: Cambridge University Press 2004, p. 105. This differs to some extent from the wording chosen by the Commission. According to the Guidelines on Article 81(3) EC [now Article 101(3) TFEU], an "*agreement must not afford the undertakings concerned the possibility of eliminating competition in respect of a substantial part of the products concerned*".

No.	Elimination of competition	No elimination of competition
1[1073]	When long-term losses outweigh short-term efficiency gains, the less likely a party satisfies the fourth condition in Article 101(3) TFEU.	When long-term losses do not outweigh short-term efficiency gains, the more likely a party satisfies the fourth condition in Article 101(3) TFEU.
2[1074]	If efficiency-related benefits flowing from anticompetitive conduct are ancillary to the protection of competition and rivalry, the less likely a party satisfies the fourth condition in Article 101(3) TFEU.	If efficiency-related benefits flowing from anticompetitive conduct are not ancillary to the protection of competition and rivalry, the more likely a party satisfies the fourth condition in Article 101(3) TFEU.
3[1075]	The greater the likelihood that anticompetitive conduct will reduce competition in a market and the more the degree of competition was already weakened prior to the adoption of a nonlegal measure, the less likely a party satisfies the fourth condition in Article 101(3) TFEU.	The less likely that anticompetitive conduct will reduce competition in a market and the lesser the degree of competition was already weakened prior to the adoption of a nonlegal measure, the more likely a party satisfies the fourth condition in Article 101(3) TFEU.
4[1076]	The more aggregated market power of the colluding actors, the less likely a party satisfies the fourth condition in Article 101(3) TFEU.	The less aggregated market power of the colluding actors, the more likely a party satisfies the fourth condition in Article 101(3) TFEU.

Whether or not the researched trade associations and their members pertaining to the anticompetitive extrajudicial measures which restrict Article

1073 A. Jones and B. E. Sufrin, "*EC Competition Law: Text, Cases, and Materials*", Oxford: Oxford University Press 2008, p. 281. In my opinion, such a rule is impracticable, vague and even platitudinous.

1074 Communication from the Commission – Notice – Guidelines on the application of Article 81(3) of the Treaty [now Article 101(1) TFEU] of 27 April 2004, [OJ 2004, No. C 101/97], para. 105.

1075 Ibid., para. 107.

1076 Even though Article 102 TFEU is specifically tailored to prevent the abuse of market power, a market power analysis is permissible under the fourth condition in Article 101(3) TFEU. In particular, because the "no elimination of competition" criterion is an autonomous concept of EU law. See R. Whish and D. Bailey, "*Competition Law: Eight Edition*", Oxford: Oxford University Press 2015, p. 174; The concept of the "elimination of competition" is narrower than the existence of a dominant position under Article 102 TFEU. See CFI 28 February 2002, Case T-395/94 (Atlantic Container Line AB et al v. Commission of the European Communities), [2002] ECR II-595, para. 330 and CFI 30 September 2003, joined cases T-191/98, T-212/98 to T-214/98 (Atlantic Container Line AB et al v. Commission of the European Communities), [2003] ECR II-3275, para. 939; However, this does not mean that when all the four conditions in Article 101(3) TFEU are fulfilled, scrutiny under Article 102 TFEU is not possible. See ECJ 16 March 2000, joined cases C-395/96P, C-396/96P (Compagnie Maritime Belge Transports SA et al v. Commission of the European Communities),

101(1) TFEU by effect, but are structured in such a way that they are indispensable to lower transaction costs can provide evidence that the fourth condition of Article 101 (3) TFEU is fulfilled, much will depend on whether the above-mentioned benchmarks exonerate both actors. Consequently, the following table will apply these criteria to [i] the dissemination of the names of wrongdoers in a blacklist; [ii] withdrawals of membership; [iii] refusals to regain membership following an expulsion on the basis of an additional entry condition; and [iv] inadequate access to public courts prior to arbitral proceedings and after an award. For reasons of simplicity and logic, the extrajudicial measures will be discussed together and not separately.

No.	Do the extrajudicial measures eliminate competition?
1	No. All of the extrajudicial measures generate lower transaction costs by ensuring the success of specialized commercial arbitration. These efficiency gains are not of a short-term nature.
2	No. Lowering transaction cost is more important than punishing disloyal actors. This can best be explained by the overarching rule of utilitarianism (*i.e.* the principle of "utility").[1077] According to this theory, the option that produces the greatest good for the greatest number must always be chosen. Given that regulatory sanctioned industry actors are only small in numbers compared to the members of the trade associations researched, it is very unlikely that rivalry and competition are significantly reduced and impaired.
3	No. There is a not a great likelihood that anticompetitive conduct will reduce competition in the commodities markets. Only disloyal industry actors are targeted. A weakened degree of competition before the adoption of the extrajudicial measures is also improbable.

[2000] ECR I-1365, para. 130; Moreover, Article 101(3) TFEU cannot exempt an abuse of a dominant position under Article 102 TFEU. See, for example, CFI 30 September 2003, joined cases T-191/98, T-212/98 to T-214/98 (Atlantic Container Line AB et al v. Commission of the European Communities), [2003] ECR II-3275, para. 1456; See also Routledge, "Code-Sharing Agreements in Scheduled Passenger Air Transport–The European Competition Authorities' Perspective", *European Competition Journal* 2006, p. 279. The Commission takes into account (i) market shares; (ii) opposing market power from competitors; (iii) actual or potential competition; and (iv) market access/barriers to entry.

1077 B. Gert, "*Morality: Its Nature and Justification*", New York/Oxford: Oxford University Press 1998, p. 120;
M. Mendonca and R. N. Kanungo, "*Ethical Leadership*", New York: Open University Press 2007, p. 15. The theory of utilitarianism was made famous by *David Hume* and suggests that the "end justifies the means". Much criticism can be raised against such an approach. In particular, because it fails to determine the righteousness and morality of acts; P. Tittle, "*Ethical Issues in Business: Inquiries, Cases, and Readings*", Petersborough: Peg Tittle 2000, p. 41. However, it is the most suitable yardstick to compare alternatives.

4	Yes. The trade associations researched and their members on each respective market hold significant market power.

Even though the market power of the trade associations researched and their members suggests that extrajudicial measures could eliminate competition, this argument – standing alone – is insufficient to prevent any other conclusion than to say that the fourth requirement pursuant to Article 101(3) TFEU is fulfilled. Extrajudicial measures when structured in the least restrictive manner, so that they fulfil the third requirement of Article 101(3) do not eliminate competition.

V. Conclusion

When a trade association and its members disseminate the names of wrongdoers in a blacklist, withdraw membership, deny readmission of expelled members to membership on the basis of an additional entry condition, and limit adequate access to public courts prior to arbitral proceedings and after an award, albeit that these extrajudicial measures infringe Article 101(1) TFEU, both actors can successfully make a justification defence under Article 101(3) TFEU. The reason for this is this method of enforcement lowers transaction costs and passes on this efficiency to final consumers. Moreover, when structured in the least restrictive manner, these measures are also indispensable to lower such costs. Lastly, these measures do not eliminate competition.

D. Key findings

An immediate, far-reaching and very much noticeable consequence for a violation of Article 101(1) TFEU concerns the fact that an anticompetitive agreement is automatically null and void pursuant to the second paragraph of Article 101(1).[1078] Bearing in mind that the nullity can be relied upon by everyone and has retroactive and prospective effects, the trade associations researched and their members must try to persuade the Commission (and, when relevant, in appeal, the CJEU) that their role in anticompetitive collusion/nonlegal sanctioning can be exempted. This impunity can happen in two ways: first, when the agreement falls within the safe

1078 See Part III, Chapter 10, A.

harbour of the RDBER and SABER. Second, when the collusive conduct satisfies the four-step assessment pursuant to Article 101(3) TFEU.

With regard to both BERs, the trade associations researched and their members are not eligible to exculpate themselves.[1079] In particular, because both actors do not carry out joint research and development and do not participate in any form of specialization agreement for the production and distribution of goods. Unfortunately, such a conclusion cannot be nearly as easily drawn in relation to the balancing clause enshrined in Article 101(3) TFEU, which exonerates anticompetitive agreements/extrajudicial measures that bring improvements in the production or distribution of goods, or promote technical or economic progress.[1080] At first glance, the provisions of Article 101(3) seem applicable owing to the assumption that the increased economic benefits for the members of the trade association researched appear to overshadow the negative harm done to extrajudicially targeted industry actors. Whether this is true depends on the balancing of all extrajudicial measures which restrict Article 101(1) TFEU by effect against the four requirements enshrined in the third paragraph of Article 101(3).

The first condition that must be satisfied refers to the notion of "efficiency gains".[1081] This requires that the role of the trade associations researched and their members in disseminating the names of wrongdoers in a blacklist, withdrawing membership, denying former members readmission to membership on the basis of an additional entry condition, and limiting adequate access to public courts prior to arbitral proceedings and after an award reduces transaction costs. Fortunately, this can be confirmed on the basis of two reasons: First, all of these extrajudicial measures achieve appreciable objective advantages, because without them specialized commercial arbitration would be ineffective.[1082] Second, there is also a sufficient link between nonlegal sanctions and lowered transaction costs.[1083] As a result, the first requirement under Article 101(3) TFEU is fulfilled.

The second requirement that must be fulfilled to set aside the nullity flowing from the anticompetitive extrajudicial measures concerns the concept of a "fair share for consumers".[1084] This entails that consumers must

1079 See Part III, Chapter 10, B.
1080 See Part III, Chapter 10, C.
1081 See Part III, Chapter 10, C, I.
1082 See Part III, Chapter 10, C, I, 1.
1083 See Part III, Chapter 10, C, I, 2.
1084 See Part III, Chapter 10, C, II.

have sufficiency benefitted from the lowered transaction costs. In the absence of nonlegal sanctions to punish disloyal behaviour, higher prices will be passed on to final consumers.[1085] The reasons are three-fold: First, the cost of doing business for members of the trade associations researched increases without an efficient system of specialized commercial arbitration. Second, these members sell products which consumers desire. Third, a change of the quality of products following a price increase is unmerited. Due to the lowering of distribution costs for consumers, the trade associations researched and their members fulfil the second requirement pursuant to Article 101(3) TFEU.

The third condition that must be satisfied requires that the extrajudicial measures be indispensable to lower transaction costs.[1086] This requires that it must be assiduously assessed with regard to each measure if it is reasonably necessary to achieve this efficiency, or if there is a less restrictive alternative available. Disseminating the names of disloyal industry actors in a blacklist seems to correspond with this requirement, if this document is only accessible for the members of the relevant trade association.[1087] The reason is that there are no effective less restrictive measures to enforce arbitral awards from specialized commercial arbitration. Reprimands and penalties are ineffective. Interestingly, a comparison with online evaluation forums is unfounded.[1088] None of the current rules of the trade associations researched and their members with regard to withdrawals of membership are indispensable to lower transaction costs.[1089] This is because there is a less restrictive way of structuring this nonlegal sanction. This is by setting up a procedure based on clearly defined, transparent, non-discriminatory reviewable criteria that allows for cumulative penalties enforceable in national courts, with a final threat of suspension, or, in the worst case scenario when non-compliance is combined with other misconduct, an indefinite expulsion provided that the trade association has objective, reasonable and legitimate reasons for doing so based on fair and neutral criteria (*e.g.* do not favour certain members of others). Furthermore, expelled members should be allowed the possibility of an internal appeal against an expulsion decision and be advised of the possibility of recourse in public courts.

1085 See Part III, Chapter 10, C, II, 3.
1086 See Part III, Chapter 10, C, III.
1087 See Part III, Chapter 10, C, III, 1.
1088 See Part III, Chapter 10, C, III, 1, a.
1089 See Part III, Chapter 10, C, III, 2, a.

With regard to refusing a reapplication for membership following an expulsion by a Board of Directors or when a period of two years following an expulsion has not elapsed, both barriers are not indispensable to lower transaction costs. Denying a reapplication for membership should be done on the basis of clearly defined, equally applicable, transparent, non-discriminatory criteria, such as (i) the current liquidity status of the former member; (ii) an unwillingness to pay the penalty for non-compliance with the arbitral award; and (iii) evidence of probable disloyalty in the future.[1090] Furthermore, preliminary approval pending a full examination would reduce the harmful effects for expelled former members of a trade association. A waiting period of two years is too long and restrictive. It would be better to impose a six-month standstill period following non-payment of an award, or if this is combined with other misconduct, a one-year period. If these changes are introduced, the third requirement pursuant to Article 101(3) TFEU is fulfilled.

Concerning limiting adequate access to public courts prior to arbitral proceedings and after an award, this measure is indispensable to guarantee the success of specialized commercial arbitration.[1091] If parties could go to public court in both scenarios, this carries the risk of making arbitration redundant. Yet, access to public courts must be at least equal to the standards provided in the Arbitration Act 1996. If so, the third requirement pursuant to Article 101(3) TFEU is fulfilled.

The fourth and last requirement that must be observed necessitates that the extrajudicial measures imposed by the trade associations researched and executed by their members must not be able to substantially eliminate competition.[1092] Fortunately, this condition does not raise any concern. The extrajudicial measures lower transaction costs, which situation is not of a short-term nature. This efficiency outweighs the harm inflicted on disloyal industry actors by applying the theory of utilitarianism and there is a slight likelihood that competition on the market will be reduced. A weakened degree of competition before the adoption of the extrajudicial measures is also unlikely.

In sum, all of the regulatory measures fulfil the four conditions pursuant to Article 101(3) TFEU insofar as they are modified to a certain extent where relevant.[1093] As they stand now, it is unlikely that the Commission

1090 See Part III, Chapter 10, C, III, 2, b.
1091 See Part III, Chapter 10, C, III, 3.
1092 See Part III, Chapter 10, C, IV.
1093 See Part III, Chapter 10, C, V.

and in appeal the CJEU will leave them untouched. This can result in hazardous consequences, given that then the nullity of Article 101(2) TFEU applies.[1094]

1094 B. Thorson, "*Individual Rights in EU Law*", Oslo: Springer International 2016, p. 131.

Chapter 11: Abuse of a Dominant Position under Article 102 TFEU

A. Introduction

When imposing nonlegal sanctions on disloyal industry actors, the trade associations researched (and not their members since their role in the execution of such measures does not fit within the required description of collective dominance or an oligopoly)[1095] can also act inconsistently with Ar-

1095 The members of the trade associations researched (which consist of many industry actors) do not hold collective dominant positions in the second-tier commodities markets because they do not qualify as oligopolies. This is because an oligopoly (*i.e.* collective dominance) can only emerge in concentrated markets with few market competitors. See N. Dunne, "*Competition Law and Economic Regulation: Making and Managing Markets*", Cambridge: Cambridge University Press 2015, p. 177; Despite the concept of oligopoly (or collective dominance) finding its origin in Merger Control, the CJEU explained that this concept has the same meaning within Article 102 TFEU. More specifically, the CJEU applied the tripartite modified Airtours test as developed in CFI 6 June 2002, Case T-342/99 (Airtours plc. v. Commission of the European Communities), [2002] ECR II-2585, para. 62 (emphasis added) to Article 102 TFEU. See CFI 26 January 2005, Case T-193/02 (Laurent Piau v. Commission of the European Communities), [2005] ECR II-209, para. 111; For a reiteration, even though relating to different circumstances, see ECJ 10 July 2008, Case C-413/06P (Bertelsmann AG and Sony Corporation of America v. Independent Music Publishers and Labels Association (Impala)), [2008] ECR I-4951, para. 124: For more information on how to substantiate collective dominance, see M. Lorenz, "An Introduction to EU Competition Law", Cambridge: Cambridge University Press 2013, p. 208. In his view, this requires a connection between the undertakings to jointly infringe Article 102 TFEU (i) when two or more economic entities (read: undertakings) are united by economic links and are collectively dominant on a specific market (CFI 10 March 1992, joined cases T-68/89, T-77/89 and T-78/89 (Società Italiana Vetro SpA, Fabbrica Pisana SpA and PPG Vernante Pennitalia SpA v. Commission of the European Communities), [1992] ECR II-01403, para. 35); (ii) if the undertakings are united so that they adopt the same conduct on the market (ECJ 27 April 1994, Case C-393/92 (Municipality of Almelo et al v. NV Energiebedrijf Ijsselmij), [1994] ECR I-1477, para. 42); and (iii) the existence of collective dominance may "*flow from the nature and terms of an agreement, from the way in which it is implemented and, consequently, from the links or facts which give rise to a connection. Nevertheless, the existence of an agreement or of other links in law is not indispensable to a*

ticle 102 TFEU relating to an abuse of a dominant position.[1096] Although Article 102 is mutually applicable in conjunction with Article 101 TFEU (*i.e.* the concurrence of legal provisions), it provides distinctive requirements[1097] and consequences that derive from a divergent narrative.[1098] Whereas in Article 101 TFEU the focus is on anticompetitive collusion, Article 102 TFEU applies where certain conduct is engaged in unilaterally by a trade association.[1099] In other words, Article 102 encompasses a monopoly position held by a trade association.[1100] While this may appear a very broad definition, one can spotlight and derive two major require-

---

finding of a collective dominant position; such a finding may be based on other connecting factors and would depend on an economic assessment and, in particular, on an assessment of the structure of the market in question" (ECJ 16 March 2000, joined cases C-395/96P, C-396/96P (Compagnie Maritime Belge Transports SA et al v. Commission of the European Communities), [2000] ECR I-1365, para. 45).

1096 Article 102 TFEU is a directly applicable provision of EU law, enforceable in national courts of EU Member States. See, *inter alia*, CFI 10 July 1990, Case T-51/89 (Tetra Pak Rausing SA v. Commission of the European Communities), [1990] ECR II-309, para. 42; ECJ 19 January 2004, Case C-453/00 (Kühne & Heitz NV v. Produktschap voor Pluimvee en Eieren), [2004] ECR I-837, para. 20.

1097 Articles 101 and 102 TFEU can be applied to the same anticompetitive conduct. See N. Foster, "*Foster on EU Law*", Oxford: Oxford University Press 2015, p. 381.

1098 However, akin to Article 101 TFEU, the protection of competition in the interest of consumers is also the core objective of Article 102 TFEU. See, for example, ECJ 21 February 1973, Case 6-72 (Europemballage Corporation and Continental Can Company Inc. v. Commission of the European Communities), [1973] ECR 215, para. 26.

1099 D. Leczykiewicz and S. Weatherill, "*The Involvement of EU Law in Private Law Relationships*", in: O. Odudu (ed), "Competition Law and Contract: The EU Defence", Oxford/Portland: Hart Publishing 2013, p. 395.

1100 Article 102 TFEU also includes the participation in an oligopolistic market. However, this will not be of interest in this Chapter; For more information on oligopolies, see N. Dunne, "*Competition Law and Economic Regulation: Making and Managing Markets*", Cambridge: Cambridge University Press 2015, p. 177. Oligopolies emerge in concentrated markets with few market competitors; Other characteristics of oligopolies include (i) high barriers to entry; (ii) high degree of interdependence between market competitors; (iii) homogenous or highly differentiated products; and (iv) price stability within the market. See R. Jayaram and N. R. Kotwani, "*Industrial Economics and Telecommunication Regulations*", New Delhi: PHI Learning Private Limited 2012, p. 41; Many markets are oligopolistic. See R. Whish and D. Bailey, "*Competition Law: Eight Edition*", Oxford: Oxford University Press 2015, p. 595; Despite the concept of oligopoly (or collective dominance) finding its origin in Merger Control, the

ments from the wording of Article 102 TFEU. First, the existence of a dominant position in the relevant product market. Second, the abuse of such a dominant position.[1101]

When applying the two-part test to determine the anti-competitiveness of extrajudicial measures imposed on wrongdoers by the trade associations researched, the first step is to investigate whether or not these associations hold dominant positions (Paragraph B). This can be done by outlining the general framework of what constitutes a dominant position. Subsequently, whether these associations abuse their dominant positions (Paragraph C) will be determined. Here, understanding the historical roots of Article 102 TFEU, the wording of this provision, case law of the CJEU and modern economic thinking provide guidance.[1102] Furthermore, the Commission's Guidance on the Commission's enforcement priorities in applying Article 82 of the EC Treaty[1103] [now Article 102 TFEU] to abusive exclusionary

---

CJEU explained that this concept has the same meaning within Article 102 TFEU. More specifically, the CJEU applies the tripartite modified Airtours test as developed in CFI 6 June 2002, Case T-342/99 (Airtours plc. v. Commission of the European Communities), [2002] ECR II-2585, para. 62 (emphasis added) to Article 102 TFEU. See CFI 26 January 2005, Case T-193/02 (Laurent Piau v. Commission of the European Communities), [2005] ECR II-209, para. 111; For a reiteration, even though relating to different circumstances, see ECJ 10 July 2008, Case C-413/06P (Bertelsmann AG and Sony Corporation of America v. Independent Music Publishers and Labels Association (Impala)), [2008] ECR I-4951, para. 124.

1101 In more detail, perhaps the most fitting test to gain a thorough grasp of what amounts to an abuse of a dominant position pursuant to Article 102 TFEU can be found in M. Lorenz, "*An Introduction to EU Competition Law*", Cambridge: Cambridge University Press 2013, p. 189. *Lorenz* explains that "*it follows from the wording of Article 102 TFEU that the following conditions are met to establish a violation: (i) a dominant position on the relevant market must be held by one or more undertakings; (ii) the position must be held in the internal market or a substantial part of it; (iii) abuse of the dominant position; (iv) actual or potential effect on trade between Member States*".

1102 For a similar approach, see P. Akman, "*The Concept of Abuse in EU Competition Law: Law and Economic Approaches*", Oxford/Portland: Hart Publishing 2012, [Abstract].

1103 The text of Article 82 EC and Article 102 TFEU are similar, with one minor distinction. The archaic reference to "incompatible with the common market" is changed by the current wording "incompatible with the internal market". See C. Ehlermann and M. Marquis, "*European Competition Law Annual 2007: A Reformed Approach to Article 82 EC*", Oxford/Portland: Hart Publishing 2008, p. xxv. Although this book dates from before the TFEU, it compared Article 82 EC with Article 102 TFEU before Article 102 entered into force.

conduct by dominant undertakings (the "Commission's Guidance") will be analysed, as well as its post-reform decisional practice.[1104] After that, three categories of objective justifications for the trade associations researched to not violate Article 102 TFEU are discussed. The first category is relevant when anti-competitive conduct results in efficiencies for the members of the trade associations researched and a net gain for the consumers of these industry actors. The second category relates to the protection of a legitimate commercial interest and, the third category concerns the objective necessity defence. This Chapter ends with a conclusion (Paragraph D).

B. *The existence of a dominant position in the relevant market which impacts the EU territory*

To assess whether the trade associations researched hold dominant positions in the relevant markets for regulation and private ordering which impact the EU territory, the concept of "paramount market position" and "market shares" must be considered.[1105] Therefore, the case law of the CJEU and the Commission's Discussion Paper on the application of Article 82 of the Treaty [now Article 102 TFEU] to exclusionary abuses (the "Discussion Paper") must be examined.[1106] This Paragraph is structured as follows: first, dominance is defined based on the guidance given by CJEU and the decisional practice of the Commission (Paragraph I). Second, dominance is clarified on the basis of the Discussion Paper (Paragraph II). Third, whether the trade associations researched are dominant within the meaning of Article 102 TFEU is discussed (Paragraph III).

1104 Communication from the Commission — Guidance on the Commission's enforcement priorities in applying Article 82 of the EC Treaty [now Article 102 TFEU] to abusive exclusionary conduct by dominant undertakings of 24 February 2009, [OJ 2009, No. C 45].

1105 M. Mackenrodt, B. C. Gallego, and S. Enchelmaier, "*Abuse of Dominant Position: New Interpretation, New Enforcement Mechanisms?*", in: P. Këllezi (ed), "Abuse below the Threshold of Dominance? – Market Power, Market Dominance, and Abuse of Economic Dependence", Berlin/Heidelberg: Springer 2008, p. 88.

1106 European Commission, "DG Competition discussion paper on the application of Article 82 of the Treaty [now Article 102 TFEU] to exclusionary abuses", *European Commission* 2005.

I. Guidance by the CJEU and the decisional practice of the Commission

The definition of dominance was considered in detail by the ECJ in *United Brands (Chiquita)*.[1107] In that judgment, the Court interpreted this criterion as "*A position of economic strength enjoyed by an undertaking which enables it to prevent effective competition being maintained on the relevant market by affording it the power to behave to an appreciable extent independently of its competitors, customers and ultimately of its consumers*".[1108] In other words, according to *Joelson*, it follows from this wording that undertakings which are able to behave in a market in a strategically independent way and have considerably greater market shares than that of competitors are dominant.[1109] In *Hoffman-La Roche*, the ECJ even argued that "*very large shares are in themselves and save in exceptional circumstances evidence of the existence of a dominant position*".[1110] Following this case, it seems that a high market share is sufficient to show dominance in a market which impacts the EU territory. Nonetheless, the Court disqualified this statement in two important ways.[1111] First, it stated that market shares are not necessarily decisive and must be considered in conjunction with other factors.[1112] Second, a large amount of market shares must exist for "some time".[1113]

1107 ECJ 14 February 1978, Case 27/76 (United Brands Company and United Brands Continental BV v. Commission of the European Communities), [1978] ECR 207.

1108 Ibid., para. 38.

1109 This conclusion was drawn by *Joelson* in M. R. Joelson, "*An International Antitrust Primer: A Guide to the Operation of United States, European Union and Other Key Competition Laws in the Global Economy*", Alphen aan den Rijn: Kluwer Law International 2006, p. 371.

1110 ECJ 13 February 1979, Case 85/76 (Hoffman-La Roche & Co. AG v. Commission of the European Communities), [1979] ECR 461, para. 41.

1111 M. M. Dabbah, "*EC and UK Competition Law: Commentary, Cases and Materials*", Cambridge: Cambridge University Press 2004, p. 330.

1112 ECJ 14 February 1978, case 27/76 (United Brands Company and United Brands Continental BV v. Commission of the European Communities), [1978] ECR 207, par. 66; ECJ 13 February 1979, case 85/76 (Hoffman-La Roche & Co. AG v. Commission of the European Communities) [1979] ECR 461, par. 39, 48. Other factors include the absence of potential competition, a technological lead over competitors and the existence of an elaborate sales network; ECJ 9 November 1983, case C-322/81 (NV Nederlandsche Banden Industrie Michelin v Commission of the European Communities), [1983] ECR 3461, par. 37. In determining the position of dominance, the structure of demand and supply in the market as well as competitive conditions must be contemplated.

In later case law, the Commission and the CJEU described more precisely how many market shares are required to establish a presumption of dominance. Both institutions also explained when such a presumption can be rebutted by presumed dominant undertakings. In line with this reasoning, to understand whether the trade associations researched (which qualify as undertakings within the meaning of Article 102 TFEU) are dominant in their relevant markets for regulation and private ordering which impact the EU territory, it is fundamental to quantify the amount of market shares needed to establish dominance. To this end, a brief overview of the Commission's decisional practice and the case law of the CJEU can be found in the following table:

EU Market Shares	Case	Dominant Position
< 10%	*Metro II*[1114]	Too small to be capable of establishing a dominant position in the absence of exceptional circumstances
20-40%	*Hoffmann-La Roche*[1115]	A dominant position cannot be ruled out when additional factors are present. However, it is very unlikely that a dominant position can be established
39.2%	*Virgin/ British Airways*[1116]	Dominant position, because the closest competitor only had 5.5% market shares.

1113 The requirement that a large amount of shares must exist for „some time" will not be discussed. In particular, because the researched trade associations have a relatively steady amount of market shares.

1114 ECJ 22 October 1986, Case 75/84 (Metro SB-Großmärkte GmbH & Co. KG v. Commission of the European Communities), [1986] ECR 3021, para. 85-86.

1115 See European Commission, IXth Report on Competition Policy, para. 22. This report explains whether an undertaking that has market shares between 20-40% is dominant; Reference is made to ECJ 13 February 1979, Case 85/76 (Hoffman-La Roche & Co. AG v. Commission of the European Communities) [1979] ECR 461, para. 57-58 (emphasis added). In this case, Roche (*i.e.* an undertaking) had an approximate market share of 20-40%. In its judgment, "*the Court felt that there was inadequate evidence of dominance*". The Commission interpreted this wording to mean that an undertaking can be dominant, when other factors are present.

1116 Commission Decision of 14 July 1999 relating to a proceeding under Article 82 of the EC Treaty [now Article 102 TFEU], Case No IV/D-2/34.780 (Virgin/ British Airways), para. 87-88, 90-91; According to *Blanco*, this is the lowest amount of market shares where dominance was established. See L. O. Blanco, "*Market Power in EU Antitrust Law*", Oxford/Portland: Hart Publishing 2011, p. 56. However, given the fact that the market shares that are required to establish a dominant position is rather arbitrary, future decisional practice of the Commission and the CJEU can change this amount of market shares.

40-45%	*United Brands*[1117]	Although these market shares on their own are insufficient to establish dominance, certain additional factors (on the basis of thorough economic analysis) can substantiate a dominant position.
> 50%	*Akzo*[1118]	Strong presumption of dominance, except in exceptional circumstances
70-80%	*Hilti*[1119]	Clear indication of dominance

II. The Discussion Paper

The Commission tends to follow the case law of the CJEU in the Discussion Paper, even though the intention was not to restate the law, but to steer the Commission's approach.[1120] According to this document, "*market shares provide useful first indications of the market structure and of the competitive importance of various undertakings on the market*".[1121] When elucidating at which market shares dominance can be established, the Commission explained that an undertaking which holds more than 50% EU market shares is considered dominant.[1122] Importantly, this presumption requires that competitors active within the same relevant market hold a much smaller market share within the EU. In the event an undertaking holds below 40% EU market shares, even though below this threshold it is more unlikely that dominance is found compared to market shares between 40% and 50%, such an undertaking can still be dominant.[1123] One thing is clear, when an undertaking has below 25% market shares, it is unlikely that dominance can be attributed to that company.[1124]

1117 ECJ 14 February 1978, Case 27/76 (United Brands Company and United Brands Continental BV v. Commission of the European Communities), [1978] ECR 207, para. 108, 113-117.
1118 ECJ 3 July 1991, Case C-62/86 (AKZO Chemie BV v. Commission of the European Communities), [1991] ECR I-3359, para. 60.
1119 CFI 12 December 1991, Case T-30/89 (Hilti AG v. Commission of the European Communities), [1991] ECR II-1439, para. 92.
1120 J. Basedow and W. Wurmnest, "*Structure and Effects in EU Competition Law: Studies on Exclusionary Conduct and State Aid*", Alphen aan den Rijn: Kluwer Law International 2011, p. 71.
1121 European Commission, "DG Competition discussion paper on the application of Article 82 of the Treaty [now Article 102 TFEU] to exclusionary abuses", *European Commission* 2005, para. 29.
1122 Ibid., para. 31.
1123 Ibid.
1124 Ibid.

That being said, the explanation given by the Commission corresponds with the case law of the CJEU. However, *Jones & Sufrin* consider it contentious due to two misrepresentations.[1125] First, whilst the ECJ in *Akzo* explains that only "exceptional circumstances" can rebut dominance, when an undertaking has more than 50% market shares, the Commission narrows this down to one circumstance: the market shares of competitors should not be low. Second, the Discussion Paper did not rule out dominance below 40% market shares contrary to the general trend in the case law of the CJEU.

III. The unequivocal dominance of the trade associations researched in the EU markets for regulation and private ordering

Now that the concept of dominance has been defined by considering both the CJEU's and the Commission's approach, it is necessary to examine whether the trade associations researched hold dominant positions on the markets for regulation and private ordering which impact the EU territory. Fortunately, this is relatively straightforward and uncomplicated due to the worldwide (and, therefore, EU-wide) pre-eminent position of most of these trade associations, supported by high amounts of market shares. More specifically, the two trade associations with the highest amount of global market shares are the LME and FOSFA, with market shares of 80% and 85% respectively. Even though empirical evidence regarding Community market shares is lacking and despite the complexity of interchangeability, they provide a clear indication that the ECJ's developed threshold of 70-80% EU-wide market shares in *Hilti* is exceeded. At EU level, there are no other associations active that can be considered competitive in the same markets for regulation and private ordering with these associations. Accordingly, there is a clear indication of dominance in relation to Article 102 TFEU. A multi-factor analysis is redundant.

Similarly, albeit a bit less clear, a strong presumption of dominance can be established for the ICA. This can be substantiated by the fact that the market shares of this association is probably above the 50% Community market share threshold as developed in *Akzo,* but below the required 70% *Hilti* threshold. This is because this trade association holds 60% global market shares in the global market for regulation and private ordering.

1125 A. Jones and B. E. Sufrin, "*EC Competition Law: Text, Cases, and Materials*", Oxford: Oxford University Press 2008, p. 404.

Whereas transposing global market shares to substantiate Community shares must be treated with a certain amount of caution, a lack of EU competitors substantiates that the 50% EU-wide market share threshold is achieved. Hence, there is a strong presumption of dominance. Exceptional circumstances that allow for a refutation are vague, doubtful and impractical. This is because of two main reasons: first, exceptional circumstances are not defined following *Akzo*. Second, only a non-binding (*i.e.* soft law) Discussion Paper described that exceptional circumstances apply to the situation when rivals hold a more than low percentage of market shares.

For GAFTA and the FCC, neither empirical evidence regarding global nor Community market shares can be found. Yet, it is rather obvious that both associations hold a strong position within their respective EU market for regulation and private ordering. With regard to GAFTA, no serious competitors exist and, with regard to the FCC, virtually all international contracts are performed on the basis of that association's bylaws. Despite it being unclear whether both associations fulfil the 70% *Hilti* threshold, it deserves no further examination that at least the 50% *Akzo* threshold is exceeded. For the purposes of this research, the dominance of GAFTA and the FCC is unequivocally presumed in their respective EU markets for regulation and private ordering.

With regard to the DDC, it is unlikely that this association holds an amount of EU market shares which is required to establish dominance. The reason being that the FBDB is the dominant association on the EU territory in the market for regulating and private ordering.

C. The existence of an abuse of a dominant position in the market

Article 102 TFEU does not prohibit bare dominance (*e.g.* constituted by large market shares held by the trade associations researched), but seeks to prevent the abuse of a dominant position that is incompatible with the internal market.[1126] This concept is not easy to define, as it is both con-

---

1126 A. Bavasso, "*Communications in EU Law: Antitrust Market Power and Public Interest*", The Hague: Kluwer Law International 2003, p. 164; S. D. Anderman, "*The Interface Between Intellectual Property Rights and Competition Policy*", Cambridge: Cambridge University Press, p. 40. Although this book is about intellectual property rights, *Anderman*, irrespective of this area of law, interpreted the abuse requirement pursuant to Article 102 TFEU by stating that "*the mere possession of extensive market power, if lawfully acquired, does not amount to an abuse*".

tentious, vague[1127] and subject to change from the outset.[1128] Accordingly, to understand whether the trade associations researched abused their dominant positions, the current understanding of this concept must first be explained (Paragraph I). This must be done through an ordoliberal lens. At the end of this Paragraph, the proof required for finding an exclusionary abuse is discussed. Subsequently, whether the imposition of nonlegal sanctions by the trade associations researched is synonymous with the exclusionary abuse of a refusal to grant access to an essential facility is examined (Paragraph II). Lastly, a discussion follows of whether there is a sufficient causal connection between the dominance of the trade associations researched on the EU markets for regulation and private ordering and the imposition of an exclusionary abuse on adjacent second-tier commodities markets (Paragraph III).

I. The current understanding of the "abuse" concept through an Ordoliberal lens

The earliest inclusion of the abuse (of a dominant position) concept can be found in Article 86 of the Treaty Establishing the European Economic Community (the "Rome Treaty" or "EEC").[1129] This provision can be traced back, even though it is not generally agreed, to the ideas of German

1127 P. Behrens, "The ordoliberal concept of "abuse" of a dominant position and its impact on Article 102 TFEU", *Econstor* 2015, p. 5.

1128 P. L. Parcu, G. Monti, and M. Botta, "*Abuse of Dominance in EU Competition Law: Emerging Trends*", Cheltenham/Northampton: Edward Elgar Publishing 2017, p. 2.

1129 The Treaty Establishing the European Economic Community of 25 March 1957; K. Davies, "*Understanding European Union Law*", Abingdon/New York: Routledge 2016, p. 54. The Rome Treaty is a primary source of EU law; G. W. Comanor, K. Jacquemin, and A. Jenny, "*Competition Policy in Europe and North America*", New York: Hardwood Academic Publishers GmbH 1990, p. 231. According to Article 86 EEC, the abuse of a dominant position is prohibited. Dominance – standing alone – is not sufficient to substantiate a violation of this Article; Great Britain. Dept. of Trade and Industry, "*Abuse of Market Power: A Consultative Document on Possible Legislative Option*", Richmond: H.M. Stationery Office 1992, p. 7. The aim of such a prohibition system is to declare conduct automatically unlawful, when undertakings abuse their dominant position.

Ordoliberalism.[1130] When looking at the wording of Article 86 EEC, four examples can be found when an abuse of a dominant position can be substantiated. These refer to "*(a) the direct or indirect imposition of any inequitable purchase or selling prices or of any other inequitable trading conditions; (b) the limitation of production, markets or technical development to the prejudice of consumers; (c) the application to parties to transactions of unequal terms in respect of equivalent supplies, thereby placing them at a competitive disadvantage; or (d) the subjecting of the conclusion of a contract to the acceptance, by a party, of additional supplies which, either by their nature or according to commercial usage, have no connection with the subject of such contract*". Given that in that time it was unclear whether or not this list was exhaustive and how an abuse could be defined, much depended on how the Commission and the CJEU articulated this concept.[1131] This insecurity almost lasted for two decades after the adoption of the Rome Treaty.

1130 W. Möschel, "Competition Policy from an Ordo Point of View", *German Neo-Liberals and the Social Market Economy* 1989, p. 146. The main objective of German ordoliberalism concerns the protection of economic freedom of action of all market players; P. Marsden, "*Handbook of Research in Trans-Atlantic Antitrust*", Cheltenham: Edward Elgar 2006, p. 268. The influence of this philosophical school on the concept of abuse pursuant to Article 86 EEC is a much debated topic in the literature. Even though it deserves a thorough analysis, this would deflect attention from the central focus of this research. Therefore, summary arguments for and against the influence of German Ordoliberalism on Article 102 TFEU will be given by the, in my opinion, most important authors; D. J. Gerber, "Law and Competition in Twentieth Century Europe: Protecting Prometheus", Oxford: Oxford University Press 1998, p. 264. *Gerber* stated that EU Competition Law can be traced back to German Ordoliberalism, because of three main reasons: first, the German influence of the competition law provisions in the Rome Treaty. Second, Article 86 EEC was related to ordoliberal thought. Third, *Hans von der Groeben*, who was clearly a German Ordoliberal, was appointed the first Commissioner for Competition Policy of the Commission; P. Akman, "*The Concept of Abuse in EU Competition Law: Law and Economic Approaches*", Oxford/Portland: Hart Publishing 2012, p. 59, 63. *Akman*, however, denied that an ordoliberal viewpoint had an influence on the concept of abuse. In particular, because ordoliberalism contravenes efficiency, which is the core principally in relation to Article 102 TFEU. This can be derived from the *travaux préperatoires* of the Rome Treaty; P. Behrens, "The ordoliberal concept of "abuse" of a dominant position and its impact on Article 102 TFEU", *Econstor* 2015, p. 20. *Behrens* explains that it is without doubt that ordoliberal thinking influenced Article 102 TFEU.

1131 P. I. Colomo, "The Law on Abuses of Dominance and the System of Judicial Remedies", *Yearbook of European Law, Vol. 32, No. 1* 2013, p. 389; L. Warlouzet, "The Centralization of EU Competition Policy: Historical Institutional-

Fortunately, in *Continental Can* the ECJ finally gave much needed clarification.[1132] In is judgment, the Court stated that the four examples laid down in Article 86 EEC are a non-exhaustive enumeration of what constitutes an abuse of a dominant position.[1133] The Court went on to explain that an abuse may occur when an undertaking used its dominant position to fetter competition, irrespective of the aim and procedure by which it is achieved.[1134] Despite that fact that this wording, though clearly corresponding with German Ordoliberalism,[1135] must be understood in light of the system and objectives of the Rome Treaty, as well as the spirit, general scheme and wording of Article 86 EEC, it is rather vague and broad.[1136]

1. The proof required for finding an exclusionary abuse

Within a decade after *Continental Can*, the ECJ in *Hoffman La Roche*[1137] and *Michelin 1*[1138] elaborated the abuse concept by focusing on exclusion-

---

ist Dynamics from Cartel Monitoring to Merger Control (1956–91)", *Journal of Common Market Studies, Vol. 54, No. 3* 2016, p. 731.

1132 ECJ 21 February 1973, Case 6-72 (Europemballage Corporation and Continental Can Company Inc. v. Commission of the European Communities), [1973] ECR 215. One must take into consideration that this case concerned a merger between two horizontally competing undertakings and was decided before the Merger Control Regulation was adopted. In light of current law, it is very well possible that a different outcome would be reached. Regardless of this unpredictability, the ECJ provided guidance on how the concept of abuse needs to be interpreted. In my opinion, it can be considered as a highly relevant yardstick nowadays.

1133 Ibid., para. 26.

1134 Ibid., para. 26-27.

1135 Q. Wu, "*Competition Laws, Globalization and Legal Pluralism: China's Experience*", Oxford/Portland: Hart Publishing 2013, p. 28; A. Jones and B. E. Sufrin, "*EU Competition Law: Text, Cases, and Materials*", Oxford: Oxford University Press 2016, p. 37. By protecting an „effective competition structure" Article 86 EEC reflects the ordoliberal view to foster economic freedom by means of safeguarding competition in the internal market and protecting competitors.

1136 Ibid., para. 22.

1137 ECJ 13 February 1979, Case 85/76 (Hoffman-La Roche & Co. AG v. Commission of the European Communities) [1979], ECR 461.

1138 ECJ 9 November 1983, Case 322/81 (NV Nederlandsche Banden Industrie Michelin v. Commission of the European Communities), [1983] ECR 3461.

ary abuses.[1139] In *Hoffman La Roche*, the ECJ formulated three criteria to establish an abuse: first, the conduct must be capable of influencing the structure of the market.[1140] Second, there must be "*recourse to methods different from those which condition normal competition in products or services on the basis of the transactions of commercial operators*".[1141] Third, the conduct must be able to have "*the effect of hindering the maintenance of the degree of competition still existing in the market or the growth of that competition*".[1142] Although the Court's reasoning offered guidance when conduct is capable of restricting competition, it failed to offer a clear yardstick as to what type of exclusionary effect is required.[1143] Despite this legal uncertainty still remaining unsolved today, *Hoffman La Roche* is the leading decision concerning exclusionary abuses pursuant to Article 102 TFEU (formerly known as Article 82 EC, or Article 86 EEC).[1144]

However, the effect on trade criteria (*i.e.* the third criteria) has to some extent been broadened and clarified. In *Michelin 1*, the ECJ stated that an undertaking has a "*special responsibility not to allow its conduct to impair gen-*

1139 M. Mackenrodt, B. C. Gallego, and S. Enchelmaier, "*Abuse of Dominant Position: New Interpretation, New Enforcement Mechanisms?*", in: H. K. S. Schmidt (ed), "Private Enforcement – Is Article 82 EC special?", Berlin/Heidelberg: Springer 2008, p. 151; M. Andenas, P. Marsden, and M. Hutchings, "*Current Competition Law Volume II*", London: British Institute of International and Comparative Law 2004, p. 359.

1140 ECJ 13 February 1979, Case 85/76 (Hoffman-La Roche & Co. AG v. Commission of the European Communities), [1979] ECR 461, para. 91. "*The concept of abuse is an objective concept relating to the behaviour of an undertaking in a dominant position which is such as to influence the structure of a market as a result of the very presence of the undertaking in question, the degree of competition is weakened*".

1141 Ibid; J. Bourgeois and D. Waelbroeck, "Ten years of effects-based approach in EU competition law State of play and perspectives", in: A. Meij and T. Baum, "Balancing Object and Effect Analysis in Identifying Abuses of a Dominant Position under Article 102 TFEU", Brussels: Groupe de Boeck 2013, p. 164. Even today, this notion of "competition on the merits" can be considered vague and largely unclear.

1142 Ibid.

1143 R. Nazzini, "*The Foundations of European Union Competition Law: The Objective and Principles of Article 102*", Oxford: Oxford University Press 2011, p. 170.

1144 J. Bourgeois and D. Waelbroeck, "*Ten years of effects-based approach in EU competition law State of play and perspectives*", in: A. Meij and T. Baum, "Balancing Object and Effect Analysis in Identifying Abuses of a Dominant Position under Article 102 TFEU", Brussels: Groupe de Boeck 2013, p. 162.

uine undistorted competition on the common market".[1145] Moreover, in *Michelin II*, the CFI found that abuse does not need to have an "actual effect" on the internal market, but must be "capable" of having that effect.[1146] This has been reiterated by the CFI in *British Airways*.[1147] *Ullrich* calls such a move towards an increased emphasis on the effects of an abuse, the shift from a form-based approach to a full-fledged effects-based approach.[1148] Albeit that the CFI's line of reasoning has been followed by the Commission in its guidance on Article 102 TFEU, it is necessary to make a distinction between the object and effect of an exclusionary abuse.[1149] An example of a case that focused on the object of an exclusionary abuse is the judgment by the GC in *AstraZeneca*.[1150] In this judgment, the Court ruled that be-

---

1145 ECJ 9 November 1983, Case 322/81 (NV Nederlandsche Banden Industrie Michelin v. Commission of the European Communities), [1983] ECR 3461, para. 57.

1146 CFI 30 September 2003, Case T-203/01 (Manufacture française des pneumatiques Michelin v. Commission of the European Communities), [2003] ECR II-4071, para. 239; See also, in appeal, ECJ 15 March 2007, Case C-95/04P (British Airways plc v. Commission of the European Communities), [2007] ECR I-2331, para. 77.

1147 CFI 17 December 2003, Case T-219/99 (British Airways plc v. Commission of the European Communities), [2003] ECR II-05917, par. 293. The CFI stated that "*It is sufficient* […] *to demonstrate that the abusive conduct of the undertaking in a dominant position tends to restrict competition, or, in other words, that the conduct is capable of having, or likely to have, such an effect*".

1148 H. Ullrich, "*The Evolution of European Competition Law: Whose Regulation, Which Competition?*", Cheltenham/Northampton: Edward Elgar Publishing 2006, p. 348.

1149 Communication from the Commission — Guidance on the Commission's enforcement priorities in applying Article 82 of the EC Treaty [now Article 102 TFEU] to abusive exclusionary conduct by dominant undertakings of 24 February 2009, [OJ 2009, No. C 45], para. 22. This approach, like Article 101(1) TFEU, must be followed with regard to the finding of an exclusionary abuse. The Commission stated that "*There may be circumstances where it is not necessary for the Commission to carry out a detailed assessment before concluding that the conduct in question is likely to result in consumer harm. If it appears that the conduct can only raise obstacles to competition and that it creates no efficiencies, its anti-competitive effect may be inferred. This could be the case, for instance, if the dominant undertaking prevents its customers from testing the products of competitors or provides financial incentives to its customers on condition that they do not test such products, or pays a distributor or a customer to delay the introduction of a competitor's product*".

1150 GC 1 July 2010, Case T-321/05 (AstraZeneca AB and AstraZeneca plc v. European Commission), [2010] ECR II-2805.

haviour that by its object restricts competition,[1151] supported by evidence in view of an economic or regulatory context[1152] is sufficient to establish an abuse of a dominant position, irrespective of its effect on competition.[1153]

II. The exclusionary abuse of refusal to grant access to an essential facility when the trade associations researched impose nonlegal sanctions

The most relevant type of exclusionary abuse to determine the anti-competitiveness of extrajudicial measures imposed by the trade associations researched concerns the "refusal to grant access to an essential facility". By disciplining disloyal industry actors, especially by (i) blacklisting; (ii) withdrawing membership; (iii) denying reapplication for membership on the basis of an additional entry barrier; and (iv) instructing members to refuse to deal with expelled members, one could argue that given the dominance of the associations and the impact of these measures which leads to market foreclosure by making access to the services provided by these associations impossible (*i.e.* (ii) and (iii)), or more difficult (*i.e.* (i) and (iv)), the role of the trade associations researched in the imposition of each type of nonlegal sanction amounts to exclusionary abuse by denying an essential facility.[1154] Whether this is indeed true depends on the applicability of three condi-

1151 Ibid., para. 360.
1152 Ibid., para. 824.
1153 Ibid., para. 826.
1154 Entering the premises of a recalcitrant industry actor without a warrant and limiting adequate access to public courts prior to arbitral proceedings and after an award do not constitute exclusionary abuses within the meaning of Article 102 TFEU. The first measure is not severe enough to foreclose market access and the second measure does not result in market foreclosure for a wrongdoer. With regard to refusing an essential facility, see V. Hagenfeld, "*EC Competition Law - the Essential Facilities Doctrine: To what extent is the Essential Facilities Doctrine established in Community law and how has its application under Article 82 EC evolved over time*", Munich: GRIN Verlag GmbH 2009, p. 3; P. A. McNutt, "*Law, Economics and Antitrust: Towards a New Perspective*", Cheltenham/ Northampton: Edward Elgar Publishing 2005, p. 136. *McNutt* explains that the aim of the essential facility doctrine is to prevent, in practice, "*insuperable barriers to entry for competitors*".

tions.[1155] First, the existence of a "facility" (*i.e.* the nature and characteristics of the facility). Second, the "essentiality" of the facility. Third, whether "competition is eliminated" with regard to the four extrajudicial measures, if imposed by one of the trade associations researched. Unfortunately, this is not an easy task. According to *Dabbah*, the essential facility doctrine is highly controversial.[1156]. In addition, *Lorenz* argued that the refusal to grant access to an essential facility does not apply to extrajudicial measures imposed by a trade association, but refers to market hindrance on a downstream market.[1157]

1. Nature and characteristics of the facility

To determine whether the trade associations researched have abused their dominant position, the first condition that must be fulfilled necessitates that their services offered can be classified as a "facility". From an antediluvian comprehension of this concept, especially by looking at early decisional practice of the Commission, a restrictive interpretation was favoured. Only when (parts of) infrastructure, or valuable and hard to duplicate raw material is offered by a dominant undertaking, can the existence of a facility be established.[1158] Some examples include airports,[1159]

1155 The additional condition that the facility must be used for a 'new' product is not a workable condition and, hence, will not be discussed. Especially, because such a condition was not considered in relation to the imposition of nonlegal sanctions by a trade association, but was mentioned only by the ECJ pertaining to the licensing of intellectual property rights. See ECJ 29 April 2004, Case C-418/01 (IMS Health GmbH & Co. OHG v. NDC Health GmbH & Co. KGIMS), [2004] ECR I-05039, para. 37, 47.

1156 M. M. Dabbah, "*EC and UK Competition Law: Commentary, Cases and Materials*", Cambridge: Cambridge University Press 2004, p. 351.

1157 M. Lorenz, "*An Introduction to EU Competition Law*", Cambridge: Cambridge University Press 2013, p. 237.

1158 M. M. Dabbah, "*Module B: Abuse of a dominant position*", London: University of London Press 2012, p. 33; V. Hatzopoulos, "The EU essential facilities doctrine", *College of Europe* 2006, p. 19.

1159 *E.g.* Commission Decision of 26 February 1992 relating to a procedure pursuant to Articles 85 and 86 of the EEC Treaty [now Articles 101 and 102 TFEU], Case No IV/33.544 (British Midland v. Aer Lingus), para. 5, 26-27.

railways,[1160] seaports,[1161] intangible networks (*e.g.* distribution network)[1162] and tangible networks (*e.g.* pipelines).[1163] In the course of time, due to privatization and market liberalization, the Commission and the CJEU relaxed the restrictive definition of facility in three proceedings.[1164] First, in *GVG/FS* the Commission explained that not only a railway structure was considered a facility, but also other assets at stake.[1165] These include, *inter alia*, staff, drivers and trains. Second, in the ECJ's judgment in *IMS Health*, the Court argued that also the structure of a database falls

1160 For a recent example, see Commission, press release IP/ 17/3622 of 2 October 2017 "Commission fines Lithuanian Railways €28 million for hindering competition on rail freight market" (to access: http://europa.eu/rapid/press-release_IP-17-3622_en.htm).

1161 *E.g.* Commission Decision of 21 December 1993 relating to a proceeding pursuant to Article 86 of the EC Treaty [now Article 102 TFEU], Case No IV/34.689 (Sea Containers v. Stena Sealink), para. 66, 75; T. Jiang, "*China and EU Antitrust Review of Refusal to License IPR*", Antwerp: Maklu-Publishers 2015, p. 88. *Sea Containers v. Stena Sealink* was the first case concerning the essential facility doctrine; Commission Decision of 21 December 1993 relating to a proceeding pursuant to Article 86 of the EC Treaty [now Article 102 TFEU], Case No IV/34.689 (Sea Containers v. Stena Sealink), para. 12.

1162 *E.g.* ECJ 26 November 1998, Case C-7/97 (Oscar Bronner GmbH & Co. KG v. Mediaprint Zeitungs- und Zeitschriftenverlag GmbH & Co. KG, Mediaprint Zeitungsvertriebsgesellschaft mbH & Co. KG and Mediaprint Anzeigengesellschaft mbH & Co. KG), [1998] ECR I-07791, para. 24, 37.

1163 *E.g.* Commission, press release IP/01/1641 of 23 November 2001 "Commission settles Marathon case with Thyssengas" (to access: http://europa.eu/rapid/press-release_IP-01-1641_en.htm); Commission, press release IP/04/573 "Commission settles Marathon case with Gaz de France and Ruhrgas" (to access: http://europa.eu/rapid/press-release_IP-04-573_e.htm).

1164 V. Hatzopoulos, "The EU essential facilities doctrine", *College of Europe* 2006, p. 20; The CJEU has never expressly used the term essential facility, unlike the Commission. See V. Hagenfeld, "*EC Competition Law - the Essential Facilities Doctrine: To what extent is the Essential Facilities Doctrine established in Community law and how has its application under Article 82 EC evolved over time*", Munich: GRIN Verlag GmbH 2009, p. 3; C. Graham, F. Smith, and F. M Smith, "*Competition, Regulation and the New Economy*", in: E. Derclaye (ed), "Abuse of a dominant Position and IP Rights", Oxford/Portland: Hart Publishing 2004, p. 74.

1165 Commission Decision of 27 August 2003 relating to a proceeding pursuant to Article 82 of the EC Treaty [now Article 102 TFEU], Case No COMP/37.685 (GVG/FS), para. 132, 141, 152.

within this term.[1166] Third, in *Microsoft* the Commission and the CFI found that even a server operating system could be classified as a facility.[1167]

That being said, by broadening the concept of facility a bit of a catch-all term emerged. Subsequently, it is unconvincing to argue that the services provided by the trade associations researched do not fall within its scope. There are two reasons for this: first, depriving the Commission and the CJEU of a useful method to address the potential anti-competitiveness of imposing extrajudicial measures by the trade associations researched pursuant to Article 102 TFEU should be prevented at all cost. Second, legal doctrine presupposes the formation of general broad principles to include situations that are not covered by a specific rule.[1168]

2. The essentiality, indispensability or objective necessity of the facility

The next condition which needs to fall within the scope of the essential facility doctrine necessitates that the services offered by the trade associations researched are essential, indispensable, or objectively necessary. Here, the interpretation provided by the Organisation for Economic Co-operation

1166 ECJ 29 April 2004, Case C-418/01 (IMS Health GmbH & Co. OHG v. NDC Health GmbH & Co. KGIMS), [2004] ECR I-05039, para. 46. Although the Court discussed the essentiality of a facility, this implies that a facility is present.

1167 Commission Decision of 24 May 2004 relating to a proceeding pursuant to Article 82 of the EC Treaty [now Article 102 TFEU] and Article 54 of the EEA Agreement against Microsoft Corporation, Case No COMP/C-3/37.792 (Microsoft), para. 18; CFI 17 September 2007, Case T-201/04 (Microsoft Corp. v. Commission of the European Communities), [2007] ECR II-3601, para. 1313 (emphasis added). By denying work group server operating systems access to information to operate their software on Windows desktop PCs, a facility can be established; M. Stoyanova, "*Competition Problems in Liberalized Telecommunications: Regulatory Solutions to Promote Effective Competition*", Alphen aan den Rijn: Kluwer Law International 2008, p. 144. *Stoyanova* interprets the Microsoft decision by describing that a facility can be established by a wide range of factual circumstances that show strategic behaviour of a dominant undertaking.

1168 E. Zamir and D. Teichman, "*The Oxford Handbook of Behavioral Economics and the Law*", Oxford: Oxford University Press 2014, p. 440. This argument should be applied with caution. On the grounds that legal doctrine is not self-evident, it is unsustainable to determine general principles axiomatically.

and Development (the "OECD") and the Commission are guiding.[1169] With regard to the OECD, a facility is considered indispensable or essential, "*if without access there is, in practice, an insuperable barrier to entry for competitors of the dominant company, or if without access competitors would be subject to a serious, permanent and inescapable competitive handicap which would make their activities uneconomic*".[1170] In contrast, when there is an economic alternative, no such barriers exist and the facility is considered non-essential.[1171] For the Commission, the essentiality of a facility can be substantiated if a potential substitute in the downstream market can counterbalance negative consequences of the refusal in the long-term.[1172]

In consideration of the foregoing, it is clear that the facilities offered by the trade associations researched are essential, indispensable, or objectively necessary.[1173] Due to their market dominance and the absence of viable economic alternatives, an insuperable barrier to entry befalls extrajudicially sanctioned industry actors operating on second-tier commodities mar-

---

1169 I. Haracoglou, "*Competition Law and Patents: A Follow-on Innovation Perspective in the Biopharmaceutical Industry*", Cheltenham/Northampton: Edward Elgar Publishing 2008, p. 135.

1170 Organisation for Economic Co-operation and Development, "The Essential Facilities Concept", *OCDE/GD(96)113* 1996, p. 97.

1171 Ibid; A comparable approach was embraced by the Commission relating to the telecommunications sector. More specifically, in the Notice on the application of the competition rules to access agreements in the telecommunications sector of 22 August 1998 [OJ 1998, No. C265/02], para. 68, a facility that cannot be replicated by reasonably means and is essential for reaching consumers (and for competitors to carry out their business) is essential.

1172 Communication from the Commission — Guidance on the Commission's enforcement priorities in applying Article 82 of the EC Treaty [now Article 102 TFEU] to abusive exclusionary conduct by dominant undertakings of 24 February 2009, [OJ 2009, No. C 45], para. 83.

1173 One can reach a different conclusion when examining, exclusively, early decisional practice. One example is the Commission Decision of 21 December 1993 relating to a proceeding pursuant to Article 86 of the EC Treaty [now Article 102 TFEU], Case No IV/34.689 (Sea Containers v. Stena Sealink), para. 41. In this Decision, the Commission defined an essential facility as "*a facility or infrastructure, without access to which one cannot provide services to their customers*". When applying this legal rule to the situation of the researched trade associations, the essentiality of a facility cannot be proven. This is because absent access, extrajudicially sanctioned industry actors can still provide service to their customers, albeit in a less economic manner.

kets if access to the services of these institutions were to become more difficult or impossible.[1174]

3. Elimination of (effective) competition

The third condition that is required to determine whether the trade associations researched violate the essential facilities doctrine requires that the self-regulatory measures function as "bottlenecks" to gain access to an essential facility (*i.e.* eliminate competition).[1175] To ascertain how much proof is required to establish such an infringement, the Commission and the CJEU developed two different approaches. First, the rigid approach, which calls for an elimination of "all" competition in the downstream market.[1176] Second, the more flexible approach, which underlines the like-

1174 Interestingly, according to the ECJ 26 November 1998, Case C-7/97 (Oscar Bronner GmbH & Co. KG v. Mediaprint Zeitungs- und Zeitschriftenverlag GmbH & Co. KG, Mediaprint Zeitungsvertriebsgesellschaft mbH & Co. KG and Mediaprint Anzeigengesellschaft mbH & Co. KG), [1998] ECR I-07791, para. 43, alternatives must be contemplated, regardless of whether they are economically less advantageous; In my opinion, this formulation is unwise from an economic perspective, because the term essentially presupposes the most important facility rather than an economically lesser option. This entails for the trade associations researched that, although extrajudicially sanctioned industry actors can get access to other trade associations active on the market, given the overwhelming dominance of the associations researched this would be unwise; For support of this conclusion, see P. Areeda, "Essential Facilities: An Epithet in Need of Limiting Principles", *Antitrust Law Journal, Vol. 58, No. 3* 1989, p. 853. *Areeda* explains that it is decisive whether practical alternatives can be established rather than imperfect ones. Please be aware that his argumentation refers to US Antitrust Law and should be transposed to the EU essential facility doctrine with due diligence; S. P. Waller, "Areeda, Epithets, and Essential Facilities", *Wisconsin Law Review* 2008, p. 368. This theory can be considered influential.

1175 The necessity of this condition is not commonly accepted. *O'Donoghue* and *Padilla* argue that it is superfluous to assess whether there is an elimination of competition, because once a facility is essential, indispensable or objectively necessary such a finding is obvious. See R. O'Donoghue and A. J. Padilla, "*The Law and Economics of Article 82 EC*", Oxford: Hart Publishing 2006, p. 440-442.

1176 ECJ 6 April 1995, joined cases C-241/91P and C-242/91P (Radio Telefis Eireann (RTE) and Independent Television Publications Ltd (ITP) v. Commission of the European Communities), [1995] ECR I-00743, para. 56-57; ECJ 26 November 1998, case C-7/97 (Oscar Bronner GmbH & Co. KG v. Mediaprint Zeitungs- und Zeitschriftenverlag GmbH & Co. KG, Mediaprint Zeitungsvertriebsgesellschaft mbH & Co. KG and Mediaprint Anzeigengesellschaft mbH

lihood to eliminate effective competition in the market (*i.e.* the risk of an elimination of competition).[1177] Despite both approaches having been developed with regard to a refusal to license intellectual property rights/ information, the impact of this measure differed. With regard to the first approach, as decided in *Magill*, *Bronner* and *IMS Health*, all effective competition on the downstream market was eliminated immediately or within a few days after the refusal of access.[1178] With regard to the second approach, in line with the Commission's decision and CFI's judgment in *Microsoft*, even though there were other operators left on the market, competitors were placed at a negative disadvantage. [1179] In other words, they were effectively eliminated from the market.

Against this background, the latter approach is of importance to determine whether nonlegal sanctions imposed by the trade associations researched eliminate competition by hindering access to an essential facility pursuant to Article 102 TFEU.[1180] Subsequently, it will be established for each of these measures whether Article 102 is infringed.

& Co. KG), [1998] ECR I-07791, para. 41; Strikingly, in the more recent ECJ 29 April 2004, Case C-418/01 (IMS Health GmbH & Co. OHG v. NDC Health GmbH & Co. KGIMS), [2004] ECR I-05039, para. 38 the ECJ explained that the exclusion of "any" competition should be used as a yardstick.

1177 Commission Decision of 24 May 2004 relating to a proceeding pursuant to Article 82 of the EC Treaty [now Article 102 TFEU] and Article 54 of the EEA Agreement against Microsoft Corporation, Case No COMP/C-3/37.792 (Microsoft), para. 589, 984; CFI 17 September 2007, case T-201/04 (Microsoft Corp. v. Commission of the European Communities), [2007] ECR II-3601, para. 105, 275, 280; This is closely related to the CFI's judgments in *Michelin II* and *British Airways*, in which the Court explained that an exclusionary abuse does not need to have an actual effect on the internal market, but must be capable of having that effect.

1178 T. Jiang, "*China and EU Antitrust Review of Refusal to License IPR*", Antwerp: Maklu-Publishers 2015, p. 141. *Jian* only refers to *Magill* and *IMS Health*, but this should also include the ECJ's judgment in *Bronner*.

1179 CFI 17 September 2007, Case T-201/04 (Microsoft Corp. v. Commission of the European Communities), [2007] ECR II-3601, para. 442.

1180 Although the stringent and more flexible approach to interpret the elimination of competition concept was developed in light of the licensing of intellectual property rights and, therefore, bears no resemblance to the situation of foreclosing access to the services of the trade associations researched by imposing nonlegal sanctions, it does provide a general theory that can (but not necessarily must) be considered applicable to assess these measures. However, one must be cognizant of the dangers of law in a vacuum (*i.e.* infringing the principle of legal certainty). See, for example, A. Ottow, "*Market and Competition Authorities: Good Agency Principles*", Oxford: Oxford University Press 2015, p. 154.

a. Blacklisting

Once a disloyal industry actor is blacklisted by one of the researched trade associations, it will be difficult to find a member of that institution who or that is willing to conduct trade with him or it. As a result, access to specialized commercial arbitration, which is the core service provided by such an institution, is made more difficult. This is because once an industry cannot enter into a standardized contract with a member of a relevant trade association, potential future conflicts cannot be solved in specialized commercial arbitration. This forecloses market access to an essential facility and is likely to eliminate effective competition in the relevant second-tier commodities market.[1181]

1181 The decisional practice of the Commission and the case law of the CJEU in *Compagnie Maritime Belge* provide some support for this conclusion. However, (i) both institutions refrained from explicitly mentioning the essential facility doctrine; and (ii) blacklists were drawn up to coordinate different behaviour compared to the dissemination of market information by the trade associations researched. More specifically, in *Compagnie Maritime Belge* blacklists were drawn up to ensure 100% loyalty with the shipping conference Cewal. This was done by depriving disloyal shippers, who used the services of a competing shipping conference, from getting access to its adequate services. The Commission and the CJEU argued that such a practice to ensure loyalty resulted in an exclusionary abuse pursuant to Article 102 TFEU. Contrarily, with regard to the situation of the trade associations researched, names of disloyal industry actors were disseminated after not conforming with an arbitral award from specialized commercial arbitration. Despite this disparity, in my opinion, although one cannot overlook that both blacklists have a similar exclusionary aim, it is uncertain whether the ruling in *Compagnie Maritime Belge* can be used to illustrate that the dissemination of the names of wrongdoers in a blacklist by the trade associations researched eliminated competition by refusing access to an essential facility. In particular, because Cewal's practice of blacklisting disloyal shippers was only found in breach of Article 102, since it aggravated even further the terms imposed under the loyalty contract. Standing alone, it was found insufficient to constitute an abuse. In my view, when reading the *ratio decidendi* it is apparent that blacklisting is a factor to establish an abuse pursuant to Article 102 TFEU. Given that the trade associations researched also withdraw membership and one even coerces members not to deal with excluded members, it may very well be possible that a similar conclusion can be reached. See CFI 8 October 1996, joined cases T-24/93, T-25/93, T-26/93 and T-28/93 (Compagnie Maritime Beige Transports SA and Compagnie Maritime Belge SA v. Commission of the European Communities), [1996] ECR 11-1201, para. 170, 172, 182, 185; Opinion of the Advocate-General Fennelly of 29 October 1998, joined cases C-395/96P, C-396/96P (Compagnie Maritime Belge Transports SA et al v. Commission of the European Communities), [2000]

b. Membership rules and barriers for market access

i. Withdrawal of membership

Once one of the six trade associations researched imposes withdrawal of membership on a recalcitrant industry actor, this undertaking or individual member will be denied access to all the services provided by the association. Obviously, such a measure eliminates effective competition in the relevant second-tier commodities market. This is because such an industry actor is placed at a competitive disadvantage.

ii. Denial of readmission to membership of expelled members on the basis of an additional entry condition

If an expelled former member of a trade association wishes to be readmitted to membership and that association denies an application for membership on the basis of an additional entry barrier, access to its services/essential facility is again denied. This eliminates effective competition in the relevant second-tier commodities market, because it places a targeted industry actor at a competitive disadvantage.

c. Refusal to deal with an expelled member

In the event a trade associations instructs its member to refuse to deal with an expelled member, the expelled member will not be able to have access to the services/essential facility of this association due to the expulsion, but will also most likely not be able to conduct trade on the basis of a standardized contract with any member. Subsequently, future conflicts will not be resolved in specialized commercial arbitration. This places a targeted industry actor at a competitive disadvantage and is likely to eliminate effective competition in the relevant second-tier commodities market. Irrespective of the fact that object restrictions are not discussed by the Commission and the CJEU with regard to a refusal to deal with an essential fa-

ECR I-1365, para. 143, 144, 151, 152, 162; Commission Decision of 30 April 2004 relating to a proceeding under Article 82 of the EC Treaty [now Article 102 TFEU], Case No COMP/D/32.448 and 32/450 (Compagnie Maritime Belge), para. 35-36.

cility, the legal rule adopted by the GC in *AstraZeneca*, which suggests that exclusionary abuses can also restrict Article 102 TFEU by object, is sufficient to establish that an instruction of a trade association to refuse to deal with an expelled member restricts Article 102 in such a manner.

III. Existence of a causal connection between market power of the trade associations researched and an exclusionary abuse on adjacent second-tier commodities markets

The trade associations researched, except for the DDC, hold dominant positions in the EU markets for regulation and private ordering, which aim to represent the interests of their members active in adjacent second-tier commodities markets. By imposing nonlegal sanctions on disloyal industry actors by the trade associations researched, not the former markets, but the latter markets are impacted.[1182] This raises the ensuing question: Does an exclusionary abuse that is committed in the market where dominance was established, but has effects in a non-dominated second-tier market, have a sufficient causal link?[1183] Although no express guidance can be found in the wording of Article 102 TFEU to necessitate that dominance and an abuse of a dominant position must be held and felt within the same market, the case law of the CJEU provides sufficient elucidation. In *Tetra Pak* the ECJ held that dominance in one market and an abuse felt in a distinct, but associated market is sufficient when special circumstances exist.[1184] Even though the Court failed to explain in detail what such circumstances

1182 According to *Monti*, this is also relevant with regard to leveraging and tying. For an explanation, see G. Monti, "*EC Competition Law*", Cambridge: Cambridge University Press 2007, p. 192; An overview of scenarios involving adjacent markets pursuant to Article 102 TFEU can also be found in R. Whish and D. Bailey, "*Competition Law: Eight Edition*", Oxford: Oxford University Press 2015, p. 175.

1183 R. Nazzini, "*The Foundations of European Union Competition Law: The Objective and Principles of Article 102*", Oxford: Oxford University Press 2011, p. 185. There must be a link between dominance and an abuse.

1184 ECJ 14 November 1996, Case C- 333/94 P (Tetra Pak International SA v. Commission of the European Communities), [1996] ECR I-5951, para. 27; A. Ezraichi, "*Article 82 EC: Reflections on its Recent Evolution*", Oxford/Portland: Hart Publishing 2009, p. 124. *Ezraichi* reiterates the ECJ's ruling in *Tetra Pak* by explaining that an abuse could not only occur in the market where dominance was established, but also in a related (secondary) market.

are, it was careful to stress that when two markets are linked, a causal connection is established.[1185]

That being said, regardless of the fact that such a link *prima facie* exists between the EU markets for regulation and private ordering on which the trade associations researched are active and the adjacent second-tier commodities markets on which their members operate, two reasons deny the existence of a causal connection. First, these associations do not hold market shares on the adjacent second-tier commodities markets. Second, the associations offer representation services as opposed to providing products (*i.e.* different product features). However, in my opinion, these rebuttal factors can be ignored altogether. Specialized commercial arbitration provided by the trade associations researched is quintessential for their members to operate on their relevant adjacent second-tier commodities markets. In contrast, representing the interests of their members by the associations is redundant and impossible when there are no members active in the relevant commodities markets. Accordingly, a sufficient link exists between the markets on which the trade associations researched are active and the neighbouring commodities markets on which their members operate.

IV. "Objective justification" of the refusal to grant access to the facilities offered by the trade associations researched

Even though a written exception to excuse a refusal of access to an essential facility offered is omitted from the wording of Article 102 TFEU,[1186] the

1185 ECJ 14 November 1996, Case C- 333/94 P (Tetra Pak International SA v. Commission of the European Communities), [1996] ECR I-5951, para. 31; For further guidance, see the Opinion of the Advocate-General Ruiz-Jarabo Colomer of 27 June 1996, Case C-333/94P ((Tetra Pak International SA v. Commission of the European Communities), [1996] ECR I-5951, para. 57. The link between the dominated market and the abuse on the associated market must be a close one. It must be established on a case-by-case basis, by taking into account: the (i) market share of the dominant undertaking on the secondary market; (ii) characteristics of the products; (iii) use of the dominant position of the undertaking in one market to penetrate the associated market; (iv) supply and demand structure of the markets; and (v) the dominant undertaking's degree of control on the linked market.

1186 W. Sauter, "*Coherence in EU Competition Law*", Oxford: Oxford University Press 2016, p. 101. Opinion of the Advocate-General Jacobs of 28 October 2004, Case C-53/03 (Synetairismos Farmakopoion Aitolias & Akarnanias

Commission and the CJEU have explained that conduct that can be "objectively justified" does not constitute an abuse.[1187] There are three categories of justifications which must be considered.[1188] First, an efficiency defence.[1189] Second, the protection of a legitimate commercial interest and, third, the objective necessity of an abuse. The goal of this Paragraph is to determine which category is most suitable to justify a denial of access to the services/essential facility of the trade associations researched in the event such these associations impose nonlegal sanctions on disloyal industry actors. Therefore, a balancing exercise must be conducted between the abusiveness of such a refusal and compensating positive effects.

1. Efficiency defence: lower transaction and distribution costs?

According to the Discussion Paper, an efficiency defence is permissible when efficiencies (i) are realized or are likely to be realized as a result of the conduct concerned; (ii) are indispensable; (iii) benefit consumers; and (iv) do not eliminate competition.[1190] Whereas this test is modelled after Article 101(3) TFEU, it is possible to similarly argue that indeed the denial of an essential facility following an imposition of nonlegal sanctions by the

---

(Syfait) et al v. GlaxoSmithKline plc und GlaxoSmithKline AEVE), [2005] ECR I-4609, para. 72. AG Jacobs also explains that the abuse under Article 102 TFEU suggests that a negative conclusion has already been reached, as opposed to the more neutral terminology concerning Article 101 TFEU, which requires the prevention, distortion or prevention of competition. Therefore, it is unwise to talk about an exemption, but rather that certain conduct does not fall within the category of abuse.

1187 See, for example, ECJ 14 February 1978, Case 27/76 (United Brands Company and United Brands Continental BV v. Commission of the European Communities), [1978] ECR 207, para. 168, 208, 236.

1188 R. O'Donoghue and A. J. Padilla, "*The Law and Economics of Article 82 EC*", Oxford: Hart Publishing 2013, p. 282-283.

1189 This parallels the exemption possibility under Article 101 (3) TFEU, as explained in I. E. Wendt, "*EU Competition Law and Liberal Professions: an Uneasy Relationship?*", Leiden: Koninklijke Brill NV 2013, p. 384; See also N. Kroes, EC Commissioner for Competition, "Preliminary Thoughts on Policy Review of Article 82", Speech, 23 September 2005, p. 5 (http://europa.eu/rapid/press-release_SPEECH-05-537_en.htm?locale=en).

1190 European Commission, "DG Competition discussion paper on the application of Article 82 of the Treaty [now Article 102 TFEU] to exclusionary abuses", *European Commission* 2005, par. 84. These four conditions are similar to Article 101 (3) TFEU.

trade associations researched is legitimate. This is because an efficient system of specialized commercial arbitration in which awards are enforced by nonlegal sanctions lowers transaction and distribution costs and outweighs any potential anticompetitive effects placed upon targeted industry actors.[1191]

Unfortunately, this finding is not unanimously shared in legal doctrine. *Gormsen*, *inter alia*, argues that the idea of an efficiency defence is debatable.[1192] She starts her thought-provoking analysis with explaining that the test for efficiency is about whether the conduct "eliminates effective competition" and not whether conduct is efficient.[1193] She then argues that such a standard entails that an efficiency defence is meaningless if Article 102 TFEU is exclusively understood – which is most likely – to protect economic freedom.[1194] Weighting efficiencies is then beyond the bounds of possibility, in practice. In my opinion, however, the overarching goal of EU Competition Law must be to benefit consumers rather than to protect economic freedom. This is in line with the general understanding of how

1191 Communication from the Commission — Guidance on the Commission's enforcement priorities in applying Article 82 of the EC Treaty [now Article 102 TFEU] to abusive exclusionary conduct by dominant undertakings of 24 February 2009, [OJ 2009, No. C 45], para. 27. Interestingly, the term "defence" has been removed by the Commission; However, N. Kroes, EC Commissioner for Competition, "Exclusionary abuses of dominance - the European Commission's enforcement priorities", Speech, 25 September 2008, p. 4 refers to the term efficiency defence (http://europa.eu/rapid/press-release_SPEECH-08-457_en.htm?locale=en).

1192 L. L. Gormsen, "*A Principled Approach to Abuse of Dominance in European Competition Law*", Cambridge: Cambridge University Press 2010, p. 56-57; For a denial of an efficiency defence, see also CFI 30 September 2003, joined cases T-191/98, T-212/98 to T-214/98 (Atlantic Container Line AB et al v. Commission of the European Communities), [2003] ECR II-3275, para. 1112. This judgment was, however, adopted before the Discussion Paper and the Commission's guidance on Article 102 TFEU.

1193 Communication from the Commission — Guidance on the Commission's enforcement priorities in applying Article 82 of the EC Treaty [now Article 102 TFEU] to abusive exclusionary conduct by dominant undertakings of 24 February 2009, [OJ 2009, No. C 45], para. 29; See also ECJ 21 February 1973, Case 6-72 (Europemballage Corporation and Continental Can Company Inc. v. Commission of the European Communities), [1973] ECR 215, para. 26. In that judgment, the ECJ explains that the strengthening or using of a dominant position must not eliminate effective competition.

1194 L. L. Gormsen, "*A Principled Approach to Abuse of Dominance in European Competition Law*", Cambridge: Cambridge University Press 2010, p. 56.

to perceive EU Competition Law.[1195] Accordingly, an efficiency defence that encompasses similar conditions as Article 101(3) TFEU must be endorsed.[1196] The trade associations researched can justify any refusal of access to their essential facilities (with the exception of a refusal to deal with expelled members) once they impose nonlegal sanctions on wrongdoers by invoking such a defence, unless these measures are not structured in the least restrictive manner.[1197]

2. The protection of a legitimate commercial interest

The trade associations researched pursue their members' collective economic interests by lowering transaction costs and benefit consumers by reducing distribution costs. However, it is debatable whether such benefits empower these associations to invoke the second category of defence, namely the protection of a legitimate commercial interest. Criticism to refute an application is based on three arguments: first, contrary to the ECJ's ruling in *United Brands*, the trade associations researched do not protect an "own" commercial interest, but safeguard the interests of their members.[1198] Second, the protection of a legitimate commercial interest has

---

1195 J. Drexl, W. Kerber, and R. Podszun, "*Competition Policy and the Economic Approach: Foundations and Limitations*", in: D. Zimmer (ed), "Consumer welfare, economic freedom and the moral quality of competition law – comments on Gregory Werden and Victor Vanberg", Cheltenham/Northampton: Edward Elgar Publishing 2011, p. 72.

1196 Nonetheless, one can argue whether the existence of an efficiency defence must assessed after an abuse is established pursuant to Article 102 TFEU, or amidst the appraisal of this condition; *Paulis* explains that the burden of proof is on the persons invoking an efficiency defence. This seems to suggest that efficiencies must be considered after a finding of an abuse of a dominant position pursuant to Article 102 TFEU. See E. Paulis, Deputy Director for the Directorate-General for Competition, "The Burden of Proof in Article 82 cases", Speech, 6 September 2006, p. 5 (http://ec.europa.eu/competition/speeches/text/sp2006_014_en.pdf).

1197 This must be done on the basis of the recommendations pertaining to the third condition of Article 101(3) TFEU. See Part III, Chapter 10, C, III.

1198 ECJ 14 February 1978, Case 27/76 (United Brands Company and United Brands Continental BV v. Commission of the European Communities), [1978] ECR 207, para. 189. The ECJ refers to an own commercial interest. See also, *inter alia*, CFI 8 October 1996, joined cases T-24/93, T-25/93, T-26/93 and T-28/93 (Compagnie Maritime Beige Transports SA and Compagnie Maritime Belge SA v. Commission of the European Communities), [1996] ECR 11-1201,

never been accepted by the Commission and the CJEU to justify nonlegal sanctions imposed by a trade association. Most decisional practice and case law relates to a refusal to supply. Third, the principle of proportionality has been infringed upon when a trade association does not organize a nonlegal sanction in the least restrictive manner.[1199]

Despite clear evidence against the application of a protection of a legitimate commercial interest defence, these three arguments can be contradicted. With regard to the first refutation, the requirement that an "own" business interest must be protected must be interpreted more flexibly. This is because these trade associations are not able to justify their refusal to grant access to an essential facility under a traditional understanding of this defence. In my opinion, due to the close proximity of the market on which the trade associations researched are active and the second-tier commodities markets on which their members are active, safeguarding an "own" commercial interest also encompasses the protection of the interests of the member undertakings. The associations are merely a vehicle through which their members collectively protect their business interests.

With regard to the second refutation, the mere fact that most cases relate to a refusal to supply does not preclude the possibility that a protection of a commercial interest defence can be made by the trade associations researched. Law is in constant motion and it may very well be possible that the Commission or the CJEU will – at least – consider such a defence.[1200]

---

para. 107; ECJ 16 September 2008, joined cases C-468/06 to C-478/06 (ot. Lélos kai Sia EE et al v.
GlaxoSmithKline AEVE Farmakeftikon Proionton, formerly Glaxowellcome AEVE), [2008] ECR I-7139, para. 50; CFI 9 September 2009, Case T-301/04 (Clearstream Banking AG and Clearstream International SA v. Commission of the European Communities), [2009] ECR II-3155, para. 132.

1199 The concept of proportionality was introduced by the ECJ in ECJ 14 February 1978, Case 27/76 (United Brands Company and United Brands Continental BV v. Commission of the European Communities), [1978] ECR 207, para. 190; The best definition of this concept was given in the Opinion of the Advocate-General Kirschner of 21 February 1990, Case T-5I/89 (Tetra Pak Rausing SA v. Commission of the European Communities), [1990] ECR II-309, para. 68. Proportionality is given when "*the undertaking in a dominant position may act in a profit-oriented way, strive through its efforts to improve its market position and pursue its legitimate interests. But in so doing it may employ only such methods as are necessary to pursue those legitimate aims. In particular it may not act in a way which, foreseeably, will limit competition more than is necessary.*"

1200 While obvious, the constant motion of law is, for example, confirmed by A. Barak, "*The Judge in a Democracy*", Princeton/Woodstock: Princeton University Press 2006, p. 113.

Last, when nonlegal sanctions are structured in the least restrictive manner, they do not go beyond the goal to ensure the protection of a commercial interest. Hence, these self-regulatory measures seem justified.

In sum, arguments can be made both for and against potential application of the protection of a legitimate commercial interest defence. It is uncertain how the Commission and the CJEU would deal with such a request. As a result, focusing on an efficiency defence seems more appropriate. However, this does not mean that the second type of defence becomes completely redundant. Every shred of evidence or argumentation in support of an exemption should be used.

3. The objective necessity of an abuse

The objective necessity defence was introduced by the ECJ in *Centre belge d'études de marché.*[1201] Although the Court failed to provide sufficient guidance on how to interpret this category of exemption, two decades later the Commission in its Discussion Paper provided much needed clarification.[1202] By referring to the CJEU judgments of *Hilti* and *Tetra Pak,* the Commission argued that health and safety considerations can offset the negative effects of an abuse [of an essential facility].[1203] That being said, the imposition of nonlegal sanctions by the trade associations researched does not attain one or both public interest considerations. Consequently, no ob-

1201 ECJ 3 October 1985, Case 311/84 (Centre belge d'études de marché - Télémarketing (CBEM) v. SA Compagnie luxembourgeoise de télédiffusion (CLT) and Information publicité Benelux (IPB), [1985] ECR 3261, para. 27.

1202 European Commission, "DG Competition discussion paper on the application of Article 82 of the Treaty [now Article 102 TFEU] to exclusionary abuses", *European Commission* 2005, para. 80.

1203 CFI 12 December 1991, Case T-30/89 (Hilti AG v. Commission of the European Communities), [1991] ECR II-1439, para. 118; CFI 6 October 1994, Case T-83/91 (Tetra Pak International SA v. Commission of the European Communities), [1994] ECR II-00755, para. 83-84, 138; More recently, for example, in the Commission Decision of 22 June 2011 relating to a proceeding under Article 102 of the Treaty on the Functioning of the European Union (TFEU), Case No COMP/39.525 (Telekomunikacja Polska), para. 874 no clarification was given which public interests can result in an objective necessity defence. The Commission only defined this category of defence in vague terms by stating that "*A given conduct is objectively necessary where the dominant undertaking is able to show that the alleged abusive conduct is actually necessary on the basis of objective factors external to the dominant undertaking and is proportionate*".

jective necessity defence can be made. Whether or not other public interests such as the wellbeing of end-consumers can change this conclusion is unlikely.[1204] Furthermore, to date, neither the Commission nor the ECJ has exempted an abuse of an essential facility under Article 102 TFEU by arguing that conduct was objectively necessary.[1205]

D. *Key findings*

Unlike the members of the trade associations researched which cannot be held accountable for their role in the execution of nonlegal sanctions in the absence of collective dominance (oligopolies), it is not inconceivable that the imposition of nonlegal sanctions by the trade associations researched could be classified as abuses of dominant positions in violation of Article 102 TFEU.[1206] This is particularly true when these measures infringe the goal of maintaining effective and undistorted competition within the EU.[1207] At first reading, this provision manifests itself as a simple rule of law, since it would appear that only two requirements are needed, namely dominance and an abuse of a dominant position. Furthermore, Article 102 contains an easy to comprehend non-exhaustive enumeration of conduct which may be abusive. However, by taking a closer look, it is not so straightforward as to provide evidence that extrajudicial measures imposed by the trade associations researched qualify as abuses of dominant positions. Difficulties arise in at least four respects: first, it is difficult to measure how many market shares are required to substantiate dominance with regard to the trade associations researched. Second, it is difficult to establish if the imposition of nonlegal sanctions constitute exclusionary abuses. Third, it is uncertain whether dominance on the EU markets for regulation and private ordering on which the trade associations researched are active and the abuse of these positions, which has an impact on non-dominated adjacent second-tier commodities markets on which their

1204 One can make an argument that since the regulatory measures are necessary to ensure an efficient allocation of products, the wellbeing of end-consumers is fostered. This is because end-consumers benefit from lower prices.

1205 A. Jones and B. E. Sufrin, "*EU Competition Law: Text, Cases, and Materials*", Oxford: Oxford University Press 2016, p. 372.

1206 See Part III, Chapter 11, A.

1207 ECJ 21 February 1973, Case 6-72 (Europemballage Corporation and Continental Can Company Inc. v. Commission of the European Communities), [1973] ECR 215, para. 25.

members are active is sufficiently causal. Fourth, there is no possibility of obtaining an exemption when reading the wording of Article 102 TFEU, even though decisional practice and guidance offered by the Commission and case law of the CJEU permit some defences to justify an abuse of a dominant position.

To understand whether or not these difficulties are sufficiently addressed at EU level and whether extrajudicial measures imposed by the trade associations researched violate Article 102 TFEU, three components are of importance. These are the existence of (i) dominance; (ii) an exclusionary abuse; and (iii) possible justifications. With regard to the establishment of dominance, it is necessary to establish whether the trade associations researched hold dominant positions in their EU markets for regulation and private ordering.[1208] Put differently, these associations must hold a high degree of market power that is referred to as "dominance". According to the ECJ judgments in *United Brands* and *Hoffman-La Roche*, such a position of strength can be substantiated by calculating market shares.[1209] Due to the worldwide (and, therefore, EU-wide) pre-eminent position of most of the trade associations researched, regardless of the fact that there is no concrete evidence of market shares held in the EU markets for regulation and private ordering and that economic models to measure market power are notoriously difficult to apply and fathom, this is unproblematic.[1210] All of the trade associations researched, except for the DDC, hold a dominant position in these markets. To be more concrete, this Chapter divided these associations into four classes. The first class contains the trade associations researched that each hold more than 80% global market shares in their markets for regulation and private ordering, which are interchangeable with EU market shares. These include the LME and FOSFA. Such high amounts of market shares exceed the 70-80% Community market share threshold as was decided by the CFI in *Hilti*. As a consequence, irrespective of opposing facts, dominance is established. The second class encompasses those trade associations that do not exceed the standard developed in *Hilti*, but hold more than 50% EU market shares. This class comprises the ICA. While this association holds more than 50% global market shares, also here, these shares were seen as interchangeable with Community shares. Hence, there is a strong presumption that the ICA is dominant in accordance with the ECJ's judgment in *Akzo* and the Com-

1208 See Part III, Chapter 11, B.
1209 See Part III, Chapter 11, B, I.
1210 See Part III, Chapter 11, B, III.

mission's Discussion Paper. A rebuttal of this presumption should not be contemplated. Exceptional circumstances such as "a more than low market share of competitors" are absent and can be considered ill-defined.

With regard to the third and most controversial class of the trade associations researched, namely GAFTA and the FCC, no evidence of global and Community market shares can be determined. While some may consider an absence of such a market power indicator too uncertain to establish dominance, in my opinion, such a viewpoint can be contradicted. Due to the strong market position of both associations, supported with evidence that suggests that they are market leaders, it is very likely that at least the 50% Community market share threshold as was developed in *Akzo* is fulfilled. Accordingly, both associations hold dominant positions in their respective EU markets for regulation and private ordering. The fourth and last class concerns the DDC, which clearly does not have a dominant position in the relevant EU market for regulation and private ordering. The FBDB is the leading trade association in that market.

Regarding the second component, which requires that nonlegal sanctions imposed by the dominant trade associations researched must be abusive within the meaning of Article 102 TFEU,[1211] the ECJ in *Hoffman La Roche*, *Michelin I* and the CFI in *Michelin II* and *British Airways* provide guidance.[1212] Similar to the aim of self-regulatory sanctioning by the trade associations researched to punish disloyal behaviour, the focus of the CJEU was on exclusionary behaviour. The CJEU explained that this can be substantiated when (i) conduct is capable of influencing the structure of the market; (ii) there is recourse to methods different from those which condition normal competition in products or services on the basis of the transactions of commercial operators; and (iii) conduct is able to have, or capable of having, the effect of hindering the maintenance of the degree of competition still existing in the market or the growth of that competition. Be that as it may, this Chapter has decided not to assess whether nonlegal sanctions imposed by the trade associations researched fulfil this tripartite test. This is because nonlegal sanctions do not really fit within the three partite test, but are better qualified as denials of an essential facility.[1213]

Once the dominant trade associations researched impose nonlegal sanctions on wrongdoers, access to the services of these associations is made more difficult, or impossible, depending on the type of extrajudicial mea-

---

1211 See Part III, Chapter 11, C.
1212 See Part III, Chapter 11, C, I.
1213 See Part III, Chapter 11, C, II.

sure. Although the essential facility doctrine has never been employed by the Commission and the CJEU under similar circumstances, the imposition of nonlegal sanctions on disloyal industry actors qualifies as denial of an essential facility when three requirements are fulfilled.[1214] First, the services offered by these associations must be classified as a facility.[1215] Whereas from an older perspective, the focus was on airports, railways, seaports, intangible networks and tangible networks, in more recent times a broader understanding of this criterion is favoured. Examples include the ECJ's judgment in *IMS Health* and the Commission's and CFI's reasoning in *Microsoft*. On the basis of these cases, one can argue that the services offered by the dominant trade associations researched qualify as a facility. Moreover, two arguments in favour of such an attribution can be given. First, it is irrational to deprive the Commission and the CJEU of a useful method to analyse an infringement of Article 102 TFEU by applying a more restrictive comprehension of a facility. Second, the content of a norm (here: the wording of a facility) can change over time. Hence, previously unknown situations could fall within the scope of a facility.

The second requirement that must be fulfilled under the essential facility doctrine requires that the services offered by the dominant trade associations researched be indispensable, essential, or objectively necessary.[1216] This requires that access to a facility must be refused resulting in an insuperable barrier to obtain access to an essential facility, or a serious, permanent and inescapable competitive handicap (*i.e.* trading on non-economic grounds). It is clear that when access to the services of the dominant trade associations researched is made more difficult, or impossible, and given their market dominance and the absence of viable economic alternatives, an insuperable barrier befalls extrajudicially sanctioned industry actors operating on the second-tier commodities markets. This places such industry actors at an inescapable competitive handicap. As a result, the services/facility offered by the trade associations researched are essential, indispensable, or objectively necessary.

1214 V. Hagenfeldt, "*EC Competition Law - the Essential Facilities Doctrine: To what extent is the Essential Facilities Doctrine established in Community law and how has its application under Article 82 EC evolved over time?*", Munich: Grin Verlag 2009, p. 4. The application of the essential facility doctrine should be of an exceptional nature, subject to conditions and meticulous contemplation.

1215 See Part III, Chapter 11, C, II, 1.

1216 See Part III, Chapter 11, C, II, 2.

Third, the extrajudicial measures must eliminate competition in a substantial part of the internal market.[1217] To substantiate evidence as to whether this condition is fulfilled, two approaches are guiding: the rigid approach, which entails that all competition must be eliminated and the more flexible approach, which requires that competition is "effectively" eliminated. Despite both approaches having been developed pertaining to a refusal to license intellectual property rights/information, they can be tailored to function as a yardstick to determine whether the imposition of nonlegal sanctions by the dominant trade associations researched eliminates competition by hindering access to an essential facility pursuant to Article 102 TFEU. The dissemination of the names of wrongdoers in a blacklist makes access to the services of the responsible dominant trade association more difficult, because members of this association are more unwilling to conduct trade with a blacklisted disloyal industry actor on the basis of a standardized contract.[1218] As a result, potential future disputes are not resolved in specialized commercial arbitration. This eliminates effective competition. Withdrawals of membership and denials of readmission to membership for an expelled member on the basis of an additional entry condition ensure that a targeted industry actor has no access to the services of the relevant dominant trade association.[1219] This clearly eliminates effective competition. A refusal to deal with an expelled member carries in its wake that such an industry actor cannot conduct trade with a member of the relevant dominant trade association.[1220] This makes it impossible to enter into a standardized contract and clearly places a targeted wrongdoer at a competitive disadvantage. While one can argue that this eliminates effective competition in the relevant second-tier commodities market, along the lines of the GC in AstraZeneca – arguably –a refusal to deal with members can even restrict competition by object.

It is without doubt that nonlegal sanctions qualify as refusals of access to an essential facility. Yet, there is a causation problem: Can the dominance felt by the trade associations researched in their EU markets for regulation and private ordering and the imposition of nonlegal sanctions by these associations on wrongdoers active in (non-dominated) adjacent second-tier commodities markets be seen as sufficiently causal?[1221] This question must

1217 See Part III, Chapter 11, C, II, 3.
1218 See Part III, Chapter 11, C, II, 3, a.
1219 See Part III, Chapter 11, C, II, 3, b, i and ii.
1220 See Part III, Chapter 11, C, II, 3, c.
1221 See Part III, Chapter 11, C, III.

be answered in the affirmative. According to the ECJ in *Tetra Pak*, a causal relationship can be established regardless of whether dominance and an abuse are felt within different, but associated markets when there are special circumstances. Along the lines of this case, it is inconceivable to deny causation between the EU markets for regulation and private ordering and the adjacent second-tier commodities markets. The reason is that the dominant trade associations researched optimize the functioning of their members on each relevant commodities market by, in particular, coordinating and facilitating a system of specialized commercial arbitration. In addition, the proximity of both markets can also be corroborated by converse argument. As an illustration, when in the unlikely event, but by assuming for the sake of argument that, all members of the dominant trade associations researched leave their relevant markets, it is clear that also these associations will disappear. On that premise, since the trade associations cannot exist without their members, both markets can be seen as intrinsically close. Accordingly, a "hypothetical" *conditio sine qua non* nexus can be established between the dominance of these associations and the abuse felt in the closely-related commodities markets. Consequently, every time one of the dominant trade associations researched imposes a nonlegal sanction on a recalcitrant industry actor, it refuses access to an essential facility in violation of Article 102 TFEU.

Justifications for a violation of Article 102 TFEU relate to three different categories.[1222] The first category can be invoked when efficiency compensates for the distortion of competition.[1223] Despite some authors suggesting that Article 102 TFEU is more about the protection of economic freedom as opposed to protecting consumers, unlike Article 101(3) TFEU an efficiency defence should consist of the same conditions with reference to Article 101(3). Since the dominant trade associations researched lower transaction and distribution costs, the extrajudicial measures described above (with the exception of a refusal to deal with expelled members) can be justified when they are structured in the least restrictive manner possible.

The second category that allows for a justification requires that when the dominant trade associations research impose nonlegal sanctions on wrongdoers, and, hence, refuse access to an essential facility, they have done so to protect an "own" legitimate commercial interest.[1224] It appears that nonlegal sanctions cannot be justified by invoking such a defence be-

1222 See Part III, Chapter 11, C, IV.
1223 See Part III, Chapter 11, C, IV, 1.
1224 See Part III, Chapter 11, C, IV, 2.

cause of three reasons. First, these associations do not protect an own legitimate commercial interest, but that of their members. Second, protection of an own commercial interest has never been used by the Commission and the CJEU to justify similar exclusionary abuses. Third, the principle of proportionality has been infringed when a trade association does not organize a nonlegal sanction in the least restrictive manner. After extensive review, however, all three arguments can be refuted. First, given that the markets on which the associations and their members operate are closely related, it is conceivable to relax the terminology of an "own" legitimate commercial interest to also include that of such industry actors. Second, an absence of decisional practice by the Commission and case law of the CJEU does not entail that both institutions deny the presence of such a defence. Third, when a trade association imposes nonlegal sanctions in the least restrictive manner, the principle of proportionality has been complied with. Whichever line of reasoning is favoured by the Commission and the CJEU is open for debate. It is highly recommended to at least provide evidence to both institutions so that the second category of defence is satisfied. The third and last category of defence which explains that health and safety reasons in line with the CJEU's judgments in *Hilti* and *Tetra Pak* can justify an abuse, is not applicable with regard to the imposition of nonlegal sanctions on wrongdoers resulting in refusals of access to an essential facility.[1225]

In sum, nonlegal sanctions imposed by the trade associations researched on recalcitrant industry actors violate Article 102 TFEU when such measures are not structured in the least restrictive manner. Because wrongdoers lose access to the services of the relevant trade associations, these associations refuse access to an essential facility every time they impose a nonlegal sanction. Notwithstanding, it seems that the efficiency defence and to a lesser extent the protection of an own legitimate interest defence provide escape routes.

1225 See Part III, Chapter 11, C, IV, 3.

Part IV: Summary, Conclusions and Best Practice Guidelines

Chapter 12: A Succinct Summary of the Research

A. *A case study based review of present-day PLSs*

History underpins that many forms of private initiatives, or early PLSs, existed prior to their modern-day encapsulation.[1226] Examples that support this observation can be found by reference to the system of self-regulation within the Oikos in classical Athens,[1227] the flexibility and risk allocation with regard to lease contracts in the agriculture sector in the Roman Empire,[1228] *Lex Mercatoria* in Middle Ages,[1229] and the nonlegal sanctioning of disloyal workers by industrialists from the late 18th through the 19th century in Europe (*i.e.* the Industrial Revolution).[1230] While some might argue that these precedents are merely anomalies and that opting out of the public legal system is a mere fallacy, in this day and age PLSs can be found in over 50 industries.[1231] In each of them, industry actors have established a trade association with the aim to protect their collective interest, specifically through the adoption of bylaws and rules applicable to all members, the formulation of standardized contracts and, most importantly, instead of being subject to adjudication in public courts, a system of specialized commercial arbitration to resolve disputes between members and sometimes between a member and a non-member.

This research has narrowed down these industries by focusing on six trade associations which represent the interests of their members that operate in specific commodities industries, such as the cotton, diamond, grain and feed, cocoa, metal, and oils and fats industry. These are the ICA, the DDC, GAFTA, the FCC, the LME and FOSFA. Interestingly, all of them have two crucial features in common: First, they have set up a system of specialized commercial arbitration and, second, they have introduced nonlegal sanctions to punish non-conformance with their awards. By doing so,

---

1226 See Part I, Chapter 1, A.
1227 See Part I, Chapter 1, A, I.
1228 See Part I, Chapter 1, A, II.
1229 See Part I, Chapter 1, A, III.
1230 See Part I, Chapter 1, A, IV.
1231 See Part I, Chapter 2, A.

these trade associations as well as their members and – arguably – non-members operate PLSs as substitutes for the public court system.[1232]

B. Similarities and differences between the trade associations researched

Before a statement on the limits of nonlegal sanctioning and the introduction of the central research question, this research has then provided a broad overview of the differences and similarities of these associations.[1233] This is because not all of the trade associations researched are structured in the same way and such a broad discussion is a necessary bulwark against unclarity relating to an incoherent conception of how they function, how they have set up a system of specialized commercial arbitration, the types of nonlegal sanctions available to ensure compliance with arbitral awards, and the reasons to impose such extrajudicial measures. This was done by focusing on seven distinct but related features. First, with regard to their legal structure, four out of six of the trade associations researched are UK-based not-for-profit "private limited liability companies by guarantee", whereas the other two are either a not-for-profit UK-based "private company limited by shares", or a not-for-profit New York-based "incorporated company".[1234] Second, with reference to entry requirements, all of the six trade associations researched have three entry conditions in place: First, candidates need to be able to substantiate some form of connection/experience to the commodities traded in the relevant industry.[1235] Second, candidates must file an application for membership, including an explanation, *inter alia*, under which membership category they fall. Third, candidates must pay an entry/registration fee. Furthermore, two of the trade associations researched require additional entry conditions such as the proposal by at least two members of the relevant trade association, a minimum of two years' experience in the particular commodities trade and an approval by the Board of Directors.

Third, concerning the structure and composition of the arbitration tribunal, all have introduced a system of specialized commercial arbitration which is applicable when disputes arise out of standardized contracts provided by these trade associations, even though one of these institutions

1232 See Part I, Chapter 3, A.
1233 See Part I, Chapters 2 and 3.
1234 See Part I, Chapter 3, B.
1235 See Part I, Chapter 3, C.

favours mediation over arbitration.[1236] With regard to first-tier arbitration, the trade associations can be divided into two groups.[1237] The first group consists of those trade associations which are solely responsible for appointing the arbitration panel of three qualified arbitrators. The second group of trade associations allows both parties to agree to sole arbitration, or allows either party to name an arbitrator. In this aspect, the naming of a third arbitrator differs: Some allow this arbitrator to be selected by the relevant trade association, whereas others either instruct the associations to do so when one party requests this and at least one arbitrator deems this necessary, or only permit the naming of a referee in the event of disagreement between the two arbitrators. Concerning second-tier arbitration, five out of the six trade associations researched provide a possibility of internal appeal to review an arbitral award.[1238] However, the number of arbitrators differs: a tribunal is typically comprised of five, three, or between two and four arbitrators. Regardless of whether first- or second-tier arbitration is applicable, the majority of trade associations require that arbitrators are members, have practical experience in the industry, and have completed exams.[1239]

Fourth, pertaining to the place or arbitration and applicable law, specialized commercial arbitration is held at the place in the country in which the trade association is established, its premises, or exceptionally where the parties subject to arbitration opt for.[1240] For the trade associations researched this is either England and Wales, or the premises of the trade association in London/Liverpool/New York. The applicable law is determined by the place of arbitration. Considering the trade associations researched, this is either England or New York. Fifth, with regard to the finality of arbitration or the possibility of (some) legal redress in public courts, the trade associations researched differ in terms of restrictiveness.[1241] Two UK-based trade associations only allow for judicial review by public courts when consensus between the parties is reached, or to obtain security of an arbitral award. This does not comply with the Arbitration Act 1996, because it goes below the standard provided in this law. This Act allows a broader basis to seek legal redress at a public court both prior to

---

1236 See Part I, Chapter 3, D.
1237 See Part I, Chapter 3, D, I.
1238 See Part I, Chapter 3, D, II.
1239 See Part I, Chapter 3, D, III.
1240 See Part I, Chapter 3, E.
1241 See Part I, Chapter 3, E, III.

the commencement of arbitral proceedings (*i.e.* when a defence to negate a stay of proceedings is justifiable and when the arbitration tribunal has no substantive jurisdiction) and after an arbitral award is provided (*i.e.* when there is a lack of substantive jurisdiction of the arbitration tribunal, when proceedings were unfair and –arguably – if the arbitration clause in the standardized agreements insufficiently refers to a broader arbitration agreement and when a full review of the arbitrator's factual and legal determinations is permissible). With regard to two other UK-based trade associations, this is more difficult to say, despite their explicitly permitting a review by public courts to ensure the enforcement of an award at the English High Court and to replace an arbitrator in first- or second-tier arbitration at the English Court. The reason is that both associations remain silent about the possibilities to ask for recourse in a public court. The remaining UK-based trade association is in conformity with the Arbitration Act 1996 and the New York based trade association probably corresponds with Article 75 of the CPLR and the FAA.

Sixth, concerning the types of nonlegal sanctions, six nonlegal sanctions can be detected in the bylaws and rules of the trade associations researched to punish wrongdoers for not complying with an arbitral award from specialized commercial arbitration.[1242] These are (i) the dissemination of the names of disloyal industry actors in blacklists; (ii) withdrawals of membership (iii) denials for re-admittance to membership for expelled members on the basis of an additional entry barrier; (iv) refusals to deal with an expelled member; (v) entering the premises of wrongdoers without a warrant; and although not an extrajudicial measure, but included for reasons of structure (vi) limiting adequate access to public courts prior to arbitral proceedings and after an award. Yet, not all the trade associations researched have included these measures and have structured them in the same way. With regard to the practice of blacklisting, all of the six trade associations have included this measure.[1243] The majority of them do so on a publicly available section of the trade association's website/on the wall of the trading hall, and one does this on a section of the website which is only accessible for its members. Furthermore, half of the trade associations researched are obligated to do so following non-compliance with an award, the other half "may" impose such a measure. Concerning the withdrawal of membership, five out of six of the trade associations researched permit

1242 See Part I, Chapter 3, G.
1243 See Part I, Chapter 3, G, I.

such an extrajudicial sanction.[1244] In this regard, the directors/Board of Directors/Council (whichever is the relevant body) may impose an expulsion and sometimes may or must, although the majority of associations do not, publish this decision on the website of the relevant trade association. Only one of the trade associations researched permits an internal appeal against a withdrawal of membership. With regard to subsequent denials for readmission to membership for expelled members on the basis of an additional entry barrier, only one trade association has barriers in place.[1245] These relate to the necessity to ask a Board of Directors to reinstate membership and the lapse of a period of two years following a withdrawal of membership. About a refusal to deal with an expelled member, only one of the trade associations researched can impose such a sanction following the dissemination of a member's name in a blacklist, or an expulsion.[1246] Along the same lines, but different given an absence of specific requirements, only one trade association has included the possibility to enter the premises of a wrongdoer without a warrant.[1247]

Seventh, considering the reasons for nonlegal sanctions, the trade associations researched must be divided into two groups.[1248] The first group comprises five of the six trade associations researched which represent members active in commodities markets in which futures play a significant role. The second group consists of one of the trade associations which represents its members active on a commodities market in which trust is even more important. With regard to the first group, to hedge this risk of usual price fluctuations, these associations provide standardized contracts/terms for their members (and sometimes even non-members) to exchange a specific quantity of commodities at a predetermined price and specified time in the future.[1249] This can be problematic if the buyer and the seller were to negotiate an average price and in the future, owing to a scarcity/abundance of the commodities, the latter/former industry actor would gain more profit by selling to another buyer/buying from a different seller. Then, a contract deviation cannot be excluded when expected legal fees do not offset this monetary advance. The enforcement of arbitral awards from specialized commercial arbitration by imposing nonlegal sanctions pro-

1244 See Part I, Chapter 3, G, II.
1245 See Part I, Chapter 3, G, III.
1246 See Part I, Chapter 3, G, IV.
1247 See Part I, Chapter 3, G, V.
1248 See Part I, Chapter 3, H.
1249 See Part I, Chapter 3, H, I.

vides a much better alternative. Another reason to explain why extrajudicial sanctioning is a better option for the first group of trade associations relates to the New York Convention. Because industry actors which contract on the basis of futures are often active in different States, if an awards need to be enforced in public court, the court located in one country must enforce the award and the court located in the other country must recognize that enforcement decision in accordance with the New York Convention. This procedure takes too long and bears the risk that the second court would refuse to recognize the enforcement decision. Nonlegal sanctioning does not raise such problems.

In consideration of the remaining trade association which represents the interests of industry actors in a market in which trust is essential, the reasons for nonlegal sanctioning to ensure compliance with arbitral awards from specialized commercial arbitration relate to the necessity to have trustworthy traders even more so than in relation to the first group of trade associations.[1250] The reasons are three-fold: First, the value of the commodities traded is very high. Second, commodities transactions are expeditious. Third, members are part of a close-knit society.

C. *The antitrust limits of nonlegal sanctioning*

By taking these features of the trade associations researched into account, much of the success of specialized commercial arbitration must be attributed to nonlegal sanctions. Without such extrajudicial measures, compliance with arbitral awards is insufficiently guaranteed. Furthermore, these measures are necessary to resolve the prisoner's dilemma of the adverse impact of opportunistic behaviour.[1251] However, nonlegal sanctions also negatively affect the commercial reputation (and sometimes even social standing) of targeted industry actors.[1252] Given that all of the trade associations researched are major players and represent the interests of industry actors that operate in commodities markets, nonlegal sanctions can result in a loss of access to these markets for such undertakings and/or individuals. Despite some viewing these measures as laudable, their relatively severe impact on wrongdoers when imposed by the trade associations researched and executed by their members and non-members could be banned under

1250 See Part I, Chapter 3, H, II.
1251 See Part I, Chapter 4, B.
1252 See Part I, Chapter 4, A.

the two most influential systems of competition law in the world, namely US Antitrust Law and EU Competition Law.[1253] In particular, the role of the three actors in the imposition and execution of nonlegal sanctions could violate Sections 1 of the Sherman Act when these nonlegal sanctions classify as contracts in restraint of trade or commerce among US states or foreign nations.[1254] Furthermore, the trade associations researched could be held accountable for their imposition of nonlegal sanctions when these measures qualify as anticompetitive monopolization, or an unlawful attempt to monopolize under Section 2 of the Sherman Act. Section 2 can also attribute liability for members of trade associations in the execution of extrajudicial enforcement when they fall within the description of illegal conspiracies to monopolize any part of the trade or commerce among US states or foreign nations. In addition, the role of the trade associations researched, their members and non-members in the imposition and execution of extrajudicial measures can classify as illegal anticompetitive agreements pursuant to Article 101 TFEU.[1255] Moreover, the imposition of such measures by the trade associations researched and the execution of these measures by their members could attribute liability for both actors when these measures qualify as abuses of dominant positions in violation of Article 102 TFEU.

Even though, to date, the FTC, US courts, the Commission, or the CJEU have yet to even considered the anti-competitiveness of nonlegal sanctioning by assessing the role of the three actors, this does not mean that the participation of all three actors in extralegal sanctioning is permissible.[1256] It may very well be possible that antitrust scrutiny and subsequent findings of illegality are just a matter of time. To overcome this lack of clarity, the research question was formulated as follows: "*Do the trade associations researched, their members and non-members, for their role in the imposition and execution of nonlegal sanctions, infringe US Antitrust Law and EU Competition Law and, if yes, can they justify these extrajudicial measures?*" Answering this question will clearly contribute to the general understanding of whether trade associations, their members and non-members involved in nonlegal sanctioning should fear they are in violation of competition law (*i.e.* guidance for compliance with competition law).[1257] Furthermore, it promotes

1253 See Part I, Chapter 4, C.
1254 See Part I, Chapter 4, A, I.
1255 See Part I, Chapter 4, A, II.
1256 See Part I, Chapter 4, D.
1257 See Part I, Chapter 5, D, I.

transparency for these three actors[1258] and will clarify what the actors that infringe US Antitrust Law and EU Competition Law must do to escape antitrust liability under both legal regimes by formulating best practice guidelines.[1259]

D. Restraint of trade or commerce under Section 1 of the Sherman Act

To reach the conclusion that the trade associations researched and their members and non-members, for their role in the imposition and execution of nonlegal sanctions, violate Section 1 of the Sherman Act, first, all three actors must qualify as a corporation or individual.[1260] Second, there must be a concurrence of wills. Third, it must be assessed whether the role of the three actors in the imposition and execution of nonlegal sanctions is inherently illegal or qualifies for a rule-of-reason defence. Fourth, it must be discussed whether anticompetitive extrajudicial measures can be justified under a rule-of-reason analysis.

With regard to the qualification as an individual or undertaking, the members of the trade associations researched and non-members easily fall within this description.[1261] Regardless of the fact that this is a bit more troublesome for these associations, they qualify as undertakings within the meaning of Section 1 of the Sherman Act. This follows from the 10th US Circuit Court of Appeals in *Gregory v. Port Bridger Rendezvous Association*, because they as well as their members are engaged in unilateral conduct, namely the imposition and execution of nonlegal sanctions.

Concerning the requirement that there must be a concurrence of wills, the imposition of nonlegal sanctions by the trade associations researched and the execution of these sanctions by their members and non-members must qualify as a contract, a combination in the form of trust or otherwise or a conspiracy.[1262] Whichever form of collusion is suitable to define the conduct of the three actors varies. The execution of nonlegal sanctions by members of the trade associations researched amounts to a contract, because this group of actors has agreed to the bylaws and rules of these asso-

1258 See Part I, Chapter 5, D, II.
1259 See Part I, Chapter 5, D, III.
1260 See Part II, Chapter 6, A.
1261 See Part II, Chapter 6, B, I.
1262 See Part II, Chapter 6, C.

ciations when obtaining membership.[1263] This is particularly true when members conduct trade under a standardized contract which refers to these bylaws and rules which include nonlegal sanctions. A non-member can also enter into a contract, but only to the extent this industry actor conducts trade with a member of a relevant trade association on the basis of a standardized contract provided by that relevant trade association. A combination in the form of trust is suitable to define the role of the trade associations researched in the imposition of nonlegal sanctions.[1264] While appearing to be not applicable at first glance, the word combination serves as a catch-all concept and includes the trade associations researched, since they protect the interests of their members by providing services on a not-for-profit basis. For non-members, such argumentation is not plausible. The third form of collusion, namely the existence of conspiracy, is inappropriate to describe the forms of collusion of the trade associations researched and their members.[1265] Non-members also do not typically fall within the constraints of this concept due to a lack of intent. However, for the purpose of this research, they have conspired.

With regard to the imposition of nonlegal sanctions by the trade associations researched and the execution of those measures by their members and non-members, the trade associations and their members – separately – violate Section 1 of the Sherman Act[1266] when disseminating of the names of wrongdoers in a blacklist,[1267] withdrawing membership,[1268] denying readmission to membership of expelled former members on the basis of an additional entry condition,[1269] and refusing to deal with ostracized members.[1270] These extrajudicial measures harm the commercial reputation (and sometimes social standing) of targeted industry actors and result in financial harm. The main reason is that the involvement of the trade associations researched and their members in the imposition and execution of nonlegal sanctions on disloyal industry actors forecloses their access to the relevant commodities markets. While some could argue that the extrajudicial measures described constitute per se violations of Section 1 of the Sherman Act, three arguments rebut this assertion in favour of a more le-

1263 See Part II, Chapter 6, C, I.
1264 See Part II, Chapter 6, C, II.
1265 See Part II, Chapter 6, C, III.
1266 See Part II, Chapter 6, D.
1267 See Part II, Chapter 6, D, I.
1268 See Part II, Chapter 6, D, II, 1.
1269 See Part II, Chapter 6, D, II, 2
1270 See Part II, Chapter 6, D, III.

nient approach, namely that the measures violate Section 1, but that their impact on targeted wrongdoers must be weighed against their generated procompetitive benefits (*i.e.* rule-of-reason analysis). First, the trade associations researched and their members classify as joint ventures, which are typically subject to a rule-of-reason analysis. Second, there has been a paradigm shift in how to treat collective boycotts. Whereas in the past the more stringent per se violation approach was favoured, the focus is now on the more lenient rule-of-reason analysis. Third, nonlegal sanctions appear necessary to operate a system of specialized commercial arbitration as efficiently as possible, a system which lowers transaction and distribution costs. Albeit that refusals to deal with ostracized members are very severe and it is quite obvious that the other extrajudicial measures are less restrictive, this measure that violates Section 1 of the Sherman Act was also discussed in a rule-of-reason analysis. In contrast, the participation of all three actors in entering the premises of a recalcitrant member of a trade association without a warrant and limiting adequate access to public courts prior to arbitral proceedings and after an award does not attribute liability to them under Section 1.

In deploying a rule-of-reason analysis to assess whether it is feasible that the pro-competitive benefits related to the imposition of nonlegal sanctions by the trade associations researched and the execution of those measures by their members outweigh the anticompetitive harm placed on targeted recalcitrant industry actors,[1271] it must be discussed for each nonlegal sanction – separately – that such a measure is reasonably necessary to ensure the success of specialized commercial arbitration which lowers transaction and distribution costs[1272] and in turn benefits total welfare and consumer welfare.[1273] With regard to the dissemination of the names of wrongdoers in a blacklist, even though this is the least restrictive extrajudicial measure to guarantee compliance with an arbitral award, since penalties and reprimands are ineffective, the majority of the trade associations researched and their members can structure it in a less intrusive way for targeted industry actors.[1274] Especially five safeguards are necessary to reduce the reputational harm placed on blacklisted industry actors. First, blacklists should not be made publicly available, but accessible for members only. Second, it would be better to allow a third party to collect, han-

1271 See Part II, Chapter 6, E.
1272 See Part II, Chapter 6, E, II.
1273 See Part II, Chapter 6, E, II, 1.
1274 See Part II, Chapter 6, E, II, 2, a.

dle and disseminate the names of wrongdoers in a blacklist, instead of a trade association which is often biased. Third, the dissemination of the names of disloyal industry actors in a blacklist should only occur after the lapse of clear deadlines and a final warning. Fourth, when the effect of blacklisting also targets an industry actor's social standing, more reluctance should be shown. Fifth, every blacklisted member should be given the opportunity to ask for an internal appeal to object to such decision. Once a trade association and, in particular, its members do not structure the method of blacklisting in the bylaws and rules of the trade association in keeping with these safeguards, the dissemination of the names of wrongdoers in a blacklist cannot be justified by referring to its necessity to ensure an effective system of specialized commercial arbitration which benefits consumer welfare and total welfare. Then, the negative harm placed upon blacklisted industry actors outweighs these benefits. In contrast, once a trade association and its members abide by these blacklists, Section 1 of the Sherman Act is not violated.

A withdrawal of membership, on the other hand, is a bit more stringent than the dissemination of the name of a disloyal industry actor in a blacklist.[1275] Despite its restrictiveness for targeted members of a relevant trade association, such an extrajudicial measure is reasonably necessary to ensure the effectiveness of specialized commercial arbitration which benefits total welfare and consumer welfare. However, as it stands, none of the trade associations researched and their members structure it in the least restrictive manner. This would necessitate a procedure based on clearly defined, transparent, non-discriminatory reviewable criteria that allows for cumulative penalties enforceable in national courts, with a final threat of a suspension, or in the worst case scenario when non-compliance is combined with other misconduct, an indefinite expulsion provided that the trade association has objective, reasonable and legitimate reasons for doing so which are based on fair and neutral criteria (*e.g.* do not favour certain members over others). In addition, expelled members should be given the chance to ask an internal appeal tribunal to review such a decision and must be advised of the possibility to request recourse in public courts. If these changes are introduced, the trade associations researched and their members, when imposing and executing withdrawals of membership, would not violate Section 1 of the Sherman Act.

With regard to denying readmission to membership of an expelled member, because a period of two years following a withdrawal of member-

1275 See Part II, Chapter 6, E, II, 2, b, i.

ship has not elapsed, or a Board of Directors declines readmission, the trade associations researched and their members cannot justify such an extrajudicial method of sanctioning if it is structured in this manner.[1276] However, if a two-year period is changed to a six-month standstill (or if this is combined with other misconduct, a one-year) period following nonpayment of an award, the trade associations researched and their members would comply with Section 1 of the Sherman Act. Similarly, when instead of a Board of Directors, an independent third-party panel (not connected with the relevant trade association) denies a reapplication for membership on the basis of clearly defined, equally applicable, transparent, non-discriminatory criteria, such as (i) the current liquidity status of the former member; (ii) an unwillingness to pay the penalty for non-compliance with the arbitral award; and (iii) evidence of probable disloyalty in the future, a refusal to reobtain membership for expelled members is necessary to ensure the success of specialized commercial arbitration which benefits total welfare and consumer welfare and does not outweigh the harm placed on targeted industry actors. If preliminary approval pending a full examination is also provided, the trade associations researched and their members would not violate Section 1 of the Sherman Act.

A refusal to deal with an ostracized member in no way can be justified under a rule-of-reason analysis under Section 1 of the Sherman Act.[1277] Such a measure ensures that a targeted industry can no longer conduct business with members of the relevant trade association, which results in a dramatic loss of market access and tremendous reputational damage. This violates the principle of proportionality and is not necessary to safeguard an efficient system of specialized commercial arbitration which benefits total welfare and consumer welfare.

E. *Monopolization of any part of trade or commerce under Section 2 of the Sherman Act*

Another provision which is of importance to assess the anti-competitiveness of nonlegal sanctions can be found in Section 2 of the Sherman Act. Section 2 provides an alternative legal basis to hold the trade associations researched and their members accountable for a violation of this Section when the trade associations have unlawfully "monopolized" or have "at-

1276 See Part II, Chapter 6, E, II, 2, b, ii.
1277 See Part II, Chapter 6, E, II, 2, c.

tempted to monopolize" and their members have committed an illegal "conspiracy to monopolize".[1278]

It is without doubt that the trade associations researched hold monopoly positions in the relevant US markets for regulation and private ordering.[1279] Despite nonlegal sanctions being felt by targeted disloyal industry actors active on adjacent second-tier commodities markets, on the basis of the theory of monopoly leveraging, this does not matter.[1280] The trade associations researched participate in illegal monopolies insofar as they disseminate the names of wrongdoers in blacklist, withdraw membership, deny readmission to membership of an expelled member if a two-year period following a withdrawal of membership has not elapsed, or a Board of Directors of the relevant trade association refuses to readmit the former member, and instruct members to refuse to deal with an ostracized member.[1281] When these measures are not structured in a similar manner as compared to the rule-of-reason analysis under Section 1 of the Sherman Act, they do not comply with the four theories to measure such harm.[1282] These are the effects-balancing test, the profit sacrifice and no-economic-sense tests, the equally efficient competitor test and the disproportionality test. Furthermore, with regard to withdrawals of membership and refusals on the basis of additional entry conditions, the trade associations researched refuse access to an essential facility.[1283]

However, in the unlikely event that at least one of the trade associations researched does not possess a monopoly position, any anticompetitive attempt to monopolize is also illegal under Section 2 of the Sherman Act.[1284] This concept serves as a safety net when the required amount of monopoly power is not reached. As a requirement, three conjunctive elements need to be fulfilled by such a residual trade association. These are: the existence of anticompetitive conduct,[1285] a specific intent to monopolize,[1286] and a dangerous probability of achieving monopoly power.[1287] Whereas the first two requirements are without any doubt met, the same cannot be said

1278 See Part II, Chapter 7, A.
1279 See Part II, Chapter 7, B, I, 2 and 3.
1280 See Part II, Chapter 7, B, II, 1.
1281 See Part II, Chapter 7, B, II, 2.
1282 See Part II, Chapter 7, B, II.
1283 See Part II, Chapter 7, B, II, 2, b, i and ii.
1284 See Part II, Chapter 7, C.
1285 See Part II, Chapter 7, C, I.
1286 See Part II, Chapter 7, C, II.
1287 See Part II, Chapter 7, C, III.

about the last requirement. This is because even though it is presumed that any residual trade association has a near monopoly position in the relevant market for regulation and private ordering concerning the US territory, when this association imposes anticompetitive nonlegal sanctions, the effects are not felt in the same market, but by disloyal industry actors operating on an adjacent second-tier relevant commodities market. This is where the theory of monopoly leveraging plays a central role. This theory requires that in such a situation, the near monopoly position in the first market must create a dangerous probability of a monopoly in the second market. While it is unclear whether such a position is held on the second market, it depends on whether its members are dependent on the services of a relevant residual trade association to speak of a near monopoly position. If yes, the dangerous probability of achieving monopoly power is satisfied and the residual trade association can be held accountable for an illegal attempt to monopolize pursuant to Section 2 of the Sherman Act when imposing anticompetitive nonlegal sanctions.

When the trade associations researched impose nonlegal sanctions on disloyal industry actors, their members can also be held accountable for violation of Section 2 of the Sherman Act.[1288] This group of actors has then conspired to monopolize, because they have entered into a written agreement,[1289] have a specific intent to monopolize,[1290] and took part in overt acts in furtherance of the agreement.[1291]

Comparable to Section 1 of the Sherman Act, a similar rule-of-reason analysis can exempt the trade associations researched and their members for a violation of Section 2 of the Sherman Act. This entails that with regard to the dissemination of the names of wrongdoers in blacklists, blacklists should not be made publicly available, but accessible for members only. Furthermore, it would be better to allow a third party to collect, handle and disseminate the names of wrongdoers in a blacklist, after the lapse of clear deadlines and a final warning, instead of a trade association which is often biased. Last, every blacklisted member should be given the opportunity to ask for an internal appeal to object to such a decision and when blacklisting also targets an industry actor's social standing, more reluctance should be shown.

1288 See Part II, Chapter 7, D.
1289 See Part II, Chapter 7, D, I.
1290 See Part II, Chapter 7, D, II.
1291 See Part II, Chapter 7, D, III.

For withdrawals of membership, to ensure that trade associations and their members escape antitrust liability under Section 2 of the Sherman Act, this would necessitate a procedure based on clearly defined, transparent, non-discriminatory reviewable criteria that allows for cumulative penalties enforceable in national courts, with a final threat of suspension, or in the worst case scenario when non-compliance is combined with other misconduct, an indefinite expulsion provided that the trade association has objective, reasonable and legitimate reasons for doing so which are based on fair and neutral criteria (*e.g.* do not favour certain members over others). Furthermore, expelled members should be given the chance to ask an internal appeal tribunal to review such a decision and must be advised of the possibility to request recourse in public courts.

Pertaining to denying readmission to membership of expelled members for the reasons that a period of two years following a withdrawal of membership has not elapsed, or a Board of Directors declines to readmit the former member, any trade association as well as their members should implement the following changes. Instead of empowering a Board of Directors to refuse a reapplication for membership, an independent third-party panel (not connected with the relevant trade association) should be tasked with doing this by taking clearly defined, equally applicable, transparent, non-discriminatory criteria into account, such as (i) the current liquidity status of the former member; (ii) an unwillingness to pay the penalty for non-compliance with the arbitral award; and (iii) evidence of probable disloyalty in the future. In addition, a two-year period should be changed to a six-month standstill (or if this is combined with other misconduct, a one-year) period. Refusals to deal with expelled members can never be justified under Section 2 of the Sherman Act.

F. The applicability of Articles 101 and 102 TFEU

To assess whether the trade associations researched, their members and non-members for their role in the imposition and execution of nonlegal sanctions on disloyal industry actors for non-compliance with an award can be held accountable under the two most important provisions of EU Competition Law, namely Articles 101 and 102 TFEU, these actors must trigger their scope of application.[1292] As a requirement, a legal boundary and multiple economic boundaries must be fulfilled.

1292 See Part III, Chapter 8, B.

The legal boundary is exceeded by the members of the trade associations researched and non-members pursuant to Articles 101 and 102 TFEU.[1293] Industry actors belonging to both groups of actors are undertakings within the meaning of both provisions, because they engage in economic activities. This is not true when they are not entities, but private individuals. Then, the legal boundary is not met. With regard to the trade associations researched, they are associations of undertakings within the meaning of Article 101 TFEU.[1294] However, this concept does not exist pertaining to Article 102 TFEU. Therefore, it must be established that the trade associations researched are undertakings. Given their functioning as umbrella organizations for different undertakings, such a qualification is not problematic. An absence of profit maximization as an underlying motive when providing services to their members also does not change this outcome. Whereas one could argue that services provided by the trade associations researched which include specialized commercial arbitration guaranteed under the threat of nonlegal sanctions are excluded from the scope of Article 102 TFEU, because they fall within the essential prerogatives of the State (*i.e.* essential function of the State), in my opinion, they do not. The trade associations researched were formed to accommodate the needs of globally active industry actors that operate in specific commodities markets. Hence, they are detached from the State and operate within a PLS. In addition, due to the harmful effects for extrajudicially sanctioned disloyal industry actors, it would be imprudent to treat the trade associations researched as public undertakings. This would prevent an antitrust review on the merits. Consequently, the trade associations researched are undertakings within the meaning of Article 102 TFEU.

Whether the three actors exceed the economic boundaries (*i.e.* the concept of the effect on inter-State trade) is a more difficult task for the Commission.[1295] The main reason is that this EU Competition Law enforcement institution must consider the interpretation of this concept given by the CJEU which is profoundly less specific with regard to the appreciability standard.[1296] The Commission must explain that the nonlegal sanctions imposed by the trade associations researched and executed by their members and non-members are capable of having the effect to hinder trade.[1297]

1293 See Part III, Chapter 8, C, I.
1294 See Part III, Chapter 8, C, II.
1295 See Part III, Chapter 8, D.
1296 See Part III, Chapter 8, D, I.
1297 See Part III, Chapter 8, D, II.

As a requirement, according to the Guidelines on Inter-State Trade, three elements need to be fulfilled to trigger the scope of application of Articles 101 and 102 TFEU. First, the Commission must establish that the three groups of actors are engaged in cross-border activity.[1298] It deserves no further explanation that this requirement is fulfilled. Second, the imposition and execution of nonlegal sanctions must be capable of having a direct or indirect, actual or potential, influence on the pattern of trade between Member States.[1299] Given that little evidence is needed to satisfy this requirement and only once in the history of the CJEU was this requirement not fulfilled, nonlegal sanctioning by the trade associations researched, their members and non-members can potentially influence Community trade. When a member of a trade association gets punished for disloyal behaviour, this will result in a loss of market access and, hence, inter-State trade is impeded. Furthermore, member undertakings of the trade associations researched can resolve disputes in the most efficient manner via specialized commercial arbitration which lowers transaction and distribution costs. This also has an influence on Community trade.

Third, the last concept to fall within the reach of the effects on inter-State trade doctrine necessitates that the trade associations researched, their members and non-members fulfil the "appreciability" (*i.e.* de minimis) requirement.[1300] With regard to Article 102 TFEU such an examination is not necessary, because the Commission must consider this criterion under the dominance requirement. However, pertaining to Article 101 TFEU, the concept of appreciability is crucial which is described in the De Minimis Notice. Here, a distinction must be made between restrictions by object and by effect in order to establish when nonlegal sanctions imposed by the trade associations researched and executed by their members and non-members satisfy this requirement.[1301]

If an extrajudicial measure is classified as a restriction by object, the appreciability requirement is automatically satisfied. This follows from the Commission's decision in *Expedia*. Conversely, when a nonlegal sanction has an effect on trade this is not so obvious. The Commission must then examine whether the members of the trade associations researched possess – jointly – more than 10% market shares in each relevant commodities on the territory of the EU. In addition, they must generate more than 40 mil-

1298 See Part III, Chapter 8, D, III, 1.
1299 See Part III, Chapter 8, D, III, 2.
1300 See Part III, Chapter 8, D, III, 3.
1301 See Part III, Chapter 8, D, III, 3, a.

lion euro annual turnover on that market. Notwithstanding an absence of evidence, the members of the trade associations researched, with the exception of the DDC, satisfy both thresholds. This is because the majority of industry actors prefer to belong to the most important trade association which ensures efficiency gains to them. Non-members also fulfil both requirements when they have entered into an agreement. With regard to the researched trade associations, even though they operate on the EU markets for regulation and private ordering and not on the second-tier adjacent commodities markets on which their extrajudicial measures take effect, these associations of undertakings meet the appreciability requirement. Any other conclusion would deprive the Commission of conducting an antitrust scrutiny.

In sum, nonlegal sanctions imposed by the trade associations researched and executed by their members and non-members trigger the scope of application of Articles 101 and 102 TFEU. This is because the legal and economic boundaries are satisfied. Put differently, the Commission is empowered to carry out an antitrust review to ensure that both Articles vis-à-vis guaranteeing market freedom and benefiting consumers are complied with.

G. *Anticompetitive agreement under Article 101(1) TFEU*

Every time one of the trade associations researched imposes a nonlegal sanction on a wrongdoer, that trade association as well as its members and non-members risk transgressing the bounds of the Article 101(1) TFEU. Despite the fact that, to date, neither the Commission nor the CJEU has ever ruled on the anti-competitiveness of extrajudicial measures to punish disloyal industry actors for not complying with an arbitral award, many parallels exist between this situation and prior decisional practice and guidance given by them. In more detail, to violate Article 101(1) TFEU two conditions must be satisfied: first, the trade associations researched, their members and non-members must have colluded. Second, their participation in nonlegal sanctions must violate Article 101(1) by object or effect. [1302]

With regard to the requirement of collusion, it is sufficient to qualify as a decision by an association of undertakings within the meaning of Article 101(1) TFEU when one of the trade associations researched imposes a non-

1302 See Part III, Chapter 9, A.

legal sanction on a wrongdoer that operates in a specific commodities market.[1303] This is because such a measure (i) comes from the governing bodies of a trade association; (ii) is formal (*i.e.* the bylaws); and (iii) imposes a certain market economic behaviour on its members. Following imposition of a nonlegal sanction by one of the trade associations researched, due to their role in the execution of this measure, members have also cooperated. Their faithful expression of the joint intention in writing classifies as an agreement between undertakings.[1304] Along the same lines, when a non-member conducts trade with a member of a relevant trade association on the basis of a standardized contract which is linked to a broader arbitration agreement which includes that nonlegal sanctions and the member is extrajudicially sanctioned, the non-member has also participated in the agreement between undertakings. However, if a trade association imposes a nonlegal sanction on a wrongdoer, also non-members that have not entered into a standardized contract with a member of a trade association have a role in its enforcement. Given that they break all commercial ties with a targeted industry actor, some form of collaboration exists, without having reached the stage than an agreement has been concluded. [1305] This qualifies as a concerted practice within the meaning of Article 101(1) TFEU.

With regard to the second requirement, it is necessary to establish that each nonlegal sanction violates Article 101(1) by object or effect.[1306] This dichotomy is of importance, because only the latter less severe form of restriction is eligible for a justification under Article 101(3) TFEU, whereas the former form of violation, which is about when an agreement by its nature and all readily ascertainable circumstances is apt to seek effect, does not. With regard to the dissemination of the names of wrongdoers in a blacklist, when one of the trade associations researched imposes this measure, a restriction by effect can be found.[1307] This follows from the ECJ's judgment in *Asnef-Equifax/Ausbanc*, because despite factual differences,[1308] these trade associations possess high levels of market power in the EU markets for regulation and private ordering and can oust a targeted industry actor from the relevant second-tier adjacent commodities market.[1309] In ad-

1303 See Part III, Chapter 9, B, II.
1304 See Part III, Chapter 9, B, I.
1305 See Part III, Chapter 9, B, III.
1306 See Part III, Chapter 9, C.
1307 See Part III, Chapter 9, C, II, 1.
1308 See Part III, Chapter 9, C, II, 1, c.
1309 See Part III, Chapter 9, C, II, 1, a.

dition, the Commission's and CJEU's judgments in *Compagnie Maritime Belge* provide guidance, following which (despite differences) the practice of blacklisting has exclusionary effects, since it ensures that targeted wrongdoers can no longer compete with other industry actors active on the relevant market.[1310] The members of the trade associations researched can also be held accountable for a violation of Article 101(1) TFEU by effect insofar as these trade associations disseminate the names of wrongdoers in a blacklist. [1311] Because of the competence of the members of a trade association to abolish a blacklisting clause in the bylaws of these associations, when the members do not, they execute an illegal collective boycott. Non-members cannot be held accountable for a violation of Article 101(1).[1312]

With regard to a withdrawal of membership, any expulsion imposed by one of the trade associations researched amounts to an illegal boycott, because the expulsion prevents market access and forecloses future commerce through the signalling of untrustworthiness of other merchants.[1313] Furthermore, the majority of the trade associations researched provide insufficient recourse to public courts following an expulsion and have no internal appeal procedure in place. All things combined, a withdrawal of membership violates Article 101(1) TFEU by effect. Similarly, their members also violate Article 101(1) for their role in the execution of this measure.[1314] When they abstain from abolishing a withdrawal of membership clause in the bylaws of the relevant trade association, they participate in a collective boycott which restricts Article 101(1) TFEU by effect. Non-members have no role in the execution of an expulsion of a member of one of the trade associations researched.[1315]

With reference to the denial of readmission to membership after a withdrawal on the basis of an additional entry condition, decisional practice and guidance of the Commission and case law of the CJEU explain that rules relating to the admission of members must be easily discernible and voluntary based on clear, objective and qualitative criteria, without being too restrictive to not infringe Article 101(1) TFEU by effect.[1316] When one of the trade associations researched imposes a lapse of a two-year period

1310 See Part III, Chapter 9, C, II, I, b.
1311 See Part III, Chapter 9, C, II, 2.
1312 See Part III, Chapter 9, C, II, 3.
1313 See Part III, Chapter 9, C, III, 1, a.
1314 See Part III, Chapter 9, C, III, 1, b.
1315 See Part III, Chapter 9, C, III, 1, c.
1316 See Part III, Chapter 9, C, III, 2, a.

following an expulsion, or permits its Board of Directors to arbitrarily deny a reapplication for membership, this rule is not complied with. In combination with an absence of an internal appeal possibility against an expulsion decision and given that reasons for a denial are not given, this association violates Article 101(1) TFEU by effect. When its members did not abolish a clause which empowers the relevant trade association to deny a reapplication for membership on the basis of an additional entry condition, they participate in an illegal group boycott in violation of Article 101(1) TFEU by effect.[1317] Non-members do not violate this provision.

Concerning the instruction of a trade association to its members not to conduct business with an ostracized member, following the Commission's decision in *Centraal Bureau voor de Rijwielhandel*, this instruction violates Article 101(1) TFEU by object.[1318] Violation of this provision can then also be attributed to the members of such a trade association, because without abolishing a clause which permits such an association from instructing its members to refuse to deal with an expelled member, they are also liable.[1319] Non-members do not violate Article 101(1) TFEU. About entering the premises of a recalcitrant industry actor without a warrant, the trade associations researched, their members and non-members do not violate Article 101(1) TFEU.[1320] This is irrespective of the fact that such a measure can hamper the reputation of a targeted wrongdoer. Taking into account limiting adequate access to public courts prior to arbitral proceedings and after an award, the trade associations researched can be held accountable for a violation of Article 101(1) TFEU by effect.[1321] This is because the requirement that arbitration must not take away the possibility of recourse to national courts, as formulated by the Commission in its notice on the *FIA* case and its guidance on *FIFA*, is not complied with by all the trade associations researched. Two trade associations are clearly in violation of this rule, two trade associations remain silent and one trade association complies with the rule. Anytime a trade association does not offer recourse to public courts, its members can also be held accountable for a violation of Article 101(1) TFEU by effect. This is because they possess the competence to change the bylaws of a trade association and guarantee an ad-

1317 See Part III, Chapter 9, C, III, 2, b.
1318 See Part III, Chapter 9, C, IV, 1.
1319 See Part III, Chapter 9, C, IV, 2.
1320 See Part III, Chapter 9, C, V.
1321 See Part III, Chapter 9, C, VI.

equate access to public courts. Non-members clearly do not violate Article 101(1).

Unlike Section 1 of the Sherman Act, a full-fledged rule-of-reason balancing exercise is not permitted at this stage with regard to restrictions by effect. [1322] The reasons are two-fold: First, Article 101(1) TFEU does not contain exemption grounds in its wording. Second, the Commission in its 1999 White Paper and the CJEU in *Metropole*, *van den Bergh* and *O2* explains that Article 101(1) TFEU should be interpreted grammatically and does not leave room for any form of balancing.[1323] Even though the ECJ in *Wouters* and *Meca Medina* ruled that legal and economic factors must be taken into account when an agreement restricts Article 101(1) TFEU "by effect", this research has exclusively considered justification grounds with regard to the dissemination of the names of wrongdoers in a blacklist, withdrawals of membership, denials of readmission to membership following an expulsion on the basis of an additional entry barrier, and limiting adequate access to public courts prior to arbitral proceedings under Article 101(3) TFEU.

H. Exemption under Article 101(3) TFEU

Any agreement in violation of Article 101(1) is automatically null and void pursuant to Article 101(2) TFEU, unless the safe harbour laid down in the RDBER, the SABER, or the justification embodied in Article 101(3) TFEU is applicable.[1324] This entails that for each anticompetitive nonlegal sanction, when it is imposed by one of the trade associations researched and executed by their members, it must be established whether both actors can persuade the Commission (and, when relevant, in appeal the CJEU) that their role can be exempted.

Even though the RDBER and the SABER are not appropriate to exculpate the behaviour of the trade associations researched and their members, since both actors do not carry out joint research and development and do not participate in any form of specialization agreement for the production and distribution of goods,[1325] this is different in relation to the balancing clause enshrined in Article 101(3) TFEU, which exonerates anticompetitive

1322 See Part III, Chapter 9, D.
1323 See Part III, Chapter 9, D, II.
1324 See Part III, Chapter 10, A.
1325 See Part III, Chapter 10, B.

agreements/extrajudicial measures that infringe Article 101(1) TFEU by effect and bring improvements to the production or distribution of goods, or promote technical or economic progress.[1326] While it may appear that nonlegal sanctions are reasonably necessary to ensure an efficient system of specialized commercial arbitration which in turn benefits economic and consumer welfare, each measure must satisfy the four-tier test enshrined in Article 101(3) TFEU.

The first requirement that must be satisfied refers to the notion of "efficiency gains".[1327] This necessitates that the trade associations researched and their members for their role in the dissemination of the names of wrongdoers in a blacklist, withdrawals of membership, denials of readmission to membership of former members on the basis of an additional entry condition following an expulsion, and limiting adequate access to public courts prior to arbitral proceedings and after an award reduce transaction costs. Fortunately, establishing this is not complicated for two reasons: first, all of these extrajudicial measures achieve appreciable objective advantages, because without them specialized commercial arbitration would be ineffective.[1328] Second, there is also a sufficient link between nonlegal sanctions and lowered transaction costs.[1329] Subsequently, the first requirement under Article 101(3) TFEU is fulfilled.

The second requirement that must be satisfied pertains to the concept of a "fair share for consumers".[1330] This requires that consumers must have sufficiently benefitted from the lowered transaction costs. Fortunately, also this condition is rather straightforward. Without the nonlegal sanctions which infringe Article 101(1) TFEU by effect, higher prices will be passed on to end consumers.[1331] The reasons are three-fold: first, the cost of doing business for members of the trade associations researched increases in the absence of an efficient system of specialized commercial arbitration. Second, these members sell products which consumers desire. Third, a change of the quality of products following a price increase is not likely. Given that nonlegal sanctions lower the distribution costs of consumers, the trade associations researched and their members fulfil the second requirement pursuant to Article 101(3) TFEU.

1326 See Part III, Chapter 10, C.
1327 See Part III, Chapter 10, C, I.
1328 See Part III, Chapter 10, C, I, 1.
1329 See Part III, Chapter 10, C, I, 2.
1330 See Part III, Chapter 10, C, II.
1331 See Part III, Chapter 10, C, II, 3.

The third requirement that must be fulfilled necessitates that the extrajudicial measures which restrict Article 101(1) TFEU by effect are indispensable to lower transaction costs.[1332] Here, each nonlegal sanction must be reasonably necessary to achieve this efficiency and must be structured in the least restrictive manner. Obviously, this bears similarities with the rule-of-reason analysis under Section 1 of the Sherman Act pertaining to the nonlegal sanctions which have the effect to restrict this provision. With regard to dissemination of the names of disloyal industry actors in a blacklist, the majority of the trade associations researched and their members can structure it in a less intrusive way for blacklisted disloyal industry actors, despite such a measure being the least restrictive nonlegal sanction to ensure the success of specialized commercial arbitration.[1333] Especially five safeguards are necessary to reduce the reputational harm placed on blacklisted industry actors. First, blacklists should not be made publicly available, but accessible for members only. Second, it would be better to allow a third party to collect, handle and disseminate the names of wrongdoers in a blacklist, instead of a trade association which is often biased. Third, the dissemination of the names of disloyal industry actors in a blacklist should only occur after the lapse of clear deadlines and a final warning. Fourth, when the effect of blacklisting also targets an industry actor's social standing, more reluctance should be shown. Fifth, every blacklisted member should be given the opportunity to ask for an internal appeal to object to such a decision. When the trade associations researched and their members disseminate the name of a wrongdoer in a blacklist without respecting these safeguards, both actors most likely do not fulfil the third requirement under Article 101(3) TFEU. In contrast, when they adhere to these changes it is likely that the practice of blacklisting is indispensable to lower transaction costs. IN this regard, a comparison with online evaluation forums is unfounded.[1334]

In relation to withdrawals of membership, none of the trade associations researched and their members organize expulsions in a manner which is indispensable to lower transaction costs.[1335] This is because there is a less restrictive way of structuring this nonlegal sanction. This is done by setting up a procedure based on clearly defined, transparent, non-discriminatory reviewable criteria that allows for cumulative penalties enforceable in na-

1332 See Part III, Chapter 10, C, III.
1333 See Part III, Chapter 10, C, III, 1.
1334 See Part III, Chapter 10, C, III, 1, a.
1335 See Part III, Chapter 10, C, III, 2, a.

tional courts, with a final threat of a suspension, or in the worst case scenario when non-compliance is combined with other misconduct, an indefinite expulsion provided that the trade association has objective, reasonable and legitimate reasons for doing so which are based on fair and neutral criteria (*e.g.* do not favour certain members of others). Furthermore, expelled members should be given the possibility of an internal appeal against an expulsion decision and must be advised of the possibility to seek recourse in public courts. When the trade associations researched and their members introduce these changes, any withdrawal of membership fulfils the third requirement under Article 101(3) TFEU.

With regard to denying readmission of former expelled members to membership when a two-year period has not elapsed following a withdrawal of membership, or when the relevant Board of Directors of a trade association denies a reapplication for membership, both barriers are not indispensable to lower transaction costs. Instead of allowing a Board of Directors to capriciously deny a reapplication for membership, a refusal should be done on the basis of clearly defined, equally applicable, transparent, non-discriminatory criteria, such as (i) the current liquidity status of the former member; (ii) an unwillingness to pay the penalty for non-compliance with the arbitral award; and (iii) evidence of probable disloyalty in the future.[1336] Furthermore, preliminary approval pending a full examination should be introduced. A waiting period of two years is also too long and restrictive. It would be better to impose a six-month standstill period following non-payment of an award, or if this is combined with other misconduct, a one-year period. If these changes are adhered to, any trade association which refuses a reapplication for membership of an expelled member on the basis of an additional entry barrier as well as its members comply with the third requirement pursuant to Article 101(3) TFEU.

In consideration of limiting adequate access to public courts prior to arbitral proceedings and after an award, this measure is indispensable to guarantee the success of specialized commercial arbitration.[1337] If parties could go to a public court in both scenarios, this could make arbitration merely a hollow concept. Yet, access to public courts must be at least equal to the standards provided in the Arbitration Act 1996. If this is the case, the third requirement pursuant to Article 101(3) TFEU is fulfilled.

The fourth and last requirement that must be complied with requires that the nonlegal sanctions imposed by the trade associations researched

1336 See Part III, Chapter 10, C, III, 2, b.

1337 See Part III, Chapter 10, C, III, 3.

and executed by their members are not able to substantially eliminate competition.[1338] While efficiency outweighs the harm placed on disloyal industry actors by applying the theory of utilitarianism and given that there is a small likelihood that competition on the market will be reduced, this requirement is satisfied. All of the extrajudicial measures ensure the long-term success of specialized commercial arbitration, which lowers transaction costs, and a weakened degree of competition prior to the adoption of the extrajudicial measures is unlikely.

In sum, the trade associations researched and their members for their role in the imposition and execution of nonlegal sanctions can satisfy the four conditions pursuant to Article 101(3) TFEU insofar as they are structured in the least restrictive manner.[1339] However, as they are currently used, it is unlikely that the Commission and in appeal the CJEU would not consider them as anti-competitiveness. If so, they are null and void pursuant to Article 101(2) TFEU.

I. Abuse of a dominant position under Article 102 TFEU

Regardless of the fact that the members of the trade associations researched cannot be held accountable for their role in the execution of nonlegal sanctions, especially since they do not hold collective dominant positions (*i.e.* oligopolies) in the second-tier commodities markets, the same cannot be said for the trade associations themselves.[1340] This group of actors can infringe the two-tier test laid down in Article 102 TFEU which requires the presence of dominance and an abuse of a dominant position. Yet, four difficulties prevent an easy review. First, it is unsure what the sizes of the market shares are required to prove dominance for the trade associations. Second, it is not easy to establish that the imposition of nonlegal sanctions qualifies as exclusionary abuse. Third, it is questionable whether potential dominance held by the trade associations researched in the EU markets for regulation and private ordering and the abuse felt on adjacent second-tier commodities markets is sufficiently causal. Fourth, Article 102 TFEU does not contain grounds for justification, despite the fact that the decisional practice of and guidance given by the Commission and the case law of the CJEU permit defences to justify an abuse of a dominant position pursuant

1338 See Part III, Chapter 10, C, IV.
1339 See Part III, Chapter 10, C, V.
1340 See Part III, Chapter 11, A.

to Article 102. Solving these uncertainties at EU level is crucial to establish the imposition of nonlegal sanctions by the trade associations researched is illegal under Article 102 TFEU. Subsequently, three components must be addressed. These are the existence of: (i) dominance; (ii) an exclusionary abuse; and (iii) possible justifications.

With regard to the establishment of dominance for the trade associations researched, it is necessary to establish whether they hold dominant positions (*i.e.* a high degree of market power) in the EU markets for regulation and private ordering.[1341] This must be done by calculating market shares in line with the ECJ judgments in *United Brands* and *Hoffman-La Roche*.[1342] Albeit that economic models are difficult to apply, owing to the worldwide (and, therefore, EU-wide) importance of the trade associations researched, with the exception of the DDC, the requirement of dominance is satisfied.[1343] Two of the trade associations researched, the LME and FOSFA, hold more than 80% global market shares in the relevant EU markets for regulation and private ordering, which are interchangeable with EU market shares. As a result, they satisfy the dominance requirement in line with the CFI judgment in *Hilti*. The remaining three trade associations either hold more than 50% global market shares (the ICA), which is equivalent to EU market shares, or do not provide any evidence of global and EU market shares (GAFTA and the FCC), despite being the only actual trade association. Because there is a strong presumption of dominance, especially since the ECJ's judgment in *Akzo* and the Commission's Discussion Paper are adhered to, dominance can be established.

With reference to the second requirement, the ECJ's judgments in *Hoffman La Roche*, *Michelin I* and the CFI in *Michelin II* and *British Airways* provide guidance[1344] to assess whether the nonlegal sanctions imposed by the dominant trade associations researched are abusive pursuant to Article 102 TFEU.[1345] The CJEU focuses on exclusionary behaviour on the basis of a well-known test, which consists of three elements. First, conduct must be capable of influencing the structure of the market. Second, there cannot be recourse to methods different from those which condition normal competition in products or services on the basis of the transactions of commercial operators. Third, conduct must not be able to have or capable of having

1341 See Part III, Chapter 11, B.
1342 See Part III, Chapter 11, B, I.
1343 See Part III, Chapter 11, B, III.
1344 See Part III, Chapter 11, C, I.
1345 See Part III, Chapter 11, C.

the effect of hindering the maintenance of the degree of competition still existing in the market or the growth of that competition. Irrespective of the importance of this tripartite test, nonlegal sanctions do not really fit in the approach of this test. They much more qualify as denials of an essential facility.[1346] This is because when dominant trade associations impose nonlegal sanctions on a wrongdoer, access to the services of these associations is made more difficult, or impossible, depending on the type of extrajudicial measure. Even though the essential facility doctrine has never been employed by the Commission and the CJEU under similar circumstances, the imposition of such measures qualifies as denial of an essential facility when three requirements are fulfilled. The first requirement necessitates that the services offered by these associations must fall within the definition of a facility.[1347] Whereas from an older perspective, the focus was on airports, railways, seaports, intangible networks and tangible networks, in more recent judgments such as the ECJ's ruling in *IMS Health* and the Commission's and CFI's rulings in *Microsoft* the definition of what constitutes a facility has been broadened. Subsequently, it is likely that the services of the dominant trade associations researched qualify as a facility. In addition, two arguments support this conclusion. First, the content of a norm (here: the wording of a facility) can change over time which entails that previously unknown situations could fall within the scope of a facility. Second, it is unwise to prevent the Commission and the CJEU from applying a useful tool to establish an infringement of Article 102 TFEU by using a more restrictive understanding of the term facility.

The second requirement that must be satisfied under the essential facility doctrine necessitates that the services offered by the dominant trade associations researched are indispensable, essential, or objectively necessary.[1348] As a requirement, nonlegal sanctions must cause insuperable barriers to obtain access to an essential facility for targeted wrongdoers, or a serious, permanent and inescapable competitive handicap (*i.e.* trading on non-economic grounds) for such industry actors. Given the importance of membership of the trade associations researched in the wake of insufficient alternatives, this is not problematic. The facilities/services offered by the trade associations researched are essential, indispensable, or objectively necessary.

1346 See Part III, Chapter 11, C, II.
1347 See Part III, Chapter 11, C, II, 1.
1348 See Part III, Chapter 11, C, II, 2.

The third requirement demands proof of an elimination of competition in a substantial part of the internal market.[1349] Here, two approaches provide guidance. First, the rigid approach, which entails that all competition must be eliminated. Second, the more flexible approach, which requires that competition is "effectively" eliminated. Albeit both approaches specifically pertain to a refusal to license intellectual property rights/information, they are useful to determine whether nonlegal sanctions eliminate competition by hindering access to an essential facility pursuant to Article 102 TFEU. With regard to the dissemination of the names of disloyal industry actors in a blacklist, such a measure makes access to the services of the responsible dominant trade associations more difficult. The reason is that members of these associations are more reluctant to conduct trade with blacklisted market participants on the basis of a standardized contract.[1350] Hence, they lose access to specialized commercial arbitration which eliminates effective competition. For withdrawals of membership and subsequent denials of readmission to membership on the basis of an additional entry condition, this is even clearer, because targeted members lose all access to the services of the relevant dominant trade association.[1351] With regard to a refusal to deal with ostracized members, this extrajudicial measure makes it impossible to enter into a standardized contract and, hence, excludes access to the system of specialized commercial arbitration provided by the relevant dominant trade association.[1352] This eliminates competition in the relevant second-tier commodities market and, according to the GC in *AstraZeneca* (albeit debatable) can even be considered as a restriction by object.

Taking into account that all three requirements are fulfilled, these nonlegal sanctions block access to an essential facility. Yet, there is one problem: the trade associations researched hold dominant positions in the EU markets for regulation and private ordering whereas the imposition of nonlegal sanctions takes effect in adjacent (non-dominated) second-tier commodities markets.[1353] This raises the following question: Does this entail that there is insufficient causation? In line with the ECJ's judgment in *Tetra Pak,* this question can be answered in the affirmative. A causal relationship can be established regardless of whether dominance and an abuse

---

1349 See Part III, Chapter 11, C, II, 3.
1350 See Part III, Chapter 11, C, II, 3, a.
1351 See Part III, Chapter 11, C, II, 3, b, i and ii.
1352 See Part III, Chapter 11, C, II, 3, c.
1353 See Part III, Chapter 11, C, III.

are felt within different markets, as long as they are associated and special circumstances are present. In particular, two reasons corroborate that there is sufficient causation between dominance felt by the trade associations researched in the EU markets for regulation and private ordering and the abuses felt in the adjacent second-tier commodities markets. First, the dominant trade associations researched coordinate and facilitate a system of specialized commercial arbitration for their members. Second, if the trade associations researched did not have any members, they would also disappear. Because a lack of causation is unproblematic, every time one of the dominant trade associations researched imposes one of the nonlegal sanctions mentioned above on a disloyal industry actor, it refuses access to an essential facility in violation of Article 102 TFEU.

To escape antitrust liability under Article 102, three defences can justify refusals to an essential facility.[1354] To invoke the first defence, which is comparable to the analysis under Article 101(3) TFEU, the trade association must substantiate that nonlegal sanctions are necessary to ensure the success of specialized commercial arbitration which produces efficiencies and serves as a compensation for the distortion of competition.[1355] Fortunately, this is relatively straightforward. Because nonlegal sanctions lower transaction and distribution costs, the extrajudicial measures described above, with the exception of refusal to deal with expelled members, can be justified when they are structured in the least restrictive manner possible. A second defence that can be used by the trade associations researched to justify imposition of nonlegal sanctions necessitates that they have done so to protect an "own" legitimate commercial interest.[1356] Yet, its application is open to debate. Three reasons prevent its application. First, these associations do not protect an own legitimate commercial interest, but that of their members. Second, the protection of an own commercial interest has never been used by the Commission and the CJEU to justify similar exclusionary abuses. Third, the principle of proportionality has been infringed when a trade association does not organize a nonlegal sanction in the least restrictive manner. However, three arguments counter these arguments in favour of the second defence. First, since the markets on which the associations and their members operate are closely related, the terminology of an "own" legitimate commercial interest should be relaxed to also include that of such industry actors. Second, a lack of decisional practice by the

1354 See Part III, Chapter 11, C, IV.
1355 See Part III, Chapter 11, C, IV, 1.
1356 See Part III, Chapter 11, C, IV, 2.

Commission and case law of the CJEU does not mean that both institutions do not allow the second defence. Third, the principle of proportionality has been complied with if a trade association imposes nonlegal sanctions in the least restrictive manner. Because it is uncertain how the Commission and the CJEU would treat these arguments, trade associations should always provide evidence in favour of this defence when relevant. The third and last defence which establishes that health and safety reasons may warrant a defence is not applicable to justify the imposition of nonlegal sanctions.[1357]

In sum, every time one of the trade associations researched, except for the DDC, disseminates the names of a wrongdoer in a blacklist, withdraws membership and denies reapplication for membership following an expulsion on the basis of an additional entry condition, an infringement of Article 102 TFEU is likely if such measures are not structured in the least restrictive manner. Yet, when a trade association instructs is members to refuse to deal with an expelled member, a breach of Article 102 TFEU is established irrespective of its form. The efficiency defence and to a lesser extent the protection of an own legitimate interest defence provide escape routes for the first three nonlegal sanctions.

1357 See Part III, Chapter 11, C, IV, 3.

Chapter 13: Conclusions and Best Practice Guidelines

A. *An answer to the central research question*

This research was designed and carried out to answer the central research question, which is worded as follows: "*Do the trade associations researched, their members and non-members, for their role in the imposition and execution of nonlegal sanctions, infringe US Antitrust Law and EU Competition Law and, if yes, can they justify these extrajudicial measures?*" Answering this question was done by comparing the illegality of all three actors for their role in the imposition and execution of nonlegal sanctions under both legal systems on the basis of two methods, namely the library-based legal research method (*i.e.* gathering information from reported comparable decisional practice and case law, legislation and academic publications) and the comparative research method (*i.e.* comparing US and EU antitrust law). Put simply, although a trade association and its members violate the core provisions of US Antitrust Law (Sections 1 and 2 of the Sherman Act) and EU Competition Law (Articles 101 and 102 TFEU) when (i) a trade association instructs its members to refuse to deal with an expelled member; (ii) both a trade association and its members are involved in the dissemination of the names of disloyal industry actors in a blacklist; (iii) both a trade association and its members withdraw membership; and (iv) both a trade association and its members deny readmission of an expelled member to membership on the basis of an additional entry requirement, they do not necessarily violate these Articles. When measures (ii) – (iv) are structured in the least restrictive form (which is now not the case), the relevant trade association and its members guarantee an efficient system of specialized commercial arbitration which benefits total welfare and consumer welfare. This justifies any trade association and its members orchestrating one of these measures to ensure compliance with arbitral awards from specialized commercial arbitration. Both a trade association and its members violate Article 101 TFEU if, when they limit adequate access to public courts prior to arbitral proceedings and after an award, this conduct is not structured in the least restrictive form. Although this is not a nonlegal sanction but is treated as such throughout this research for reasons of structure, trade associations and their members cannot be held accountable for a violation of Sections 1 and 2 of the Sherman Act.

B. Introductory comments to draft best practice guidelines for compliance with US Antitrust Law and EU Competition Law

Trade associations are often scrutinized by the Commission and the FTC on account of suspicions that they are acting as a conduit for anti-competitive behaviour between members. Furthermore, members of such associations are frequently subject to antitrust inspection for entering into illegal anti-competitive agreements. Despite the fact that a system of specialized commercial arbitration achieves far greater efficiency than adjudication in public courts, the method of enforcement of awards, which takes the form of nonlegal sanctions, can attribute liability to trade associations and their members pursuant to Sections 1 and 2 of the Sherman Act and Articles 101 and 102 TFEU. This is problematic, as any violation of any of these provisions may have serious consequences. A trade association and each individual member can be held subject to excessive fines and (senior executives) could even face criminal charges and imprisonment.

To keep these negative consequences from happening, it is crucial that these trade associations as well as their members do not infringe US Antitrust Law and EU Competition Law when they impose and execute nonlegal sanctions. Therefore, it is necessary to recommend best practice guidelines for both actors which will enable them to escape antitrust liability under Sections 1 and 2 of the Sherman Act and Articles 101 and 102 TFEU. This will also help to minimize risks of infringement.

I. Differences between US Antitrust Law and EU Competition Law

Owing to the many similarities between US Antitrust Law and EU Competition Law, it is not necessary to recommend two separate guidelines for both legal systems. However, some differences between both legal systems must be taken into account when drafting best practice guidelines. These can be found in the following table.

Differences	US Antitrust Law	EU Competition Law
The subject of antitrust law	Undertakings and private individuals.	Undertakings only.
Refusal to deal with expelled members	A violation of Section 1 of the Sherman Act by effect. A justification is unsuccessful.	A violation of Article 101(1) TFEU by object. A justification under Article 101(3) TFEU is unnecessary.

Limiting adequate access to public courts prior to arbitral proceedings and after an award	Cannot infringe Section 1 of the Sherman Act.	Can infringe Article 101(1) TFEU.
Justification of nonlegal sanctions	Rule-of-reason analysis under Section 1 of the Sherman Act.	Separate and more extensive four-tier justification test under Article 101(3) TFEU.
Monopolization and abuse of dominance	Members of a trade association for their role in the execution of nonlegal sanctions can be held accountable under Section 2 of the Sherman Act.	Members of a trade association for their role in the execution of nonlegal sanctions cannot be held accountable under Article 102 TFEU.

II. Outline of the best practice guidelines

The core provisions of US Antitrust Law and EU Competition Law, namely Sections 1 and 2 of the Sherman Act and Articles 101 and 102 TFEU, treat extrajudicial measures imposed by trade associations and executed by their members in a largely similar manner. This is because when these measures are structured in the least restrictive way possible (with the exception of refusals to deal with expelled members), they are permissible.[1358] That being said, Paragraphs C and D include best practice guidelines for trade associations and their members engaged in nonlegal sanctioning to not infringe Sections 1 and 2 of the Sherman Act and Article 101 and 102 TFEU. This will be done on the basis of tables which inform both actors about what they should do (DOs) and refrain from doing (DON'Ts) for each legal sanction.

C. Best practice guidance for trade associations

I. The dissemination of the names of wrongdoers in a blacklist

When a trade association disseminates the names of an industry actor in a blacklist, the following precautions should be followed:

1358 With regard to inadequate access to public courts prior to arbitral proceedings and after an award, the approach under Section 1 of the Sherman Act and under Article 101(1) TFEU differ.

DOs	DON'Ts
DO disseminate the names of wrongdoers in a members-only non-public blacklist. This will reduce the reputational harm placed on a wrongdoer.	DON'T disseminate the names of wrongdoers in a public blacklist. This will place additional unnecessary harm on a wrongdoer.
DO allow an independent third party to collect, handle and disseminate the names of wrongdoers in a blacklist.	DON'T allow a specific body in a trade association to disseminate the names of wrongdoers in a blacklist.
DO provide a disloyal industry actor with clear deadlines and a final warning before disseminating that actor's name in a blacklist.	DON'T disseminate the name of a wrongdoer in a blacklist without first establishing clear deadlines and issuing a final warning.
DO show more reluctance (*e.g.* longer deadlines for payment of an award) when blacklisting an industry actor also targets his social standing.	DON'T forget that the practice of blacklisting can also infringe EU Competition Law and US Antitrust Law when it only affects the commercial reputation of an industry rather than also his social standing.
DO allow targeted wrongdoers with an internal appeal procedure to reassess whether dissemination of a wrongdoer's name in a blacklist is justified.	DON'T take away the possibility for blacklisted wrongdoers to allow a reassessment in an internal appeal procedure.
DO be aware that the dissemination of the names of wrongdoers in a blacklist should change depending on the future development of the internet. If the internet becomes less private than it now is, blacklisting industry actors should be more limited. If it becomes more private, blacklisting disloyal industry actors is more acceptable.	DON'T overlook future progress of the internet with regard to the practice of blacklisting.
DO understand that online valuation forums are inherently different than the dissemination of the names of disloyal industry actors in blacklist.	DON'T refer to online valuation forums to justify the practice of blacklisting by the trade associations researched.

II. Withdrawal of membership

When a trade association expels a member, the following recommendations should be followed:

DOs	DON'Ts
DO only withdraw membership when there are objective, reasonable and legitimate reasons for doing so and the rules and criteria are fair and neutral (*i.e.* do not favour certain members over others).	DON'T expel a member when others in a similar situation would not be targeted.
DO only use a withdrawal of membership as a last resort to ensure payment of an award. If penalties and blacklisting are ineffective, withdrawal of membership should be considered.	DON'T automatically withdraw membership of a recalcitrant industry actor.

DO consider a suspension before imposing expulsion on a disloyal member.	DON'T arbitrarily impose a suspension or an indefinite expulsion.
DO withdraw membership without publishing a decision of such measure.	DON'T publish the decision to withdraw the membership of a wrongdoer. This will add unnecessary reputational harm to such an individual or undertaking.
DO allow expelled members the possibility of an internal appeal procedure to review a withdrawal of membership.	DON'T reject an internal appeal possibility for expelled members.

III. Denial of readmission of expelled members to membership on the basis of an additional entry requirement

When a trade association refuses a reapplication for membership on the basis of additional entry barriers following an expulsion, the following recommendations should be followed:

DOs	DON'Ts
DO allow an independent third-party panel (not connected with the relevant trade association) to review/deny a reapplication for membership on the basis of clearly defined, equally applicable, transparent, non-discriminatory criteria, such as (i) the current liquidity status of the former member; (ii) an unwillingness to pay the fine for non-compliance with the arbitral award; and (iii) evidence of probable disloyalty in the future.	DON'T allow a Board of Directors of a trade association to arbitrarily deny a reapplication for membership of an expelled former member.
DO apply the reapplication criteria equally to all expelled members. Put differently, eliminate any subjectivity in the decision whether to accept or refuse a reapplication for membership.	DON'T give the impression that one or more expelled members are being singled out for special treatment to be readmitted to membership.
DO allow preliminary approval pending a full examination.	DON'T automatically deny a reapplication for membership without considering all circumstances.
DO impose a six-month standstill period following non-payment of an award, or if this is combined with other misconduct, a one-year period.	DON'T deny a reapplication when a period of two years following an expulsion has not elapsed.
DO allow the possibility of an internal appeal when membership is refused on the basis of an additional entry barrier.	DON'T refuse an internal appeal procedure to reconsider a denial of readmission to membership on the basis of an additional entry barrier.

IV. Refusal to deal with an expelled member

When a trade association instructs its members to refuse to deal with an expelled member, the following recommendations should be followed:

DOs	DON'Ts
DO understand that instructing members to refuse to deal with an expelled member is in violation of EU Competition Law and US Antitrust Law.	DON'T instruct members to refuse to deal with an expelled member.
DO understand that instructing members to refuse to deal with an expelled member is unnecessarily injurious to ostracized members and in no way should be seen as proportionate to not complying with an arbitral award.	DON'T justify a refusal to deal with expelled members on the ground that it is necessary to deter disloyal members of a trade association when penalties, the dissemination of the names of industry actors in a blacklist and withdrawals of membership are ineffective.
DO expect that circulating a decision to refuse to deal with an expelled member to the general public is an even more severe violation.	DON'T make things worse by making a decision to refuse to deal with an expelled member publicly available.

V. Entering the premises of a recalcitrant industry actor without a warrant

When officers of a trade association enter the premises of a disloyal member to search for information in order to establish why this industry actor did not comply with an arbitral award, the following recommendations should be followed:

DOs	DON'Ts
DO expect entering the premises of a disloyal industry actor without a warrant to be of interest under US Antitrust Law and EU Competition Law. Criminal law is a more appropriate legal basis to assess such conduct.	DON'T let a potential violation of US Antitrust Law and EU Competition Law function as a deterrent to not enter the premises of a recalcitrant industry actor without a warrant.
DO instruct the responsible officers who carry out entering the premises of a disloyal industry actor to limit the reputational harm of targeted wrongdoers as much as possible.	DON'T instruct the responsible officers to carry out entering the premises of a disloyal industry actor without considering its reputational consequences
DO ensure that no decision following entering the premises of a recalcitrant industry actor is published.	DON'T publish a decision to enter the premises of a disloyal market participant, and that the decision has been carried out.

VI. Limiting adequate access to public courts prior to arbitral proceedings and after an award

When a trade association provides limits adequate access to public courts prior to arbitral proceedings and after an award, the following recommendations should be followed:

DOs	DON'Ts
DO forecast that limiting adequate access to public courts prior to arbitral proceedings and after an award does not infringe Section 1 of the Sherman Act. A rule-of-reason analysis is unnecessary.	DON'T combine limiting adequate access to public courts prior to arbitral proceedings and after an award with other anticompetitive conduct. Then, such a measure could potentially violate Section 1 of the Sherman Act.
DO expect that it is unlikely that limiting adequate access to public courts prior to arbitral proceedings and after an award is in violation of Article 101 TFEU, unless the safeguards laid down in the Arbitration Act 1996 are not respected.	DON'T go below the standards of access to public courts laid down in the Arbitration Act 1996.

D. Best practice guidance for the members of a trade association

I. The dissemination of the names of wrongdoers in a blacklist

With regard to the dissemination of the names of an industry actor in a blacklist by a trade association, to prevent liability under US Antitrust Law and EU Competition Law for its members for their role in the execution of such an extrajudicial measure, the members should adhere to the following recommendations:

DOs	DON'Ts
DO change the bylaws to remove any clause in the bylaws and rules that empowers the relevant trade association to disseminate the name of a recalcitrant industry actor in a publicly available blacklist.	DON'T use a trade association as a vehicle to drive disloyal competitors out of the relevant commodities market by allowing this association to disseminate that competitor's name in a publicly available blacklist.
DO instruct the relevant trade association to put a clause in the bylaws and rules in place that allows an independent third party to collect, handle and disseminate the names of wrongdoers in a blacklist	DON'T empower the relevant trade association to allow a specific body in a trade association to disseminate the names of wrongdoers in a blacklist.

DO instruct the relevant trade association to put a clause in the bylaws and rules in place that provides a disloyal industry actor with clear deadlines and a final warning before disseminating that actor's name in a blacklist.	DON'T empower the relevant trade association to disseminate the name of a wrongdoer in a blacklist without issuing clear deadlines and a final warning.
DO change the bylaws and rules of the relevant trade association to ensure that disloyal industry actors that operate in a market in which social relationships are close, more reluctance (*e.g.* longer deadlines for payment of an award) is shown when blacklisting such a wrongdoer.	DON'T change a blacklisting clause in such a manner under the presumption that EU Competition Law and US Antitrust Law cannot be infringed when this extrajudicial measure affects only the commercial reputation of an industry and not also his social standing.
DO instruct the relevant trade association to introduce the possibility of an internal appeal procedure for blacklisted industry actors.	DON'T leave a clause in the bylaws and rules which prohibits or does not grant blacklisted wrongdoers the possibility of an internal appeal against the dissemination of the wrongdoer's name in a blacklist.
DO inform other members that future developments may require that the blacklisting clause included in the bylaws and rules of the relevant trade association be altered.	DON'T be silent with other members about the future progress of the internal appeal procedure with regard to the practice of blacklisting.

II. Withdrawals of membership

With regard to a withdrawal of membership imposed by a trade association, to prevent liability under US Antitrust Law and EU Competition Law for the role of its members in the execution of such an extrajudicial measure, the members should adhere to the following recommendations:

DOs	DON'Ts
DO include a clause in the bylaws and rules of the relevant trade association which empowers the association to terminate membership when there are objective, reasonable and legitimate reasons for doing so and the rules and criteria are fair and neutral (*i.e.* do not favour certain members over others).	DON'T insert an expulsion clause in the bylaws and rules of the relevant trade association which grants the association the arbitrary power to expel a member when others in a similar situation would not be targeted.
DO ensure that the expulsion clause laid down in the bylaws and rules of the relevant trade association only empowers the association to withdraw membership as a last resort to ensure payment of an award. Furthermore, this clause should state that only when penalties and blacklisting are ineffective, withdrawals of membership should be considered.	DON'T allow the continuance of a clause in the bylaws and rules of the relevant trade association which empowers the association to expel a disloyal member automatically following non-compliance with an award.

DO change the expulsion clause in the bylaws and rules of the relevant trade association in such a manner so that a suspension must be considered first before the imposition of an expulsion on a disloyal member.	DON'T permit a clause in the bylaws and rules of the relevant trade association which empowers the association to arbitrarily impose a suspension or an indefinite expulsion.
DO ensure that the expulsion clause laid down in the bylaws and rules of the relevant trade association stipulates that the association only withdraws membership, but does not publish a decision of such a measure.	DON'T allow an expulsion clause in the bylaws and rules of the relevant trade association which instructs the association to publish the decision to withdraw the membership of a wrongdoer.
DO ensure that the expulsion clause laid down in the bylaws and rules of the relevant trade association stipulates that expelled members can seek relief in an internal appeal procedure to review a withdrawal of membership.	DON'T permit a clause in the bylaws and rules of the relevant trade association that bars the possibility of an internal appeal for expelled members.

III. Additional entry barriers to being readmitted to membership after an expulsion

With regard to denial of a reapplication for membership on the basis of additional entry barriers following an expulsion, to prevent liability under US Antitrust Law and EU Competition Law for its members for their role in the execution of such an extrajudicial measure, the members should adhere to the following recommendations:

DOs	DON'Ts
DO include a clause in the bylaws and rules of the relevant trade association which instructs an independent third-party panel (not connected with this association) to review/deny a reapplication for membership on the basis of clearly defined, equally applicable, transparent, non-discriminatory criteria, such as (i) the current liquidity status of the former member; (ii) an unwillingness to pay the penalty for non-compliance with the arbitral award; and (iii) evidence of probable disloyalty in the future.	DON'T permit a clause in the bylaws and rules of the relevant trade association which empowers a Board of Directors of this association to arbitrarily deny a reapplication for membership of an expelled former member.
DO ensure that the additional re-entry barrier clause in the bylaws and rules of the relevant trade association applies reapplication criteria equally to all expelled members. Put differently, this clause should eliminate any subjectivity in the decision whether to accept or deny a reapplication for membership.	DON'T leave room for the relevant trade association to allow that one or more expelled members receive special treatment to be readmitted to membership, and others do not.
DO insert a clause in the bylaws and rules of the relevant trade association which allows for preliminary approval pending a full examination.	DON'T allow the existence of a clause in the bylaws and rules of the relevant trade association which empowers th association to automatically deny a reapplication for membership without considering all circumstances.

DO change a re-entry barrier clause in the bylaws and rules of the relevant trade association which instructs the association to impose a six-month standstill period following non-payment of an award, or if this is combined with other misconduct, a one-year period.	DON'T permit the existence of a re-entry barrier clause in the bylaws and rules of the relevant trade association which empowers the association to deny a reapplication when a period of two years following an expulsion has not elapsed.
DO insert a clause in the bylaws and rules of the relevant trade association which allows the possibility of an internal appeal when membership is denied on the basis of an additional entry barrier.	DON'T allow the existence of a clause in the bylaws and rules of the relevant trade association that does not provide an internal appeal procedure to review a denial of readmission to membership on the basis of an additional entry barrier.

IV. Refusal to deal with an expelled member

With regard to an instruction by a trade association to refuse to deal with other members, to prevent liability under US Antitrust Law and EU Competition Law for its members for their role in the execution of such an extrajudicial measure, the members should adhere to the following recommendations:

DOs	DON'Ts
DO delete any clause in the bylaws and rules of the relevant trade association which empowers the association to instruct its members to refuse to deal with an expelled member.	DON'T allow any clause in the bylaws and rules of the relevant trade association which empowers the association to instruct its members to refuse to deal with an expelled member.
DO inform the relevant trade association of a concerted unwillingness to refuse to deal with an expelled member in order not to violate US Antitrust Law and EU Competition Law.	DON'T adhere to an instruction of the relevant trade association to refuse to deal with an expelled member despite the consequences.
DO inform the relevant trade association that instructing members to refuse to deal with an expelled member is unnecessarily injurious to ostracized members and in no way should be seen as proportionate to non-compliance with an arbitral award.	DON'T accept that the relevant trade association justifies a refusal to deal with expelled members on the ground that it is necessary to deter disloyal members of a trade association when penalties, the dissemination of the names of industry actors in a blacklist, and withdrawals of membership are ineffective.
DO delete any clause in the bylaws and rules of the relevant trade association which empowers the association to circulate a decision to refuse to deal with an expelled member to the general public. This is an even more severe violation.	DON'T be negligent to inform the relevant trade association that making a decision to refuse to deal with an expelled member publicly available is particularly injurious for a targeted industry actor.

V. Entering the premises of a recalcitrant industry actor without a warrant

With regard to the situation when officers of a trade association enter the premises of a disloyal member without a warrant to search for information in order to establish why this industry actor did not comply with an arbitral award, to prevent liability under US Antitrust Law and EU Competition Law for its members for their role in the execution of such an extrajudicial measure, the members should adhere to the following recommendations:

DOs	DON'Ts
DO expect that entering the premises of a disloyal industry actor without a warrant is of no interest with regard to US Antitrust Law and EU Competition Law. Criminal law is a more appropriate legal basis to assess such conduct.	DON'T misinform other members and the relevant trade association that a potential violation of US Antitrust Law and EU Competition Law should function as a deterrent to not enter the premises of a recalcitrant industry actor without a warrant.
DO change the "entering the premises" clause in the bylaws and rules of the relevant trade association in such a manner so that it instructs the responsible officers of the association to carry out entering the premises of a disloyal industry actor with a warrant in such away as to limit the reputational harm of targeted wrongdoers as much as possible.	DON'T allow a clause in the bylaws and rules of the relevant trade association which instructs the responsible officers of the association to carry out entering the premises of a disloyal industry actor without a warrant without considering reputational consequences of such an action.
DO ensure that the "entering the premises" clause in the bylaws and rules of the relevant trade association does not authorize the association to publish a decision of this measure.	DON'T allow a clause in the bylaws and rules of the trade association which empowers the association to publish a decision that entering the premises of a disloyal market participant without a warrant has been carried out.

VI. Limiting adequate access to public courts prior to arbitral proceedings and after an award

With regard to limiting adequate access to public courts prior to arbitral proceedings and after an award, to prevent liability under US Antitrust Law and EU Competition Law for its members for their role in the execution of such an extrajudicial measure, the members should adhere to the following recommendations:

DOs	DON'Ts
DO realize that members of the relevant trade association do not violate Section 1 of the Sherman Act when this association limits adequate access to public courts prior to arbitral proceedings and after an award.	DON'T conclude that in combination with other misconduct, members of the relevant trade association do not violate Section 1 of the Sherman Act when the association limits adequate access to public courts prior to arbitral proceedings and after an award.
DO ensure that the "recourse to public courts" clause in the bylaws and rules of the relevant trade association respects the safeguards laid down in the Arbitration Act 1996. Then, members of this association do not violate Article 101 TFEU.	DON'T allow a "recourse to public courts" clause in the bylaws and rules of the relevant trade association when it goes below the standards of access to public courts laid down in the Arbitration Act 1996.

Bibliography

ARTICLES

Adanacioglu, H, "The Futures Market in Agricultural Products and an Evaluation of the Attitude of Farmers: A Case Study of Cotton Producers in Aydin Province in Turkey", *New Medit, No. 2* 2011, 58.

Adkinson, Jr., WF, Grimm, KL, and Bryan, CN, "Enforcement of Section 2 of the Sherman Act: Theory and Practice", *FTC Working Paper* 2008, p. 3-4.

Akman, P, ""Consumer" versus "Customer": the Devil in the Detail", *ESRC Centre for Competition Policy Working Paper No. 08-34* 2008, p. 8.

Areeda, P, "Essential Facilities: An Epithet in Need of Limiting Principles", *Antitrust Law Journal, Vol. 58, No. 3* 1989, p. 853.

Armstrong, Jr., NA, Carroll, JD, and Yook, CC, "Sherman Act Section 1 Fundamentals", *LexisNexis* 2019, p. 3.

Association of Legal Administrators, "Antitrust Guide: For Members of the Association of Legal Administrators", *Association of Legal Administrators* 2019, p. 1.

Attorney General's National Committee to Study the Antitrust Laws, "Report of the Attorney General's National Committee to Study the Antitrust Laws", *Attorney General's National Committee to Study the Antitrust Laws* 1955, p. 1, 3.

Aviram, A, "The Paradox of Spontaneous Formation of Private Legal Systems", *John M. Olin Law & Economics Working Paper No. 192* 2003, p. 1-72.

Barber, CF, "Refusals to Deal under the Federal Antitrust Laws", *University of Pennsylvania Law Review, Vol. 103, No. 7* 1955, p. 847.

Behrens, P, "The ordoliberal concept of "abuse" of a dominant position and its impact on Article 102 TFEU", *Econstor* 2015, p. 5, 20.

Bernstein, L, "Opting out of the Legal System: Extralegal Contractual Relations in the Diamond Industry", *The Journal of Legal Studies, Vol. 21, No. 1* 1992, p. 115, 124, 126.

Bernstein, L, "Private Commercial Law in the Cotton Industry: Creating Cooperation Through Rules, Norms, and Institutions", *Michigan Law Review* 2001, p. 7.

Bird, CC, "Sherman Act Limitations on Noncommercial Concerted Refusals to Deal", *Duke Law Journal, Vol. 1970, No. 2* 1970, p. 253-254.

Blair, RD, and Sokol, DD, "The Rule of Reason and the Goals of Antitrust: An Economic Approach", *UF Law Scholarship Repository* 2012, p. 476, 480.

Bork, RH, "Legislative Intent and the Policy of the Sherman Act", *The Journal of Law and Economics, Vol. 9* 1966.

Bossone, B, "The Role of Trust in Financial Sector Development", *Policy Research Working Paper 2200* 1999, p. 18.

Brodley, JF, "Antitrust Analysis of Joint Ventures: An Overview", *American Bar Association, Vol. 66, No. 3,* 1998, p. 1526.

Bruce, AB, "Baillière's Encyclopædia of Scientific Agriculture", *Baillièr, Tindall and Cox* 1931, p. 520.

Calliess, G, and Zumbransen, P, "*Rough Consensus and Running Code: A Theory of Transnational Private Law*", Oxford/Portland: Hart Publishing 2010, p. 2110.

Calliess, G, "Lex Mercatoria", *Zentra Working Papers in Transnational Studies No. 52 / 201* 2015, p. 1-15.

Calliess, G, "Lex mercatoria", *Encyclopedia of Private International Law* 2017, p. 1119-1129.

Chaplan, B, "The Economics of Non-State Legal Systems", *Libertarian Alliance* 1997, p. 2, 13.

Charny, D, "Nonlegal Sanctions in Commercial Relationships", *Harvard Law Review* 1993, p. 392-393.

Cheung, CMK, and Lee, MKO, "Online Consumer Reviews: Does Negative Electronic Word-of-Mouth Hurt More?", *Association for Information Systems* 2008, p. 2.

Colomo, PI, "The Law on Abuses of Dominance and the System of Judicial Remedies", *Yearbook of European Law, Vol. 32, No. 1* 2013, p. 389.

Cucu, C, "Agreements, Decisions and Concerted Practices: Key Concepts in the Analysis of Anti-competitive Agreements", *Lex ET Scientia International Journal, Vol. 20, Issue 1* 2013 p. 222.

Dammann, J, and Hansmann, H, "Globalizing Commercial Litigation", *Cornell Law Review, Vol. 94, No. 1* 2008, p. 1.

Drahozal, CR, "Private Ordering and International Commercial Arbitration", *Penn State Law Review, Vol. 113:4* 2009, p. 1032.

European Commission, "DG Competition discussion paper on the application of Article 82 of the Treaty [now Article 102 TFEU] to exclusionary abuses", *European Commission* 2005, para. 29, 31, 80, 84.

Food and Agriculture Organization of the United Nations and World Health Organization in collaboration with the National Institute for Public Health and the Environment (Netherlands), "Development of Criteria for Acceptable Previous Cargoes for Fats and Oils", *Food and Agriculture Organization of the United Nations and World Health Organization in collaboration with the National Institute for Public Health and the Environment (Netherlands)* 2007, p. 20.

Geradin, D, and Petit, N, "Price Discrimination under EC Law: The Need for a Case-by-Case Approach", *Coleurope* 2005, p. 15.

Gerard, D, "Effects-based enforcement of Article 101 TFEU: the "object paradox"", Kluwer *Competition Law Blog* 2012, p. 1.

Goldman, B, "*Frontières du Droit et Lex Mercatoria*", *Arch. De Philosophie Du Droit* 1964, p. 177-192.

Gomtsian, S, Balvert, A, Hock, B, and Kirman, O, "Between the Green Pitch and the Red Tape: The Private Legal Order of FIFA", *TILEC Discussion Paper* 2017, p. 8, 12.

Haddock, GB, "The Right of Trade Associations to Deny Membership and to Expel Members", *Antitrust Bulletin Vol. 13* 1968, p. 555-556.

Harwell, JL, "The Relevant Market Concept in Conspiracy to Monopolize Cases under Section 2 of the Sherman Act", *The University of Chicago Law Review* 1977, p. 808-812.

Hatzopoulos, V, "The EU essential facilities doctrine", *College of Europe* 2006, p. 19-20.

Hennig-Thurau, T, Gwinner, KP, Walsh, G, and Gremler, DD, "Electronic Word-of-mouth via Consumer-Opinion Platforms: What Motivates Consumers to Articulate Themselves on the Internet", *Wiley Periodicals* 2004, p. 39.

Heyer, K, "Consumer Welfare and the Legacy of Robert Bork", *The University of Chicago Press* 2014, p. 20.

Hibner, Jr., DT, "Litigation as an Overt Act in Furtherance of an Attempt to Monopolize", *Ohio State Law Journal, Vol. 38, Nr. 2* 1977, p. 246.

Hovenkamp, HJ, "The Rule of Reason", *Penn Law: Legal Scholarship Repository* 2018, p. 96.

ICN Advocacy Working Group, "Explaining the Benefits of Competition to the General Public", *International Competition Network* 2017, p. 3.

Jones, TT, and Pickering, JF, "The Consumer's Interest in Competition Policy", *Journal of Consumer Studies and Home Economics* 1979, p. 98.

Jones, A, "The Boundaries of an Undertaking in EU Competition Law", *European Competition Journal* 2015, p. 302.

Kahn, AE, "Market Power and Economic Growth: Guides to Public Policy", *Antitrust Bulletin, Vol. 8* 1963.

Katz, ED, "Private Order and Public Institutions", *Michigan Law Review, Vol. 98, No. 8* 2000, p. 2482.

Kauper, TE, "The Report of the Attorney General's National Committee to Study the Antitrust Laws: A Retrospective", *Michigan Law Review Vol. 100, No. 7* 2002, p. 1867.

Kirchner, C, and Picot, A, "Transaction Cost Analysis of Structural Changes in the Distribution System: Reflections on Institutional Developments in the Federal Republic of Germany", *Journal of Institutional and Theoretical Economics, Vol. 143* 1987, p. 64.

Kube, S, and Traxler, C, "The interaction of legal and social norm enforcement", *Journal of Public Economic Theory* 2010, p. 1.

Lao, M, "Search, Essential Facilities, and the Antitrust Duty to Deal", *Northwest Journal of Technology and Intellectual Property, Vol. 11, Is. 5* 2013, p. 298-304.

Lévesque, G-H, "The Concrete Characteristics of Laissez-Faire Capitalism", *Relations industrielles / Industrial Relations, Vol. 5, No. 5,* 1950, p. 41-42.

Lörcher, T, Pendell, G, and Lowery, W, "CMS Guide to Arbitration, Vol. 1", *CMS Legal Services EEIG* 2012, p. 521.

Lowe, P, "The design of competition policy institutions for the 21st century — the experience of the European Commission and DG Competition", *Competition Policy Newsletter No. 3* 2008, p. 6.

Mark, W, and Weidemaier, C, "Toward a Theory of Precedent in Arbitration", *William & Mary Law Review, Vol. 51, Is. 5* 2010, p. 1901.

Mazzacano, P, "The Lex Mercatoria as Autonomous Law", *Comparative Research in Law & Political Economy Research Paper No.* 29 2008, p. 1.

McMillan, J, and Woodruf, C, "Private Order under Dysfunctional Public Order", *Michigan Law Review, Vol. 98, No. 8* 2000, p. 2421.

Michaels, R, "The True Lex Mercatoria: Law Beyond the State", *Indiana Journal of Global Legal Studies 14* 2007, p. 448.

Möschel, W, "Competition Policy from an Ordo Point of View", *German Neo-Liberals and the Social Market Economy* 1989, p. 146.

Newman, JM, "Procompetitive Justifications in Antitrust Law", *Social Science Research Network* 2017, p. 7.

Nicolaides, P, "The balancing myth: The Economics of Article 81(1) & (3)", *Legal Issues of Economic Integration* 2005, p. 134-143.

Nunnenkamp, P, "Short Note: Biased Arbitrators and Tribunal Decisions Against Developing Countries: Stylized Facts on Investor-state Dispute Settlement", *Journal of International Development* 2017, p. 851.

Oliar, D, "There's No Free Laugh (anymore): The Emergence of Intellectual Property Norms and the Transformation of Stand-up Comedy", *Virginia Law Review, Vol. 94, No. 8* 2008, p. 1789, 1791.

Organisation for Economic Co-operation and Development, "The Essential Facilities Concept", OCDE/GD(96)113 1996, p. 97.

Organisation for Economic Co-operation and Development, "Latin American Competition Forum", *DAF/COMP/LACF* 2011, p. 21.

Ottervanger, T, "Socially Responsible Competition: Competition law in a changing society", *Markt & Mededinging* 2010, p. 9.

Peyt, H, and Nørager, N, "Current Developments in Member States", *European Competition Journal 4* 2008, p. 332.

Polovets, I, Smith, M, and Terry, B, "GAFTA Arbitration as the Most Appropriate Forum for Disputes Resolution in Grain Trade", *Arizona Journal of International & Comparative Law Vol. 30, No. 3* 2013, p. 571-572, 580.

Ponsoldt, JF, "The Application of the Sherman Act Antiboycott law to Industry Self-Regulation: An Analysis Integrating Nonboycott Sherman Act Principles", *Bepress* 1981, p. 13.

Post, RC, "The Social Foundations of Defamation Law: Reputation and the Constitution", *California Law Review, Vol. 74, No. 691* 1986, p. 692.

Pritchard, JR, "Oilseed quality requirements for processing", *Journal of the American Oil Chemists' Society* 1983, p. 322.

Prüfer, J, "Business Associations and Private Ordering", *TILEC Discussion Paper* 2012, p. 4.

Richman, BD, "Community Enforcement of Informal Contracts: Jewish Diamond Merchants in New York", *The Harvard John M. Olin Discussion Paper, No. 384* 2002, p. 0 (abstract), 17, 102.

Richman, BD, "How Community Institutions Create Economic Advantage: Jewish Diamond Merchants in New York", *Law & Social Inquiry, Vol. 31, Is. 2* 2006, p. 18, 395, 398.

Richman, BD, "The Antitrust of Reputation Mechanisms: Institutional Economics and Concerted Refusals to Deal", *Virginia Law Review, Vol. 95:325* 2009, p. 332-334, 340, 349.

Richman, BD, "An Autopsy of Cooperation: Diamond Dealers and the Limits of Trust-based Exchange",*Journal of Legal Analysis, Vol. 9, No. 2* 2017, p. 279.

Routledge, "Code-Sharing Agreements in Scheduled Passenger Air Transport–The European Competition Authorities' Perspective", *European Competition Journal* 2006, p. 279.

Salop, SC, "Exclusionary Conduct, Effect on Consumers, and the Flawed Profit-Sacrifice Standard", *73 Antitrust L. J.* 2006, p. 330.

Saputelli, G, "The European Union, the Member States, and the Lex Mercatoria", *Notre Dame Journal of International & Comparative Law: Vol. 8, Is. 2, Article 3* 2018, p. 3.

SBD, "De Belgische Diamentnijverheid", *Algemene vergadering van SBD* 2014, p. 7.

Sherwin, P, Roesser, JD, Miller, PL, and Loughery, V, "Proskauer on International Litigation and Arbitration: Managing, Resolving, and Avoiding Cross-Border Business or Regulatory Disputes", *Proskauer Rose LLP* 2007, chapter 21.

Slaughter and May, "An overview of the EU competition rules – A general overview of the European Competition rules applicable to cartels, abuse of dominance, forms of commercial cooperation, merger control and State aid", *Slaughter and May* 2016, p. 8, 14.

Stucke, ME, "Does the Rule of Reason Violate the Rule of Law?", *U.C. Davis Law Review, Vol. 42* 2009, p. 1422.

Sussman, E, and Wilkinson, J, "Benefits Of Arbitration for Commercial Disputes", *Dispute Resolution Magazine* 2012.

The Yale Law Journal Company, "Intra-Enterprise Conspiracy under the Sherman Act", *The Yale Law Journal Company, Vol. 63, No. 3* 1954, p. 372.

TradeAssociationForum, "The Benefits of Trade Associations", *TradeAssociationForum* 2009, p. 2, 4.

Trenz, M, and Berger, B, "Analyzing Online Customer Reviews – An Interdisciplinary Literature Review and Research Agenda", *ECIS* 2013, p. 2.

U.S. Department of Justice, "Competition and Monopoly: Single-firm Conduct under Section 2 of the Sherman Act", *U.S. Department of Justice* 2008, p. 5, 34, 39.

van Cleynenbreugel, P, "Single Entity Tests in US Antitrust and EU Competition Law", *Orbi* 2011, p. 6.

van Erp, J, "Reputational Sanctions in Private and Public Regulation", *Erasmus Law Review, Vol. 1, Is. 5* 2009, p. 146.

Velkar, A, "'Deep' integration of 19th century grain markets: coordination and standardisation in a global value chain", *London School of Economics* 2010, p. 24.

Waller, SP, "Areeda, Epithets, and Essential Facilities", *Wisconsin Law Review* 2008, p. 368.

Warlouzet, L, "The Centralization of EU Competition Policy: Historical Institutionalist Dynamics from Cartel Monitoring to Merger Control (1956–91)", *Journal of Common Market Studies, Vol. 54, No. 3* 2016, p. 731.

Weitbrecht, A, "From Freiburg to Chicago and Beyond—the First 50 Years of European Competition Law", *European Competition Law Review* 2008, p. 85.

Williams, KD, "Ostracism", *Annual Review of Psychology* 2007, p. 428.

Willis Towers Wadson, "Preserving Your Reputation", *Willis Alert, Issue 17* 2011, p. 3.

Woods, D, "Hybrid Single Entities and the Market Power Requirement for Conspiracies to Monopolize Following Fraser: Are Courts Putting Form over Substance?", *University of Illinois Law Review* 2004, p. 1262.

Zirhlioglu, E, "The Diamond Industry and the Industry's Dispute Resolution Mechanisms", *Arizona Journal of International and Comparative Law* 2013, p. 4.

Zito Jr., AS, "Refusals to Deal: The Sherman Antitrust Act and the Right to Customer Selection", *The John Marshall Law Review, Vol. 14, Is. 2* 1981, p. 357.

BOOKS

Ackermann, T, "*Art. 85 Abs. 1 EGV und die rule of reason - Zur Konzeption der Verhinderung, Einschränkung oder Verfälschung des Wettbewerbs*", Cologne/Berlin/Bonn/ Munich: Heymanns 1997, p. 21 ff, 211 ff.

Akman, P, "*The Concept of Abuse in EU Competition Law: Law and Economic Approaches*", Oxford/Portland: Hart Publishing 2012, [abstract], p. 59, 63, 127.

Al-Ameen, A, "*Antitrust: The Person-centred Approach*", Heidelberg/New York/ Dordrecht/London: Springer International Publishing, Switzerland 2014, p. 73.

Albors-Llorens, A, "*EC Competition Law and Policy*", Abingdon: Routledge 2002, p. 152.

Alford, S, Barrow, J, and Nigel Hall, SJD, "*Northern History*", in: N Hall (ed), "The governance of the Liverpool raw cotton market, c. 1840-1914", Abingdon: Taylor & Francis, Vol. 153, Is. 1, 2016, p. 98.

Allensworth, RH, "The Commensurability Myth in Antitrust", *Vanderbilt Law Review, Vol. 69, No. 1* 2016, p. 5 (citation 7).

American Bar Association, "*Jury Instructions in Criminal Antitrust Cases, 1976-1980: A Compilation of Instructions Given by United States District Courts*", Chicago: American Bar Association 1982, p. 311.

American Bar Association, "*Antitrust & Trade Associations: How Trade Regulation Laws Apply to Trade and Professional Associations*", Chicago: American Bar Association 1996, p. 62.

American Bar Association, "*Model Jury Instructions in Civil Antitrust Cases*", Chicago: American Bar Association 2005, p. C-35.

American Bar Association, "*Joint Ventures: Antitrust Analysis of Collaborations Among Competitors*", Chicago: American Bar Association 2006, p. 102.

American Bar Association, "*Antitrust and Associations Handbook*", Chicago: American Bar Association 2009, p. 64, 68-69.

American Bar Association, "*Model Jury Instructions in Criminal Antitrust Cases*", Chicago: American Bar Association 2009, p. 71-75.

American Bar Association, "*Antitrust Health Care Handbook, Fourth Edition*", Chicago: American Bar Association 2010, p. 50-51.

American Bar Association, "*Federal Antitrust Guidelines for the Licensing of Intellectual Property*", Chicago: American Bar Association 2010, p. 71.

American Bar Association, "*Proof of Conspiracy under Federal Antitrust Laws*", Chicago: American Bar Association 2010, p. 24.

Andenas, M, Marsden, P, and Hutchings, M, "*Current Competition Law Volume II*", London: British Institute of International and Comparative Law 2004, p. 359.

Anderman, SD, "*The Interface Between Intellectual Property Rights and Competition Policy*", Cambridge: Cambridge University Press, p. 40.

Ando, C, and Rüpke, J, "*Public and Private in Ancient Mediterranean Law and Religion*", Berlin/Munich/Boston: Walter de Gruyter GmbH 2015, p. 37-41.

Andrews, N, "*Arbitration and Contract Law*", Basel: Springer International Publishing 2016, p. 130, 140.

Ankersmit, L, "*Green Trade and Fair Trade in and with the EU: Process-based Measures within the EU Legal Order*", Cambridge: Cambridge University Press 2017, p. 208.

Anonymous, "*How to Deal with Negative Electronic Word-Of-Mouth?*", Norderstedt: GRIN Verlag 2011, p. 4.

Antwerp World Diamond Centre, "Antwerp Diamond Masterplan – Diamonds love Antwerp 2020", *Antwerp World Diamond Centre* 2012, p. 5, 69, 148, 154.

Applewhite, TH, "*Proceedings of the World Conference on Lauric Oils: Sources, Processing, and Application*", Champaign: AOCS Press 1994, p. 29.

Areeda, PE, and Hovenkamp, H, "*Antitrust Law –Vol. 3*", New York: Aspen Publishers 2008, p. 446.

Aspen Publishers, "*Antitrust: Keyed to Pitofsky, Goldschmid, and Wood's Trade Regulation: Cases and Materials Fifth Edition*", New York: Aspen Publishers 2004, p. 71.

Aspen Publishers, "*Antitrust*", New York: Aspen Publishers 2004, p. 38.

Atkin, M, "*The International Grain Trade*", Abington: Woodhead Publishing 1995, p. 111, 113.

Atkinson, B, and John, S, "*Studying Economics*", Basingstoke/New York: Palgrave Macmillan 2001, p. 9.

Baffes, J, Larson, DF, and Varangis, P, "*Commodity Market Reforms: Lessons of Two Decades*", Washington: The International Bank for Reconstruction 2001, p. 38.

Baker, HD, and Jursa, M, "*Documentary Sources in Ancient Near Eastern and Greco-Roman Economic History*", Oxford/Philadelphia: Oxbow Books 2014, p. 147.

Baldwin, AR, "*World Conference on Emerging Technologies in the Fats and Oils Industry*", in: E.C. Campbell (ed.), "Trade Association Rules - Impact on International Trade", Urbana: American Oil Chemists' Society 1986, p. 24.

Banks, E, "*Exchange-Traded Derivatives*", Chichester: John Wiley & Sons 2003, p. 105-106.

Barak, A, "*The Judge in a Democracy*", Princeton/Woodstock: Princeton University Press 2006, p. 113.

Barnard, C, and Peers, S, "*European Union Law*", Oxford: Oxford University Press 2017, p. 521.

Barton, J, and Smith, RH, "*The Handbook for the New Legal Writer*", New York: Wolters Kluwer 2019, p. 345.

Basedow, J, and Wurmnest, W, "*Structure and Effects in EU Competition Law: Studies on Exclusionary Conduct and State Aid*", Alphen aan den Rijn: Kluwer Law International 2011, p. 15, 71.

Bavasso, A, "*Communications in EU Law: Antitrust Market Power and Public Interest*", The Hague: Kluwer Law International 2003, p. 164.

Beckert, S, "*Empire of Cotton: A Global History*", New York: Vintage Books 2014, p. 40.

Beckett, ST, "*Industrial Chocolate Manufacture and Use – Fourth Edition*", Hoboken: Blackwell Publishing 2009, p. 25.

Beckett, ST, Fowler, MS, and Ziegler, GR, "*Beckett's Industrial Chocolate Manufacture and Use – Fifth Edition*", Hoboken: Wiley-Blackwell 2017, p. 28.

Beggs-Humphreys, M, Gregor, H, and Humphreys, D, "*The Industrial Revolution*", Abingdon: Routledge 1959, p. 27.

Berman, HJ, "*Law and Revolution: The Formation of the Western Legal Tradition*", Cambridge/London: Cambridge University Press 1983, p. 519.

Berman, PS, "*Global Legal Pluralism: A Jurisprudence Of Law Beyond Borders*", New York: Cambridge University Press 2012, p. 13.

Bernholz, P, and Vaubel, R, "*Explaining Monetary and Financial Innovation: A Historical Analysis*", Heidelberg/New York/Dordrecht/London: Springer International Publishing 2014, p. 267.

Berry, E, Homewood, M, J, Bogusz, B, "*Complete EU Law: Text, Cases, and Materials*", Oxford: Oxford University Press 2017, p. 596, 610.

Bhatia, V, K, Garzone, G, and Degano, C, "*Arbitration Awards: Generic Features and Textual Realisations*", Newcastle upon Tyne: Cambridge Scholars Publishing 2012, p. 177.

Binmore, K, "*Game Theory and the Social Contract: Playing Fair*", Cambridge/London: The MIT Press 1994, p. 112.

Bittman, JB, "*Trading and Hedging with Agricultural Futures and Options*", Hoboken: John Wiley & Sons 2013, p. 2.

Blair, RD, and Sokol, DD, "*The Oxford Handbook of International Antitrust Economics – Vol. 2*", Oxford: Oxford University Press 2015, p. 156.

Blanco, LO, "*Shipping Conferences under EC Antitrust Law: Criticism of a Legal Paradox*", Portland: Hart Publishing 2007, p. 375.

Blanco, LO, "*Market Power in EU Antitrust Law*", Oxford/Portland: Hart Publishing 2011, p. 22, 56, 104, 106-107

Block, MJ, "The Benefits of Alternate Dispute Resolution for International Commercial and Intellectual Property Disputes", *The Digital Journal of Rutgers School of Law, Vol. 44* 2016, p. 7-8.

Bogart, JH, "*Circuit Conflicts in Antitrust Litigation*", Chicago: American Bar Association 2009, p. 34.

Boisson de Chazournes, L, Kohen, M, and Viñuales, JE, "*Diplomatic and Judicial Means of Dispute Settlement*", Leiden/Boston: Koninklijke Brill NV 2013, p. 273.

Bouckaert, B, and de Geest, G, "*Encyclopedia of Law and Economics*", in: S. G. Medema (ed), RO Zerbe, "The Coase Theorem", Cheltenham: Edward Elgar 2000, p. 837-838, in: S. Panther (ed), "Non-Legal Sanctions", Aldershot: Edward Elgar 2000, p. 1000.

Bourgeois, J, and Waelbroeck, D, "*Ten years of effects-based approach in EU competition law - State of play and perspectives*", in: A Meij, and T Baum, "Balancing Object and Effect Analysis in Identifying Abuses of a Dominant Position under Article 102 TFEU", Brussels: Groupe de Boeck 2013, p. 162, 164, in: H Zenger, and M Walker (ed) "Theories of Harm in European Competition Law: A Progress Report", Brussels: Groupe de Boeck 2013, p. 195.

Branch, AE, "*International Purchasing and Management*", London: Thomson 2000, p. 63.

Brunet, E, Brunet, E,J, Speidel, RE, Sternlight, JE, Ware, SH, and Ware, SJ, "*Arbitration Law in America: A Critical Assessment*", New York: Cambridge University Press 2006, p. 124.

Bussani, M, and Sebok, AJ, "*Comparative Tort Law: Global Perspectives*", Cheltenham/Northampton: Edward Elgar Publishing 2015, p. 18.

Cafaggi, F, "*Enforcement of Transnational Regulation: Ensuring Compliance in a Global World*", Cheltenham/Northampton: Edward Elgar Publishing 2012, p. 218.

Cahill, D, Power, V, and Connery, N, "*European Law*", New York: Oxford University Press 2011, p. 164.

Camerer, CF, "*Behavioral Game Theory: Experiments in Strategic Interaction*", Princeton/Woodstock: Princeton University Press 2003, p. 445.

Cartledge, P, Millett, P, and von Reden, S, "*Kosmos: Essays in Order, Conflict and Community in Classical Athens*", Cambridge/New York/Melbourne: Cambridge University Press 1998, p. 1.

Carter, JH, and Fellas, J, "*International Commercial Arbitration in New York*", New York: Oxford University Press 2010, p. 16.

Candlin, CN, "*Discourse and Practice in International Commercial Arbitration: Issues, Challenges, and Prospects*", London/New York: Routledge 2016, p. 265.

Castleman, M, "*The New Healing Herbs: The Classic Guide to Nature's Best Medicines*", Emmaus: Rodale 2001, p. 140.

Chander, K, "*Encyclopaedic Dictionary of Commerce: Volume 3*", New Delhi: Sarup & Sons 1999, p. 780.

Chatnani, NN, "*Commodity Markets: Operations, Instruments, and Applications*", New Delhi: Tata McGraw Hill 2010, p. 4.

Chen, K, and Fadlalla, A, "*Online Consumer Protection: Theories of Human Relativism: Theories of Human Relativism*", New York: IGI Global 2009, p. 278.

Chew, DH, "*Corporate Risk Management*", New York: Columbia University Press 2008, p. 28.

Cirace, J, "*Law, Economics, and Game Theory*", London: The Rowman & Littlefield Publishing Group 2018, p. 113-119, 238.

Clarke, J, "*Managing Better: Becoming a Limited Company*", Dublin: Combat Poverty Agency 1996, p. 2, 371.

Colino, SM, "*Cartels and Anti-Competitive Agreements, Volume 1*", in: C Callery (ed), "Should the European Union Embrace or Exorcise Leegin's "Rule of Reason"?", Abingdon/New York: Routledge 2012, p. 101.

Colino, SM, "*Competition Law of the EU and UK*", Oxford: Oxford University Press 2019, p. 393.

Crooks, E, "*The Unrelenting Machine: A Legacy of the Industrial Revolution*", Morrisville: Lulu 2012, p. 65.

Cross, FB, and Miller, RL, "*The Legal Environment of Business: Text and Cases – Tenth Edition*", Boston: Cengage Learning 2018, p. 571.

Cruz, JB, "*Between Competition and Free Movement*", Oxford/Portland: Hart Publishing 2002, p. 89.

Currie, W, "*Value Creation from E-Business Models*", in: N Madeja, and D Schoder, "Value creation from Corporate websites: how different features contribute to success in e-Business", Oxford: Elsevier 2004, p. 216.

Czaprack, K, "*Intellectual Property and the Limits of Antitrust: A Comparative Study of US and EU Approaches*", Chelthenham/Northampton: Edward Elgar Publishing 2009, p. 32.

Dabbah, MM, "*EC and UK Competition Law: Commentary, Cases and Materials*", Cambridge: Cambridge University Press 2004, p. 69, 105, 330, 351.

Dabbah, MM, "*International and Comparative Competition Law*", Cambridge: Cambridge University Press 2010, p. 71.

Dabbah, MM, "*Module B: Abuse of a dominant position*", London: University of London Press 2012, p. 33

Dand, R, "*The International Cocoa Trade*", New York: Woodhead Publishing 1996, p. 82-83.

Dand, R, "*The International Cocoa Trade*", Cambridge/Philadelphia/New Delhi: Woodhead Publishing 2011, p. 97-98.

Davies, K, "*Understanding European Union Law*", Abingdon/New York: Routledge 2016, p. 54.

Diebold, NF, "N*on-Discrimination in International Trade in Services: 'Likeness' in WTO/GATS*", Cambridge: Cambridge University Press 2010, p. 277.

Dietz, T, "*Global Order Beyond Law: How Information and Communication Technologies Facilitate Relational Contracting in International Trade*", Oxford/Portland: Hart Publishing 2016, p. 192.

DiMatteo, LA, "*International Business Law and the Legal Environment: A Transactional Approach*", Abingdon: Routledge 2016, p. 251.

DiMatteo, LA, "*International Business Law and the Legal Environment: A Transactional Approach*", New York/London: Routledge 2017, p. 127.

Dixit, AK, "*Lawlessness and Economics: Alternative Modes of Governance*", Princeton: Princeton University 2004, p. 4, 60-61.

Dolmans, M, "*The Dominance and Monopolies Review*", London: Law Business Research Ltd 2014, p. 368, 373.

Dominicé, C, "*Etudes de droit international en l'honneur de Pierre Lalive*", in: B Goldman (ed), "Nouvelles Riflexions sur la Lex Mercatoria", Basel/Frankfurt am Main: Helbing Lichtenhahn Verlag 1993, p. 241-256.

Drexl, J, Grimes, WS, and Jones, CA, "*More Common Ground for International Competition Law?*", Chelthenham/Northampton: Edward Elgar Publishing 2011, p. 52.

Drexl, J, Kerber, W, and Podszun, R, "Competition Policy and the Economic Approach: Foundations and Limitations", in: D Zimmer (ed), "Consumer welfare, economic freedom and the moral quality of competition law – comments on Gregory Werden and Victor Vanberg", Cheltenham/Northampton: Edward Elgar Publishing 2011, p. 72.

Drexl, J, and Di Porto, F, "*Competition Law as Regulation*", Chelthenham/ Northampton: Edward Elgar Publishing 2015, p. 296.

Dubowski, T, "*Białystok Law Books 2 Constitutional Law Of The European Union*", Bialystok: Temida 2 2011, p. 116-120.

Duncan, R, "*Agricultural Futures and Options: A Guide to Using North American and European markets*", Abington: Woodhead Publishing 1992, p. 53-54, 109.

Dunne, N, "*Competition Law and Economic Regulation: Making and Managing Markets*", Cambridge: Cambridge University Press 2015, p. 177.

Duns, J, Duke, A, and Sweeney, B, "*Comparative Competition Law*", Cheltenham/ Northampton: Edward Elgar Publishing 2015, p. 172.

Duval, A, and van Rompuy, B, "*The Legacy of Bosman: Revisiting the Relationship Between EU Law and Sport*", in: K Pijetlovic (ed.), "EU Competition Law and Organisational Rules", T.M.C. Asser Press 2016, p. 148.

Ehlermann, C, and Gosling, L, "*European Competition Law Annual 1998: Regulating Communications Markets*", Portland: Hart Publishing 2000, p. 476.

Ehlermann, C, and Atanasiu, I, "*European Competition Law Annual 2000: The Modernisation of EC Antitrust Policy*", Portland: Hart Publishing 2000, p. 141.

Ehlermann, C, and Atanasiu, I, "*European Competition Law Annual 2002: Constructing the EU Network of Competition Authorities*", Oxford/Portland: Hart Publishing 2004, p. 261.

Ehlermann, C, and Atanasiu, I, "*European Competition Law Annual 2004: The Relationship Between Competition Law and the (Liberal) Professions*", Portland: Hart Publishing 2006, p. 454.

Ehlermann, C, and Marquis, M, "*European Competition Law Annual 2007: A Reformed Approach to Article 82 EC*", Oxford/Portland: Hart Publishing 2008, p. xxv.

Elcin, M, "*Lex Mercatoria in International Arbitration Theory and Practice*", Vol. 1, Florence: Mert Elcin 2012, p. 5.

Ellison, T, "*The Cotton Trade of Great Britain: including a history of the Liverpool cotton market and of the Liverpool Cotton Brokers' Association*", London: Effingham Wilson 1886, p. 181–182, 184.

Enaux, C, "*Effiziente Marktregulierung in der Telekommunikation: Möglichkeiten und Grenzen der Ruckführung sektorspezifischer Sonderregulierung in das allgemeine Wettbewerbsrecht*", Münster: Lit Verlag 2004, p. 148, 156.

Epstein, RA, "*Contract - Freedom and Restraint: Liberty, Property, and the Law*", New York/Abingdon: Routledge 2000, p. 393, 363-364, 369.

Erickson, DR, "*Practical Handbook of Soybean Processing and Utilization*", Urbana: AOCS Press 1995, p. 50.

Ezraichi, A, "*Article 82 EC: Reflections on its Recent Evolution*", Oxford/Portland: Hart Publishing 2009, p. 124.

Ezrachi, A, "*EU Competition Law: An Analytical Guide to the Leading Cases*", Oxford/Portland: Hart Publishing 2014, p. 33.

Fatur, A, "*EU Competition Law and the Information and Communication Technology Network Industries*", Oxford: Hart Publishing 2012, p. 112

Ferretti, F, "*EU Competition Law, the Consumer Interest and Data Protection: The Exchange Consumer Information in the Retail Financial Sector*", Heidelberg/New York/Dordrecht/London: Springer 2014, p. 47.

Food and Agriculture Organization of the United Nations, "*Proceedings of the FAO Rice Conference 2004: Rice in Global Markets*", Rome: Food and Agriculture Organization of the United Nations 2005, p. 56.

Foster, N, "*Blackstone's EU Treaties and Legislation 2014-2015*", Oxford: Oxford University Press 2014, p. 609.

Foster, N, "*Foster on EU Law*", Oxford: Oxford University Press 2015, p. 381.

Frederick, DA, "*Antitrust Status of Farmer Cooperatives: The Story of the Capper-Volstead Act*", Washington, DC: United States Department of Agriculture 2002, p. 84.

Frenz, W, "*Handbook of EU Competition Law*", Berlin/Heidelberg: Springer Verlag Berlin Heidelberg 2016, p. 270.

Frohloff, J, "*Verletzung von Schiedsvereinbarungen: Eine Untersuchung des deutschen Schiedsverfahrensrechts zu den Pflichten der Schiedsparteien und den Rechtsfolgen ihrer Verletzung*", Tübingen: Mohr Siebeck 2017, p. 50

Gabel, D, and Weiman, DF, "*Opening Networks to Competition: The Regulation and Pricing of Access*", New York: Springer Science+Business Media 1998, p. 190.

Galgano, F, "*Lex mercatoria: storia del diritto commerciale*", Munich: Il Mulino 1993.

Geradin, D, Layne-Farrar, A, and Petit, N, "*EU Competition Law and Economics*", Oxford: Oxford University Press 2012, p. 1-134.

Gerber, DJ, "*Law and Competition in Twentieth Century Europe: Protecting Prometheus*", Oxford: Oxford University Press 1998, p. 264.

Gert, B, "*Morality: Its Nature and Justification*", New York/Oxford: Oxford University Press 1998, p. 120.

Gessner, V, "*Contractual Certainty in International Trade: Empirical Studies and Theoretical Debates on Institutional Support for Global Economic Exchanges*", in: W Konradi (ed), "The Role of Lex Mercatoria in Supporting Globalised Transactions", Oxford/Portland: Hart Publishing 2009, p. 67, 70.

Gharavi, H, and Liebscher, C, "*The International Effectiveness of the Annulment of an Arbitral Award*", The Hague: Kluwer law International 2002, p. 34.

Gideon, A, "*Higher Education Institutions in the EU: Between Competition and Public Service*", Liverpool/Singapore: T.M.C. Asser Press 2017, p. 74, 75 (note 159).

Givens, RA, "*Antitrust: An Economic Approach*", New York: Law Journal Press 2005, p. 4-48.28.

Comanor, GW, Jacquemin, K, and Jenny, A, "*Competition Policy in Europe and North America*", New York: Hardwood Academic Publishers GmbH 1990, p. 231.

Gorham, M, and Singh, N, "*Electronic Exchanges: The Global Transformation from Pits to Bits*", London: Elsevier 2009, p. 4.

Gormsen, LL, "*A Principled Approach to Abuse of Dominance in European Competition Law*", Cambridge: Cambridge University Press 2010, p. 56-57.

Goss, BA, "*Futures Markets (Routledge Revivals): Their Establishment and Performance*", in: BA Goss (ed.), "The Forward Pricing Function of the London Metal Exchange", London/Sydney: Croom Helm 1986, p. 157.

Goyder, DG, "*EC Competition Law, 3rd Edition*", Oxford: Oxford University Press 1998, p. 145.

Graham, C, Smith, F, and Smith, FM, "*Competition, Regulation and the New Economy*", in: E Derclaye (ed), "Abuse of a Dominant Position and IP Rights", Oxford/Portland: Hart Publishing 2004, p. 74.

Great Britain. Dept. of Trade and Industry, "*Abuse of Market Power: A Consultative Document on Possible Legislative Option*", Richmond: H.M. Stationery Office 1992, p. 7.

Grivetti, LE, and Shapiro, H, "*Chocolate: History, Culture, and Heritage*", in: JH Momsen and P Richardson (ed), "Caribbean Cocoa: Planting and Production", Hoboken: John Wiley & Sons 2009, p. 481.

Hagenfeld, V, "*EC Competition Law - the Essential Facilities Doctrine: To what extent is the Essential Facilities Doctrine established in Community law and how has its application under Article 82 EC evolved over time*", Munich: GRIN Verlag GmbH 2009, p. 3-4.

Hall, KL, "*Oxford Companion to the Supreme Court of the United States, Second Edition*", Oxford: Oxford University Press 2005, p. 145.

Haracoglou, I, "*Competition Law and Patents: A Follow-on Innovation Perspective in the Biopharmaceutical Industry*", Cheltenham/Northampton: Edward Elgar Publishing 2008, p. 135.

Harris, B, Planterose, R, and Tecks, J, "*The Arbitration Act 1996: A Commentary*", Oxford/Malden/Melbourne: Blackwell Publishing 2007, p. 47, 309.

Hawk, BE, "*International Antitrust Law & Policy: Fordham Corporate Law 2003*", Huntington: Juris Publishing 2004, p. 423.

Hawkins, C, "*Roman Artisans and the Urban Economy*", Cambridge: Cambridge University Press 2016, p. 120.

Heckman, JJ, Nelson, RL, and Cabatingan, L, "*Global Perspectives on the Rule of Law*", in: F Allen, and J Qian, "Comparing Legal and Alternative Institutions in Finance and Commerce", Abingdon/New York: Routledge 2010, p. 128.

Henderson, WO, "*The Lancashire Cotton Famine 1861 - 65*", New York: Augustus M. Kelley 1969, p. 34.

Hendrickson, KE, "*The Encyclopedia of the Industrial Revolution in World History*", Band 3, London: Rowmann & Littlefield 2015, p. 103.

Heremans, T, "*Professional Services in the EU Internal Market: Quality Regulation and Self-Regulation*", Oxford: Hart Publishing 2012, p. 327.

Hibbert, C, Weinreb, B, and Keay, J, "*The London Encyclopaedia (3rd Edition)*", London: Macmillan London Limited 1983, p. 505.

Hildebrand, D, "*The Role of Economic Analysis in the EC Competition Rules*", Alphen aan den Rijn: Kluwer Law International 2009, p. 301.

Hilty, RM, and Früh, A, "*Lizenzkartellrecht: Schweizer Recht gespiegelt am US-amerikanischen und europäischen Recht*", Bern: Stämpfli Verlag AG 2017, p. 64.

Historic Society of Lancashire and Cheshire, "*Transactions of the Historic Society of Lancashire and Cheshire*", in: N Hall (ed) "A 'Quaker Confederation'? The great Liverpool cotton speculation of 1825 reconsidered", Liverpool: Historic Society of Lancashire and Cheshire, Vol. 151 2002, p. 1, 99.

Hobbes, T, "*Philosophicall Rudiments Concerning Government and Society (De Cive)*", London: J.C. for R. Royston 1651, p. 85.

Hoffmann, G, "*The Chemistry and Technology of Edible Oils and Fats and Their High Fat Products*", London/San Diego: Academic Press 1989, p. 201.

Hofstadter, R, "*The Paranoid Style in American Politics and Other Essays*", Cambridge: Harvard University Press 1965.

Hope, E, "*Competition and Trade Policies: Coherence or Conflict*", London/New York: Routledge 2005, p. 61.

Horn, J, Rosenband, LN, and Smith, MR, "*Reconceptualizing the Industrial Revolution*", Cambridge/London: The MIT Press 2010, p. 157.

Horspool, M, and Humphreys, M, "*European Union Law*", Oxford: Oxford University Press 2012, p. 438, 439

Hovenkamp, H, "*The Antitrust Enterprise: Principle and Execution*", Cambridge/London: Harvard University Press 2005, p. 2

Huang, J, "*Interregional Recognition and Enforcement of Civil and Commercial Judgments*", Oxford/Portland: Hart Publishing 2014, p. 58-59.

Huszar, ML, "*Rohstoffe als Investmentklasse: Eine theoretische und empirische Analyse*", Hamburg: Diplomica Verlag GmbH 2008, p. 4-5.

Hylton, KN, "*Antitrust Law and Economics*", Cheltenham: Edward Elgar Publishing 2010, p. 24, 33, 50.

Imwinkelried, EJ, and Friedman, RD, "*The New Wigmore: A Treatise on Evidence: Evidentiary Privileges*", Aspen: Aspen Law & Business Publishers 2002, p. 763.

International Business Publications, "*US: Importing into the Unites States Practical Guide*", Washington; International Business Publications 2008, p. 186.

Ioannidou, M, "*Consumer Involvement in Private EU Competition Law Enforcement*", Oxford: Oxford University Press 2015, p. 34.

Jacobson, JM, "*Antitrust Law Developments (sixth)*", Chicago: American Bar Association, Vol. 1, 2007, p. 433.

Jänig, R, "*Commercial Law: Selected Essays on the Law of Obligation, Insolvency and Arbitration*", Göttingen: Universitätsverlag Göttingen 2012, p. 125.

Jayaram, R, and Kotwani, NR, "*Industrial Economics and Telecommunication Regulations*", New Delhi: PHI Learning Private Limited 2012, p. 41.

Jentzsch, N, "*Financial Privacy: An International Comparison of Credit Reporting Systems*", Berlin/Heidelberg: Springer-Verlag 2006, p. 89-94.

Jiang, T, "*China and EU Antitrust Review of Refusal to License IPR*", Antwerp: Maklu-Publishers 2015, p. 88, 141.

Joelson, MR, "*An International Antitrust Primer: A Guide to the Operation of United States, European Union and Other Key Competition Laws in the Global Economy*", Alphen aan den Rijn: Kluwer Law International 2006, p. 371.

Joliet, R, "*The Rule of Reason in Antitrust Law*", The Hague: Martinus Nijhof 1967, p. xx-198.

Jones, A, and Sufrin, BE, "*EC Competition Law: Text, Cases, and Materials*", Oxford: Oxford University Press 2008, p. 281, 404.

Jones, A, and Sufrin, BE, "*EU Competition Law: Text, Cases, and Materials*", Oxford: Oxford University Press 2014, p. 259, 1073.

Jones, A, and Sufrin, BE, "*EU Competition Law: Text, Cases, and Materials*", Oxford: Oxford University Press 2016, p. 22, 37, 163, 247, 372.

Jung, T, and tom Dieck, MC, "*Augmented Reality and Virtual Reality: Empowering Human, Place and Business*", Cham: Springer International Publishing AG 2018, p. 148.

Kaczorowska, A, "*European Union Law*", Abingdon/New York: Routledge-Cavendish 2008, p. 774.

Kaysen, C, and Turner, DF, "*Antitrust Policy: An Economic and Legal Analysis*", Cambridge: Harvard University Press 1959.

Kehoe, DP, and McGinn, T, "*Ancient Law, Ancient Society*", Ann Arbor: University of Michigan Press 2017, p. 126.

King, R, "*Jehovah Himself Has Become King*", Bloomington: AuthorHouse 2010, p. 252.

Kingston, S, "*Greening EU Competition Law and Policy*", Cambridge: Cambridge University Press 2012, p. 280.

Kobrin, R, and Teller, A, "*Purchasing Power: The Economics of Modern Jewish History*", Philadelphia: University of Pennsylvania Press 2015, p. 201-202.

Kokkoris, I, and Lianos, I, "*The Reform of EC Competition Law: New Challenges*", Alphen aan den Rijn: Kluwer Law International 2010, p. 402-403.

Kolmar, M, "*Principles of Microeconomics: An Integrative Approach*", Cham: Springer International Publishing AG 2017, p. 140.

Komninos, A, "*EC Private Antitrust Enforcement: Decentralised Application of EC Competition Law by National Courts*", Portland: Hart Publishing 2008, p. 151.

Lafave, WR, and Scott, Jr., AW, "*Substantive Criminal Law - 2nd Edition*", St. Paul: West Publishing Company 1986, p. 549.

Lambert, L, "*Spirituality, Inc.: Religion in the American Workplace*", New York/ London: New York University Press 2009, p. 73.

Landolt, PL, "*Modernised EC Competition Law in International Arbitration*", The Hague: Kluwer Law International 2006, p. 46, 237.

Lanni, A, "*Law and Order in Ancient Athens*", New York: Cambridge University Press 2016, p. 1-27, 34.

LaRue, PH, Applebaum, HM, Calvani, T, Collins, WD, Halverson, JT, Johnston, TW, Jones, JA, Rill, JF, Sayre, WM, Schlitt, L, and Whiting, RA, "*The Robinson-Patman Act: Policy and Law – Vol. 1*", Chicago: American Bar Association 1989, p. 25.

Leczykiewicz, D, and Weatherill, S, "*The Involvement of EU Law in Private Law Relationships*", in: O Odudu (ed), "Competition Law and Contract: The EU Defence", Oxford/Portland: Hart Publishing 2013, p. 395.

Leczykiewicz, D, and Weatherill, S, "*The Images of the Consumer in EU Law: Legislation, Free Movement and Competition Law*", Oxford/Portland: Hart Publishing 2016, p. 70.

Lee, I, "*Encyclopedia of E-Commerce Development, Implementation, and Management, Band 1*", Hershey: IGI Global 2016, p. 1985.

Lees, FA, "*Financial Exchanges: A Comparative Approach*", New York/Abingdon: Routledge 2012, p. 164.

Leser, HG, "*Gesammelte Schriften*", Band 1, Tübingen: J.C.B. Mohr (Paul Siebeck) 1968, p. 11.

Lew, JDM, Mistelis, LA, and Kröll, SM, "*Comparative International Commercial Arbitration*", The Hague/London/New York: Kluwer Law International 2003, p. 332.

Li, S, "*Managing International Business in Relation-Based versus Rule-Based Countries*", New York: Business Expert Press, LCC 2009, p. 49-50.

Lianos, I, and Geradin, D, "*Handbook on European Competition Law: Substantive Aspects*", Cheltenham/Northampton: Edward Elgar Publishing 2013, p. 160.

Lista, A, "*International Commercial Sales: The Sale of Goods on Shipment Terms*", Abingdon/New York: Routledge 2017, p. 4, 10-11.

Looijestijn-Clearie, A, Rusu, CS, and Veenbrink, M, "*Boosting the Enforcement of EU Competition Law at the Domestic Level*", Newcastle upon Tyne: Cambridge Scholars Publishing 2017, p. 2.

Lorenz, M, "*An Introduction to EU Competition Law*", Cambridge: Cambridge University Press 2013, p. 45, 51-52, 76, 189, 208, 237.

Lytras, MD, Damiani, E, Carroll, JM, Avison, D, Tennyson, RD, Dale, A, Naeve, A, Lefrere, P, Tan, F, Sipior, J, and Vossen, G, "*Visioning and Engineering the Knowledge Society - A Web Science Perspective*", Berlin/Heidelberg: Springer-Verlag 2009, p. 501.

Mack, CS, "*The Executive's Handbook of Trade and Business Associations: How They Work-and How to Make Them Work Effectively for You*", New York/Westport/Connecticut/London: Quorum Books 1991, p. 14.

Mackenrodt, M, Gallego, BC, and Enchelmaier, S, "*Abuse of Dominant Position: New Interpretation, New Enforcement Mechanisms?*", in: P Këllezi (ed), "Abuse below the Threshold of Dominance? – Market Power, Market Dominance, and Abuse of Economic Dependence", Berlin/Heidelberg: Springer 2008, p. 88, in: HKS Schmidt (ed), "Private Enforcement – Is Article 82 EC special?", Berlin/Heidelberg: Springer 2008, p. 151.

Madhavan, KS, "*Business & Ethics - An Oxymoron?*", Bangalore: KS Madhavan, p. 40.

Mallard, G, and Sgard, J, "*Contractual Knowledge: One Hundred Years of Legal Experimentation in Global Markets*", Cambridge: Cambridge University Press 2016, p. 157.

Malloy, RP, "*Law in a Market Context: An Introduction to Market Concepts in Legal Reasoning*", Cambridge: Cambridge University Press 2004, p. 132.

Mansell, R, "*The International Encyclopedia of Digital Communication and Society, 3 Volume Set, Volume 1*", Hoboken: Wiley-Blackwell 2015, p. 79.

Mäntysaari, P, "*The Law of Corporate Finance: General Principles and EU Law - Volume II: Contracts in General*", Berlin/Heidelberg: Springer 2010, p. 159.

Marciano, A, "*Law and Economics: A Reader*", in: TJ Zywicki (ed), "The Rise and Fall of Efficiency in the Common Law: A Supply-Side Analysis", Abingdon/New York: Routledge 2009, p. 364.

Mark, J, Strange, R, and Burns, J, "*The Food Industries, Vol. XXVIII*", London: Chapman & Hall 1993, p. 236.

Marsden, P, "*Handbook of Research in Trans-Atlantic Antitrust*", Cheltenham: Edward Elgar 2006, p. 268.

Martínez, JP, "*Net Neutrality: Contributions to the Debate*", Madrid: Fundación Telefónica 2011, p. 139.

Marx, K, "*Pre-Capitalist Economic Formations*", New York: International Publishers 1965, p. 30, 37, 104 [edited version by E. J. Hobsbawm].

Mathis, K, "*Law and Economics in Europe: Foundations and Applications*", Dordrecht: Springer 2014, p. 374.

Mattli, W, and Dietz, T, "*International Arbitration & Global Governance: Contending Theories and Evidence*", Oxford: Oxford University Press 2014, p. 190.

McGinn, TAJ, "*Obligations in Roman Law: Past, Present, and Future*", Ann Arbor: University of Michigan Press 2012, p. 201.

McNutt, PA, "*Law, Economics and Antitrust: Towards a New Perspective*", Cheltenham/Northampton: Edward Elgar Publishing 2005, p. 136.

Meisel, JW, ""*Now" or Never: Is There Antitrust Liability for Noncommercial Boycotts?*", Columbia Law Review, Vol. 80, No. 6 1980, p. 1317.

Mendonca, M, and Kanungo, RN, "*Ethical Leadership*", New York: Open University Press 2007, p. 15.

Merkin, R, and Flannery, L, "*Arbitration Act 1996*", Abingdon, Oxon: Informa Law 2014, p. 24, 32-33.

Miller, R, and Jentz, G, "*Cengage Advantage Books: Business Law Today: The Essentials*", Mason: Thomson West 2008, p. 674.

Miller, RL, "*Business Law Today, Comprehensive: Text and Cases: Diverse, Ethical, Online, and Global Environment – 10th Edition*", Stamford: Cengage Learning 2015, p. 886.

Miller, RL, "*Cengage Advantage Books: Business Law Today, The Essentials: Text and Summarized Cases – 11th Edition*", Boston: Cengage Learning 2015, p. 617.

Mitchell, CE, "*Contract Law and Contract Practice: Bridging the Gap between Legal Reasoning and Commercial Expectation*", Oxford/Portland: Hart Publishing 2013, p. 30.

Molenaar, C, "*E-Marketing: Applications of information technology and the internet within marketing*", Abingdon: Routledge 2012, p. 105.

Monti, G, "*EC Competition Law*", Cambridge: Cambridge University Press 2007, p. 99, 192, 486.

Morgan, J, "*Contract Law Minimalism: A Formalist Restatement of Commercial Contract Law*", Cambridge/ New York: Cambridge University Press 2013, p. 208.

Morgan, J, "*Great Debates in Contract Law*", London: Palgrave 2015, p. 88.

Musmann, AC, "*Recht und soziale Sanktionen: Eine Untersuchung am Beispiel des grenzüberschreitenden Baumwollhandels*", Baden-Baden: Nomos 2018.

Nazzini, R, "*The Foundations of European Union Competition Law: The Objective and Principles of Article 102*", Oxford: Oxford University Press 2011, p. 170, 185.

Nee, I, "*Managing Negative Word-of-Mouth on Social Media Platforms: The Effect of Hotel Management Responses on Observers' Purchase Intention*", Bremen: Springer Fachmedien Wiesbaden 2016, p. 2.

Neergaard, U, Szyszczak, E, van de Gronden, JW, and Krajewski, M, "*Social Services of General Interest in the EU*", The Hague: T.M.C. Asser Press 2013, p. 280.

Newmann, P, "*The New Palgrave Dictionary of Economics and the Law: Three Volume Set*", London: Palgrave Macmillan 2002, p. 93.

Nguyen, B, and Wait, A, "*Essentials of Microeconomics*", Abingdon/New York: Routledge 2016, p. 77.

Nistor, L, "*Public Services and the European Union: Healthcare, Health Insurance and Education Services*", The Hague: T.M.C. Asser Press 2011, p. 183.

Norman, P, "*The Risk Controllers: Central Counterparty Clearing in Globalised Financial* Markets", Chichester: John Wiley & Sons 2011, p. 60.

Nygh, PE, "*Autonomy in International Contracts*", Oxford: Oxford University Press 1999, p. 92.

O'Donoghue, R, and Padilla, AJ, "*The Law and Economics of Article 82 EC*", Oxford: Hart Publishing 2006, p. 440-442.

O'Donoghue, R, and Padilla, AJ, "*The Law and Economics of Article 82 EC*", Oxford: Hart Publishing 2013, p. 282-283.

Oltuski, A, "*Precious Objects: A Story of Diamonds, Family, and a Way of Life*", New York: Scribner 2011, p. 76.

Oswald, LJ, "*The Law of Marketing – 2th Edition*", Mason: South-Western Cengage Learning 2010, p. 112.

Ottow, A, "*Market and Competition Authorities: Good Agency Principles*", Oxford: Oxford University Press 2015, p. 154.

Oxford Corpus, "*Shorter Oxford English Dictionary: Sixth Edition*", Oxford: Oxford University Press 2007.

Papadopoulos, AS, "*The International Dimension of EU Competition Law and Policy*", Cambridge: Cambridge University Press 2010, p. 272.

Parcu, PL, Monti, G, and Botta, M, "*Abuse of Dominance in EU Competition Law: Emerging Trends*", Cheltenham/Northampton: Edward Elgar Publishing 2017, p. 2.

Pareto, V, "*Manual of Political Economy*", New York: Kelley 1906.

Parker, R, "*Polytheism and Society at Athens*", Oxford: Oxford University Press 2005, p. 9.

Patel, KK, and Schweitzer, H, "*The Historical Foundations of EU Competition Law*", Oxford: Oxford University Press 2013, p. 209.

Perelman, C, "*Justice, Law, and Argument: Essays on Moral and Legal Reasoning*", Dordrecht: D. Reidel Publishing Company 1980, p. 59.

Perle, EG, Fischer, MA, and Williams, JT, "*Perle and Williams on Publishing Law*", Austin/Boston/Chicago/New York: Wolters Kluwer Law & Business 2009, p. 10-11.

Polinsky, AM, and Shavell, S, "*Handbook of Law and Economics: Volume 2*", Amsterdam: Elsevier 2007, p. 1604.

Posner, RA, "*Law and Social Norms*", Cambridge/London: Harvard University Press 2000, p. 172.

Posner, RA, "*Antitrust Law, Second Edition*", Chicago: University of Chicago Press 2001, p. 194-195.

Posner, RA, "*Economics Analysis of Law*", New York: Wolters Kluwer Law & Business 2014, para. 8.6.

Redfern, A, and Hunter, M, "*Law and Practice of International Commercial Arbitration*", London: Sweet & Maxwell 2004, p. 24, 387.

Revuelta, MB, "*Mineral Resources: From Exploration to Sustainability Assessment*", Cham: Springer International Publishing AG 2018, p. 44.

Richman, BD, "*Stateless Commerce: The Diamond Network and the Persistence of Relational Exchange*", Cambridge/London: Harvard University Press 2017, p. 14, 42-43, 77.

Richman BD, et al, "*Journal of Legal Analysis, Vol. 9, Is. 2*", in: B. D. Richman (ed), "An Autopsy of Cooperation: Diamond Dealers and the Limits of Trust-based Exchange", Oxford: Oxford University Press 2017, p. 251, 255-256.

Rißmann, K, "*Die kartellrechtliche Beurteilung der Markenabgrenzung*", Munich: Herbert Utz Verlag 2008, p. 108.

Ritter, L, and Braun, WD, "*European Competition Law: A Practitioner's Guide*", The Hague: Kluwer Law International 2005, p. 249.

Robbins, D, "*Handbook of Public Sector Economics*", Boca Raton: CRC Press 2005, p.185.

Robbins, P, "*Stolen Fruit: The Tropical Commodities Disaster*", London/New York: Zed Books 2003, p. 167.

Robinson, Jr., L, "*Marketing Dynamism & Sustainability: Things Change, Things Stay the Same*", Heidelberg/Dordrecht/New York/London: Springer 2012, p. 304.

Roche, J, "*The International Cotton Trade*", Cambridge: Woodhead Publishing 1994, p. 17.

Rubino-Sammartano, M, "*International Arbitration: Law and Practice, Third Edition*", New York: JurisNet 2014, p. 1085-1086.

Saferstein, HI, and Everett, JC, "*State Antitrust Practice and Statutes (Fourth)*", Chicago: American Bar Association 2009, p. 10-3, 10-4.

Sanchez-Taínta, AS, "*The Prevention of Cardiovascular Disease through the Mediterranean Diet*", London/San Diego/Cambridge/Oxford: Elsevier 2018, p. 49.

Šarčević, P, "*Essays on International Commercial Arbitration*", London/Dordrecht/Boston: Graham & Trotman/Martinus Nijhoff 1989, p. 69.

Sauter, W, "*Coherence in EU Competition Law*", Oxford: Oxford University Press 2016, p. 75-87, 101, 256.

Schmitthoff, CM, "*The Unification of the Law of International Trade*", London: Sweet & Maxwell 1968.

Schofield, NC, "*Commodity Derivatives: Markets and Applications*", Hoboken: John Wiley & Sons 2007, p. 75.

Schoon, N, "*Modern Islamic Banking: Products and Processes in Practice*", Chichester: John Wiley & Sons 2016, p. 117.

Shaffer, BD, "*In Restraint of Trade*", Cranbury/London/Mississauga: Associated University Presses 1997, p. 64.

Shemtov, N, "*Beyond the Code: Protection of Non-Textual Features of Software*", Oxford: Oxford University Press 2017, p. 65.

Shield, RS, "*Diamond Stories: Enduring Change on 47th Street*", London: Cornell University Press 2002, p. 92, 190-192.

Slot, PJ, and Farley, M, "*An Introduction to Competition Law*", Oxford/London/Portland: Hart Publishing 2017, p. 56.

Sörling, SU, et al., "*Studies presented to Pontus Hellström*", in: BL Sjöberg, "The Greek oikos: a space for interaction, revisited and reconsidered", Uppsala: S. U. Sörling et al. 2014, p. 315.

Stein, U, "*Lex mercatoria: Realität und Theorie*", Band 28, Frankfurt am Main: Vittorio Klostermann 1995 p. 188.

Stoyanova, M, "*Competition Problems in Liberalized Telecommunications: Regulatory Solutions to Promote Effective Competition*", Alphen aan den Rijn: Kluwer Law International 2008, p. 144.

Stuyck, J, Gilliams, H, and Ballon, E, "*Modernisation of European Competition Law: The Commission's Proposal for a New Regulation Implementing Articles 81 and 82 EC*", Antwerp/Oxford/New York: Intersentia 2002, p. 108.

Subrin, S, and Woo, MYK, "*Litigating in America: Civil Procedure in Context*", New York: Aspen Publishers 2006, p. 165.

Sullivan, ET, "*Nonprice Predation under Section 2 of the Sherman Act*", Chicago: American Bar Association 1991, p. 55, 58.

Sumangla, R, and Panwar, A, "*Capturing, Analyzing, and Managing Word-of-Mouth in the Digital Marketplace*", Hershey: IGI Global 2016, p. 172

Sutherland, EE, "*Law Making and the Scottish Parliament*", Edinburgh: Edinburgh University Press 2011, p. 314.

Terlinden, U, "*City and Gender: Intercultural Discourse on Gender, Urbanism and Architecture*", Opladen: Leske + Budrich 2003, p. 43.

Thorson, B, "*Individual Rights in EU Law*", Oslo: Springer International 2016, p. 131.

Tietje, C, and Brouder, A, "*Handbook of Transnational Economic Governance Regimes*", Leiden/Boston: Martinus Nijhoff Publishers 2009, p. 656-657, 659.

Tittle, P, "*Ethical Issues in Business: Inquiries, Cases, and Readings*", Petersborough: Peg Tittle 2000, p. 41.

Todd, JA, "*The Cotton World: A Survey of the World's Cotton Supplies and Consumption*", London: Sir I. Pitman & Sons 1927, p. 91.

Townley, C, "*Article 81 EC and Public Policy*", Portland: Hart Publishing 2009, p. 64, 273.

Townsend, T, "*Cotton Trading Manual*", Cambridge: Woodhead Publishing Limited 2005, p. iii.

Travaux du Comité français de droit international privé, "*Droit international privé:*", in: B Goldman (ed), "La lex mercatoria dans les contrats et l'arbitrage internationaux: réalité et perspectives", Paris: Travaux du Comité français de droit international privé 1979, p. 221-270.

Ullrich, H, "*The Evolution of European Competition Law: Whose Regulation, Which Competition?*", Cheltenham/Northampton: Edward Elgar Publishing 2006, p. 348.

Union Internationale Des Advocats, "*Arbitrage International Commercial, Vol. II*", Leiden: Martinus Nijhoff 1960, p. 393.

Vakerics, TV, "*Antitrust Basics*", New York: Law Journal Press 2006, p. , 5-3, 6-40.

van Bael & Bellis (firm), "*Competition Law of the European Community*", The Hague: Kluwer Law Internationaal 2005, p. 52, 101, 438.

van Boom, WH, Giesen, I, and Verheij, AJ, "*Gedrag en privaatrecht: Over gedragspresumpties en gedragseffecten bij privaatrechtelijke leerstukken*", in: J van Erp, "Naming en shaming in het contractenrecht? Het reputatie-effect van schadevergoedingen tussen ondernemingen", The Hague: Boom Juridische Uitgevers 2008, p. 166.

van der Hof, S, van den Berg, B, and Schermer, B, "*Minding Minors Wandering the Web: Regulating Online Child Safety*", The Hague: T.M.C. Asser Press 2014, p. 136.

Vishny, PH, "*Guide to International Commerce Law*", New York: McGraw-Hill Inc. 1984, p. 2.

Waters, TJ, and Morse, RH, "*Antitrust & Trade Associations: How Trade Regulation Laws Apply to Trade and Professional Associations*", Chicago: American Bar Association 1996, p. 58, 65.

Watson, L, and Watson, P, "*Juvenal: Satire 6*", Cambridge: Cambridge University Press 2014, 196.

Welch, PJ, and Welch, GF, "*Economics: Theory and Practice – Ninth Edition*", Hoboken: John Wiley & Sons 2010, p. 408.

Wendt, IE, "*EU Competition Law and Liberal Professions: an Uneasy Relationship?*", Leiden: Koninklijke Brill NV 2013, p. 220, 269, 384, 512.

Wengler, S, "*Key Account Management in Business-to-Business Markets: An Assessment of Its Economic Value*", Berlin: Deutscher Universitäts-Verlag 2006, p. 112.

Wesseling, R, "*The Modernisation of EC Antitrust Law*", Oxford/Portland: Hart Publishing 2000, p. 116-117.

Whish, R, and Bailey, D, "*Competition Law: Eighth Edition*", Oxford: Oxford University Press 2015, p. 54, 174-174, 595.

Williamson, OE, "*The Economic Institutions of Capitalism*", New York: Macmillan 1985, p. 20.

Wu, Q, "*Competition Laws, Globalization and Legal Pluralism: China's Experience*", Oxford/Portland: Hart Publishing 2013, p. 28.

Zamir, E, and Teichman, D, "*The Oxford Handbook of Behavioral Economics and the Law*", Oxford: Oxford University Press 2014, p. 440.

US CASE LAW

Standfacts Credit Services, Inc. v. Experian Information, 405 F.Supp.2d 1141 (C.D. Cal. 2005).

Hecht v. Pro-Football, Inc., 570 F.2d 982, 992 (D.C. Cir. 1977).

United States v. Microsoft Corp., 253 F.3d 34, 59 (D.C. Cir. 2001).

Covad Communications Company v. Bell Atlantic Corp., 398 F.3d 666, 672 (D.C. Cir. 2005).

United States v. King, 229 F. 275 (D. Mass. 1915).

United States v. Kansas City Star Company, No. 18444 (D. Kans. 1953).

Pretz v. Holstein Friesian Ass'n, 698 F. Supp. 1531, 1539 (D. Kans. 1988).

United States v. Otter Tail Power Co., 331 F. Supp. 54, 61 (D. Minn. 1971).

Charleton v. Vt. Dairy Herd Improvement Ass'n, 782 F. Supp. 926, 932 (D. Vt. 1991).

In re Educ. Testing Serv. Litig., 429 F. Supp. 2d 752, 759 (E.D. La. 2005).

McElhinney v. Medical Protective Co., 549 F. Supp. 121, 132 (E.D. Ky. 1982).

Bennett v. Cardinal Health Marmac Distribs., 2003-2 Trade Cas. (CCH) 74, 137 (E.D.N.Y. 2003).

Intergraph Corp. v. Intel Corp., 195 F.3d 1346, 1356, 1357 (Fed. Cir. 1999).

Blalock v. Ladies Professional Golf Association, 359 F. Supp. 1260, 1265-1266 (N.D. Ga. 1973).

Choiceparts v. General Motors Corporation, No. 01 C 0067 (N.D. Ill. 2005), para. 12.

Aetna Life & Casualty Co. v. Slekardis, 34 N.Y.2d 182 (N.Y. App. Div. 1974).

Matarasso v. Continental Casualty Co., 56 N.Y.2d 264 (N.Y. App. Div. 1982).

Rabinowitz v. Olewski, 473 N.Y.S. 2d 232, 234 (N.Y. App. Div. 1984).

Goldfinger v. Lisker, 500 N.E.2d 857, 858 (N.Y. App. Div. 1986).

Abraham v. Diamond Dealers, 896 N.Y.S. 2d 848 (N.Y. App. Div. 2010).

Antco Shipping Co., Ltd. v. Sidermar S. p. A., 417 F. Supp. 207 (S.D.N.Y. 1976), para. 215.

United States v. Western Winter Sports Representatives Ass'n, Inc., 1962, Trade Cas. (CCH) 74,263 (W.D. Penn. 1973).

Clamp-All Corp. v. Cast Iron Soil Pipe Institute, 851 F.2d 478, 490, 492 (1st Cir. 1988).

Fraser v. Major League Soccer, 284 F.3d 47, 59 (1st Cir. 2002).

Stop & Shop Supermarket Co. v. Blue Cross & Blue Shield of R.I., 373 F.3d 57, 61 (1st Cir. 2004).

United States v. Consolidated Laundries Corp., 291 F.2d 563, 572-573 (2nd Cir. 1961).

Volvo North America Corp. v. Men's Int'l Prof'l Tennis Council, 857 F.2d 55, 74 (2nd Cir. 1988).

Worldcrisa Corp. v. Armstrong, 129 F.3d 71 (2d Cir. 1997), para. 74.

Bogan v. Hodgkins, 166 F.3D 509, 515 (2nd Cir. 1999).
Smith/Enron Cogeneration Ltd. P'ship. v. Smith Cogeneration Int'l Inc., 198 F.3d 88 (2nd Cir.1999), para. 49.
Satellite Television & Associated Resources, Inc. v. Continental Cablevision, 714 F.2d 351, 358 (4th Cir. 1983).
Heattransfer Corp. v. Volkswagenwerk, A.G., 553 F.2d 964, 981 (5th Cir. 1977).
United States v. Cont'Group 603 f.2d 444, 463 (5th Cir. 1979).
United States v. Realty Multi-List Inc., 629 F.2d 1351 (5th Cir. 1980), para. 107.
Adjusters Replace-A-Car, Inc. v. Agency Rent-A-Car, Inc., 735 F.2d 884, 887-888 (5th Cir. 1984).
United States v. American Airlines, Inc., 743 F.2D, 1114, 1116-1117 (5th Cir. 1984).
Brown v. Pacific Life Ins. Co., 462 F.3d 384, 396 (5th Cir. 2006).
Spirit Airlines v. Northwest Airlines, 431 F.3d 917, 935-936 (6th Cir. 2005).
MCI Communications Corp. v. AT&T, 708 F.2d 1081, 1113, 1132, 1143 (7th Cir. 1982).
Ball Memorial Hospital, Inc. v. Mutual Hospital Insurance, Inc., 784 F.2d 1325, 1338-1339 (7th Cir. 1986).
Great Escape, Inc. v. Union City Body Co., 791 F.2d 532, 540-541 (7th Cir. 1986).
Blue Cross & Blue Shield v. Marshfield Clinic, 65 F.3d 1406, 1411 (7th Cir. 1995)
United States v. Empire Gas Corp., 537 F.2d 296 (8th Cir. 1976).
Trace X Chemical v. Canadian Industries, 738 F.2d 261, 266, 268 (8th Cir. 1984).
Conoco, Inc. v. Inman Oil Company, Inc. 774 F.2d 895, 905 (8th Cir. 1985).
General Industries Corp., 810 F.2d 795, 801 (8th Cir. 1987).
City of Malden v. Union Elec. Co., 887 F.2d 157, 160 (8th Cir. 1989)
Craftsmen Limousine v. Ford Motor Co., 491 F.3d 380, 389 (8th Cir. 2007).
Deesen v. Professional Golfers' Association of America, 358 F. 2d 165 (9th Cir. 1966).
Hunt-Wesson Foods, Inc. v. Ragu Foods, Inc., 627 F.2d 919, 926 (9th Cir. 1980).
Ferguson v. Greater Pocatello Chamber of Commerce, Inc., 848 F.2d 976, 983 (9th Cir. 1988).
City of Anaheim v. S. Cal. Edison Co., 955 F.2d 1373, 1380 (9th Cir. 1992).
Nova Designs, Inc. v. Scuba Retailers Association, 202 F.3d 1088, 1092 (9th 2000).
County of Tuolumne v. Sonora Cmty. Hosp., 236 F.3d 1148, 1155 (9th Cir. 2001), para. IV, A, I.
Paladin Assoc., Inc. v. Mont. Power Co., 328 F.3d 1145, 1158 (9th Cir. 2003).
Nagrampa v. MailCoups, Inc., 469 F.3d 1257 (9th Cir. 2006), para. 43.
Olsen v. Progressive Music Supply, Inc., 703 F.2d 432, 438 (10th Cir. 1983).
Gregory v. Fort Bridger Rendezvous Ass'n, 448 F.3d 1195, 1201 (10th Cir. 2006).
CHA-Car, Inc. v. Calder Race Source, Inc., 752 F.2D 609, 613 (11th Cir. 1985).
McGahee v. N. Propane Gas Co., 858 F.2d 1487, 1505 (11th Cir. 1988).

Key Enterprises of Delaware v. Venice Hosp, 919 F.2d 1550, 1564 (11th Cir. 1990).
Thompson v. Metro. Multi-List, Inc. 934 F.2d 1566, 1582 (11th Cir. 1991).
Bailey v. Allgas, Inc., 284 F.3d 1237, 1250 (11th Cir. 2002).
Morris Communications Corp. v. PGA Tour, 364 F.3d 1288, 1294 (11th Cir. 2004).
Brief for the United States As Amici Curiae Supporting Petitioners, Reiter, 442 U.S. 330 (1979) (No. 78-690), 1979 WL 213494, para. 12.
Montague & Co. v. Lowry, 193 U.S. 38, 44 (1904).
Standard Oil Co. of New Jersey v. United States, 221 U.S. 1, 62 (1911).
United States v. American Tobacco Company, 221 U.S. 106 (1911).
United States v. Terminal R.R. Ass'n, 224 U.S. 383 (1912).
Eastern States Lumber Assn. v. United States, 234 U. S. 600, 601, 605, 608, 614 (1914).
United States v. United States v. Colgate & Co., 250 U.S. 300 (1919).
American Column & Lumber Co. v. United States, 257 U.S. 377 (1921).
United States v. American Linseed Oil Co., 262 U.S. 371 (1923).
Interstate Circuit, Inc. v. United States, 306 U.S. 208, 227 (1939).
Fashion Originators' Guild v. Federal Trade Comm'n, 312 U. S. 457, 458, 465, 468 (1941).
American Medical Assn. v. United States, 317 U.S. 519, 535-536 (1943).
Associated Press v. United States, 326 U.S. 1, 2, 23 (1945).
American Tobacco v. United States, 328 U.S. 781, 809 (1946).
United States v. Griffith, 334 U.S. 100, 107-108 (1948).
Kiefer-Stewart Co. v. Seagram & Sons, 340 U. S. 211, 214 (1951).
Times-Picayune Publishing Co. v. United States, 345 U. S. 594, 625 (1953).
Yates v. United States 354 U.S. 298, 334 (1957).
Northern Pacific R. Go. v. United States, 356 U. S. 1, 5 (1958).
Klor's, Inc. v. Broadway-Hale Stores, Inc., 359 U.S. 207, 212-213 (1959).
Radiant Burners, Inc. v. Peoples Gas Co., 364 U.S. 656, 659 (1961).
Silver v. New York Stock Exch. 373 U.S. 341 (1963).
United States v. Grinnell Corp., 384 U.S. 563, 570 (1966).
Fed. Maritime Comm'n v. Aktiebolaget Svenska Amerika Linien, 390 U.S. 238, 250 (1968).
Broadcast Music, Inc. v. CBS, Inc., 441 U.S. 1 (1979), para. E.
Reiter v. Sonotone Corp., 442 U.S. 330 (1979).
Mid-Texas Communications v. Am. Tel. Tel., 615 F.2d 1372, 1389 n. 13 (5th Cir. 1980).
Moses H. Cone Mem'l Hosp. v Mercury Constr. Corp., 460 U.S. 1, 24-27 (1983) and Southland Copperweld v. Independence Tube, 467 U.S. 752 (1984), para. III.
Corp. v. Keating, 465 U.S. 1, para. 12 (1984).

Monsanto Co. v. Spray-Rite Serv. Corp., 465 U.S. 752, 764, 768 (1984).

Monsanto Co. v. Spray-Rite Svc. Corp., 465 U.S. 752, 768 (1984).

Mitsubishi Motors Corp. v. Soler Chrysler-Plymouth, Inc., 473 U.S. 614 (1985).

NW Wholesale Stationers v. Pac. Stationery, 472 U.S. 284, 287, 293-297 (1985).

Matsushita v. Zenith Radio Corp., 475 U.S. 574 (1986).

Spectrum Sports, Inc. v. McQuillan, 506 U.S. 447, 456 (1993).

NYNEX Corp. v. Discon, Inc., 525 U.S. 128, 134 (1998).

California Dental Ass'n v. Federal Trade Commission, 526 U.S. 756, 763, 780 (1999).

Verizon Commc'ns Inc. v. Law Offices of Curtis V. Trinko, LLP, 540 U.S. 398, 407 (2004).

Buckeye Check Cashing, Inc. v. Cardegna, 546 U.S. (2006) [J. Thomas, dissenting], para. 8.

Leegin Creative Leather Prods., Inc. v. PSKS, Inc., 551 U.S. 877 (2007).

UK CASE LAW

Rhone Mediterranee v. Achille Lauro [1983] 712 F. 2nd 50.

Federal Bulk Carriers v C Itoh & Co default [1989] 1 Lloyd's Rep 103.

Aughton Limited (formerly Aughton Group Limited) v. M.F. Kent Services Limited, [1991] 57 BLR 1.

Trygg Hansa Insurance Co. Ltd. v. Equitas Ltd, [1998] 2 Lloyd's Rep. 439.

Azov Shipping co. v. Baltic Shipping co. [1999] 1 Lloyd's Rep. 68, para. 5 and 31

Vale Do Rio Doce Navegacao SA & Anor v Shanghai Bao Steel Ocean Shipping Co Ltd. [2000] EWHC 205 (Comm), para. 45.

Competition Appeal Tribunal 19 March 2002, case 1005/1/101 (Aberdeen Journals Limited v. Director General of Fair Trading), [2002] CAT 4, para. 96-97.

Downing v. Al Tameer Establishment [2002] EWCA Civ 721.

Mackley & Co Ltd v Gosport Marina Ltd [2002] EWHC 1315, para. 20, 22, 39.

Esso Exploration and Production UK Ltd v. Electricity Supply Board [2004] EWHC 787 (Comm).

Welex AG v. Rosa Maritime Ltd [2003] EWCA Civ 938.

Albon v. Naza Motor Trading Sdn Bhd (No 3) [2007] Lloyd's Rep. L.

Sea Trade Maritime Corporation v. Hellenic Mutual War Risks Association (Bermuda) Ltd (The "Athena") (No 2), [2007] 1 Lloyd's Rep. 280, para. 64-65.

Stretford v. The Football Association Ltd et al (CA) [2007] EWCA Civ 238, para. 38, 67.

Sukuman Ltd v. Commonwealth Secretariat [2007] EWCA Civ 243, para. 36.

Fulham Football Club (1987) Ltd v. Richards [2011] EWCA Civ 855.

Ust-Kamenogorsk Hydropower Plant JSC (Appellant) v. AES Ust-Kamenogorsk Hydropower Plant LLP (Respondent), [2011] EWCA Civ 647.

Joint Stock Company "Aeroflot Russian Airlines" v. Berezovsky et al [2012] EWHC 1610 (Ch), para. 73.

Lombard North Central plc et al. v. GATX Corporation [2012] EWHC 1067 (Comm), para. 21.

Assaubayev et al v. Michael Wilson and Partners Ltd, [2014] EWCA Civ 1491.

Toyota Tsusho Sugar Trading Ltd v. Prolat S.R.L [2014] EWHC 3649 (Comm), para. 2.

EU DECISIONAL PRACTICE AND CASE LAW

Commission, Competition in a media sector, press releases RAPID "Dutch fishermen allowed to land and auction catches in foreign ports following Commission action" (to access: http://europa.eu/rapid/press-release_IP-01-84_en.htm?locale=EN).

Commission, Competition in a media sector, press releases RAPID "Commission closes investigations into FIFA regulations on international football transfers" (to access: http://europa.eu/rapid/press-release_IP-02-824_en.htm?locale=EN); "Commission, concerning Case IV / 36 583-SETCA-FGTB / FIFA" (to access: http://ec.europa.eu/competition/antitrust/cases/dec_docs/36583/36583_54_3.pdf).

Commission, Competition in a media sector, press releases RAPID "Antitrust: Commission welcomes steps taken by collective rights management bodies in Hungary and Romania to improve competition" (to access: http://europa.eu/rapid/pressReleasesAction.do?reference=IP/11/284&format=HTML&aged=0&language=EN).

Commission, press release IP/ 17/3622 of 2 October 2017 "Commission fines Lithuanian Railways €28 million for hindering competition on rail freight market" (to access: http://europa.eu/rapid/press-release_IP-17-3622_en.htm).

Commission, press release IP/ 17/3622 of 2 October 2017 "Commission fines Lithuanian Railways €28 million for hindering competition on rail freight market" (to access: http://europa.eu/rapid/press-release_IP-17-3622_en.htm).

Commission, press release IP/01/1641 of 23 November 2001 "Commission settles Marathon case with Thyssengas" (to access: http://europa.eu/rapid/press-release_IP-01-1641_en.htm).

Commission, press release IP/04/573 "Commission settles Marathon case with Gaz de France and Ruhrgas" (to access: http://europa.eu/rapid/press-release_IP-04-573_e.htm).

Commission Decision of 18 July 1975 relating to a proceeding under Article 85 of the EEC Treaty [now Article 101 TFEU], Case No IV/21.353 (Kabelmetal-Luchaire), para. 11.

Commission Decision of 21 November 1975 relating to a proceeding under Article 85 of the EEC Treaty [now Article 101 TFEU], Case No IV/256 (Bomée-Stichting), para. II.

Commission Decision of 2 December 1977 relating to a proceeding under Article 85 of the EEC Treaty [now Article 101 TFEU], Case No IV/28.948 (Cauliflowers), para. II (4).

Commission Decision of 2 December 1977 relating to a proceeding under Article 85 of the EEC Treaty [now Article 101 TFEU], Case No IV/147 (Centraal Bureau voor de Rijwielhandel), para. 6, 28-29, 36.

Commission Decision of 20 July 1978 relating to a proceeding under Article 85 of the EEC Treaty [now Article 101 (1) TFEU], Case No IV/28.852 (GB-Inno-BM/Fedetab), Case No IV/29.127 (Mestdagh-Huyghebaert/Fedetab), Case No IV/29.149 (Fedetab Recommendation), para. 123.

Commission Decision of 5 December 1979 relating to a proceeding under Article 85 of the EEC Treaty [now Article 101 TFEU], Case No IV/29.011 (Rennet), para. 30.

Commission Decision of 9 July 1980 relating to a proceeding under Article 85 of the EEC Treaty [now Article 101 TFEU], Case No IV/27.958 (National Sulphuric Acid Association), para. 47.

Commission Decision of 10 July 1985 relating to a proceeding under Article 2 of Council Regulation (EEC) No 1017/68 applying rules of competition to transport by rail, road and inland waterway, Case No IV/31.029 (French inland waterway charter traffic: EATE levy), para. 51.

Commission Decision of 13 December 1985 relating to a proceeding under Article 85 of the EEC Treaty [now Article 101 TFEU], Case No IV/27.590 (London Sugar Futures Market Limited).

Commission Decision of 13 December 1985 relating to a proceeding under Article 85 of the EEC Treaty [now Article 101 TFEU], Case No IV/27.591 (London Cocoa Terminal Market Association Limited).

Commission Decision of 13 December 1985 relating to a proceeding under Article 85 of the EEC Treaty [now Article 101 TFEU], Case No IV/27.592 (Coffee Terminal Market Association of London Limited).

Commission Decision of 13 December 1985 relating to a proceeding under Article 85 of the EEC Treaty [now Article 101 TFEU], Case No IV/27.593 (London Rubber Terminal Market Association Limited).

Commission Decision of 10 December 1986 relating to a proceeding under Article 85 of the EEC Treaty [now Article 101 TFEU], Case No IV/29.688 (The London Grain Futures Market).

Commission Decision of 10 December 1986 relating to a proceeding under Article 85 of the EEC Treaty [now Article 101 TFEU], Case No IV/30.176 (The London Potato Futures Association Limited).

Commission Decision of 10 December 1986 relating to a proceeding under Article 85 of the EEC Treaty [now Article 101 TFEU], Case No IV/31.614 (The London Meat Futures Exchange Limited), para. 12, 18.

Commission Decision of 10 December 1986 relating to a proceeding under Article 85 of the EEC Treaty [now Article 101 TFEU], Case No IV/29.036 (The GAFTA Soya Bean Meal Futures Association).

Commission Decision of 4 December 1986 relating to a proceeding under Article 85 of the EEC Treaty [now Article 101 TFEU], Case No IV/30.439 (Petroleum Exchange of London Limited).

Commission Decision of 18 July 1988 relating to a proceeding under Article 86 of the EEC Treaty, Case No IV/30.178 (Napier Brown - British Sugar).

Commission Decision of 28 October 1988 relating to a proceeding pursuant to Article 85 of the EEC Treaty [now Article 101 TFEU], Case No IV/B-2/31.424, Hudson's Bay-Dansk Pelsdyravlerforening, para. 1 (a), 9, 10, 11.

Commission Decision of 12 December 1988 relating to a proceeding under Article 85 of the EEC Treaty [now Article 101 TFEU], Case No IV/27.393 and IV/27.394 (Publishers Association - Net Book Agreements), para. 73.

Commission Decision of 26 February 1992 relating to a procedure pursuant to Articles 85 and 86 of the EEC Treaty [now Articles 101 and 102 TFEU], Case No IV/33.544 (British Midland v. Aer Lingus), para. 5, 26-27.

Commission Decision of 23 December 1992 relating to a proceeding pursuant to Articles 85 [now Article 101 TFEU], Case No IV/32.448 and IV/32.450 (Cewal, Cowac and Ukwal) and 86 [now Article 102 TFEU], Case No IV/32.448 and IV/32.450 (Cewal) of the EEC Treaty, para. 86.

Commission Decision of 11 June 1993 relating a proceeding pursuant to Article 85 of the EEC Treaty [now Article 101 TFEU], Case No IV/32.150 (EBU/Eurovision System), para. 59-67.

Commission Decision of 21 December 1993 relating to a proceeding pursuant to Article 86 of the EC Treaty [now Article 102 TFEU], Case No IV/34.689 (Sea Containers v. Stena Sealink), para. 12, 41, 66, 75.

Commission Decision of 13 July 1994 relating to a proceeding under Article 85 of the EC Treaty [now Article 101 TFEU], Case No IV/C/33.833 (Cartonboard).

Commission Decision of 30 November 1994 relating to a proceeding under Article 85 of the EC Treaty [now Article 101 TFEU], Case No IV/33.126 and 33.322 (Cement).

Commission Decision of 11 March 1998 relating to a proceeding under Articles 85 and 86 of the EC Treaty [now Articles 101 and 102 TFEU], Case No IV/34.073, IV/34.395 and IV/35.436 (Van den Bergh Foods Limited), para. 224.

Commission Decision of 24 January 1999 relating to a proceeding under Article 81 of the EC Treaty [Article 101 TFEU] and Article 53 of the EEA Agreement, Case No IV.F.1/36.718 (CECED), para. 55-57.

Commission Decision of 14 July 1999 relating to a proceeding under Article 82 of the EC Treaty [now Article 102 TFEU], Case No IV/D-2/34.780 (Virgin/British Airways), para. 87-88, 90-91

Commission Decision of 31 July 2001 relating to a proceeding under Article 81 of the EC Treaty [now Article 101 TFEU] and Article 53 of the EEA Agreement, Case No COMP/37.462 (Identrus), para. 46.

Commission Decision of 5 December 2001, Case No IV/37.614/F3 PO (Interbrew and Alken-Maes), para. 223.

Commission Decision of 27 August 2003 relating to a proceeding pursuant to Article 82 of the EC Treaty [now Article 102 TFEU], Case No COMP/37.685 (GVG/FS), para. 132, 141, 152.

Commission Decision of 30 April 2004 relating to a proceeding under Article 82 of the EC Treaty [now Article 102 TFEU], Case No COMP/D/32.448 and 32/450 (Compagnie Maritime Belge), para. 35-36.

Commission Decision of 24 May 2004 relating to a proceeding pursuant to Article 82 of the EC Treaty [now Article 102 TFEU] and Article 54 of the EEA Agreement against Microsoft Corporation, Case No COMP/C-3/37.792 (Microsoft), para. 18, 589, 984.

Commission Decision of 16 July 2008 relating to a proceeding under Article 81 of the EC Treaty [now Article 101 TFEU] and Article 53 of the EEA Agreement, Case No COMP/C2/38.698 (CISAC), para. 18, 125.

Commission Decision of 8 July 2009 relating to a proceeding under Article 81 of the EC Treaty [now Article 101 TFEU], Case No 39.401 (E.ON/GDF), para. 265.

Commission Decision of 14 October 2009 relating to a proceeding under Article 81 of the EC Treaty [now Article 101 TFEU] and Article 53 of the EEA Agreement, Case No COMP/39.416 (Ship classification), para. 3 (f) (g).

Commission Decision of 22 June 2011 relating to a proceeding under Article 102 of the Treaty on the Functioning of the European Union (TFEU), Case No COMP/39.525 (Telekomunikacja Polska), para. 874.

Commission Decision of 23 January 2013 relating to a proceeding under Article 101 of the Treaty on the Functioning of the European Union, Case No COMP/39.839 (Telefónica/Portugal Telecom), para. 444.

Commission Decision of 19 June 2015 relating to a proceeding under Articles 101 and 102 TFEU, Case No AT.39864 (BASF), para. 26.

Order of the President of the CFI of 21 January 2004, case T-245/03R (Fédération Nationale des Syndicats d'Exploitants Agricoles (FNSEA) et al v. Commission of the European Communities), [1996] ECR I-4971, para. 45.

Order of the President of the CFI of 14 December 2000, case T-5/00 R (Nederlandse Federatieve Vereniging voor de Groothandel op Elektrotechnisch Gebied v. Commission of the European Communities), [2000] ECR II-4121, para. 56, 64.

Order of the President of the CFI of 21 January 2004, case T-217/03R (Federation nationale de la coopération bétail v. Commission of the European Communities), [2004] ECR II-241, para. 52-54.

Opinion of the Advocate-General Kirschner of 21 February 1990, case T-5I/89 (Tetra Pak Rausing SA v. Commission of the European Communities), [1990] ECR II-309, para. 68, 72.

CFI 10 July 1990, Case T-51/89 (Tetra Pak Rausing SA v. Commission of the European Communities), [1990] ECR II-309, para. 42.

CFI 12 December 1991, Case T-30/89 (Hilti AG v. Commission of the European Communities), [1991] ECR II-1439, para. 92, 118.

CFI 10 March 1992, joined cases T-68/89, T-77/89 and T-78/89 (Società Italiana Vetro SpA, Fabbrica Pisana SpA and PPG Vernante Pennitalia SpA v. Commission of the European Communities), [1992] ECR II-01403, para. 35.

CFI 2 July 1992, Case T-61/89 (Dansk Pelsdyravlerforening v. Commission of the European Communities), [1992] ECR II-1931, para. 64, 78.

CFI 22 April 1993, Case T-9/92 (Automobiles Peugeot SA and Peugeot SA v. Commission of the European Communities), [1993] ECR II-493, para. 27.

CFI 23 February 1994, joined cases T-39/92 and T-40/92 (Groupement des Cartes Bancaires "CB" and Europay International SA v. Commission of the European Communities), [1994] ECR II-49113, para. 114.

CFI 15 July 1994, Case T-17/93 (Matra Hachette SA v. Commission of the European Communities), [1994] ECR II-595, para. 85, 135.

CFI 6 October 1994, Case T-83/91 (Tetra Pak International SA v. Commission of the European Communities), [1994] ECR II-00755, para. 83-84, 138.

CFI 6 April 1995, Case T-141/89 (Tréfileurope Sales SARL v. Commission of the European Communities), [1995] ECR II-791, para. 96.

CFI 8 October 1996, joined cases T-24/93, T-25/93, T-26/93 and T-28/93 (Compagnie Maritime Beige Transports SA and Compagnie Maritime Belge SA v. Commission of the European Communities), [1996] ECR 11-1201, para. 107, 170, 172, 182-183,185.

CFI 15 September 1998, joined cases T-374/94, T-375/94, T-384/94 and T-388/94 (European Night Services Ltd (ENS) et al v. Commission of the European Communities), [1998] ECR II-1533, para. 203.

CFI 27 November 1998, Case T-290/94 (Fort James France, formerly Kaysersberg SA v. Commission of the European Communities), [1997] ECR II-2137, para. 178–179.

CFI 15 March 2000, joined cases T-25/95, T-26/95, T-30/95, T-31/95, T-32/95, T-34/95, T-35/95, T-36/95, T-37/95, T-38/95, T-39/95, T-42/95, T-43/95, T-44/95, T-45/95, T 46/95, T-48/95, T-50/95, T-51/95, T-52/95, T-53/95, T-54/95, T-55/95, T-56/95, T-57/95, T-58/95, T-59/95, T-60/95, T-61/95, T-62/95, T-63/95, T-64/95, T-65/95, T-68/95, T-69/95, T-70/95, T-71/95, T-87/95, T-88/95, T-103/95 and T-104/95 (Cimenteries CBR et al v. Commission), [2000] ECR II-491.

CFI 21 March 2001, Case T-206/99 (Métropole Television SA v. Commission of the European Communities), [2001] ECR II-1057, para. 37.

CFI 18 September 2001, Case T-112/99 (Métropole télévision (M6) et al v. Commission of the European Communities), [2001] ECR II-2459, para. 74, 76.

CFI 28 February 2002, Case T-395/94 (Atlantic Container Line AB et al v. Commission of the European Communities), [2002] ECR II-595, para. 330.

CFI 6 June 2002, case T-342/99 (Airtours plc. v. Commission of the European Communities), [2002] ECR II-2585, para. 62.

CFI 30 September 2003, joined cases T-191/98, T-212/98 to T-214/98 (Atlantic Container Line AB et al v. Commission of the European Communities), [2003] ECR II-3275, para. 239, 939, 1112, 1456.

CFI 23 October 2003, Case T-65/98 (Van den Bergh Foods Ltd v. Commission of the European Communities), [2003] ECR II-4653, para. 84, 107, 139.

CFI 17 December 2003, Case T-219/99 (British Airways plc v. Commission of the European Communities), [2003] ECR II-05917, para. 293.

CFI 26 January 2005, Case T-193/02 (Laurent Piau v. Commission of the European Communities), [2005] ECR II-209, para. 111.

CFI 27 July 2005, joined cases T-49/02 to T-51/02 85 (Brasserie nationale SA (formerly Brasseries Funck-Bricher and Bofferding) et al v. Commission of the European Communities), [2005] ECR II-3033, para. 85.

CFI 2 May 2006, Case T-328/03 (O2 (Germany) GmbH & Co. OHG v. Commission of the European Communities), [2006] ECR II-1231, para. 66, 69, 71, 73.

CFI 27 September 2006, Case T-204/03 (Haladjian Frères v Commission), [2006], ECR II-03779, para. 28, 34, 36.

CFI 12 December 2006, Case T-155/04 (SELEX Sistemi Integrati SpA v. Commission of the European Communities), [2006] ECR II-04797, para. 50.

CFI 17 September 2007, Case T-201/04 (Microsoft Corp. v. Commission of the European Communities), [2007] ECR II-3601, para. 105, 275, 280, 442, 482, 1313.

CFI 1 July 2008, case T-276/04 (Compagnie Maritime Belge SA v. Commission of the European Communities), [2008] ECR II-1277.

CFI 9 September 2009, Case T-301/04 (Clearstream Banking AG and Clearstream International SA v. Commission of the European Communities), [2009] ECR II-3155, para. 47, 132.

GC 1 July 2010, Case T-321/05 (AstraZeneca AB and AstraZeneca plc v. European Commission), [2010] ECR II-2805, para. 360, 824, 826.

GC 23 November 2011, Case T-320/07 (Jones et al v. Commission), [2011], ECR II-00417, para. 115.

GC 24 May 2012, Case T-111/08 (MasterCard, Inc. et al v. European Commission), [2012] ECR II-000, para. 87.

GC 12 April 2013, Case T-442/08 (International Confederation of Societies of Authors and Composers (CISAC) et al v. European Commission), [2013] 5 CMLR, para. 12, 20.

Opinion of the Advocate-General Darmon of 20 November 1986, case 45/85 (Verband der Sachversicherer v. Commission of the European Communities), [1987] ECR 405, p. 438.

Opinion of the Advocate-General Lenz of 16 June 1994, Case C-360/92P (The Publishers Association v. Commission of the European Communities), [1995] ECR I-23, para. 43, 47.

Joined Opinion of the Advocate-General Tesauro of 12 September 1995, joined cases C-319/93, C-40/94, C-224/94, and C-399/93 (Dijkstra v Friesland (Frico Domo) Coöperatie BA and Cornelis van Roessel et al v. De coöperatieve vereniging Zuivelcoöperatie Campina Melkunie VA and Willem de Bie et al v. De Coöperatieve Zuivelcoöperatie Campina Melkunie BA), [1995] ECR I-4515, para. 10, 31.

Opinion of the Advocate-General Ruiz-Jarabo Colomer of 27 June 1996, Case C-333/94P (Tetra Pak International SA v. Commission of the European Communities), [1996] ECR I-5951, para. 57.

Opinion of the Advocate-General Fennelly of 29 October 1998, joined cases C-395/96P, C-396/96P (Compagnie Maritime Belge Transports SA et al v. Commission of the European Communities), [2000] ECR I-1365, para. 143, 144, 151, 152, 162.

Opinion of the Advocate-General Jacobs of 28 January 1999, joined cases C-115/97, C-116/97 and C-117/97 and Case C-219/97 (Albany International BV v. Stichting Bedrijfspensioenfonds Textielindustrie), [1999] ECR I-5751, para. 272.

Opinion of the Advocate-General Jacobs of 28 October 2004, Case C-53/03 (Synetairismos Farmakopoion Aitolias & Akarnanias (Syfait) et al v. GlaxoSmithKline plc und GlaxoSmithKline AEVE), [2005] ECR I-4609, para. 72.

Opinion of the Advocate-General Poiares Maduro of 23 May 2007, Case C-438/05 (International Transport Workers' Federation v. Viking Line ABP et al), [2008] IRLR 143, para. 7.

Opinion of the Advocate General of 19 February 2009, case C-8/08 (T-Mobile Netherlands BV et al v. Raad van bestuur van de Nederlandse Mededingingsautoriteit), [2009] ECR I-04529, para. 55.

ECJ 30 June 1966, Case 56/65 (Société Technique Minière (L.T.M.) v. Maschinenbau Ulm GmbH (M.B.U.)), [1966] ECR 235, p. 249.

ECJ 13 July 1966, joined cases 56 and 58-64 (Établissements Consten S.à.R.L. and Grundig-Verkaufs-GmbH v. Commission of the European Economic Community) [1966] ECR 299, p. 249, 341-342, 348.

ECJ 12 December 1967, Case C-23/67 (SA Brasserie de Haecht v. Consorts Wilkin-Janssen), [1967] ECR 525, p. 415.

ECJ 9 July 1969, Case 5-69 (Franz Völk v S.P.R.L. Ets J. Vervaecke), [1969] ECR 295, para. 5-7.

ECJ 25 November 1971, Case 22-71 (Béguelin Import Co. v. S.A.G.L. Import Export), [1971] ECR 949, para. 17, 29.

ECJ 14 July 1972, Case 48/69 (Imperial Chemical Industries Ltd. v. Commission of the European Communities), [1972] ECR 619, para. 64.

ECJ 21 February 1973, Case 6-72 (Europemballage Corporation and Continental Can Company Inc. v. Commission of the European Communities), [1973] ECR 215, para. 25-27.

ECJ 26 November 1975, Case 73-74 (Groupement des fabricants de papiers peints de Belgique et al v. Commission of the European Communities), [1975] ECR 1491, para. 32.

ECJ 16 December 1975, joined cases 40 to 48, 50, 54 to 56, 111, 113 and 114-73 (Coöperatieve Vereniging "Suiker Unie" UA et al v. Commission of the European Communities), [1975] ECR 1663, para. 174.

ECJ 25 October 1977, Case 26-76 (Metro SB-Großmärkte GmbH & Co. KG v. Commission of the European Communities), [1977] ECR 1875, para. 20, 47.

ECJ 14 February 1978, Case 27/76 (United Brands Company and United Brands Continental BV v. Commission of the European Communities), [1978] ECR 207, para. 10, 38, 108, 113-117, 168, 189-190, 208, 236.

ECJ 13 February 1979, Case 85/76 (Hoffman-La Roche & Co. AG v. Commission of the European Communities), [1979] ECR 461, para. 41, 57-58, 91.

ECJ 20 February 1979, Case C-120/78 (Rewe Zentrale v. Bundesmonopolverwaltung für Branntwein), [1979] ECR 649.

ECJ 12 July 1979, joined cases 32/78, 36/78 to 82/78 (BMW Belgium SA et al v. Commission of the European Communities), [1979] ECR 2435, para. 36.

ECJ 29 October 1980, joined cases 209 to 215 and 218/78 (Heintz van Landewyck SARL et al v. Commission of the European Communities), [1980] ECR 3125, para. 88, 183, 185.

ECJ 8 June 1982, Case 258/78 (L.C. Nungesser KG and Kurt Eisele v. Commission of the European Communities), [1982] ECR 2015.

ECJ 9 November 1983, Case 322/81 (NV Nederlandsche Banden Industrie Michelin v. Commission of the European Communities), [1983] ECR 3461, para. 57.

ECJ 17 January 1984, joined cases 43/82 and 63/82 (Vereniging ter Bevordering van het Vlaamse Boekwezen, VBVB, and Vereniging ter Bevordering van de Belangen des Boekhandels, VBBB, v. Commission of the European Communities), [1984] ECR 19, para. 52.

ECJ 28 March 1984, joined cases 29 and 30/83 (Compagnie Royale Asturienne des Mines SA and Rheinzink GmbH v. Commission of the European Communities), [1984] ECR 1979, para. 26.

ECJ 30 January 1985, Case 123/83 (Bureau national interprofessionnel du cognac v. Guy Clair), [1985] ECR 391, para. 22.

ECJ 11 July 1985, Case 42/84 (Remia BV et al v. Commission of the European Communities), [1985] ECR 2566, para. 22.

ECJ 3 October 1985, Case 311/84 (Centre belge d'études de marché - Télémarketing (CBEM) v. SA Compagnie luxembourgeoise de télédiffusion (CLT) and Information publicité Benelux (IPB), [1985] ECR 3261, para. 27.

ECJ 28 January 1986, Case 161/84 (Pronuptia de Paris GmbH v. Pronuptia de Paris Irmgard Schillgallis), [1986] ECR 353.

ECJ 22 October 1986, Case 75/84 (Metro SB-Großmärkte GmbH & Co. KG v. Commission of the European Communities), [1986] ECR 3021, para. 85-86.

ECJ 20 May 1987, Case 272/85 (Association nationale des travailleurs indépendants de la batellerie (ANTIB) v. Commission of the European Communities), [1987] ECR 2201, para. 25, 27-38.

ECJ 16 June 1987, Case 118/85 (Commission of the European Communities v. Italian Republic), [1987] ECR 2599, para. 7.

ECJ 23 April 1991, Case C-41/90 (Klaus Höfner and Fritz Elser v. Macrotron GmbH), [1991] ECR I-1979, para. 21.

ECJ 3 July 1991, Case C-62/86 (AKZO Chemie BV v. Commission of the European Communities), [1991] ECR I-3359, para. 60.

ECJ 31 March 1993, joined cases C-89/85, C-104/85, C-114/85, C-116/85, C-117/85, C-125/85, C-126/85, C-127/85, C-128/85 and C-129/85 (Ahlström Osakeyhtiö et al v. Commission), [1993] ECR I-01307.

ECJ 27 April 1994, Case C-393/92 (Municipality of Almelo et al v. NV Energiebedrijf Ijsselmij), [1994] ECR I-1477, para. 42.

ECJ 15 December 1994, Case C-250/92 (Gøttrup-Klim Grovvareforening et al v. Dansk Landbrugs Grovvareselskab AmbA (DLG)), [1994] ECR I-5641, para. 14, 35.

ECJ 6 April 1995, joined cases C-241/91P and C-242/91P (Radio Telefis Eireann (RTE) and Independent Television Publications Ltd (ITP) v. Commission of the European Communities), [1995] ECR I-00743, para. 56-57.

ECJ 16 November 1995, Case C-244/94 (Federation Française des Sociétés d'Assurance, Société Paternelle Vie, Union des Assurances de Paris-Vie, Caisse d'Assurance et de Prévoyance Mutuelle des Agriculteurs and Ministère de l'Agriculture et de la Pêche), [1995] ECR I-4013, para. 14.

ECJ 12 December 1995, Case C-399/93 (H. G. Oude Luttikhuis et al v. Verenigde Coöperatieve Melkindustrie Coberco BA), [1995] ECR I-4515, para. 3.

ECJ 14 November 1996, Case C- 333/94 P (Tetra Pak International SA v. Commission of the European Communities), [1996] ECR I-5951, para. 27, 31.

ECJ 18 March 1997, Case C-343/95 (Cali e Figli), [1997] ECR I-1547, para. 22-23.

ECJ 17 July 1997, Case C-219/95P (Ferriere Nord SpA v. Commission of the European Communities), [1997] ECR I-04411, para. 19.

ECJ 11 December 1997, Case C-55/96 (Job Centre coop. arl.), [1997] ECR I-7119, para. 21.

ECJ 28 May 1998, C-7/95P John Deere Ltd v. Commission of the European Communities), [1998] ECR I-311, para. 77.

ECJ 18 June 1998, Case C-35/96 (Commission of the European Communities v. Italian Republic), [1998] ECR I-3851, para. 36.

ECJ 26 November 1998, Case C-7/97 (Oscar Bronner GmbH & Co. KG v. Mediaprint Zeitungs- und Zeitschriftenverlag GmbH & Co. KG, Mediaprint Zeitungsvertriebsgesellschaft mbH & Co. KG and Mediaprint Anzeigengesellschaft mbH & Co. KG), [1998] ECR I-07791, para. 24, 37, 41, 43.

ECJ 21 January 1999, Case C-216/96 (Carlo Bagnasco et al v. Banca Popolare di Novara soc. coop. arl. (BNP) et al), [1999] ECR I-135, para. 48.

ECJ 1 June 1999, Case 126/97 (Eco Swiss China Time Ltd v. Benetton International NV), [1999] ECR I-3055, para 37.

ECJ 8 July 1999, Case C-49/92P (Commission of the European Communities v. Anic Partecipazioni SpA) [1999] ECR I-4125, para. 112, 132, 133.

ECJ 8 July 1999, case C-199/92P (Hüls AG v. Commisson of the European Communities), [1999] ECR I-4287, para. 163-166.

ECJ 16 March 2000, joined cases C-395/96P, C-396/96P (Compagnie maritime belge transports SA et al v. Commission of the European Communities), [2000] ECR I-1365, para. 45, 130.

ECJ 19 February 2002, Case C-309/99 (J. C. J. Wouters, J. W. Savelbergh and Price Waterhouse Belastingadviseurs BV v. Algemene Raad van de Nederlandse Orde van Advocaten, intervener: Raad van de Balies van de Europese Gemeenschap), [2002] ECR I-1577, para. 46, 97, 110.

ECJ 2 October 2003, Case C-194/99P (Thyssen Stahl AG v. Commission of the European Communities), [2003] ECR I-10821, para. 59, 60, 62-63, 84.

ECJ 6 January 2004, joined cases C-2/01 P and C-3/01P (Bayer v. Commission), [2004] ECR I-23, para. 101-102.

ECJ 7 January 2004, joined cases C-204/00 P, C-205/00 P, C-211/00 P, C-213/00 P, C-217/00 P and C-219/00 P, (Aalborg Portland et al v. Commission of the European Communities), [2004] ECR I-123, para. 78, 81.

ECJ 19 January 2004, Case C-453/00 (Kühne & Heitz NV v. Produktschap voor Pluimvee en Eieren), [2004] ECR I-837, para. 20.

ECJ 29 April 2004, Case C-418/01 (IMS Health GmbH & Co. OHG v. NDC Health GmbH & Co. KGIMS), [2004] ECR I-05039, para. 37-38, 46-47.

ECJ 28 June 2005, joined cases C-189, 202, 205-208 and 213/02P (Dansk Rørindustri A/S et al v. Commission of the European Communities), [2005] ECR I-5425, para. 145.

ECJ 11 July 2006, Case C-205/03P (Federación Española de Empresas de Tecnología Sanitaria (FENIN) v. Commission of the European Communities, [2006] ECR I-6295, para. 25.

ECJ 18 July 2006, Case C-519/04P (David Meca-Medina and Igor Majcen v. Commission of the European Communities), [2006] ECR I-6991, para. 42, 45.

ECJ 21 September 2006, Case C-167/04P (JCB Service v. Commission of the European Communities), [2006] ECR I-8935, para. 162-163.

ECJ 23 November 2006, Case C-238/05 (Asnef-Equifax, Servicios de Información sobre Solvencia y Crédito, SL and Administración del Estado v. Asociación de Usuarios de Servicios Bancarios (Ausbanc)), [2006] ECR I-11125, para. 7, 46-48, 58, 70.

ECJ 25 January 2007, Case C-407/04P (Dalmine SpA v. Commission of the European Communities), [2007] ECR I-829, para. 90.

ECJ 15 March 2007, Case C-95/04P (British Airways plc v. Commission of the European Communities), [2007] ECR I-2331, para. 77.

ECJ 10 July 2008, Case C-413/06P (Bertelsmann AG and Sony Corporation of America v. Independent Music Publishers and Labels Association (Impala)), [2008] ECR I-4951, para. 124.

ECJ 16 September 2008, joined cases C-468/06 to C-478/06 (ot. Lélos kai Sia EE et al v. GlaxoSmithKline AEVE Farmakeftikon Proionton, formerly Glaxowellcome AEVE), [2008] ECR I-7139, para. 50.

ECJ 20 November 2008, Case C-209/07 (Competition Authority v. Beef Industry Development Society Ltd and Barry Brothers (Carrigmore) Meats Ltd.), [2008] ECR I-8637, para. 21.

ECJ 4 June 2009, Case C-8/08 (T-Mobile Netherlands BV, KPN Mobile NV, Orange Nederland NV and Vodafone Libertel NV v. Raad van Bestuur van de Nederlandse Mededingingsautoriteit), [2009] ECR I-4529, para. 27, 36.

ECJ 10 September 2009, Case C-97/08P (Akzo Nobel NV et al v. Commission of the European Communities), [2009] I-08237, para. 54.

ECJ 6 October 2009, joined cases C-501/06P (GlaxoSmithKline Services Unlimited v. Commission of the European Communities), C-513/06P (and Commission of the European Communities v. GlaxoSmithKline Services Unlimited), C-515/06P (European Association of Euro Pharmaceutical Companies (EAEPC) v. Commission of the European Communities), and C-519/06P (Asociación de exportadores españoles de productos farmacéuticos (Aseprofar) v. Commission of the European Communities), [2009] ECR I-09291, para. 7.

ECJ 23 March 2010, joined cases C-236/08 to C-238/08 (Google Inc. v. Louis Vuitton Malletier SA et al.), [2010] ECR I-02417, para. 3.

ECJ 13 December 2012, Case C-226/11 (Expedia Inc. v. Autorité de la concurrence et al), [2012] ECR I-795, para. 16-17, 35-37.

ECJ 7 February 2013, Case C-68/12 (Protimonopolný úrad Slovenskej republiky v. Slovenská sporiteľňa a.s), ECLI:EU:C:2013:71, para. 17.

ECJ 28 February 2013, Case C-1/12 (Ordem dos Técnicos Oficiais de Contas v. Autoridade da Concorrência), [2013] 4 CMLR 20, para. 99.

ECJ 11 September 2014, Case C-382/12P (MasterCard Inc. et al v. European Commission), [2014] ECLI:EU:C:2014:2201, para. 242.

ECJ 6 October 2015, Case C-23/14 (Post Danmark A/S v. Konkurrencerådet), [2015] 651, p. 70-73.

LEGISLATION

Article 281 of the Mainland CPL.

The Companies Act 2006 (to access: http://www.legislation.gov.uk/ukpga/2006/46/pdfs/ukpga_20060046_en.pdf).

The Human Rights Act 1988 (to access: http://www.legislation.gov.uk/ukpga/1998/42/contents).

The Arbitration Act 1996 of 17 June 1996.

The Companies Act (to access: http://www.oas.org/juridico/english/mesicic3_jam_companies.pdf).

The Companies Act of 1989 (to access: http://www.legislation.gov.uk/ukpga/1989/40/contents).

The Arbitration Act 1996 (to access: http://www.legislation.gov.uk/ukpga/1996/23/contents).

Chapter 8 of the Consolidated Laws of the State of New York of 1909 (Civil Practice Law & Rules) (to access: https://www.nysenate.gov/legislation/laws/CVP).

Zivilprozessordnung (to access: https://dejure.org/gesetze/ZPO).

Gesetz gegen Wettbewerbsbeschränkungen of 2017 (to access: https://www.gesetze-im-internet.de/gwb/BJNR252110998.html).

Gesetz gegen den unlauteren Wettbewerb of 2019 (to access: https://dejure.org/gesetze/UWG).

United Nations Convention on the Recognition and Enforcement of Foreign Arbitral Awards of 1958 (to access: https://www.uncitral.org/pdf/english/texts/arbitration/NY-conv/New-York-Convention-E.pdf).

New York Consolidated Laws, Civil Practice Law and Rules of 1962 (to access: https://www.nysenate.gov/legislation/laws/CVP).

UNCITRAL Model Law on International Commercial Arbitration of 1985 (with amendments adopted in 2006) (to access: https://www.uncitral.org/pdf/english/texts/arbitration/ml-arb/07-86998_Ebook.pdf).

United Nations Convention on the Recognition and Enforcement of Foreign Arbitral Awards of 1958 (to access: https://www.uncitral.org/pdf/english/texts/arbitration/NY-conv/New-York-Convention-E.pdf).

Federal Arbitration Act of 1947 (to access: https://sccinstitute.com/media/37104/the-federal-arbitration-act-usa.pdf).

Sherman Antitrust Act of 1890 (to access: https://www.justice.gov/atr/file/761131/download).

The Treaty Establishing the European Economic Community of 25 March 1957.

Council Regulation No 17/62, First Regulation Implementing Articles 85 and 86 of the Treaty [now Articles 101 and 102 TFEU], [OJ 1962, No 87 28].

Council Regulation (EEC) No 2821/71 of the Council of 20 December 1971 on application of Article 85(3) of the Treaty [now Article 101(3) TFEU] to categories of agreements, decisions and concerted practices, [OJ 1971, No. L 285].

Commission Notice on the definition of relevant market for the purposes of Community competition law of 9 December 1997 [OJ 1997, No. C 372/5].

Notice on the application of the competition rules to access agreements in the telecommunications sector of 22 August 1998 [OJ 1998, No. C265/02].

Notice pursuant to Article 19(3) of Council Regulation No 17 (Î) of 9 January 1999 concerning Case No IV/F-1/36.160 (International Dental Exhibition).

Commission, "White Paper on Modernisation of the Rules implementing Article 85 and 86 of the EC Treaty [now Articles 101 and 102 TFEU]" of 28 April 1999, [OJ 1999, No. C 132/01].

Notice published pursuant to Article 19(3) of Council Regulation No 17 of 13 June 2001 concerning Case No COMP/35.163 (Notification of FIA Regulations), Case No COMP/36.638 (Notification by FIA/FOA of agreements relating to the FIA Formula One World Championship), and Case No COMP/36.776 (GTR/FIA), sect. 6.

Council Regulation (EC) No 1/2003 of 16 December 2002 on the implementation of the rules on competition laid down in Articles 81 and 82 of the Treaty [now Article 101 and 102 TFEU] [OJ 2003, No L 001].

Commission Recommendation concerning the definition of micro, small and medium-sized enterprises or any future recommendation replacing it of 20 May 2003, [OJ 2003, No. L 124].

The Commission – Notice – Guidelines on the application of Article 81(3) of the Treaty [now Article 101 (3) TFEU] of 27 April 2004, [OJ 2004, No. C 101/97], para. 20.

Commission Notice — Guidelines on the effect on trade concept contained in Articles 81 and 82 of the Treaty [now Articles 101 and 102 TFEU] of 27 April 2004, [OJ 2004, No. C 101/07].

Communication from the Commission — Guidance on the Commission's enforcement priorities in applying Article 82 of the EC Treaty [now Article 102 TFEU] to abusive exclusionary conduct by dominant undertakings of 24 February 2009, [OJ 2009, No. C 45].

Commission Regulation (EU) No 1217/2010 of 14 December 2010 on the application of Article 101(3) of the Treaty on the Functioning of the European Union to certain categories of research and development, [OJ 2010, No. L 335/36].

Commission Regulation (EU) No 1218/2010 of 14 December 2010 on the application of Article 101(3) of the Treaty on the Functioning of the European Union to certain categories of specialisation agreements, [OJ 2010, No. L 335/43].

Guidelines on the applicability of Article 101 of the Treaty on the Functioning of the European Union to horizontal co-operation agreements of 14 January 2011, [OJ 2011, No. C 11/01].

Commission Notice on Agreements of Minor Importance which do not Appreciably Restrict Competition under Article 101(1) TFEU (de minimis) of 30 August 2014 [OJ 2014, No. C 291/1].

GUIDANCE

European Commission, IXth Report on Competition Policy, para. 22.

National British Cattle and Sheep Breeders' Association, Twenty-second Report on Competition Policy 1992, Annex III, p. 416.

M. Monti, EC Commissioner for Competition, "The Future for Competition Policy in the European Union", Speech, 9 July 2001, p.2 (europa.eu/rapid/press-release_SPEECH-01-340_en.pdf);

N. Kroes, EC Commissioner for Competition, "European Competition Policy – Delivering Better Markets and Better Choices", Speech, 15 September 2005, p. 2 (http://europa.eu/rapid/press-release_SPEECH-05-512_en.htm).

N. Kroes, EC Commissioner for Competition, "Preliminary Thoughts on Policy Review of Article 82", Speech, 23 September 2005, p. 5 (http://europa.eu/rapid/press-release_SPEECH-05-537_en.htm?locale=en).

E. Paulis, Deputy Director for the Directorate-General for Competition, "The Burden of Proof in Article 82 cases", Speech, 6 September 2006, p. 5 (http://ec.europa.eu/competition/speeches/text/sp2006_014_en.pdf).

N. Kroes, EC Commissioner for Competition, "Exclusionary abuses of dominance - the European Commission's enforcement priorities", Speech, 25 September 2008, p. 4 (http://europa.eu/rapid/press-release_SPEECH-08-457_en.htm?locale=en).

BYLAWS AND RULES OF THE TRADE ASSOCIATIONS RESEARCHED

The Site Terms and Conditions of Use (to access: https://www.nyddc.com/terms--conditions.html).

DDC Bylaws (1999) (not publicly available).

The World Federation of Diamond Bourses By-laws and Inner Rules (2016).

The Articles of Association of the International Cotton Association (to access: https://www.ica-ltd.org/wp-content/uploads/2018/10/Articles_Nov2018.pdf).

Bylaws and Rules of the International Cotton Association Limited of 2018 (to access: https://www.ica-ltd.org/media/layout/documents/rulebooks/2018-11-rulebook-en.pdf).

The General Rules and Regulations Applicable to All Members of 2017 (to access: https://www.gafta.com/write/MediaUploads/Membership/General_Rules_and_RegulationsApplicable_to_All_Members_2017.pdf).

The General Rules and Regulations Applicable to all Members of 2017 (to access: https://www.gafta.com/write/MediaUploads/Membership/General_Rules_and_Regulations_Applicable_to_All_Members_2017.pdf).

The Arbitration Rules No. 125 of 2018 (to access: https://www.gafta.com/write/MediaUploads/Contracts/2018/125_2018.pdf).

Gafta Rules - Mediation Rules & Agreement of 2014 (to access: https://www.gafta.com/write/MediaUploads/Contracts/2014/128_2014.pdf).

Simple Disputes Arbitration Rules No. 126 of 2010 (to access: https://www.gafta.com/write/MediaUploads/Contracts/2010/126.pdf).

Arbitration Rules No.127 For use with Charter Parties or Other Forms of Maritime Transport of 2014 (to access: https://www.gafta.com/write/MediaUploads/Contracts/2014/127_2014.pdf).

Rules and Code of Conduct for Qualified Arbitrators & Qualified Mediators (to access: https://www.gafta.com/Rules-and-Code-of-Conduct-for-Qualified-Arbitrators-Qualified-Mediators).

Guidelines for GAFTA Appointment of Arbitrators (to access: https://www.gafta.com/Guidelines-for-Gafta-Appointment-of-Arbitrators).

Mediation Rules No. 128 of 2012 (to access: https://www.gafta.com/write/MediaUploads/Contracts/2012/128.pdf).

The Contract for the Delivery of Goods Central and Eastern Europe in Bulk or Bags No. 49 of 2018 (to access: https://www.gafta.com/write/MediaUploads/Contracts/2018/49_2018.pdf).

The FCC Articles of Association (2017) (to access: https://www.cocoafederation.com/dashboard/documents/download/371).

The FCC Arbitration and Appeal Rules of 2017 (to access: https://www.cocoafederation.com/dashboard/documents/freecontent/rules/arbitration-and-appeal/arbitration-appeal-rules/ENG).

The Application Procedure to Join the FCC Arbitration and Appeal Panel of 2017 (to access: https://www.cocoafederation.com/dashboard/documents/download/382).

Dispute Resolution Service: A Guide to FCC Arbitration of 2015 (to access: https://www.google.de/url?sa=t&rct=j&q=&esrc=s&source=web&cd=2&ved=2ahUKEwjjrYja14HhAhWCyqQKHVmID60QFjABegQICRAC&url=https%3A%2F%2Fwww.cocoafederation.com%2Fdashboard%2Fdocuments%2Fdownload%2F211&usg=AOvVaw38QHl1n8pHknBUKlz_6uof).

The London Metal Exchange Rules and Regulations of 2019 (to access: https://www.lme.com/LME-Clear/Rules-and-regulations).

The LME Articles of Association of 2013 (to access: https://www.lme.com/-/media/Files/LME-Clear/Governance/Approved-LMEC-Articles-of-Association.pdf?la=en-GB).

The LME Rulebook of 2019 (to access: https://www.lme.com/-/media/Files/Regulation/Rulebook/Full-Rulebook/Rulebook-as-of-January-2019.pdf?la=en-GB).

FOSFA Rules and Regulations of 2018 (to access: https://www.fosfa.org/about-us/rules-and-regulations/).

FOSFA Rules of Arbitration and Appeal of 2018 (to access: https://www.fosfa.org/document-library/rules-of-arbitration-and-appeal-april-2018/).

The FOSFA Rules of Brokerage Commission and Interest (2018) (to access: https://www.fosfa.org/document-library/rules-for-brokerage-commissions-and-interest-april-2018/). https://www.fosfa.org/arbitration/directory-of-fosfa-arbitrators/).

FOSFA Code of Practice for Arbitrators of 2018 (to access: https://www.fosfa.org/content/uploads/2018/03/Code-of-Practice-for-Arbitrators-and-Time-Sheet-April-2018.pdf).

FOSFA Guide to Arbitrations and Appeals of 2018 (to access: https://www.fosfa.org/content/uploads/2018/03/FOSFA-Guide-to-Arbitrations-and-Appeals-April-2018.pdf).

GAFTA Contract No. 1 – General Contract for Shipment of Feeding Stuffs in Bags Tale Quale – CIF/CIFFO/C&F/C&FFO Terms of 2018. (to access: https://www.gafta.com/write/MediaUploads/Contracts/2018/1_2018.pdf).

ICA, ICA membership directory, incorporating annual review.

The London Metal Exchange, "A Guide to the LME", *The London Metal Exchange* 2013.

The London Metal Exchange, "A Guide to Trading LME", The London Metal Exchange 2016.

MISCELLANEOUS

http://www.ica-ltd.org/.

http://www.nyddc.com/.

http://www.gafta.com/.

http://www.cocoafederation.com/.

https://www.lme.com/.

http://www.fosfa.org/.

http://www.cicca.info/.

https://www.ica-ltd.org/about-ica/our-board/.

https://www.ica-ltd.org/about-ica/.

https://www.ica-ltd.org/safe-trading/member-search/.

https://www.ica-ltd.org/arbitration/.

https://www.ica-ltd.org/advanced-level-arbitrator-training/.

https://www.ica-ltd.org/basic-level-arbitrator-training/.

https://www.ica-ltd.org/safe-trading/loua-part-one/.

https://www.nyddc.com/contact-us.html.

https://www.diamondintelligence.com/magazine/magazine.aspx?id=9862.

https://www.nyddc.com/terms--conditions.html.

https://www.nyddc.com/membership.html.

https://www.nyddc.com/arbitration.

https://www.wfdb.com/diamond-dealers-club.

https://www.nyddc.com/officers.html.

https://www.nyddc.com/membership.html.

https://www.nyddc.com/membership.html.

http://www.nyddc.com/uploads/2/3/7/3/23730718/ddc_membership_application.pdf.

https://www.wfdb.com/.

https://www.wfdb.com/wfdb-bourses.

https://www.nytimes.com/1979/05/06/archives/the-citys-most-exclusive-club.html.

https://www.diamonds.net/News/NewsItem.aspx?ArticleID=49902&ArticleTitle=New+York+Adapting+to+Changing+Diamond+Market.

https://www.gafta.com/about.

https://www.gafta.com/Membership.

https://www.gafta.com/Council.

https://www.gafta.com/Staff/75508. https://www.gafta.com/write/MediaUploads/Arbitration/Gafta_Qualified_Arbitrator_Status_201.pdf.

https://www.gafta.com/Gafta-Professional-Development-GPD.

https://www.gafta.com/Distance-Learning-Programme.

https://www.gafta.com/Trade-Diploma.

https://www.gafta.com/Gafta-Qualified-Arbitrators-Annual-Continuing-Professional-Development-GPD-Policy.

https://www.gafta.com/about.

https://www.gafta.com/write/MediaUploads/Arbitration/Defaulters/Defaulters_on_Gafta_Awards_of_Arbitration_2011-present.pdf.

https://www.cocoafederation.com/fcc/members.

https://www.cocoafederation.com/membership/categories-of-membership.

https://www.cocoafederation.com/services/arbitration/arbitration.

https://www.cocoafederation.com/dashboard/documents/download/211.

https://www.cocoafederation.com/services/arbitration/defaulters.

https://www.lme.com/en-GB/Trading/Trading-venues/Ring#tabIndex=0.

https://www.lme.com/en-GB/Trading/Systems/LMEselect#tabIndex=0.

https://www.lme.com/en-GB/Trading/Access-the-market/Membership-categories#tabIndex=0.

https://www.lme.com/en-GB/About/Regulation/Arbitration#tabIndex=0.

https://www.lme.com/About/Regulation/Arbitration/Arbitration-panel.

https://www.lme.com/About/Regulation/Arbitration#tabIndex=1).

https://uk.globaldatabase.com/company/federation-of-oils-seeds-and-fats-associations-limited.

http://www.datalog.co.uk/browse/detail.php/CompanyNumber/00926329/CompanyName/FEDERATION+OF+OILS+SEEDS+AND+FATS+ASSOCIATIONS+LIMITED.

https://www.fosfa.org/about-us/officers-of-the-federation/.

https://www.fosfa.org/membership/categories-of-membership/.

https://www.fosfa.org/document-library/rules-for-small-claims-single-tier-april-2018/.

https://www.fosfa.org/arbitration/posted-companies/.

https://www.ica-ltd.org/media/layout/documents/publications/lca_econtract.pdf.

https://www.gafta.com/write/MediaUploads/Contracts/2018/1_2018.pdf.

https://www.cocoafederation.com/dashboard/documents/freecontent/rules/cocoa-beans/contract-rules-for-cocoa-beans/ENG.

https://www.lme.com/-/media/Files/Metals/Precious-Metals/LMEprecious/LMEprecious-Contract-Specifications.pdf.

https://www.lme.com/en-GB/About/Regulation/Arbitration#tabIndex=2.

http://www.rheinische-warenboerse.de/upload/Contract_No_26_2822.pdf.

https://www.wfdb.com/media-news-press/news-headlines/370-ddc-announces-new-initiative-to-safeguard-diamond-transactions.

www2.ef.jcu.cz/~sulista/pages/kdfp/BUEN1-1.pdf.

https://thebusinessprofessor.com/knowledge-base/the-sherman-act-antitrust-law/.

https://www.ica-ltd.org/safe-trading/loua-part-one/.

http://www.africotton.org/aca/en/.

http://english.china-cotton.org/.

http://acsa-cotton.org/).

http://www.cicca.info/member_associations.php.

http://www.liverpoolmuseums.org.uk/maritime/exhibitions/cotton/traders/trading-rules.aspx.

https://www.nyddc.com/about-the-ddc.html.

http://articles.latimes.com/1985-08-18/business/fi-1708_1_diamond-prices.

http://www.heritagediamonds.net/antwerp-diamond-bourse/.

https://www.auction-house.ru/en/news_analytics/rynok-almazov-mira/.

https://www.icco.org/about-cocoa/trading-a-shipping.html.

https://www.justice.gov/atr/case-document/brief-united-states-and-federal-trade-commission-amici-curiae-supporting-0.

https://www.nyddc.com/ddc-news--events/rapaport-qa-with-david-lasher-managing-director-of-the-new-york-diamond-dealers-club.

https://www.nyddc.com/ddc-news—events.

Decision n° 98-D-73 of 25 November 1998 on a referral and a request for interim measures submitted by the National Employers' Union of dental technicians.

Decision N°05-D-33 of 27 June 2005 on practices implemented by Ilec., p. 6.

Danish Competition Council of 30 January 2008, (Lokale Pengeinstitutter (the Association of Local Banks, Savings Banks and Cooperative Banks in Denmark; the Association) Pharmaceutische Handelsconventie' (PHC), Eighth Report on Competition Policy 1978, p. 73.